CHRONOLOGIES
IN OLD WORLD
ARCHAEOLOGY

Contributors

WILLIAM F. ALBRIGHT

DONALD F. BROWN

KWANG-CHIH CHANG

GEORGE F. DALES

ROBERT H. DYSON, JR.

ROBERT W. EHRICH

MARIJA GIMBUTAS

DONALD P. HANSEN

HELENE J. KANTOR

MACHTELD J. MELLINK

EDITH PORADA

HOMER L. THOMAS

PATTY JO WATSON

SAUL S. WEINBERG

CHRONOLOGIES IN OLD WORLD ARCHAEOLOGY

Edited by

ROBERT W. EHRICH

THE UNIVERSITY OF CHICAGO PRESS
CHICAGO AND LONDON

Chronologies in Old World Archaeology supersedes the earlier *Relative Chronologies in Old World Archeology*, published by The University of Chicago Press in 1954

THE UNIVERSITY OF CHICAGO PRESS, CHICAGO 60637
The University of Chicago Press, Ltd., London

Published 1965. Fourth Impression 1971. Printed in the United States of America

ISBN: 0-226-19443-4 (clothbound); 0-226-19444-2 (paperbound)

Library of Congress Catalog Card Number: 65-17296

Foreword

Since the appearance of Relative Chronologies in Old World Archeology in 1954, so much intensive research has gone forward that in the light of present information the earlier volume can no longer fulfill its purpose. At the prompting of several colleagues, the editor undertook to explore the possibilities of bringing it up to date. The University of Chicago Press expressed interest in such a project, and the Wenner-Gren Foundation for Anthropological Research not only provided the funds necessary to bring together the participants in a new symposium but also organized the meeting and provided the facilities for it.

The group met at the Foundation's headquarters in New York for an intensive working session on April 10 and 11, 1964. The participants had prepared drafts or working papers, which had been duplicated by the Foundation, and these served as the basis for an exchange of ideas and information and for planning, with the understanding that all contributions were to be revised and ready for the press by midsummer. Thus, although the meeting can quite properly be called a symposium, it can also be described as a working conference. The resulting volume, although in spirit a second edition of Relative Chronologies, is actually a replacement. The change in title, brought about by eliminating the word Relative, reflects the emergence of radiocarbon determinations which, despite spotty and uneven distribution as of the present, do seem to provide more secure patterns of relative dates, and presumably a closer approximation to absolute ones. The emphasis, of course, remains on cultural sequences, cross-ties between them, and the floating network of relative chronologies. Once these are firmly established, any further revisions of radiocarbon analysis, with resultant shifting of dates, can be easily assimilated.

Although many of the cross-datings and chronological equations of the original volume are still valid, even the four participants in the first symposium have drastically rewritten their papers. The full publication of the Tarsus material by Hetty Goldman and that from the Amuq by Robert J. Braidwood have permitted their inclusion in a wider context in the current papers by Machteld Mellink and by Patty Jo Watson. Edith Porada and Donald Hansen include new data in their reworking of Ann

Perkins' earlier excellent contribution, which can still be read with profit. Robert Dyson completely reformulates and redates material treated in the earlier essay by Donald McCown. Kwang-chih Chang takes issue with the late Lauriston Ward's treatment of the West-to-East diffusion of Neolithic elements from the Middle East to China. Robert W. Ehrich and Saul Weinberg have completely rewritten their pieces. George F. Dales, Donald F. Brown, Homer L. Thomas, and Marija Gimbutas deal with areas either not covered or referred to only briefly in the previous work, and thus extend the range of interlocking patterns.

The general arrangement is the same in both volumes: the first seven papers begin with Egypt and in succession move northward and eastward to take in the Middle East north of Arabia as far as and including the Indus Valley. The sequence then resumes with the Aegean as the branching-off point, and, after moving to the northwest Mediterranean, reverses itself and progresses eastward from western and northern Europe across east central and eastern Europe and includes China.

Although the area of Poland falls between western, northern, central, northeastern, and eastern Europe, and although its internal regionalization is well marked during the various periods, it is omitted from separate consideration only because it proved impossible to arrange for an adequate treatment. Some cross-references to western and southeastern Poland appear in the Thomas and Gimbutas papers, respectively. In like vein, Dorothy Libby attempted to provide coverage for central Asia, but her results could not be fitted into the rest of the volume.

The time span covered in each area begins with the earliest known appearance of Neolithic culture and extends to the most convenient breaking point in the early part of the second millennium B.C. There is, of course, considerable diversity of approach and outlook among the contributors, but for the most part the established aim of co-ordinating the sequences from region to region has been successful. Despite some discrepancies in interpretation, different degrees of faith in radiocarbon dating, and adherence not only to theoretical considerations of cultural diffusion but also to high or low chronological systems, the successive treatments with attention to areas of contact should provide a workable base line for further integration.

In the interest of compatibility, most of the radiocarbon determinations have been adjusted from the figures as originally published in order to utilize various proposed corrections. Of particular importance is the change from 5570 ± 30 to 5730 ± 40 as the most accurate figure yet obtained for the half life of radiocarbon itself. As indicated in the Editorial Statement of Radiocarbon V, 1963, such changes, effected by multiplying B.P. dates by 1.03 and subtracting 1950 to convert them to B.C. values, must be considered as tentative, pending an agreement among the laboratories. After this and other uncertainties are resolved, it is proposed that all dates will be recalculated and republished. In the present volume, each contributor specifies the half-life figure he employs.

Although the editor received some criticism for not having provided a one-man synthesis of the contributions in the first volume, he has again deliberately refrained from doing so. The purpose of this book is to present, in series, the chronologies of various contiguous areas as they appear in 1964 to the eyes of regional specialists. Despite the new information, the over-all situation is still fluid, and forthcoming data will render some conclusions obsolete, possibly even before this volume appears in print. Furthermore, the archaeological picture is much sketchier in some regions than in others, and this unevenness suggests that there will be marked differences in the rates and degrees of future change. It hardly needs to be said that one of the purposes of this effort is to provide a reference for each region, treated so that one can keep abreast of, or himself make, such alterations and reformulations as may become necessary. If one regards these papers as the working documents they are intended to be, any attempt on the part of the editor to pull them into a single grand design would be nothing short of an impertinence.

In general, the included bibliographies are more extensive than those of the previous volume and show a heavy reliance on recent publications. In this regard it is worth remembering Weinberg's statement to the effect that the older an excavation report, the less reliable it is likely to be.

There are two further points, stressed in the Foreword of Relative Chronologies, that deserve mention but that do not need elaboration here. The first of these is that the term "culture," in its particularistic sense, can be used with relation to societies of differing orders of magnitude and complexities of organization—in short, that it is a categorical device that is usable on various levels of abstraction, provided that the level on which it is used is made explicit. The second is that, although there may seem to be an undue emphasis on pottery, the contributors are well aware that a pottery style of itself is not a culture, but that it is our most sensitive medium for perceiving shared aesthetic traditions in the sense that they define ethnic groups, for recognizing culture contact and culture change, and for following migration and trade patterns.

Even more so than was true of Relative Chronologies, the present work can be described as a collaborative and co-ordinated venture. Not only did our meeting in New York provide more time for discussion and consultation between specialists dealing with contiguous areas, but many of the authors remained in close touch thereafter.

On behalf of my colleagues and myself, I wish to express our deepest appreciation to the Wenner-Gren Foundation for the support of our working session, and to the Director of Research, Mrs. Lita Fejos, and to her staff, for the management and technical assistance which they provided, and for their most graceful hospitality. As organizer and editor, I also wish to thank my colleagues for their unfailing co-operation in the preparation of this volume, and in making possible its prompt publication.

Brooklyn College of the City University of New York

Robert W. Ehrich

Editor's Note

In the preparation of this volume, early publication has seemed far more important than stylistic regularity or uniformity at the price of delay. In general the practices of the University of Chicago Press have been followed, but since spelling, transliteration, punctuation, capitalization, bibliographical citation, and the like tend to vary from area to area and also according to language, the authors have followed differing usages. Insofar as possible, diversities and discrepancies have been brought together in a very full index, which should help to reduce confusion. For what remains awkward or unclear, and for any irregularities, the editor assumes full responsibility.

The Relative Chronology of Egypt and Its Foreign Correlations before the Late Bronze Age

Helene J. Kantor
Oriental Institute
University of Chicago

THE CHRONOLOGICAL FRAMEWORK IN EGYPT

Unlike many other areas of the Near East, Egypt during the past decade has not yielded a large amount of new material pertinent to our problems here. Although elsewhere entire previously blank cultural areas have been filled in or significant new data discovered, in Egypt progress has been limited chiefly to further analysis or assessment of finds largely made many years ago. Unfortunately, the final reports of some highly important excavations remain unpublished. Accordingly, insofar as materials found in Egypt itself are concerned, my task is to refine results presented ten years ago or to appraise them in the light of either subsequent studies or discoveries outside the country.

The absolute chronology of Egypt relies upon indigenous historical traditions organized in the third century B.C. by the priest Manetho into a framework of thirty-one dynasties, stretching from the beginning of historical times through the Persian period. The details of this chronology are based on king lists with regnal years, various types of contemporary documents, and astronomical and calendrical data (Drioton and Vandier, 1952, pp. 10-13, 156, 159, 627-32, and *passim*; W. S. Smith, 1960, pp. 193-202; Gardiner, 1961, pp. 61-68, 429-53, and *passim*; Hayes, Rowton, and Stubbings, 1962, pp. 3-23). The dates for the Twelfth Dynasty and later periods are known with only a relatively small margin of error (Parker, 1950, pp. 63-69). The uncertain length of the First Intermediate period entails a larger margin of error for its dates and those of the preceding periods.

Except for phases of change and decline in the First and Second Intermediate periods and in the Late period, when rival dynasties ruled in a divided land, Egypt was from the time of the First Dynasty a unified country both politically and culturally. Thus, in contrast to western Asia, the difficult chronological problems of co-ordinating the dynastic sequences of contemporary states do not exist, except for the periods of decline. In addition to the general simplicity of the historical framework, the archaeological material from Egypt has a peculiar character distinguishing it from that of most of the rest of the ancient Near East (for geographical setting, cf. Butzer, 1959; for distribution of sites, see Fig. 1). In Egypt, with certain rare exceptions, we do not have excavated stratified village or city sites, each with a sequence of levels which must be correlated in order to arrive at the internal archaeological chronology of the country. The mass of archaeological remains in Egypt, except for the great temples and a limited number of settlement sites, consists of cemeteries—aggregations of separate units—which must be arranged in sequence by the association of the individual grave groups with inscribed material and by typological study. Fortunately, sufficient evidence exists to make the general picture of cultural development clear, despite the uncertainties sometimes arising as to the exact position of specific graves or deposits.

Only in the predynastic period are there major problems of internal relative chronology. The most difficult of these is the correlation of the cultural sequence of the Nile Valley proper (that is, southern and middle Egypt) originally established by Flinders Petrie with that of the Delta. In historical times Egypt had a unified culture with only at periods strong local variations in specific features; yet the striking political and administrative persistence of separate Upper and Lower Egyptian kingdoms unified only by joint allegiance to the pharaoh points back to the predynastic period when, as archaeological evidence shows, culturally also the two lands were distinct. The few sites known around the southern periphery of the Delta are sufficient to prove the existence in the north of a cultural tradition differing widely from that of the south. Thus, these sites are of the utmost importance, although in both space and time they are scattered and isolated; they are not sufficiently numerous to constitute a continuous cultural sequence. They are also outlying, rural settlements, not exemplifying the full range of the prehistoric Delta kingdoms, which political and religious data suggest were fully as advanced as the southern ones. Our ignorance of the archaeology of the Delta capitals has left full scope for theory. It has been assumed that they were the cultural leaders of Egypt in prehistoric times, a position against which Baumgartel has reacted so strongly that she reverses the situation, considering northern sites culturally backward and later than comparable southern ones (Baumgartel, 1955, Chapter III and Appendix).

In contrast to our limited knowledge of the Delta, the southern prehistoric sequence is relatively well known and very rich (Fig. 2). The culture of the First Dynasty is directly derived from the last clearly differentiable Upper Egyptian phase—that is, Gerzean. This circumstance corresponds to the political development which inaugurated Egyptian history—the conquest of the north and the unification of the country by an Upper Egyptian dynasty. However, the unified culture of the First Dynasty was apparently not abruptly imposed on Lower Egypt. The most certain north-south correlation—that of Gerzean with Maadi—shows that the culture of the north, assuming Maadi to be a typical sample, was growing increasingly like that of Upper Egypt. Gerzean sites were not distant, so the sherds of imported Decorated ware, an Upper Egyptian slate palette, and footed basalt jars found at Maadi did not have far to travel. The dark-on-light painting and the ovoid vessels with well-shaped necks and rims characteristic of local Maadi pottery are analogous to traits diagnostic for Gerzean.

The pre-Gerzean stages as set up by Petrie and Brunton are Amratian, Badarian, and Tasian. The consecutiveness of Badarian and Amratian has been taken for granted, largely because Badarian is typologically simpler than Amratian and contains numerous features related and presumably antecedent to important Amratian ones, while Amratian sherds lie above Badarian in the stratified village of Hemamieh. This sequence has been challenged by Werner Kaiser, who proposes that in its area Badarian was contemporary with Amratian elsewhere (Kaiser, 1956, pp. 96-97). Among other points, Kaiser argues that Amratian is thinly represented in the Qau-Matmar region and at Hemamieh village and that some pottery of Amratian type occurs with Badarian sherds in the famous breccia-sealed lowest Badarian level at Hemamieh. Although detailed discussion of the many factors involved is impossible, it should be noted that some are susceptible of varying interpretations. For example, Badarian-Amratian similarities which Kaiser interprets as exchanges between contemporary cultures seem better explained as survivals showing a genetic link. Above all, I would stress the cultural development from Badarian to Amratian attested by varied categories of crafts—not only various main classes of ceramic wares as well as persisting individual types (shallow and deep rounded bowls, S-curved bowls, carinated bowls, squat beaker, bag-shaped vessels, bottle, tall S-sided jar, rimmed storage jars), but also the making of slate palettes, ivory spoons, and animal-topped combs, and the carving or modeling of human and animal figures (cf. also Arkell and Ucko, 1965) (Fig. 2). My continued adherence here to Brunton's dating of Badarian (cf. also ibid.) is based further on the likelihood that Badarian also existed upstream at Armant (Mond, 1937, pp. 3, 61, 176, 229) and Hierakonpolis (Brunton, 1932, p. 274) as well as on the difficulty of visualizing a fragmentation of the narrow and relatively unified upper Nile Valley into contemporary local cultures (cf. remarks of Kaiser, 1956, p. 96, note 4); the burden of proof still seems to lie with those who would reconstruct several regional contemporary cultures.

Tasian was tentatively defined by Brunton on the basis of forty graves and eight town groups from the Qau-Matmar area with the angled bowl as the principal diagnostic character. No further evidence to substantiate the existence of the period has come to light; the present consensus of opinion is that Tasian represents at most an early stage of Badarian.

Three cultural entities or phases of the Upper Egyptian sequence are clear: Badarian, Amratian, and Gerzean. Petrie's subdivision of Amratian and Gerzean into sequence dates has been examined by Kaiser, who substitutes a system of eleven groups arrived at by analysis of the cemetery at Armant (Kaiser, 1957). There is no scope here for evaluation of Kaiser's system nor need to concern ourselves with subdivisions of the main predynastic periods except for one major instance. Although Gerzean is a fairly homogeneous culture, an earlier and later phase can be distinguished, that is those graves belonging to Petrie's Sequence Dates 40 to 50 and those ranging from Sequence Dates 50 to approximately 65. The later phase is marked by: the degeneration of the wavy handles (Petrie, 1921, Pls. 28-29, Wavy 8-27); the occurrence, in addition to the normal Decorated ware, of vases with simplified patterns (ibid., Pl. 37, Decorated 78 A-F; Keimer, 1944, Pls. 1, 2); elaborate ivory and stone carvings (Bénédite, 1916, 1918; Capart, 1904, pp. 224-25, Figs. 155-56, Pl. 1; Kantor, 1944).

Available for correlation with the pre-Gerzean Upper Egyptian sequence in the north are El Omari, Merimde, and Fayum A. Of El Omari little has been published; its excavator considered it a link between Maadi and the typologically earlier culture of Merimde (De Bono, 1946, pp. 53-54; Hayes, 1964, pp. 242-48). Merimde, on the edge of the western Delta, had several stratified layers, all representing the same culture but with increasingly dense settlement and some shifting pottery traits (Junker, 1945). Merimde is much poorer in its range of features than the Upper Egyptian cultures, but its round houses, carinated bowls, and, in particular, the unusual and specific type of bowl supported by human feet modeled in clay, place it in the general time range of Amratian (Fig. 2).

Fayum A, established typologically as the earliest of the known northern cultures, is also typologically similar to Tasian/Badarian, but without the more elaborate features, such as ivory carving or modeling in clay, of the Upper Egyptian complex. In the Fayum culture various analogies with Tasian (angled bowls, varyingly profiled polished red rectangular bowls, and roughly rectangular palettes) or Badarian (squarish and round bag jars, sherds with densely set knobs, and solid based cups—the rims and bases widely splayed in the Fayum and only slightly in the Badarian) are somewhat too generalized to be binding comparisons (Fig. 2). Nonetheless, they suggest that Fayum A may be placed at the beginning of the northern sequence, approximately opposite Tasian/Badarian.

Unfortunately, the C-14 dates for Fayum A and other prehistoric Egyptian periods listed below (Libby, 1955, pp. 77-79, using a half life of 5,568 years, retained here following editorial policy of Radiocarbon; cf. Editorial Statements, vols. 4-6, 1962-1964) are neither sufficiently numerous nor uncontaminated—those from Upper Egypt were determined from samples stored in England for years after excavation—to give indications of absolute date or correlations between northern and southern Egypt (cf. also Arkell and Ucko, 1965, *passim*; Larsen, 1957, pp. 50-51; H. S. Smith, 1964).

Fayum A:	C-457: Average	6095 ± 250	(=4145 B.C. ± 250)
	C-550, C-551:	6391 ± 180	(=4441 B.C. ± 180)
El Omari:	C-463:	5256 ± 230	(=3306 B.C. ± 230)
Amratian:	C-810:	5744 ± 300	(=3794 B.C. ± 300)
	C-814:	5577 ± 310	(=3627 B.C. ± 310)
Gerzean:	C-812:	5020 ± 290	(=3070 B.C. ± 290)
	C-811:	5619 ± 280	(=3669 B.C. ± 280)
	C-813:	4720 ± 310	(=2770 B.C. ± 310)

Two C-14 dates for Merimde, 5531 ± 100 (=3580 B.C. ± 100) and 6130 ± 110 (=4180 B.C. ± 110), additional to the prehistoric Egyptian dates given by Libby, are quoted and discussed by Larsen, 1960, pages 49 ff.

Despite the tentativeness of pre-Gerzean Upper and Lower Egyptian correlations, the general relationship of the prehistoric Egyptian periods is clear. Already in prehistoric times, and even more in the dynastic period, the clear-cut sequence of Egyptian phases provides a gauge helpful in establishing the chronology, both relative and absolute, of various other parts of the ancient Near East.

THE PREDYNASTIC PERIOD

At various western Asiatic sites it is possible to trace the crucial period in which agriculture and the domestication of animals were developing or just appearing. In Egypt materials of a comparable period are unknown, perhaps being hidden far below Nile silt. It has also been suggested that these features of neolithic economy may have been introduced from outside. Whatever may have been the eventual sources of the agricultural economy in Egypt or the affinities of the earliest known village cultures—Tasian/Badarian and Amratian in the south, Fayum A and Merimde in the north (cf. Arkell and Ucko, 1965; Hayes, 1964)—Egypt appears as an isolated corner of the Near East. Its local cultures flourished without any particular outside stimulation; even within the country, contacts between north and south do not seem to have been active. It is likely that the affinities of these early Egyptian cultures will be found to lie with other African assemblages, such as those beginning to be known from the Sudan and Kharga oasis, although it is perhaps premature to make a precise statement about the relationships of these groups.

Imported materials—such as shells from the Red Sea, turquoise and copper presumably from Sinai, and even pine, cedar, cypress, and juniper from Syria (cf. Brunton, 1928, pp. 41, 62 f.)—show that the early villagers were not completely isolated. However, objects indisputably foreign, in manufacture or type, are almost nonexistent in early contexts. Brunton suggested that an unusual four-handled, narrow-necked vessel from a Badarian grave might be foreign (ibid., p. 24; Pls. XVI, _7_; XXVI, Group 569). Its shape is similar to some Ghassulian vessels (Perrot, 1961, p. 75, Fig. 39, _7_-_9_; cf. Kaplan, 1959, who suggests also a few other Ghassulian parallels). The possibility of some kind of connection between Ghassulian and Amratian has been raised by the important finds of Perrot in the outskirts of Beersheba, where ivories similar to typical Amratian ones in elongation, shape of ankles and face, and use of drill holes (but different in many other details) have been found. Perrot suggests a derivation from some substratum common to both the African and Palestinian cultures (Perrot, 1959, pp. 18-19; Perrot, 1963, p. 93). Beersheba also revealed an active copper-casting industry, which recalls the circumstance that early in Gerzean elaborate metallurgical techniques were established in Egypt, as indicated by the Matmar ax (Brunton, 1948, p. 21; Pl. XV1, 47). To what extent were these two metallurgical techniques independent? It is tempting to imagine some sort of cultural influence linking the Ghassulian inhabitants of Palestine and the Amratians in Upper Egypt. Although this may be possible from the chronological point of view, the tenuousness or generality of the similarities and the problem as to the mechanism of connection preclude any firm establishment of the connection. We may note also that attempts to derive the painted pottery of Amratian—the White Cross-lined ware—from the painted wares of various Mesopotamian and Iranian cultures seem unfounded (Baumgartel, 1947, pp. 54-71; Kantor, 1949, pp. 78-79).

The situation in Gerzean and the contemporary Maadian was in the sharpest contrast to that prevailing earlier. For the first time there were unmistakable foreign relations, which mark Gerzean as a period of greatly widening horizons. Three classes of connections can be differentiated: imitations of foreign pottery vessels in native wares, imported pottery vessels or other objects, and imitations of elaborate foreign features. These did not all occur at the same time. In addition to the distinctions between Early and Late Gerzean already cited, a further, and important, difference is that the foreign connections of the earlier phase were of the first type—that is, relatively frequent imitations of alien features—while in the later phase of Gerzean they were of the second and third types. Late Gerzean contacts with foreign countries were more frequent and presumably more rapidly accomplished than those of the preceding phase.

Prominent features of Gerzean, distinguishing it from the parent Amratian culture, are the classes of light-faced Qena pottery. First and foremost are the ledge-handled jars. The earlier types from Egypt tend to be relatively squat and to have well-shaped wavy or thumb-indented handles (Fig. 3, 50); they are comparable to Early Bronze I (Late Chalcolithic) types in Palestine. In Egypt such vessels and handles have no prototypes, but in Palestine primitive ledge handles already appear in the Early Chalcolithic of Jericho VIII and Beth Shan XVIII (Garstang,

1936, Pl. 32, 28, 29 A, B; Fitzgerald, 1935, Pl. 2, 13, 14). By the beginning of Early Bronze I several developed forms of ledge handles, both thumb-indented and wavy, were used on different types of vessels. Palestine must have been the source from which the ledge-handled jar reached Egypt. It is interesting to note that the connection was sufficiently strong to stimulate the development of an entire class of Gerzean pottery in which the alien jar and handle shapes were gradually degraded.

In addition to the ledge handles, two other pottery elements of Early Gerzean are attributable to foreign influence. Among the Decorated pot shapes are relatively large jars with three or four triangular lug handles on the shoulder. These lugs are reminiscent of those which were already in use on Mesopotamian pottery in the Ubaid period and which became particularly typical and frequent on Protoliterate pottery (Frankfort, 1932, Table I; Delougaz, 1952, p. 39). Since the general shape of the vessels with the triangular lugs does not closely resemble any particular Mesopotamian type, the Mesopotamian origin of the lugs is suggested here with considerable reserve. More convincing are the vessels with tilted spouts (Figs. 3, 51, 52; 4, N, O, T). Although made in the old, indigenous Polished Red ware, the spouts are completely un-Egyptian; as a whole these jugs resemble Mesopotamian ones of the earlier part of the Protoliterate period (Fig. 4, P, Q, U). How such prototypes may have influenced Egyptian potters is difficult to determine. Similar spouts (Fig. 4, R), associated with reserve slip, occur in the Amuq area during Phase G, corresponding to a time when that region was a western outpost of strong Protoliterate influence. Since some spouted vessels of the Early Bronze I in Palestine (Fig. 4, S, V) are similar in shape and spouts to both Protoliterate and Gerzean examples, it is possible that the type diffused from northern Syria southward; however, even more likely is the alternative direct route, as we shall see below.

All three types of vessels discussed above occur fairly commonly in Egypt, and continued to be used in the Late Gerzean period; note, for example the variations of the spouted type in Late Gerzean (Figs. 3, 44; 4, J), Early Bronze I Palestine (Fig. 4, M), and Late Protoliterate (K and L). Such comparatively wide adoption, particularly marked in the case of the ledge-handled jars, suggests rather intensive outside connections, though probably not any large-scale foreign immigrations. It is unlikely that such contacts could have begun suddenly; they must have carried on from more sporadic connections of earlier times for which we have no certain evidence, and they provide the basis for the very active foreign connections of the following phase. Insofar as a relative chronology is concerned, the ledge-handled and spouted jars equate the earlier part of Gerzean with the Early Bronze I period in Palestine and the Early Protoliterate (A and B) in Mesopotamia.

Several Palestinian pottery types—bowls with conoid projections (Fig. 3, 43); a lug-handled pot (Fig. 3, 41); loop-handled cup and another lugged pot with vertical painted bands (Fig. 3, 37, 40)—occur in tombs assigned to the Late Gerzean phase. A painted flask with similar decoration found at Abusir el Meleq in a tomb of the beginning of the First Dynasty may well be only an instance of persistence rather than a true synchronism (Fig. 3, 32). These types are represented either by one or a few examples, and are scattered from Abusir el Meleq in the north to Naqada in the south. It can hardly be doubted that these vessels were imports. Ten years ago, using this evidence, I equated Late Gerzean with Early Bronze I in Palestine and Early Gerzean with Palestinian Late Chalcolithic, but suggested the possibility that such a neat correlation might be an oversimplification. This does, indeed, seem to be the case. Materials accumulating from Palestine indicate that the burnished Esdraelon ware, which has been taken as diagnostic for a Late Chalcolithic phase, does not occur in deposits sharply separated from materials hitherto classified as Early Bronze I (cf. Wright, 1961, p. 82). The solution at the moment seems to be to consider the Esdraelon ware as characteristic for the earlier part of Early Bronze I in Palestine and to await the detailed analysis of recently excavated materials in Palestine before attempting a more precise correlation of individual phases of Early Bronze I with the Egyptian sequence.

The situation at Maadi is strikingly different from that at the Gerzean sites nearby or farther south. At Maadi the published unpainted lugged pots and loop-handled cup (Fig. 3, 33-35), analogous to those cited above, as well as ledge-handled vessels (Fig. 3, 36) are only some examples of a number of un-Egyptian shapes. Moreover, all these vessels, as I was able, through the kindness of Professor Mustafa Amer, to observe in the excavation store rooms at Maadi, are of drab-colored, friable ware filled with many grits—quite un-Egyptian but typical of Palestine. In other words, there is in Maadi a considerable body of imported Eastern pottery apparently representing Early Bronze I. To the implications of Maadi for the interpretation of prehistoric Egyptian foreign relations we will return below.

The items demonstrating early Mesopotamian connections with Egypt are now well known, but, thanks in part to some recent unpublished Oriental Institute excavations at Chogha Mish in Khuzestan, we can now date certain Mesopotamian imports into Egypt more accurately than was possible ten years ago, allowing us to refine Mesopotamian-Egyptian correlations. Of the three Mesopotamian pots from Egypt, only the brown, four-lugged pot from Matmar occurred in a datable context (Fig. 4, B); it indicates that the red-polished and cream-slipped examples from Badari and Mostagedda also belong to Late Gerzean (Fig. 4, F, A). In all probability likewise imported were four cylinder seals (Fig. 8; Kantor, 1952, p. 247), while witness to the intensity of contacts are the Mesopotamian motifs adopted by Egyptian artists. To the items established by Frankfort—high-hulled ships (Fig. 3, 39), interlacing serpents (Fig. 3, 47), serpent-necked panthers (Fig. 3, 46), masters of animals (Fig. 3, 48), headdress and long robe (Frankfort, 1951, Appendix), Amiet has added the horizontal-winged griffin typical of Susa seals (Fig. 3, 49; Amiet, 1957, p. 126 and Figs. 5-6).

Since these Mesopotamian features provide a basic correlation with Egypt, their date is of great importance. They all belong to that initial period of classical Mesopotamian civilization in which writing, cylinder seals, elaborate art, and political organization first appeared. Delougaz, having distinguished the nature and fundamental importance of the cultural features testifying to this development, which mark it off clearly from the preceding prehistoric phases, termed the period "Protoliterate" after what was probably its most revolutionary invention—writing (Delougaz and Lloyd, 1942, p. 8, n. 10).

The Protoliterate period is divided into several phases (for architectural and ceramic assemblages of the later part, cf. Delougaz and Lloyd, 1942, *passim*, and Delougaz, 1952, *passim*; for glyptic assemblages, Frankfort, 1955, *passim*). The four seals from Egypt represent the Jemdet Nasr style typical for Protoliterate C and D. The evidence available in 1954 suggested that the four-lugged pots should also be dated to Late Protoliterate. These Late Protoliterate dates for the imported seals and pottery conflicted with the Early Protoliterate date of the artistic motifs borrowed by the Egyptians. In 1954, the impasse was solved by the assumption that some kind of cultural lag delayed the appearance of the motives in Egypt. The situation now looks different. The Chogha Mish excavations show that both the four-lugged vessels of Figure 4, A and B, and the red-polished example with knobbed and incised decoration (Fig. 4, F), for which ten years ago there was only an unstratified parallel from Tello, are characteristic of Early Protoliterate. Further, these same excavations have indicated also that seal types with fish, typical of the Jemdet Nasr style, began earlier than has hitherto been thought. Accordingly, it now seems that Late Gerzean is contemporary with the final part of Protoliterate B and the beginning of Protoliterate C. Implicit in this correlation is the assumption that there was little, if any, cultural lag, so that Mesopotamian objects and artistic models reached Egypt promptly—an assumption that is closely tied to the problem of the route and character of Mesopotamian-Gerzean connections.

The existence of a direct sea route around the Arabian peninsula and up the Red Sea to Upper Egypt (Frankfort, 1951, pp. 110-11; Kantor, 1952, p. 250; Wainwright, 1963) has recently been strongly opposed by Helck (1960, pp. 6-9), who maintains that there were no direct confrontations between Egyptians and Sumerians. Instead, according to Helck, Mesopotamian influence, limited on the whole to imported cylinder seals with various designs, entered the country through trading cities of the western Delta after having traveled the long overland route across northern Mesopotamia to the Syro-Palestinian littoral, whence the objects in question were transshipped to the Delta. Only from there did Mesopotamian features finally percolate into southern Egypt. If this were actually the way in which Mesopotamian features reached the south, they would provide only a very approximate synchronism, allowing much possibility of lag. Accordingly, it is necessary briefly to summarize Helck's persuasively presented arguments and my reasons for rejecting them.

1. Period at which Mesopotamian influences began. Helck, accepting Kaiser's still debatable subdivisions of Gerzean and claim that the culture reached its northern confines only relatively late, emphasizes that only then, when physically contiguous to the Delta trading cities, did Mesopotamian features appear. However, spouted vessels, as well as the less indisputably Mesopotamian triangular lugs, occurred as early as the beginning of the Gerzean period.

2. Ship types. On the basis of a high-hulled boat on an Amratian sherd and Winckler's dating of Eastern Desert rock drawings with such

ships, Helck considers the high-hulled, reputedly Mesopotamian type to be actually an Egyptian form appearing as early as Amratian. However, the ship on the Amratian sherd is both incomplete and not clearly Mesopotamian in type (Brunton, 1937, pp. 83-84, Pl. 38, 4), while Winckler's dating of the rock drawings in question to Amratian (Winckler, 1938, pp. 26-27, 35-39, Pls. 37 ff.) is tenuous when examined in detail. On the other hand, certain Egyptian ship renderings, including a few from the Eastern Desert, are overwhelmingly similar to Mesopotamian ones and unlike standard Gerzean representations.

3. Practical problems of the direct sea route. No specific evidence exists to disprove Helck's claim that the early Sumerian ships were not sufficiently seaworthy to make the trip through the Persian Gulf and the Red Sea. However, in view of the apparently large and elaborate ships on Protoliterate seals (Amiet, 1961, Pls. 13 bis, E; 46, 655) and the modern exploits of Arab dhows in ranging along the Arabian, African, and Indian coasts (Villiers, 1940, pp. 6-10 and *passim*; *New York Times*, April 12, 1964), it is highly unlikely that similar journeys would have been beyond Mesopotamian capacity. As for the problem of water supply, even a small ship could have carried water sufficient for a considerable period in a few skins. Such modern ports as Gizan and Jiddah suggest the existence of ancient predecessors which could have provided revictualling stops. It should also be noted that predynastic graves and village debris have been traced along the Wadi Hammamat from the port area of Kosseir to Koptos, indicating that this well-known historical route between the Red Sea and the Nile Valley was already in use in predynastic times (De Bono, 1951).

4. Absence of Sumerian references to such voyages, although trips to Magan and Meluhha are recorded. This is not surprising, since the Egyptian voyages were undertaken at a time when writing was just developing and apparently used chiefly for economic notations. Further, the Protoliterate period was a time of particular Mesopotamian vigor, and trips made then may not all have been continued later as regular trade routes.

5. Absence of evidence for direct Mesopotamian-Egyptian confrontation, which would imply a sea route. Helck disposes of the prime evidence for such confrontation by denying the existence of a Mesopotamian ship type in Egypt and the Mesopotamian origin of Egyptian niched-brick architecture (Frankfort, 1951, Appendix). Egyptologists have long

hesitated to accept the idea that such a significant feature of Egyptian civilization could have been borrowed from abroad (for example, Ricke, 1944, p. 46 and comments of Frankfort, 1953, pp. 161-62), but the evidence set forth by Frankfort is receiving increasing acceptance (Baumgartel, 1960, p. 139; Emery, 1961, pp. 31, 177, 189) and seems indisputable, particularly when considered together with all the other signs of Mesopotamian connections.

A further consideration favoring a direct Mesopotamian-Egyptian sea route is the distribution and nature of Protoliterate features in Egypt, Syria, and Palestine. The Mesopotamian elements known from predynastic contexts are all from Upper Egyptian sites, which would fit in well with an entry through the Wadi Hammamat. Undue reliance cannot, of course, be placed upon this circumstance, which new discoveries may alter. However, less likely to be the result of accidental preservation or discovery is the fact that in Syria and Palestine Protoliterate influence, as shown by pottery and some Jemdet Nasr cylinder seals, is strong only in the Amuq and the northern Orontes Valley. Even Ras Shamra, relatively far north on the coast, does not share these influences to the same extent, although it has yielded one Uruk-style cylinder seal (Amiet, 1963, p. 67, Fig. 12). Apparently diffusion of Mesopotamian influence in the Protoliterate period was strong up the Euphrates and across to the mouth of the Orontes, but beyond thinned out so markedly that the area south of Amuq does not seem a good intermediary for spreading such influences still farther. Further, nowhere in Syria or Palestine is there yet any hint of the rich complex of Mesopotamian features traceable in Egypt, or even of the finer varieties of Protoliterate lugged pots such as those occurring in Upper Egypt. Accordingly, the most likely assumption is that Mesopotamian influence was carried to Egypt by sea. In fact, Amiet, pointing out that such features as entwined snakes with rosettes and horizontal-winged griffins are apparently limited to the Susa Plain, proposes that many, at the least, of the foreign influences in Egypt were specifically Susian (Amiet, 1957, pp. 126-29; 1961, pp. 38-39). In contrast, Syro-Palestinian raw materials and objects must have reached Egypt from the north, presumably in part through Delta ports, though we have no archaeological evidence of their existence. It is, however, unlikely that all Syro-Palestinian connections were by sea. The imported pottery at Maadi strongly suggests that this site was a center of diffusion for Palestinian elements into Egypt; in historical times the usual road from Egypt to Palestine, as indicated by texts, passed directly by Maadi and across the eastern Delta and Sinai (Rizkhana, 1952, p. 123; cf. also Helck, 1962, pp. 13, 17). As Rizkhana has emphasized, this was probably already the case in predynastic times. Maadi was probably one of the entrepôts which handled Palestinian trade and from which isolated Palestinian pots of the Early Bronze I period filtered into upstream areas in the Late Gerzean period. At the beginning of the period, Lower Egyptian sites of analogous character perhaps served as intermediaries introducing and facilitating the adoption of ledge-handled jars by Upper Egyptian potters.

The definition of the different routes by which foreign influences entered Egypt enables us to be more confident in setting up precise chronological correlations. The existence of good reasons for postulating a direct Mesopotamian-Egyptian sea route means that the Mesopotamian objects in Egypt provide a direct synchronism, independent of the Syro-Palestinian evidence and providing a check for it. The Early Bronze I of Syria and Palestine, the Late Gerzean of Egypt, and the transition from Early to Late Protoliterate in Mesopotamia were contemporary.

THE PROTODYNASTIC PERIOD

With the First Dynasty we enter a new phase. Mesopotamian connections, so active in the preceding period, seem now to have tapered off and to consist mainly of the survival, in rapidly Egyptianizing forms, of some of the features introduced earlier. The few persisting examples of motifs were relatively inconspicuous, with the exception of the serpent-necked panthers on the Narmer palette. The foreign cylinder seal had been fully acclimatized by the substitution of Egyptian motifs for the foreign ones. As far as pottery is concerned, some cut-ware braziers or stands known in Mesopotamia in the Protoliterate and Early Dynastic periods may be connected with Egyptian braziers of the First Dynasty (Delougaz, 1952, p. 134; Frankfort, 1924, Fig. 13; Petrie, 1921, Pl. 51, Late 84b, 85). Among the rapidly Egyptianizing forms can be included the niched-brick architecture, which appears for the first time at the beginning of the dynasty in forms more reminiscent of Early Protoliterate architecture than that of later phases. As Frankfort has shown (1951, Appendix), the elaborately recessed brick tombs in Memphite cemeteries (Fig. 3, 31) and at Naqada—the earliest monumental constructions in

Egypt—closely resemble Protoliterate temples in their exterior plan and in the construction of the niches. In Mesopotamia the prototypes of such niched buildings can be traced early in the Ubaid period, far back in prehistoric times. In Egypt, niched tombs appear suddenly without any antecedents (the primitive bricks from Merimde and Maadi can hardly be construed as such) at the beginning of the First Dynasty, immediately after the Mesopotamian connections of the Late Gerzean period. Presumably among the Mesopotamians reaching Egypt in Late Gerzean were adventurers or skilled craftsmen who introduced the knowledge of such building, even though no examples occur until later. Important though the niched-brick architecture is for cultural development, it provides no chronological synchronism between Egypt and Mesopotamia as did the earlier materials.

Very different is the situation as regards Syria and Palestine. In strong contrast to Egypt's relations with Mesopotamia, its cultural peer, here there was a more prosaic situation, the exploitation of the resources of a peripheral area by a now centralized power. Masses of imported Syro-Palestinian pottery vessels, presumably oil or perfume containers, from both royal and private tombs of the First Dynasty testify to intensive trade connections and provide one of the best-authenticated comparative correlations—that of the Syro-Palestinian Early Bronze II period with the First Dynasty (Helck, 1962, pp. 31-38; Amiran, 1963, pp. 84 ff.).

Three distinct wares occur: (1) Red-polished, with gritty drab or brown paste, fired at relatively low temperatures; represented chiefly by flasks, usually one-handled, with flat or stump bases (cf. Fig. 3, *26*, *27*, *29*, *30*). (2) Light-faced or white-slipped, similar in paste and low firing to the first type, painted in brown or red with geometric designs or, exceptionally, a bird; most common form is the one-handled flask, but variously shaped jars are also known (cf. Figs. 3, *28*; 5; possible example, Capart and Werbrouck, 1960, p. 199, Fig. 192). (3) Metallic ware characterized by high firing and consequent metallic clink; paste usually well levigated, though grits may be present; color ranges from light pink or brown through red to purplish or blackish gray; interior often characterized by dents from finger impressions; divisible into subcategories according to the surface treatment—(*a*) plain; (*b*) burnished, sometimes in vertical streaks; (*c*) lattice burnished, sometimes so deeply that bands are slightly impressed; (*d*) combed—wide variety of forms, including ordinary or narrow-based flasks and thin or fat two-handled jars (cf. Fig. 3, 24, 25).

The rarest of these wares is the light-faced painted one, though this may be accidental. Increasing examples of it are being found in Palestine, where it may have originated, rather than in Syria, as suggested by Frankfort many years ago (1924, pp. 108-10). The ware occurs, albeit infrequently, in Phase G of the Amuq sites (Braidwood and Braidwood, 1960, p. 288, Fig. 227). The red-polished and metallic wares are diagnostic for Palestine (Engberg and Shipton, 1934, pp. 9, 11 f.), Byblos (Dunand, 1960, Pl. CCVI), and other southern Syrian sites (A. M. H. Ehrich, 1939, Pls. VIII, XV, XVI) in the Early Bronze II period, but relatively rare in Amuq G (Braidwood and Braidwood, 1960, p. 269, Fig. 207, 9; p. 271, Fig. 211, 11-15; p. 275, Fig. 217, 2-5; p. 293, Fig. 233, 11, 12). Apparently this complex of ceramics was particularly typical for Palestine and coastal Syria—both closely linked to Egypt by sea and land routes. Excavations in Israel—as at Khirbet Kerak (= Beth Yerah), Tell Arad (Aharoni and Amiran, 1964), and Tell Gath, as well as the hoard of copper implements from Tell Monash (Hestrin and Tadmor, 1963)—are revealing the Palestinian reverse of the discoveries made in Egypt. The existence in southern Palestine of such important Early Bronze II sites as Tell Arad and Tell Gath is significant in connection with the situation in prehistoric times when Maadi seemed to be the Egyptian end of an overland route. In particular, Tell Gath has yielded one of the most unexpected and outstanding discoveries of recent Near Eastern excavation. A mass of imported Egyptian pottery vessels, including a fragment incised with the serekh of Narmer (Yeivin, 1960, pp. 194-203; Pls. 23-24; Yeivin, 1963) testifies to very intimate relations with Egypt—even closer than those enjoyed by Byblos, which, despite all its Egyptian or Egyptianizing objects, can provide no such comparable phenomenon for the beginning of the First Dynasty. Egyptian links with southern Palestine must have been especially active.

Ten years ago it seemed unlikely that the active connections attested to in Egypt by numerous Syro-Palestinian imports were interrupted suddenly at the end of the First Dynasty, particularly since the Asiatic side has yielded a stone vessel fragment with the name of the Second Dynasty King Khasekhemui from Byblos (Dunand, 1939, pp. 26-27, Pl. 39, 1115) and from Ai in southern Palestine an Egyptianizing ivory knife handle (Kantor, 1956, p. 157) and Egyptian stone vessels (cf. Albright, below). Nor was there any interruption in the availability of the timber indispensable for ambitious building projects. Now, at least one flask from a Second Dynasty context, a tomb at Helwan, has been published (Fig. 3, 23A). The absence of other Second or Third Dynasty examples is probably to a great extent due to the relatively small number of graves available from the later Protodynastic period. In fact, the connections indicated by the ubiquitous Syro-Palestinian imports of the First Dynasty continued during the Old Kingdom.

THE OLD KINGDOM (FOURTH-SIXTH DYNASTIES)

The tomb deposits of the Old Kingdom at Giza, many specifically dated to an individual reign or phase of a dynasty, provide the major part of the imported Syro-Palestinian pottery of this period (Reisner and Smith, 1955, pp. 62-65, 73-76; Figs. 80, 95-98). However, more modest graves at Saqqara and upstream at Matmar prove that such equipment was not limited to the nobility. No trace remains of the light-faced painted ware prominent in the First Dynasty. The scene is dominated by metallic one-handled flasks and two-handled jars, frequently combed and cream-slipped. These types correspond closely to metallic ware vessels from Early Bronze III contexts in Palestine and Ras Shamra (Schaeffer, 1949, Fig. 99, 8, 9, 12; 1962, Fig. 16; Fig. 22, H), even in such details as the cylinder-seal rolling on a Giza jar comparable to those found at Khirbet Kerak in the past and in 1963 by an Oriental Institute excavation and at Byblos (Reisner and Smith, p. 75, Fig. 95, Pl. 53, a, b; Prausnitz, 1955). It is the vessels continuing the standard Early Bronze ceramic tradition of Syria and Palestine and adapted to the transport of liquids that were imported to Egypt. The exotic Khirbet Kerak ware from the northeast, which is also a diagnostic feature of the Syro-Palestinian Early Bronze III period, does not appear. The vessel with the most remote origin to be found at Giza during the Old Kingdom is a flask of typical Cilician Early Bronze III type (Goldman, 1954, p. 73; Reisner and Smith, 1955, pp. 73-74; reign of Khufu) (Fig. 3, 22).

Early Bronze III is represented in the Antioch Plain sites excavated by the Oriental Institute by Phase H, which is characterized by various wares traditional to the general area, including some rare metallic-ware sherds (Braidwood and Braidwood, 1960, p. 369, Fig. 286, 13, 14; p. 371, Fig. 288) and by Khirbet Kerak ware. Although in general Amuq H can be classified as Early Bronze III and correlated with the Old

Kingdom, some problems of synchronization exist in connection with both Amuq H and the preceding Phase G. Thus, the light-faced painted ware typical of Early Bronze II occurs not only in Amuq G but also in Amuq H, where in fact it appears to be slightly more common than earlier ("0-2%" of the selected pottery samples as opposed to "0-1%"; Braidwood and Braidwood, 1960, pp. 287, 358, 359, Fig. 279). Its appearance as late as Early Bronze III, synchronous with Khirbet Kerak ware, conflicts sharply with the painted ware's limitation to the First Dynasty in Egypt and to Early Bronze II in Palestine. The Amuq H occurrences of the painted sherds should be re-examined to determine whether they are actually stratified alongside Khirbet Kerak sherds (cf. Tadmor, 1964).

Further, some reassessment or refinement of Amuq G may be in order. As it now stands, this phase contains pottery that elsewhere must be divided into two distinct and successive periods. Amuq G contains, in addition to Early Bronze II painted, red-polished, and metallic wares synchronous with the First Dynasty, other ceramic types—triangular lug handles (Fig. 4, I), crooked spouts combined with reserve slip—comparable to typical Protoliterate features. Accordingly, the question arises as to whether Amuq G is really a coherent archaeological assemblage. Detailed examination of the factors involved falls outside the scope of this paper. Fortunately, despite these problems, the synchronism of the Fourth to Sixth Dynasties with the third stage of the Syro-Palestinian Early Bronze period is clear. Egyptian foreign relations of this time are illustrated, not only by actual pottery imports and the record on the Palermo stone of a timber-collecting expedition of Snefru, but also by reliefs from the funerary temple of Sahure at Abusir. Ships returning from an Asiatic journey as well as part of the cargo—bears and one-handled flasks (Fig. 3, 23)—are shown. It is likely that the commerce with the East was exclusively carried on by state expeditions at this time (Helck, 1962, p. 39; for political relations, cf. pp. 13-27).

The Old Kingdom was followed by a period of change and decline—the First Intermediate period—which brought a break in Egypt's connections with Syria and Palestine. This interruption can be attributed, not only to the breakdown of the central Egyptian government into small rival kingdoms, but also to the disturbances which brought to a close the Early Bronze period in Palestine and Syria. Its end is now often interpreted as a result of the immigrations of new, "Amorite" settlers.

In Egypt, too, the turmoil throughout the land was apparently heightened, as suggested by the Admonitions of Ipuwer, by incursions of Asiatics. However, attempts to trace their presence in Egypt by archaeological means have not been successful. No unmistakably foreign types of objects are known from the graves of the First Intermediate period, although stamp seals appear for which parallels outside have been sought (cf. Goldman, 1954, p. 73; Weinberg, 1954, p. 90). The synchronization of the First Intermediate period with the Middle Bronze I of Syria and Palestine is not established by specific archaeological correlations. These periods fall into place opposite each other merely as the successors of the Old Kingdom and the Early Bronze period.

THE TWELFTH DYNASTY AND THE SECOND INTERMEDIATE PERIOD

Not until the height of the Middle Kingdom, during the Twelfth Dynasty, are clear evidences for foreign connections again found within the borders of Egypt. These foreign objects can be fully evaluated only when taken together with the Egyptian small objects and inscribed statues found in Crete, Palestine, Syria, and even as far north as Anatolia (Porter, Moss, and Burney, 1951, pp. 381, 386-87, 392-93; Pendlebury, 1930, p. 115). The range and intensity of connections now seem greater than in the Early Bronze period. The question has even arisen as to what extent Egypt may have established some sort of organized rule in Palestine and Syria (cf. Helck, 1962, pp. 43-91, for discussion of all types of evidence for the various facets of Middle Kingdom foreign relations). Nonetheless, there is no reappearance of large-scale Syro-Palestinian pottery imports into Egypt until another period of turmoil —the Second Intermediate period. Middle Kingdom materials do not provide any such direct and highly satisfactory Syro-Palestinian correlations as do Old Kingdom finds. In fact, the synchronism of the Twelfth Dynasty with the Middle Bronze IIA period must be substantiated by discoveries made outside Egypt, such as the Byblos tombs and temple dated by the names of the Twelfth Dynasty Pharaohs Amenemhet III and IV and by the circumstance that the following Middle Bronze IIB period is again directly correlated with Egypt.

Several important finds of foreign objects, all involving relations with Crete, have been made in Twelfth Dynasty contexts. Earliest in date are the four bronze chests dedicated by Amenemhet II in the Montu temple at Ṭod, south of Luxor. This treasure consisted of hundreds of crushed, thin silver vessels and a silver stamp seal of Minoan type, as well as numerous other small objects, the majority made of lapis lazuli (de la Roque, 1950; de la Roque, Contenau, and Chapouthier, 1953). The character of the treasure can only be understood if we regard it not as a series of objects selected as worthy of royal presentation to the temple, but rather as a collection of precious materials made up by objects of exceedingly varied origin and date. The collection included many Mesopotamian Early Dynastic elements (hair-curl inlays; pendants in the forms of double-bull protomes, simplified spread-wing birds, couchant bovines, frogs, and flies; trapezoidal spacers; petal inlay), possibly even some Protoliterate ones (petal inlay, four-way lozenge beads), as well as Protoliterate geometric, Akkadian, Guti, Third Dynasty of Ur, and Old Babylonian cylinder seals (cf. Landsberger, 1954, p. 119). If this motley stock of jewelers' materials was put together in one place, the Syro-Palestinian littoral seems the most likely spot; it has been suggested that the treasure was booty taken by Amenemhet II (Vandier, 1937; de la Roque, Contenau, and Chapouthier, 1953, pp. 32-34). In any case, chronological correlations can be based on the treasure only by assuming that the latest cylinder seals—the Old Babylonian ones—and the silver vessels were added shortly before the hoard was buried. As far as Mesopotamia is concerned, one thus arrives at an approximate correlation of the Old Babylonian period with the Twelfth Dynasty.

The Ṭod silver vessels are the earliest known objects of Minoan style so far found in Egypt. They seem also to be the first actual examples of those Minoan metal vessels hitherto known only from pottery imitations of the Middle Minoan IIA and later periods (for Chapouthier's discussion, cf. de la Roque, Contenau, and Chapouthier, 1953, pp. 21-29). Characteristic forms for the delicate Kamares ware of Middle Minoan IIA are bowls and cups similar in shape to the Ṭod silver vessels and with painted designs patterned after the plain or torsional fluting of metallic models (Evans, 1921, p. 241, Fig. 181; Pl. 2, a; Sup. Pl. 3, b; Evans, 1935, p. 132, Fig. 100; compare de la Roque, 1950, Pls. 12, 70580; 13, 70583; 16, 70619; 17, 70623, 70624, 70627, 70629). Also found at Ṭod was a cup with Vaphio handle, for which the earliest known Minoan parallel is a Middle Minoan IIIA imitation in pottery of a metal prototype (Evans, 1921, Fig. 183, b, 1, facing p. 242); we must rely upon the Ṭod specimen itself as proof that this typical Minoan handle type was already known in Middle Minoan II. Ten years ago the similarities between the Ṭod silver vessels and Middle Minoan IIA pottery ones seemed sufficient for them to be considered contemporary, thus enabling the treasure to be used as indication that the first phase of Middle Minoan II existed as early as the reign of Amenemhet II in Egypt (cf. now Chapouthier, in de la Roque, Contenau, and Chapouthier, 1953, pp. 21-29, 34). Although there is disagreement on this question (Albright, 1954, pp. 32-33; Åstrom, 1957, pp. 259-60), such a conclusion still seems likely.

If accepted, the Minoan-Egyptian correlation provided by the Ṭod treasure supplements the information provided by the three much discussed occurrences of Middle Minoan II pottery in Egypt (Pendlebury, 1939, pp. 144-45; S. Smith, 1945, pp. 1-3; Matz, 1950, pp. 173-74), pushing back the existence of Middle Minoan IIA to at least a period contemporary with Amenemhet II. Previously, the earliest known date for the importation of Minoan objects was the reign of Amenemhet II's son Sesostris II. Middle Minoan IIA sherds from Harageh were found in isolated shallow dumps of town debris, not associated with any houses (Fig. 3, 17). Aside from certain coarse Twelfth Dynasty pottery types, the only datable object in the dumps was a stone with the name of Sesostris II, whose pyramid and pyramid town lie in the neighborhood. The second Egyptian site with Minoan pottery is in the south, at Abydos, an indication of the wide distribution of Minoan ceramics in Egypt; the bridge-spouted jar in question, of a transitional Middle Minoan IIA-B type (Fig. 3, 18), unfortunately comes from a shaft in a disturbed tomb, other shafts of which contained cylinder seals with the names of Sesostris III and Amenemhet III, whose dates cannot be assigned with certainty to the Minoan vessel.

The third find of Minoan pottery—in this case belonging to the Middle Minoan IIB phase (Fig. 3, 12, 13)—was made both in a room within, and in rubbish heaps outside, the pyramid city of Sesostris II at Kahun, a settlement occupied not only during the reign of that king but also in the Second Intermediate period. The various Kahun deposits contain a Middle Cypriote White Painted III-IV Pendent Line jug and various Syrian sherds of types that can hardly be earlier than the Second Intermediate period. This evidence contradicts Petrie's belief that the external rubbish heaps must have belonged to the reign of Sesostris II, that is, at a time when the city was still fully occupied, so that debris had to be dumped outside the settlement instead of into empty houses, and that the deposits in the town dated to the Twelfth Dynasty. The Kahun heaps and the village itself contained also black, incised and white-filled Tell el Yahudiyah ware, which usually occurs in the form of juglets. In Egypt, this ware was most common during the Second Intermediate period. There has been considerable uncertainty as to when it first appeared both in Egypt, where only some isolated juglets have been attributed to the Twelfth Dynasty (Fig. 3, 11; Randall-MacIver and Woolley, 1911, Pl. 92, 10869, 10875), and in the East, where there are only a few possible examples in Middle Bronze IIA (Engberg, 1939, pp. 26-28; Säve-Söderbergh, 1941, pp. 124-26). These finds are not sufficient to establish an early date for the ware, so that its appearance at Kahun supports a Second Intermediate dating for the various pottery deposits (cf. detailed lists and discussion in Åstrom, 1957, pp. 233-39). Despite the imprecision surrounding the Kahun deposits (ibid., pp. 212-13), they do suggest a Second Intermediate context for the Middle Bronze IIB sherds found there. Altogether, the evidence available from Egypt points to a general synchronization of Middle Minoan IIB with the end of that dynasty and a part of the Second Intermediate period.

It would perhaps be misleading to say that in the Second Intermediate period Egypt's connections with Syria and Palestine gained a new intensity. There had already been intimate connection in the Twelfth Dynasty, but then the relationship was that of a dominating power, traces of whose influence are found in client areas (statues of Egyptian officials and princesses, Egyptian gifts in royal tombs at Byblos, and the like), while in Egypt itself there are only instances of imported luxury objects (silver vessels, thin Kamares ware). Now, in the Second Intermediate period, the situation is altered. In this period of political instability and foreign domination, we have the beginnings of widespread commerce linking Egypt, Palestine, Syria, and Cyprus. Thus in many Egyptian and Nubian sites there are examples of Middle Bronze IIB Syro-Palestinian pottery—Tell el Yahudiyah juglets (Fig. 3, 6, 7), plain red polished juglets (Fig. 3, 5), painted juglets (Fig. 3, 3, 4) and flasks (Fig. 3, 2), and vessels closely related to Cypriote White Painted V ware (Figs. 3, 1; 7, A). In addition to these normally found foreign types, there occur in Egypt a few vessels painted with designs characteristic of the Tell el Ajjul ware in Asia (Säve-Söderbergh, 1951, p. 58; Heurtley, 1939) but not executed in bichrome paint (Fig. 7, B-E). In Egypt such vessels can be assigned to the latest part of the Second Intermediate period; one of them (Fig. 7, C) was described by Petrie as a "Syrian flask of the XVIIIth dynasty" (Petrie, 1914, p. 12). Since the Tell el Ajjul ware in Palestine, Syria, and Cyprus is typical of Late Bronze I, the pots of Figure 7, B-E, show evidence that the beginning of Late Bronze I in western Asia overlapped the end of the Second Intermediate period in Egypt, a synchronism not indicated in Figure 3 for lack of space. All the vessels cited, both the actual imports and those showing the influence of foreign prototypes, illustrate the beginning of that intense international trade and communication which was typical of the Late Bronze period and was not checked until the catastrophic incursions of Sea Peoples at the end of the Nineteenth Dynasty.

Perhaps the most remarkable of the foreign vessels assignable to the Second Intermediate period is a jar from the excavations of the Metropolitan Museum of Art at Lisht, not yet published in detail. A tomb shaft (879) near the northern, Amenemhet I, pyramid, apparently made during the Twelfth Dynasty and containing some Twelfth Dynasty types of material, seems to have been either reused in the Second Intermediate period or contaminated by pottery from the Second Intermediate period village that existed in the area. The shaft contained, in addition to Tell el Yahudiyah juglet fragments, a vase unique in Egypt but belonging to a typical Palestinian and Syrian type known at the end of the Middle Bronze IIA period but common in Middle Bronze IIB (Fig. 6, D-F). This vase is not merely a normal import from Palestine, however, but is outstanding for its decoration—decoration utterly unparalleled in both Egypt and Palestine (Fig. 6, A, B). The designs are executed in a red wash, with borders and interior details incised and filled with white pigment. Although the ungainly geese seem unparalleled, the dolphins are somewhat clumsy imitations of Middle Minoan IIIB dolphins, motifs borrowed from wall paintings by the Minoan pot painters. In technique the Lisht dolphins have affinities both with their white-outlined Minoan prototypes and with the incised, white-filled decoration of Tell el Yahudiyah juglets. The synchronism between the Second Intermediate period in Egypt, Middle Minoan III in Crete, and the Middle Bronze IIB in Palestine is, of course, already well established by other finds in Egypt and elsewhere, but the dolphins of the Lisht jar are the first Middle Minoan III feature to be discovered in Egypt. Thus they form a most welcome counterblanace to the evidence for Egyptian, and also Syrian, influence on the development of the representational art of Middle Minoan III. The Lisht find provides what might hardly have been expected, the epitomization on a single vase of the intimacy of connections between Egypt, Syria-Palestine, and Crete in the final phase of Middle Bronze.

With the end of the Middle Bronze period, we have reached a time when the archaeological evidence for comparative chronology is, except for the Aegean area, but a supplement for the detailed synchronisms given by written historical sources, a situation in strong contrast to the earlier periods surveyed here, during which archaeological evidence is the primary source for relative chronology.

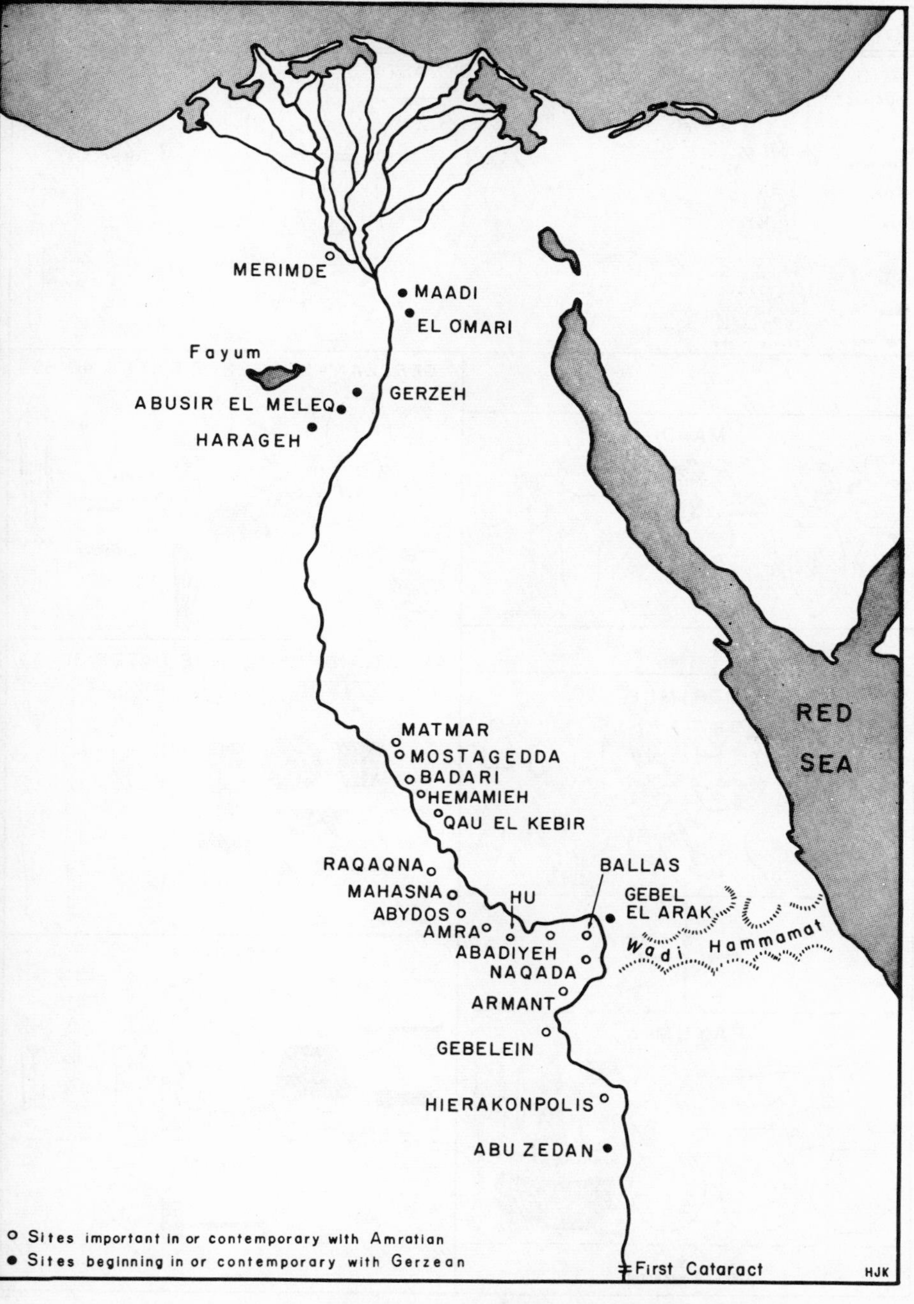

Fig. 1.—Sketch Map of Egypt, Showing the Distribution of Important Prehistoric Sites.

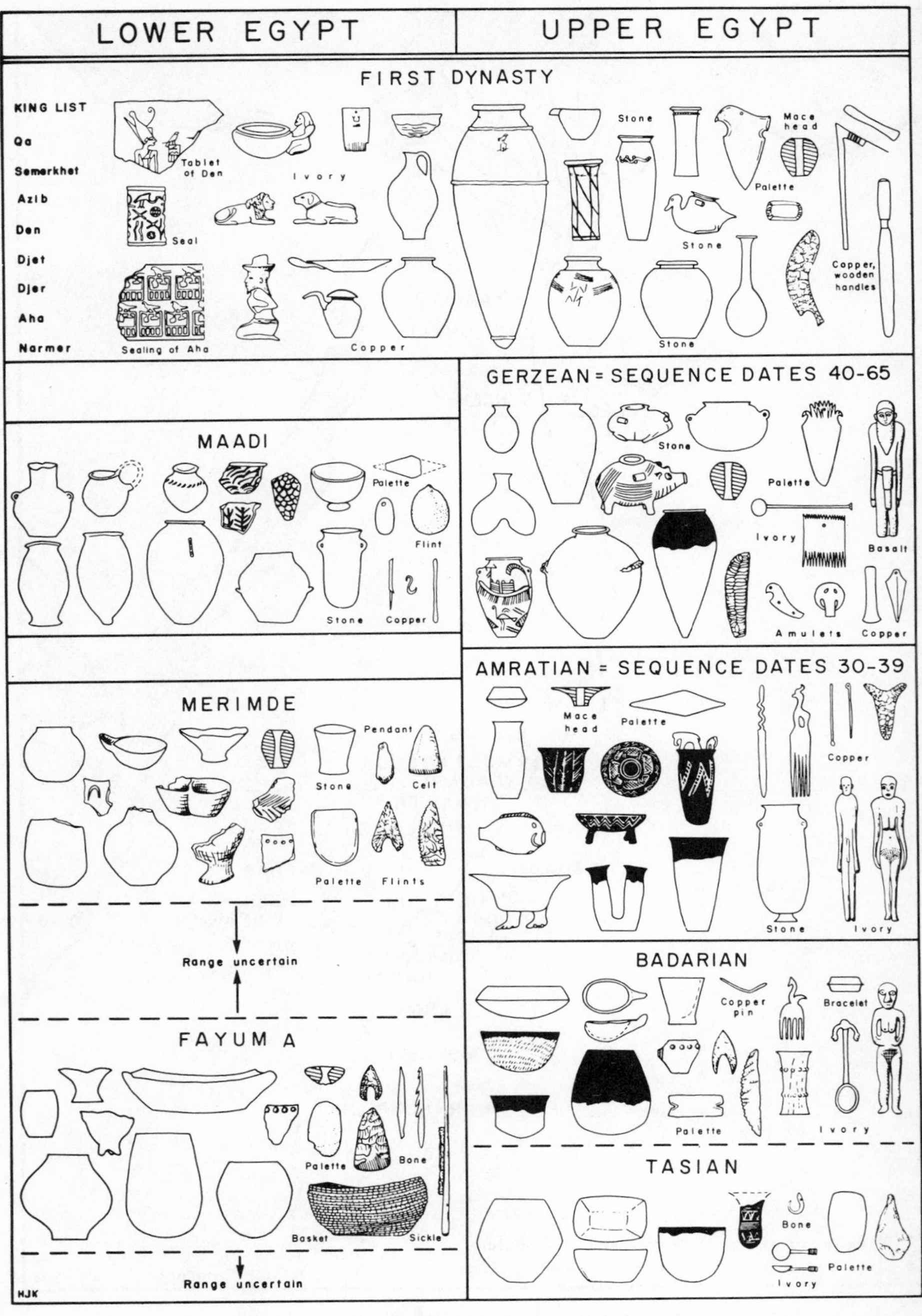

Fig. 2.—Assemblage Chart of the Cultures of Egypt in the Predynastic Periods and the First Dynasty.

FOREIGN FEATURES IN EGYPT	PAL. SYRIA	MES-POT.	CRETE
1570 B.C.			
SECOND INTERMEDIATE PERIOD = DYNASTIES XIII–XVII (1, 2, 3, 4, 5, 6, 7, 8)	MB II B	OLD BABY-LONIAN & ISIN LARSA	MM III A+B
1786 B.C.			
DYNASTY XII (9, 10, 11, 12, 13, 14, 15, 16, 17, 18)	MB II A	UR III	B MM II A / MIDDLE MINOAN I
1991 B.C.			
FIRST INTERMEDIATE PERIOD (DYNS. VII–X) & DYNASTY XI	MB I Amuq I–J	AKKADIAN	EM III
Ca. 2160 B.C.			
DYNASTIES IV–VI (19, 20, 21, 22, 23)	EB III Amuq H Ugarit III, 3 Byblos IV	ED III	EM II
Ca. 2620 B.C.			
DYNASTIES II–III (23 A)	EB II	ED II	EM I
Ca. 2900 B.C.			
DYNASTY I (24, 25, 26, 27, 28, 29, 30, 31)	Amuq G Byblos III	ED I	SUB & LATE NEOLITHIC
Ca. 3100 B.C.			
MAADI (33, 34, 35, 36) / LATE GERZEAN — ca. S.D. 50–65 (32, 37, 38, 39, 40, 41, 42, 43, 44, 45, 46, 47, 48, 49)	Amuq G Byblos II / EB I	PL C+D	
EARLY GERZEAN — ca. S.D. 40–50 (50, 51, 52)	Amuq F	PL A+B	
MERIMDE / AMRATIAN	GHASSULIAN		
FAYUM A / BADARIAN			
TASIAN			HJK

Fig. 3.—The Relative Chronology of Egypt and Other Parts of the Near East through the Middle Bronze Period.

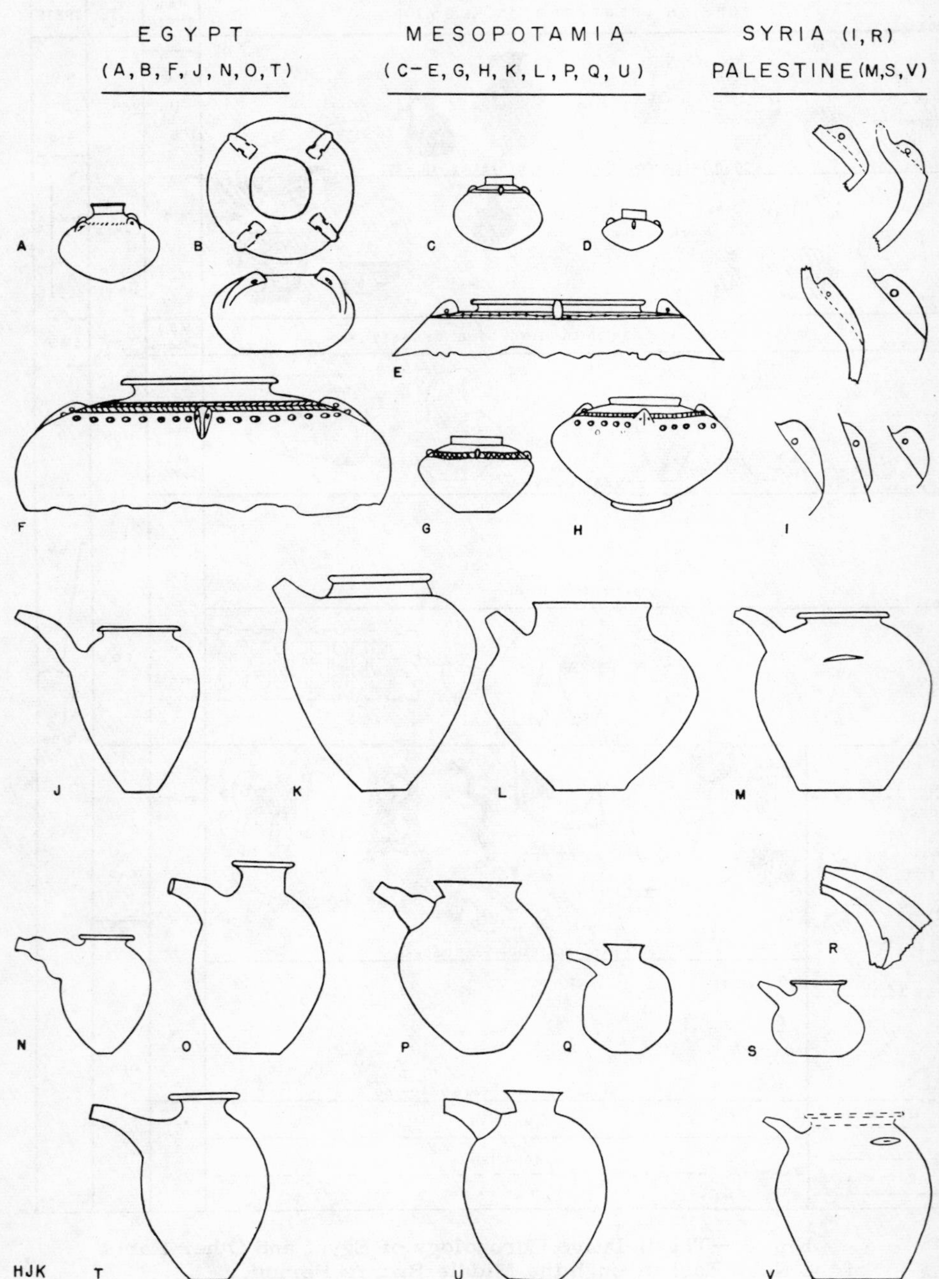

Fig. 4.—Mesopotamian Pottery Types in Prehistoric Egypt, Syria, and Palestine.

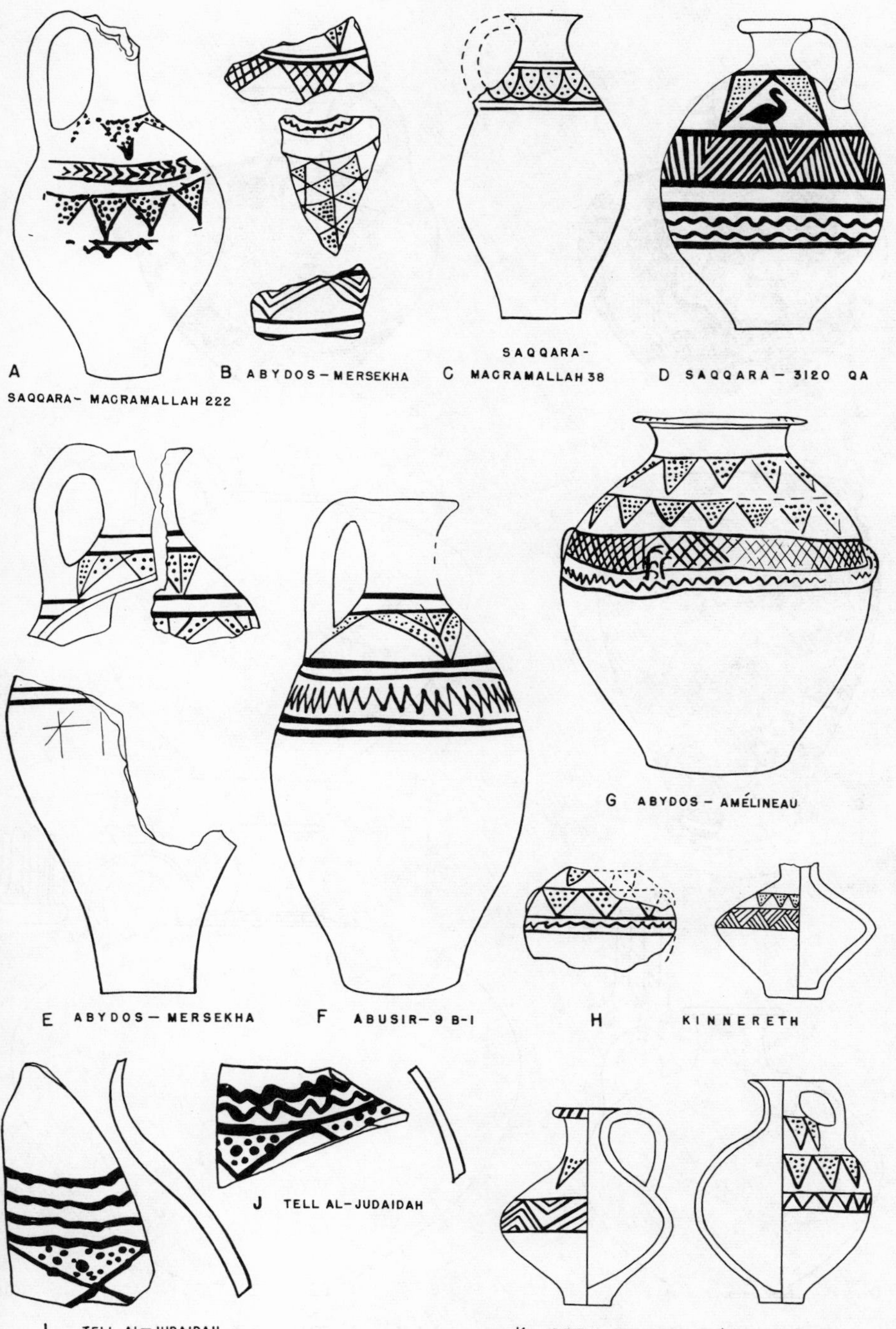

Fig. 5.—Light-Faced Painted Ware of the Early Bronze II Period.

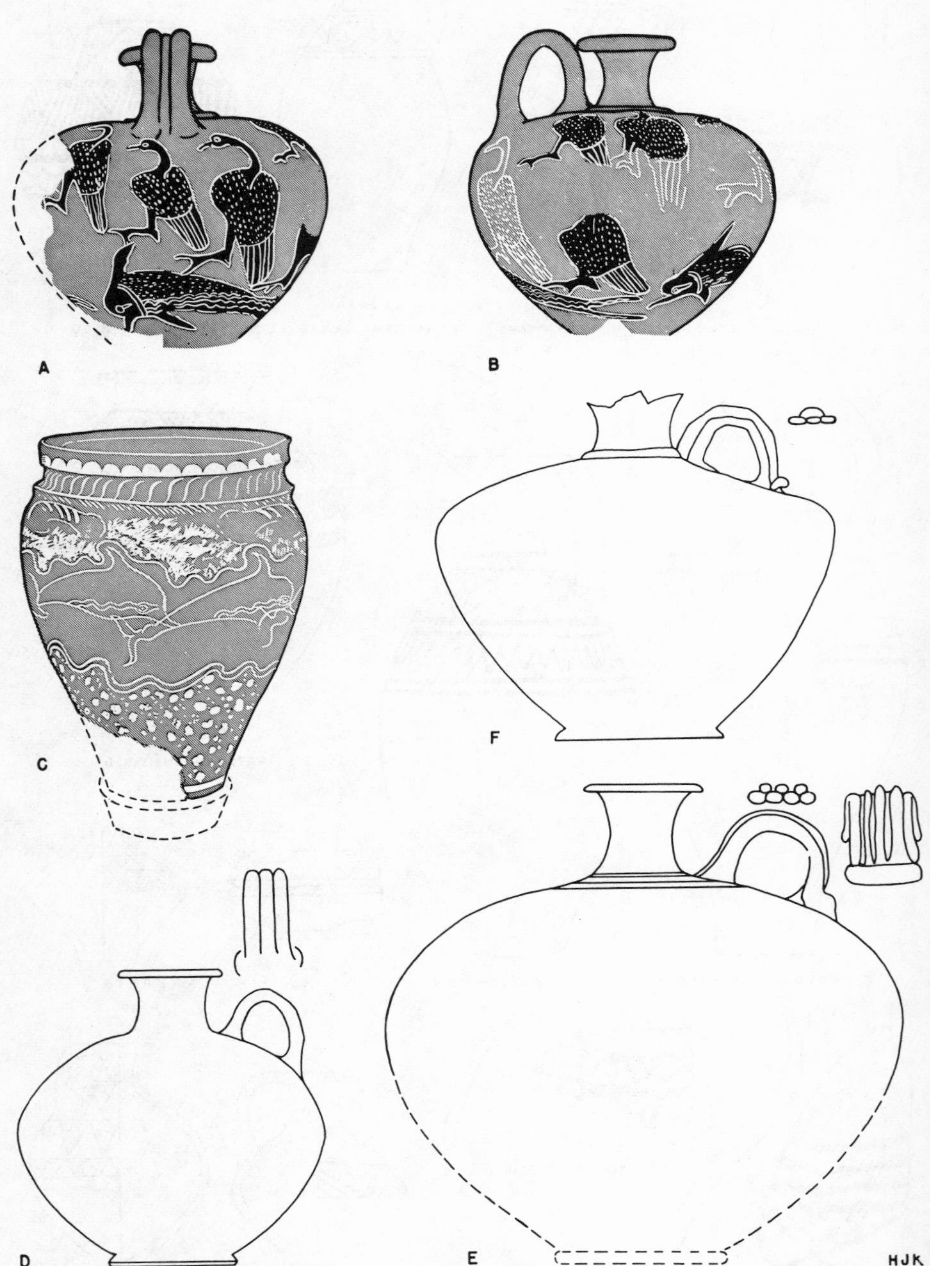

Fig. 6.—A Decorated Jar from Lisht (A, B) and Related Vessels.

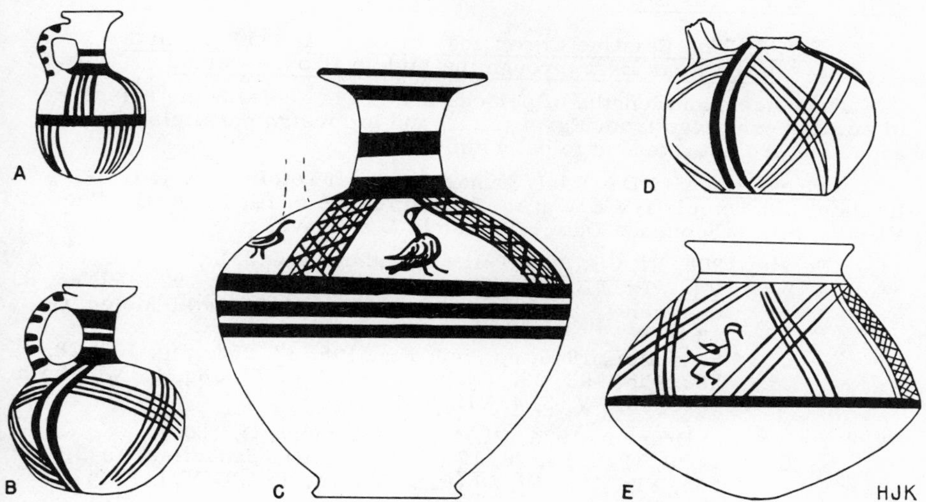

Fig. 7.—Vessels from Egypt Related to the Tell Ajjul Ware of Late Bronze I.

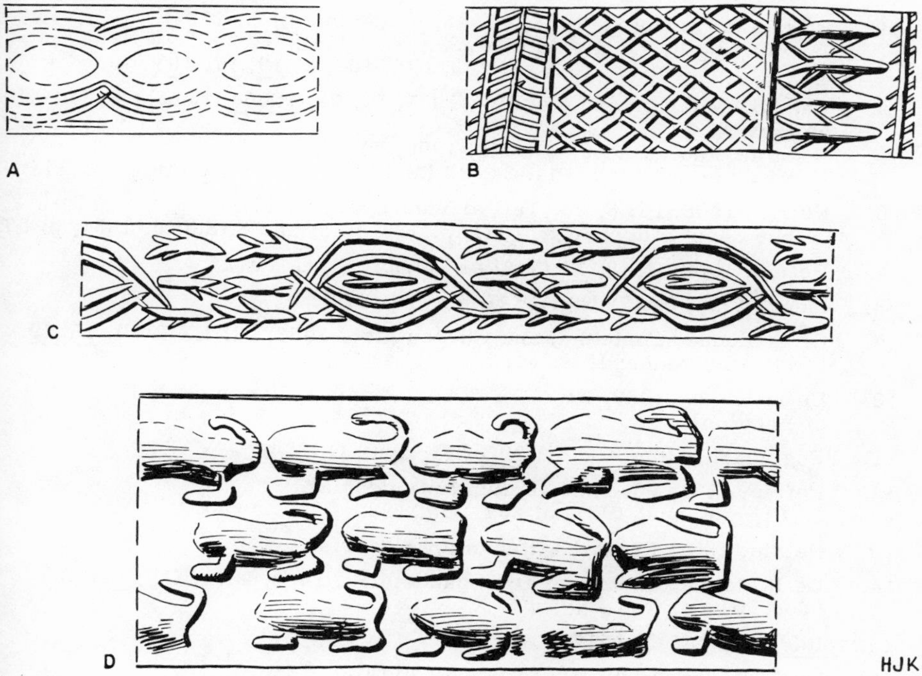

Fig. 8.—Protoliterate Cylinder Seals from Egypt.

Sources of Figures 3-8

Fig. 3: The Relative Chronology of Egypt and Other Parts of the Near East through the Middle Bronze Period

The objects and lengths of periods are not to scale. Some references to similar examples from Egypt (Sim.) and to foreign parallels (Cf.) are added but are not intended to be complete.

Abbreviations: ED = Early Dynasty; PL = Protoliterate (PL C-D = Khafaje, Sin Temple I-V & Warka, Archaic Stratum III; PL A-B = Warka, VII-IV); S.D. = Sequence Date; T = Tomb; G = Grave.

1. Petrie, 1906, Pl. 8B, 101 (Tell el Yahudiyah, G.52).
   Sim.: Ibid., Pl. 8B, 99, 102. Petrie and Brunton, 1924, Pl. 45, 69 (Sedment). Scharff, 1926, Pl. 76, 4 (Abusir el-Meleq, G. 48 g 7).
   Cf.: Schaeffer, 1949, pp. 249, Fig. 105, 37; 253, Fig. 107, 28; 255, Fig. 108, 23. Gjerstad, 1926, p. 72, Jug. 1. Westholm, 1939, Pls. V, 3, 4; VII, 3, 4.
2. Petrie and Brunton, 1924, Pl. 41, 16 (Sedment, G. 1300).
   Cf.: Loud, 1948, Pl. 26, 17 (Megiddo XII). Schaeffer, 1949, p. 255, Fig. 108, 19, 20 (Ras Shamra, T. LXXXV).
3. Randall-MacIver and Woolley, 1911, Pl. 49, 10501 (Buhen).
   Cf.: Guiges, 1938, Pl. 3, x, d; p. 44, Fig. 67, z. Ory, 1947-48, p. 79, Fig. 7.
4. Petrie and Brunton, 1924, Pl. 45, 67 (Sedment, G. 1262).
   Sim.: Ibid., Pl. 45, 68 (Sedment, G. 1254).
   Cf.: Schaeffer, 1949, p. 253, Fig. 107, 2, 10, 17, 18.
5. Randall-MacIver and Woolley, 1911, Pl. 92, 10864 (Buhen, K 44; red polished).
   Sim.: Ibid., Pl. 49. Petrie, 1906, Pl. VIII.
   Cf.: Loud, 1948, Pls. 24, 23 (Megiddo XII); 41, 6 (Megiddo X).
6. Petrie, 1906, Pl. 8, 50 (Tell el Yahudiyah, G. 37).
   See Säve-Söderbergh, 1941, p. 125, n. 5; and S. Smith, 1951, p. 57.
7. Petrie, 1906, Pl. 7, 13 (Tell el Yahudiyah, G. 407).
8. Mace, 1921, p. 17, Fig. 18 (Lisht, Pit 879).
9. De la Roque, Contenau, and Chapouthier, 1953, Pl. LXXXIII, 15160 (Ṭod; Amenemhet II; silver).
10. De la Roque, 1950, Pl. XIX, 70647 (Lapis cylinder seal; First Dyn. of Babylon).
11. Engelbach, 1923, Pl. 41, 99D (Harageh, G. 354).
12. Petrie, 1891, Pl. 1, 13 (Kahun town debris).
    Cf.: Evans, 1921, p. 267, Fig. 198.
13. Petrie, 1891, Pl. 1, 13 (Kahun town debris).
14. De la Roque, Contenau, and Chapouthier, 1953, Pl. XXXI, 15148 (Ṭod; silver).
15. Ibid., Pl. XXXI, 15172.
16. De la Roque, 1950, Pl. XVIII, 70630 (Ṭod; silver).
17. Evans, 1928, Pl. 9, g (Harageh).

18. Evans, 1921, p. 268, Fig. 199; see also Garstang, 1913, pp. 107-11.
    Cf.: Evans, 1921, p. 268.

19. Reisner, 1942, p. 437, Fig. 256 (Giza 2140A).
    Sim.: Ibid., pp. 467, Fig. 282; 468, Fig. 283; 472, Fig. 285; 476, Fig. 287; 489, Fig. 297, a; 509, Fig. 312. Brunton, 1948, Pl. 37, 2 (Matmar, G. 3209; Dyn. IV). Jequier, 1929, p. 26, Fig. 25 (South Saqqara; Dyn. VI).
    Cf.: Garstang, 1932, Pl. 6, 15-17 (Jericho, T. A). Schaeffer, 1949, p. 237, Fig. 99, 7, 9 (Ras Shamra III).

20. Reisner, 1942, p. 410, Fig. 234, c (Giza 1233A).

21. Ibid., p. 449, Fig. 274 (Giza 2170A).
    Cf.: Garstang, 1932, Pl. 27, 10 (Jericho, T. A).

22. Reisner, 1942, p. 410, Fig. 234 c, left (Giza 1233).
    Cf.: below, p. 74.

23. Schäfer and Andrae, 1942, p. 254, 2 (Asiatic booty, Mortuary Temple of Sahure, Abusir; Dyn. V).

23a. Saad, 1957, Pl. XXXIV, 3 (cf. also p. 60 and Plan J; T. 419 H8).

24. Petrie, 1902, Pl. 8, 2 (Abydos, T. of Djer).
    Sim.: Petrie et al., 1925, Pl. 4, 9, 10 (Abydos).
    Cf.: Garstang, 1932, Pl. 2, 11. Garstang, 1935, Pl. 31, 20.

25. Macramallah, 1940, Pl. 46, S_4 (Saqqara).
    Sim.: Petrie, 1902, Pl. 8, 8 (Abydos, T. of Djer).
    Cf.: De Vaux and Steve, 1948, p. 555, Fig. 4 (Tell el Fara near Nablus). Garstang, 1932, Pls. 12, 8; 20, b.

26. Petrie, 1902, Pl. 8, 2 (Abydos, T. of Djer).
    Sim.: Emery, 1949, p. 153, Fig. 86, G2. Emery, 1938, Pl. 26, left. Macramallah, 1940, Pl. 46, S_1.
    Cf.: Garstang, 1935, Pl. 27, 24.

27. Petrie, 1902, Pl. 8, 5 (Abydos, T. of Djer).
    Sim.: Ibid., Pl. 8, 4. Petrie et al., 1923, Pl. 53, 97, C, D, E (Bashkatib). Emery, 1938, Pl. 26, right. Emery, 1949, p. 152, Fig. 86, G1. Macramallah, 1940, Pl. 46, $S_{2,3,5,6}$.
    Cf.: Maisler, 1942, Pl. 1, 39 (Kinnereth; also many unpublished examples). Dunand, 1950, Pl. XXVI (Byblos). Engberg and Shipton, 1934, Chart, 11A, 11B.

28. Bonnet, 1928, Pl. 27, middle (Abusir, G. 9 B-1).

29. Macramallah, 1940, Pl. 46, S.

30. Petrie, 1901, Pl. 54 (Abydos, T. of Mersekha).
    Sim.: Petrie, 1902, Pl. 6, 17.
    Cf.: Engberg and Shipton, 1934, Chart, 8C. Garstang, 1935, Pl. 29, 12, 13.

31. Emery, 1939, Pl. I (Saqqara, plan of elaborately niched, brick mastaba).
    See: Frankfort, 1951, Appendix.

32. Scharff, 1926, Pl. 13, 59 (Abusir el-Meleq, G. 1019; beginning of Dyn. I).
    Cf.: Marquet-Krause, 1949, Pls. 71, 774; 72, 824.

33. Menghin, 1934, Pl. 19, c, f (Maadi).
    Cf.: Marquet-Krause, 1949, Pls. 70, 674; 89, 862. Fitzgerald, 1935, Pl. 5, 26 (Beth Shan XV).

34. Menghin and Amer, 1932, Pl. 34, 2 (Maadi).

35. Menghin, 1934, Pl. 19, c, 5.
    Cf.: Garstang, 1936, Pl. 36, 2 (Jericho VI). Rowe, 1935, Pl. 3.

36. Menghin and Amer, 1932, Pl. 32, 4.

37. Petrie, 1921, Pl. 19, Fancy 99 (Gerzeh; G. 94; S.D. 47-70).
    Cf.: Macalister, 1912, Pl. 44, 2. Sukenik, 1948, Pl. 12, 13.

38. Petrie, 1921, Pl. 28, Wavy 14.

39. Frankfort, 1924, Pl. 13, 1 (ship on jar of the simplified "Decorated" style, British Museum).
    Cf.: Heinrich, 1936, Pl. 17, a.

40. Brunton and Caton-Thompson, 1928, Pl. 40, Decorated 67p (Badari, G. 1728; S.D. 46-57[?]).
    Cf.: Garstang, 1935, Pl. 36, 2 (Jericho VI). Sukenik, 1948, Pl. 12, 14. Vincent, 1911, Pl. 9, 1.

41. Brunton, 1937, Pl. 36, Rough 28 (Mostagedda, G. 11719).
    Sim.: Petrie, 1921, Pl. 13, Polished red 79.

42. Brunton, 1928, Pl. 40, Decorated 59w.

43. Scharff, 1926, Pl. 41, 5 (Abusir el-Meleq, G. 7 g 5).
    Sim.: Petrie, 1921, Pl. 15, Fancy 5a and 5b (Naqada). Brunton, 1937, Pl. 39, 15.
    Cf.: Engberg and Shipton, 1934, Chart, 18A (Megiddo, Stages VII-IV). Fitzgerald, 1935, Pl. 5, 28 (Beth Shan XV). Macalister, 1912, Vol. III, Pl. 48 (Gezer, Cave VII). Sukenik, 1948, Pl. 12, 2. Wampler, 1947, Pl. 52, 1124 (T. 67).

    Two stone examples of bowls with conoid projections are known: one from an "early deposit" at Megiddo (Engberg and Shipton, 1934, p. 63, Fig. 17), and another from the Step Pyramid complex of Djoser at Saqqara (Lauer, 1939, Pl. 17, 10). The great deposits of stone vessels of the Step Pyramid included examples made in the First Dynasty. The knobbed bowl may be assigned to that period or perhaps even to a slightly earlier time. It was apparently, like the Egyptian one-handled pitchers of stone (Lauer, 1939, Pls. 17, 12; 18, 6; Emery, 1949, p. 144, Fig. 77, DD1), an imitation in stone of a foreign pottery type. The Badarian and Fayum A sherds with small knobs (Brunton, 1937, Pl. 18, Miscellaneous 39, 40; Caton-Thompson and Gardner, 1934, Pl. 17, 24, 25) do not provide Egyptian prototypes for the knobbed bowls, since they are of quite different character.

44. Petrie, 1921, Pl. 18, Fancy 58K.

45. Brunton, 1937, Pl. 35, Miscellaneous 24.

46. Quibell and Green, 1902, Pl. 28 (from Small Hierakonpolis palette).
    Cf.: Frankfort, 1939, Pls. 4, d, f, h; 5, h. Heinrich, 1937, Pl. 15, i.

47. Capart, 1904, p. 68, Fig. 33 (from gold handle of Gebel Tarif ripple-flaked flint knife; cf. Amiet, 1957, p. 129, Figs. 7, 8.

48. Schäfer and Andrae, 1942, p. 185, 2 (from ivory handle of Gebel el-Arak ripple-flaked flint knife).
Cf.: Frankfort, 1939, Pl. 4, 1. Heinrich, 1936, Pl. 15, b. Schäfer and Andrae, 1942, p. 471.

49. Petrie, 1953, Pl. F (from Small Hierakonpolis palette).

50. Petrie, 1921, Pl. 28, Wavy 3 (Naqada; S.D. 45, 53).
Cf.: Engberg and Shipton, 1934, Chart, 12P, 14G, H (Megiddo, Stage VII). Fitzgerald, 1935, Pl. 2, 1-5, 7-9 (Beth Shan XVII-XVI). De Vaux and Steve, 1949, p. 113, Fig. 1, 26 (Tell el Fara, T.3).

51. Petrie, 1921, Pl. 18, Fancy 58a.

52. Ibid., Pl. 18, Fancy 58B.

Fig. 4: Mesopotamian Pottery Types in Prehistoric Egypt, Syria, and Palestine

Note that certain Egyptian vessels—crudely made bowls of the "Rough" and "Late" classes with angular rims (Petrie, 1921, Pls. 38, 26 B, C; 45, 7 D, E, G)—have been identified with the famous Mesopotamian beveled-rim bowls characteristic of the Protoliterate period (Baumgartel, 1947, p. 93; Burton-Brown, 1951, pp. 247 and n. 12, 263, 266; Burton-Brown, 1946, pp. 36-37, also quoted Protodynastic and Old Kingdom bread pots as pertinent). This correlation must be emphatically denied. Any seeming similarity between the two classes of bowls is purely illusory, possibly a misapprehension caused by comparison of simplified line drawings. In their thickness, broad beveled rims, and specific formation (Delougaz, 1952, pp. 39, 127-128; Pls. 21, 168, G.002.210), the Mesopotamian bowls are completely unlike any bowls known from Egypt. So far, the Amuq and Hama remain the farthest western areas yielding beveled-rim bowls (Delougaz, 1952, Pl. 168, C.002.210).

A. Brunton, 1937, Pl. 35, 24 (Mostagedda, G. 1837; no date).

B. Brunton, 1948, Pl. 12, Decorated 22 (Matmar, G 5112; S.D. 58).

C. Mackay, 1931, Pl. 64, 6 (Jemdet Nasr).

D. Ibid., Pl. 64, 4.

E. Mackay, 1931, Pl. 64, 3.

F. Brunton, 1928, Pl. 40, Decorated 59w (Badari, Area 3800; no date).

G. Mackay, 1931, Pl. 64, 12.

H. De Genouillac et al., 1939, Pl. 25, 2 (Telloh; cf. ibid., p. 35 and Pl. A, bottom).

I. Braidwood, 1960, p. 272, Fig. 213, 1-7 (Amuq, Phase G).

J. Petrie, 1921, Pl. 18, Fancy 58K (Diospolis, G. U 187A; S.D. 61).

K. Delougaz, 1952, Pl. 182, C 535.242 (Khafaje; two examples, one PL C, one PL D).

L. Ibid., Pl. 182, C 334.222 (Khafaje: two examples, one PL C, one PL D).

M. Iliffe, 1936, p. 121, No. 63 (Ras el Ain; EB I).

N. Brunton, 1928, Pl. 38, Fancy 581 (Badari, Area 4600; no date).

O. Petrie, 1921, Pl. 18, Fancy 59B (Naqada, G.1619; S.D. 38).

P. Nöldeke et al., 1932, Pl. 19, B, z (Warka VI; PL A).

Q. Ibid., Pl. 19, B, w (Warka VI; PL A).

R. Braidwood, 1960, p. 272, Fig. 213, 18 (Amuq, Phase G).

S. De Vaux, 1951, p. 584, Fig. 12, 2 (Tell el Fara, T. 12; Early Bronze

T. Petrie, 1921, Pl. 18, Fancy 58a (Naqada, G.1211; not dated; Petrie's range for type is S.D. 40-58).

U. Nöldeke, et al., 1932, Pl. 19, D, ć (Warka V; PL B).

V. De Vaux, 1951, p. 584, Fig. 12, 4 (Tell el Fara, T. 12; Early Bronze

Fig. 5: Light-faced Painted Ware of the Early Bronze II Period

A. Macramallah, 1940, Pl. 50, 2 (Saqqara, G. 222).

B. Petrie, 1901, Pl. 54 (Abydos, T. of Mersekha).

C. Macramallah, 1940, p. 32, Fig. 28, 5 (Saqqara, T. 38).

D. Emery, 1949, p. 124, Fig. 68 (Saqqara, Archaic Cemetery, T. 3120; reign of Qa).

E. Petrie, 1901, Pl. 54, top middle (Abydos, T. of Mersekha).

F. Bonnet, 1928, Pl. 27, middle (Abusir, G. 9 B-1).

G. Amélineau, 1899, Pl. 13, lower row, pot 4 (Abydos, no find spot).

H. Maisler, 1942, Pl. 1, 45 and Amiran, 1963, p. 87, Pl. 17, 7 (Kinnere

I,J. Braidwood, R. J. and L. S., 1960, pp. 359, Fig. 279, 1 (Amuq H); 288 Fig. 227, 5 (Amuq G).

K. Fitzgerald, 1931, Pl. XXX, 1 (Beth Shan, Terrace).

L. Kenyon, 1960, p. 88, Fig. 25, 34 (Jericho, T. A 127).

Fig. 6: A Decorated Jar from Lisht (A, B) and Related Vessels

A,B. Mace, 1921, p. 17, Fig. 18 (Lisht, Pit 879; Hayes, 1959, pp. 12-13). I am much indebted to Dr. W. C. Hayes for information concerning Pit 879 and for the photographs from which these drawings were made.

C. Evans, 1921, p. 608, Fig. 477a (Pachyammos).

D. Loud, 1948, Pl. 31, 6 (Megiddo XI).

E. Garstang, 1934, Pl. 21, 13 (Jericho, Palace). Ory, 1947-48, p. 81, Fig. 14 (Dharat el Humaraiya, G 14).

F. Garstang, 1934, Pl. 23, 4 (Jericho, Palace, storeroom 44).

Fig. 7: Vessels from Egypt Related to the Tell Ajjul Ware of Late Bronze I

A. Petrie and Brunton, 1924, Pl. 45, 69 (Sedment, G. 1289).
Cf.: Fig. 3, 1.

B. Ibid., Pl. 45, 70 (Sedment, G. 1289).
Cf.: Guy, 1938, Pl. 41, 27 (Megiddo, T. 77). Heurtley, 1939, Pl. 8, h (Tell el Ajjul). Westholm, 1939, Pl. 7, 9 (Milia, T. 15).

C. Petrie, 1914, Pl. 9, 25 (Tarkhan, G. 821).

D. Petrie and Brunton, 1924, Pl. 45, 71 (Sedment, G. 1270).
Cf.: Schaeffer, 1949, p. 233, Fig. 98, 15 (Ras Shamra, T. XXXV). Heurtley, 1939, Pls. 8, d, e, f (Tell el Ajjul); 23, h (Milia).

E. Brunton, 1930, Pl. 16, 55P (Qau, G. 902).

Fig. 8: Protoliterate Cylinder Seals from Egypt

A. Kantor, 1952, p. 243, Fig. 1, A (Naqada, Grave T. 29; ca. S.D. 48-66).

B. Ibid., Fig. 1, B (Naga ed-Der G. 7304; ca. S.D. 55-60).

C. Ibid., Fig. 1, D (purchased in Luxor).

D. Ibid., Fig. 1, E (Berlin 20099).

Bibliography

Åstrom, P.

1957 The Middle Cypriote Bronze Age. Lund.

Aharoni, Y., and Amiran, R.

1964 "Arad: A Biblical City in Southern Palestine," Archaeology XVII: 43-53.

Amélineau, E.

1899 Les nouvelles fouilles d'Abydos, 1895-1896. Paris.

Amiet, P.

1957 "Glyptique susienne archaique," Revue d'assyriologie LI: 121-29.
1961 La glyptique mésopotamienne archaique. Paris.
1963 "La glyptique syrienne archaique," Syria XL: 57-83.

Amiran, R.

1963 Hakiramika hakadima shel Eretz-Israel (The Ancient Pottery of Eretz Yisrael). Jerusalem.

Arkell, A. J., and Ucko, P. J.

1965 "Review of Predynastic Development in the Nile Valley," Current Anthropology VI: 145-66.

Baumgartel, E. J.

1947 The Cultures of Prehistoric Egypt. Vol. I. (Rev. ed., 1955) Oxford.
1960 Ibid. Rev. ed., Vol. II. Oxford.

Bénédite, G. A.

1916 "Le Couteau de Gebel el-'Arak," Commission de la Fondation Piot, Monuments et mémoires XXII: 1-34.
1918 "The Carnarvon Ivory," Journal of Egyptian Archaeology V: 1-15.

Bonnet, H.

1928 Ein frühgeschichtliches Gräberfeld bei Abusir. Leipzig.

Bono, F. de

1945 "Helouan-El Omari: Fouilles du Service des Antiquités, 1934-1935," Chronique d'Égypte XXI: 50-54.
1951 "Expédition archéologique royale au désert oriental (Keft-Kosseir): Rapport préliminaire sur la campagne 1949," Annales du Service des Antiquités de l'Egypte LI, Part I: 59 ff.

Braidwood, R. J., and L. S.

1960 Excavations in the Plain of Antioch, Vol. I: The Earlier Assemblages: Phases A-J. Chicago.

Brunton, G.

1932 "The Predynastic Town-site at Hierakonpolis," Studies presented to F. Ll. Griffith, pp. 272-76. London.
1937 Mostagedda and the Tasian Culture. London.
1948 Matmar. London.

Brunton, G., and Caton-Thompson, G.

1928 The Badarian Civilization and Predynastic Remains near Badari. London.

Burton-Brown, T.

1946 Studies in Third Millennium History. London.
1951 Excavations in Azarbaijan, 1948. London.

Butzer, K. W.

1959 Die Naturlandschaft Ägyptens während der Vorgeschichte und der dynastischen Zeit, Abhandlungen der Akademie der Wissenschaften, Mainz, Math-Naturwissen. Kl., No. 2.

Capart, J.

1904 Les Débuts de l'art en Égypte. Brussels.

Capart, J., and Werbrouck, M.

1930 Memphis à l'ombre des pyramides. Brussels.

Caton-Thompson, G., and Gardner, E. W.

1934 The Desert Fayum. London.

Chehab, M.

1939 "Tombes phéniciennes, Sin el Fil," Mélanges syriens offert à M. René Dussaud, Vol. II. Paris.

Delougaz, P.

1952 Pottery from the Diyala Region. Chicago.

Delougaz, P., and Lloyd, S.

1942 Pre-Sargonid Temples in the Diyala Region. Chicago.

Drioton, E., and Vandier, J.

1952 Les Peuples de l'Orient méditerranéen, Vol. II: L'Égypte. 3d ed. Paris.

Dunand, M.

1939 Fouilles de Byblos, Vol. I. 1926-1932. Paris.
1950 Fouilles de Byblos, Vol. II. 1933-1938. Paris.

Ehrich, A. M. H.

1939 Early Pottery of the Jebeleh Region. Philadelphia.

Emery, W. B.

1938 Excavations at Saqqara: The Tomb of Hemaka. Cairo.
1939 Excavations at Saqqara, 1937-1938: Hor-Aha. Cairo.
1949 Great Tombs of the First Dynasty, Vol. I. Cairo.
1961 Archaic Egypt. Harmondsworth.

Engberg, R. M.

1939 The Hyksos Reconsidered. Chicago.

Engberg, R. M., and Shipton, G. M.

1934 Notes on the Chalcolithic and Early Bronze Pottery of Megiddo. Chicago.

Evans, A.

1921 The Palace of Minos, Vol. I. London.
1928 The Palace of Minos, Vol. II. London.
1930 The Palace of Minos, Vol. III. London.
1935 The Palace of Minos, Vol. IV. London.

Fitzgerald, G. M.

1931 Beth-Shan Excavations 1921-1923. Philadelphia.
1935 "The Earliest Pottery of Beth Shan," The Museum Journal, University Museum, University of Pennsylvania XXIV: 5-22.

Frankfort, H.

1924 Studies in Early Pottery of the Near East. London.
1932 Archaeology and the Sumerian Problem. Chicago.
1939 Cylinder Seals. London.
1951 The Birth of Civilization in the Near East. Bloomington, Ind.
1953 "Pyramid Temples and the Religion of the Old Kingdom," Bibliotheca orientalis X: 157-62.
1955 Stratified Cylinder Seals from the Diyala Region. Chicago.

Gardiner, A.

1961 Egypt of the Pharaohs. Oxford.

Garstang, J.

1913 "Note on a Vase of Minoan Fabric from Abydos (Egypt)," Liverpool Annals of Archaeology and Anthropology V: 107-11.
1932 "Jericho: City and Necropolis, Second Report," ibid. XIX: 3-22.
1933 "Jericho: City and Necropolis, Third Report," ibid. XX: 3-42.
1934 "Jericho: City and Necropolis, Fourth Report," ibid. XXI: 99-1
1936 "Jericho: City and Necropolis, Sixth Report," ibid. XXIII: 67-10

Genouillac, H. de, et al.

1934 Fouilles de Telloh, Vol. I: Époques présargoniques. Paris.

Gjerstad, E.

1926 Studies on Prehistoric Cyprus. Uppsala.

Goldman, H.

1954 "The Relative Chronology of Southeastern Anatolia." In Relative Chronologies in Old World Archeology, pp. 69-85. Ed. by R. W. Ehrich. Chicago.

Guiges, P. E.

1938 "Lébéa, Kafer-Ğarra, Qraye: nécropoles de la région sidonienne," Bulletin du Musée de Beyrouth II: 27-72.

Guy, P. L. O.

1938 Megiddo Tombs. Chicago.

Hayes, W. C.

1959 The Scepter of Egypt, Part II. Cambridge, Mass.

1964 "Most Ancient Egypt: Chapter III: The Neolithic and Chalcolithic Communities of Northern Egypt," Journal of Near Eastern Studies XXIII: 217-72.

Hayes, W. C., Rowton, M. B., and Stubbins, F. H.

1962 "Chronology: Egypt; Western Asia; Aegean Bronze Age." In The Cambridge Ancient History. Cambridge.

Heinrich, E.

1936 Kleinfunde aus den archäischen Tempelschichten in Uruk. ("Ausgrabungen der Deutschen Forschungsgemeinschaft in Uruk-Warka," Vol. I.) Berlin.

Helck, W.

1962 Die Beziehungen Ägyptens zu Vorderasien im 3. und 2. Jahrtausend v. Chr. Wiesbaden.

Hestrin, R., and Tadmor, M.

1963 "A Hoard of Tools and Weapons from Kfar Monash," Israel Exploration Journal XIII: 265-88.

Heurtley, W. A.

1939 "A Palestinian Vase Painter of the Sixteenth Century B.C.," Quarterly of the Department of Antiquities in Palestine VIII: 21-37.

Iliffe, J. H.

1936 "Pottery from Ras el 'Ain," Quarterly of the Department of Antiquities in Palestine V: 113-26.

Jéquier, G.

1929 Tombeaux de particuliers contemporaines de Pepi II. Cairo.

Junker, H.

1945 Report of Service des Antiquités on Seventh Season (1939) at Merimde, Chronique d'Egypte XX: 74-75.

Kaiser, W.

1956 "Stand und Problem der ägyptischen Vorgeschichtsforschung," Zeitschrift für ägyptische Sprache und Altertumskunde, LXXXI: 87-109.

1957 "Zur inneren Chronologie der Naqadakultur," Archaeologia Geographica, VI: 69-77.

Kantor, H. J.

1944 "The Final Phase of Predynastic Culture: Gerzean or Semainean (?)," Journal of Near Eastern Studies III: 110-36.

1947 Review of Baumgartel (1947) in American Journal of Archaeology LIII: 76-79.

1952 "Further Evidence for Early Mesopotamian Relations with Egypt," Journal of Near Eastern Studies XI: 239-50.

1956 "Syro-Palestinian Ivories," Journal of Near Eastern Studies XV: 153-74.

Kaplan, J.

1959 "The Connections of the Palestinian Chalcolithic Culture with Prehistoric Egypt," Israel Exploration Journal IX: 134-36.

Keimer, L.

1944 Études de égyptologie, No. VI. Cairo.

Kenyon, K.

1960 Excavations at Jericho, Vol. I. Jerusalem.

Landsberger, B.

1954 "Assyrische Königsliste und 'Dunkles Zeitalter,'" Journal of Cuneiform Studies VIII: 31-73, 106-33.

Larsen, H.

1957 "Verzierte Tongefässescherben aus Merimde Benisalame" Orientalia Suecana VI: 3-53.

Lauer, J.-P.

1939 La Pyramide à dégres, Vol. III: Compléments. Cairo.

Libby, W. F.

1955 Radiocarbon Dating, 2d ed. Chicago.

Loud, G.

1948 Megiddo II: Seasons of 1935-39. Chicago.

Macalister, R. S.

1912 The Excavation of Gezer. London.

Mace, A. C.

1921 "The Egyptian Expedition, 1920-21: Excavations at Lisht," Bulletin of the Metropolitan Museum of Art XVI, Dec., Part II, 5-19.

Mackay, E.

1931 Report on Excavations at Jemdet Nasr, Iraq. Chicago.

Macramallah, R.

1940 Un Cimetière archaïque de la classe moyenne du peuple à Saqqarah. Cairo.

Maisler, B.

1942 "An Early Bronze Age Tomb Found at Kinnereth," Bulletin of the Jewish Palestine Exploration Society X, No. 1.

Marquet-Krause, J.

1949 Les Fouilles de 'Ay (et-Tell), 1933-1935. Paris.

Matz, F.

1950 "Zur ägäischen Chronologie der frühen Bronzezeit," Historia I: 173-94.

Menghin, O.

1934 "Die Grabung der Universität Kairo bei Maadi: Drittes Jahrgang," Mitteilungen des Deutschen Instituts für ägyptische Altertumskunde in Kairo, Vol. V.

Mond, R.

1937 The Cemeteries of Armant. London.

New York Times

1964 "Zanzibar Arabs Shipped to Oman: 400 Refugees Jammed into Three Dhows for 2,000-Mile Trip." Apr. 12.

Nöldeke, A., et al.

1932 "Vierter vorläufige Bericht über die von der Notgemeinschaft der Deutschen Wissenschaft in Uruk unternommenen Ausgrabungen (1931-32)," Abhandlungen der Preussischen Akademie der Wissenschaften, Phil-hist. Kl., No. 6.

Ory, J.

1947-48 "A Bronze-Age Cemetery at Dhahrat el Humraiya," Quarterly of the Department of Antiquities in Palestine XIII: 75-91.

Parker, R. A.

1950 The Calendars of Ancient Egypt. Chicago.

Pendlebury, J. D. S.

1930 Aegyptiaca: A Catalogue of Egyptian Objects in the Aegean Area. Cambridge.

1939 The Archaeology of Crete. London.

Perrot, J.

1959 "Statuettes en ivorie et autres objets en ivorie et en os provenant des gisements préhistoriques de la région de Béershéba," Syria XXXVI: 8-19.

1961 "Une tombe à ossuaires du IVe millenaire à Azor, pres de Tel Aviv," 'Atiqot: Journal of the Israel Department of Antiquities III: 1-83.

1963 "Les ivories de la 7e campagne de fouilles à Safadi pres de Beersheva," Ersetz-Israel VII: 92-93.

Petrie, F.

1891 Illahun, Kahun, and Gurob 1889-1890. London.
1901 The Royal Tombs of the First Dynasty, Vol. II. London.
1902 Abydos I. London.
1906 Hyksos and Israelite Cities. London.
1914 Tarkhan II. London.
1921 Corpus of Prehistoric Pottery and Palettes. London.
1953 Ceremonial Slate Palettes. London.

Petrie, F., and Brunton, G.

1924 Sedment I. London.

Petrie, F., et al.

1912 The Labyrinth, Gerzeh, and Mazghuneh. London.
1923 Lahun II. London.
1925 Tombs of the Courtiers and Oxyrhynkhos. London.

Porter, B., Moss, R. L. B., and Burney, E. W.

1951 Topographical Bibliography of Egyptian Hieroglyphic Texts, Reliefs, and Paintings, Vol. VII: Nubia, the Deserts, and Outside Egypt. Oxford.

Prausnitz, M.

1955 "Note on a Cylinder Seal Impression," 'Atiquot: Journal of the Israel Department of Antiquities I: 139.

Quibell, J. E., and Green, F. W.

1902 Hierakonpolis II. London.

Randall-MacIver, P., and Woolley, C. L.

1911 Buhen. Philadelphia.

Reisner, G. A.

1942 A History of the Giza Necropolis, Vol. I. Cambridge, Mass.

Reisner, G. A., and Smith, W. S.

1955 A History of Giza Necropolis, Vol. II: The Tomb of Hetepheres, the Mother of Cheops. Cambridge, Mass.

Ricke, H.

1944 Bemerkungen zur ägyptischen Baukunst des Alten Reichs, I ("Beiträge zur ägyptischen Bauforschung und Altertumskunde, Heft 4). Zurich.

Rizkana, I.

1952 "Centres of Settlement in Prehistoric Egypt in the Area between Helwan and Heliopolis," Bulletin de l'Institut Fouad Ier du Désert II: 117-30.

Roque, Bisson de la

1950 Trésor de Tod ("Catalogue Général du Musée du Caire"). Cairo.

Roque, Bisson de la, Contenau, G., and Chapouthier, F.

1953 Le trésor de Tod ("Documents de fouilles de l'Institut francais d'Archéologie orientale du Caire, XI). Cairo.

Rowe, A.

1935 "The 1934 Excavations at Gezer," Palestine Exploration Fund Quarterly Statement: 19-33.

Saad, Zaki

1957 Ceiling Stelae in Second Dynasty Tombs from the Excavations at Helwan ("Supplement aux Annales du Service," No. 21). Cairo.

Säve-Söderbergh, T.

1941 Ägypten und Nubien. Lund.
1951 "The Hyksos Rule in Egypt," Journal of Egyptian Archaeology XXXVII: 53-71.

Schäfer, H., and Andrae, W.

1942 Die Kunst des alten Orients. 3d ed. Berlin.

Schaeffer, C. F. L.

1949 Ugaritica II. Paris.

Scharff, A.

1926 Das vorgeschichtliche Gräberfeld von Abusir el-Meleq. Leipzig.

Smith, H. S.

1964 "Egypt and C14 Dating," Antiquity XXXVIII: 32-37.

Smith, S.

1945 "Middle Minoan I-II and Babylonian Chronology," American Journal of Archaeology XLIX: 1-24.

Smith, W. S.

1952 Ancient Egypt as Represented in the Museum of Fine Arts, Boston. 3d ed. Boston.

Sukenik, E. L.

1948 Archaeological Excavations at Affula Conducted on Behalf of the Hebrew University. Jerusalem.

Tadmor, M.

1964 Review of Braidwood, 1960, Israel Exploration Journal XIII (in press).

Vandier, J.

1937 "A propos d'un dépôt de provenance asiatique trouvé à Tod," Syria XVIII: 174-82.

Vaux, R. de

1949 "La troisième campagne de fouilles à Tell el-Far'ah près Naplouse," Revue biblique LVI: 102-38.

Vaux, R. de, and Steve, A. M.

1948 "La deuxième campagne de fouilles à Tell el-Far'ah, près Naplouse," Revue biblique LV: 544-80.

Villiers, A. J.

1940 Sons of Sinbad. New York.

Vincent, P.

1911 Underground Jerusalem: Discoveries on the Hill of Ophel (1901-11). London.

Wainwright, G. A.

1947 "Early Magan," Antiquity XXXVII: 307-9.

Wampler, J. C.

1947 Tell en Naṣbeh, Vol. II: The Pottery. Berkeley and New Haven.

Weinberg, S. S.

1954 "The Relative Chronology of the Aegean in the Neolithic Period and the Early Bronze Age." In Relative Chronologies in Old World Archeology, pp. 86-107. Ed. by R. W. Ehrich. Chicago.

Westholm, A.

1939 "Some Late Cypriote Tombs at Milia," Quarterly of the Department of Antiquities of Palestine VIII: 1-20.

Winkler, H. A.

1938 Rock-Drawings of Southern Upper Egypt, Vol. I. London.

Wright, G. E.

1961 "The Archaeology of Palestine," In The Bible and the Ancient Near East, pp. 73-112. Ed. G. E. Wright. Garden City.

Yeivin, S.

1960 "Early Contacts between Canaan and Egypt," Israel Exploration Journal X: 193-203.

1963 "Further Evidence of Narmer at 'Gat,'" Oriens Antiquus II: 205-13.

Some Remarks on the Archaeological Chronology of Palestine before about 1500 B.C.

William F. Albright
Johns Hopkins University

During the decade since the publication of Relative Chronologies in Old World Archeology (1954), there has been an extraordinary increase in chronological precision, thanks to radiocarbon dating. In spite of still unexplained contradictions between various sets of data and isolated counts from many sources, the results are highly satisfactory as long as one avoids pinpointing early chronology too closely.

The most serious chronological conflicts among Palestinian archaeologists have arisen over the relation between the geographical diffusion of cultural assemblages and a severely stratigraphical approach, as represented by J. Kaplan and with modifications by G. Ernest Wright. According to the French school, as formerly represented by L. H. Vincent, A. Mallon, and especially by R. Neuville, much more flexibility must be allowed for local developments and particularly for geographical zones (e.g., Transjordan, the Negeb, the hill country of western Palestine, and the coastal plain). This approach is now illustrated by the work of Jean Perrot, E. Anati, and to some extent by that of Kathleen Kenyon and members of her school; it must, however, be noted that Perrot and Anati have been modifying their positions of late, and that their approach and that of the stratigraphical school are closer together than they were formerly.

There are many serious objections to exaggerating the differences between coeval areas of material culture in such a small country as Palestine. We must recall that the distance in a straight line from Dan to Beersheba is only about 150 miles and that the east-west distance from the coast of the Mediterranean to the frontier of the Syrian Desert varies only from about seventy to about a hundred miles. Except for a few higher hilltops and exceptionally high contiguous areas, the elevation varies from 2,700 feet above sea level to 1,300 feet below it, at the Dead Sea, for a total range of 4,000 feet. Even more important is the fact that Palestine was one of the principal land bridges of the ancient world, with trading caravans crossing it along various routes from north to south.

Anati (1962) has recently demonstrated that the walled town of Jericho would be inconceivable in Pre-Pottery Neolithic except as the place where the mineral wealth of the Dead Sea Valley was collected for export to other regions. In an agricultural and pastoral community, the wealth of the town would be just as incredible as the riches of Maryab and Timna' in south Arabia would be without the spice trade. In addition to such general considerations, we have ample proof of rather intensive trade between Mesopotamia and Egypt in the Djemdet Nasr period, about 3000 B.C. (low chronology). (There is no serious evidence for sea trade between Babylonia and Egypt at that time.) We know also that there was intensive land trade between Egypt and Palestine through most of the Old Kingdom (see below), in addition to the sea trade between Egypt and the Phoenician ports during the same period. It can now be proved that there was intensive caravan trade between Asia and Egypt during the Twelfth Dynasty.

In short, it has become absurd to treat ancient Palestine as though it were a land with little movement of trade. It is even more absurd to assume that there was little movement of population. For one thing, almost all major migrations and military invasions which passed over the land bridge of Palestine had to affect the entire country during the Neolithic and Bronze ages, before there were any strong native states. For another thing, the more broken up into tribes and clans Palestine was, the more reciprocal raiding there was bound to be, judging from its history in later ages. The different geographical zones were, furthermore, too small and too easy of access to allow for a situation in which there was little or no exchange of goods. Under such conditions the relative proportion of different types of artifact might change considerably, but there would always be some circulation and usually quite enough for cross-dating purposes.

It follows that when even such an eminent authority as Kathleen Kenyon suggests that the different Late Chalcolithic pottery of Jericho and of Tell Abu 'Ala'iq less than three miles away represents contemporary settlements, or that the different assemblages of Early Bronze-Middle Bronze reflect coexisting regional cultures or even different aspects of one culture, she must furnish proof of an otherwise improbable situation. This does not mean that there were no relatively local assemblages, or that the advancing front of one culture did not stop short at a natural or political boundary, but simply that there has been a vast amount of exaggeration, as when the Ghassulian of the fourth millennium was thought to be contemporary with the Early Bronze of the third millennium by nearly all archaeologists, while I was considered as an archaeological maverick because I protested consistently against such an impossible view.

We owe the high level of our present knowledge of the early Holocene of Palestine chiefly to the brilliant excavations of Kathleen Kenyon at Jericho. Here she found a relatively undisturbed sequence of levels and deposits, beginning with Natufian and continuing through Basal Neolithic, Pre-Pottery Neolithic A and B, Pottery Neolithic of Stratum IX (=Jerichoan), Chalcolithic of Stratum VIII (=Yarmukian), Late Chalcolithic. The only important known period which is so far entirely missing is the Ghassulian, although it is well represented in the Jordan Valley and many other parts of Palestine (except in the hill country, where it is extremely rare).

Without becoming involved in details—for which I refer particularly to Kaplan (1959), Wright (1961), de Contenson (1963), Anati (1963), as well as to the survey of contiguous lands by Helene Kantor and Patty Jo Watson in this volume—I offer the following table, arranged in "historical" sequence, to illustrate the chronology which seems most plausible to me at this time.

Kebaran Stage (food-gathering)	To ninth millennium B.C.
Natufian (incipient food-producing)	Ninth to early seventh millennium B.C.
Pre-Pottery Neolithic	Early seventh to late sixth millennium B.C.
Pottery Neolithic	Late sixth to end of fifth millennium B.C.
"Chalcolithic"	End of fifth to end of fourth millennium B.C.
Jericho VIII, etc.	Between 4000 and 3600 B.C.
Ghassulian	Between 3700 and 3300 B.C.
Late Chalcolithic	Between 3400 and 3000 B.C.

When we come to the Late Chalcolithic and Early Bronze I periods, we find ourselves in an obscure and controversial situation. It is now certain that, at least in southern Palestine, the end of E.B. I fell between the reign of Narmer, founder of the First Dynasty in Egypt, and the end of the reign of Athothis (Djer)—that is, at some time during the twenty-ninth century B.C. (minimal chronology). This fact is established by the excavations of S. Yeivin at Gath, where an Egyptian jar bearing the name of Narmer (Menes) was found (1959) in an E.B. I level with quantities of Egyptianizing ware (Yeivin, 1960, pp. 193-203). It had long been known that Palestinian (or coastal Syrian) pottery of early E.B. II type is often found in the royal tombs of the middle and late First Dynasty (see the summary in Helck, 1963, pp. 31 ff.), and consequently it may be inferred that the critical shift from E.B. I to E.B. II took place during the first third of the dynasty. This inference has now been confirmed by the discovery (1964) of many vases of the same "Abydos" type in the large E.B. II town at Arad on the southern end of the hill country of Judah, about thirty miles southeast of Gath. The continued excavation of this magnificent site by Ruth Amiran is certain to bring much clarification of ceramic chronology.

At this point it is necessary to insert some remarks about the chronology of the Proto-Dynastic period (Dynasties I and II). Already published studies (e.g., Scharff, 1927, 1950; Stock, 1949) have forced a drastic reduction of Old Kingdom dates; the beginning of the Sixth Dynasty is now set by most recent writers in the late twenty-fourth century or even as late as 2300, whereas the beginning of the Third Dynasty can be fixed by dead reckoning at about 2600. These reductions are further confirmed by still unpublished finds. Although the dates proposed for Menes by Scharff (*ca*. 2850) and Stock (*ca*. 2830) are probably too low, we may safely follow the data furnished by Edwards (1964) and allow about three centuries for the first two dynasties; Menes may then be placed safely about 2900 B.C., with some reduction more likely than scaling upward. It may be noted that I have insisted on a date for the beginning of Egyptian dynastic history between 3000 and 2800 ever since 1920 (*Journal of Egyptian Archaeology*, VI, 89-98).

It follows that in southern Palestine we must date the appearance of typical E.B. II pottery not later than the end of the reign of Athothis, Narmer's second successor, about the second half of the twenty-ninth century. This close link between the pottery chronology of southern Palestine and Dynastic Egypt provides us with a *point de repère* which is found nowhere else in southwestern Asia at so early a date. Since the same pottery, with the same Abydos ware, is also known from the extreme north of Palestine, there can be little doubt that the civilization of the country was quite homogeneous at that time.

I do not, however, think that Wright (1961, p. 81 f.) is justified in changing his views and combining Late Chalcolithic and E.B. I into one long period of four hundred or more years. Much of the evidence for this point of view comes from poorly stratified sites and tombs which may have been used for several generations. The well-stratified acropolis mound at Beth-shan fails us precisely at this point, and the site may have been unoccupied during most of the first half of the third millenium. The soundings in the mound itself at Megiddo were too limited in extent and too mixed stratigraphically to be of much value, although the previous soundings on the eastern slope had yielded valuable, well-published material (Engberg and Shipton, 1934). My present opinion is that there is a gap at both Megiddo and Beth-shan covering E.B. I, at least in large part. When the results of the excavations at Beth-yerah on the Sea of Galilee and of Gath and Arad in the south have been published, the now accessible material will fall into line. In short, Wright's original view (1937), sharply distinguishing the gray-burnished bowls and grain-slip ware in the north from the Ophel and Ai pottery in the south, was quite correct—except that it should have been recognized that the latter was later than the former, not contemporary with it. In fact, the well-known E.B. I sites in the south (but naturally found elsewhere as well) should be dated in the thirty-first to twenty-ninth centuries, and the Esdraelon phase in the thirty-third to thirty-first centuries, roughly speaking. As is now well known (see Kantor, this volume), the excavations of Mustafa Amr at Ma'adeh south of Cairo have yielded pottery characteristic of Late Chalcolithic (e.g., at Esdraelon, Tell el-Far'ah in the north). This is apparently Middle Gerzean, and should be dated in the thirty-first century (plus or minus) and not in the E.B. I period at all. In other words, it seems that there was no such sharp distinction between the cultures of northern and southern Palestine as has been supposed. It also seems probable that most of the present confusion will be eliminated after more publication of completed excavations and more extensive excavations in both old and new sites. Incidentally, a relatively clear break between "Chalcolithic" and Early Bronze can be made about 3000 B.C. or a little earlier. This is of course a matter of terminology, not a far-reaching change of culture.

Early Bronze III is the best known and best dated period of E.B. It ran concurrently with the Egyptian Pyramid Age, and may safely be dated between the twenty-sixth and twenty-third centuries B.C. Three phases may be distinguished: (A) before the introduction of Khirbet Kerak ware; (B) during the domination of Khirbet Kerak ware in the north; (C) after the decline of the Khirbet Kerak culture and during the Egyptian Sixth Dynasty. Phases (A) and (B) correspond roughly to Wright's 1937 category E.B. IIIA, and (C) is in part equivalent to his 1937 phase E.B. IIIB and partly to his later phase E.B. IV. (Note that the latter two designations include the first part of Kenyon's E.B.-M.B.) The new classification is proposed for convenience and without any expectation that it will be adopted in the suggested form.

The best example of phase (A) is the latest occupation of Bronze Age Ai (Marquet-Krause, 1949), dated by a large collection of alabaster plates and bowls about the Third Dynasty—that is, about the twenty-sixth century B.C. Since the French excavations found no trace of Khirbet Kerak or contemporary wares (although J. L. Kelso has found Khirbet Kerak sherds at Bethel, two miles away by air), it follows with certainty that (A) is to be dated before the main southward sweep of this pottery about 2500 B.C. (Albright, 1961). (B) probably covered about a century (ibid.), between the late twenty-sixth and the early twenty-fourth centuries. In my opinion, there must have been a massive irruption from Asia Minor into Syria-Palestine, bringing with it still unidentified Anatolians, to have produced the observed phenomena, which do not accord with gradual diffusion through commerce. (C) can be assigned to the Sixth Dynasty (twenty-third century) by common pottery and ceramic forms (Albright, 1962).

The following period, between about 2200 and about 1800, is again the subject of controversy, since there are few synchronisms to assist. The end of the period came suddenly, at least in southern Palestine, probably toward the end of the nineteenth century (see below). Since the pottery between the end of E.B. III(C) and developed Middle Bronze was wholly unrecognized before I found it in good stratigraphic sequence during the 1930 and 1932 campaigns at Tell Beit Mirsim, there was no basis elsewhere for sound stratigraphic chronology. I named it "Middle Bronze I," dating it in the twenty-first to nineteenth centuries and distinguishing two phases which differed chiefly in having envelope ledge handles in the lower stratum "I" (Eye) and apparently none at the end of the stratum above, "H." Subsequently the same pottery, which I termed "caliciform" to emphasize its resemblance to Syrian pottery from the end of the third millennium, has been found in many excavated sites and tombs, as well as on the surface of hundreds of sites in Transjordan and the Negeb (explored by Nelson Glueck). South of Esdraelon, "M.B. I" is astonishingly homogeneous; north of Esdraelon, especially at Khirbet Kerak on the Sea of Galilee, it is intermediate in type between the former and the incised ware that follows caliciform in northern Syria. Since the excavations of H. Ingholt and his colleagues at Hama (Fugmann, 1958), Hama J, with its eight phases and its consistent radiocarbon chronology, has become standard for the period. At first I was still influenced by the erroneous impression that the caliciform of Syria and the cruder "M.B. I" of Palestine were nearly contemporary, as a result of which I considered the radiocarbon dates too high (Albright, 1961). I now recognize that they are substantially correct, but a shift upward or downward to accord with improved estimates of half life may become necessary. Following are the three dates (Fugmann, 1958, pp. 281 f.):

K-530	From J_6	2310 ± 140 B.C.	Before about 2170
K-531	From J_5	2230 ± 120 B.C.	Before about 2110
K-533	From $J_{4/5}$	2210 ± 120 B.C.	Before about 2090

These dates agree well with my present estimate of a total duration for J_{8-1} from before 2200 to after 2000 (Albright, 1962).

Where does the "M.B.I" of Palestine fit into this picture? Obviously it must follow Hama J, for stylistic reasons alone. Recently Amiran has provided us with a satisfactory classification, although for quite objective reasons she first arranged her three groups wrong. Having proved convincingly that the pottery of my "M.B. I" (Tell Beit Mirsim I-H) goes back ultimately to Mesopotamian prototypes of the Accad period (24th-22nd centuries B.C.), she placed it first, with B and C later. These two groups are not nearly so abundant as "M.B. I" and, on the basis of the relatively scanty data, seem to be less homogeneous. However, they do go back unmistakably to E.B. III prototypes (pushed-up and folded ledge handles, etc.), and are typologically earlier (at least in Palestine) than her group A. Moreover, it may easily be shown that her group A arose from a late phase of the Syrian caliciform (see above), which did not directly influence B and C. It follows, as seen independently by Tufnell and recognized by Amiran herself, that B and C are earlier than A; they must, in fact, be dated respectively about the twenty-second and the twenty-first to the twentieth centuries B.C. (Albright, 1962). The envelope handle of Tell Beit Mirsim "I" (Eye) is a direct development from the folded ledge handle of C, and should presumably be dated about the twentieth century B.C.

The bearing of this discussion on Kenyon's "Early Bronze-Middle Bronze" is clear: my "M.B. I" (Amiran's A) is only the second (but longer) part of her period. All Kenyon's pottery belongs to Amiran's group A, but the tomb pottery is less diversified and more crudely made, on the whole, than the contemporary pottery from the town. (For the pottery, see Kenyon, 1960; Amiran, 1960, p. 224, n. 252.) The use of the term "nomadic" to describe this culture is not particularly felicitous, but there can be no doubt that the diffusion of its pottery was closely related to the extraordinary development of the donkey caravan trade during the Third Dynasty of Ur and the Twelfth Dynasty in Egypt (Albright, 1961, pp. 36-43). As for nomenclature, I suggest provisionally that we use Wright's E.B. IV to designate Amiran's groups B and C of the "Early Bronze-Middle Bronze" and continue to employ my designation M.B. I for Amiran's group A. After all, the use of the terms "Early Bronze" and "Middle Bronze" was introduced for chronological, not for typological, purposes. The division would fall about 2000 B.C. in any event.

The following initial phase of carinated pottery, which I first isolated in Tell Beit Mirsim strata G and F, has been called M.B. IIA in my own writings and those of many others; it is termed M.B. I by Kenyon. This latter designation does seem to exaggerate the difference between this late pre-Hyksos ceramic phase and the following Hyksos phases, which can now be safely dated between the end of the eighteenth and the end of the sixteenth century B.C. Thanks to Tufnell's important recent study (1962), it is possible to form a clear idea about the spread of this pottery in Palestine. There has not, however, been any recent analysis of the close resemblances between this ceramic phase in Palestine and the pottery of the four royal tombs of Byblos (Montet, 1928-29), to which I have called attention since 1933 but which has never been thoroughly investigated. The ceramic parallels are numerous and close, including identically profiled (and characteristic) jar rims, carinated bowls, caliciform goblets without feet, and elongated one-handled jugs with small flat bases ("dippers").

Since 1945 I have insisted on dating the royal tombs of Byblos in the eighteenth century, but the chronological spread of their contents has been impossible to establish exactly. In Tombs I and II were found a number of hieroglyphic inscriptions, including an object from I inscribed with the name of Amenemmes III (Parker: 1842-1797), one from II with the name of Amenemmes IV (Parker: 1798-1790), a third from II with the name of an Amenemmes, a sword from II bearing the name of the prince of Byblos, Yapi-shemu-abi son of Abi-shemu, as well as a pendentive (from II?) with the name of Yapi-shemu-abi. Montet reasonably conjectured that Abi-shemu was the occupant of Tomb I. Since there is no inscription stating the relation of the Byblian princes to their Egyptian suzerains, it is perfectly possible that the burials did not take place until after about 1800 B.C. Whatever may have been the dates of some of the precious objects, it is obvious that none of the pottery need be dated before 1800, especially since the Byblian princes may have outlived the pharaohs in question by many years. (It must be remembered that there is no evidence for autonomous Byblian princes during the Twelfth Dynasty itself.)

It is, however, no longer necessary to toy with an earlier dating for any of these tombs, which are so closely related in situation and pottery content that they cannot be separated. During the preparation of this study I have discovered that the name of the Byblian prince buried in Tomb IV is preserved on a broken alabaster vase from this tomb (Montet, 1928, p. 196; 1929, Pl. CXVII). The excavator originally read the last two consonants correctly (Montet, 1924, p. 8), but four years later he was led astray by an impossible combination. A re-examination of the inscription is conclusive: the name of the prince of Byblos is 'NTN, now well known from several scarabs and a broken stone inscription from Byblos, published by Dunand in 1937 and discussed by me in detail (Albright, 1945). The latter inscription makes it certain that Entin (or Yantin) of Byblos was contemporary with the Egyptian Pharaoh Neferhetep, who reigned for eleven years between about 1740 and 1730. The fact that the same Entin or Yantin is obviously a normal abbreviated form of the name of Yantin'ammu, contemporary of Zimri-Lim of Mari (Albright, 1945; Helck, 1962, pp. 64 ff.), makes it almost certain that Yantin outlived Neferhetep and died no earlier than about 1725 B.C. In other words, the characteristic M.B. IIA (Kenyon's M.B. I) of Tombs I-IV was still in use near the end of the eighteenth century. A date for the entire phase (which presumably spread from Phoenicia to Palestine) between the late nineteenth and the end of the eighteenth centuries is therefore established on a solid basis by astronomically fixed Egyptian synchronisms (which are, incidentally, in full agreement with the low

Mesopotamian chronology which I follow).

The following period (Tell Beit Mirsim E, Megiddo XII-XI) is characterized by the wealth which poured into Palestine from Egypt, then under Hyksos rule. The pottery of this period probably cost more in labor than that of any other period, and the tombs of the nobility are strikingly rich in imported objects. It was in the beginning of this phase that the fortifications of terre pisée were constructed. The numerous Hyksos ramparts of this age were certainly used in part to protect the chariotry, which continued to expand rapidly during the seventeenth century B.C. The most recently discovered enclosing pisé rampart was found at Achzib north of Acre in the summer of 1964; it is not far from the partly excavated pisé fortifications of Tell Kisan (Achshaph), erected over remains of my M.B. IIA. My M.B. IIB may thus be provisionally dated from the end of the eighteenth to the early sixteenth century B.C., when Hyksos wealth began to shrink.

Finally, my M.B. IIC (Kenyon's M.B. IIB), best exemplified at Megiddo X and Tell Beit Mirsim D, represents the twilight of Hyksos power, and may be safely dated in the sixteenth century B.C. A valuable check on relative chronology is provided by the general destruction of towns in the hill country of Palestine by the Egyptians after their capture of the southern base at Sharuhen (Tell el-Far'ah, south of Gaza) following a three-year blockade toward the end of the reign of Amosis I—1557-1532, according to the latest proposal of Parker (Albright, 1964), or 1552-1527, according to Helck (1962, p. 99). The destruction of a large number of Palestinian towns about this time (in late M.B. II and before the spread of bichrome paneled ware) would then have to be placed between about 1540 as the earliest reasonable date and about 1520 as the latest. Shortly afterward, the bichrome pottery came into use; it appears at Tell el-'Ajjul and elsewhere along the coast and in the low hill country before the end of M.B. IIC, as pointed out most recently by S. Yeivin (see Albright, 1938, and Yeivin, 1960). A date for the effective end of M.B. II may then be set at the end of the sixteenth century—about 1500. This date agrees extremely well with Åström's 1963 date for the end of Middle Minoan III—about 1525 B.C.

The following table illustrates the sequence of Bronze Age periods and their approximate dates.

Early Bronze I	between about 3100 and 2850 B.C.
Early Bronze II	between about 2900 and 2600 B.C.
Early Bronze IIIA	between about 2650 and 2500 B.C.
Early Bronze IIIB	between about 2550 and 2350 B.C.
Early Bronze IIIC	between about 2400 and 2250 B.C.
Early Bronze IV	about 23rd to 21st centuries
Middle Bronze I	before 2000 to before 1800
Middle Bronze IIA	about 18th century
Middle Bronze IIB	about 17th and early 16th centuries
Middle Bronze IIC	about 1575-1500 B.C.

Postscript: For details with respect to the Byblian evidence for dating M.B. IIA (Tell Beit Mirsim G-F) between the end of the nineteenth and the end of the eighteenth century B.C., see my paper, "The Eighteenth-Century Princes of Byblos and the Chronology of Middle Bronze" (BASOR 176: 38-46). My Egyptological conclusions have been endorsed by W. Helck (letter of April 24, 1965).

Bibliography

Albright, William F.

1933 "The Excavation of Tell Beit Mirsim, IA: The Bronze Age Pottery of the Fourth Campaign," AASOR XVII: 55-127.

1935 "Palestine in the Earliest Historical Period," Journal of the Palestine Oriental Society XV: 193-234.

1938a "The Excavation of Tell Beit Mirsim, II: The Bronze Age," AASOR: XVII.

1938b "The Excavation of a South Palestinian City: Tell el-'Ajjul," American Journal of Semitic Languages LV: 337-59.

1945 "An Indirect Synchronism between Egypt and Mesopotamia, cir. 1730 B.C.," BASOR 99: 9-18.

1960 The Archaeology of Palestine (latest, partly revised, edition). Harmondsworth: Penguin.

1961a "Abram the Hebrew: A New Archaeological Interpretation," BASOR 163; 36-54, especially pp. 36-40.

1961b Review of A. Goetze, Kleinasien, American Journal of Archaeology LXV: 399-400.

1962 "The Chronology of Middle Bronze I (Early Bronze-Middle Bronze)," BASOR 168: 36-42.

1964a "Prehistory." In The World History of the Jewish People, First Series, Vol. I, pp. 65-80. Ed. E. A. Speiser. Tel-Aviv: Massadah Publishing House.

1964b Review of S. Yeivin, A Decade of Archaeology in Israel, Bibliotheca Orientalis XXI: 65-66.

Amiran, Ruth

1960 "The Pottery of the Middle Bronze Age I in Palestine," Israel Exploration Journal X: 204-25.

1963 The Ancient Pottery of Eretz Yisrael: From Its Beginnings in the Neolithic Period to the End of the First Temple. Jerusalem: Bialik Institute. [In Hebrew, but lavishly illustrated.]

Anati, Emmanuel

1962 "Prehistoric Trade and the Puzzle of Jericho," BASOR 167: 25-31.

1963 Palestine before the Hebrews: A History from the Earliest Arrival of Man to the Conquest of Canaan. New York: Knopf.

Åström, Paul

1963 "Remarks on Middle Minoan Chronology," Kretika Chronika, 137-50.

Contenson, Henri de

1963 "New Correlations between Ras 'Shamra and al-'Amuq," BASOR 172: 35-40.

Dunand, Maurice

1937 Fouilles de Byblos, Texte, pp. 197 ff. Atlas, Pl. XXX.

Edwards, I. E. S.

1964 The Early Dynastic Period in Egypt. Advance separate publication of Cambridge Ancient History, Revised Edition, Vol. I, Chapter XI. Cambridge: University Press.

Engberg, Robert M., and Shipton, Geoffrey M.

1934 Notes on the Chalcolithic and Early Bronze Age Pottery of Megiddo. ("Studies in Ancient Oriental Civilization," No. 10.) Chicago: University of Chicago Press.

1939 Notes on the Megiddo Pottery of Strata VI-XX. ("Studies in Ancient Oriental Civilization," No. 17.) Chicago: University of Chicago Press.

FitzGerald, G. M.

1935 "The Earliest Pottery of Beth-shan," The Museum Journal (University of Pennsylvania) XXIV, No. 1.

Fugmann, E. Hama

1958 Fouilles et Recherches de la Fondation Carlsberg 1931-1938: L'architecture des périodes pré-hellenistiques. Copenhagen: National Museum.

Helck, Wolfgang

1962 Die Beziehungen Ägyptens zu Vorderasien im 3. und 2. Jahrtausend v. Chr. Wiesbaden: Otto Harrassowitz.

Kaplan, J.

1959 "The Neolithic Pottery of Palestine," BASOR 156: 15-22.

Kenyon, Kathleen

1957 Digging up Jericho. London: Ernest Benn.

1960a Archaeology in the Holy Land. London: Ernest Benn.

1960b Excavations at Jericho. I: The Tombs Excavated in 1952-54. London: British School of Archaeology in Jerusalem.

Marquet-Krause, Judith

1949 Les fouilles de 'Ay (et-Tell) 1933-1935. Paris: Geuthner.

Montet, Pierre

1924 "L'art phénicien au XVIIIe siècle avant J.-C," Monuments et Mémoires publié par l'Académie des Inscriptions et Belles Lettres XXVII: 1-29.

1928 Byblos et l'Egypte, Texte. Paris: Geuthner.

1929 Byblos et l'Egypte, Atlas. Paris: Geuthner.

Scharff, Alexander

1927 Grundzüge der ägyptischen Vorgeschichte. ("Morgenland," No. 12.) Leipzig.

Scharff, Alexander, and Moortgat, Anton

1950 Ägypten und Vorderasien im Altertum. Munich: Bruckmann.

Stock, Hanns

1949 Studia Aegyptiaca II: Die erste Zwischenzeit Ägyptens. ("Analecta Orientalia," 31.)

Tufnell, Olga

1962 "The Courtyard Cemetery at Tell el-'Ajjul, Palestine," Bulletin of the University of London Institute of Archaeology, III.

Wright, G. Ernest

1937 The Pottery of Palestine from the Earliest Times to the End of the Early Bronze Age. New Haven: American Schools of Oriental Research.

1961 "The Archaeology of Palestine." In The Bible and the Ancient Near East. Essays in Honor of William Foxwell Albright. Garden City: Doubleday.

Yeivin, Sh.

1960 A Decade of Archaeology in Israel, 1948-1958. ("Publications de l'Institut historique et archéologique néerlandais de Stamboul," VIII.)

The Chronology of North Syria and North Mesopotamia from 10,000 B.C. to 2000 B.C.[1]

Patty Jo Watson
Oriental Institute
University of Chicago

THE TERMINAL FOOD-COLLECTING, INCIPIENT FOOD-PRODUCING, AND EARLIEST ESTABLISHED FOOD-PRODUCING SETTLEMENTS OF NORTH SYRIA AND NORTH MESOPOTAMIA

In the past several years our knowledge of Pleistocene prehistory in the Near East has increased considerably. For Anatolia, Esin and Benedict have recently provided a convenient detailed summary (Esin and Benedict, 1963), and see also Mellink's chapter in this volume. The terminal food-collecting era is represented by caves yielding blade industries (some with and some without microliths). The era of incipient food-production is not well known for Anatolia, but is possibly represented by level C of the Beldibi rock shelter (Bostanci, 1959). The earliest Anatolian material pertaining to the era of established food production is that found in the basal ("Aceramic") levels of Hacılar near Burdur in southwestern Anatolia (Mellaart, 1961_a_). The earliest occurrences of pottery in Anatolia are those of level B at the Beldibi rock shelter and levels IX-X at Chatalhüyük East in the Konya Plain (Mellaart, 1962, 1963_a_, 1964_a_ and _b_). At Beldibi a flint industry characterized by geometric microliths was said to be accompanied by sherds of an early kind of pottery, which closely resembles that from Chatalhüyük IX-X (Mellaart, 1964_a_), but at the latter site there is an entirely different type of chipped-stone industry (Bialor, 1962).

---

1. I should like to thank Professor Robert J. Braidwood for his help in preparing this paper, and especially for providing unpublished data from the 1963-64 Joint Prehistoric Project of Istanbul University and the University of Chicago's Oriental Institute (J.P.P.I.C.) in southeastern Turkey, which he co-directed with Professor Halet Çambel of Istanbul University. The material in this paper is organized according to 'Amuq phases A to J. For an outline of the geography of this north Syrian-north Mesopotamian region, see Braidwood, pp. 34-35, and Perkins, pp. 42-43, _in_ Ehrich, 1954.

Following the Middle and Upper Pleistocene industries of such sites as Hazer Merd and Shanidar in Iraq, Yabrud in Syria, and the Mount Carmel caves in Palestine, the terminal food-collecting stage in these areas is represented by flint industries, such as the Kebaran in Palestine and the Zarzian in Iraq, which include both microlithic and normal-sized blade tools. The Zarzian has been found at Zarzi, Palegawra, in Shanidar B 2 (all rock shelters in northern Iraq: Garrod, 1930; Braidwood and Howe, et al., 1960, pp. 28-29, 57-59, 155-57; Solecki, 1955), and also in western Iran at Gar Warwasi (Braidwood, 1960, 1961, pp. 5-6).

The era of incipient food-production is represented by the Natufian sites of Palestine and, in Iraq, by such sites as Karim Shahir, Melefa'at, Gird Chai, Zawi Chemi Shanidar (Braidwood and Howe, et al., 1960, pp. 50-55, 157-59; Solecki, 1957; Solecki and Rubin, 1958). Perrot mentions surface finds in Syria of materials typologically similar to the Palestinian Natufian (Perrot in Braidwood and Willey, 1962, p. 153); at least two Iranian sites of this stage are also now known (Tepe Asiab near Kermanshah; Braidwood, 1960, 1961, p. 6; and Ali Kosh in the Deh Luran Valley; Hole, 1962).

Since the first edition of this volume, the pre-ceramic phase of the early food-producing stage has become much better known. It has been clear for some time that this stage is not only far older but also much more complex than had been thought (as indicated by such sites as basal Jericho (Tell es-Sultan), basal Hacılar, Ras Shamra V, the reassessment of the old Libby dates for Jarmo, the discovery of non-ceramic levels in Aegean sites). To judge from present evidence, the earliest effective village-farming communities must have been established at least as early as the first half of the seventh millennium B.C. In the north Syrian-north Mesopotamian area under consideration in this paper, five excavated sites are pertinent to this pre-ceramic range, none of them in the 'Amuq: Ras Shamra V C (Néolithique Ancien), Tell Muraibet, Çayönü, basal Jarmo, and basal Shemshara. There are also a number of Syrian surface sites which may pertain to this time range, the most important of which at present seems to be Tell Ramad (van Liere and Contenson, 1963).

Preliminary excavations at both Tell Muraibet and Çayönü were made in the late spring and summer of 1964. Muraibet, lying west of Raqqa on the east bank of the Euphrates, was sounded by Dr. Maurits van Loon's Columbia University expedition and revealed a substantial pre-ceramic sequence capped by a Protoliterate settlement. Flints from the lower levels included sickle blades and skillfully retouched, tanged projectile points of the Syro-Cilician type as well as a few of the notched-base types known from Palestine (personal communication, Dr. Maurits van Loon).

Çayönü, near Ergani in the Diyarbekir vilayet of southeastern Turkey, was sounded by the J.P.P.I.C. (see above, p. 61, n. 1). The following remarks are a personal communication from Robert J. Braidwood: "Two preliminary radiocarbon assays for the pre-ceramic levels indicate a placement of about 8500 years ago. The Çayönü ground stone industry appears to pertain to the Jarmo tradition for this category (as do a few figurines), the flint and obsidian appear to link more closely with Syro-Cilicia. The site showed a rather remarkable architectural complexity, and there was a significant occurrence of small artifacts of free copper and of malachite."

Ras Shamra V C is the apparent local predecessor of the Syro-Cilician early-village culture represented by 'Amuq A-B (this culture may have originated in southwestern Anatolia; see Mellink, 1962, pp. 220-21). Ras Shamra <u>Néolithique Ancien</u> has been found by Schaeffer and his colleagues, Kuschke and Contenson, at levels varying from 9.60 m. to 17.15 m. below the surface in four sondages (those of 1934, 1935, 1955, and 1960; Schaeffer, 1962, p. 163). The chipped-stone industry (flint and obsidian) seems generally similar to that of 'Amuq A-B, basal Mersin, and that of Chatalhüyük East in Anatolia in that it includes lance heads and other projectile points—some with distinct tangs—punches, burins, and finely denticulated sickle blades, and in that there is an absence of microliths. There are also limestone vessels and a schematic female figurine (see the useful summary by Contenson, 1963). Architecture did not include plastered floors, but such floors were found in the <u>Néolithique Moyen</u> (level V B) and in the <u>Néolithique Récent</u> (level V A). In the most recent soundings (Kuschke's of 1955 and Contenson's of 1960; Schaeffer, 1962), debris of the pre-pottery settlement has been found to be about two meters deep. Schaeffer believes that the settlement was large (Schaeffer, 1962, pp. 157-60), but Contenson (1963, p. 35) disagrees with this interpretation.

Basal Jarmo was an unfortified small village of this pre-ceramic range (Braidwood and Howe, <u>et al</u>., 1960, pp. 26-27, 38-50). The site reveals a continuous development from pre-ceramic levels to pottery-bearing strata with no abrupt stratigraphic break accompanying the introduction of this new trait. The pre-ceramic assemblages of Jarmo and Ras Shamra have few items in common. The Jarmo chipped stone consists of a blade and microlith industry with a complete lack of projectile points; architecture is in touf (pisé or packed mud); Jarmo ground stone—vessels, bracelets, balls, full-ground celts, pendants and other small items—is abundant, distinctive, and masterfully worked; Jarmo clay animal and female figurines are well modeled and numerous.

Material in some ways comparable to that of Jarmo has been reported to exist at the base of Tell Shemshara, a site in the Dokan area of northern Iraq (Ingholt, 1957; Mortensen, 1962). The sequence of levels in basal Shemshara is as follows: levels 9 to 13 with Samarran and Hassunan pottery; levels 14 to 16 with no pottery but with the same types of ground and chipped stone as in the upper prehistoric levels. Mortensen thinks the basal, pre-ceramic levels of Shemshara (14 to 16) are contemporary with early Hassunan at the mound of Hassuna, but there are close parallels to Jarmo in the chipped and ground stone industries, and—at this time—the question cannot be completely resolved.

Other sites with non-ceramic early village materials are now known in various parts of the Near East: basal Hacılar in Anatolia, Seyl Aqlat and basal Jericho in Jordan, Perrot's new site of Munhatta in Israel, Tepe Guran (see "Archaeological News," p. 290, in Archaeology, Vol. 16, No. 4) and Ali Kosh in Iran. Seyl Aqlat and Munhatta levels 4 to 6 are similar to the PPN B assemblage of Jericho. Similarly, the red-burnished, plastered floors of Hacılar Aceramic levels recall the plastered floors of PPN B Jericho.

Pottery first appears at Ras Shamra in level V B. In Iraq, no pottery is yet known earlier than that of upper Jarmo, which certainly seems to have been introduced from some other place. The site of Ali Agha near Girdamamik on the Greater Zab may be contemporaneous with upper Jarmo and basal Hassuna (Braidwood and Howe, et al., 1960, pp. 26, 37-38.

In Palestine, the earliest published pottery seems to be that of Sheikh Ali, Telulyot Batashi, Kfar Giladi, Shaar ha-Golan, and Jericho Pottery Neolithic AB (Prausnitz, 1958; Kaplan, 1958, 1959; Stekelis, 1950-51; Perrot in Braidwood and Willey, 1962, p. 159). Perrot says similar pottery occurs in his new Israeli site of Munhatta (personal communication). This material, however, is relatively late, being approximately contemporary with 'Amuq D or a little later. It is separated by a gap of unknown length from the earlier part of the Palestinian sequence that begins with the Kebaran, continues with the Natufian and the Late Natufian developments (the latter seen in various aspects at Nahel Oren, al-Khiam, and—a special instance in a peculiar environment—Jericho PPN A), and concludes with the influx of Syro-Anatolian traits in the Jericho PPN B-Seyl Aqlat-Munhatta 4 to 6 horizon. (This interpretation is based on a personal communication from Jean Perrot).

In southwestern Anatolia, the earliest appearances of pottery yet known are in the Beldibi rock shelter and in levels IX-X of Chatalhüyük East (see above).

Present evidence suggests communication along the entire eastern coast of the Mediterranean at the pre-'Amuq A and 'Amuq A time level. From southwestern Anatolia (Hacılar and Chatalhüyük) to Phoenicia (Ras Shamra V C and V B) to Palestine (Jericho PPN B and Munhatta) similar traits are found: rectangular buildings (often of stone) with plastered floors, crude vessels of plaster or mortar (not known from Anatolia but found at several sites in Syria and Palestine, see below, p. 66), the manufacture of tanged projectile points, elaborate treatment of the dead.

Phase A

Phase A in the 'Amuq is represented by what was certainly a well-developed early village type of assemblage, though it is not yet well known archaeologically. Stratified Phase A materials come only from Judeideh in the 'Amuq, and include three kinds of pottery: Coarse Simple Ware, Washed Impressed Ware, and Dark-Faced Burnished Ware, the latter being by far the most common. There is also a distinctive blade industry in chipped stone (mostly flint but with some obsidian) characterized by numerous well-made projectile points of the javelin head or lance head type, and by short, narrow, finely denticulated sickle blades. Other items include stone vessels, full-ground celts, stone beads (including a double ax form), stamp seals incised with linear designs,[2] and possibly sling missles. The architecture is unknown because of flooding by ground water in these lowest levels.

Outside the 'Amuq, the closest parallels occur at Yümük Tepe, Mersin, in the pre-XXVII levels. Braidwood includes Yümük Tepe with Ju-

2. For detailed information on these and other seals, see the paper by Porada in this volume, and the forthcoming "Corpus of Western Asiatic Stamp Seals" by Edith Porada and B. W. Buchanan.

deideh as equally representing the essential Syro-Cilician Dark-Faced Burnished Ware assemblage.

Dark-Faced Burnished Ware occurs also at Gözlü Kule, Tarsus, together with remains of polished wall plaster (Goldman, 1956, pp. 5, 65 ff.). There is Dark-Faced Burnished Ware (some with impressed or excised decoration) at Ras Shamra in levels IV C (with Halafian painted ware), V A, and V B, but both V A and B include pattern burnish which does not appear until Phase B in the 'Amuq. Ras Shamra V A (Néolithique Récent) includes the plastered and red painted ware referred to below as well as Hassunan husking trays (Contenson in Schaeffer, 1962, p. 502, Fig. 25; cf. Lloyd and Safar, 1945, Pl. XVIII, 1, Fig. 3, 8-10), and is thought by Contenson to be approximately equivalent to 'Amuq B. Ras Shamra V B (Néolithique Moyen) has Dark-Faced Burnished ware (Contenson in Schaeffer, 1962, p. 503; Contenson, 1963; Schaeffer, 1962, p. 162), including some pattern burnish and some impressed and incised wares. There is also a strange ware (plastered and red painted) rare at Ras Shamra but found also in the Byblos Néolithique Ancien (Contenson, 1963), and some sand-and-limestone plaster vessels also present at basal Tell Sukas, Tell Ramad (Syria), Byblos, and in Palestine at Munhatta (Riis, 1961-62; van Liere and Contenson, 1963; Perrot, personal communication). Contenson parallels this Ras Shamra V B material with 'Amuq A; if this assumption is correct, then pattern burnish is earlier at Ras Shamra than in the 'Amuq. The flints of both Ras Shamra V A and V B seem to be much like those of the 'Amuq A-B range: blades and carefully retouched projectile points, often with tangs, burins, and perforators (Schaeffer, 1962, pp. 285, 289, Pls. XI and XIII, p. 508, Fig. 34 A). Plastered floors are characteristic of V B (Contenson, 1963).

Material comparable to 'Amuq A has recently been reported from Tell Sukas on the Syrian coast between Banias and Jebeleh (Riis, 1961, 1961-62).

To the east, Dark-Faced Burnished Ware has been found at Chagar Bazar 13-15 (Mallowan, 1936, pp. 10-11), Tell Halaf (Oppenheim, 1943, pp. 25-31), the Jabbul Plain between Aleppo and the Euphrates (Maxwell-Hyslop, et al., pp. 24-26), Carchemish (Woolley, 1952, pp. 227-28), and Yunus (Woolley, 1934, p. 154). At all these places, however (and also in Ras Shamra IV C), except possibly Tell Halaf, the Dark-Faced Burnished Ware occurs with Halafian style painted pottery and is therefore later than 'Amuq A. In its surface surveys in the Sürt and Diyarbekir vilayets in southeastern Turkey, the J. P. P. I. C. found Dark-Faced Burnished Ware—usually of somewhat coarser and clumsier manufacture than that of Syro-Cilicia—to be quite common. Some surface occurrences were clearly without Halafian painted ware, others included it.

Dark-Faced Burnished Ware is also recorded for Hama M (with red polished wall plaster), Tabbat al-Hammam, and (with plastered floors) for basal Byblos (Ingholt, 1940, p. 11; Fugmann, 1958, p. 12; Braidwood and Braidwood, 1940, pp. 196-203, 222, 226; Hole, 1959, pp. 149-83; Dunand, 1949-50, 1950b, 1955; Cauvin, 1962). The chipped-stone industries of both Byblos *Néolithique Ancien* and Tabbat al-Hammam include some items, such as projectile points, which tie them to the Palestinian tradition (Cauvin, 1962; Hole, 1959).

Dark-Faced Burnished Ware has recently been reported from a few Israeli sites—Telulyot Batashi (Kaplan, 1958, Fig. 8), Kfar Giladi (Kaplan, 1959), Sheikh Ali (Prausnitz, 1959)—mixed with Jericho Pottery Neolithic AB type painted sherds; however, these far southern occurrences must be post 'Amuq A-B (Perrot, 1962, p. 156; and pp. 64-65, above).

In the northern Iraq sequence, Dark-Faced Burnished Ware appears (evidently as a minor complement in the total ceramic industry) at Arpachiyah, Hassuna, and Nineveh (Mallowan and Rose, 1935, p. 174; Lloyd and Safar, 1945, Pl. XIV, 1; Mallowan, 1933, p. 150). Two projectile points like those from Chatalhüyük East and Syro-Cilicia were found in Hassuna Ia (Lloyd and Safar, 1945, Fig. 22, 9-10).

Phase B

Materials of Phase B in the 'Amuq, like those of Phase A, come only from Judeideh. Architectural traces suggest rectilinear buildings with stone-founded mud-brick or *touf* walls. The chipped-stone and ground-stone industries are the same as those of Phase A. In pottery, Dark-Faced Burnished Ware is still important; pattern burnish first appears in this category in Phase B and continues through Phase E. Incised decoration is now found on the Coarse Simple Ware. There is a minor increment of painted pottery, the Brittle Painted Ware.

Again, the closest parallels are with Yümük Tepe, Mersin, specifically levels XXVII—where painted sherds first appear (Garstang, 1953, pp. 39, 58)—to XXIV. Chatalhüyük West seems to fit into the end 'Amuq B-early C range according to Mellaart's parallels with Mersin XXIV-XXII (Mellaart, 1961b, p. 178).

Braidwood (Braidwood and Braidwood, 1960, p. 506) feels that the Dark-Faced Burnished occurrences at Carchemish and Chagar Bazar are contemporary with Phase B at the earliest, and that the Yunus material is contemporary with Phase C. He notes a few sherds from Tell Halaf which, he thinks, are Phase B Brittle Painted Ware (Oppenheim, 1943, Pl. XCVIII, 1-3). Another sherd could be Hassunan incised ware, and a third is a fragment of a husking tray (Oppenheim, 1943, Pl. XCVIII, 4, and p. 30, *textabb*. 2).

Phase B type materials are perhaps represented by the lowest levels at Sakje Geuzi (Coba Hüyük) where pattern burnish occurs with Dark-Faced Burnished Ware, but the chipped-stone industry is different from that of 'Amuq A-B.

Level XII of Tell esh-Sheikh is said to have yielded plain black pottery with occasional burnishing, which pottery persists into level XI where Halafian sherds appear (Woolley, 1953, p. 26). Hence, level XII may belong to 'Amuq Phase B.

Perrot feels that Tabbat al-Hammam and Byblos *Néolithique Ancien* are contemporary with 'Amuq B (Perrot, 1962, p. 156). Hole suggests that Tabbat al-Hammam at least may be earlier than 'Amuq B (Hole, 1959, p. 178). Cauvin says that he cannot be certain whether to equate Tabbat al-Hammam with Byblos *Néolithique Ancien* or *Néolithique Moyen* (Cauvin, 1962). However, until further excavation at Tabbat al-Hammam, the basal levels may be provisionally placed near the 'Amuq B range.

As noted above, Ras Shamra level V A with Dark-Faced Burnished Ware and husking trays is probably more or less equivalent to 'Amuq B, according to Contenson (1963).

The northern Iraq counterpart of 'Amuq A-B is the Hassunan. Occurrences of this particular early-village assemblage are detailed in Perkins (1949, Chap. I), to which may be added the sites of al-Khan, on the Khazir River between Erbil and Mosul, and Tell Shemshara with three near-by sites all in the vicinity of Rania (Broman *in* Braidwood, 1954*b*, pp. 129-30; Braidwood and Howe, *et al*., 1960, pp. 25, 35; Ingholt, 1957; Mortensen, 1962). The J. P. P. I. C. found no clear traces of Hassunan materials in its recent surveys in southeastern Turkey.

The Samarran—defined almost exclusively on the basis of painted pottery—is at present a somewhat enigmatic phenomenon (see Braidwood and Howe, *et al*., 1960, p. 161; Kleindienst, 1960[3]). The recent

---

3. In note 2, p. 70, Kleindienst refers to Samarran ware at Bana-

work by the Iraq Directorate of Antiquities at Umm as-Suwan (or Tell as-Suwan) near Samarra should help to clarify the question because the site apparently has a sequence beginning with Hassunan or even pre-Hassunan remains and terminating in a Samarran occupation. In any case, it is no longer generally thought that the Samarran painted pottery style owes its origin to influence from Iran (Oates, 1960, p. 47; Le Breton, 1957, p. 86). The classic Samarran style is largely contemporary with at least the early part of the Halafian style, and it is at about this time that pottery-producing villages are first known in southern Iraq (basal Eridu, Haji Mohammad, Ras al-'Amiya). There are no finds of true Samarran or Halafian sherds in southern Iraq, but the earliest pottery which does occur there was certainly produced by people familiar with both styles, especially the Samarran (Le Breton, 1957, pp. 84, 86; Oates, 1960, pp. 42-43). Significantly enough, there were pieces of Hassunan husking trays in Eridu levels XIX, XVII, and XV (Lloyd and Safar, 1948, p. 125 and Pl. III), and Oates refers to a large Haji Mohammad jar type which resembles those so characteristic of Hassuna and Matarrah (Oates, 1960, p. 43; Lloyd and Safar, 1945, Fig. 6, top rows, and Pl. XIII, 1; Braidwood, Braidwood, Smith, and Leslie, 1952, Pl. V, 1-3).

Phase C

Materials of Phase C in the 'Amuq come from Tell Kurdu and the First Mixed Range at Judeideh, and are not abundant. However, it is clear that this is the time when Halafian pottery was introduced into the area, and this well-known painted style provides links to many sites in Syro-Cilicia, Syria, and northern Iraq.

Halafian style painted pottery appears in levels XIX-XVII at Mersin (Garstang, 1953, p. 80 and Chap. VI), but Braidwood suggests that there may be local imitations of Halafian motifs as early as Mersin XXIV (Braidwood and Braidwood, 1960, p. 509) and that by level XIX sherds comparable to 'Amuq D are present. There is Halafian pottery at Ras Shamra in IV A, IV B, and IV C; IV A painted pottery may be transitional to the Ubaidian style; moreover, a red ware like that of 'Amuq D occurs here, and this level at Ras Shamra must be equated at

hilk. This statement was based on information from me, but since the writing of her paper (1956), more detailed work on the Banahilk pottery has indicated that the few sherds earlier thought to be of Samarran type are not demonstrably so.

least in part with 'Amuq D (Schaeffer, 1961, p. 222, and Contenson *in* Schaeffer, 1962, p. 494; Contenson, 1963). In Ras Shamra IV C, there is also an "archaic painted ware" which Contenson compares with the painted ware of Mersin XXIV-XX and the "non-brittle painted ware" of late 'Amuq B (Contenson, 1963). In Ras Shamra IV B, local Halafian style painted ware predominates, and the red wash ware of IV A (and 'Amuq D) makes its first appearance.

Other sites with Halafian style painted pottery are: Sakje Geuzi levels II and III (Taylor, *et al*., 1950, pp. 86-94); Tabbat al-Hammam—two possible sherds only (Braidwood and Braidwood, 1940, pp. 201-2); Hama L—but Hama L has also Ubaid pottery and even some possible Ninevite 5 ware (Fugmann, 1958, pp. 22-23; Ingholt, 1940, pp. 13-14); Tell esh-Sheikh XI (Woolley, 1953, p. 26), Tell Ailun and Tell Rifa'at in northern Syria (Moortgat, 1957, p. 25; Seton-Williams, 1961); basal Tell Halaf (Oppenheim, 1943); levels 3 and 4 at Turlu, a site found by Jean Perrot in 1962 which lies 45 km. east of Gaziantab and about 35 km. from Yunus-Carchemish (personal communication, Jean Perrot); Mallowan's north Syrian sites of Chagar Bazar, Brak, Tell Aswad (Mallowan, 1936, 1937*a*, 1946, 1947); and Tilkitepe on Lake Van (Reilly, 1940). Halafian pottery also occurred in various of the surface collections made by the J. P. P. I. C. in the Sürt-Diyarbekir area of southeastern Turkey. Except for the newer site of Banahilk near Diyana in Iraq (Braidwood and Howe, *et al*., 1960, pp. 25, 33-35; the final report on Banahilk is scheduled to appear in a forthcoming publication of the Oriental Institute), all the important Iraqi and Syrian occurrences of Halafian style painted pottery are fully detailed in Perkins' study (Perkins, 1949). (See also the map by Mellaart on p. 64 of *The Dawn of Civilization*, Piggott, ed., and refer to Weinberg's paper in this volume for Aegean relationships of Halafian type pottery). At some of the Syro-Cilician sites—such as Kurdu, Ras Shamra IV C, Yunus, and Carchemish (see above, p. 66), Dark-Faced Burnished Ware persists together with Halafian style pottery. There are also late occurrences of Dark-Faced Burnished Ware in Palestine on the Jericho Pottery Neolithic AB horizon (p. 67, above).

The Phase C chipped-stone industry in the 'Amuq is different from that of Phases A-B, the most striking divergences being in the sickle blade category and in the absence of the characteristic projectile points of A-B (Braidwood and Braidwood, 1960, pp. 150-54, 525-30). Braidwood notes a possible resemblance to the 'Amuq C flints at Tell Zaidan on the

Balikh River (Albright, 1926), but there the associated sherds seem to be of Ubaidian type; consequently, the site is more likely to be contemporary with 'Amuq E than C (the chipped-stone industry of 'Amuq C persists through D and E). This 'Amuq C chipped-stone industry also seems to occur at Sakje Geuzi (Braidwood and Braidwood, 1953, p. 292; Braidwood and Braidwood, 1960, p. 507; Taylor, et al., 1950, pp. 126-30).

Phase D

Phase D materials were found (in context) only at Tell Kurdu in the 'Amuq. Besides the Dark-Faced Burnished Ware, Red-Wash Ware and examples of both Halafian and Ubaidian painted wares as well as local styles of painted pottery occur. New forms in the unpainted pottery include bow-rims (for instance, Braidwood and Braidwood, 1960, Fig. 127, 4 and 5), one fragment of a pierced pedestal base (ibid., Fig. 123, 17), small triangular-sectioned jar handles (ibid., Fig. 123, 7). Non-ceramic remains are scant, but the flint and obsidian tools seem to be of the same industry as those of C and E.

There are parallels to the 'Amuq D pottery in Ras Shamra IV A (red ware and Halafian painted ware) and III C (red ware). In Ras Shamra III B, local Ubaid wares are present, but the red wash ware gives way to wares "with a general resemblance to 'Amuq F," and Canaanean blades are included in the chipped-flint industry (Contenson, 1963).

Other comparable sites are Byblos Néolithique Moyen (Dunand, 1961, pp. 77, 81-82; Cauvin, 1962); Tell Halaf, where bow-rim jars also appear (Oppenheim, 1943, Fig. 88, p. 50, Pl. XIV, 1-5, 10); and levels 5 and 6 at Perrot's new site of Turlu (also with a few bow-rims). Other important ties indicated by the pottery are to Palestine: to Jericho Pottery Neolithic AB (cf. Garstang's Jericho VIII; Wright, 1951), to Shaar ha-Golan (Stekelis, 1950-51), and to Batashi and Sheikh Ali (Kaplan, 1959; Prausnitz, 1959).

The complexities of the relations among 'Amuq D, Jericho Pottery Neolithic AB, and basal Byblos (i.e., Byblos Énéolithique A or simply Byblos A of the older literature, which is the same as Byblos Néolithique or Néolithique Ancien of the more recent Byblos reports) have been diagrammed and fully discussed by Dyson in his review of the 'Amuq publication (Dyson, 1961, pp. 634-36). The situation has now been considerably clarified (see Perrot, 1962, pp. 156-57; Cauvin, 1962). The pottery of Jericho VIII is equivalent to Kenyon's Pottery Neolithic B, but Perrot groups Kenyon's Pottery Neolithic A and B together because, he says, the distinction is only a typological one. Both kinds of pottery occur in the same pits at Jericho and in Munhatta 2, Batashi, and Sheikh Ali, and consequently they are actually contemporary (Perrot, 1962, p. 157, n. 5). Perrot equates this Jericho pottery AB with 'Amuq D and with the Byblos Néolithique Moyen (see also Cauvin, 1962).

Phase E

Phase E is a time of strong Ubaidian influence on the painted pottery of the 'Amuq. Phase E remains (in context) come only from Tell Kurdu. Besides the large quantity of local Ubaid-inspired Monochrome Painted Ware, there were traces of rectangular mud-brick structures in the sondage. This is also the final stage of the Dark-Faced Burnished Ware. Other items in the assemblage are clay sling missiles, whorls, human and animal figurines, implements of chipped flint and obsidian which fit with the general Phase C to E industry, stone vessels, full-ground celts, a shaft-hole adz, stamp seals with geometric designs, and bone awls.

Pottery from three other 'Amuq mounds pertains in some way to Phase E, although the nature of the relationship (transitional to E, late to post E, or some kind of local variation of E) is not clear. The three mounds are Karaca Khirbet Ali, Tell esh-Sheikh, and Tabara al-Akrad.

Ubaid type painted pottery also occurs at Mersin, especially levels XVI A-XV, and possibly begins as early as level XIX (see above, p. 69; Garstang, 1953, p. 175). It has been found in Ras Shamra III B, as already noted. Contenson (in Schaeffer, 1962, p. 485) feels that the Ras Shamra Ubaid painted style is the same as that of Tell esh-Sheikh and that this style is different from that of 'Amuq E.

Although little is yet known of it, the Byblos Néolithique Récent (Dunand, 1961, pp. 75-78, 82) should somehow be pertinent to the 'Amuq E- Ubaid time range, because Byblos Néolithique Moyen is equivalent to 'Amuq D and Byblos Énéolithique B is approximately equivalent to 'Amuq F.

Other contemporary strata are Hama L (Fugmann, 1958, p. 22), Yunus (Woolley, 1934), Tell Ahmar (Thureau-Dangin and Dunand, 1936, Pls. XXXV-XXXVI), Tell Zaidan (Albright, 1926), and possibly Arslan Tepe-Malatya across the border in Turkey (Braidwood and Braidwood, 1960, p. 511, n. 85). Surface collections made by the J. P. P. I. C. indicate several contemporary sites in southeastern Turkey. One sherd in the Kurdu Phase E materials suggests connections with Palestine, since it seems to be a fragment of a Ghassulian churn (Braidwood and Braidwood, 1960, Fig. 137, 20; Perrot, 1955, p. 82 and Pl. 14 C).

Perkins has catalogued the available Ubaidian occurrences in Iraq (Perkins, 1949, Chap. III). To these may be added the site tested by the 1956 Japanese expedition, Telul eth-Thalathat (Egami, 1958), which lies in the Jazira region 60 km. west of Mosul. Mound II has Ubaid and Uruk occupations, and there is also mention of pre-Ubaid material (Egami, 1958, p. iii of Preface; see also Lloyd, 1938, p. 135).

The Ubaidian pottery style originated and flowered most dramatically in southern Iraq (see the account by Porada in this volume). As noted by Perkins (1949, p. 90), there is a tie to the north Iraq Ubaid of Tepe Gawra in the presence in both Eridu VIII-XII and Gawra XVII-XIX of a peculiar lenticular or "tortoise" jar with a long tubular spout. Gawra XVII-XIX is transitional (from Halaf to Ubaid) and early Ubaid. The Eridu ware of XV-XIX at Eridu is at least partly contemporary with the Hassunan and Halafian of northern Iraq: husking trays occur in levels XIX, XVII, and XV, and there are numerous parallels with Halafian forms and designs. Le Breton (1957) suggests that his Susiana *a* (Jefferabad I) may be contemporary with the Hassunan and earlier than the earliest wares at Eridu. Oates (1960) does not agree with this suggestion, but feels rather than Jefferabad and Jowi may be interpreted as provincial variants of Haji Mohammad type pottery. Oates and Le Breton agree that there is no evidence to suggest that the earliest southern Mesopotamian painted pottery style derived from Iran.

Phase F

Phase F is known from Tell Judeideh, Chatal Hüyük, and Tell Dhahab in the 'Amuq. It includes traces of mud-brick buildings, beveled-rim bowls, and occurrences of wheel-made pottery, some metal tools, sickle flints made of Canaanean blade sections, full-ground celts, stone vessels, stone stamp seals with representational designs on a few for the first time, and stone "studs." Braidwood's general conclusion is that 'Amuq F is a western version of the northern Iraq Gawran, but lacks the gray burnished ware.

The gray burnished ware is found at Mersin XIV-XIII (Garstang, 1953, p. 173), at Tarsus (Mellink *in* Goldman, 1956, pp. 79-81) and at Tabara al-Akrad in level V (Hood, 1951, pp. 127-28, 130). Pottery similar to that of 'Amuq F occurs at Tell Halaf, Carchemish, the Jabbul Plain, Arslan Tepe, possibly at Şamiramalti-Tilkitepe, and in northern Iraq (Oppenheim, 1943, pp. 94 ff.; Woolley, 1952, pp. 217-18; Maxwell-Hyslop, *et al.*, 1942, pp. 24-26; Braidwood and Braidwood, 1960, p. 511, n. 85; *ibid.*, p. 514; Mellink, 1962, p. 221). The J. P. P. I. C. found beveled-rim bowls and blade fragments which were probably of Canaanean type fairly generally throughout its survey regions in southeastern Turkey. To the south, Phase F pottery also occurs at Qala'at er-Rus 19-17 (A. Ehrich, 1939) and Hama K (Braidwood and Braidwood, 1960, p. 514). Beveled-rim bowls seem to be present in the 'Amuq at the end of Phase F and the beginning of G (ibid., p. 234 and n. 10). This vessel form is well known from Warkan and Protoliterate levels in southern Mesopotamia (see below).

At both Mersin and Tarsus, Canaanean blades are later than the 'Amuq F type pottery which occurs in the Late Chalcolithic levels of Tarsus, but is represented at Mersin only by gray burnished bowls in levels XIV-VIII (Goldman, 1956, pp. 82-86; Garstang, 1953, p. 173). At Tarsus, Canaanean blades first appear in E. B. I context (Goldman, 1956, p. 257), at Mersin in level XII (Garstang, 1953, Fig. 77, 1), and they are also reported for Ras Shamra III B (Contenson, 1963). At Tepe Deshawar in Iran, Canaanean blades have been found with Uruk-Protoliterate pottery (Braidwood, 1960).

At Tarsus, metal first appears in an E. B. I context, and in the 'Amuq there is none in certain context earlier than Phase F. However, copper tools are present in earlier levels at a number of other sites, and traces of copper occur at Chatalhüyük East (see Mellink, in this volume), and at Çayönü (see p. 63, above). A copper pin was found in Mersin XXII (Garstang, 1953, pp. 76, 83), one in XXI (ibid., pp. 76, 84), a chisel and a (possibly intrusive) stamp seal in XVII (ibid., p. 108), some roll-headed pins, a chisel, and two axes in XVI (ibid., p. 139). In Siyalk I were found 2 awls, a pin, and a needle (Ghirshman, 1938, pp. 16-17, Pl. LII, 49, 53-56, 58); in level II were some tanged awls, a pin, a bracelet, and a fragment of a spatula (ibid., p. 30, Pl. LII, 46-48, 50-52, 57, 59). In Ras Shamra III B (or uppermost IV A) was found a copper knife (Kuschke in Schaeffer, 1962, diagram on p. 252, p. 257), 3 metal awls (Courtois in Schaeffer, 1962, p. 353, Fig. 21, K, p. 358, Fig. 25, P, Q), and two roll-headed pins (ibid., p. 411, Fig. 51, A, p. 358, Fig. 25, R; see also section diagram on p. 390, Fig. 49). Awls also occur in Ubaid or slightly post-Ubaid context at Sakje Geuzi (level IV C, Taylor, et al., 1950, Fig. 33, 4, and p. 123) and in an early Gawran level (XI) at Tepe Gawra (Tobler, 1950, Pl. XCVIII, a, 3). There is a copper bead in Chagar Bazar XII (Mallowan, 1936, p. 26) and, finally, a series of needles (or pins) and awls plus a possible dagger blade from the Late Chalcolithic of Beycesultan—said to be of general late Halaf-Ubaid time range but with a radiocarbon date of from 3000-2700 B.C.—(Lloyd and Mellaart, 1962, p. 281; cf. Mellink in this volume).

According to Perkins' analysis (Perkins, 1949, Chaps. IV-V), the Warka period and the early part of the Protoliterate period in south Mesopotamia are contemporary with a somewhat heterogenous group of wares in northern Iraq which she has labeled Gawran. Gawran materials are known from Tepe Gawra XI A-VIII B (wheel-made pottery appears in Gawran VIII), Nineveh 4, Nuzi (Yorgan Tepe) IX-VIII, Grai Resh IV-II. There are ties with southern Mesopotamia (Perkins, 1949, pp. 194-97): for instance, the presence of beveled-rim bowls in Nineveh 3 and 4 (Mallowan, 1933, p. 168), Nuzi (Starr, 1937, Pl. 50 A), Grai Resh (Lloyd, 1940, Pl. III, Fig. 7, 13), Brak (Mallowan, 1947, p. 222 and Pl. LXVI, 4); "Uruk gray" burnished ware at Tepe Gawra (XI-X A), Nineveh 3, Grai Resh, and many other sites in the Sinjar area (Tobler, 1950, p. 155; Lloyd, 1938, 1940; Perkins, 1949, p. 170, note 116). Nineveh has also Reserved-Slip Ware (Mallowan, 1933, Pl. LII, 12, and p. 167).

Perkins treats the Gawran and succeeding Ninevite periods in detail (Perkins, 1949, Chap. V). To her account may be added the site of Telul eth-Thalathat in the Sinjar region (Egami, 1958; see above, p. 73).

Phase G

Phase G materials come from Judeideh, and make up a well-developed assemblage which includes the first substantial appearance of metal. This is accompanied by a decline in numbers of flint and groundstone implements, although the types of implements are much the same as in Phase F. Braidwood notes that much of the pottery has almost a "factory-made" look (Braidwood and Braidwood, 1960, p. 259). Architecture included rectangular mud-brick structures as well as a circular mud-brick wall. The several pottery types of Phase G include Reserved-Slip Ware and Multiple-Brush Painted Ware. Metal work includes four striking human figurines as well as a range of copper pins and reamers. Stamp seals and the first cylinder seals occur. There are several piriform mace heads, including one fluted example. In bone, there are awls, pins, and an incised tube made of a lion femur.

The most important external connections for this material are with southern Mesopotamia in the late Protoliterate period—whereas relations with Cilicia cannot be well documented (Mellink, 1962, p. 223)—and include: Reserved-Slip Ware, a trait which continues into the Mesopotamian Early Dynastic (Braidwood and Braidwood, 1960, p. 277, Fig. 218,

p. 278, Fig. 219, Pl. 29, Pl. 85, 1, 7; cf. Delougaz, 1952, Pl. 17, 1, and see Perkins, 1949, pp. 104, 109, for examples at Khafajah and Ur); drooping spouts (Braidwood and Braidwood, 1960, p. 272, Fig. 213, 18, 19, p. 277, Fig. 218, 10), cf. Warka VII-VI (Perkins, 1949, p. 100) and Jemdat Nasr (Mackay, 1931, Pl. LXIII, 26); beveled-rim bowls which probably belong to the end of F and the beginning of G in the 'Amuq (Braidwood and Braidwood, 1960, p. 234, n. 10), cf. Warka XII-IV (Nöldeke, et al., 1932, p. 41, Pl. 18 A c) and Khafajah (Delougaz, 1952, Pl. 21); piriform mace heads (Braidwood and Braidwood, 1960, p. 323, Fig. 250); see Perkins, 1949, p. 148, for similar mace heads at Warka, Ur, Telloh, and Farah in south Mesopotamia; Jemdat Nasr style cylinder seals (Braidwood and Braidwood, 1960, p. 332, fig. 254); a pendant similar to eyed figurines ("spectacle idols") of Brak and of south and north Iraq (Braidwood and Braidwood, 1960, p. 328, Fig. 252, 35; Mallowan, 1947, Pls. XXV-XXVI; Tobler, 1950, Pl. LII b).

There are also connections with Egypt. The Phase G (and H) Syrian bottle (Braidwood and Braidwood, 1960, p. 270) is a form discovered in First Dynasty context in Egypt (Petrie, 1902, Pl. VIII 6; Kantor, 1942, pp. 193-94, 198; for its occurrence in E.B. II context in Palestine, see Wright, 1937, pp. 69-72). One sherd of comb-impressed ware in 'Amuq G is paralleled by finds in Egyptian First Dynasty context (Braidwood and Braidwood, 1960, p. 293, Fig. 233, 12; Kantor, 1942, pp. 196, 198-99). There are also drooping spouts in the Egyptian Gerzean and in the Palestinian Late Chalcolithic-E.B. I range (Kantor in Ehrich, 1954, pp. 4-5). Palestinian E.B. I-E.B. II platters are paralleled in 'Amuq G (Braidwood and Braidwood, 1960, p. 274-75, Fig. 216; Wright, 1937, pp. 58, 69-70).

Some pottery in Hama L is said to be like the incised Ninevite 5 ware (Fugmann, 1958, p. 22), and there are beveled-rim bowls in Hama K (ibid., Fig. 37, 5 B 840; Fig. 46, 4 A 882) as well as "spectacle idols" (ibid., Fig. 30, 5 B 23 TC; Fig. 37, 4 B 603 34; Fig. 46, 4 C 623; the last examples are the hollow-based ceramic type, like those of Gawra XII-IX (Tobler, 1950, Pl. LXXXVI) and Grai Resh IV-II (Lloyd, 1940, Pl. III, Fig. 7, 1, and p. 19). There are also Jemdat Nasr period (late Protoliterate) cylinder seals in Hama K (Ingholt, 1940, pp. 22-23) and cylinder seal impressions of the same period in the Byblos *première installation urbaine* (Dunand, 1950b, pp. 595, 600).

There is possible Reserved-Slip Ware at Carchemish (Woolley, 1952 pp. 228-29 and Pl. 58 c), Arslan Tepe (Braidwood and Braidwood, 1960, p. 511) and Gözlü Kule Early Bronze II (Goldman, 1956, pp. 107, 117). Moortgat reports some Ninevite 5 ware from Tell Ailun (Moortgat, 1957), and says it continues until the Akkadian levels there.

The Brak Eye Temples are contemporary with 'Amuq G, but are much more closely tied to southern Mesopotamia than to the western part of the area (Mallowan, 1947).

The J. P. P. I. C. surveys found evidence that some complex of roughly Phase G type (with or without the persistence of beveled-rim bowls, and including Reserved-Slip Ware and drooping-spouted jars) must have been well established in the more level plains of the Urfa, Diyarbekir, and Sürt vilayets. At Sögüt Tarlasi, capping an occurrence of Upper Paleolithic materials of his own interest, Bruce Howe encountered the remains of a small village of this complex, including—as well as the pottery—an "eye-goddess" amulet.

In northern Mesopotamia, the Ninevite period, characterized by Ninevite 5 incised ware, is contemporary with late Protoliterate in southern Mesopotamia and hence more or less with 'Amuq G. The known sites and levels are Nineveh 5, Gawra VIII A-VII (the 'Amuq G chalice is similar in form to a painted example from Gawra VII; Braidwood and Braidwood, 1960, p. 269, Fig. 207, 7; Speiser, 1935, Pls. XXIX a, LXV, 58; Perkins *in* Ehrich, 1954, p. 47), Nuzi VII, Billa 6-7, Grai Resh I, Chagar Bazar 4-5 (Perkins, 1949, Table 1).

Phase H

Materials of Phase H were found on Chatal Hüyük, Judeideh, Ta'yinat, and Dhahab. The most distinctive aspect of the assemblage is the appearance of Red-Black Burnished Ware (or Khirbet Kerak Ware, as it is often called). Brittle Orange Ware also makes its first appearance, Reserved-Slip Ware continues. The flint industry is the same as that of Phases F-G. Architecture was in mud brick, and included rectangular buildings, benches, and carefully prepared floor basins. Other items in the assemblage include the somewhat enigmatic baked-clay andirons, animal figurines in clay, a number of objects in cupreous metal (including reamers, knot-headed pins, a lugged ax, and a poker-butted spear), piriform mace heads, stamp seals, cylinder seals, a number of beads and pendants, an engraved bovid femur reminiscent of the engraved lion bone from Phase G, and some bone awls and pins.

The characteristic "cyma profiled" cups of Phase H Simple Ware (Braidwood and Braidwood, 1960, p. 352) are similar to some from Chagar Bazar 5 (Mallowan, 1936, Fig. 10, 16-17).

Red-Black Burnished (or Khirbet Kerak) Ware occurs at: Tabara al-Akrad I-IV (Hood, 1951), Ras Shamra III A 2 and III A 3, with engraved ox bones in III A 3 much like the 'Amuq ones and in association with combed ware like that of 'Amuq H and J (Braidwood and Braidwood, 1960, p. 369, Fig. 286, 14, and pp. 441-42, Fig. 341, 6; Schaeffer, 1962, pp. 204-12 and Chap. VI); Qala'at er-Rus levels 7-8, with an engraved ox bone in level 8 and combed ware in level 6 (Forrer's Appendix II *in* A. Ehrich, 1939, p. 123, Fig. 3; Schaeffer, 1948, p. 41); Tell Sukas level 5, also with combed ware (Schaeffer, 1962, p. 209), Hama K 5 to K 1 (Fugmann, 1958, pp. 37 ff.; Ingholt, 1940, pp. 20-21). Red-Black Burnished Ware is also apparently present at Arslan Tepe and at a site somewhere near Kharput in the Elazig area (Braidwood and Braidwood, 1960, pp. 511, n. 85, 519); Braidwood notes that andirons occur with a similar burnished pottery from Georgia (*ibid*., p. 519; and see Dzhaparidze, 1964).

Khirbet Kerak Ware is well known as a foreign ceramic imported into Palestine during the E.B. III period (Wright, 1937, p. 72; 1961, p. 34; Amiran, 1952; for discussions of its place of origin, see Mellink, 1962, p. 224; and Dzhaparidze, 1964).

Brittle Orange Ware is not abundant in 'Amuq H; because the clay is unique according to Matson's analysis, Braidwood suggests that this ware may have been imported into the 'Amuq. Mellaart relates it to his metallic ware category, and suggests the Konya Plain as the place of origin for the metallic ware (Mellaart, 1963*b*, pp. 231-32). Brittle Orange Ware occurs also in E.B. II levels at Gözlü Kule (Mellink *in* Goldman, 1956, pp. 108-9); however, the same strata yield a type of truncated conical cup found in Phase I of the 'Amuq, and consequently Gözlü Kule E. B. II may be somewhat later than 'Amuq H. There is an association of Brittle Orange Ware with Canaanean blades and a few sherds of Red-Black Burnished Ware at Telmen Hüyük near Zincirli (shown to Braidwood by Bahadir Alkim, personal communication from Braidwood, 1963), and Brittle Orange Ware also occurs at Zincirli itself (Braidwood and Braidwood, 1960, p. 518; and see Mellink, 1962, p. 224).

Several of the parallels with southern Iraq mentioned for Phase G are true also for H: Reserved-Slip Ware, incised and piriform mace heads, cylinder seals (Braidwood and Braidwood, 1960, pp. 516, 519). Northern Iraq is not well known during this time interval (see Perkins *in* Ehrich, 1954, pp. 47-48).

Phase I

Phase I materials come from Chatal Hüyük, Tell Judeideh, and Tell Ta'yinat. The assemblage includes some of the same pottery types as Phase H (Red-Black Burnished Ware, Brittle Orange Ware, Reserved-Slip Ware) as well as some types appearing in this phase for the first time (a Painted Simple Ware, Smeared-Wash Ware). Architecture is poorly known, but was perhaps not greatly different from that of Phase H. The andirons persist into this phase from H. A human figurine in clay is thought to be an example of the monster-headed or pinch-faced figurines which are later widely distributed in Syria. A few metal objects were found: reamers, pins, and a needle. Flint implements (no obsidian was found) still seem to be part of the tradition that began with Phase F, and are characterized by Canaanean blades. Miscellaneous items include a cylinder seal with representative design and some segmented fayence beads.

Smeared-Wash Ware is present at Tell Brak in the Sargonid levels (Mallowan, 1947, Pl. XLIII, 1-4, and p. 191) and a few sherds in E.B. III at Gözlü Kule (Mellink in Goldman, 1956, p. 163, 743), but Braidwood thinks both these are probably Phase J type rather than I. He states that the general I-J Simple Ware tradition can be seen at Gözlü Kule (Goldman, 1956, Pl. 245, 178-184, are truncated conical cups from E.B. II levels; Pl. 268, 517-518, 520, 523, are goblets), Til-Barsib among the hypogeum pottery (Thureau-Dangin and Dunand, 1936, Pls. 99 and XX), Carchemish graves (Woolley, 1914, Pl. XXII, 6), Hama J (Fugmann, 1958, pp. 49-83), several of du Buisson's sites (Khan Sheikhoun, Tell 'As tombs, Mishrifé Tomb 4; Du Mesnil du Buisson, 1932, 1935), Qala'at er-Rus and Tell Sukas (A. Ehrich, 1939), Tell Simiryan and Tabbat al-Hammam (Braidwood and Braidwood, 1940). The recent sondages at Ras Shamra have produced fragments of goblets and truncated conical cups of 'Amuq I-J Simple Ware type (Schaeffer, 1962, 435, Fig. 23, upper rows; p. 334, Fig. 5, A, B, E, G, H; p. 239, Fig. 31, at right).

The one cylinder seal from Phase I was thought by Frankfort to be peripheral E.D. III; he also considered one of the sealings on the Hama J goblets to be E.D. II or III and probably peripheral (Braidwood and Braidwood, 1960, p. 521). Mallowan has noted the similarity of the Til-Barsib metals to those from the Ur Royal Cemetery, now generally thought to be E.D. III in date (Mallowan, 1937b).

Miscellaneous comparisons among sites outside the 'Amuq include the Til-Barsib tripod bowl (Thureau-Dangin and Dunand, 1936, Pl. XXV, 4), which is paralleled at Chagar Bazar level 5 (Mallowan, 1936, p. 31, Fig. 10, 12), and an amphora with handles (Thureau-Dangin and Dunand,

1936, Pl. XXVI, 1) also found in the Sargonid levels of Brak and in a Sargonid grave at Tell Jidle (Mallowan, 1947, Pl. LXVIII, 15; 1946, Fig. 9, 13). The Painted Simple Ware of 'Amuq I-J is probably related to the Khabur Ware of north Syria (Braidwood and Braidwood, 1960, p. 520; Mallowan, 1937a, pp. 102-4; 1947, pp. 23-25; Hrouda, 1957).

Phase J

Knowledge of the Phase J assemblage is almost completely based on material from Tell Ta'yinat, and is largely defined by the sharp decline in quantity of the Red-Black Burnished (or Khirbet Kerak) Ware. Architecture is not well known. Parts of rectilinear mud-brick buildings were found; nearly all were probably private houses. Much of the pottery of Phase J is of a Simple Ware style which began in Phase I, a goblet form being especially popular. Otherwise Painted Simple Ware continues (with one innovation: incising a design through dark paint) as does Smeared-Wash Ware. There are two types of imported pottery: a two-handled cup and some sherds of gray burnished bottles. A few sherds of Brittle Orange Ware were found in the lower levels. Other items of the assemblage include a baked clay mold for casting metal tools, one large fragment of an andiron different from those of H and I, and several metal objects (toggle pins, needles, a dagger blade, a shaft-hole ax). Only three pieces of chipped stone were found, and ground-stone objects were nearly as rare.

The cup with double handles mentioned above is a Troy IV type; the bottles are comparable to finds from Woolley's site of Amarna (Woolley, 1914, pp. 91-92, Pl. XXIII, 12) and from Tell Chuera in northern Syria (Moortgat, 1960b, Abb. 6), Brak (Mallowan, 1947, Pl. LXXI, pp. 230-31), and Gözlü Kule (Mellink in Goldman, 1956, Pl. 268, 617; and see also Mellink, 1962, pp. 225-26). Braidwood agrees with Mallowan that this kind of pottery may relate to the gray ware of Shah Tepe and other north Iranian sites. A third link between Brak and the 'Amuq J materials (the other two being Smeared-Wash Ware and the gray ware bottles) is the Phase J goblet form, which compares with some vessels occurring only in the Sargonid to Ur III levels at Brak (Mallowan, 1947, Pl. LXXV, 15-17, and pp. 235-36). It does not appear, from the results of the J. P. P. I. C. surface surveys in southeastern Turkey, that the western type of I-J assemblage was very strongly evidenced in this region. However, some simple goblet bases and the Smeared-Wash Ware did occur.

White-on-black decoration occurs at Hama on goblets of G II type in level J (but this is after Khirbet Kerak Ware has disappeared there; Ingholt, 1940, p. 30). The earliest pottery from a sondage at Tell Kazel on the Syrian coast seems to include goblet forms at least and possibly other parallels to 'Amuq I-J (Dunand and Saliby, 1957, Pl. VI, lower).

There are ceramic parallels to the Palestinian Middle Bronze Age in the Phase J assemblage also. Goblets and "teapots" with white-on-black decoration occur at Megiddo, as do toggle pins (Braidwood and Braidwood, 1960, p. 522).

Moortgat's excavations at Tell Chuera have revealed remains of the Ur III to Akkadian time range (Moortgat, 1960a, 1960b). There are parallels with Mesopotamia—a cylinder seal, temple architecture—(Moortgat, 1960a, pp. 83-85) and with the 'Amuq (gray ware bottle mentioned above).

Braidwood notes that an impressive catalogue of metals could be made from the sites of the 'Amuq I-J range: Til-Barsib (the hypogeum, Thureau-Dangin and Dunand, 1936), Carchemish, Tell Kara Hasan, and the Hammam graves (Woolley, 1952, Pls. 60-61; 1914, Pl. XIX c, XXI c), Gözlü Kule Early Bronze II and III (Goldman, 1956), Mishrifé Tomb IV (Du Mesnil du Buisson, 1935, Pl. XLVII), Tell 'As tombs I-III (Du Mesnil du Buisson, 1932), Hama J (Fugmann, 1958, pp. 49-83). To this may be added Ras Shamra III A (Courtois in Schaeffer, 1962, Chaps. V, VI). The metal objects found at these sites indicate a standard industry, and include such items as pins (in several varieties, the toggle pin being most characteristic), needles, chisels, reamers, axes (shaft-hole, lugged, and plain), poker-butted and socketed spearheads, daggers, and swords.

Ras Shamra II, which overlies Ras Shamra III A, is securely placed, by means of inscribed Egyptian objects found there (Schaeffer, 1962, pp. 212-25), as beginning about 2000 B.C. This, together with the radiocarbon dates for Hama J (see below), indicates that Braidwood's estimate of 2000 B.C. for the end of 'Amuq J (in Ehrich, 1954, p. 38) is probably correct.

A number of items from the 'Amuq I-J range, Chagar Bazar II-III, and the Brak Sargonid levels also have parallels in Akkadian levels of Mesopotamia (Perkins in Ehrich, 1954, pp. 48-49: for instance, tea-pots, toggle pins, poker-butted spearheads). In north Iraq and north Syria, cuneiform writing appears for the first time (Nuzi V-III, Brak Sargonid, Chagar Bazar II-III).

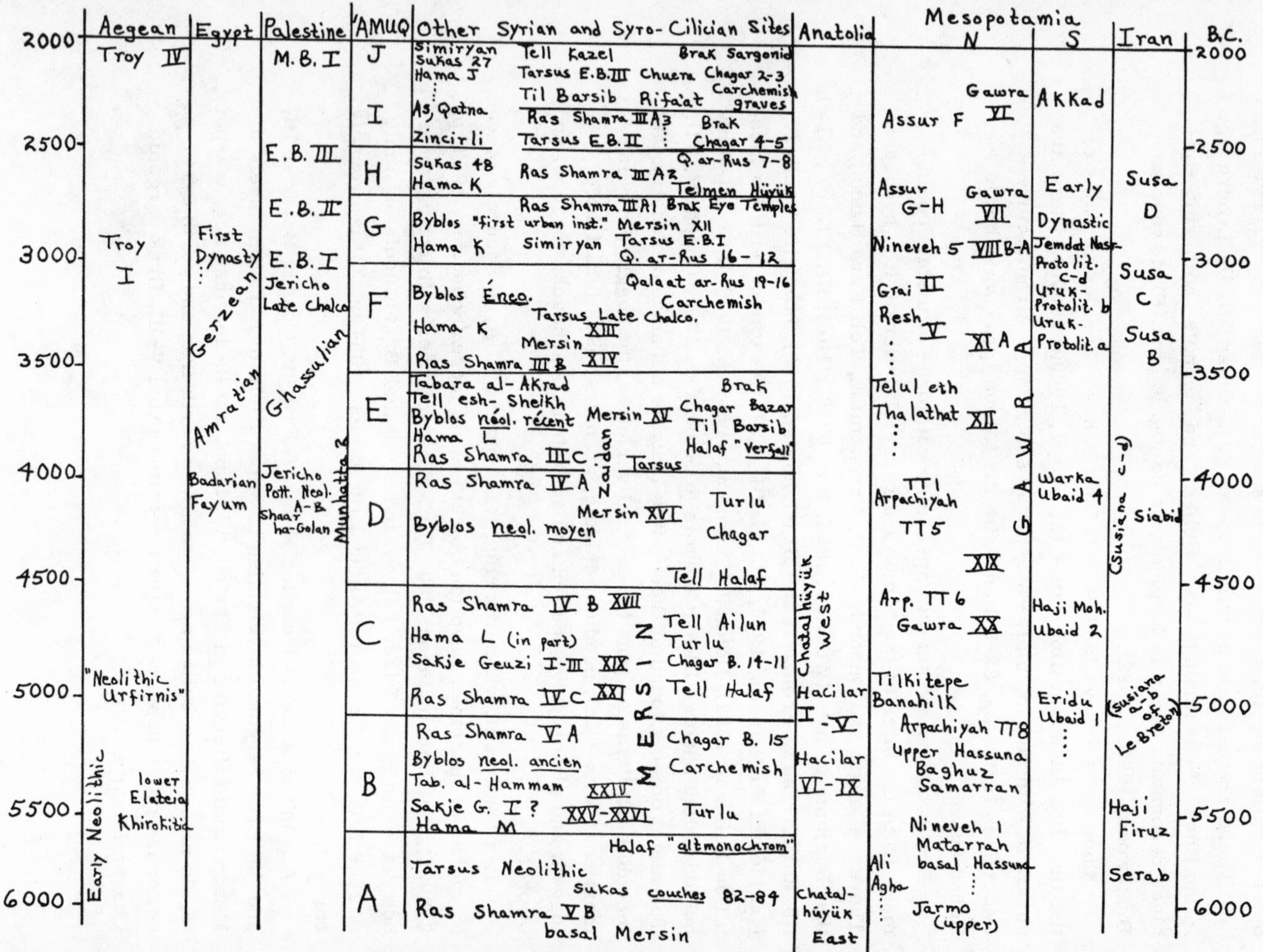

B.C.	Aegean	Egypt	Palestine	'AMUQ	Other Syrian and Syro-Cilician Sites	Anatolia	Mesopotamia N	Mesopotamia S	Iran	B.C.
2000	Troy IV		M.B. I	J	Simiryan; Sukas 27; Hama J; Tell Kazel; Tarsus E.B.III; Chuera; Brak Sargonid; Chagar 2-3; Til Barsib; Rifa'at; Carchemish graves		Gawra VI	Akkad		2000
				I	As, Qatna; Zincirli; Ras Shamra III A3; Tarsus E.B.II; Brak; Chagar 4-5		Assur F			
2500			E.B. III	H	Sukas 48; Hama K; Ras Shamra III A2; Q. ar-Rus 7-8; Telmen Hüyük		Assur G-H; Gawra VII	Early Dynastic	Susa D	2500
3000	Troy I	First Dynasty	E.B. II; E.B. I	G	Byblos "first urban inst."; Hama K; Ras Shamra III A1; Brak Eye Temples; Mersin XII; Simiryan; Tarsus E.B.I; Q. ar-Rus 16-12		Nineveh 5; Gawra VIII B-A	Jemdat Nasr-Protolit. c-d		3000
		Gerzean	Jericho Late Chalco	F	Byblos Énéo.; Hama K; Ras Shamra III B; Qalaat ar-Rus 19-16; Carchemish; Tarsus Late Chalco.; Mersin XIII; XIV		Grai II; Resh V; Gawra XI A	Uruk-Protolit. b; Uruk-Protolit. a	Susa C; Susa B	
3500		Amratian	Ghassulian	E	Tabara al-Akrad; Tell esh-Sheikh; Byblos néol. récent; Hama L; Ras Shamra III C; Mersin XV; Brak; Chagar Bazar; Til Barsib; Halaf "Verfall"; Tarsus; Zaidan		Telul eth Thalathat; XII; GAWRA		(Susiana c-d)	3500
4000		Badarian; Fayum	Jericho Pott. Neol. A-B; Shaar ha-Golan; Munhatta 2	D	Ras Shamra IV A; Byblos néol. moyen; Mersin XVI; Turlu; Chagar; Tell Halaf		TT1 Arpachiyah TT5; XIX	Warka Ubaid 4	Siabid	4000
4500	"Neolithic Urfirnis"			C	Ras Shamra IV B XVII; Hama L (in part); Sakje Geuzi I-III XIX; Ras Shamra IV C XXI; Tell Ailun; Turlu; Chagar B. 14-11; Tell Halaf; MERSIN	Chatal hüyük West; Hacilar I-V	Arp. TT6; Gawra XX; Tilkitepe; Banahilk	Haji Moh. Ubaid 2; Eridu Ubaid 1	(Susiana a-b of Le Breton)	4500
5000	lower Elateia; Khirokitia			B	Ras Shamra V A; Byblos neol. ancien; Tab. al-Hammam XXIV; Sakje G. I ?; Hama M; XXV-XXVI; Chagar B. 15; Carchemish; Turlu	Hacilar VI-IX	Arpachiyah TT8; Upper Hassuna; Baghuz; Samarran; Nineveh 1		Haji Firuz	5000
5500	Early Neolithic			A	Halaf "altmonochrom"; Tarsus Neolithic; Sukas couches 82-84; Ras Shamra V B; basal Mersin	Chatal-hüyük East	Ali Agha; Matarrah; basal Hassuna; Jarmo (upper)		Serab	5500
6000										6000

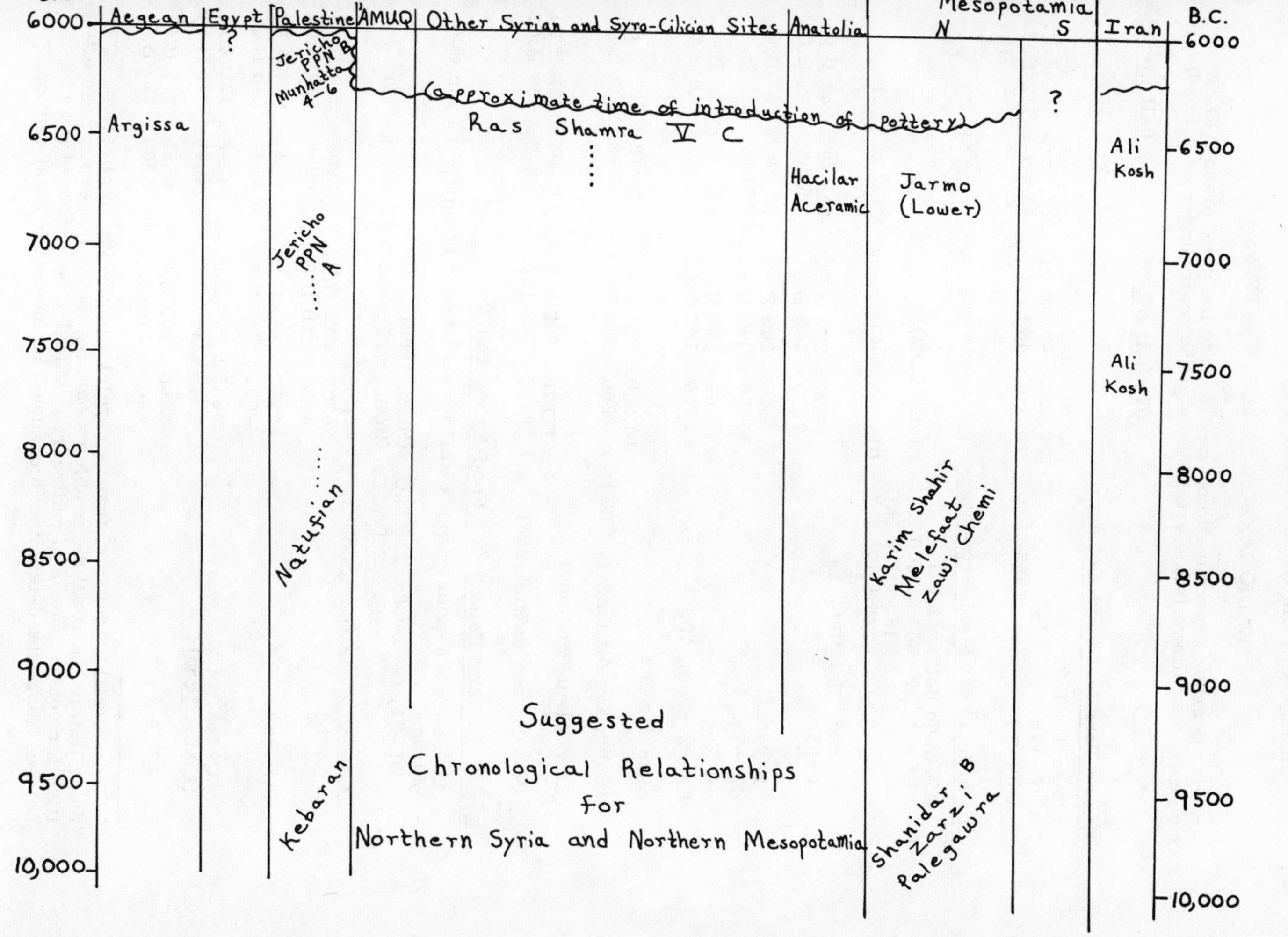
B.C.
Aegean
Egypt
Palestine
AMUQ
Other Syrian and Syro-Cilician Sites
Anatolia
Mesopotamia
N
S
Iran
B.C.
6000
6500
7000
7500
8000
8500
9000
9500
10,000
?
Jericho PPN B
Munhatta 4–6
(approximate time of introduction of pottery)
?
Argissa
Ras Shamra V C
Ali Kosh
Hacilar Aceramic
Jarmo (Lower)
Jericho PPN A
Ali Kosh
Natufian
Karim Shahir
Melefaat
Zawi Chemi
Kebaran
Shanidar
Zarzi B
Palegawra
Suggested
Chronological Relationships
for
Northern Syria and Northern Mesopotamia

RADIOCARBON DETERMINATIONS

Radiocarbon determinations[4] pertinent to the pre-'Amuq A time range are as follows (sites are listed alphabetically under each heading):

	5,570 half life	5,730 half life
Era of Terminal Food-Collecting		
Shanidar B 2	(Lower Zarzian)	
W-179	12,000 ± 400 B.P.	12,360 ± 412 B.P.
(Rubin and Suess, 1955)	10,050 ± 400 B.C.	10,410 ± 412 B.C.
Era of Incipient Food-Production		
Ali Kosh bottom level		
DL-21, #9	6448 ± 200 B.C. (Hole, 1962)	
	6465 ± 180 B.C.	
	6290 ± 175 B.C. (Hole and Flannery, 1962, p. 115)	
Jericho "Natufian"		
F-69	9850 ± 240 B.P.	10,146 ± 247 B.P.
	7800 ± 240 B.C.	8196 ± 247 B.C.
F-72	9800 ± 240 B.P.	10,094 ± 247 B.P.
(Kenyon, 1959)	7850 ± 240 B.C.	8144 ± 247 B.C.
P-376	11,166 ± 107 B.P.	11,501 ± 110 B.P.
(Stuckenrath, 1963)	9216 ± 107 B.C.	9551 ± 110 B.C.
Shanidar B 1		
W-681	10,600 ± 300 B.P.	10,918 ± 309 B.P.
(Rubin and Alexander, 1960)	8650 ± 300 B.C.	8968 ± 309 B.C.
Zawi Chemi Shanidar		
W-681	10,870 ± 300 B.P.	11,196 ± 309 B.P.
(Solecki and Rubin, 1958)	8920 ± 300 B.C.	9246 ± 309 B.C.
Era of Earliest Established Food-Production		
Ali Kosh, pre-pottery brick wall levels (second occupation from the bottom)		
DL-21, #4	6888 ± 210 B.C. (Hole, 1962)	
	5810 ± 330 B.C. (Hole and Flannery, 1962, p. 115)	
Jarmo, lower and middle (pre-pottery)		
C-113	6707 ± 320 B.P.	6908 ± 330 B.P.
	4757 ± 320 B.C.	4958 ± 330 B.C.
C-742	6606 ± 330 B.P.	6804 ± 340 B.P.
	4656 ± 330 B.C.	4854 ± 340 B.C.
C-743	6695 ± 360 B.P.	6896 ± 371 B.P.
(Libby, 1955)	4745 ± 360 B.C.	4946 ± 371 B.C.
F-44	6650 ± 170 B.P.	6850 ± 175 B.P.
	4700 ± 170 B.C.	4900 ± 175 B.C.

4. It will be obvious, from a careful study of the implications of these listings, that all the problems bearing on the numerous possibilities for contamination of radiocarbon samples have not yet been resolved. Hence the determinations should be used with great caution.

F-45 (Braidwood, 1958)	6570 ± 165 B.P. 4620 ± 165 B.C.	6767 ± 170 B.P. 4815 ± 170 B.C.
H-551/491 (Braidwood, 1959)	8525 ± 175 B.P. 6575 ± 175 B.C.	8781 ± 180 B.P. 6831 ± 180 B.C.
W-607	9040 ± 250 B.P. 7090 ± 250 B.C.	9311 ± 258 B.P. 7361 ± 258 B.C.
W-608	7750 ± 250 B.P. 5800 ± 250 B.C.	7983 ± 258 B.P. 6033 ± 258 B.C.
W-651	8830 ± 200 B.P. 6880 ± 200 B.C.	9095 ± 206 B.P. 7145 ± 206 B.C.
W-652	7950 ± 200 B.P. 6000 ± 200 B.C.	8189 ± 206 B.P. 6239 ± 206 B.C.
W-657	11,240 ± 300 B.P. 9290 ± 300 B.C.	11,577 ± 309 B.P. 9627 ± 309 B.C.
W-665 (Rubin and Alexander, 1960)	11,200 ± 200 B.P. 9250 ± 200 B.C.	11,536 ± 206 B.P. 9586 ± 206 B.C.
Jericho, Pre-pottery Neolithic A		
F-39 (Kenyon, 1959)	8800 ± 160 B.P. 6850 ± 160 B.C.	9064 ± 165 B.P. 7114 ± 165 B.C.
F-40 (two different pretreatments)	8725 ± 210 B.P. 6775 ± 210 B.C.	8987 ± 216 B.P. 7037 ± 216 B.C.
(Kenyon, 1957)	8805 ± 210 B.P. 6855 ± 210 B.C.	9069 ± 216 B.P. 7119 ± 216 B.C.
P-377	9582 ± 89 B.P. 7632 ± 89 B.C. PPN A, first level	9869 ± 92 B.P. 7919 ± 92 B.C.
P-378	9775 ± 110 B.P. 7825 ± 110 B.C. PPN A, after construction of defenses	10,068 ± 113 B.P. 8118 ± 113 B.C.
P-379 (Stuckenrath, 1963)	9655 ± 84 B.P. 7705 ± 84 B.C. PPN A, later than phase VI of defenses	9945 ± 87 B.P. 7995 ± 87 B.C.
BM-105	10,250 ± 200 B.P. 8300 ± 200 B.C. PPN A, after construction of defenses	10,558 ± 206 B.P. 8608 ± 206 B.C.
BM-106	10,300 ± 200 B.P. 8350 ± 200 B.C. PPN A, phase VI of defenses	10,609 ± 206 B.P. 8659 ± 206 B.C.
BM-110 (Barker and Mackey, 1963)	10,180 ± 200 B.P. 8230 ± 200 B.C. PPN A, destruction of defenses	10,485 ± 206 B.P. 8535 ± 206 B.C.
Jericho Pre-pottery Neolithic B		
GL-28	8200 ± 200 B.P. 6250 ± 200 B.C.	8446 ± 206 B.P. 6496 ± 206 B.C.

GL-38 (Zeuner, 1956)	7800 ± 200 B.P. 5850 ± 200 B.C.	8034 ± 207 B.P. 6084 ± 206 B.C.
F-38	7800 ± 160 B.P. 5850 ± 160 B.C.	8034 ± 165 B.P. 6084 ± 165 B.C.
F-40 (same sample as F-38, different pre-treatments)	8670 ± 200 B.P. 6720 ± 200 B.C.	8930 ± 206 B.P. 6980 ± 206 B.C.
GR-942	8900 ± 70 B.P. 6950 ± 70 B.C.	9167 ± 72 B.P. 7217 ± 72 B.C.
GR-963 (de Vries and Waterbolk, 1958)	8785 ± 100 B.P. 6835 ± 100 B.C.	9049 ± 106 B.P. 7099 ± 106 B.C.
P-380	8610 ± 75 B.P. 6660 ± 75 B.C. PPN B, first level	8868 ± 77 B.P. 6918 ± 77 B.C.
P-381	8658 ± 101 B.P. 6708 ± 101 B.C. early PPN B	8918 ± 104 B.P. 6968 ± 104 B.C.
P-382 (Stuckenrath, 1963)	8956 ± 103 B.P. 7006 ± 103 B.C. mid-PPN B	9225 ± 106 B.P. 7275 ± 106 B.C.
BM-111 (Barker and Mackey, 1963)	9170 ± 200 B.P. 7220 ± 200 B.C. mid-PPN B	9445 ± 206 B.C. 7425 ± 206 B.C.

Ras Shamra V C, Néolithique Ancien (pre-pottery)

P-460	8364 ± 101 B.P. 6414 ± 101 B.C.	8615 ± 104 B.P. 6665 ± 104 B.C.
P-459 (Stuckenrath, 1963)	8142 ± 100 B.P. 6192 ± 100 B.C.	8386 ± 103 B.P. 6436 ± 103 B.C.

Radiocarbon determinations pertinent to the 'Amuq A-B range are as follows:

Bakun B

P-438	5990 ± 81 B.P. 4040 ± 81 B.C.	6170 ± 83 B.P. 4220 ± 83 B.C.

Byblos Néolithique Ancien

W-627 (Rubin and Alexander, 1960)	6550 ± 200 B.P. 4600 ± 200 B.C. Néolithique Ancien, upper	

GR- ? 5043 ± 80 B.C.
(Dunand, 1961) Néolithique Ancien, middle

Elateia (central Greece), Early Neolithic, Monochrome pottery

GR-2973	5520 ± 70 B.C. near bottom of deposit
GR-3037	5400 ± 90 B.C.
GR-3041	5230 ± 100 B.C. more developed Early Neolithic ware

GR-3502 5080 ± 130 B.C.
first painted pottery

GR-2933 6280 ± 75 B.C.
(Weinberg, 1962) Late Neolithic (excavator's comment: GR-2933 is too early)

Hacılar
BM-48 7550 ± 180 B.P. 7777 ± 185 B.P.
5600 ± 180 B.C. 5827 ± 185 B.C.
(Barker and Mackey, 1960) level VI, end Late Neolithic

P-314 7340 ± 94 B.P. 7560 ± 97 B.P.
5390 ± 94 B.C. 5610 ± 97 B.C.
level IX, Late Neolithic

P-313A 7350 ± 85 B.P. 7571 ± 88 B.P.
5400 ± 85 B.C. 5621 ± 88 B.C.
(Ralph and Stuckenrath, 1962) level VI, end Late Neolithic

Haji Firuz
P-455 7269 ± 86 B.P. 7487 ± 89 B.P.
5319 ± 86 B.C. 5537 ± 89 B.C.

P-502 6895 ± 83 B.P. 7162 ± 86 B.P.
(Stuckenrath, 1963) 4945 ± 83 B.C. 5212 ± 86 B.C.

Hassuna
W-660 7040 ± 200 B.P. 7251 ± 206 B.P.
5090 ± 200 B.C. 5301 ± 206 B.C.
(Rubin and Alexander, 1960) level V

Khirokitia non-ceramic
St- 414, 415, 416 averaging ca. 7600 ± 150 B.P.
5650 ± 150 B.C.
(Perrot, 1962, p. 155)

Knossos, Early Neolithic
BM-124 8050 ± 180 B.P. 8292 ± 185 B.P.
6100 ± 180 B.C. 6341 ± 185 B.C.

BM-126 7000 ± 180 B.P. 7210 ± 185 B.P.
5050 ± 180 B.C. 5260 ± 185 B.C.
(Barker and Mackey, 1963) Knossos 5, near top of Early Neolithic levels

Matarrah, middle
W-623 7570 ± 250 B.P. 7797 ± 258 B.P.
(Rubin and Alexander, 1960) 5620 ± 250 B.C. 5847 ± 258 B.C.

Mersin, basal
W-617 7950 ± 250 B.P. 8189 ± 257 B.P.
(Rubin and Alexander, 1960) 6000 ± 250 B.C. 6239 ± 257 B.C.

Nea Nicomedeia, W. Macedonia
Q-655 8180 ± 150 B.P. 8425 ± 155 B.P.
(Godwin and Ellis, 1962) 6230 ± 150 B.C. 6475 ± 155 B.C.

Ras Shamra V B, Néolithique Moyen		
P-458	7686 ± 112 B.P. 5736 ± 112 B.C.	7917 ± 115 B.P. 5967 ± 115 B.C.
V A, Néolithique Récent		
P-457 (Stuckenrath, 1963)	7184 ± 84 B.P. 5234 ± 84 B.C.	7400 ± 87 B.P. 5450 ± 87 B.C.
Tepe Serab		
P-465	7605 ± 96 B.P. 5655 ± 96 B.C.	7833 ± 99 B.P. 5883 ± 99 B.C.
P-466	7956 ± 98 B.P. 6006 ± 98 B.C.	8195 ± 101 B.P. 6245 ± 101 B.C.
P-467 (Stuckenrath, 1963)	7644 ± 89 B.P. 5694 ± 89 B.C.	7873 ± 92 B.P. 5923 ± 92 B.C.

Radiocarbon determinations pertinent to the 'Amuq C-D-E range are as follows:

'Amuq C range

Dalma Tepe		
P-503 (Stuckenrath, 1963)	5986 ± 87 B.P. 4036 ± 87 B.C.	6166 ± 90 B.P. 4216 ± 90 B.C.
Hacılar Chalcolithic		
P-316	7170 ± 134 B.P. 5220 ± 134 B.C. level II, early Chalcolithic	7385 ± 138 B.P. 5432 ± 138 B.C.
P-315 (Ralph & Stuckenrath, 1962)	6090 ± 121 B.P. 5040 ± 121 B.C. level Ia, Early Chalcolithic	7200 ± 125 B.P. 5250 ± 125 B.C.
Tell Halaf GR-2660 (Vogel and Waterbolk, 1964)	7560 ± 35 B.P. 5620 ± 35 B.C. Near "altmonochrome" level, maybe early stage of Halaf	7787 ± 36 B.P. 5837 ± 36 B.C.

'Amuq D-E range

Beycesultan		
P-297	4690 ± 62 B.P. 2740 ± 62 B.C. level XXVIII, Late Chalcolithic	4831 ± 64 B.P. 2881 ± 64 B.C.
P-298 (Ralph and Stuckenrath, 1962)	4960 ± 58 B.P. 3010 ± 58 B.C.	5109 ± 60 B.P. 3159 ± 60 B.C.
Tal-i-Gap		
GaK-198	5440 ± 120 B.P. 3490 ± 120 B.C.	5603 ± 124 B.P. 3653 ± 124 B.C.
GaK-197 (Kigoshi and Endo, 1963)	5870 ± 160 B.P. 3920 ± 160 B.C.	6046 ± 165 B.P. 4096 ± 165 B.C.
Tepe Gawra, levels 17/18		
C-817 Average (Libby, 1955)	5400 ± 800 B.P. 3450 ± 800 B.C.	

Site / Sample	Date	Corrected date
Pisdeli		
P-157 (Ralph, 1959)	5460 ± 160 B.P. 3510 ± 160 B.C.	5624 ± 164 B.P. 3674 ± 164 B.C.
P-505	5638 ± 85 B.P. 3688 ± 85 B.C.	5807 ± 88 B.P. 3857 ± 88 B.C.
P-504 (Stuckenrath, 1963)	5518 ± 81 B.P. 3568 ± 81 B.C.	5684 ± 83 B.P. 3734 ± 83 B.C.
Ras Shamra		
P-389 (Stuckenrath, 1963)	6134 ± 173 B.P. 4184 ± 173 B.C. early Ubaid	6319 ± 178 B.P. 4369 ± 178 B.C.
Warka		
H-138/123 (Münnich, 1957)	6070 ± 160 B.P. 4120 ± 160 B.C. reeds from deepest strata in Eanna precinct, on virgin soil	6252 ± 165 B.P. 4302 ± 165 B.C.
<u>'Amuq F range</u>		
Grai Resh		
P-469	5169 ± 64 B.P. 3219 ± 64 B.C.	5324 ± 66 B.P. 3374 ± 66 B.C.
P-468 (Stuckenrath, 1963)	4939 ± 75 B.P. 2989 ± 75 B.C.	5087 ± 77 B.P. 3137 ± 77 B.C.
Jericho Chalcolithic		
GL-24 (Zeuner, 1956)	5210 ± 110 B.P. 3260 ± 110 B.C.	5366 ± 113 B.P. 3416 ± 113 B.C.
<u>'Amuq G range</u>		
Byblos <u>prémiere installation urbaine</u>		
C-819 (Libby, 1955)	5317 ± 300 B.P. 3367 ± 300 B.C.	5477 ± 309 B.P. 3527 ± 309 B.C.
<u>'Amuq H-I-J range</u>		
Beycesultan Early Bronze		
P-273 (Ralph and Stuckenrath, 1962)	3980 ± 97 B.P. 2030 ± 97 B.C. likened to Troy I by the excavators	
Ur "Royal Cemetery"		
BM-64	3920 ± 150 B.P. 1970 ± 150 B.C. skeleton of Mes-Kalam-Shar	4038 ± 155 B.P. 2088 ± 155 B.C.
BM-70	4030 ± 150 B.P. 2080 ± 150 B.C. burned bone from clay coffin	4151 ± 155 B.P. 2201 ± 155 B.C.
BM-76 (Barker and Mackey, 1961)	3990 ± 150 B.P. 2040 ± 150 B.C. skeleton of Queen Shub-Ad	4110 ± 155 B.P. 2160 ± 155 B.C.

Hama J		
K-530	4260 ± 140 B.P. 2310 ± 140 B.C.	4388 ± 144 B.P. 2438 ± 144 B.C.
K-531	4180 ± 120 B.P. 2230 ± 120 B.C.	4305 ± 124 B.P. 2355 ± 124 B.C.
K-533 (Tauber, 1960)	4160 ± 120 B.P. 2210 ± 120 B.C.	4285 ± 124 B.P. 2335 ± 124 B.C.

Tell Sukas, Early Bronze Age levels

Couche 48
about 2500 ± 120 B.C.

Couche 27
about 2260 ± 120 B.C. (Riis, 1961-62)

Bibliography

Albright, W. F.

1926 "Proto-Mesopotamian Painted Ware from the Balikh Valley," Man XXVI: 41-42.

Amiran, Ruth B. K.

1952 "Connections between Anatolia and Palestine in the Early Bronze Age," Israel Exploration Journal 2: 89-103.

Barker, H., and Mackey, J.

1960 "British Museum Natural Radiocarbon Measurements II," Radiocarbon II: 26-30.
1961 "British Museum Natural Radiocarbon Measurements III," ibid. III: 39-45.
1963 "British Museum Natural Radiocarbon Measurements IV," ibid. V: 104-8.

Bialor, P. A.

1962 "The Chipped Stone Industry of Chatal Hüyük," Anatolian Studies XII: 67-110.

Bostanci, E.

1959 "Researches on the Mediterranean Coast of Anatolia, a New Paleolithic Site at Beldibi near Antalya. Preliminary Report," Anatolia 4: 129-78.

Braidwood, R. J.

1954a "A Tentative Relative Chronology of Syria from the Terminal Food-gathering Stage to ca. 2000 B.C." In Ehrich, 1954, pp. 34-41.
1954b "The Iraq-Jarmo Project," Sumer X: 120-38.
1955 "The Earliest Village Materials of Syro-Cilicia," Proceedings of the Prehistoric Society for 1955 XXI: 72-76.
1958 "Near Eastern Prehistory," Science 127: 1419-30.
1959 "Über die Anwendung der Radiokarbon-Chronologie fur das Verständnis der ersten Dorfkultur-Gemeinschaften in Südwestasien," Osterreichischen Akademie der Wissenschaften, Phil.-hist. Kl., 1958: 249-59.
1960 "Seeking the World's First Farmers in Persian Kurdistan: a Full-Scale Investigation of Prehistoric Sites near Kermanshah," Illustrated London News 237: 695-97.
1961 "The Iranian Prehistoric Project, 1959-1960," Iranica Antiqua I: 3-7.
1962 "The Earliest Village Communities of Southwestern Asia Reconsidered," Atti del VI Congresso Internazionale delle Scienze Preistoriche e Protostoriche, I: 115-26.

Braidwood, R. J., and Braidwood, L.

1940 "Report on Two Sondages on the Coast of Syria, South of Tartous," Syria XXI: 183-226.
1953 "The Earliest Village Communities of Southwestern Asia," Journal of World History I: 278-310.

1960 Excavations in the Plain of Antioch, Vol. I. ("Oriental Institute Publications," Vol. LXI.) Chicago: University of Chicago Press.

Braidwood, R. J., Braidwood, L., Smith, J., and Leslie, C.

1952 "Matarrah," Journal of Near Eastern Studies XI: 1-75.

Braidwood, R. J., Howe, B., et al.

1960 Prehistoric Investigations in Iraqi Kurdistan. ("Studies in Ancient Oriental Civilization," No. 31.) Chicago: University of Chicago Press.

Braidwood, R. J., and Willey, G., eds.

1962 Courses toward Urban Life. ("Viking Fund Publications in Anthropology," No. 32.) New York: Wenner-Gren Foundation.

Burney, C. A.

1958 "Eastern Anatolia in the Chalcolithic and Early Bronze Age," Anatolian Studies VIII: 157-209.

Cauvin, J.

1962 "Les Industries Lithiques du Tell de Byblos (Liban)," L'Anthropologie 66: 488-502.

Contenson, H. de.

1963 "New Correlations between Ras Shamra and al-'Amuq," Bulletin of the American Schools of Oriental Research 172: 35-40.

de Vries, H. and Waterbolk, H. T.

1958 "Groningen Radiocarbon Dates III," Science 128: 1550-56.

Delougaz, P.

1952 Pottery from the Diyala Region. ("Oriental Institute Publications," Vol. LXIII.) Chicago: University of Chicago Press.

Du Mesnil du Buisson.

1932 "Une Campagne de Fouilles á Khan Sheikhoun," Syria XIII: 171-88.

1935 Le Site Archéologique de Mishrifé-Qatna. Paris: E. de Bocca

Dunand, M.

1949-50 "Rapport Préliminaire sur les Fouilles de Byblos en 1948," Bulletin du Musée de Beyrouth IX: 53-64.

1950a "Rapport Préliminaire sur les Fouilles de Byblos en 1949," ibid. X: 65-74.

1950b "Chronologie des plus anciennes installations de Byblos," Revue Biblique 57: 583-603.

1955a "Rapport préliminaire sur les fouilles de Byblos en 1950," Bulletin du Musée de Beyrouth XII: 7-20.

1955b "Rapport préliminaire sur les fouilles de Byblos en 1952," ibid. XII: 21-23.

1961 "Rapport préliminaire sur les fouilles de Byblos en 1957, 1958, 1959," ibid. XVI: 69-85.

Dunand, M., and Saliby, N.

1957 "À la recherche de Simyra," Annales Archéologiques de Syrie VII: 3-16.

Dyson, R. H.

1961 Review of Braidwood and Braidwood, 1960. In American Anthropologist 63: 630-41.

Dzhaparidze, O. M.

1964 "The Cultures of Early Agricultural Tribes in the Territory of Georgia," VII International Congress of Anthropological and Ethnological Sciences (Moscow, August, 1964). Moscow: Nauka Publishing House.

Egami, N.

1958 Telul eth-Thalathat. The Excavation of Tell II. Tokyo: The Institute for Oriental Culture.

Ehrich, Ann M. H.

1939 Early Pottery of the Jebeleh Region. ("Memoirs of the American Philosophical Society," Vol. XIII.) Philadelphia.

Ehrich, R. W., ed.

1954 Relative Chronologies in Old World Archeology. Chicago: University of Chicago Press.

Esin, Ufuk, and Benedict, P.

1963 "Recent Developments in the Prehistory of Anatolia," Current Anthropology 4: 339-46.

Fugmann, E.

1958 Hama. Fouilles et Recherches 1931-1938. L'Architecture des Périodes pre-Hellénistiques. ("Nationalmuseets Skrifter Større Beretninger," Vol. IV.) Copenhagen.

Garrod, D. A. E.

1930 "The Palaeolithic of Southern Kurdistan: Excavations in the Caves of Zarzi and Hazar Merd," Bulletin of the American School of Prehistoric Research, 6: 8-43.

Garstang, J.

1953 Prehistoric Mersin. Oxford: Clarendon Press.

Ghirshman, R.

1938 Fouilles de Sialk près de Kashan 1933, 1934, 1937. Paris: Geuthner.

Godwin, H.

1962 "The Half-Life of Radiocarbon 14," Nature 195: 984.

Godwin, H., and Ellis, E. H.

1962 "Cambridge University Natural Radiocarbon Measurements V," Radiocarbon IV: 57-70.

Goldman, Hetty

1956 Excavations of Gözlü Kule, Tarsus. Vol. II. From the Neolithic through the Bronze Age. Princeton: Princeton University Press

Hole, F.

1959 "A Reanalysis of Basal Tabbat al-Hammam, Syria," Syria XXXVI: 149-83.

1962 "Archeological Survey and Excavation in Iran, 1961," Science 137: 524-26.

Hole, F., and Flannery, K.

1962 "Excavations at Ali Kosh, Iran, 1961," Iranica Antiqua II, 97-148.

Hood, S.

1951 "Excavations at Tabara El Akrad, 1948-49," Anatolian Studies I: 113-47.

Hrouda, B.

1957 Die bemalte Keramik des Zweiten Jahrtausends in Nordmesopotamien und Nordsyrien. Berlin: Verlag Gebr. Mann.

Ingholt, H.

1940 "Rapport Préliminaire sur Sept Campagnes de Fouilles à Hama en Syrie (1932-1938). ("Det Kgl. Danske Videnskabernes Selskab. Archaeologisk-kunsthistoriske Meddelelser," Vol. III, 1.) Copenhagen.

1957 "The Danish Dokan Expedition," Sumer XIII: 214-15.

Kantor, H. J.

1942 "The Early Relations of Egypt with Asia," Journal of Near Eastern Studies I: 174-213.

1954 "The Chronology of Egypt." In Ehrich, 1954, pp. 1-27.

Kaplan, J.

1958 "The Excavations at Telulyot Batashi in the Vale of Sorek," Eretz Israel 5: 9-24, 83-84.

1959 "The Neolithic Pottery of Palestine," Bulletin of the American Schools of Oriental Research, 156: 15-21.

Kenyon, K.

1957 "Excavations at Jericho, 1956," Palestine Exploration Quarterly, pp. 101-7.

1959 "Earliest Jericho," Antiquity XXXIII: 5-9.

Kigoshi, K., and Endo, K.

1963 "Gakushuin Laboratory (Japan) Natural Radiocarbon Measurements II," Radiocarbon V: 109-17.

Kirkbride, Diane

1960 "The Excavation of a Neolithic Village at Seyl Aqlat, Beidha, near Petra," Palestine Exploration Quarterly, pp. 136-45.

Kleindienst, M. R.

1960 "Notes on a Surface Survey at Baghouz (Syria)," Anthropology Tomorrow VI: 65-72.

Lamb, W.

1954 "The Culture of North-East Anatolia and its Neighbors," Anatolian Studies IV: 21-32.

Le Breton, L.

1957 "The Early Periods at Susa, Mesopotamian Relations," Iraq XIX: 79-124.

Libby, W.

1955 Radiocarbon Dating. Chicago: University of Chicago Press.

Lloyd, S.

1938 "Some Ancient Sites in the Sinjar District," Iraq V: 123-42.

1940 "Iraq Government Soundings at Sinjar," Iraq VII: 13-21.

1960 "Ur-Al Ubaid, Uqair and Eridu: An Interpretation of Some Evidence from the Flood Pit," Iraq XXII: 23-31.

Lloyd, S., and Mellaart, J.

1962 Beycesultan. Vol. I. ("Occasional Publications of the British Institute of Archeology at Ankara," No. 6.) London.

Lloyd, S., and Safar, F.

1945 "Tell Hassuna," Journal of Near Eastern Studies IV: 255-89.

1948 "Eridu: Second Season's Excavations, 1947-48," Sumer IV: 115-25.

Mackay, E.

1931 Report on Excavations at Jemdat Nasr, Iraq. ("Field Museum of Natural History. Anthropology, Memoirs" I,3.) Chicago.

Mallowan, M. E. L.

1933 "The Prehistoric Sondage of Nineveh, 1931-32," University of Liverpool, Annals of Archaeology and Anthropology XX: 127-86.

1936 "The Excavations at Tall Chagar Bazar, and an Archaeological Survey of the Habur Region, 1934-35," Iraq III: 1-59.

1937a "The Excavations at Tall Chagar Bazar, and an Archaeological Survey of the Habur Region, Second Campaign, 1936," Iraq IV: 91-177.

1937b "The Syrian City of Til-Barsib," Antiquity XI: 328-39.
1946 "Excavations in the Balih Valley, 1938," Iraq VIII: 111-62.
1947 "Excavations at Brak and Chagar Bazar," Iraq IX:

Mallowan, M. E. L., and Rose, J.

1935 "Excavations at Tall Arpachiyah, 1933," Iraq II: 1-178.

Maxwell-Hyslop, R., Taylor, J. duPlat, Seton-Williams, M. V., and Waechter, J. D'a.

1942 "An Archaeological Survey of the Plain of Jabbul, 1939," Palestine Exploration Quarterly, pp. 8-40.

Mellaart, J.

1956 "The Neolithic Site of Ghrubba," Annual of the Department of Antiquities of Jordan III: 25-40.
1958 "Excavations at Hacılar. First Preliminary Report," Anatolia Studies VIII: 127-56.
1961a "Excavations at Hacılar. Fourth Preliminary Report, 1960," Anatolian Studies XI: 39-75.
1961b "Early Cultures of the South Anatolian Plateau," Anatolian Studies XI: 159-84.
1962 "Excavations at Chatal Hüyük. First Preliminary Report, 1961," Anatolian Studies XII: 41-65.
1963a "Excavations at Chatal Hüyük, 1962. Second Preliminary Report," Anatolian Studies XIII: 43-103.
1963b "Early Cultures of the South Anatolian Plateau II," Anatolian Studies XIII: 199-236.
1964a "Earliest of Neolithic Cities: The Origins of Pottery in Anatolian Chatal Hüyük," Illustrated London News 244: 232-34.
1964b "A Neolithic City in Turkey," Scientific American 210: 94-104.

Mellink, M.

1962 "The Prehistory of Syro-Cilicia," Bibliotheca Orientalis XIX: 219-26.

Moortgat, A.

1957 "Archaeologische Forschungen der Max Frhr. von Oppenheim Stiftung im Noerdlichen Mesopotamien 1956," Annales Archéologiques de Syrie VII: 17-30.
1960a "Vorläufiger Bericht uber eine Grabungskampagne der M. Frhr. von Oppenheim-Stiftung in Nordmesopotamien 1958," ibid. X: 73-86.
1960b "Tell Chuera in Nordost-Syrien. Vorläufiger Bericht uber die zweite Grabungskampagne 1959," Schriften der Max Freiherr von Oppenheim Stiftung, Heft 4.

Mortensen, Peder

1962 "On the Chronology of Early Village-Farming Communities in Northern Iraq," Sumer XVIII: 73-80.

Münnich, K. O.

1957 "Heidelberg Natural Radiocarbon Measurements I," Science 126: 194-99.

Nöldeke, A., et al.

1932 "Vierter Vörlaufiger Bericht uber die von der Notgemeinschaft der deutschen Wissenschaft in Uruk unternommenen Ausgrabungen," Abhandlungen der Akademie der Wissenschaften Berlin, Phil.-hist. Kl., No. 6.

Oates, J.

1960 "Ur and Eridu, the Prehistory," Iraq XXII: 32-50.

Oppenheim, Max Freiherr von

1943 Tell Halaf, Vol. I. Die Prahistorische Funde. Bearbeitet von Hubert Schmidt. Berlin: Walter de Gruyter and Co.

Perkins, Ann

1949 The Comparative Archeology of Early Mesopotamia. ("Studies in Ancient Oriental Civilization," No. 25.) Chicago: University of Chicago Press.

1954 "The Relative Chronology of Mesopotamia." In Ehrich, 1954, pp. 42-55.

Perrot, J.

1952 "Le Néolithique d'Abou Gosh," Syria XXIX: 120-45.

1955 "The Excavations at Tell Abu Matar near Beersheba," Israel Exploration Journal V: 73-84.

1962 "Palestine-Syria-Cilicia." In Braidwood and Willey, 1962.

Petrie, W. M. Flinders

1902 Abydos I. ("Egyptian Exploration Fund Memoir," Vol. XXII.) London.

Piggot, S., ed.

1962 The Dawn of Civilization. London: Thames and Hudson.

Prausnitz, M. W.

1958 "Khirbet Sheikh 'Ali," Revue Biblique 65: 414.

1959 "The First Agricultural Settlements in Galilee," Israel Exploration Journal 9: 166-74.

Ralph, E.

1959 "University of Pennsylvania Radiocarbon Dates III," Radiocarbon I: 45-58.

Ralph, E., and Stuckenrath, R.

1962 "University of Pennsylvania Radiocarbon Dates V," Radiocarbon IV: 144-59.

Reilly, E. B.

1940 "Test Excavations at Tilkitepe (1937)," Türk Tarih Arkeologya ve Etnografya Dergisi IV: 145-65.

Riis, P. J.

1960 "L'Activité de la Mission Archéologique Danoise sur la Côte Phenicienne en 1959," Annales Archéologiques de Syrie X: 111-32.

1961 "Excavations in Phoenicia," Archaeology 14: 215-16.

1961-62 "L'Activité de la Mission Archéologique Danoise sur la Côte Phenicienne en 1960," Annales Archéologiques de Syrie XI: 133-44.

Rubin, M., and Alexander, C.

1960 "U. S. G. S. Radiocarbon Dates V," Radiocarbon II: 129-85.

Rubin, M., and Suess, H. E.

1955 "U. S. G. S. Radiocarbon Dates II," Science 121: 481-88.

Schaeffer, C. F. A.

1948 Stratigraphie Comparée et Chronologie de l'Asie Occidentale. Oxford: Oxford University Press.

1961 "Les Fondements Pré- et Protohistoriques de Syrie du Néolithique Préceramique au Bronze Ancien," Syria XXXVIII: 7-22.

1962 Ugaritica IV. ("Institut Français d'Archéologie de Beyrouth, Bibliotheque Archéologique et Historique," Tome LXXIV.) Paris: Geuthner.

Seton-Williams, M. V.

1961 "Preliminary Report on the Excavations at Tell Rifa'at," Iraq XXIII: 68-87.

Solecki, R.

1955 "Shanidar Cave, a Paleolithic Site in Northern Iraq," Annual Report of the Smithsonian Institution, 1954, pp. 389-425.

1957 "The 1956 Season at Shanidar," Sumer XIII: 165-71.

Solecki, R., and Rubin, M.

1958 "Dating of Zawi Chemi Shanidar, an Early Village Site at Shanidar, Northern Iraq," Science 127: 1446.

Speiser, E. A.

1935 Excavations at Tepe Gawra, Vol. I. Philadelphia: University of Pennsylvania Press.

Starr, R. F. S.

1937-39 Nuzi. Cambridge, Mass.: Harvard University Press.

Stekelis, M.

1950-51 "A New Neolithic Industry: the Yarmukian of Palestine," Israel Exploration Journal 1: 3-20.

Stekelis, M., and Haas, G.

1952 "The Abu Usba Cave (Mount Carmel)," Israel Exploration Journal 2: 15-47.

Stekelis, M., and Yizraely, T.

1963 "Excavations at Nahal Oren. Preliminary Report," Israel Exploration Journal 13: 1-12.

Stronach, D.

1961 "Excavations at Ras al 'Amiya," Iraq, XXIII: 95-137.

Stuckenrath, R.

1963 "University of Pennsylvania Radiocarbon Dates VI," Radiocarbon V: 83-103.

Tauber, H.

1960 "Copenhagen Radiocarbon Dates IV," Radiocarbon II: 12-25.

Taylor, J. duPlat, Seton-Williams, M. V., and Waechter, J.

1950 "The Excavations at Sakçe Gözü," Iraq XII: 53-138.

Thureau-Dangin, F., and Dunand, M.

1936 Til-Barsib. Paris: Geuthner.

Tobler, A. J.

1950 Excavations at Tepe Gawra. Vol. II. Philadelphia: University of Pennsylvania Press.

van Liere, J., and Contenson, H. de.

1963 "A Note on Five Early Neolithic Sites in Inland Syria," Annales Archéologiques de Syrie XIII: 175-209.

Vogel, J. C., and Waterbolk, H. T.

1964 "Groningen Radiocarbon Dates V," Radiocarbon VI: 349-69.

Weinberg, S.

1962 "The Neolithic Period in Greece," Current Anthropology, 4: 377.

Woolley, C. Leonard

1914 "Hittite Burial Customs," University of Liverpool, Annals of Archeology and Anthropology VI: 87-98.
1934 "The Prehistoric Pottery of Carchemish," Iraq I: 146-62.
1952 Carchemish, Vol. III. London: British Museum.
1953 A Forgotten Kingdom. Baltimore: Penguin.

Wright, G. E.

1937 "The Pottery of Palestine from the Earliest Times to the End of the Early Bronze Age." Ph.D. Dissertation, Johns Hopkins University.

1951 "An Important Correlation between Palestinian and Syrian Chalcolithic," Bulletin of the American Schools of Oriental Research 122: 52-55.

1961 "The Archaeology of Palestine." In The Bible and the Ancient Near East, G. E. Wright, ed. New York: Doubleday.

Zeuner, F. E.

1956 "The Radiocarbon Age of Jericho," Antiquity XXX: 195-97.

Addendum:

Since this volume went to press, an important summary account of the stratigraphic succession at Ali Kosh in Iran has appeared:

Hole, F., Flannery, K., and Neely, J.

1965 "Early Agriculture and Animal Husbandry in Deh Luran, Iran." Current Anthropology 6: 105-6.

Anatolian Chronology

Machteld J. Mellink
Bryn Mawr College

Anatolia, being on the immediate periphery of Mesopotamia, had the advantage of early contacts with documented history. The archaeologist's work is not confined to a laborious tracing of relative synchronisms, but he can anchor part of the network of interrelations with the aid of chronological fixed points and thus determine the tempo of otherwise ageless developments.

Anatolia probably entered the historical record at the time of the Akkadian dynasty in Mesopotamia, although the historicity of this entry will remain somewhat dubious until excavations will have proved the reality of Akkadian commercial establishments and military campaigns on the soil of Asia Minor. For the Old Assyrian period, contacts are abundantly documented and Anatolian chronology is firmly tied in to the Mesopotamian sequence. Tablets from Kültepe, Boğazköy, and Alişar give a range of dates corresponding to the reigns from Erišum I to Šamši-Adad I in the Assyrian king list (Goetze, 1957, pp. 69-81; Balkan, 1955, 1957; Garelli, 1963, pp. 31-79). Native history begins with the recorded activities of King Anitta of Kuššar, who is attested in stratified records from Kültepe and Alişar and remembered in the historical tradition of the later Hittite archives. The Old Hittite Kingdom has left its record in Hittite and Akkadian tablets at Boğazköy which complement the tradition of the Babylonian chronicles. Thus early Hittite history is co-ordinated with events in north Syria, the Hurrian lands, and Mesopotamia (the destruction of Babylon by a Hittite raid under the leadership of Muršili I). The Hittite Empire, from Šuppiluliuma on, is amply documented in the local archives at Boğazköy, the Amarna tablets, the Ugarit archives, and to a lesser extent in Mesopotamian records, down to its destruction about 1190 B.C.

The pre-Akkadian sequence of Anatolian archaeological material is not completely free-floating, and has the advantage of potential synchronization with the historical developments in the literate Near East. Specifically, the period of the earliest contact between Egypt and Mesopotamia (discussed by Helene J. Kantor in this volume) can be used as an important hinge in Near Eastern relative chronology. This contact is known to have occurred at the beginning of literacy, and is dated just before the start of Dynasty I in Egypt. Anatolia has not produced archaeological symptoms of Mesopotamian cultural penetration such as occur at this time in Egypt, but archaeological correlation allows a determination of the southeast Anatolian levels which are contemporary with the period of Egypto-Mesopotamian contact.

The archaeology of southeast Anatolia thus can be tied into the beginning of absolute chronology in Egypt and Mesopotamia. It is immaterial whether the absolute date of the Egypto-Mesopotamian contact turns out to be about 3200, 3000, or 2800 B.C. The important dividing line between prehistory and potential history can be traced into Anatolia. Material evidence in the vicinity of this line cannot be much earlier than 3000 B.C. The reference to this hypothetical absolute date may be frowned upon in a context which sets its aims in relative terms, but it will be clear from the following that a disregard of Egyptian and Mesopotamian historical facts will lead to distortions in prehistoric chronological estimates.

Before 3000 B.C. (if we may use this symbolic figure as that of the dim beginnings of history in the Near East) Anatolian archaeological sequences can be correlated on a relative basis only. The assignment will be a local Anatolian one first of all, but again coherence will be brought into the multiple evidence if Anatolia can be connected with the known preliterate sequence of Mesopotamia which, in spite of recent revolutionary claims for the periphery, remains the provisional center of coordination for East and West.

In emphasizing the assignment of correlating Anatolian chronology with that of the Near East, and Mesopotamia in particular, we want to allow Anatolia to function as the often quoted "bridge" between East and West, in this instance, between Mesopotamia and the Aegean. Once the eastern connections of Anatolia have been fixed in the grid of correlations, the relative position of the Aegean will become clear through its neighborly contacts with coastal Anatolia.

Substantial aid is to be expected from scientific methods of time determination. C-14 at present holds out the best promise to provide archaeologists with an independent set of absolute dates and an external control over relative estimates. The results of C-14 will be left out of consideration in this discussion in order to offer a purely archaeological version of the evidence, but a list of relevant C-14 dates is appended at the end of this chapter.

The pre-3000 B.C. series

The above introduction will explain why we start our chronological analysis in the middle and work in opposite directions from there. Our earliest fixed zone, that of the Egypto-Mesopotamian contacts, will serve as a horizontal dividing line in the tabulation and be abbreviated as "*ca.* 3000 B.C."

The Mesopotamian period in question is Protoliterate C and D or the Jemdet Nasr period; the north Syrian equivalent of this phase is Amuq G, which can be correlated with the Early Bronze I phase of Cilicia at Tarsus. The preceding phase, Protoliterate A and B, Amuq F, has strong material links with the Cilician Late Chalcolithic phase. The latter is represented at Tarsus by about three meters depth of stratified material in the settlement and a number of extramural burials (Goldman, 1956, pp. 5-7, 82-91). The excavated part of Mersin has no levels belonging to this period. The correlation of Tarsus Late Chalcolithic with Amuq F is based principally on ceramic evidence. The predominant pottery in both regions is a wheel-made ware of chaff-tempered light fabric, remarkably uniform in appearance, in spite of regional variations in decoration or surface treatment. (For a detailed analysis of the Amuq-Cilicia correlations in this and other pre-3000 phases, see the paper by Watson in this volume and Mellink, 1962.)

The earlier Chalcolithic sequence of Cilicia (Garstang, 1953, pp. 45 ff.) is also recognizably related to north Mesopotamian and north Syrian developments. Both Tarsus and Mersin have stratified material of a regional Ubaid phase (Amuq E). Mersin goes through several upheavals in this long phase (levels XVI-XIIB, *ca.* 3 m.); the most important architectural evidence is provided by the burned fortress of Mersin level XVI. The architectural forms as well as some features of the pottery of this level seem to be of Anatolian character, and perhaps antedate the full impact of Ubaid traditions. Mersin levels XIX-XVII and telescoped strata at Tarsus have unmistakable contacts with Amuq C and north Mesopotamia in the form of imported and imitated Halaf pottery, sufficient to warrant synchronisms, insufficient for a further analysis of cultural interrelations.

The earliest Chalcolithic levels at Mersin (XXIV-XX) are fairly independent. The alleged Hassuna affinities of Mersin painted wares (Garstang, 1953, pp. 59, 62) will need more documentation. In architecture, Mersin has some respectable remnants of rectangular and buttressed constructions. Tarsus has no more than marginal support for this phase, which must run parallel with part of the Amuq C range.

The preceding material at Tarsus and Mersin belongs to the so-called Neolithic period. It is abundant at Tarsus, and known to be at least ten meters deep at Mersin (levels XXXII-XXV). At both sites virgin soil and possibly pre-ceramic levels have remained elusive under the ground water level. The character of the architecture is barely known. Mersin XXV had a long rectangular building. The site is large, and may well have been fortified. Tarsus yielded fragments of polished floors or wall plaster. The outstanding known industries are obsidian and pottery. Mersin XXIX-XXV yielded excellent pressure-flaked javelin heads, daggers, and other implements (Garstang, 1953, Fig. 5). The pottery is predominantly a dark burnished ware which has parallels in Amuq A-B, Ugarit, and Syrian coastal sites, forming a closely knit ceramic province quite distinct from the north Mesopotamian pottery of the Hassuna period. There are a few signs of exchange with Hassuna (Braidwood and Braidwood, 1960, p. 503, obsidian javelin head), but the pottery traditions of north Mesopotamia and Syro-Cilicia are basically separate in this early phase.

The regions of the upper Euphrates, Habur, and Tigris are known to have taken part in the general north Mesopotamian development, but, as in most of eastern Anatolia, the archaeological evidence consists principally of surface finds. Halaf and Ubaid materials are known from the excavated sites of Sakça Gözü (du Plat Taylor, 1950) and Carchemish (Yunus kilns, Woolley, 1934a), and from a sounding at Turlu near Gaziantep (Perrot, 1964). The limits of north Mesopotamian ceramic (and presumably cultural) expansion and of potentially easy chronological correlation seem to be the Taurus Mountains, the Antitaurus, and the mountains between Elâziğ and Lake Van. Occasional contacts were made with sites beyond the mountain barriers, and exports of Halaf ware have been reported for the region of Hekimhan northwest of Malatya (Burney, 1958, pp. 159-63). Ubaid ware has been claimed for Malatya (Braidwood and Braidwood, 1960, p. 511, n. 85) and for Fraktin beyond the Antitaurus (T. Özgüç, 1956, p. 70). Halaf period occupation is attested for the Lake

Van area by the relevant finds at Tilki Tepe (Reilly, 1940, pp. 158-59; Burney, 1958, p. 160). We do not know what east Anatolian cultural phase corresponds to Cilician Neolithic.

To the west and north of Cilicia, direct Mesopotamian relations are absent. Individual sequences can be built up by excavation, and regional comparisons will allow the construction of a west or central Anatolian framework of interrelations. Recent discoveries have made it clear that important early developments were taking place in southwest Anatolia and the Konya area independent of Mesopotamia. The vast complex that is being excavated in those regions will have to be analyzed in local terms and as an independent time sequence first. Typologically, it can be classified according to the traditional categories of archaeological evolution such as Palaeolithic, Mesolithic, Neolithic, Chalcolithic, and Bronze Age, or their modern replacements referring to the dietary emancipation of mankind. The precise chronological co-ordination of this material with the southeast Anatolian and Mesopotamian complex is a separate and, for the time being, still difficult assignment.

The typological classification, although based on a good deal of common sense, has the inherent danger of <u>petitio principii</u> when admitted to chronological considerations, and its criteria do not always appear equally applicable to all the parts of Anatolia within and beyond the zone of Mesopotamian contact. If enough material similarities exist, however, the incomplete nature of the parallelism need not deter us from assuming basically similar developments of culture while allowing chronological margins for unevenness in tempo.

The earliest stratified sequence of habitation levels in Anatolia is found in the caves at Karain and Beldibi near Antalya (Esin and Benedict, 1963). Typologically (i.e., judging by the categories of stone artifacts) the Karain deposits range from Early, Middle, and Late Palaeolithic to Mesolithic and a less clearly identified Neolithic. The importance of these finds, in contrast to a large number of Palaeolithic discoveries in other parts of Anatolia, lies in the continuity of the record. The recognition of clearly transitional stages from Mesolithic cave strata to Neolithic mound sites is a matter of further exploration of habitation sites near the caves. At present, several of the caves near Antalya have a good stone-tool sequence and an upper stratum with ceramic admixture. The sherds from Karain include dark burnished simple bowl fragments which typologically (shapes and fabric) can be called

Neolithic. Moreover, in comparative archaelogical terms, these sherds closely resemble the dark neolithic pottery of Cilicia. Here typology and material archaeological correlation may well coincide to advocate the chronological link: Antalya Neolithic overlaps in time with Cilician Neolithic.

The next installment of southwest Anatolian Neolithic (and its successor Chalcolithic) is available, thanks to J. Mellaart's excavations, at Hacılar near Burdur and Çatalhüyük in the Konya area.

The sequence is fragmentary at its lower end. The aceramic levels at Hacılar (Mellaart, 1961, pp. 70-73; 1964b, p. 6; seven occupation levels with a total depth of 1.50 m.) represent an important but ill-known episode in the development of Neolithic village sites. On the assumption that this stage is truly aceramic (the excavated area was fairly large), it belongs typologically early in the Neolithic phase. Its artifacts (stone bowls; chert, obsidian, and bone tools) and burnished plaster floors are in agreement with this. The houses of aceramic Hacılar are built of large mud bricks.

In 1963, a deep sounding at Çatalhüyük reached a deposit of probably aceramic type which may be comparable to the earliest levels at Hacılar (Mellaart, 1964a, p. 158; the sounding was made in a small trench to a depth of 3.50 m. below a sterile stratum at the base of level X). No archaeological tie-in is available by means of specific features, but correlation with the Antalya cave sequence will undoubtedly be possible after further analysis. Cave sites and settlements in the foothills of Cilicia should provide the stepping-stones to north Syria where aceramic Ugarit represents the nearest typological equivalent.

At Çatalhüyük the excavated Neolithic sequence so far goes down from level I to X (Mellaart, 1962a, 1963a, 1964a). Levels X-VIII are only summarily known, but contain primitive pottery. Levels VII-I have enriched our knowledge of the typology of Neolithic to an astonishing degree. The houses are now of developed form, with timber reinforcement and embellishment of the mud-brick construction. Paintings, painted reliefs, and modeled animal protomes decorate the walls, displaying an artistic symbolism also apparent in the minor arts. Apart from the standard repertoire of stone and bone tools, monochrome pottery, and fertility idols (the latter suspected for many parts of Anatolia on the basis of surface finds; Bittel, 1949-50, pp. 135-39), Çatalhüyük has a production of small stone figurines of varying, but sometimes excellent quality, especially in level VI. A clay statuette of a goddess from level II proves the existence of iconographic traditions. Terracotta seals appear in levels IV-II. Traces of copper and lead occur as early as level IX. The wealth of cultural data suggests that some of the artistic and religious material from Çatalhüyük bears a local character, thereby opening vistas for further explorations of this articulate Neolithic stage elsewhere.

At present the evidence from Neolithic Çatalhüyük stands without detailed parallels in Anatolia. The chipped-stone industry of levels VIII-II is "very similar" to that of Mersin Middle Neolithic (Bialor, 1962, pp. 104-9). An archaeological connection and a potential synchronism can be suspected.

The sequence of the Çatalhüyük levels X-I at present is not tied in with the late Neolithic levels at Hacılar. At Hacılar itself a stratigraphic and chronological hiatus separates the aceramic deposit from the later stages of Neolithic, levels IX-VI. These levels are characterized by a poor (i.e., typologically late) chipped-stone industry, traces of copper working, monochrome pottery of none too simple shapes, and clay fertility figures of artistic distinction. The architecture of Hacılar VI consists of developed domestic units built of mud brick with provisions for an upper story.

At present the chronological and geographic representation of Neolithic Anatolian materials is too incoherent for confident detailed correlation. The archaeological system of direct linkage will be applicable when more excavated sites dot the map and longer sequences become available. The correlation of the Konya Plain with Cilicia and Mesopotamia will perhaps not remain vague for long. The geographical connection of western Cilicia and the Konya district is via the Calycadnus (Göksu) valley. Materials of Mesopotamian affinity crossed the Taurus Mountains with the traffic on this route at least from Chalcolithic times on. The site of Can Hasan northeast of Karaman, now being excavated by D. H. French (French, 1962, 1963), maintained a certain amount of contact with Cilicia in the periods of Mersin XXIII-XX (Early Chalcolithic, pre-Halaf) as is attested by ceramic imports in stratified context at Can Hasan, level 2 B. Can Hasan in this level has a well-developed architectural complex consisting of rectangular mud-brick houses with interior buttresses. Painted wall plaster had fallen from an upper story. There are also some surface finds at Can Hasan of Cilician "multiple brush ware" of Mersin XVI type, so far not found in stratified context outside Cilicia. Further reconstruction of archaeological contact via the Göksu route will provide the needed link between the Mesopotamian orbit and western Anatolia, as a counterpart of similar contacts which crossed the mountain barriers of eastern Anatolia to sites on the plateau.

The independent Chalcolithic sequence of western Anatolia is also represented at Çatalhüyük West and Hacılar. Çatalhüyük West (Mellaart, 1961b, pp. 177-84; 1962a, pp. 42, 44) has produced some excavated and much unstratified surface pottery; none of this is close enough to the Chalcolithic sequence at Mersin to prove specific equations, but Can Hasan will again form a bridge. Çatalhüyük itself may produce continuity from Neolithic to Chalcolithic strata in the lower levels of the west mound.

At Hacılar, Chalcolithic strata V-I have not strictly been proved to follow immediately after the burning of Neolithic level VI. This stretch of habitation levels still floats somewhere between the end of Neolithic and the later Chalcolithic period. The painted pottery styles of Hacılar V-II are more imaginative than those of the Konya Plain Chalcolithic; there is also considerable difference in styles of figurines. The variety of material cultures is considerable, although the basic styles of living and architecture were similar in this stage. Hacılar II and Ia have solid mud-brick architecture with many domestic refinements.

The end of Hacılar (burning of the Ia "fortress," some reoccupation by squatters levels Ib-d; Mellaart, 1960, pp. 92-99) is not linked to any excavated sequence to explain its relative position with regard to the beginning of Early Bronze or the "3000" limit. On the other hand, further exploration promises to establish a chain of sites to link the Hacılar version of Chalcolithic with the west coast of Anatolia and with the Aegean (Mellaart, 1960, pp. 88-90).

In other parts of Anatolia, the existence of typologically Chalcolithic material is not safely attested. In central Anatolian archaeology the term Chalcolithic has been used for the earliest strata at Alişar, Alaca Hüyük, and some other sites. Bittel (1949/50, 1950) has pointed out that Alişar Late "Chalcolithic" could hardly antedate 3000 B.C., but he referred to the depth of the "Chalcolithic" deposit (about 6 meters below Late "Chalcolithic") as a reason for caution. Orthmann (1963, p. 10) equates all Alişar "Chalcolithic" with Early Bronze I. At the present stage there are neither strong typological indications for a true Chalcolithic at Alişar (e.g., in pottery, tools, figurines, architecture) nor demonstrable archaeological connections with the sequences discussed so far. The excavated area is, however, small, and no other central Anatolian site has given a full sampling of the material of the stage in question. Büyük Güllücek (Koşay and Akok, 1957; Orthmann, 1963, pp. 39-40) has at least produced a quantity of pottery of Central Anatolian "Chalcolithic" type, but the decorated dark burnished wares seem to have affinities to east Anatolian Early Bronze Age wares which themselves are in need of more chronological definition (cf. Orthmann, 1963, pp. 80-81).

Similar uncertainties exist about the early levels at Beycesultan in the upper Maeander valley (Lloyd and Mellaart, 1962). There is no stratigraphic or typological connection between Hacılar Id and Beycesultan level XL, and we cannot estimate the gap which separates the two. The earliest material from Beycesultan is not different typologically from the Early Bronze stage into which it merges. As at Alişar, the deep sounding covered only a small area.

It is of course possible that early settlements, unmistakably contemporary with the Neolithic and Chalcolithic periods of south Anatolia, will be discovered in the central plateau area and in the northwest (cf. French, 1961). General probability would favor a theory of early-village distribution over most of the Anatolian peninsula as far northwest as the Troad and Bosporus. Fikirtepe, a site near Istanbul-Kadiköy, is typologically early enough to be ranked as a forerunner of the Early Bronze Age (Bittel, 1942, pp. 166-70; 1960). But few such sites have been identified so far, and it is methodologically dangerous to update the known material to fill what at present seems an awkward vacuum in central and north Anatolian chronology.

The Bronze Age sequence

We follow the method of Goldman's paper in Relative Chronologies in considering Cilicia the key area for chronological correlations, especially for the Early Bronze Age (Goldman, 1954). The Tarsus stratification gives an uninterrupted sequence of levels from the crucial "3000" date and the beginning of Early Bronze to the destruction of the site at the end of Late Bronze. With the destruction we are in historical context. The attackers are the Sea Peoples, the absolute date is 1190 ± about ten years.

The traditional division of Early, Middle, and Late Bronze Age will here be maintained even for the periods which are historically identifiable by political names and absolute dates. The advantage of the neutral labels is that they are used as chronological subdivisions only and do not presuppose cultural, political, or any other kind of unity. The subdivisions of Early Bronze I, II, and III are in general use, although unfortunately not always with identical chronological meanings. Subdivision of MB and LB is desirable.

The Early Bronze Age

The Cilician EB I-III periods form a complete sequence which runs parallel with Amuq G-J, with Mesopotamian Jemdet Nasr (Protoliterate C and D), Early Dynastic, Akkadian, and probably post-Akkadian down to the end of Ur III. The correlations with the Amuq are clear in ceramic parallels for phases H (brittle orange ware of EB II type also found in the Zincirli area), I (EB III goblets), J (EB III ring-burnished gray bottles) and in some of the metal forms (Tarsus EB III, Amuq I-J). (For details, see Watson, this volume, and Mellink, 1962).

The Amuq correlation is not the only standard for Cilician EB chronology. EB I and II connections can be made with Syrian sites outside the Amuq. Wheel-made light pottery of Syrian origin, partly of finer type than the plain simple wares of Amuq G and H, occurs through Tarsus EB I (*Tarsus* II, Fig. 236, 50-52) and II (*Tarsus* II, Fig. 245, 178-87) levels. Some of this pottery is contemporary with Amuq H, which apparently did not make or import the finer light wares during the Khirbet Kerak interlude. These wheel-made wares are not closely datable elsewhere, but will serve for correlation when other north Syrian sites will become better known. There is some relevant material from Tell Sukas and Qal'at er-Rus (A.M.H. Ehrich, 1939, pp. 66-69).

Tarsus EB II has also occasional north Mesopotamian imports in the form of wheel-made, spiral-burnished bottles and jars in buff ware with mat red stripes. Fragments of bottles of this type were sealed in a safe EB II context at Tarsus (*Tarsus* II, Fig. 244, 154 *a*,*b*, text p. 114). A similar bottle was found in a grave of the Early Dynastic cemetery at Ur (Woolley, 1934*b*, pp. 466-67, PG 1273, U 12.175, now in the University Museum, Philadelphia, UM 31-17-329), presumably of ED III date. A parallel with the same squat profile comes from Fara (Istanbul Museum 5926, Fara 674, height 0.09 m.). These ring-burnished and neatly painted bottles were imports in Fara and Ur. They probably came from the upper Euphrates region, where jars of similar fabric and decoration were found by Woolley in the Amarna cemetery (Woolley, 1914, Pl. XXII). Fragments of two such jars again occurred in Tarsus EB II (Tarsus II, Fig. 263, 369-70, text p. 130).

The more common and later versions of ring-burnished ware occur principally in the form of gray bottles, some of which are related to the Akkadian series at Tell Brak. A large number of imported north Mesopotamian specimens occurred in Tarsus EB III levels. The most specific bottle shape has a double-edged rim, elongated body, and slightly pointed base (Tarsus II, Fig. 268, 617, text p. 154). These bottles are also imitated in local ware. They do not occur at the very beginning of Tarsus EB III, but perhaps should be called EB IIIB. They continue into MB I. The EB IIIB shape rarely occurs in the Amarna cemetery (Woolley, 1914, Pl. XXIII, 12). A slightly more globular variant is represented in sherds from Tell Tainat, Amuq J (Braidwood and Braidwood, 1960, p. 451, Fig. 348, rim missing).

A Cilician synchronism with Egypt is given by the reserve-slip pitcher of Cilician EB II type found in an annex to mastaba G 1233 at Giza, dated before the end of Cheops' life (Goldman, 1954, p. 73; Tarsus II, p. 60; Reisner and Smith, 1955, p. 73, early Dynasty IV).

A seal found in typical EB III context at Tarsus (Tarsus II, Fig. 393, 25, text pp. 234, 238) is of glazed steatite. Its figural handle in the shape of a crouched animal suggests a date in the First Intermediate Period, although the actual manufacture of the seal may be Syrian rather than Egyptian. The use of stamp seals and cylinder seals for the decoration of pottery is a general EB II-III phenomenon which occurs in Cilicia (Tarsus, Mersin) as well as in the Amuq (starting in phase G, it seems; Braidwood and Braidwood, 1960, pp. 295-96, Figs. 235, 7, and 236), Byblos, Hama, and other Syrian sites (Mellink, 1962, p. 223).

It is clear from the above that during the Early Bronze Age, Cilicia had foreign trade connections with northern Mesopotamia, Syria, and directly or indirectly with Egypt. There are also indications of trade with Cyprus, which are of value for the chronology of the Early Cypriote period. Several wares found in EB II context at Tarsus are of Cypriote origin: red and black streak-burnished ware (Tarsus II, Fig. 263, 371-78, text pp. 112-13) which is known as black-slip-and-combed ware from Kyra-Alonia and Philia (Dikaios, 1962, pp. 201-3); and so-called Erimi ware (Tarsus II, Fig. 263, 379-80, text p. 112), also known as red-on-white ware (Dikaios, 1962, p. 201).

The end of the EB III period in Cilicia is marked by the sudden appearance of a new ceramic tradition of Syrian origin, also characteristic of Alalakh levels XVI-VIII, MB I, Amuq K.

Central Anatolia. The expansion of the Cilician EB framework to central Anatolia is clear in general but lacks detail. The best early sequences are found at Alişar, Alaca, and now at Kültepe. Alişar Chalcolithic has no specific resemblance to Cilician EB I. Alişar Ib, "Copper Age," is again materially different from Cilician EB II, but a few correlations can be made indirectly. An imported Syrian bottle from burial dX46 below the floor of level 13T at Alişar (Von der Osten, 1937, I, 176, Fig. 168; cf. p. 147) in shape, but not in surface finish, corresponds to imported EB II bottles at Tarsus and the ED bottles from Ur and Fara quoted above (cf. Orthmann, 1963, p. 86; note the correct Alişar tomb number above).

The cylinder seal from level 8M at Alişar (Von der Osten 1937, I, 183, e455) has its closest parallel in a stratified seal from Tell Asmar, ED I (Frankfort, 1955, p. 18, No. 448), but this gives no more than a post quem indication (Bittel, 1950, p. 20).

Pottery of "Copper Age" type suddenly appears in small quantity at Tarsus at the beginning of EB III, mostly in the form of simple red bowls (Tarsus II, pp. 134-35). Even if this Tarsus version of Copper Age ware may be a late and peripheral representative of that group, the stratification of the Tarsus wares indicates that the Anatolian "Copper Age" fabric continues into the Cilician EB III period. At the end of Alişar's Copper Age an admixture of intermediate painted ware makes its appearance (level 7M); the next level, 6M, has Cappadocian painted ware in conjunction with monochrome Copper Age pottery, after which monochrome wheel-made ware is introduced and Cappadocian ware continues (5M). A single sherd of Cappadocian ware was found at Tarsus in EB IIIA context (Tarsus II, p. 163, Fig. 285, 744); this occurrence helps to correlate the start of Cappadocian painted ware and Alişar 6M with about the beginning of Cilician EB III, although we need much more documentation of the synchronism.

The sequence at Kültepe is now coming to our aid. As recently defined by the excavator (T. Özgüç in Mellink, 1963, pp. 175-76), EB I is in the process of exploration and has produced no imports so far. Kültepe EB II is of "Copper Age" type with imports of Syrian wheel-made jars and flaring corrugated cups of Tarsus EB II type. Kültepe EB III has three subdivisions. The early phase, IIIC, has Syrian imports, proto "intermediate" ware, and handmade depas cups with red cross-bands (N. Özgüç, 1957, pp. 77-80) such as occur also at Alişar in levels 6-7M. The middle phase, Kültepe EB IIIB, a level with monumental architecture including a "megaron," contains wheel-made plates of Tarsus EB III (and Troy II-IV) type; there are also a little Cappadocian ware, much intermediate ware, and Syrian imports. The Syrian gray bottles of Tarsus later EB III type begin to appear at Kültepe in the latest EB III phase, along with intermediate and Cappadocian ware. The next phase is MB I, represented at Kültepe also in Karum IV and at Alişar in 5M. Karum IV has imports of the Syrian painted ware which also marks the beginning of Cilician MB I (T. Özgüç, 1950, Pl. LXXIX, 617, p. 198).

The sequence at Alaca Hüyük presumably does not differ basically from that at Alişar and Kültepe. The earliest, "Chalcolithic," material, as stated above, is partly EB I; the "Copper Age" phase covers EB II and runs into EB III with little demarcation. The most important find group at Alaca is the Royal Tombs, an exclusive series of shaft graves set aside for the ruling families. The abundance of metal tools, weapons, ceremonial implements, statuettes, and precious jewelry suddenly reveals the potential of central Anatolian EB culture. The Alaca graves are unfortunately not precisely dated in stratigraphic terms, because of the absence of clearly recorded sections (for the most recent attempts at analysis, cf. Bittel, 1959, pp. 28-30; Orthmann, 1963, pp. 32-34). The existence of a conflagration at the end of Alaca stratum 5 is generally admitted, but the contours of this burned level and the relationship of the various tombs to the architecture of levels 5-7 cannot be reconstructed from the present record. The Royal Tombs contain pottery characteristic of the "Copper Age" period with no signs of admixture of EB III wares. Typologically the tomb pottery belongs to EB II or the beginning of EB III. From among the tomb gifts, several will be quoted for correlations with Troy II and Early Cycladic.

<u>Konya Plain</u>. The EB sequence of the Konya Plain is being explored by the excavations at Karahüyük (Sedat Alp in Mellink, 1963, pp. 177-78). The clearest correlation lies in EB II. A "metallic ware" of Konya Plain origin, made principally in the shape of beaked pitchers and two-handled jars, and decorated with a slightly glossy purple paint, is characteristic

of Karahüyük level VII (cf. also Mellaart, 1963b, pp. 228-29, Figs. 15-17) and occurs in an unmistakable series of imports in Tarsus EB II context (Tarsus II, Fig. 247). It is not yet clear that this EB II Konya ware had a predecessor in EB I which can claim ancestry to the "red gritty" ware of Tarsus EB I; the metallic ware is later and of a different fabric, and potential precursors of the EB I Cilician ware may have to be looked for in a different part of the plateau. Karahüyük levels VI-IV are also EB, with local variants of EB III painted ware and the use of red slip for cross- and rim-bands on handmade bowls.

Southwestern Anatolia. A long "Chalcolithic" and Early Bronze Age sequence was recently excavated at Beycesultan (Lloyd and Mellaart, 1962). The major characteristic of these levels is architectural continuity in the form of rectangular, megaroid houses with fixed hearths, some of elaborate appearance. The earliest levels (XL-XX, subdivided in four Late Chalcolithic phases by the excavators' analysis) have little or no contact with the known sequences from southeastern Anatolia; in consequence, it is difficult to find convincing grounds for the early estimates given by Lloyd and Mellaart (1962, pp. 112-13). The pottery repertoire of levels XL-XX is perhaps related to the tradition represented in Cilician Late Chalcolithic (Amuq F) in the negative sense (absence of beaked pitchers, preference for simple jugs); some of the cups of Beycesultan XXIII (Lloyd and Mellaart, 1962, p. 96, Fig. P.10, 9-10) could be related in profile to EB I cups from Tarsus (Tarsus II, Fig. 240, 88; Fig. 344, 59 a-c), in spite of differences in fabric. The estimates which the excavators give for the later Beycesultan levels are based on convincing correlations with the Trojan sequence: Beycesultan XIX-XVII has affinities to Yortan material and is correlated with Troy I; XVI-XIII are put in the Troy II period; XII-VIII have good parallels with Troy III-IV; VII-VI with Troy V. The position of Troy in the Anatolian EB sequence will be considered below.

The material from Kusura is less complete in sequence. The cemetery is EB I in general Anatolian terms; EB II strata were excavated on the city mound, and EB III is represented in chance finds made by the modern villagers after the excavation (Lamb, 1937; 1938).

Northwestern Anatolia.* The main site here remains Troy, most

*The material from the so-called Dorak treasure is left out of consideration. Whatever it consists of is inaccessible to scholarly and critical analysis.

extensively analyzed stratigraphically and best documented in detailed publication. As corrected by the Cincinnati excavators, the stratification now has thirty sublevels for Troy I-V, all of the Early Bronze Age. Troy I is a fortress with buildings of megaron type. Its ceramic tradition includes squat pitcher shapes with rising spouts, which did not exist before the Early Bronze Age. The relative position of Troy I can be determined only indirectly via the abundant correlations of its successor, Troy II-V.

Troy II is closely connected with EB III phenomena in Cilicia, and, to a lesser extent, in central Anatolia. The ceramic inventory of the Troy II levels has essential traits in common with Tarsus EB IIIA (and Kültepe EB IIIB). Some specific resemblances deserve to be mentioned here because of the recent tendency to correlate Troy II with Cilician EB II instead of Cilician EB III (Mellaart, 1962*b*, p. 44; Lloyd and Mellaart, 1962, p. 113; Weinberg, below).

The relevant pottery shapes are the depas (Troy A 45), the tankard (Troy A 43), the plate or platter (Troy A 1) and the plain wheel-made bowl (Troy A 2). These shapes are as characteristic of Tarsus EB III as they are of Troy II. The depas, tankard, and wheel-made bowl do not occur in Troy I or Cilician EB II, but they become profuse in the succeeding phases. Similarities between the two areas are so close that some of the descriptions of Troy II pottery can be literally applied to Tarsus (Goldman, 1956, p. 134, n. 3), although the repertoires of the "new style" are not identical in the two regions. Tarsus has a variety of depas forms unknown in Troy, and many of these are early in the EB III sequence: the bell-shaped goblet (*Tarsus* II, Fig. 226, 488-489); the one-handled tankard (*ibid*., Fig. 266, 467), also known in southwest Anatolia in the regions of Afyon, Burdur, and Elmalı, and perhaps at Beycesultan XIII (Lloyd and Mellaart, 1962, p. 190, Fig. P.46, 2-3). This shows that the new features in Tarsus EB III pottery are not necessarily derived from Troy. Nor does the fluted depas (*Tarsus* II, Fig. 285, 722) look like a Trojan import. The wheel-made bowls of A 2 type are more easily explained as a Cilician fashion which found its way to Troy than vice versa.

The numerous ceramic resemblances point to contemporaneity and suggest that intermediate geographical links are to be discovered along the coast between the Troad and Cilicia. The synchronism Troy II - Tarsus EB IIIA is confirmed by the fact that several of the ceramic traits here discussed are absent from Troy III-IV. The tankard shapes (Tarsus II, Fig. 265, 472, 480) are closely related to Troy IIg specimens (Troy I, Fig. 380, 35.558, 35.415), not to the debased version of Troy III (Troy II, Fig. 66, 33.153, if this is a tankard at all). The red polished platters of Tarsus EB IIIA early have a brilliant burnished slip (Tarsus II, p. 133) like the IIc platters from Troy (Troy I, pp. 224-25; 274-75, "particularly characteristic" of IIc); the later platters at both sites tend to have a pale, brownish, "slightly lustrous" slip (Tarsus II, p. 133) or a "very thin pink-red-tan wash" (Troy I, p. 221). These A 1 platters do not occur in Troy III-IV. Their Troy II career is reflected in detail in Tarsus EB III, where they outlast the Troy II sequence into EB IIIB.

This detailed ceramic digression will explain why the correlation Troy II = Cilician EB IIIA is maintained here. The logical consequence is that Troy I runs parallel with, and hardly starts earlier than, Cilician EB II. (Troy I, incidentally, has a depth of about 4.50 m., Tarsus EB II about 8.50 m., EB I about 7 m.). The "3000 B.C. limit" is therefore not reached by the most ancient materials at the site of Troy.

The cultural interpretation of the remarkable prehistoric relations between Troy II and Cilician EB IIIA is not a subject of discussion in this paper. The consequences of the synchronism are of particular interest to Aegean chronology, since the relative position of Early Helladic vis-à-vis the Near Eastern historical sequence depends upon it. This paper wants to advocate a careful re-examination of the Cilician-Trojan relationships before the recent higher estimates of Troy II are transmitted to the Aegean.

The accompanying chart will show the correlation Troy II = Tarsus EB IIIA = Amuq I = Akkadian. The next equation Troy III-IV = Tarsus EB IIIB = Amuq J is confirmed by the occurrence of a Troy IV type goblet in Tell Tainat phase J (Braidwood and Braidwood, 1960, pp. 450-51; Trojan type A 44, Blegen et al., 1951, Fig. 154a). A variant of the Syrian bottle shape in Anatolian imitative version becomes known in Troy IIIA (Blegen et al., 1951, p. 58, shape B5; cf. p. 27; SS 1823-1824).

The ceramic criteria also point to the synchronism Troy II-V = central Anatolian (Kültepe) EB III, although the direct connections are few (wheel-made plates, an occasional west Anatolian or Cilician style depas). More important correlations have recently been pointed out by K. Bittel who, in publishing a group of metal vessels of Troy II type, showed that there are direct affinities in cauldron shapes between the

Troy II stage of the Troad and the Royal Tombs of Alaca Hüyük (Bittel, 1959). Tomb M at Alaca contained fragments of a spouted bronze jar with basket handle of a type paralleled in Treasures B and S at Troy (Bittel, 1959, p. 24); Alaca Tomb K has a related silver vessel; another variant occurs at Kayapınar. Contemporaneity of Alaca Tomb M and the late phases of Troy II is indicated by this parallelism, which confirms that at least some of the Alaca Tombs belong to the first part of EB III rather than to the end of that period.

Another metal form, the slotted spearhead with bent tang, is characteristic of Alaca tomb T, Tarsus EB III, Troy II (Treasure A, SS 5842-44) and presumably Early Cycladic II (Amorgos). These contexts may indicate the earliest appearance of this metal form which has many regional variants (Stronach, 1957, p. 107).

Eastern Anatolia. The Early Bronze Age in the East is known to some extent from excavations near Erzurum: Karaz Hüyük (Koşay and Turfan, 1959) and Pulur and Güzelova (Mellink, 1963, pp. 179-80). The houses of this period have hearths and andirons of elaborate shapes and decoration. The distinctive pottery is dark burnished ware with fluted or grooved designs, the motifs including chevrons, spirals, and meanders. It is possible to see a gradual development in subperiods of EB I-II (Burney, 1958, p. 167).

The EB I-II culture extends from the Erzurum area east to the Araxes Valley and Lake Urmia and has its southern border in the mountain regions between Malatya and Lake Van. The special chronological interest of this east Anatolian EB material lies in its connections with the so-called Khirbet Kerak influx into the Amuq and Palestine (Amuq H, Palestinian EB III). The origin of the intrusive elements in Amuq H was undoubtedly east Anatolian, the route of invasion from the Elâziğ area lay in the east along the Euphrates Valley before it turned west to the Amuq, bypassing the Zincirli area and Cilicia. The chronological equation connects east Anatolian EB I-II with Amuq H, Cilician EB II.

The Malatya-Elâziğ area introduced a completely new style of painted pottery in what C. Burney defined as the EB III period (Burney, 1958, pp. 169-70). Malatya was also importing north Syrian spiral-burnished bottles of the type recognized in Tarsus EB IIIB, Kültepe EB III last phase, as can be seen among the sherds from Arslantepe in the Ankara Museum. The double-profiled rim is represented here.

The Middle Bronze Age

As we enter the second millennium, the center of correlation of Anatolian archaeology shifts to Cappadocia. With the foundation of Assyrian trading posts at a number of sites on the central plateau, direct historical connections are established for Anatolia, and archaeological synchronisms will have to converge upon the Mesopotamian dates available for Kültepe, Boğazköy, and Alişar.

The best archaeological device is still to maintain the neutral terminology of Middle Bronze but to make the subdivisions fit the historical divisions now known from Kültepe (T. Özgüç, 1950, 1959; T. and N. Özgüç, 1953). The unorthodox subdivision of MB I-IV recommends itself as a working hypothesis. The beginning of MB (MB I) is marked by the foundation of the Karum and the enormous expansion of the inhabited area of the city of Kanish (Karum levels IV-III). The MB II phase had best be defined as the first period of the Assyrian colonies, Karum II, co-ordinated with the Assyrian king list from about Erišum I through the rules of Sargon I and Puzur-Aššur II, possibly longer, but potentially closely datable by limu lists (Garelli, 1963, p. 79; Balkan, 1955, 1957). The MB III phase includes the reactivation of the Karum (level Ib) under Šamši-Adad I and closes with its destruction presumably by some native power. The end of MB (IV) could then be taken as the rise of the Hittite Old Kingdom under Hattušili and Muršili, with the fall of Babylon as the lower limit and the appropriate break in nomenclature between MB and LB.

Making Kültepe the center of reference has the great advantage of an abundant archaeological documentation in addition to the historical record. Both categories of material allow the interpretation of Alişar levels as follows: on the citadel mound, level 5M corresponds to Karum IV-III (MB I), with monochrome wheelmade pottery in the same context as Cappadocian ware; this level is violently destroyed; on the terrace, levels 11 and 10 run through MB I-III, with tablets of the Karum Ib period and references to Anitta found in Alişar level 10T.

Boğazköy has two main stratigraphic sequences: the citadel Büyükkale and the Unterstadt. Level 4 of the lower city produced tablets of the Karum Ib period (MB III). It is heavily burned, possibly as the result of the destruction of Hattuša which Anitta lists among his exploits. Level 3 corresponds to the beginning of the Old Kingdom (MB IV). On the citadel,

Büyükkale IVd is correlated with Unterstadt 4, Karum Ib, again destroyed by fire; IVc represents the beginning of the Old Kingdom. Similar and earlier levels were also identified in the Haus am Hang area, where levels 8b-c-d and 9 correspond to Karum II-III-IV (cf., most recently, Bittel, Beran et al., 1962).

These three sites will be the standards for comparative chronology. They offer, in addition to a historical framework, the anonymous comparative support of a stratified pottery sequence and a developing glyptic repertoire, the latter specific enough to be of aid in chronological problems. Stratified Anatolian stamp seals of Karum Ib type (N. Özgüç, 1958; Beran, 1962) and seal impressions of this level are relatively frequent at the three sites listed. In addition, Syrian and Mesopotamian imports occur. Karum II at Kültepe of course adds the richest glyptic repertoire for the earlier period of foreign trade.

Alaca Hüyük, certainly inhabited in the MB period, has no historical information to add. Pottery and seals of MB III-IV type are represented in levels 4 and 3b.

In the Konya area, Karahüyük levels III-I belong to the MB period. Level I is burned and comes to an end around the transition from MB III to IV, as the pottery forms suggest (kantharoi, beaked pitchers, grape-cluster vessels, rectangular bathtub). It contains a profusion of bullae and seals of local type in addition to fine examples of Syrian imported glyptic.

Cilicia. Cilicia is completely different from its central and west Anatolian contemporaries, but there are many archaeological correlations continuing the useful role of Tarsus and Mersin as intermediaries between north Syria and Anatolia. The MB I phase at Tarsus starts with a break in architectural continuity (Tarsus II, p. 39-40), paralleled by the introduction of a new type of pottery: north Syrian painted ware, best known from Alalakh levels XVI-VIII. The correlation with Amuq K is clear. The new style of pottery is found throughout the Cilician coastal plain. It antedates the palace level VII at Alalakh, which is historically correlated with the dynasty at Aleppo. Level VII was probably destroyed by Hattušili, so that Alalakh VII could be called MB III and first part of the MB IV period (Otten, 1958, p. 78).

The painted ware of Cilician MB I-II is found in imported specimens at Kültepe. Karum IV has the first samples, confirming the contemporaneity of Karum IV and Cilician MB I (T. Özgüç, 1950, Pl. LXXIX,

617). Other specimens occur in Karum II, some of which seem of Cilician manufacture (T. Özgüç, 1950, Pl. LXXIX, 616) and Cilician MB II type whereas others are local imitations. This painted class does not continue into Karum Ib, which instead has painted jars and pitchers with red bands representing a class of Habur ware.

There are correlations of Karum Ib pottery with some of the material classified as LB I at Tarsus, owing, undoubtedly, to the lack of a sharp demarcation between MB (Colony period) and LB (Old Hittite Kingdom) cultures at Tarsus. Goldman speaks of a transitional phase in which Hittite features assert themselves over the Syrian elements (*Tarsus* II, pp. 62-63). These new "Hittite" elements can be seen in Tarsus pottery of Karum Ib and Old Kingdom type (*Tarsus* II, Fig. 308, 1061, 1024; Fig. 309, 1031, 1012, 1013; also the hybrid 1009; Fig. 310, 1054; Fig. 311, 1044, 1045). Some of this Tarsus LB I level may have to be labeled MB III-IV in the present context, and would historically seem to belong before the treaty of Išputaḫšu of Kizzuwatna and Telepinus in the sixteenth century (LB I).

Southwestern Anatolia. Beycesultan and Kusura are the leading excavated sites here. Kusura has MB material in the level called C, some of it closely related to MB III types (Lamb, 1937, Pl. VIII). Beycesultan enters the MB Age with level V to which the burned palace on the eastern summit belongs. Wheel-made wares are predominant in this stratum, with occasional affinities in shape to central Anatolian pottery. Level IV has more of such, and contains general parallels to the Karum Ib level (Lloyd and Mellaart, 1956, p. 132, Fig. 4: 2, 4, 6, 11, 12, 13, 15, 16, 17). Strong resemblances to central Anatolian shapes continue into Beycesultan level III with its beaked pitchers and pilgrim flasks (Lloyd and Mellaart, 1956, p. 133, Fig. 5: 16, 19); level II (Lloyd and Mellaart, 1955, Pl. III*a*, IV, V, Fig. 13); and level I (Lloyd and Mellaart, 1956, p. 134, Fig. 6; cf. the bathtub, Fig. 6: 7). The final publication will show how the excavators classify this material. In spite of the geographical distance between Beycesultan and the central Anatolian sites, it would seem unlikely that MB age pottery types continued to be made in the Beycesultan region to the end of LB.

Northwestern Anatolia. Troy has a long series of building levels under the generic label of Troy VI, which is known to have lasted from some time early in the MB Age to the period of LH IIIB imports which appear before an earthquake destroyed Troy VIh. The known synchronisms of Troy VI are mostly with the Aegean area, and thus go in the direction opposite to the one with which we are concerned. This situation is presumably the result of the strong affinities of the Troy VI population to the inhabitants of the Aegean islands and the mainland of Greece. On the other hand, the lack of excavated MB material in the region between Troy and Gordion-Polatlı-Karaoğlan makes a theory of isolation uncertain.

It is at present impossible to date the beginning of Troy VI by Anatolian criteria. If we do not assume continuity from Troy V to VI, the date of Troy VIa is unattached in the range of MB I to IV, although good reasons for continuity have been stressed by Bittel (1956).

The nearest stratified sequence comes from Beycesultan (Bayraklı being unpublished), which has some affinities in shapes of pottery to Troy VI but no clear co-ordination of progress. Whereas Beycesultan as well as sites of the Ankara region (Gordion, Polatlı, Karaoğlan) maintain strong Anatolian characteristics in their ceramic repertoires (beaked pitchers, low carinations on jars; Mellink, 1956; Lloyd, 1951), Troy VI pottery has a neutral appearance (Blegen *et al.*, 1953, Figs. 292 *a*, *b*, 293-95).

We have therefore lost the thread of historical correlation in the west of Anatolia, and will have to wait for additional excavations to provide the links needed between central and western sites.

Eastern Anatolia. East of the Halys region, excavated and published sites are few. In the region of Erzurum, typical MB material has not been identified to date, undoubtedly because of a lack of excavation. In the Euphrates area, Malatya has relevant unpublished material, and farther to the south is the north Mesopotamian zone known from the Carchemish cemeteries and Habur valley sites. A potentially rich territory awaits the student of the early-second-millennium sites mentioned as caravan stations along the routes connecting Assur with Cappadocia. A comparison of hypothetical Colony period maps with excavated sites shows how much essential work remains to be done and how inadequate our stratigraphic guesses must be when written evidence is known to be buried along the ancient trade routes.

The Late Bronze Age

The situation for the LB period—that is, the historical evolution after the fall of Babylon to the end of the Hittite Empire—will be sketched only briefly here since it falls beyond the chronological limits set by this volume.

We have an interrupted, but steadily improving, record of history by means of which to analyze the stratigraphical and architectural growth of Boğazköy, including the last desperate messages concerning the threat to the established order during the rule of Šuppiluliama II (Otten, 1963).

Archaeologically, the task now is co-ordination with historically identifiable levels and events. The shift in power in central Anatolia is clear in the lack of (or scant) occupation on many of the great MB Age sites (Alişar, at least parts of Kültepe, Karahüyük near Konya, Acemhüyük near Aksaray). Alaca Hüyük continues to be inhabited and built up. In Cilicia, Tarsus is a strong representative and probably the capital of the kingdom of Kizzuwatna. Its historical documentation lies in seals and bullae of local kings and queens also known from the Boğazköy record (Išputaḫšu, Puduḫepa); the building levels form an uninterrupted sequence to the end of the Late Bronze Age and a devastation at the hands of the Sea Peoples. The abundant ceramic material of the Hittite Empire period is important for comparative purposes since few other sites are so well documented for this stage.

In the west, Kusura does not continue; the LB occupation of Beycesultan may at least be considered questionable and incomplete; Bayraklı is representative but unpublished; Miletus and Troy VI (Middle and Late, phases d-h) - VII (a-bl) are strongly tied in with the Mycenaean sequence and datable by the indirect aid of Aegean chronology.

The LB levels of important historical sites in the southeast are practically untouched (Carchemish, Malatya); the situation in eastern Anatolia remains unclear until the Urartian period.

This brief survey will emphasize how enormous are the gaps in the Anatolian record and how hazardous it is to make firm claims for correlations unsupported by a string of geographical and stratigraphical successions. We know much more about Anatolian chronology now than we did some decades ago, and we begin to see how long an evolution is involved from the bottom of the stratification at Karain to the burned archives on the citadel at Boğazköy. Excavations have produced sections of the authentic record. Strenuous surface explorations have facilitated the reconstruction of the regional development and the selection of sites for excavation. In another decade a much more coherent picture will emerge. The historical framework is generally established. Before 3000 B.C., we shall leave the determination of absolute chronology to the scientists.

Postscript, June, 1965.

In the year which has elapsed since the above paper was written, much new evidence has been published or excavated. No more than brief references can be given here. For a survey of the development in 1964, see my "Archaeology in Asia Minor," *American Journal of Archaeology* 69 (1965): 133-41, here cited as *AJA* 1965. *WVDOG* is the abbreviation for *Wissenschaftliche Veröffentlichung der Deutschen Orient-Gesellschaft*.

Pre-3000 B.C. New bibliography is available for Çatalhüyük and Can Hasan (*AJA* 1965: 137). A Neolithic site has been sampled at Suberde west of Lake Suğla (*AJA* 1965: 137, J. Bordaz). At Çayönü near Ergani east of the Euphrates, aceramic levels produced malachite beads and copper tools (*AJA* 1965: 138, Halet Çambel and R. J. Braidwood).

Early Bronze Age. New material has been excavated at Kültepe (*AJA* 1965: 135) and Karahüyük near Konya (*AJA* 1965: 136). New publications have appeared for Pulur (*AJA* 1965: 138) and Boğazköy (*AJA* 1965: 136, W. Orthmann, *WVDOG* 74). Good synchronisms come from excavations at Tilmen Hüyük and Gedikli Hüyük in the Zincirli area (*AJA* 1965: 134 and 139-40, U. Bahadır Alkım). Stratified tombs at Gedikli have correlations with Cilician EB II and IIIA (Syrian bottles and depa associated with cremations). An Akkadian synchronism with Cilician EB IIIA is discussed by me in *Anatolia* 7 (1963): 101-15. For the EB II-III site of Karataş-Semayük in Lycia (*AJA* 65: 140), see the C-14 dates listed below.

Middle and Late Bronze Ages. The most important new publication is Franz Fischer, *Die Hethitische Keramik von Boğazköy* (*WVDOG* 75, Berlin, 1963). For Kültepe Karum II and I b pottery, see Kutlu Emre in *Anatolia* 7 (1963): 87-99. New MB material comes from Acemhüyük near Aksaray (*AJA* 1965: 138, Nimet Özgüç) and Ilıca-Ayaş (*AJA* 1965: 140, W. Orthmann).

List of C-14 dates for Anatolian sites

The following dates are quoted from information kindly furnished by Elizabeth K. Ralph of the University of Pennsylvania. The list is restricted to dates determined by the laboratory of the University of Pennsylvania which has done the most extensive work on samples from prehistoric Anatolia.

The calculations are based on a half life of 5,730 years.

Çatal Hüyük		B.C. dates
P 782	level X charcoal from hearth	6385 ± 101
P 779	level IX charcoal from floor	6486 ± 102
P 778	level VII grain	5815 ± 92
P 777	level VI wall posts	5986 ± 94
P 797	level VI corner post	5908 ± 93
P 781	level VI roof beam	5800 ± 93
P 770	level VI roof beams (reused timber)	6200 ± 97
P 769	level VI grain	5781 ± 96
P 772	level VI post	5850 ± 94
P 776	level V post	5920 ± 94
P 775	level IV post (reused timber)	6329 ± 99
P 774	level III roof beam	5807 ± 94
P 796	level II grain	5797 ± 79
Hacılar		
P 314	level IX charcoal	5614 ± 92
P 313A	level VI charcoal from hearth	5620 ± 79
P 316A	level II roof beam	5434 ± 131
P 315	level Ia roof beam	5247 ± 119
Can Hasan		
P 790	level 2B charcoal	5085 ± 80
P 791	level 2B charcoal	5008 ± 82
P 792	level 2B charcoal	4921 ± 78
P 794	level 2B charcoal	5294 ± 92
P 795	level 2B roof beam	5087 ± 80
P 789	level 2A charcoal	5240 ± 81

Beycesultan		B.C. dates
P 298	level XXXVI charcoal	3163 ± 50
P 297	level XXVIII charcoal	2881 ± 54
Karataş-Semayük*		
P 917	charcoal from posthole	2398 ± 63
P 918	charcoal from floor	2304 ± 63
P 919	beam on floor	2300 ± 62
P 920	charcoal from storage pit 6 in floor	2452 ± 64
P 921	charcoal from storage pit 5 in floor	2312 ± 64
P 923	charcoal from courtyard	2405 ± 64

*This site is on the plain of Elmalı in the interior of Lycia. Campaigns were conducted by a Bryn Mawr College expedition in 1963 and 1964. The six C-14 samples come from a burned house which has archaeological correlations with the end of EB II, late Troy I. Reports on Karataş-Semayük appeared in American Journal of Archaeology 68 (1964): 269-78 and 69 (1965): 241-51.

AMUQ	MESOPOTAMIA	EGYPT	TARSUS	KÜLTEPE	BOĞAZKÖY		ALIŞAR		ALACA	KONYA KARAHÜYÜK	BEYCE SULTAN	TROY	EAST ANATOLIA
					CITY	BÜYÜK KALE	TERRACE	MOUND					
↑	FALL OF BABYLON		M.B. IV (TRANSITIONAL)		3	IV c			3 b	BURNING	↑ ? III		
VII ALALAḪ	ŠAMŠI-ADAD I		M.B. III (TRANSITIONAL)	KARUM I b TABLETS	BURNING 4 TABLETS	IV d	TABLETS 10 T ↑		¦	I	IV		
VIII ALALAḪ	PUZUR-AŠŠUR II | ERIŠUM I		M.B. II	BURNING KARUM II TABLETS					4	|	|	VI	
ALALAḪ XVI K "c. 2000 B.C."	ISIN-LARSA		M.B. I	KARUM III IV			11 T	5 M WHEEL-MADE WARES	¦	III	BURNT PALACE V		
J	UR III POST-AKKADIAN	FIRST INTERM.	E.B. III b	E.B. III a SYRIAN BOTTLES					5 6 ↑ ?	IV	VI XII	V IV III	E.B. III b MALATYA
I	AKKADIAN	PERIOD	E.B. III a	E.B. III b CAPPADOCIAN W. WHEELMADE PLS. E.B. III c INTERM. WARE			12 T	6 M CAPPAD. 7 M	ROYAL 7 TOMBS ↓	VI	XIII XVI	g II a	E.B. III a MALATYA
H	EARLY DYNASTIC III II I	DYN. IV KHEOPS ←	E.B. II	"COPPER AGE" E.B. II SYRIAN IMPORTS			13 T "COPPER AGE" 14 T	INTERM. 8 M ↓ 11 M	8 "COPPER AGE"	VII	XVII XIX	I	E.B. II KARAZHÜYÜK PULUR
G "c. 3000 B.C."	JEMDET NASR		E.B. I	E.B. I			VIRGIN SOIL	12 M ↓ 14 M	9 CHALCO-LITHIC ↓ 15		XX ↓		E.B. I KARAZHÜYÜK PULUR
F	URUK		LATE CHALCO-LITHIC					↓ ? 19 M	↓ ?		XL ↓ ?		

MESOPOTAMIA	AMUQ	CILICIA	CAN HASAN	ÇATAL HÜYÜK	HACILAR	ANTALYA CAVES	BEYCE SULTAN	CENTRAL ANATOLIA	NORTHWEST ANATOLIA	EAST ANATOLIA
JEMDET NASR PROTOLIT. C–D	G "c. 3000 B.C"	TARSUS E.B.I					LATER CHALCO-LITHIC	ALIŞAR LATE CHALCO-LITHIC	KUMTEPE ?	
URUK PROTOLIT. A–B	F	TARSUS LATE CHALCOLITHIC (GAP AT MERSIN)					EARLIEST CHALCO-LITHIC ↓ ?	EARLY CHALCO-LITHIC ↓ ?	? FIKIRTEPE	
UBAID	E	(TARSUS UBAID) MERSIN XII B | FORTRESS XVI →	SURFACE SHERDS							SAKÇAGÖZÜ TURLU MALATYA FRAKTIN
HALAF	D	MERSIN XVII (TARSUS HALAF)	LEVEL 2 A ?							YUNUS KILNS SAKÇAGÖZÜ TURLU
HALAF HASSUNA ↓	C	MERSIN XIX XX EARLY CHALCO-LITHIC XXIV →	IMPORTS LEVEL 2 B	? WEST MOUND SURFACE?	? I HACILAR ? ↓					TILKITEPE
	B	MERSIN XXV NEOLITHIC (TARSUS)		NEOLITHIC I LEVELS (MERSIN TYPE	GAP ? LATE VI NEOLITHIC LEVELS IX					
JARMO	A	XXXIII		OBSIDIAN INDUSTRY) X	GAP	NEOLITHIC SHERDS ↓				
PRE-CERAMIC	↓ ? PRE-CERAMIC	↓ ? PRE-CERAMIC		GAP ↓ SOUNDING 1963	ACERAMIC STRATA I – VIII VIRGIN SOIL	KARAIN CAVE PRE-CERAMIC ↓				

Bibliography

Balkan, Kemal

1955 Observations on the Chronological Problems of the Kārum Kaniš. Ankara: Türk Tarih Kurumu.

1957 Letter of King Anum-Hirbi of Mama to King Warshama of Kanish. Ankara: Türk Tarih Kurumu.

Beran, T.

1962 "Boğazköy 1958 und 1959, Stempelsiegel und gesiegelte Bullen," Mitteilungen der deutschen Orient-Gesellschaft zu Berlin 93: 59-68.

Bialor, Perry A.

1962 "The Chipped Stone Industry of Çatal Hüyük," Anatolian Studies 12: 67-110.

Bittel, K.

1942 Kleinasiatische Studien ("Istanbuler Mitteilungen," 5). Istanbul: Deutsches Archäologisches Institut.

1949-50 "Einige Idole aus Kleinasien," Prähistorische Zeitschrift 34-35: 135-44.

1950 "Zur Chronologie der anatolischen Frühkulturen," Reinecke Festschrift, pp. 13-25. Mainz: Schneider Verlag.

1956 Review of Troy III. Gnomon 28: 241-52.

1959 "Beitrag zur Kenntnis anatolischer Metallgefässe der zweiten Hälfte des dritten Jahrtausends v. Chr.," Jahrbuch des deutschen Archäologischen Instituts 74: 1-34.

1960 "Fikirtepe Kazısı," V. Türk Tarih Kongresi, Ankara 12-17 Nisan 1956, pp. 29-36. Ankara: Türk Tarih Kurumu.

Bittel, K., et al.

1962 "Vorläufiger Bericht über die Ausgrabungen in Boğazköy in den Jahren 1958 und 1959," Mitteilungen der deutschen Orient-Gesellschaft zu Berlin 93.

Blegen, C. W., et al.

1950 Troy I: General Introduction. The First and Second Settlements. Princeton: Princeton University Press.

1951 Troy II: The Third, Fourth and Fifth Settlements. Princeton: Princeton University Press.

1953 Troy III: The Sixth Settlement. Princeton: Princeton University Press.

Braidwood, R. J., and Braidwood, L.

1960 Excavations in the Plain of Antioch, I. ("Oriental Institute Publications," LXI.) Chicago: University of Chicago Press.

Burney, C. A.

1958 "Eastern Anatolia in the Chalcolithic and Early Bronze Age," Anatolian Studies 8: 158-209.

Dikaios, P.

1962 "The Stone Age," The Swedish Cyprus Expedition, Vol. IV, Pt. IA, pp. 1-204. Lund: Swedish Cyprus Expedition.

Du Plat Taylor, J., et al.

1950 "The Excavations at Sakce Gözü," Iraq 12: 53-138.

Ehrich, Ann M. H.

1939 Early Pottery of the Jebeleh Region. Philadelphia: American Philosophical Society.

Esin, Ufuk, and Benedict, Peter

1963 "Recent Developments in the Prehistory of Anatolia," Current Anthropology 4: 339-46.

Frankfort, H.

1955 Stratified Cylinder Seals from the Diyala Region. ("Oriental Institute Publications, Vol. LXXII.) Chicago: University of Chicago Press.

French, D. H.

1961 "Late Chalcolithic Pottery in North-West Turkey and the Aegean," Anatolian Studies 11: 99-141.

1962 "Excavations at Can Hasan," Anatolian Studies 12: 27-40.

1963 "Excavations at Can Hasan: Second Preliminary Report, 1962," Anatolian Studies 13: 29-42.

Garelli, Paul

1963 Les Assyriens en Cappadoce. ("Bibliothèque Archéologique et Historique de l'Institut français d'Archéologie d'Istanbul," No. XIX.) Paris: Adrien Maisonneuve.

Garstang, John

1953 Prehistoric Mersin. Oxford: Clarendon Press.

Goetze, Albrecht

1957 Kleinasien. ("Kulturgeschichte des alten Orients III," No. I.) 2d ed. Munich: C. H. Beck.

Goldman, Hetty

1954 "The Relative Chronology of Southeastern Anatolia." In Relative Chronologies in Old World Archeology, pp. 69-85. Ed. Robert W. Ehrich. Chicago: University of Chicago Press.

1956 Excavations at Gözlü Kule, Tarsus, II. Princeton: Princeton University Press.

Koşay, Hâmit, and Akok, Mahmut

1957 Ausgrabungen von Büyük Güllücek, 1947 und 1949. Ankara: Türk Tarih Kurumu.

Koşay, Hâmit, and Turfan, Kemal

1959 "Erzurum-Karaz Kazısı Raporu," Belleten XXIII: 349-413.

Lamb, Winifred

1937 "Excavations at Kusura near Afyon Karahisar," Archaeologia 86: 1-64.

1938 "Excavations at Kusura near Afyon Karahisar; II," ibid. 87: 217-73.

Lloyd, Seton, and Gökçe, Nuri

1951 "Excavations at Polatlı," Anatolian Studies 1: 21-62.

Lloyd, Seton, and Mellaart, James

1955 "Beycesultan Excavations: First Preliminary Report," Anatolian Studies 5: 39-92.

1956 "Beycesultan Excavations: Second Preliminary Report," ibid. 6: 101-35.

1962 Beycesultan I. London: British Institute of Archaeology at Ankara.

Mellaart, James

1960 "Excavations at Hacılar, 1959," Anatolian Studies 10: 83-104.

1961 "Excavations at Hacılar: Fourth Preliminary Report," ibid. 11: 39-75.

1962a "Excavations at Çatal Hüyük," Anatolian Studies 12: 41-65.

1962b "Anatolia c. 4000-2300 B.C.," Cambridge Ancient History. Rev. ed., Vol. I, chap. xviii. Cambridge: University Press.

1963a "Excavations at Çatal Hüyük, 1962," Anatolian Studies 13: 43-103.

1963b "Early Cultures of the South Anatolian Plateau," Anatolian Studies, 13: 199-236.

1964a "The Third Season of Excavations at Çatal Hüyük," Parts I-IV. Illustrated London News, Feb. 1, 8, 15, 22. Archaeological News Sections Nos. 2169-2172.

1964b "Anatolia before c. 4000 B.C. and c. 2300-1750 B.C.," Cambridge Ancient History. Rev. ed. Vol. I, chap. vii, §§ 11-14; chap. xxiv, §§ 1-6. Cambridge: Cambridge University Press.

Mellink, Machteld J.

1956 A Hittite Cemetery at Gordion. ("Museum Monographs.") Philadelphia: University Museum.

1962 "The Prehistory of Syro-Cilicia," Bibliotheca Orientalis 19: 219-26.

1963 "Archaeology in Asia Minor," American Journal of Archaeology 67: 173-90.

Orthmann, Winfried

1963 Die Keramik der Frühen Bronzezeit aus Inneranatolien. Berlin: Verlag Gebr. Mann.

Otten, Heinrich

1958 "Vorläufiger Bericht über die Ausgrabungen in Boğazköy.

Keilschrifttexte," Mitteilungen der deutschen Orient-Gesellschaft 91: 73-84.
1963 "Neue Quellen zum Ausklang des hethitischen Reiches," ibid. 94: 1-23.

Özgüç, Nimet

1957 "Marble Idols and Statuettes from the Excavations at Kültepe," Belleten XXI: 71-80.
1958 "Die Siegel der Schicht IB im Karum-Kaniş von Kültepe," ibid. XXII: 13-19.

Özgüç, Tahsin

1950 Ausgrabungen in Kültepe, 1948. Ankara: Türk Tarih Kurumu.
1956 "Das prähistorische Haus beim Felsrelief von Fraktin," Anatolia 1: 65-70.
1959 Kültepe-Kaniş. Ankara: Türk Tarih Kurumu.

Özgüç, Tahsin, and Özgüç, Nimet

1953 Ausgrabungen in Kültepe 1949. Ankara: Türk Tarih Kurumu.

Perrot, Jean

1964 "Turlu," American Journal of Archaeology 68: 156.

Reilly, Edward B.

1940 "Test Excavations at Tilki Tepe," Türk Tarih Arkeologya ve Etnografya Dergisi 4: 156-78.

Reisner, George A., and Smith, William S.

1955 A History of the Giza Necropolis. Vol. II. Cambridge, Mass.: Harvard University Press.

Schmidt, H.

1902 Heinrich Schliemann's Sammlung Trojanischer Altertümer. Berlin: K. und K. Museen.

Stronach, D. B.

1957 "The Development and Diffusion of Metal Types in Early Bronze Age Anatolia," Anatolian Studies 7: 89-125.

Von der Osten, H. H.

1937 The Alishar Hüyük: Seasons of 1930-32. I-II. ("Oriental Institute Publications," XXVIII, XXIX.) Chicago: University of Chicago Press, 1937.

Woolley, C. Leonard

1914 "Hittite Burial Customs," Liverpool Annals of Archaeology and Anthropology 6: 87-98.
1934a "The Prehistoric Pottery of Carchemish," Iraq 1: 146-62.
1934b Ur Excavations. II: The Royal Cemetery. Philadelphia: University Museum; London: British Museum.

The Relative Chronology of Mesopotamia. Part I.
Seals and Trade (6000-1600 B.C.)

Edith Porada
Columbia University

In the past decade, the material from excavations in the regions surrounding Mesopotamia has greatly increased. Since the relative chronology of these regions is largely dependent on the Mesopotamian sequence, it has been necessary to expand this paper and to give greater precision, wherever possible, to the divisions and subdivisions of periods or phases. For this purpose, Perkins' standard work, The Comparative Archaeology of Early Mesopotamia (1949) has been used extensively, whereas her paper in Relative Chronologies in Old World Archeology has been cited only in a few instances where her succinct wording seemed the best statement of the subject.

Donald P. Hansen has contributed an outline of the pottery sequence from the excavations at Nippur, here printed as Part II. He has also made valuable suggestions for the text and charts of Part I, especially concerning the date of the Royal Cemetery of Ur, a problem which he examined in connection with work on the votive plaques from Nippur (Hansen, 1963). Constructive criticism by Briggs Buchanan of the treatment of the early seals is gratefully acknowledged, as is his help in obtaining drawings for several of the seals reproduced in Figure VI.

In the present paper, the simplest terminology has been used. Thus Ubaid and Amuq are written without the symbol which indicates the Arabic 'ayn in the English transcription. Further, there is a conscious lack of consistency in order to use the terms most widely known. For example, Tello, the modern name of the site of ancient Girsu,* is employed unless a historical context is implied. For the same reason Uruk, which is the ancient name of the modern site of Warka, is used throughout. Moreover, the levels excavated in the Eanna precinct of Uruk which have not yet been satisfactorily equated with those of the Anu Ziggurat at the

*Tello, formerly identified with the town of Lagash, is now taken to have been Girsu, the principal town of the state of Lagash (Jacobsen, 1957, p. 114, note 49; Falkenstein, Edzard, and Bottéro, 1965, pp. 49, 75).

same site are nevertheless simply called Uruk III, IV, and so on.

The major change in the terminology—the return from Protoliterate a-d to Uruk and Jamdat Nasr—which stresses the division rather than the continuity between the two protohistoric periods, is intended to reflect the evidence for major changes between the periods shown in the architectural remains from Uruk, the principal site of the age. Moreover, such a division fits the pottery sequence at Nippur very well. However, the term Jamdat Nasr, derived from the modern Arabic name of the site where the remains of the period were first discovered, is an especially unfortunate one for the last protohistoric period and must certainly give way soon to a better term. Yet, by using accepted and known terminology, I hope that information can be gained more rapidly from the present survey. As recent experience has shown, the usefulness of otherwise needed compilations may be vitiated by a novel and unwieldy terminology (see Nagel, 1961-64; Strommenger, 1960, 1964).

GEOGRAPHY

Mesopotamia—modern Iraq—may be divided into the mountains and foothills of the northeast (generally referred to here as the north) and the central lowland (here called the south). The mountains are a part of the belt which extends from the Zagros to the Taurus and rises to its highest points along the frontiers of Iraq with Iran and with Turkey. The mountain ridges with narrow valleys between them decrease in height, whereas the distance between them increases as one moves south from the frontier, so that the Assyrian piedmont consists of widely separated ridges or hills.

The plain is composed of two regions: "the broad delta plain of the two great master rivers of Iraq, the Tigris and Euphrates, with important contributions of sediment from the Karun and Karkeh rivers of Iran; in the north is the low plain of the Jezireh, bounded by the sharp valleys of the two master rivers. Across the Euphrates the Jezireh is replaced by the Western Desert, which rises in broad low steps to the Arabian Plateau" (Wright, 1955, p. 84).

The geography of the country is reflected in its ancient history. Paleolithic man found natural shelters in the caves of the mountains of the northeast; sufficient rainfall made early farming possible in the piedmont foothills of what was later to be Assyria. These piedmont foothills, with their valleys in which farming produces a livelihood for small communities, belong to a wide arc which reaches from Iran to Turkey and Syria. Ethnic movements and cultural developments seem often to have been communicated from country to country along this mountainous arc. Oppenheim points out that "cities in this arc required a special stimulus to grow, such as a sanctuary, a seat of royal power, or trade routes, which were quite rare. The villages contained a number of families which supported themselves by cultivating adjacent fields and gardens, paying taxes collectively either to a ruler residing in a fortified palace or to an absentee owner connected by birth or feudal status with some sort of central power. The village units themselves, or the income derived from them, were negotiable within certain restrictions which varied according to time and region. They thus served as the economic basis of a feudal organization attached to ephemeral carriers of political power. By its contribution in taxes, the entire set-up readily supported superimposed power groups which, as a rule, showed little stability, extended rapidly under the leadership of an individual, were taken over smoothly by invading foreign groups, and collapsed easily whenever the faculty of the central organization to collect taxes vanished. The village community remained remarkably stable, and the obligation to pay taxes counteracted individual defections, although craftsmen often seem to have been attracted to the king's court thus helping towards the type of industrialization for which all kings of that region strove in order to strengthen their economic basis." (Oppenheim, 1957, pp. 35-36).

Although this picture of conditions in the regions from the Zagros through upper Mesopotamia to the coastal regions of the Mediterranean Sea was drawn by Oppenheim on the basis of texts of the historical periods, many features of the later social patterns of the people probably developed in prehistoric times as a result of the geography of the region.

The south developed differently from the north toward creating the Mesopotamian civilization based on agriculture, industry, and trade. Contrary to the older view that the southern plain had been an arm of the sea until Pleistocene times and has subsequently been filled like a normal delta, it has been shown that the rivers are still discharging their load of sediment into a tectonic basin and that tectonic movements are still continuing and preventing the silting of marshes and lakes (Lees and Falcon, 1952, pp. 24-39). Moreover, the shoreline of the Persian Gulf, thought to have been at one time far north of its present location and to have provided a direct outlet to the sea for towns like Ur, was more to the southeast in antiquity than it is at the present time. The harbor of Ur, like that of many other Mesopotamian towns, must have been a port on a former course of the Euphrates River (Buringh, 1957, p. 36).

TRADE AND TRADE ROUTES

In the south, lack of suitable timber, building stone, and metals—in fact, of all items of luxury above the mere level of subsistence—stimulated economic activities designed to provide such items by means of production of surplus goods for barter and organized trade. Tablets of Lagash from about the middle of the third millennium B.C. record trade by professional merchants for the <u>ensis</u> Lugalanda and Urukagina. "Pure silver," timber of various kinds, and cattle were among the principal imports from Elam (southwest Iran) (Leemans, 1950, pp. 40-41; Lambert, 1953, pp. 63-64). Later records mention bitumen, gypsum, occasionally copper, and perhaps tin (Leemans, 1950, p. 2; 1960, pp. 83-84; pp. 123-24). As early as the Third Early Dynastic period, according to texts from Lagash, copper was being imported from Tilmun, identified with reasonable certainty with the island of Bahrein in the Persian Gulf (see, however, Kramer, 1964, p. 45). Barley, oil, flour, and garments went back in exchange (Leemans, 1960, p. 116, and references in note 1). The early records list also cedar wood, obviously an item of transit trade from the Amanus in the northwest. An analysis of stones used in buildings of the Late Uruk period indicated that they came from Iran (Schüller, 1963), whereas Gudea of Lagash, who built a temple for his patron god Ningirsu about the middle of the twenty-second century B.C., did not expressly identify any stones as coming from Elam although he mentioned the carnelian which he received from Meluhha. Records from Ur, dated in the time of the Third Dynasty of that city (2113-2006 B.C.), show that at that time trade with Tilmun, Makkan, and Meluhha was carried on by seafaring merchants of Ur (Oppenheim, 1954). Makkan and Meluhha were near or beyond the Gulf of Oman. Meluhha was probably closer to India, to judge from the listed imports of ivory objects, carnelian, and other luxury goods (Leemans, 1960, pp. 159 ff.; Saggs, 1962, pp. 272 ff.). According to Oppenheim, the peak of the commercial relations with the East may have been reached early in the third millennium B.C. The presence of ships outside Sargon's capital Akkad, from or destined for Meluhha, Makkan, and Tilmun, shows that at that time trade with the East was still flourishing. The participation of the seafaring merchants of Ur at the time of the Third Dynasty and of the Dynasty of Larsa may, however, reflect the "diminishing power of expansion of the East" (Oppenheim, 1954, pp. 14-15). The terminal date of 2000 B.C. recently suggested for the Harappan culture on the basis of C-14 samples from Kalibangan and Lothal (Gosh, 1964, p. 16) would support this suggestion.

Shipping was the preferred means of transportation for goods destined not only for southern Mesopotamia but also as much as possible for the north (Hallo, 1964, passim). Salonen called the Euphrates and the Tigris the main arteries of Mesopotamia (Salonen, 1939, Vorwort). The principal river ports seem to have been Mari, Assur, Ur, and Akkad (Leemans, 1960, pp. 10-11). In Old Babylonian times, wine from Western countries was transported down the Euphrates to Mari and from there to Babylon, often via Sippar (ibid., p. 104), as were also aromatic oils and perfumes, although these were also transported overland (ibid., p. 127). Large numbers of donkeys carried copper and silver from Anatolia to Assur in the time of the Old Assyrian merchant colonies (J. Lewy, 1958, pp. 92-93; H. Lewy, 1964, p. 181) and possibly earlier. Tin, which was exported from Assur to Kültepe (Kanesh), may have come to Assur from the east or northeast—perhaps from Elam (Leemans, 1960, p. 124)—although other regions for this valuable material have also been suggested (Limet, 1960, pp. 95-97).* The evidence from Mari, which also seems to have been a center for the trade of tin, has, however, been similarly interpreted as suggesting an Eastern origin (Bottéro, 1957, pp. 293-94, 336, 359). Slaves, described as coming from Gutium (Leemans, 1960, pp. 110-12) in the Zagros mountains (Gadd, 1963, p. 30), probably walked alongside the donkeys.

Sumerian, Babylonian, and Assyrian merchants paid for goods in silver as well as with such commodities as dates, oil, corn, or with textiles such as the products of the flourishing wool industry of Sippar (Leemans, 1950, pp. 3, 103). Items of trade as well as trade centers and routes, which are becoming increasingly known from cuneiform texts, may help to determine some of the contacts and connections dimly perceived in the archaeological material.

The surplus foodstuffs—mainly wheat, barley, and dates—used for barter by the inhabitants of southern Mesopotamia were grown on land irrigated at first by means of small-scale systems. Later, at a time

*The suggestion that there was copper in the Lebanon cited by Limet was contested by Seyrig (1953, p. 48, note 4; p. 49).

when cities were already in existence, large-scale canal networks were undertaken (Adams, 1958, p. 102; 1960, pp. 154, 157).

The different environments of south and north in Mesopotamia did not prevent the two regions from being allied culturally, especially in historical times, and from "showing greater similarity with each other than either has with any other land. The central part of the country—notably the Diyala region—often shows a transitional character; although more closely tied to the south, it may possess features of the northern culture unknown in the sites farther south. In discussing the problem of relative chronology in Mesopotamia, therefore, there are always two aspects: the relation of the archaeological material from north and south and the relation of materials from either or both areas to those of other countries" (Perkins, 1954, pp. 42-43).

THE NORTH*

The Pre-Pottery Neolithic Period

In northern Iraq, the pre-pottery Neolithic period is mainly represented to date by the lowest levels of the village site of Jarmo (Braidwood and Howe, 1960, pp. 26-27, 38-50), and probably by those of Tell Shemshara—although the evidence from this site is somewhat confusing (Mortensen, 1962, pp. 79-80).

Characteristic of Jarmo is the excellent flint and obsidian blade-tool industry (Fig. II, 15). Hole noted general similarities to tools of pre-pottery levels from Ali Kosh in Khuzistan in southwestern Iran (Hole and Flannery, 1962, pp. 121 ff.). Moreover, he pointed out that the "fact that all the Jarmoan sites have obsidian tools included among their assemblages, indicates that they were all part of the same trade network."

Human and animal figurines of unbaked clay from Jarmo (Fig. II: 12, 13) seem to have been equally characteristic of this early phase, and are said closely to resemble the fragmentary ones from Ali Kosh (*ibid*., p. 120).

Ground stone objects—especially vessels of the inverted truncated

---

*The development of the early periods in northern Mesopotamia is outlined only briefly here to avoid duplication with Watson's paper (above), in which the material from this region is treated in conjunction with that from northern Syria. Considerable stress is placed here on seals, whereas Watson more extensively discusses pottery.

conical type with flaring rim (II:16) were widely used in this aceramic phase but seem to have outlasted it considerably (Mortensen, 1962, p. 79), so that no specific correlation can be based on them.

Early Painted Pottery Cultures: The Hassuna and Hassuna-Samarra Periods

Excavations at Hassuna (Lloyd and Safar, 1945) of a camp site which later developed into a *tauf** built village furnished an early pottery sequence for northern Iraq which confirmed and expanded the sequence earlier established for Nineveh (Mallowan, 1933).

One criterion of a date in the Hassuna period is the husking tray (Fig. II, 5), "a large, flat-bottomed oval dish, with outsloping sides with a corrugated or pitted surface" (Lloyd and Safar, 1945, p. 277), especially known from Level II at Hassuna although it was reported to have occurred up to Level V. Fragments of husking trays have been found from Ras Shamra on the Syrian coast to Eridu in southern Iraq (Watson, pp. 66, 68), but chronological differentiations remain to be determined. Those from Shemshara, for example, which are more superficially incised than those from Hassuna, may be later.

In Levels IV to VI at Hassuna occurred a fair amount of the fine painted pottery with multiple zones of varying running patterns (Fig. II, 1, 2), which Herzfeld had discovered in graves at Samarra and which was characterized by Perkins (1949, pp. 6-7). At Shemshara, Samarran ware predominated at Level 12, following a more modest distribution in Level 13, in which Hassuna standard and incised wares (Fig. II, 4) were more numerous. On the basis of this evidence, we tentatively set off the last part of the Hassuna period as a Hassuna-Samarra period.

Until now, Samarran pottery has appeared at various sites as a superior commodity probably imported. One may hope that the excavations at Tell as-Sawwan where this pottery seems to have been found in considerable amounts, above levels with Hassuna pottery (El Wailly, 1963, pp. 1-2), will finally yield the assemblage which must have accompanied the Samarra pottery in the village of its origin.

At Shemshara, pottery was introduced only at the time of Level IV at Hassuna, probably because of the isolated situation of the valley "only accessible by trails across the mountains and through the narrow

---

*See Braidwood and Howe, 1960, p. 40, for their preference of the term *tauf* over pisé or adobe.

gorges at the upper and lower ends" (Mortensen, 1962, p. 76). In these circumstances it is all the more interesting that this isolation did not prevent good trade relations with the Lake Van area, thought to have been the source of the obsidian used for most of the blade tools at Shemshara.

It is equally interesting that when pottery did appear at such an isolated spot as Shemshara, the types reflected knowledge of the superior wares of Hassuna; one would like to know how such knowledge of pottery types traveled.

Distinctive of the superior wares of Hassuna and other sites of northern Iraq is the light color in contrast to the dark gray and black burnished wares in the contemporary levels of Amuq A-B and other places in the Syro-Cilician area. Of these, hardly more than a dozen sherds were found at Hassuna in Levels IV and V, two or three at Nineveh (Mallowan, 1933, p. 150), and some at Arpachiyah (Mallowan and Rose, 1935, p. 174). Those published from Hassuna (Lloyd and Safar, 1945, Pl. XIV, 1, 11—Level IV; 9—Level V; here Fig. II, 3) are two vessels which are fine enough to have been highly prized imports. The same may have been true of the two projectile points from Syro-Cilicia (Lloyd and Safar, 1945, Fig. 22, 9, 10; here Fig. II, 8).

Two stamp seals found at Hassuna were probably also imports. Both have the top of what was undoubtedly a suspension loop or ledge broken off; both are bored through the sealing surfaces so that they could be worn as pendants but used less easily as seals. The one from Level II (Lloyd and Safar, 1945, Pl. XI, 2 top row, third item; here Fig. VI, 1) is almost identical with one published from Phase B in the Amuq (Braidwood, 1960, p. 95, Fig. 68, 1). Similar seals are known from later phases of the Amuq sites, and indicate that the seal from Hassuna was brought from that region. A seal from Mattarah from a mixed Samarra-Ubaid context should probably be similarly classified (Braidwood et al., 1952, Fig. 20, 10).

A second seal found in Level V at Hassuna has the button shape later favored in Iran (not recognizable in the reproduction, Lloyd and Safar, 1945, Pl. XI, Fig. 2, 1). No parallels exist at present for the Hassuna example, although it was surely brought from somewhere else and reused as a pendant.

The Halaf Period

Polychrome potsherds, probably mostly from flat plates and usually painted in vivid, lustrous colors, were among the characteristic remains of the late Halaf pottery (Fig. IV, 24-26). This pottery largely replaced Hassuna and Samarra wares from Levels VII to X at Hassuna, having begun in Level VI, which seems to have been transitional and marked by overlapping of Samarra and Halaf potteries. The Halaf period derives its name from a site in the Khabur drainage of north Syria. Perkins, who has made the most thorough analysis of the culture of the period (Perkins, 1949, pp. 16-45), believes the original home of the Halaf culture to have been the Mosul area of northern Iraq with the sites of Nineveh (Mallowan, 1933), Arpachiyah (Mallowan, 1935), and Tepe Gawra (Tobler, 1950).

The easternmost extension of Halaf pottery so far recorded was at Gird Banahilk (Watson, in Braidwood and Howe, 1960, pp. 33-35). Halaf pottery spread also to Syria and Syro-Cilicia, where it appeared in Phase C of the Amuq (see Watson, p. 69, above). A change in the chipped stone industry of this Amuq phase—the introduction of sickle blades and absence of projectile points found earlier—may have been due to influence from the Halaf culture. For several north Syrian sites, moreover, Perkins pointed to the possible presence of tholos structures such as those which characterize the architecture of Arpachiyah (Perkins, 1949, p. 41).

Female figurines of clay, varying from an elegant, slender, type (IV:28), or a naturalistic squatting one (IV:27) to stylized fiddle-idol types, occur in the Halaf levels of Arpachiyah, Tepe Gawra, and sites further west (Dales, 1960, Pls. 92-93, Nos. 8-25).

Stone seal pendants and seals engraved in an accomplished, delicate, linear style appear in north Mesopotamia in the Halaf period (e.g., Tobler, 1950, Pl. CLXXII, 17-19, all area A, Level D, Fig. VI, 2; Mallowan, 1935, Pl. VI, a; Pl. VII a, b). Few of the seals were actually found in Halaf levels; most seem to have survived into later levels. The favorite pattern of the seal pendants consists of squares with St. Andrew's crosses combined with empty squares or other linear patterns. The earliest occurrence of this distinctive pattern on seals is in Phase B of the Amuq (Braidwood, 1960, p. 95, Fig. 68, 2), where it is somewhat coarser. Perhaps the refined linear patterns on seal pendants and seals of north Mesopotamia are a further development of types evolved in the preceding period in the Amuq. Derivation of Halaf period seals of north Mesopotamia from those of the Amuq is also suggested by the shapes: a relatively thin base with rectangular or rounded outline and a suspension device on the back cut from the stone itself, usually a perforated ridge in the Amuq and a loop or roll handle in north Mesopotamia.

An animal figure, as delicately engraved as the geometric designs was found in a seal impression at Gawra (Tobler, 1950, Pl. LXXXIX, b, Pl. CLXVI, 123; here Fig. VI, 3) assigned to a Halaf level but perhaps belonging to the early Ubaid period (Perkins, 1949, p. 34). Such figured designs may have been a Mesopotamian innovation, because they are lacking among the seals of Amuq C-E, the phases contemporary with the Halaf and Ubaid periods.

The Early Northern Ubaid Period

Pottery of the early Ubaid levels in the north, where the type site is Tepe Gawra (Tobler, 1950), is characterized by bell-shaped bowls (Fig. IV, 20) with a decoration in which painted design contrasts with open background. Motifs are often continuous, permitting rapid execution of wavy lines, triangles, or chevrons which differ from the singly applied elements of many Halaf patterns. At Gawra, Ubaid elements begin as early as in Stratum XX, and Halaf ones survive until XVII, into the Ubaid period. Such periods of transition, however, must be taken for granted whenever one pottery replaces another without destruction of the preceding culture—and often even after violent interruption of life at a site. It has not been found necessary, therefore, to express such transitions in the terminology of the present paper.

Valuable for correlation of the northern Ubaid levels with those of the Ubaid period of the south are lenticular hole-mouth jars with long trumpet-shaped spouts (Fig. IV, 23)—also called "tortoise vases"—covered with dark paint and small patterns which occur in Gawra XIX-XVII and which are known from Eridu XIII-VIII and Ras al 'Amiya in the south (see below).

Other similarities include: bent clay nails used as mullers (Tobler, 1950, p. 169; here Fig. IV, 19; Stronach, 1961, p. 107); spindle whorls, of which a series from Ras al 'Amiya resembles one from Tepe Gawra (Stronach, 1961, pp. 106-7); and the tripartite plan of the temples from Gawra XIX and XVIII comparable to those of Eridu XI-VIII.

For the glyptic development of the Early Ubaid period in the north, however, good parallels are lacking in the south. A new lentoid seal shape engraved with a delicate, single antelope, like the earliest imprint (Tobler, 1950, Pl. CLXVI, 123), was found in Gawra XVIII and again in XV (ibid., Pl. CLXIV, 103, Pl. CLXV, 104). In the latter level an imprint was also found which shows human figures and animals for the first time in a composition (Tobler, 1950, Pl. CLXIV, 98; here, Fig. VI, 4); the thin, linear figures seem to float in the space which they fill with their dovetailing forms. Legs of both the animals and the humans are bent. Seal impressions found in the Well of Gawra XIII (Tobler, 1950, Pl. CLXIV, 100, 101, 102; Pl. CLXIX, 162), as well as a seal from Tell Gomel in eastern Iraq (Frankfort, 1935, p. 29, Fig. 31), also belong to this style. Often the figures stand on the circumference of the seal, causing something of a rotational movement in the design. Ubaid relations with east and west, based mainly on pottery forms, techniques, and designs, are numerous (Perkins, 1949, p. 96) but remain to be charted in detail to indicate the date of the correlations.

Female figurines of the Early Ubaid period are simplified in comparison with Halaf figurines. Especially characteristic are stumps for arms (Tobler, 1950, pl. LXXXI, c, Pl. CLIII, 4; here Fig. IV, 22). Further characteristics are the painted bands on the body, crossed on the breast and forming a girdle below (ibid., Pl. LXXXI, c, d). The ornamentation of the crossed bands was to survive in later periods from the Mediterranean to India (Dales, 1963, pp. 34-36). Another type of figurine, probably male, from Gawra, Stratum XVI (Tobler, 1950, Pl. LXXXIV, Fig. b, 2, Pl. CLVI, 58; here Fig. IV, 21), closely resembles unstratified figurines of the pre-Uruk period from Warka (Perkins, 1949, p. 62).

The Late Northern Ubaid Period

In this period, Gawra XIII, with its acropolis crowned by three elaborate temples built of excellent, well-bonded mud brick with complex stepped piers and niches, must have been the most important phase. Pottery is typified by the beaker with gently curved sides and flaring rim painted with various bold and sweeping bands and much use of negative space (Fig. IV, 18). Beakers of this general type were found in a sounding at Makhmur (Mallowan and El-Amin, 1950, p. 57, text, p. 65) although they have ring bases in contrast to those of Gawra—and beakers with related decoration but different shape were also found at Telul eth-Thalathat (Egami, 1959, Pl. 50, 2).

A distinctive type of vessel in this period is ridged and incised (Tobler, 1950, Pl. LXXVIII, c, Pl. CXXXI, 218, 220; here Fig. IV, 17) called corrugated by Lloyd, who found the same pottery at Grai Resh (Lloyd, 1940, Pl. II, Fig. 5, 29; text, p. 19).

An incense burner with architectural decoration (Tobler, 1950, Pl. LXXVIII, d; Pl. CXXXII, 228; here Fig. IV, 16) forms a welcome correlation with a painted incense burner from Eridu with related architectural decoration (Lloyd and Safar, 1947, Fig. 5 in the Arabic section; here Fig. III, 12). Despite this example, correlations between north and south on the basis of pottery are only about half as numerous as those which could be established for the Early Ubaid period (Perkins, 1949, pp. 90-93, passim). A comparison of the architecture of Gawra XIII with that of the Eridu temples, however, suggests contacts between north and south either direct or—more likely—through intermediary sites as yet undiscovered (see below, p. 152).

In the Well of Gawra XIII were found seal impressions of distinctive designs which must belong to the first part of the period before the northern temple was built (Tobler, 1950, pp. 31-32, 35). One group continues the dovetailing, rotating composition of thin figures found first in Stratum XV (ibid., Pl. CLXIV, 100, 102). Others show increasingly substantial figures concentrated in the lower part of the seal as on a base (ibid., Pl. CLXX, 173). In an imprint with a gazelle-horned demon (ibid., Pl. CLXIV, 94; here Fig. VI, 5), a more vertically directed composition is found, perhaps even an axial one if the seal is correctly reconstructed.

Most of the ornamental seal designs from the Well of Gawra XIII have patterns of parallel lines in different directions but related to a median axis (ibid., Pl. CLX, 38, 39, 43, here Fig. VI, 6; Pl. CLXI, 48). The pleasing effect of these designs seems somewhat similar to that of seals from Giyan VC (Contenau and Ghirshman, 1935, Pl. 38, 37, 33, 20). Some of the designs of imprints found in the Well and elsewhere in Stratum XIII suggests vegetal forms like leaves marked by short parallel lines (Tobler, 1950, Pl. CLXI, 64; Pl. CLXV, 105). These designs may prefigure those of the ornamental cylinder seals and imprints of Nineveh 4-5 (Mallowan, 1933, Pl. LXV, 21-35; Pl. LXVI, 3-7, 16-26).

The Early Gawra Period

Strata XII-A and XII mark a break in the architectural sequence; the temples of the preceding stratum were replaced by the secular buildings of a town. Moreover, new types appear in the seals; "hut symbols" may have begun at this time with a somewhat tentative form (Tobler, 1950, Pl. LXXXVI, 5, 6—here Fig. IV, 10), and new forms and techniques also appear in the pottery although Ubaid forms continue. There is a new "sprig ware," painted black on a thick brown or brick red slip (ibid., Pl. CXXXIII, 243—here Fig. IV, 13—, 245; Pl. CXXXVII, 294, 295; Pl. CXXXIX, 310, 311). The ware is "undoubtedly imported" (ibid., p. 147); its place of origin, however, is as yet unknown, although the colors make one think of Iranian potteries. Equally unknown elsewhere and unparalleled is the landscape urn of Stratum XII (ibid., Pl. LXXVIII, a, b—here Fig. IV, 12). A few sherds of a hard fired greenish gray pottery with incised, applied, and stamped decoration which became more plentiful in the following Middle Gawra period (ibid., Pl. LXXIX, a), are in the University Museum in Philadelphia, clearly labeled "12" (Fig. IV, 11). They were not mentioned in the publication, perhaps because they did not fit in the Ubaid pottery period to which Strata XII-A and XII were assigned. Such a date must be revised, however, in view of the many items of the later Gawra period which are prefigured in the strata here discussed for which the term Early Gawra period has been chosen.

In the seals of Gawra XII, all ornamental designs are angular and simplified. There are many small seals with simple geometric decoration based on the division of the circle (ibid., Pl. CLVIII, 14, Pl. CLIX, 16, 17, 24, 25, 27; 26—here Fig. VI, 7 was found "below XII"). Most of these seals are hemispheroids ranging from low to high and from small to medium-sized. Many of the geometrically decorated ones are said to be of white paste.

A few seals of this stratum have a single animal figure engraved on the base, usually an ibex with forelegs bent or stretched out obliquely (ibid., Pl. CLXV, 109—here Fig. VI, 8—, 110, 111). Two of these seals also have holes or grooves in the back for inlay. Holes for inlay are new features which also occur on stone studs in Amuq Phases F, G (Braidwood, 1960, p. 254, Fig. 192, 2; p. 333, Fig. 255, 2); they are also seen in kidney-shaped seal amulets from Brak, one of which was found in the Grey Brick Stratum, assigned to the earlier Jamdat Nasr period (Mallowan, 1947, Pl. XVII, 9).

Ritual and other scenes with more than one figure seem to have had their inception in Stratum XII and continued into XI. In general, glyptics fail to show the abrupt change from painted to monochrome pottery noted between Strata XII and XI A. In fact, two imprints of the same seal were found in Strata XII and XI respectively (Tobler, 1950, Pl. CLXIII, 82, 83; Amiet, 1961, Pl. 2, 44 shows a combined drawing of the two impressions). Although this may be an accidental division into levels at the time of the excavation, the general continuity in the seals from one level to the other is interesting, in view of the violent end of Stratum XII (Tobler, 1950, pp. 25-26).

The Middle Gawra Period

The new period, Strata XI-A and XI, is marked architecturally by the fact that Stratum XI-A was a fortified town with a strong inner citadel—the Round House (ibid., p. 18). In this stratum a new type of burial appears—the tomb, built of stone or mud brick—which was distinctive of Gawra to Stratum VIII-C. In Gawra XI-A the first of a series of temples was built which continued with minor variations through Stratum VIII. All these temples have the tripartite plan of the earlier temples at Gawra with a long central chamber flanked by subsidiary rooms. The corners are oriented to the cardinal points as in the south; however, a portico entrance in Temple XI, which becomes even more accentuated in the temples of Strata IX and VIII (Perkins, 1949, p. 173), seems to be a distinctive northern feature, as is the fact that the entrance is in a short wall, opposite the podium (Tobler, 1950, Pls. II, V, XXII).

A basic change occurred in the pottery of Stratum XI-A, which is mostly undecorated and includes new forms such as wide and shallow bowls with straight or incurving sides and a wide, flat base. Incised, impressed, punctured, or appliqué decoration continues from XII; painting with simple lines, cross-hatched triangles or the like is found; burnishing on gray or black vessels is the least popular (Tobler, 1950, pp. 153-55).

In the seal designs, human and demonic figures are now often completely upright and have a human gait (ibid., Pl. CLVIII, 81, 89). A significant motif is the ibex demon (ibid., Pl. CLXIII, 81—here Fig. VI, 9), comparable to that on seal impressions of Phase B at Susa (Amiet, 1961, Pl. 6, 118). Seals purchased at Tepe Giyan, which can be assigned to the same phase on stylistic grounds, also show the motif (Herzfeld, 1933,

Fig. 24, TG 2331, also on Pl. II; Fig. 25, TG 2506). Another characteristic motif of this period is that of a couple in an erotic scene, either seated and represented identically or bending over (Tobler, 1950, Pl. CLXIII, 86, 87); the latter rendering may be paralleled in a seal from the end of Giyan VC with horned figures (Contenau and Ghirshman, 1935, Pl. 38, 24; perhaps *ibid*., No. 22 represents a related motif).

Designs of disembodied heads of horned animals are another feature of the period (Tobler, 1950, Pl. CLXIX, 168, 169; Pl. CLXX, 170—here Fig. VI, 10—, 172). Susa B has intricate geometric patterns produced by heads of horned animals arranged on a cross within a circle (Le Breton, 1957, p. 102, Fig. 15, 9, 10; also reproduced in Amiet, 1961, Pl. 6, 129, 130). Probably the large stamp impression of Uruk XII (Jordan, UVB III, 1932, Pl. 19, a) should be associated with this group which may indicate approximate contemporaneity of Uruk XII and Gawra XI.

Syro-Cilician connections in Gawra XI-A are manifested by the rectangular imprint of what must have been a gable-shaped stamp seal with three large horned animals (Tobler, 1950, Pl. CLXVIII, 155; here Fig. VI, 11) engraved on the rectangular sealing surface in the manner of numerous gables from Syro-Cilicia (e.g., Hogarth, 1920, Pl. IV, 90, 91, 93), the precise date of which in Phase F or late E of the Amuq remains to be established.

The typical seal designs of Gawra XI-A and XI with numerous animals, especially saluki dogs pursuing horned animals, or standing above or below them, are paralleled at Arpachiyah (Mallowan, 1935, Pl. IX, 605, 613) and at Nineveh (Mallowan, 1933, Pl. LXIV, 13-14) but not outside northern Mesopotamia. The development of the style seems to have led toward larger and fewer figures.

The Late Gawra Period

The Late Gawra period, Strata X-A to VIII-C, is here taken to be contemporary with the Late Uruk and Jamdat Nasr period in the south. This correlation is shown mainly—rather tenuously, it is admitted—in the seal designs; architecture does not permit any specific correlations between levels, and pottery manifests only the general feature of the wheel-made technique beginning in Stratum IX and becoming common in VIII. The fabric is light buff, which is the characteristic color of the pottery in this period. Gray and red burnished examples, however, are still known from Stratum X, as they had been in XI (Tobler, 1950, p. 154), but are not mentioned for Strata IX and VIII. Beveled rim bowls, the hallmark of the Uruk period, were apparently not found at Gawra although they were present in Nineveh 3 and 4, Nuzi IX and VIII, and at Grai Resh (Perkins, 1949, pp. 57, 163, 165, 170, 199).

A tie with the south is stressed even more strongly by the few seal impressions found in Stratum IX which indicate relation with the massive modeled forms of the imprints found in Uruk IV. The closest parallel for the example here given (Tobler, 1950, Pl. CLXIX, *165*) seems to come from Uruk IVb (Lenzen, 1950, Pl. 4, *8*; note especially the stylization of the animal's legs). In a second imprint from Gawra IX, two human figures are shown in profile instead of with the earlier convention of a triangular frontal thorax. Such profile renderings are again related to the glyptic style of Uruk IV, although other details are unparalleled there.

The animals with crossed horns and necks on the seals of Stratum VIII at Gawra are only faintly reminiscent of Uruk IV motifs (Speiser, 1935, Pl. LVIII, *31-33*; Lenzen, 1950, Pl. 4, *9-11*). The principal parallels for the new small and medium-sized seals of Gawra VIII, engraved with one—at most two—horned animals or felines (Speiser, 1935, Pl. LVI, *8-14*; Pl. LVII, *15-27*), however, can be found in Brak in seals from the Gray Brick Stratum (Mallowan, 1947, Pls. XVIII-XX, *passim*), assigned to the earlier Jamdat Nasr period, and in examples from the Amuq sites from Phase G (Braidwood, 1960, p. 330, Fig. 253, *8-11*), equated with the later Protoliterate and Early Dynastic I range (*ibid.*, p. 516). Especially striking is the presence at all three sites of placing animals *tête-bêche* and of showing horned animals with three legs. Opposed pairs of volutes are also seen at all three sites. The example from Gawra is on a terracotta seal cursorily made and actually found in Stratum VII (Speiser, 1935, Pl. LVI, *6*), where it is one of the few survivals of stamp seals in a level otherwise characterized by cylinder seals. West-East influences indicated by these stamp seals are further documented by impressions of large plaques or gables found in Gawra VIII and by a fragment of an actual plaque of the same group (Speiser, 1935, Pl. LVII, 28—here Fig. VII, *4*—Pl. LVII, *29*, *30*) from Stratum VII, where it surely was a survival from VIII. Relations with Syro-Cilician gables are suggested by the size of the designs and by similarities, in the rendering of the animals and fillers, to gables from various sites in Syro-Cilicia (see especially a gable of "bronze" bought near Antioch: Hogarth, 1920, Pl. IV, *103*). Further, the serrated border which suggests aligned stag antlers resembles in that feature a hemispheroid found at Tarsus as a survival in an Early Bronze II level (Goldman, 1956, Fig. 392, 1).

An imprint of a stamp seal from Gawra (Speiser, 1935, Pl. LVIII, 38; here, Fig. VII, 1) has as one of the figures in a tightly filled, dovetailing composition a lion which seems to act like a human being. Seals and impressions in such a style with similar composition, often featuring animals acting like humans, have been assigned in Susa to the end of the Proto-Elamite period (Amiet, 1961, Pl. 39, 593-600; text pp. 42-43) and dated by Le Breton in Susa D (Le Breton, 1957, p. 117, Fig. 38, above). This relation to the Susa group suggests a terminal date in the First Early Dynastic period for Gawra VIII.

The present evidence is somewhat puzzling in that it shows that the seal cutters of Gawra tenaciously retained the stamp seal form during a period when Nineveh, situated not far from Gawra, seems to have produced cylinder seals of a type used at the end of the Jamdat Nasr period (Protoliterate D) in the Diyala sites and in Susa (see below, pp. 244-45). In Gawra, Cylinder seals seem to have been adopted only in the time of Strata VII and VI.

THE SOUTH

Early Painted Pottery Periods: Ubaid 1-4

The word "periods" used for the contemporary development in the north is here replaced by "phases" to stress the continuous indigenous development shown to have occurred in the pottery (Oates, 1960), previously thought to have been derived from Iran.

The Ubaid 1 (former Eridu) Phase

The first phase, Levels XIX to XV, was represented at Eridu by a fine monochrome, usually chocolate-colored painted ware decorated with small-scale rectilinear patterns, such as grids, small triangles, or zigzags, between horizontal lines. The patterns and their disposition are often reminiscent of Samarra style pottery (Figs. I, 1, II, 1), with which the Ubaid 1 style must be partly contemporary. The occurrence of Hassuna type husking trays in Levels XIX, XVII, and XV at Eridu (Lloyd and Safar, 1948, Pl. III, last column) confirms the early date of the phase.

Interpreted as the earliest recognizable sanctuary of this phase is a thin-walled square building of Level XVI with a deep recess in which a small pedestal probably represents an altar whereas a second similar pedestal in the center of the building was interpreted as an offering table. All the elements of the later Sumerian temple seem to have been prefigured here. The building was constructed of long prismatic mud bricks. The bricks of the following two levels, XV and XIV (the latter level corresponds to a filling of a building in XV), have a conspicuous row of thumb impressions on the upper side. Relations with similar bricks in Sialk II and with others in Jericho Pottery Neolithic B have been pointed out by Dyson (1961, p. 633).

The Ubaid 2 (former Hajji Muhammad) Phase

Levels XIV to XII are characterized at Eridu by a ware first recognized in the excavation at the Qal'at Hajji Muhammad (Ziegler, 1953). The ware usually has dark, purplish black paint, often thickly applied, resulting in a metallic luster. Patterns are often close and create dark zones on the light buff pottery. Wide bowls, not unlike the large plates of the Late Halaf period, are often painted on the interior wall with an oblique grid pattern, leaving a regular scatter of tiny squares in reserve; the center of the bowls has a pattern of alternating dark and reserved triangles, and the outer wall is circled by a band of thick paint in which tall narrow triangles are reserved (*ibid*., Pl. 14; here, Fig. III, *17*).

The Ubaid 3 Phase (former Ubaid I Period)

In Levels XI to VIII at Eridu occur the typical features of the Ubaid period, known earlier at several sites in the south: bent clay nails, clay sickles, and in pottery painting simple, often bold curvilinear designs with frequent use of negative space (Fig. III, *13-15*). The rapid production possible in this type of pottery painting assured its wide spread north of Mesopotamia: to Syria and Iran.

One of the links between Ubaid 2 and Ubaid 3 phases is formed by the "tortoise jars" (Fig. III, *16*); three occurred in Level XIII, but nineteen in Level XI; only one was found in each of Levels X and IX, and four in Level VIII. The massive occurrence in Level XI suggests that this is the most likely stage at which the type was taken to the north, hence the Early Ubaid Strata at Gawra, XIX to XVII, in all of which fragments of such jars are said to have been found (Tobler, 1950, p. 136), are correlated with Eridu Level XI. The conservative retention of Ubaid 3 decoration for this type of vessel was probably caused by its ritual use in the south (Lloyd and Safar, 1948, p. 119), perhaps in contrast to the north (Tobler, 1950, p. 136).

The thin-walled Temples XI to IX form a group. They have mud bricks of new proportions, clearly defined, regular buttresses, a platform on which the temples are raised, and a plan in which the principal unit is a cella with an altar at one end behind which was a passage. Annexed to the sanctuary chamber on the side were two smaller rooms one of which contained an offering table. It remains uncertain whether there was also an offering table in the main chamber as in Temples VIII to VI and in later temples of early Mesopotamia.

Temple VIII is dated by its pottery contents in the present phase, although it is more closely related to Temples VII and VI of Ubaid 4 in plan (see below), in the greater thickness of the walls, and in the fact that the buttresses seem to have become principally decorative pilasters. Oates seemed to ascribe the change in the plan of these Temples VIII to VI to the absorption of new stimuli at the beginning of the Ubaid 3 phase, suggesting at the same time that pottery reflected changes more rapidly than religious architecture (Oates, 1960, p. 37).

The Ubaid 4 Phase (former Ubaid II Period)

At some sites in the south, Late Ubaid pottery painting became "quite careless and uninspired, and even at Eridu the later wares are less skillfully painted" (*ibid*., p. 39). Oates suggests that the increased use of metal about this time contributed to a lessening of interest in the potter's craft, and that the appearance of the potter's wheel during the transition from the Ubaid to the Uruk period contributed to the decline and eventual disappearance of painted pottery. The simple, bold designs found in some of the grave pottery (Fig. III, *9, 10*), however, are as pleasing as those of Gawra XIII, which are probably about contemporary.

The plans of the Eridu Temples VIII to VI have often been compared to those of Gawra XIII. More specifically, comparison has centered on the Northern Temple, built in the middle of the period covered by Stratum XIII at Gawra (Tobler, 1950, p. 35), which was compared to Temple VII at Eridu (Lloyd, 1947, p. 93). Both temples are identically oriented and seem to be based on a plan which had a cella flanked by four corner rooms. There is a major recess in the façade, decorated like most of the other walls by stepped buttresses, but buttresses appear in the rear wall. Despite these similarities which suggest that the temples were indeed contemporary, there are important differences between them, especially in the position of the entrances, probably owing to different ritual requirements. Probably both temple types were derived from a common source as yet undiscovered.

Stamp seals are so far represented only by a few examples of oval or circular form with slightly raised back, engraved with a symmetrical pattern of parallel lines in different directions and small, shallow drillings. One such example was found in Uqair (VI: 6a) in a level preceding the end of the Ubaid period (Lloyd, 1943, p. 149); the others come from the Tell de l'Est in Tello (Parrot, 1948, p. 37, Fig. 7, i, j). The combination of drill holes in the center with parallel lines in different directions around them and in the margin of the sealing surface is the favored stamp seal decoration in Ubaid levels of the west; of several examples, one was found stratified in Phase E in the Amuq (Braidwood, 1960, p. 221, Fig. 167, 3, 4). Moreover, several seal impressions from the Well of Gawra XIII (which belongs to the earliest part of the period covered by the level) have effective patterns composed of parallel lines in different directions (Fig. VI, 6). These examples suggest a dating of this type of southern stamp seals in the earlier part of Ubaid 4. Others, such as a button with quartered circle design (Parrot, 1948, p. 37, Fig. 7, h) which corresponds to a seal from Giyan VC (Contenau-Ghirshman, 1935, Pl. 38, 46, description of shape, p. 42), were probably imports. The impressive series of figured stamps of the north is, however, to date absent from the repertory of the south.

In this last phase of the Ubaid development were also found clay figurines of animals (mostly bovids) and figurines (mostly female). Dales distinguished an Ur-Eridu naturalistic style with reptilian heads and natural legs (Fig. III, 11) and a Warka pillar style, the latter not well stratified; Ann Perkins rightly pointed to parallels in Gawra XVI (Perkins, 1949, p. 62) which serve to suggest a similar date for those from Warka. Relations of some of the southern figures with earlier prototypes in the north at Jarmo were pointed out by Dales (1960, pp. 187-88); the new figurines from Tell as-Sawwan furnish further prototypes for female figurines with tall headgears covered with bitumen. Such relations show that the direction of influence not only went from south to north, as suggested by the pottery, but that important cultural traits had at an earlier period traveled south from northern sites.

The Uruk Period

A new phase in the Mesopotamian sequence is marked by the appearance of a light colored, unpainted but significantly often wheel-made ware. We call this phase—first recognized in the excavation of Uruk, the modern Warka, in the deep sounding of the Eanna precinct (Jordan, UVB III, 1932, Pl. 10, Plan 1, pp. 18-19; Nöldecke, UVB IV, 1932, Pls. 2, 18-20, text pp. 37-45)—Uruk phase, in a return to an earlier terminology (see above, p. 133). The pottery of the period can be divided into Early, Middle, and Late Uruk (see Hansen, below); most of the other artifacts, however, cannot be assigned with any certainty to a time before the Late Uruk period, corresponding to Protoliterate-b.

The Early Uruk Period

The new pottery of the Early Uruk phase, called Warkan by Perkins, included not only the already-mentioned light-colored ware, which is also often handmade, but also red and gray ware, both usually slipped. A foreign origin for this pottery was suspected (Perkins, 1949, p. 98). In Level XII occurs the guiding fossil of the Uruk period, the beveled rim bowl, which spread to southwest Iran and to Syria with a massive appearance the reasons for which are as yet unexplained.

In Level XII of the deep sounding in the Eanna precinct was found an imprint of a large stamp with flat sealing surface (Jordan, UVB III, 1932, Pl. 19a). Engraved on it are sinuous-horned animal heads symmetrically disposed on either side of what could be the vertebral column of an animal. The design has been compared to a stamp seal impression from Susa B (Nagel, 1963, p. 46, Abb. 95) and to an extant seal from the same level (Amiet, 1961, Pl. 7, Fig. 140, text p. 23), with both of which it may be contemporary.

The temples of the Early Uruk phase were probably represented by the extensions of the platform at Eridu, V-II, of which the consistency and size of the bricks and the use of limestone set in gypsum mortar in II (Safar, 1947, p. 106) may provide some criteria of date.

The Middle and Late Uruk Phase

From the beginning of the Middle Uruk Phase onward (Eanna VII-VI), the new Nippur sequence (outlined below by Hansen) replaces the summaries of the pottery development and correlations so far given for the development in the south on the basis of published material. In this section of the present paper, only the pottery of the north will be mentioned together with other artifacts and architecture for its chronological value.

Architectural remains of the Late Uruk phase as revealed in buildings at Eanna show a longitudinal, tripartite plan with central cella flanked on both sides by a series of uniformly sized rooms with a stairway room on each side. This unit of cella and side rooms was frequently combined in Eanna with another to constitute the "head and trunk" (for the similes, see Lenzen, 1964, p. 128) of a building. It should be noted that none of the Eanna "temples" has an altar or any other unequivocal furnishings of a sanctuary, although the niched walls and the plan just described are generally _interpreted_ as characterizing temples. Both the single temple and the combined units show a tendency toward architectural uniformity, and imply an abandonment of the self-contained plan with stress on the four corner rooms noted in Ubaid temples. Uniformity also characterized the _Riemchen_ bricks, probably introduced in Uruk VI and lasting until Uruk III (Lenzen, UVB XX, 1964, p. 6, note 2). Brick built columns and half columns appear. They are decorated with uninterrupted cone mosaics, which are also used for the ornamentation of other walls throughout Level IV, Temple I at Eridu, where "circular or part-circular columns were incorporated in the architectural treatment," probably belongs to the same time, also on the evidence of the use of stone mosaic cones (some of the heads of these cones were covered with copper plating—Safar, 1947, p. 107). At Uqair, the painted temple was probably contemporary with Uruk IV, as suggested by the bricks with trident marks on them (Lloyd, 1943, Pl. XVI above and p. 149). The cone-decorated building excavated on the Ziggurat terrace at Ur probably also belongs to this period (Woolley, 1956, p. 28).

The chronological position of the stamp and cylinder seals of Mesopotamia in the Late Uruk period has to be re-evaluated. Several scholars have noted that stamp seals preceded cylinders in the excavations of Tello and also at Susa (Le Breton, 1957, p. 103). This is relevant for Mesopotamia, because the stylistic and iconographic development from stamp to cylinder seal is at present more extensively documented at Susa than at Uruk (Amiet, 1961, p. 37), where only one cylinder seal impression from Level V is known (Jordan, UVB II, 1931, p. 51, _Abb_. 44). The collared type of stamp seal found in Late Uruk period levels at Tello

(Amiet, 1961, Pl. 8, 156, 157; De Genouillac, 1934, Pl. 38, 1-b, c) is also represented by two examples in the Grey Eye Temple stratum at Brak (Mallowan, 1947, Pl. XX, 13, 16). The same stratum also contained animal-shaped amulets, some of which were found even in the red bricks underlying the Grey Brick stratum (e.g., *ibid.*, Pl. XI, 3, Pl. XII, 1, text pp. 103, 104). The possibility that these amulets, like the collared and other stamp seals, were already being made in the Late Uruk period (Amiet, 1961, p. 25) must be seriously considered.

Further, the division of the cylinders of the age into a carefully carved, subtly modeled Uruk style and a deteriorated style with drill hole patterns characteristic of the Jamdat Nasr period—derived from Frankfort's first classification of these early cylinders (Frankfort, 1939, pp. 15-38; Frankfort, 1955, pp. 12, 13, 17)—cannot be fully maintained in view of the evidence of excavation for more subtle divisions (Farkas, 1964). For example, the type of cylinder seal showing squatting pigtailed women with various objects was found in the Late Uruk level Inanna 15 at Nippur (Fig. VII, 6) and in a contemporary Early Protoliterate level at Chogha Mish (personal communication from H. J. Kantor; precise phase to be determined). Several styles, some with little if any mitigation of the drill holes thus seem to have been produced in various places at the time of the fine glyptic preserved in the seal impressions of Uruk IV. The subdivisions made in period IV, "a-c," by the excavators of Uruk cannot be distinguished very clearly in the cylinder seals of the level. It may be noted, however, that relations with Susa seem to have been close in Uruk IVb and Susa Ca, because it is often difficult to determine whether an impression was made with a cylinder from Uruk or Susa. One example (Lenzen, UBV XV, 1959, Pls. 28, c, 30, a, b; here Fig. VII, 5) shows the scene, common in Uruk IV b, of the torturing or killing of prisoners (Nöldecke *et al.*, UVB V, 1934, Pl. 23, a; UVB IV, 1932, Pl. 15, a). On the recently published imprint, however, some of the figures are squatting with one knee upright in a posture which is not Mesopotamian but typical of Susa and, incidentally, of Egypt.

Larger works of sculpture have not been found in Uruk IV levels, but several objects such as the great vase (Heinrich, 1936, Pls. 2, 3, 38) and the male bust (Strommenger, 1964, Pls. 19-22) have been assigned to this level on stylistic grounds.

Writing appeared on small tablets in Uruk IVa (Falkenstein, 1965,

p. 44). In contemporary Susa Ca, tablets have only numbers and seal impressions (Amiet, 1961, p. 37).

A thronelike chest, elaborately inlaid with colored stone and flanked by posts probably topped by copper cones, found in the Riemchengebäude, dated with some probability in Uruk IV (Lenzen, UVB XV, 1959, p. 23; but see Lenzen, 1964, p. 128), conveys an idea of the high level of craftsmanship available in Uruk in this age and at the same time conveys "indications of wealth, religious complexity and centralization of political power, with at least partial control over labor" (Perkins, 1954, p. 47).

The Jamdat Nasr Period

In this phase, which was probably longer than assumed until now, the excavations of Eanna provide again the most carefully observed differentiation of levels. Lenzen found a considerable intermediate layer between the destruction level of Eanna IV and the rebuilding in Eanna III. This intermediate layer is followed by three subdivisions, c-a, of which the first saw the erection of the first high terrace at Eanna. From this time on, the low terrace or platform for the temple complex seems to characterize Sumerian temple architecture (Perkins, 1949, p. 125, note 235). No temple comparable to those of Uruk IV, however, was built on the terrace in Uruk III. The platform and a supposed court southwest of it show architectural features which may have chronological implications. The northwest wall of the platform was ornamented in III-c by engaged brick columns, replaced in an enlargement of level III-b by shallow niches. The walls of the court show cone mosaics only in the recesses and sometimes framed even there with terracotta blocks and corner pieces simulating cones (Nöldecke et al., UVB VII, 1936, pp. 9-10; UVB VIII, 1937, p. 9). Another innovation in these wall decorations was animal figures or Inanna symbols, again simulating cones (UVB II, pp. 34 ff.). A single eye of stone mosaic, probably originally belonging to the stone cone temple (Lenzen, UVB XX, 1964, Pl. 19, h, text p. 25) is either part of a figure or represents the motif of a single eye or a pair of eyes, hitherto specifically associated with designs on seals and other artifacts of the Jamdat Nasr period, and may have originated earlier as indicated by the present evidence.

The variety of the buildings of Eanna in period III (see summary by Perkins, 1949, pp. 125-28; Lenzen, UVB XX, 1964, pp. 11-18) suggests some of the different functions concentrated in the Eanna precinct at that time. A large number of finds, especially animal amulets and stone vessels (e.g., Fig. III:1-4), the so-called Sammelfund (Heinrich, 1936), were made in a building dated in IIIa and referred to by Strommenger as the treasure house of level IIIa/II, unfortunately without further explanation (Strommenger, 1964, p. 384, s.v. 17 and passim). On the Anu Ziggurat, Temples D and E are assigned to the Jamdat Nasr period, and the White Temple to the very end of this period (Lenzen, 1951, p. 23; and UVB XVII, 1961, p. 18).

At Uqair, the building of a terrace enclosing the painted temple (Lloyd, 1943, pp. 145-46) must have occurred during the Jamdat Nasr period. It parallels the major architectural undertakings of the period in Uruk. Other parallels may be found in a range of semicircular buttresses parallel to the northwest façade of the temple (ibid., p. 146) and in clay corner plaques simulating cone mosaic and resembling those of Uruk IIIb (Perkins, 1949, p. 132, note 278).

The five superimposed strata of the Sin Temple at Khafaje in the Diyala region (Delougaz and Lloyd, 1942, pp. 8-40) are difficult to correlate with levels of the Eanna precinct in Uruk. Most probably they should be equated with the entire period III, which seems to have absorbed a period II earlier equated with Protoliterate-d by Lenzen (1951, p. 23). These subsequent strata of the Sin Temple reveal the adjustment of the tripartite plan to new requirements.

In Brak, the plan of the Eye Temple (Mallowan, 1947, Pl. LVII) shares with the south Mesopotamian temples the articulation of the walls by buttresses and the long cella with the altar placed against one of the short walls. The entrances through the opposite short wall assumed by Mallowan for the Eye Temple are somewhat reminiscent of the Eastern and Western Temples of Gawra VIII, although only one door was present there. Perkins compared the position of the entrances to those of the Anu Temples at Warka, but at least in the White Temple the principal entrance was on one of the long sides and the openings in the short side may not have been doors (Lenzen, 1955, p. 10; but see Heinrich in UVB VIII, 1936, p. 31). Southern influence, however, is obvious in such features as the use of cone mosaic for the decoration of the outer walls of the sanctuary of the Eye Temple and of simulated cone mosaic in stone (Mallowan, 1947, Pls. VI, III, IV) differing in the more valuable material from the clay examples in the south (see above). Although there can be no question about the date of the Eye Temple in the Jamdat Nasr period, the equation with Uruk III made on the basis of the ornamentation would place it in the earlier part, Protoliterate-c. This raises the problem of the date to be given to the underlying White, Gray, and Red Eye Temples, each of which had served as the platform for the next by being packed with bricks (like the White Temple on the Anu Ziggurat in Uruk). Mallowan ascribed only the Red Eye Temple "to the Uruk period proper" (Mallowan, 1947, p. 56), but, as mentioned above, the Grey Eye Temple, with its contents of animal amulets and other stamp seals, might also have to be retrogressed to the Uruk period—that is Protoliterate-b.

The close relations between architectural features of the Eye Temple at Brak and temples of Uruk suggests communication between the temple builders of Brak and those of southern Mesopotamia. Large-scale importation of raw materials into the latter region in the Protohistoric period probably accounts for the establishment of outposts on routes of supply and trade. Brak may have been such an outpost, lying as it does "at the cross-roads for transcontinental traffic between Syria and Mesopotamia on the one hand and Anatolia and the Euphrates on the other" (Mallowan, 1947, p. 49). Testimony for trade with the Khabur region may also come from Uruk in the form of a stamp seal from the debris layer between Levels D and C (Nöldecke *et al.*, UVB IX, 1937, Pl. 29, *d*; cf. Mallowan, 1947, Pl. XVIII, *28*).

"The incipient internationalism of the period," to use a phrase employed by Braidwood to characterize the foreign connections of Phase G in the Amuq, is well illustrated by the wide distribution of Jamdat Nasr type cylinder seals: Iran, Sialk and Susa (Amiet, 1961, Pl. 18, *292-95* and *299* ff., *passim*); Egypt (*ibid.*, Pl. 21 bis, *J-O* and the derivatives, *P-T*; see also Kantor, p. 10, above); Syria (Amiet, 1963, pp. 63-68 and references), first demonstrated by Frankfort (1939, pp. 223-27). In view of the apparently long time range of this type of cylinder (see above, p. 155), however, each occurrence will have to be individually examined and dated.

A much shorter duration may be assumed for the cylinders with geometric designs which occurred in the late Jamdat Nasr period, Protoliterate-d, in the Diyala temples (Frankfort, 1955, pp. 17-18, and Pls. 11-15). This mass of cylinders may represent devotionalia which were probably deposited soon after they had been made. Numerous examples were found in Susa and assigned to Susa Cc by Le Breton (1957, p. 108,

Fig. 26). In Nineveh, the cylinders and their imprints are described as tending to occur toward the bottom of Nineveh 5 (Mallowan, 1933, p. 138) and as occurring "with the last stages of the stratum Nin. 4 . . ." (ibid., p. 141). It is interesting that the style is represented by only one poor specimen in Gawra VII (Speiser, 1935, Pl. LIX, 46), where it was a survival, since the floruit of the style should be equated with the end of Stratum VIII. Similarly, there is in Gawra VII only one small chalice of the type of painted pottery characteristic of the painted pottery of Nineveh 5 (Speiser, 1935, Pl. LXV, 58). The most characteristic examples of that painted pottery (Campbell Thompson and Hamilton, 1932, Pls. LIII-LIX; Mallowan, 1933, Pls. LIV-LXI) show a curious combination of rows of squat birds or fish or ill-proportioned long-necked animals which too heavily fill the upper part of the chalices, jars, or bowls; the festoon-like bands, often seen in the lower part of vessels, successfully suggest more elegant ostentation (Fig. V, 20-22). The chalice shapes as well as the designs of long-necked animals are vaguely related to pottery from Hissar IIA (Schmidt, 1937, Pl. XX) with which they may be contemporary. At Nineveh, this pottery is said to have occurred together with a fine, sophisticated incised ware in which small areas of clay are cut away so that bands and panels stand out in relief (Campbell, Thompson and Hamilton, 1932, Pl. LX; Mallowan, 1933, Pls. LXII, LXIII—here Fig. V, 19). In Chagar Bazar, the two Nineveh wares are said to occur together (Mallowan, 1937, p. 95; Perkins, 1949, p. 171). In Billa, however, the painted Nineveh pottery occurs in Level 7, the incised in the subsequent Level 6 (Speiser, 1932-33, p. 267). Forms in Billa 6 have a vague resemblance to Early Dynastic pottery of the south more than to Gawra forms. Therefore the incised ware of Nineveh 5 has been tentatively taken by me to be contemporary with Early Dynastic II in the south, whereas the painted ware belongs to Early Dynastic I, possibly beginning at the end of the Jamdat Nasr period.

The Early Dynastic Period

The beginning of the Early Dynastic period in the south can be discerned in architecture by the use of plano-convex bricks (Delougaz, 1933) (although Riemchen continued to be used for a short period in the Diyala sites and at Nippur), in pottery (Delougaz, 1952, pp. 52-72; Hansen, below, pp. 208 ff.), and in cylinder seals, where the change from solid figures to flat, over-all patterns is most striking. Frankfort's

Brocade style (Frankfort, 1955, pp. 21-23), the most pleasingly organized of the cylinder seal styles of this age, does not appear in strength outside the Diyala region. Other styles which should be assigned to the same period can be discerned among the seal impressions from Ur. One style is based on signs of the cuneiform script (e.g., Legrain, 1936, Pls. 21-26, *passim*). Imprints of similarly engraved cylinders were found in Uruk in Early Dynastic levels (Nöldecke *et al.*, UVB V, 1934, Pl. 27, *c*; Heinrich, 1936, Pl. 16, *a, b*; Lenzen, *UVB* XIX, 1963, Pl. 16, *d-f*). The signs derived from the script are often combined with representational forms in dovetailing, even whirling compositions (Legrain, 1936, Pl. 21, *393, 394, 398*). Seals and imprints of Nineveh 4-5 (Mallowan, 1933, Pl. LXV, *21-36*, Pl. LXVI) show a related combination of representational forms with ornamental ones, although they are more clearly defined and organized than the over-all patterns of the later examples from Ur. The dovetailing style on seal impressions from Ur and Susa has also been mentioned above in relation to a stamp seal impression from Gawra VIII (Speiser, 1935, Pl. LVIII, *38*—here Fig. VII, *4*), dated in the First Early Dynastic period. Another link between north and south may be found in the erotic scenes of several Ur imprints (e.g., Legrain, 1936, Pl. 18, *365, 366, 368*; Pl. 19, *370*), the rendering of which recalls the representations of the subject on imprints of Gawra XI-A (Tobler, 1950, Pl. CLXIII, *86-88*). Some northern influences on the south in the First Early Dynastic period may be indicated by this evidence.

Continuation of Uruk and Jamdat Nasr styles with their substantial figures arranged in orderly compositions, now often axial, is found in a group of imprints from Ur which frequently show lions attacking ruminants (e.g., Legrain, 1936, Pl. 11, *215, 217*; Pl. 12, *231-239*). This style is also manifested in seals of the Diyala sites and should probably be assigned a date in the First Early Dynastic period (Ursula Moortgat-Correns, 1959, columns 346-48), although too little is known about the tempo of change in the styles of that time to be certain that it could not have survived into the Second Early Dynastic period.

A number of cylinders with which the Ur impressions were made had a design engraved on the base, to judge by the stamp seal impression beside that of the cylinder seal (e.g., Legrain, 1936, Pl. 15, *286, 297*). Such "stamp cylinders" were frequent also at Byblos and at other sites in Syria, Palestine, Cilicia, and at Troy (Benson, 1956, pp. 60-61). The inception of those at Byblos may have coincided with the First Early Dynastic period.

The close relationship in the major sculptural and glyptic styles of Susa with those of southern Mesopotamia, noted in the protohistoric period, continued in the Early Dynastic age, as exemplified by a steatite vase and several fragments carved in flat relief found at Khafaje and Tell Agrab in the Diyala region (Frankfort, 1954, Pl. 11, B; Frankfort, 1936, p. 434, Figs. 10, 12) but having probably originated in Susa. The equivalent sculptures found in Susa, however, cannot be dated with any precision within Susa D (e.g., Le Breton, 1957, p. 121, Fig. 43, 9).

The Second and Third Early Dynastic Periods

The Second Early Dynastic period marks the beginning of the historical age of Mesopotamia. The predominantly Sumerian records written with cuneiform signs on clay or stone are truly intelligible to scholars only from about this time onward.* Urbanization increased, and large architectural undertakings can be dated in this period: The oval at Khafaje (Delougaz, 1940) and Ubaid (Delougaz, 1938), the palace at Kish (Mackay, 1929)† and possibly that of Eridu in which the pottery belonged to the end of the Second or beginning of the Third Early Dynastic period (Safar, 1950, p. 32), the fine Square Temple at Tell Asmar (Delougaz and Lloyd, 1942, pp. 172-92), and possibly state C of the Ishtar Temple at Mari (Parrot, 1956, pp. 12-22; for the possible ED II date, see Porada, 1961, p. 161)—to mention only the more important structures known before the excavation of the Inanna precinct in Nippur (Hansen and Dales, 1962). That precinct revealed the interesting phenomenon of a typical Early Dynastic temple plan side by side with one which corresponds in its essential elements to the earliest known temple in the south: Eridu, Temple XVI.

Carved wall plaques from temples are first documented in this period. Those of Nippur (Hansen, 1963) support a division of the styles of the Second Early Dynastic period, as manifested at Nippur in Inanna Temple VIII, into an earlier abstract phase with simple, flat forms and

---

*Despite the use of Sumerian in the Early Dynastic texts of the south, several scholars in recent years have postulated the influx of an important Semitic element (the Akkadians) from the northwest (Goetze, 1961). This element would have been responsible for some of the major changes noted in this period (Falkenstein, Edzard, and Bottéro, 1965, pp. 56 ff.).

†There is no decisive evidence to date the palace later than the inlays, which were contemporary with its *floruit* (Moorey, 1965, p. 91). In my opinion, these inlays belong to the style of Early Dynastic II.

a later one with increased modeling and more complex forms. The latter trend continued into Early Dynastic IIIa (Inanna Temple VII B). In Early Dynastic IIIb the style may be said to have reached its classic expression in works from Lagash like the stele of Eannatum or the silver vase of Entemena (Frankfort, 1954, Pls. 32, 34, 35).

The stylistic development here outlined may be compared to that suggested by Moortgat, 1935, and elaborated by Strommenger, 1960 (see especially Table 3). The early abstract phase of Early Dynastic II was called by Moortgat, "Mesilim Stufe" after the sculptured macehead engraved for one of the titular kings of Kish whose date Rowton does not place much before Urnanshe of Lagash (Rowton, 1962, p. 54). With this early abstract style are linked the cylinder seal impressions of Fara with the elegant, linear style detailed by Frankfort (1939, pp. 44-50). The more naturalistic style of the latter part of Early Dynastic II was called by Strommenger "Fara Zeit." This name implies a reference to the majority of the texts from Fara and to seal impressions grouped around one with an inscription formerly read Imdugud Sukurru (Moortgat, 1940, pp. 13-14). Strommenger believes this glyptic group to be contemporary with the latter part of Early Dynastic II and with Early Dynastic IIIa. Moortgat's Meskalamdug style which follows upon the Imdugud Sukurru style (Moortgat, 1940, p. 14) and which is included by him in his "Ur I Zeit" is equated by Strommenger with Early Dynastic IIIb as is also the style from Mesanepada to Lugalanda.

The present writer's views can be read from Chart 3 where the Royal Cemetery is placed in Early Dynastic IIIa. This date which differs from that of Frankfort, who placed the Royal Cemetery in the second part of the Third Early Dynastic period, Early Dynastic IIIb, is based on the stylistic relations of the standard of Ur to a plaque of the Inanna temple VII B from Nippur which corresponds in time to Early Dynastic IIIa (Hansen, 1963, p. 166). It is based, furthermore, on the fact that the cylinders from the Royal Cemetery, inscribed with the names of Meskalamdug, Akalamdug, and Puabi (formerly Shubad) represent an earlier stylistic stage than the cylinder of Nin-banda (formerly Nin-tur), wife of Mesanepada, first recorded ruler of the First Dynasty of Ur. The chronological sequence of these royal persons was indicated by Sollberger (1960, pp. 71-73); the stylistic development of the cylinders was outlined by Moortgat (1940, pp. 14-15; elaborated by Nagel, 1959) but remains to be analyzed in greater detail. Even though the archaeological evidence for the date of Mesanepada is very tenuous, Mesanepada's date must fall before that of Eannatum of Lagash in whose reign we set the beginning of Early Dynastic IIIb. Hence the Royal Cemetery belongs to IIIa according to our definition of the divisions within the Third Early Dynastic period.

The occurrence of the above-mentioned carved plaques, which are characteristic of the Early Dynastic period and of which only few examples are known from subsequent centuries, parallels that of the statuettes of worshipers found in many temples of the Second and Third Early Dynastic periods (Frankfort, 1944, 1960; Strommenger, 1960). The distinctive Diyala style of long-haired, bearded worshipers is paralleled with only minor variations in statues found at Tell Chuera in North Syria (Moortgat, 1965; here Fig. V, 18). Mari, with its abundant statuary, has so far yielded only two examples, assigned by Strommenger to the abstract style of Early Dynastic II (Strommenger, 1960, p. 29, notes 229, 230). In general the chronology of the statuary from Mari is still uncertain despite several efforts at creating a chronological sequence (Strommenger, 1960, pp. 24-29 *et passim*).

Cylinder seals carved in the style of Early Dynastic II have been found in small numbers outside Mesopotamia, probably indicating trade relations with Susa (Le Breton, 1957, p. 117, Fig. 38, *above*: Susa D) and Syria (Hogarth, 1920, Pls. 1, 2, *passim*; von Luschan and Andrae, 1943, Pl. 39, *a*). The style is also represented by relatively many examples in Mari (Parrot, 1956, Pl. LXV, except 566, 572, 594, 657; Pl. LXVI, 545, 588, 587) and probably some of the others which are difficult to date between Early Dynastic II and IIIa.

The archaeological remains of the Third Early Dynastic period are more numerous than those of any other period of ancient Mesopotamia. All temple precincts of the earlier period were maintained, and some new temples may have been built at that time, such as the Ishtar Temple H of Assur (Andrae, 1922). The Palace at Kish, however, suffered destruction some time before Early Dynastic IIIb, when the area was used as the burial ground for the "A" cemetery (Mackay, 1929, p. 128). Such a late Early Dynastic date is suggested by the pottery found in the graves (Delougaz, 1952, p. 144).

Much of the most spectacular material datable in Early Dynastic IIIa comes from the shaft graves—presumably royal—which were found at Ur (Woolley, 1934).* Their most striking feature is the larger or smaller number of persons and ox-drawn vehicles (Dyson, 1960), introduced into the shaft before it was filled. Similar tombs existed at Susa, but were not recognized (De Mecquenem, 1943, p. 56). Since the material from the Susa graves was not published as a separate group the date of these burials remains somewhat uncertain.

In the "death-pit" of Puabi (formerly Shubad) at Ur were found two small stone vessels carved with patterns that are simplified in comparison with the more elaborate examples found whole or in fragments at several Mesopotamian sites (Delougaz, 1960; example from Khafaje, ibid., Pl. VI, a; here Fig. V, 17), at Mari, Susa, and also at Mohenjo Daro in Pakistan. The group has been related to incised pottery vessels from southeastern Iran and—less convincingly—to incised stone vessels of the Kulli culture of southern Baluchistan (Dales, p. 273). However distant these relationships may be, they suggest some trade connections between Mesopotamia and the east in the Early Dynastic IIIa period, as does the presence in the graves of Ur of etched carnelian beads identical with those of the Harappa culture (Wheeler, 1953, p. 76). Trade with the east is further documented by the dark blue lapis lazuli of many of the beads and other objects from Ur which must have come from Turkestan or Afghanistan.

Types of jewelry produced at Ur seems to have had a lasting influence on the technology of the surrounding regions (Maxwell-Hyslop, 1960). The same seems to have been true of weapons, although Deshayes would assign a more important role to the metallurgy of Susa (1960, p. 409). The style of the cylinder seals of the Third Early Dynastic period (Frankfort, 1939, pp. 50, f.) is found to have been modified according to local taste and iconography in Syria (Amiet, 1963, pp. 72-74) and in Elam (Frankfort, 1939, pp. 232-34). Since the practical use of cylinders outside the cuneiform sphere of South Mesopotamia and Susa consisted in sealing goods, the existence of widespread local groups of late Early

*The poorly recorded chariot burials from Kish (Watelin, 1934) were probably sunk deep in the pre-flood level of Area Y somewhat before the shaft graves of Ur were made, at the time of the palace of Kish, in the Second Early Dynastic period. Delougaz (1952, p. 137) pointed out that the pottery from the "Y" cemetery seems to have extended from Early Dynastic I to II. The relations of the chariot burials and of the copper objects found in them to those of Ur makes the later date seem more likely. The "A" Cemetery of Kish, on the other hand, has mainly pottery from the end of the Third Early Dynastic period (ibid., p. 144), although the cylinder seals seem to belong to the earlier part of the period.

Dynastic cylinders suggests that they were the result of active trade with the regions in which they are found.

The Akkad Period

The period named after the newly founded capital of Sargon and his dynasty is known in the south mainly by monumental sculpture and cylinder seals (Frankfort, 1954, pp. 41-46), some of them from the Sargonid graves at Ur. The only recent excavation of a level of this period at Tell al-Wilayah in southern Iraq, not far from Nippur—which seems to have had a fine Akkadian stratum between an Early Dynastic one and one from the time of the Third Dynasty of Ur—has been published only in summary manner (Madhlum, 1960). The imperial aspirations and successes of the Akkadian rulers, known from contemporary and later texts, are exemplified by the appearance of a fluted depas of the type of Troy II g in the hand of an officer on a stele found at Nasiriyah (Mellink, 1963) or in the rock reliefs of Naramsin found from Darband-i-Gawr in southern Kurdistan (Strommenger, 1963) to Pir Hussein, northeast of Diarbekr, in Turkey (Barrelet, 1959, pp. 33-34).

Some of the characteristic remains of the material culture of this period which permit us to recognize relations between different regions have been enumerated by Ann Perkins (1954, pp. 48-49) as follows:

> In the north, cuneiform tablets now appear for the first time (Nuzi V-III, Brak Sargonid, Chagar Bazar II-III) (Starr, 1937-39, pp. 21-25; Mallowan, 1947, p. 66; Mallowan, 1937, p. 95), as well as occupation levels which provide some links with Ur and with the sequence in the Diyala region.
>
> Gray burnished pottery characterizes the period in the north, and one of the most common forms is a well-made carinate bowl (e.g., Speiser, 1935, Pl. LXVII, 89); bowl and ware alike are probably developments of the gray ware of the Ninevite 5 phase, which is adequate explanation for their rarity in the south (the Diyala has a little gray ware and a few carinate bowls of somewhat similar type, but nothing very close). Bulging, wide-mouthed pots are also common in the north and relatively unknown in the south, although again the Diyala has a few in the Protoimperial-Akkadian range [here comprised in Early Dynastic IIIb] (e.g., Speiser, 1935, Pl. LXVIII; Delougaz, 1952, Pl. 162). "Teapots," rounded pots with tubular spouts (Fig. V, 16) are found in the Ur Sargonid cemetery, Diyala Akkadian levels, and Chagar Bazar II-III (Woolley, 1934, Pl. 265; Delougaz, 1952, Pl. 150; Mallowan, 1936, Fig. 15). Tall jars, ovoid or pear-shaped, usually with horizontally ribbed shoulders, are known in Gawra VI, Brak Sargonid, Nuzi VI-V, and Diyala Protoimperial-Akkadian (Speiser, 1935, Pl. LXX, 143; Mallowan, 1947, Pl. LXVIII, 16; Starr, 1937-39, Pl. 53; Delougaz, 1952, Pl. 191).

Another type which occurs in the Akkad period in north and south is a round-bodied jar with tall everted neck and profile rim, found at Nippur (see Fig. 41b, below), in the Diyala (Delougaz, 1952, Pl. 160, B. 556.540) and with more curvaceous profile and elaborately ridged rim in the Ur III and Isin Larsa periods in the Diyala, at Uruk, and other southern and northern sites (Strommenger, UVB XVII, 1961, pp. 38-39, s.v. W 19 789 e). The example from Gawra (Speiser, 1935, Pl. LXIX, 130; here Fig. V, 14) is intermediate between the Akkad and Ur III forms of the south. A squat, round bellied bottle with upright neck and beveled rim again found in Akkad period levels at Nippur (Fig. 42a, below), but in levels dated "Gutium - Ur III" in the Diyala (Delougaz, 1952, Pl. 162, B, 633, 570 b), occurs with an identical shape at Gawra (Speiser, 1935, Pl. LXIX, 126).

Decoration of jars and vases by a band of "combed pattern" of wavy lines, bordered by straight ones, is occasionally found in north and south as on shoulders of large jars of Gawra VI (Speiser, 1935, Pl. LXX, 144-46; here Fig. V, 15) on a vase from the Naramsin palace at Brak (Mallowan, 1947, Pl. LXVI, 16) and on type 235 of Ur (Woolley, 1934, Pl. 266), listed in the Sargonid grave 1127. Ruth Amiran suggested that a Middle Bronze I pottery group from the Orontes region was derived from these Mesopotamian examples of the Akkad period (Amiran, 1961, p. 224). To this inventory of pottery relations may be added the relation between the Sargonid to Ur III levels at Brak with the Amuq sites in Phase J and with Tell Chuera on the basis of gray ware bottles (Watson, p. 80, above).

Perkins (1954, pp. 48-49) drew attention to the fact that metal types which occur in the Early Dynastic III period in the south, chiefly in the Royal Cemetery of Ur, occur only in Akkadian context in the north. She gave as examples a pike-type poker-butted spear and a shaft-hole adze (Woolley, 1934, Pl. 227, types 2a, b and Pl. 229, type 3). Akkad period parallels in the north can be cited from Gawra (Speiser, 1935, Pl. XLIX, 5; here Fig. V, 10), Billa (Speiser, 1931, p. 21) and Brak (Mallowan, 1947, Pl. XXXI, 11; here Fig. V, 9).

The miniature pickax found at Gawra (Speiser, 1935, Pl. XLIX, 3; here Fig. V, 11), however, is in its proper context in the Akkadian stratum VI since a pickax from Ur (Woolley, 1934, Pl. 224, U. 9680) was found in grave 689 with cylinder seals of mature Akkad style. A similar observation was made by Moortgat in connection with a pickax found at Tell Chuera in Northeast Syria (Moortgat, 1950, pp. 6-7). The little pickax from Gawra is further dated by a virtually identical ax head from Luristan inscribed with the name of the last ruler of the Akkad dynasty (Dossin, 1962, Pl. XXII, 11; text, p. 156).

More Early Dynastic types which appear in Akkadian levels in the north, cited by Perkins are the wide chisel or ax blades or molds for casting these which appear in the Royal Cemetery, and later in Gawra VI, Brak Sargonid, and Chagar Bazar II (Woolley, 1934. Pl. 229, 2a, 2b, 3; Speiser, 1935, Pl. XLVII, A; Mallowan, 1947, Pl. XXXI, 9; Mallowan, 1937, Pl. XVIIIB and Fig. 13, 1). Furthermore, Perkins mentioned the toggle pin with simple head and upper shank, flattened for piercing which occurs in Gawra VI, Chagar Bazar III, and Brak Sargonid, and which is related to pins in the Royal Cemetery of Ur (Speiser, 1935, Pl. L, 8; Mallowan, 1937, Fig. 12, 5; Mallowan, 1947, Pl. XXXI, 3, 4; Woolley, 1934, Pl. 231, type 3 b); also the hairpin with spatulate head of which rare examples were found at Ur, including one of gold (Woolley, 1934, Pl. 159, a) and which is represented in Brak Sargonid (Mallowan, 1947, Pl. LIII, 32; here Fig. V, 8), in Billa 5 (Speiser, 1932-33, p. 268), and in forked form in Gawra VI (Speiser, 1935, Pl. L, 4). A copper pin with a bead and reel decorated shaft reproduced as belonging to Gawra VI may have actually been from the subsequent Stratum V (Speiser, 1935, Pl. L, 11; here Fig. V, 7; comments, Porada, 1958, p. 419). In that stratum it would serve for a fine correlation with pins having similarly decorated shanks from Level Ib at Kültepe (Özgüc, 1955, Figs. 46-49, 69-91, *passim*), a level which began in the time of Shamshi Adad of Assyria (*ca.* 1814-1782 B.C.). Pins with similarly decorated shanks also occur in the "Trésor du Liban" dated by the pectoral of Amenemhet III (1842-1797 B.C.), and they are known from Middle Ugarit II levels at Ras Shamra (Schaeffer, 1948, Fig. 78, f, Fig. 49, 5).

One may finally quote Perkins (1954, p. 49) for the relation of the lunate gold earrings of Nuzi and Brak Sargonid (Starr, 1937-39, Pl. 55, I; Mallowan, 1947, Pl. XXXVI, *passim*) to those from the Royal Cemetery (Woolley, 1934, Pl. 219, types 2-7). Chipped flint and occasionally obsidian arrowheads of lanceolate shape were in use in the Sargonid to Ur III periods in Gawra VI (Speiser, 1935, p. 84), at Brak (Mallowan, 1947, Pl. XXXVII—here Fig. V, 12—text pp. 181-82), in the Diyala and at Susa.

Distinctive of the Akkad period in the south is a type of simple clay figurine distinguished by Dales. It has "one hand at the chest, the other held straight down along the side of the body" (Dales, 1963, p. 23). An example from the Old Akkadian level at Nippur "from the TB house area under Level IX" (Dales, 1963, p. 24, Fig. 5 and 1960, s.v. No. 107) indicates the date of the figures, fully borne out by the style of one such figure from Susa with the folds of the garment indicated in Akkadian manner (Dales, 1960, p. 47, s.v. No. 120; reference to De Mecquenem, 1934, p. 235, Fig. 85, 9). Dales also points to figurines of this type from Brak found in the precincts of the Naramsin Palace (Mallowan, 1947, Pl. LIV, 2 a, b; Pl. XXXVIII, 1—here Fig. V, 13—text, p. 182).

The Sargonid cylinders of the south sparked local derivate styles as manifested in Gawra VI (Speiser, 1935, Pl. LX, 61; Pl. LXI, 65). In Susa, some of the Akkadian cylinder seal impressions on tablets are indistinguishable from those made in Mesopotamia (e.g., Delaporte, 1920, Pl. 47, 3) but there were also cylinders with strong local character produced in Elam in the Akkad period (Porada, 1964a).

Evidence for continued trade with India in the late Akkad period was provided by a well-stratified glazed steatite cylinder of Indian style (Frankfort, 1955, Pl. 61, 642) and by a stamp seal, etched beads, and kidney-shaped inlays—all closely paralleled at Mohenjo Daro (Frankfort, 1933, pp. 50-51). Kidney-shaped beads of red stone are known to have been presented to the goddess Ningal by grateful sailors returning from an expedition to Dilmun, as recorded in texts from Ur of the Larsa period (Oppenheim, 1954, p. 8).

Far-flung trade may also have been responsible for spreading the idea of stressing a starlike mark on the shoulder of lions in art. This feature is found prominently, but differently rendered, in an Akkadian cylinder seal, probably of the time of Naramsin (ca. 2291-2255 B.C.), in the contemporary chapel of an Egyptian queen and only slightly later on the lions pictured on the base of a throne of a goddess commissioned by Puzur Inshushinak of Susa (Porada, 1964b).

The Post Akkad Period

The period after the destruction of the Akkadian empire by the Guti is most clearly recognizable in the degenerate style of some of the cylinder seals (e.g., Frankfort, 1955, p. 33, s.v. Nos. 689-91). One of the cylinders closely resembles an example from Gawra VI (Frankfort, 1955 Pl. 64, 689; Speiser, 1935, Pl. LXI, 65). The easily recognizable style of the Post Akkad cylinders also served to date in this period the so-called Second Dynasty graves from Ur (Buchanan, 1954; Porada, 1954, p. 340).

Intrusion into Mesopotamia of foreign elements from the east, possibly Gutian, is documented by a distinctive group of small cylinder seals made of faïence, usually engraved with a male figure—with one or more horn-like protrusions emanating from its head—attacking animals, often double-headed. Such cylinders were found in Pre-Akkadian, Akkadian, Late and possibly Post Akkadian levels at Tell Asmar, Assur, Ur, Kish, and Susa, and were considered Gutian or Elamite by Frankfort (1939, p. 142, s.v. Pl. XXV, b; 1955, p. 33).

The texts of Gudea of Lagash-Tello, who lived in the last part of the Guti period, show that he carried out his large-scale imports undisturbed, bringing stone, wood, and metals from the Amanus region and also from Elam. The diorite of his statues—unparalleled elsewhere at that time—came from Makkan. (For the possible location of this area, see above, p. 136.)

The Third Dynasty of Ur

The administration of the Third Dynasty of Ur, profusely documented by cuneiform texts, encompassed suzerainty over Susa in southwest Iran (Hinz, 1963, pp. 13-17) and even over Byblos in present Lebanon (Sollberger, 1959-60). Literacy and intellectual culture reached unequaled heights (Landsberger, 1960, pp. 94 ff.).

Gigantic architectural undertakings, such as the Ziggurats of Ur, Eridu, and other towns (Lenzen, 1941), manifest financial power and ability to organize workmen. Temples were built apace: the temple of Gimilsin (now read Shusin) at Tell Asmar (Frankfort, Lloyd, and Jacobsen, 1940); the temple of Shulgi at Nippur (Crawford, 1959, p. 74); the Ishtar Temple E at Assur, dated by a tablet in the time of Amarsin of Ur (2047-2039 B.C.); and the temple of Gawra V, equated with the Ishtar Temple E on the basis of similarity in the plans. Large-scale building at this time is also evident in the temenos of Ur and in the Eanna precinct.

Few works of sculpture are known from this period aside from the stele of Urnammu (Frankfort, 1954, Pl. 53), and little except pottery and clay figurines has survived of what must have been a high level of material culture. Dales pointed out that the figurines were characterized principally by their posture with both hands at the breasts and by their mouthless faces (Dales, 1960, p. 48, s.v. No. 125). He found the Nippur figurines to show little differentiation between Ur III and Isin

Larsa types, in contrast to the Diyala figurines, where such differentiation is more clearly marked. One type of figurine from Nippur, however, modeled in one piece with the chair on which it sits, is limited to the Ur III period on stratigraphic evidence (Dales, 1960, p. 212). Relations of these "chair-figurines" to those of Assur have been pointed out by Dales (ibid., pp. 215-18). The Diyala figurines assigned stratigraphically to Ur III are pleasingly modeled with large lunate earrings and extended arms (Frankfort, Lloyd, and Jacobsen, 1940, p. 221, Fig. 109, c). The type becomes flattened, and the jewelry is exaggerated in the female figurines of "Common Larsa Type" (ibid., p. 222, Fig. 111; an example here in Fig. V, 5). In the Ur III period begins the technique of making clay plaques in an open mold, which replaced the hand-made figurines in the Old Babylonian period (an example from Mari in Fig. V, 4). Clay plaques of this latter period, however, represented not only female figurines but many other subjects (Opificius, 1961).

The numerous cylinder seals of the Third Dynasty of Ur are characterized by carefully carved scenes, usually showing the worship of a deity and an inscription giving not only the name of the seal owner but often also his position in relation to the king or to a higher official. Such seals were found in secondary use impressed on tablets as far afield as Kültepe (Kanesh) in eastern Anatolia. Opinions differ as to whether or not this indicates an extension of the commercial ventures of the Third Dynasty of Ur to that region (Garelli, 1963, pp. 31 ff.; Balkan, 1955, p. 63 and note 87 on p. 77; against Otten, 1951, p. 37; and others). In contrast to the following Isin Larsa and Old Babylonian periods, few if any imprints on Ur III tablets were made by seals of peripheral style.

The Isin Larsa and Old Babylonian Periods and the Mari Age

The multiple headings for this period—to which could be added the Old Assyrian period in the north—indicates the distribution of power in Mesopotamia among various cities. The fact that Mari rose to such prominence was due to the great importance of trade at this age. Although elaborate temples were still being built—such as the temple of Ishtar Kittitum at Ishchali (Frankfort, 1954, Pl. 55)—religious architecture does not seem to have been on the scale it was during the Third Dynasty of Ur. The palaces preserved from this age, however—especially that of Mari, which was already famous in its own time (Kupper, 1963, p. 13), and also that of Sinkashid at Uruk (Lenzen, UVB XIX, 1963, Pl.

49)—reflect the great representational and administrative needs and activities of the period.

South Mesopotamian trade still flourished, but it was based far more than before on private initiative instead of on that of king or temple (Oppenheim, 1954, p. 14) and—doubtless as a result—its geographical extension was more limited (Leemans, 1950, 1960, passim).

The probable "India trade" via Dilmun is recorded from this period on cuneiform tablets (Oppenheim, 1954). The impression on a tablet dated in the tenth year of King Gugunum of Larsa, about 1923 B.C., of a "Persian Gulf seal" of late type (Hallo and Buchanan, 1965) serves to pinpoint the date of the archaeological context in which such seals—ultimately derived from the glyptic style of the Harappa culture—were found at Bahrain, and dates the related examples found in Mesopotamia (ibid.). The Indian type of stamp seal provided one of the rare instances of foreign inspiration for a glyptic group in Mesopotamia, which may have begun as early as the late Akkad period and lasted into Larsa times (Porada, 1954, p. 340).

Although the cylinder seals of the royal courts of the Isin Larsa period continued the delicate carefully engraved style of Ur III and introduced new motifs in the form of various divine and symbolic figures and objects about the time of the inception of the First Dynasty of Babylon, the more common type of cylinder continued the worshiping scenes of Ur III in a sharply cut, simplified style (Porada, 1948, p. 37; 1950, p. 162; Nagel, 1958, p. 327). Closely related groups of cylinders were produced in the surrounding regions: the Old Elamite in Susa (Porada, 1962, pp. 39-40), the Old Assyrian and Provincial Babylonian in northern Mesopotamia (Porada, 1948, pp. 108-10), and the Early North Syrian in the west (Porada, 1957, p. 397). Such cylinders made along the arc of trade with Mesopotamia, all dated by impressions on tablets of the twentieth and nineteenth centuries B.C. probably satisfied the need for sharp, easily recognizable impressions with subjects similar to those current in Mesopotamia.

The brilliant Mari age, from Iakhdunlim to Zimrilim (Kupper, 1963, pp. 1-16, passim), with elaborately engraved cylinders used at the court (Parrot, 1959, Pls. XLI-LVI), may have encouraged higher standards. Whether or not Parrot is correct in ascribing the inception of the style particularly referred to as Syrian to the influence of Mari (Parrot, 1959, p. 249) will have to be examined in relation to the as yet mostly unpublished material from Ras Shamra-Ugarit.

Discoveries at Mari also serve to indicate the date at which the so-called Khabur ware (Mallowan, 1936, a and b) was used. It is a ware characterized by rounded forms, especially jars with narrow or wide necks and rather high bowls with strongly marked rims. The color is buff, and the decoration consists of simple bands or zones of simple designs, such as linear triangles, crosshatching in triangles, or other plain geometric forms (Fig. V, 2,3). It seems likely that the Khabur ware came into Mesopotamia from Syria, but in Mesopotamia it was applied to local forms (Perkins, 1954, p. 50). Moreover, the pottery underwent a specific development in the north, to judge by the button base types from Assur in a context which could not be earlier than the third quarter of the second millennium B.C. (Hrouda, 1957, p. 35). Excavations at Tell al Rimah yielded pottery of possible Khabur type in Level V tentatively dated in the fifteenth or sixteenth century B.C. (Carter, 1964). This indicates the long duration of this simple, pleasing ware in the north. Giyan II has a related ware and a cast ax similar to Chagar Bazar I specimens (Fig. V, 1) as well as projectile points with midrib (Perkins, 1954, p. 51; Contenau and Ghirshman, 1935, Pls. 21-24; Mallowan, 1937, Fig. 13, 10-14).

The activities along the northern trade routes must indeed have been intense to account for the diffusion of a pottery which probably did not spread with its makers since each region has its own type of Khabur ware. In the south, such intensity is manifested only in the earlier part of the period, until the end of the Larsa dynasty. Almost identical small vessels of fine gray ware of the late Larsa period with incised, pricked, and impressed decoration and remains of white incrustation and red paint were found at Susa, Tello, Nippur (Fig. V, 6), and Tell Asmar; these were probably all made in a single place of manufacture (Delougaz, 1952, p. 120). This probably also applies to the vessels of this type of which fragments were found in Nuzi (Starr, 1937-1939, Pl. 56, I-S; text p. 368).

Some trade must have still existed later, as confirmed by seal impressions of Syrian style on tablets from Sippar of the Hammurabi dynasty (Porada, 1957b; Buchanan, 1957a, 1957b). In general, however, there was a tendency—which had already made itself felt in the time of Rimsin of Larsa—to curtail the activities of the rich Old Babylonian merchants (Leemans, 1950, pp. 113-19), so that "no more great and wealthy businessmen are found during the reigns of Hammurabi and his successors . . ." (Leemans, 1950, p. 121). Together with the impoverishment of the south caused by salinization (Jacobsen, 1957, p. 139), this policy of the rulers had probably strangled the imports of luxury goods by a relatively large number of persons, as well as the resulting widespread Babylonian influence abroad, long before the destructive raid of Murshilish of Hatti and the resulting conflagration sealed the Old Babylonian level of the capital town about 1595 B.C.

After the completion of this manuscript, several works appeared which supplement the information here summarized. (See p. 200, below.) The most important of these is Adams (1965). Adams' book includes a survey of the geographical conditions mainly of the Diyala valley and also of the country as a whole (pp. 3-12). The settlement pattern in the Diyala plains from a few villages in the Ubaid period through the growth of walled towns in the Early Dynastic age, with only minor changes in the Akkad, Ur III, and Isin Larsa periods, to the decline in Old Babylonian times (pp. 34-53), furnishes a framework for the early history of at least part of the country. The Diyala region differed to some extent from other areas. For example, Central Akkad showed an increase in settlement in Old Babylonian and Cassite times (p. 174, note 32), which would imply an upsurge rather than a decline in the period of the First Dynasty of Babylon. "Because of the confusion of Old Babylonian with Cassite dating criteria" (p. 54), however, it is not impossible that such an upsurge occurred only in the Early Cassite period. A sparse settlement during the last reigns of the First Dynasty of Babylon would go far to explain the successful incursions of Hittites and Cassites which brought about its end.

Nagel's essay (1964b) on the period called Early Dynastic by us, presents a useful effort to integrate the historical sequence of some of the rulers, especially of the kings of Kish; the epigraphic evidence concerning the changes in the sign for king, l u g a l; the inscribed works of Early Dynastic sculpture; and the phases of glyptic art. The disturbingly inconsistent periodization adopted by Nagel from the one previously created by Moortgat (see above, p. 162), however, is no more acceptable to the present generations of archaeologists in the United States than it was to the generation of Henri Frankfort, who had devised the more flexible and more generally applicable terms Early Dynastic I, II, and III.

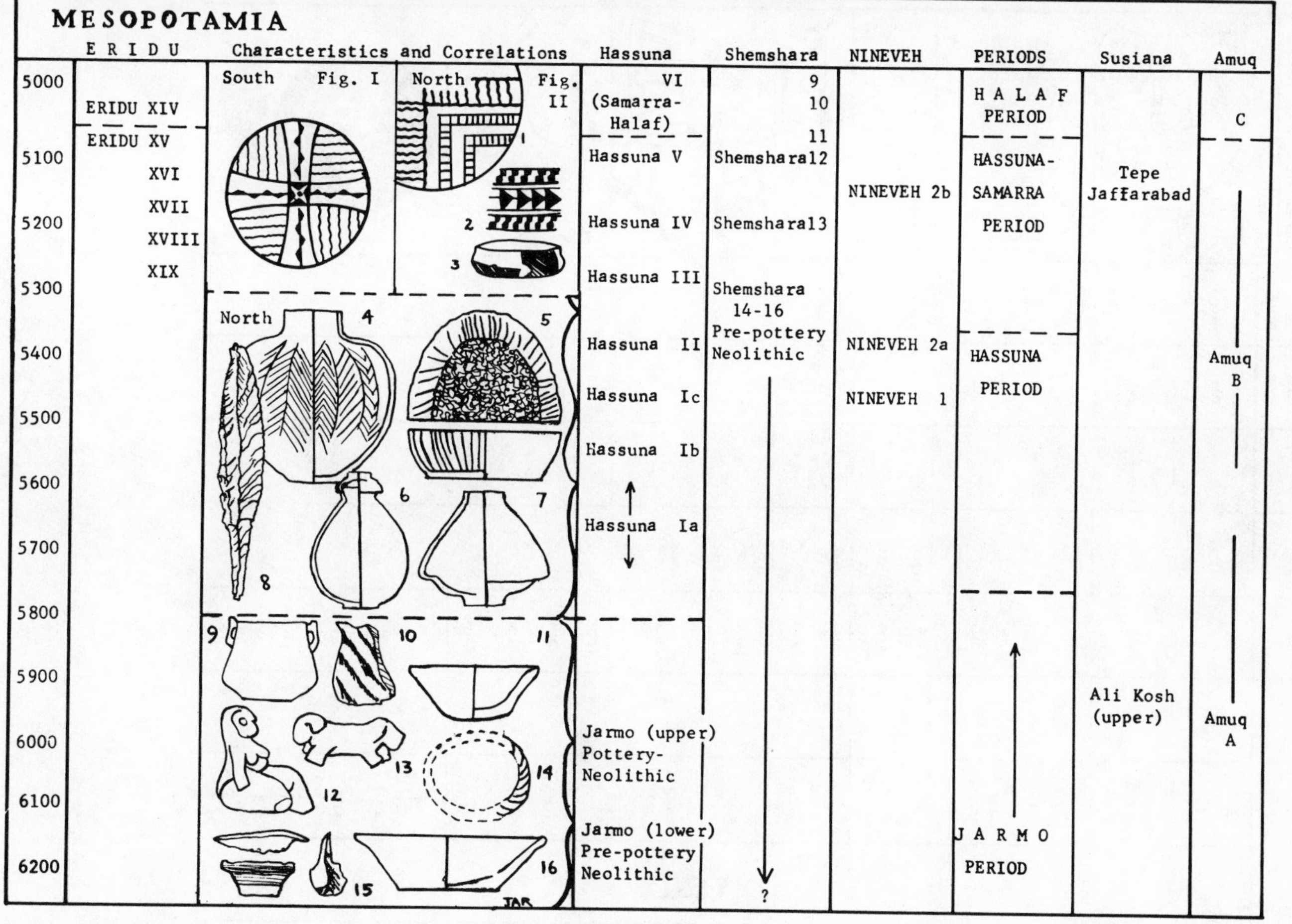
MESOPOTAMIA
ERIDU
Characteristics and Correlations
Hassuna
Shemshara
NINEVEH
PERIODS
Susiana
Amuq
5000
5100
5200
5300
5400
5500
5600
5700
5800
5900
6000
6100
6200
ERIDU XIV
ERIDU XV
XVI
XVII
XVIII
XIX
South
Fig. I
North
Fig. II
North
1
2
3
4
5
6
7
8
9
10
11
12
13
14
15
16
JAR
VI (Samarra-Halaf)
Hassuna V
Hassuna IV
Hassuna III
Hassuna II
Hassuna Ic
Hassuna Ib
Hassuna Ia
Jarmo (upper) Pottery-Neolithic
Jarmo (lower) Pre-pottery Neolithic
9
10
11
Shemshara12
Shemshara13
Shemshara 14-16 Pre-pottery Neolithic
?
NINEVEH 2b
NINEVEH 2a
NINEVEH 1
H A L A F PERIOD
HASSUNA-SAMARRA PERIOD
HASSUNA PERIOD
J A R M O PERIOD
Tepe Jaffarabad
Ali Kosh (upper)
C
Amuq B
Amuq A

MESOPOTAMIA SOUTH

	PERIODS	NIPPUR	ERIDU	URUK (Eanna)	UR	DIYALA SITES	UQAIR	Characteristics and Correlations
2900 3000	JAMDAT NASR PERIOD (PROTOLIT. C, D)	NIPPUR XII XIII XIV		URUK IIIa URUK IIIb URUK IIIc	"J N" Cemetery	Sin Temple V IV III II I	Jamdat Nasr Chapel	Fig. III
3100 3200	LATE URUK PERIOD (PROTOLIT. B)	NIPPUR XV NIPPUR XVI		URUK IVa URUK IVb URUK IVc URUK V	and Archaic III-IV		UQAIR Painted Temple ?	
3300	MIDDLE URUK PERIOD (PROTOLIT. A)	NIPPUR XVII XVIII XIX XX	ERIDU II ERIDU III	URUK VI VII VIII				For later Pottery see Part II
3400	EARLY URUK (WARKAN PERIOD)		ERIDU IV ERIDU V	URUK IX | XIV	UR UBAID III			
3500 3600 3700 3800 3900	UBAID 4 (UBAID II)		ERIDU VI ERIDU VII	URUK XV URUK XVI URUK XVII URUK XVIII	UR UBAID II			
4000 4100 4200 4300	UBAID 3 (UBAID I)		ERIDU VIII ERIDU IX ERIDU X ERIDU XI		UR UBAID I			
4400 4500 4600 4700 4800 4900	↑ UBAID 2 HAJJI MUHAMMAD ↓		ERIDU XII ERIDU XIII ERIDU XIV |					

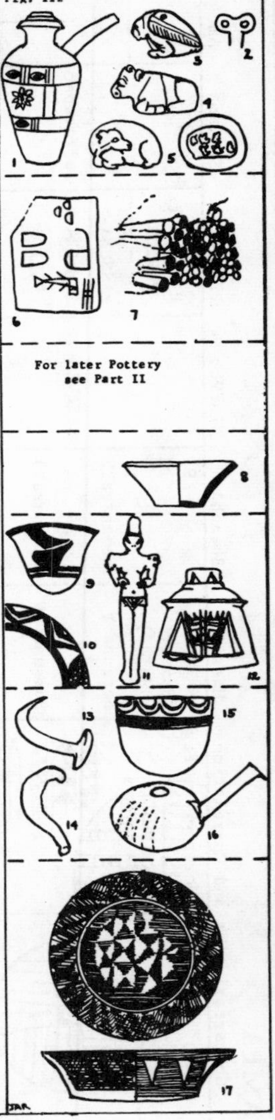

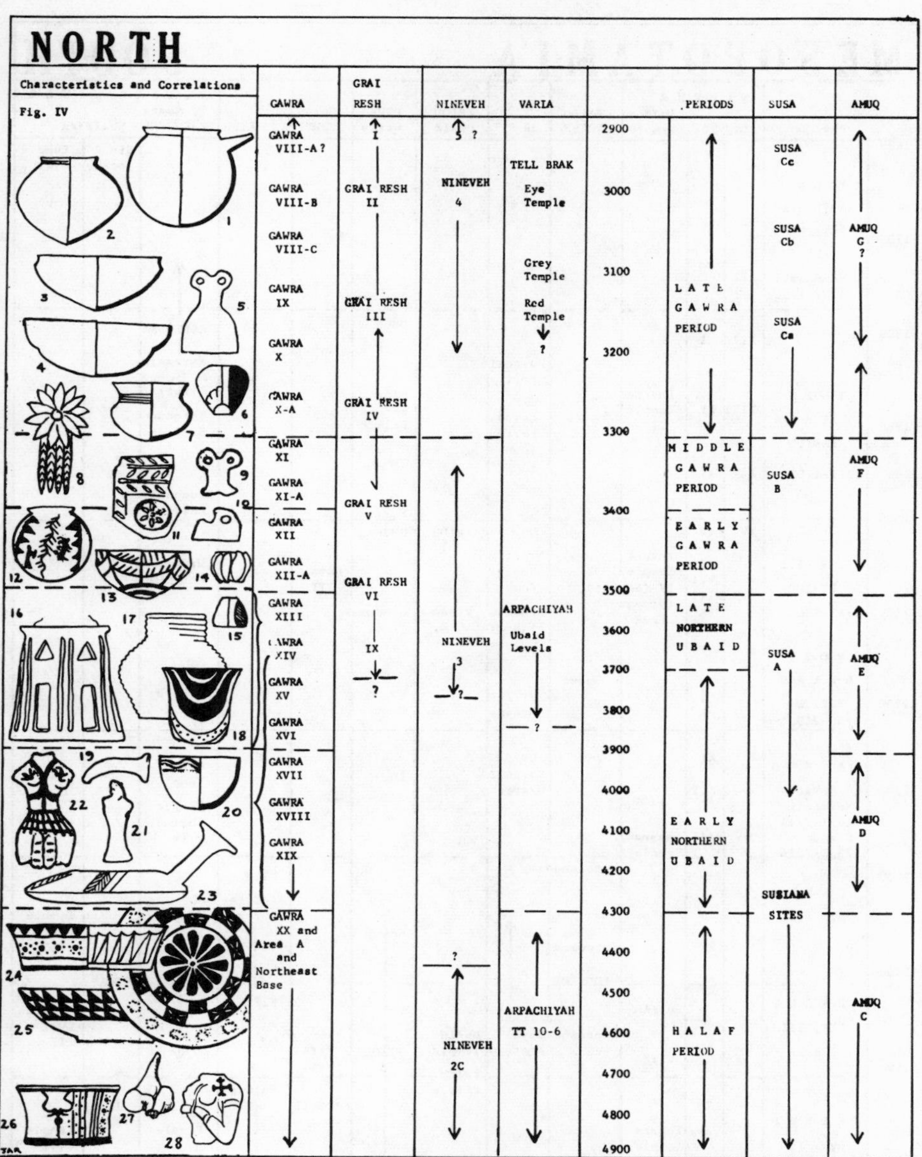
NORTH
Characteristics and Correlations
Fig. IV
GAWRA
GRAI RESH
NINEVEH
VARIA
PERIODS
SUSA
AMUQ
GAWRA VIII-A ?
GAWRA VIII-B
GAWRA VIII-C
GAWRA IX
GAWRA X
GAWRA X-A
GAWRA XI
GAWRA XI-A
GAWRA XII
GAWRA XII-A
GAWRA XIII
GAWRA XIV
GAWRA XV
GAWRA XVI
GAWRA XVII
GAWRA XVIII
GAWRA XIX
GAWRA XX and Area A and Northeast Base
I
GRAI RESH II
GRAI RESH III
GRAI RESH IV
GRAI RESH V
GRAI RESH VI
IX
5 ?
NINEVEH 4
NINEVEH 3
NINEVEH 2C
TELL BRAK
Eye Temple
Grey Temple
Red Temple
ARPACHIYAH
Ubaid Levels
ARPACHIYAH TT 10-6
2900
3000
3100
3200
3300
3400
3500
3600
3700
3800
3900
4000
4100
4200
4300
4400
4500
4600
4700
4800
4900
LATE GAWRA PERIOD
MIDDLE GAWRA PERIOD
EARLY GAWRA PERIOD
LATE NORTHERN UBAID
EARLY NORTHERN UBAID
HALAF PERIOD
SUSA Cc
SUSA Cb
SUSA Ca
SUSA B
SUSA A
SUSIANA SITES
AMUQ G ?
AMUQ F
AMUQ E
AMUQ D
AMUQ C

MESOPOTAMIA SOUTH

	PERIODS	NIPPUR TA	NIPPUR TB	NIPPUR Inanna Temple	Tello LAGASH	UR	ERIDU Ubaid	URUK Warka	Fara SHURUPPAK	KISH	DIYALA SITES T. Asmar ESHNUNNA	DIYALA SITES Khafajah Sin Temple	DIYALA SITES Khafajah Temple Oval
1600													
	OLD	IX	C?										
	BABYLONIAN	X	D										
1700	PERIOD 1792-1600												
	Hammurabi 1792-1750	XI	E								↑		
1800		XII	I			UR		URUK			ESHNUNNA		
						Waradsin Fort					Naramsin Audience Hall		
	ISIN LARSA	XIII	II	Inanna Temple III?		Larsa Period Town		Sin-kashid Palace			Ibiqadad S. Bldg.		
1900	PERIOD												
	2017-1763	XIV	III								Ilushuilia Palace		
2000		XV	IV V			UR	ERIDU	URUK					
	UR III PERIOD		VI VII VIII	Inanna Temple IV (Shulgi)		Amarsin Shulgi Tombs			Fara III		Shusin Temple		
2100	2113-2006		IX	(Urnammu) Ekur		Urnammu Ziqqurrat	Urnammu Z.	Urnammu Z.					
	POST AKKAD		↑		Gudea								
2200	PERIOD 2230-2130		X?			Ur II Graves							
	AKKAD		XI			UR Sargonid Graves					Abu Temple		
2300	PERIOD Naramsin 2291-2255 Sargon 2371-2316		XII XIII	Inanna Temple V?							Single Shrine IV		
2400	EARLY DYN. III b				Lugalanda	↑		↑		KISH A Cemetery ↓	Abu Temple		Temple Oval III
				VI	Entemena						Single Shrine III-I	Sin Temple	
2500					Eannatum	UR							
	EARLY DYN. III a			VIIA		Aanipada				KISH	↓	X	Temple Oval II
					Urnanshe	Royal Cemetery	Ubaid Temple						
2600				VIIB			ERIDU Palace		"Fara texts"			↑	
	EARLY DYN. II			Inanna Temple VIII					Fara II	Palace ↑	Abu Temple	IX	Temple Oval I
2700									"Fara-style" Seals		Square Temple III-I	VIII	
				IX		UR		URUK		KISH		Sin Temple VII	
2800	EARLY DYN. I			X		Seal Impression Stratum SIS 8-4		FRÜH DYN. ↓		Area Y Graves	Abu Temple Archaic Shrine IV-I		
2900				XI								VI	

NORTH

Date	MARI	Tell Brak	ASSUR	Tepe Gawra	Tell Billa	Tell al Rimah	PERIODS	SUSA	Amuq	Characteristics and Correlations
1600 1700			ASSUR C	Gawra IV ↓	Billa 4		DARK AGE		Amuq L	Fig. V 1, 2, 3, 4
1800	Zimri-lim 1779-61		Shamshi-Adad 1812-1797	↕		LEVEL ? mudbrick walls	MARI AGE	E		
1900 2000	Iaggid-lim Ishtup-ilum		ASSUR D	Gawra V			OLD ASSYRIAN PERIOD	OLD ELAMITE	Amuq K	5, 6
2100	MARI Palace Temples		ASSUR E	↓			UR III DYNASTY			7, 8, 9, 10, 11, 12
2200			↑	↕			POST AKKAD PERIOD		↑	13, 14
2300	MARI Ninhursag & other Temples	SARGONID	↕ ASSUR F ASSUR G	Gawra VI ↓	Billa 5	NINEVEH	AKKAD PERIOD		Amuq J	15, 16
2400 2500	MARI Ishtar Temple A	?	ASSUR H ↕	↕	↑	↑	EARLY DYN. III B	SUSA De SUSA Dd	↑ Amuq I	17, 18
2600	MARI Ishtar Temple B	?		Gawra VII	?		EARLY DYN. III A	SUSA Dc	↕	
2700	MARI Ishtar Temple C ?	?			Billa 6 ?		EARLY DYN. II	SUSA Db	Amuq H	19, 19b
2800 2900		?		Gawra VIIIa ↓	Billa 7 ? ↓	NINEVEH V ↓	EARLY DYN. I	SUSA Da	↑ Amuq G ↓	20, 21, 22

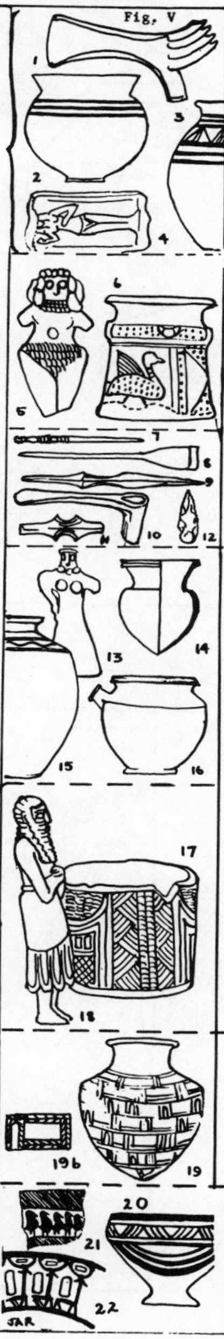

FIG. VI

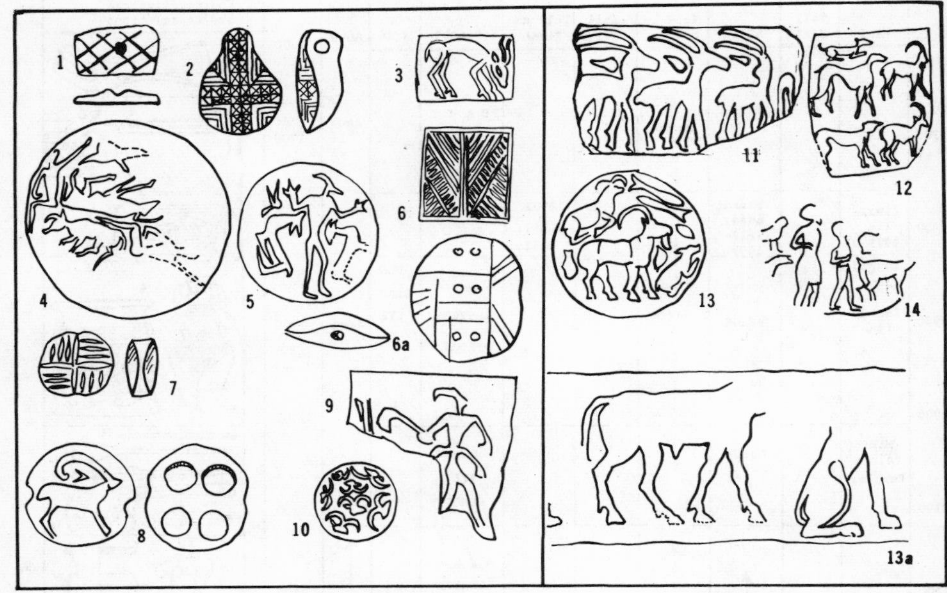

FIG.VII

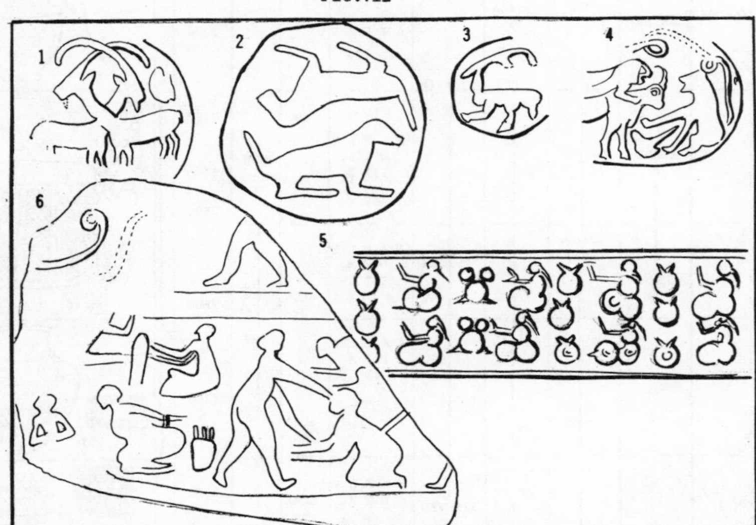

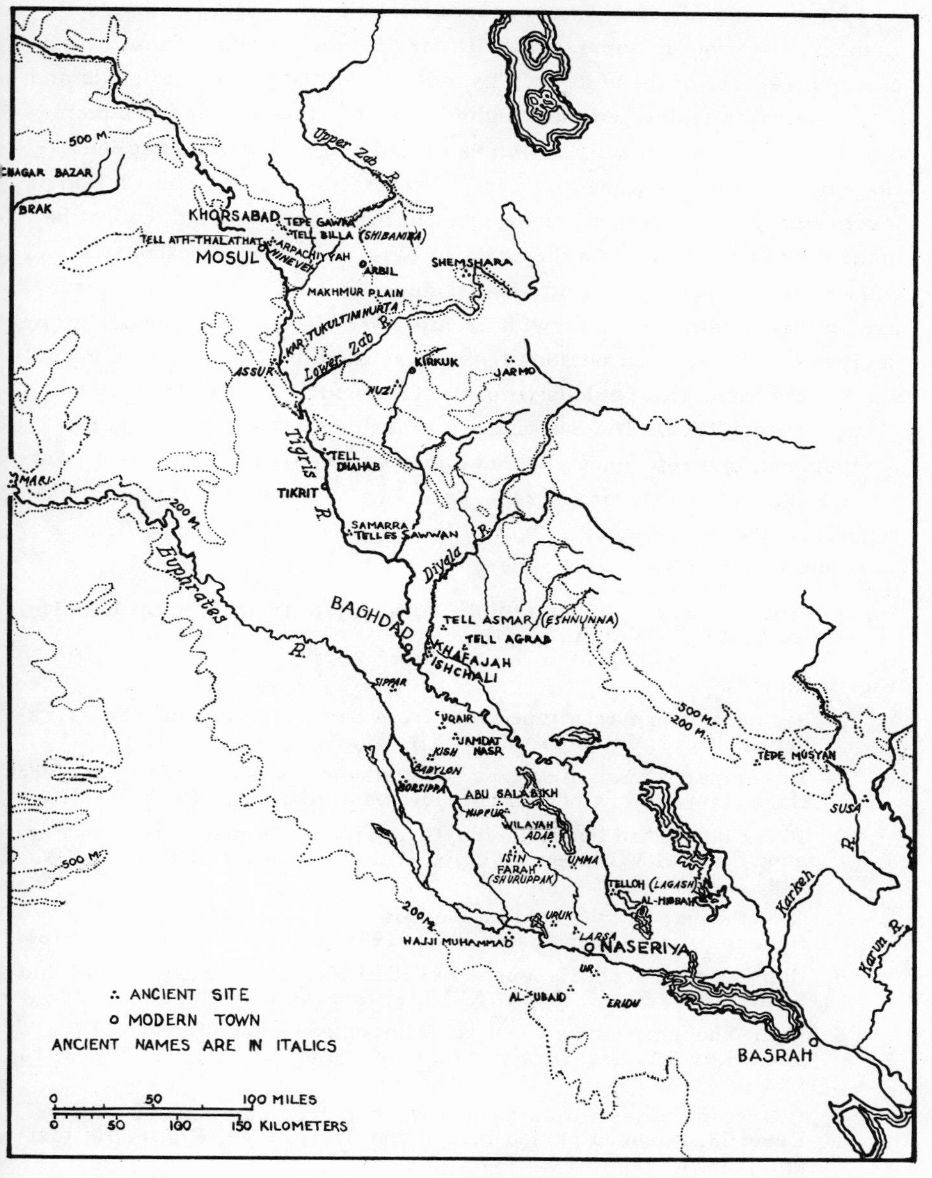

500 M.
CHAGAR BAZAR
BRAK
KHORSABAD
TEPE GAWRA
TELL BILLA (SHIBANIBA)
TELL ATH-THALATHAT
ARPACHIYYAH
MOSUL
NINEVEH
ARBIL
SHEMSHARA
Upper Zab R.
MAKHMUR PLAIN
KAR TUKULTININURTA
Lower Zab R.
ASSUR
KIRKUK
JARMO
NUZI
Tigris R.
TELL DHAHAB
TIKRIT
MARI
200 M.
Euphrates R.
SAMARRA
TELL ES SAWWAN
Diyala R.
BAGHDAD
TELL ASMAR (ESHNUNNA)
TELL AGRAB
KHAFAJAH
ISHCHALI
SIPPAR
'UQAIR
JAMDAT NASR
KISH
BABYLON
BORSIPPA
ABU SALABIKH
NIPPUR
WILAYAH
ADAB
ISIN
FARAH (SHURUPPAK)
UMMA
TELLOH (LAGASH)
AL-HIBBAH
500 M.
200 M.
TEPE MUSYAN
SUSA
Karkeh R.
Karun R.
500 M.
200 M.
URUK
LARSA
HAJJI MUHAMMAD
NASERIYA
UR
AL-'UBAID
ERIDU
BASRAH
∴ ANCIENT SITE
o MODERN TOWN
ANCIENT NAMES ARE IN ITALICS
0 50 100 MILES
0 50 100 150 KILOMETERS

Sources of Figures

Sites chosen for schematic representation are those with long sequences, observed in some detail. Illustrations were taken from the excavation reports of these sites. The objects were not drawn to scale and had to be much simplified, serving only as an aid to the reader's memory. Levels are arbitrarily shown as of uniform duration unless indications to the contrary were given in the excavation report. Correlation of levels, though schematically suggested in the present charts, cannot be made with any certainty on the basis of even several distinctive traits. Sequences of levels in test pits are assumed to have covered a shorter period than levels connected with architecture. Dates are approximations derived for the earliest periods from an average of the radiocarbon dates and for the historical periods from the Cambridge Ancient History (especially Rowton, 1962). The Susiana and Amuq sequences are shown for comparison, and reference should be made to the detailed charts of Watson (pp. 82-83) and Dyson (p. 249). Relations between Mesopotamia and Egypt are shown in Kantor's figures (pp. 27-28). The following figures were drawn by Judith A. Rosenberg.

Fig. I (South). Pattern (much simplified) on plate from Eridu. Ubaid I phase (Oates, 1960, Pl. V, 24).

Fig. II (North).

1. Segment of Samarra type plate from Samarra. Hassuna-Samarra period (Herzfeld, 1930, p. 44, Fig. 78, No. 88).
2. Lower part of Samarra type patterns on a potsherd from Matarrah Hassuna-Samarra period (Braidwood et al., 1952, Pl. VIII, 8).
3. Black burnished bowl of Syro-Cilician type, Amuq A-B from Hassunna, Level V. Hassuna period (Lloyd and Safar, 1945, Pl. XIV, Fig. 1, 9; text pp. 265, 278).
4. Globular jar of standard incised ware from Hassuna, Level Ic. Hassuna period (Lloyd and Safar, 1945, Fig. 4, 4; text pp. 279-81).
5. Husking tray from Hassuna, Level III Hassuna period. (Lloyd and Safar, 1945, Fig. 3, 8; Pl. XVIII, 1; text pp. 277-78).
6. Pear-shaped, coarse ware jar with saucer-shaped lid from Hassuna, Level Ib. Hassuna period (Lloyd and Safar, 1945, Fig. 6, 13; text p. 277).
7. Coarse ware jar with a base in double-ogee curve from Hassuna, Level Ia. Hassuna period (Lloyd and Safar, 1945, Fig. 6, 10; text pp. 276-77).
8. Projectile point, probably imported from Syro-Cilicia, Hassuna, Level Ia. Hassuna period (Lloyd and Safar, 1945, Fig. 22, 9; text p. 269).

9. Jar profile from Jarmo. Jarmo to Hassunan phase (Braidwood and Howe, 1960, Pl. 15, 18; text p. 44).
10. Potsherd with oblique blobbed lines from Jarmo, lower floors. Jarmo period (Braidwood and Howe, 1960, Pl. 15, 12; text p. 43).
11. Simple ware bowl from Jarmo, upper floors. Jarmo period (Braidwood and Howe, 1960, Pl. 15, 9).
12. Female figurine from Jarmo. Jarmo period (Braidwood and Howe, 1960, Pl. 16, 7; text p. 44).
13. Dog, clay figurine from Jarmo. Jarmo period (Braidwood and Howe, 1960, Pl. 16, 2).
14. Fragment of ground marble bracelet from Jarmo. Jarmo period (Braidwood and Howe, 1960, Pl. 21, 4; text p. 46).
15. Chipped flint and obsidian tools, borer, microlithic trapezoid and triangle from Jarmo. Jarmo period (Braidwood and Howe, 1960, Pl. 18, A, B; text p. 45).
16. Bowl of inverted truncated conical form. Jarmo period (Braidwood and Howe, 1960, Pl. 21, 14; text p. 45).

Fig. III (South).

1. Spouted jar of hard, gray stone with shell inlays from Uruk-Warka, Sammelfund. Jamdat Nasr period (Heinrich, 1936, Pl. 26, W 14819g; text p. 35).
2. Top of hut symbol(?) of greenish stone from Uruk-Warka, Sammelfund. Jamdat Nasr period (Heinrich, 1936, Pl. 33q W 15051; text p. 43).
3. Lion-headed eagle of white crystalline limestone, animal amulet from Uruk-Warka, Sammelfund. Jamdat Nasr period (Heinrich, 1936, Pl. 13, d W 14766 c3; text p. 26).
4. Recumbent young bull of yellowish white limestone, animal amulet from Uruk-Warka, Sammelfund. Jamdat Nasr period (Heinrich, 1936, Pl. 10, e W 14806 c3; text p. 21).
5. Recumbent gazelle, stamp seal probably of stag horn. Bought near Warka. Jamdat Nasr period or earlier (Heinrich, 1936, Pl. 12, i W 14829; text p. 25).
6. Tablet from Uruk-Warka, Level IV. Late Uruk period (Falkenstein, 1936, Pl. 1, 30; text p. 102, 2).
7. Clay cones forming patterns, from the Pillar Terrace at Uruk, Level IVb. Late Uruk period (Jordan, UVB II, 1931, p. 31, Fig. 17).
8. Typical beveled rim bowl, Uruk Levels XII-IV and many other sites. Early to Late Uruk period (e.g., Delougaz, 1952, Pl. 21).
9. Goblet from Eridu Cemetery. Ubaid 4 phase (Lloyd and Safar, 1948, Pl. IX, lower right; text, p. 117, s.v. Pl. III, type 1).
10. Segment of plate from Eridu Cemetery. Ubaid 4 phase (Lloyd and Safar, 1948, Pl. II, left side; text p. 117, s.v. Pl. II and III, type 5).
11. Female figurine from Ur. Ubaid 4 phase (Woolley, 1955, Pl. 20, U. 15385).

12. Incense burner, with painted architectural decoration from Eridu. Ubaid 4 phase (Lloyd and Safar, 1947, Fig. 5, Arabic section).
13. Clay nail from Eridu. Ubaid 3 or 4 phase (Lloyd and Safar, 1948, Pl. VII, left side).
14. Clay sickle from Uqair. Ubaid 3 or 4 phase (Lloyd, 1943, Pl. XXVIII, B; text p. 149).
15. Painted pot of greenish overbaked clay. Ubaid 3 or 4 phase (Lloyd, 1943, Pl. XXV, 8; description, p. 154).
16. "Tortoise jar" from Eridu. Probably Ubaid 3 phase (Lloyd and Safar, 1948, Pl. VII, upper right, and Pl. III, type 15; text p. 123).
17. Large dish of Hağği Mohammed type. Ubaid 2 phase (Ziegler, 1950, Pl. 14).

Fig. IV (North).

1. Globular spouted jar with rolled rim from Gawra, Stratum VIII-A. Late Gawra period (Speiser, 1935, Pl. LXIII, 37; text p. 44).
2. Mildly carinated jar with grooved rim, from Gawra, Stratum VIII-B, C. Late Gawra period (Speiser, 1935, Pl. LXIV, 44; text p. 43).
3. Bowl with curved rim from Gawra, Stratum VIII. Late Gawra period (Speiser, 1935, Pl. LXIII, 20; text p. 42).
4. Bowl with grooved rim and double-curved body from Gawra, Stratum VIII. Late Gawra period (Speiser, 1935, Pl. LXIII, 21; text p. 42).
5. "Hut symbol" of marble, from Gawra, probably Stratum IX. Late Gawra period (Speiser, 1935, Pl. XLIV, c; text pp. 99-100).
6. Pear-shaped mace head of black limestone from Gawra, Stratum IX. The type begins in Stratum XII and lasts until VIII and later, thus covering the entire Gawra and subsequent periods (Tobler, 1950, Pl. CLXXVII, 35; text p. 203).
7. Cup with flaring rim from Gawra, Stratum XI. Middle Gawra period (Tobler, 1950, Pl. CXLV, 388; description, p. 240).
8. Gold rosette with pendant ribbon from Gawra, Tomb 110, Stratum X. Late Gawra period (Tobler, 1950, Pl. LVIII, Fig. a, 3; text p. 90).
9. "Hut symbol" of terra cotta from Gawra, Stratum XI-A. Middle Gawra period (Tobler, 1950, Pl. LXXXVI, Fig. a, 9; text p. 171).
10. "Hut symbol" of terra cotta from Gawra, Stratum XII. Early Gawra period (Tobler, 1950, Pl. LXXXVI, Fig. a, 5; text p. 171).
11. Potsherd with decoration of incised bands and circular appliqués, stamped with rosette design from Gawra, Stratum XII. Early Gawra period (unpublished).
12. "Landscape jar" from Gawra, grave under Stratum XII. Early Gawra period (Tobler, 1950, Pl. LXXVIII, a, b; Pl. CXXXIX, 309; text p. 150).
13. "Sprig-ware" bowl from Gawra, Stratum XII. Early Gawra period (Tobler, 1950, Pl. CXXXIII, 243; text p. 147).

14. Bossed marble mace head from Gawra, Stratum XII. Early Gawra period (Tobler, 1950, Pl. CLXXVII, 30; text p. 203).
15. Mace head, greenstone, from Gawra, Stratum XIII. Late Northern Ubaid period (Tobler, 1950, Pl. CLXXVII, 36; text p. 203).
16. Incense burner from Gawra, Eastern Shrine of Stratum XIII. Late Northern Ubaid period (Tobler, 1950, Pl. LXXVIII, d and Pl. CXXXII, 228; text p. 144).
17. Jar with incised rope pattern, also called "corrugated" ware from Gawra, Stratum XIII. Late Northern Ubaid period (Tobler, 1950, Pl. LXXVIII, c and Pl. CXXXI, 220; text p. 144.
18. Beaker with slightly recurving sides from Gawra, Stratum XIII. Late Northern Ubaid period (Tobler, 1950, Pl. CXXIX, 199; text p. 142).
19. "Nail-shaped muller" from Gawra, Stratum XIX and later, mostly from Stratum XIII. Northern Ubaid period (Tobler, 1950, Pl. CLVI, 47; text p. 169).
20. Hemispherical bowl from Gawra, grave below XVII. Early Northern Ubaid period (Tobler, 1950, Pl. CXXI, 94; text p. 135).
21. Male figurine of terra cotta, called "gaming piece" from Gawra, Stratum XVI Early Northern Ubaid period (Tobler, 1950, Pl. LXXXIV, Fig. b, 2, text p. 170, but cf. Perkins, 1949, p. 62).
22. Female figurine of terra cotta from Gawra, Stratum XVII. Early Northern Ubaid period (Tobler, 1950, Pl. LXXXI, c and Pl. CLIII, 4; text p. 164).
23. "Tortoise jar" from Tepe Gawra, Stratum XVII. Early Northern Ubaid period (Tobler, 1950, Pl. LXXV, e and Pl. CXXIII, 113; text p. 136).
24. Outside and inside decoration on the walls of a plate from Arpachiyah, probably level TT 7-8. Halaf period (Mallowan, 1935, Fig. 58, 4).
25. Simplified design of the pattern on a polychrome plate from Arpachiyah, levels TT 5-6. Halaf period (Mallowan, 1935, Pl. XV; text p. 111).
26. Bowl with bucranium design from Arpachiyah, before TT 10. Halaf period (Mallowan, 1935, Fig. 76, 2; text p. 155).
27. Abbreviated female figurine of terra cotta from Arpachiyah. Halaf period (Mallowan, 1935, Fig. 47, 2; text, p. 82).
28. Torso of slender female figure of terra cotta with hollow body from Arpachiyah. Halaf period (Mallowan, 1935, Fig. 45, 10; text p. 81).

Fig. V.

The characteristics and correlations here illustrated are mainly shown in objects from northern or northwestern sites (like Mari). Only a few are represented by examples from the south: the steatite vase from Khafaje, No. 17, the incised gray ware jar from Nippur, No. 6, and the clay figurine from Tell Asmar, No. 5. Owing to lack of space, material of the Early Dynastic II period appears in the box of Early Dynastic III.

1. Ax from Chagar Bazar, found in grave under platform with tablets of Shamshi Adad and Hammurabi. After 1750 B.C. (Mallowan, 1947, Pl. XLI, 1; Pl. LV, 15; text pp. 187-88).
2. Painted jar of early Khabur ware from Chagar Bazar. "1700-1600" (Mallowan, 1947, Pl. LXXXII, 6; text p. 251).
3. Painted jar of early Khabur ware from Mari. Mari Age (Parrot, 1959, Pl. XXXVI, 1584; p. 134, Fig. 92, c; text pp. 133-34).
4. Molded plaque with nude female figure from Mari. Mari Age (Parrot, 1959, Pl. XXIX, 982; p. 71, Fig. 56, 982: text pp. 71-72).
5. Female figurine of common Larsa type from Tell Asmar. Isin Larsa period (Frankfort, 1946, Fig. 111, f; text p. 207).
6. Gray ware jar with incised decoration from Nippur. Isin Larsa period (unpublished).
7. Copper pin with bead and reel decorated shaft from Gawra, Stratum V or VI. Probably Ur III period (Speiser, 1935, Pl. L, 11; listed as from Stratum V on p. 114 but as from Stratum VI on p. 196; s.v. Pl. L, 11 and text p. 110).
8. Hairpin with spatulate head (racquet pin) from Tell Aswad, near Brak. Akkad period (Mallowan, 1947, Pl. LIII, 32; text p. 213).
9. Pike type, poker-butted spear from Brak. "Date probably Sargonid" (Mallowan, 1947, Pl. XXXI, 11; text pp. 169-70).
10. Adze from Gawra, Stratum VI. Akkad period (Speiser, 1935, Pl. XLIX, 5; text p. 105).
11. Miniature pickax from Gawra, Stratum VI. Akkad period (Speiser, 1935, Pl. XLIX, 3; text p. 106).
12. Lanceolate, chipped flint arrowhead from Brak. Akkad period (Mallowan, 1947, Pl. XXXVII, 22; text pp. 181-82).
13. Female figurine of terra cotta from Brak, Naramsin Palace. End of Akkad period (Mallowan, Pl. XXXVIII, 1; text p. 182).
14. Tall-necked, round-bodied jar with grooved, collared rim from Gawra, Stratum VI. Akkad period (Speiser, 1935, Pl. LXIX, 130, text p. 54).
15. Jar with combed wavy line on the shoulder, from Gawra, Stratum VI. Akkad period (Speiser, 1935, Pl. LXX, 146; text p. 55).
16. "Teapot" with tubular spout from Brak Naramsin Palace. Akkad period (Mallowan, 1947, Pl. LXIX, 8; text p. 229).
17. Steatite vase with representation of structure from Khafaje, Sin Temple IX. Early Dynastic II period (Delougaz, 1960, Pl. VI, a).
18. Statuette of worshiper from Tell Chuera. Early Dynastic II or IIIa period (Moortgat, 1965, in press).
19. Round-bodied jar with incised panels and bands in relief from Yarmiyah, near Nineveh, Nineveh 5 type. Probably Early Dynastic II period (Mallowan, 1933, Pl. LXIII, B).
20. Chalice of Nineveh 5 type. Early Dynastic I period (Campbell Thompson, 1932, Pl. LIV, 3).

21,22. Patterns of birds and bovine animals of Nineveh 5 type. Early

Dynastic I period (Mallowan, 1933, Pl. LVII, 21; Campbell Thompson, 1932, Pl. LVI, 7. Q 5 (B) (only partly drawn here).

Fig. VI.

1. Stamp seal from Hassuna, Level II. Hassuna period (Lloyd and Safar, 1945, Pl. XI, 2: 3; description, p. 289; side view after drawing by B. Buchanan).
2. Delicate linear style design on pendant from Gawra, Area A. Halaf period (Tobler, 1950, Pl. CLXXII, 19).
3. Stamp seal impression with antelope from Gawra, Area A. Halaf period (Tobler, 1950, Pl. LXXXIX, b; Pl. CLXVI, 123).
4. Stamp seal impression with human figures and animals from Gawra, Stratum XV. Early Northern Ubaid period (Tobler, 1950, Pl. CLXIV, 98; drawing corrected after Buchanan).
5. Stamp seal impression with gazelle-horned demon from Gawra, Stratum XIII. Late Northern Ubaid period (Tobler, 1950, Pl. CLXIV, 94; drawing corrected after Buchanan).
6. Stamp seal impression with ornamental design from Gawra, Well of XIII. Late Northern Ubaid period (Tobler, 1950, Pl. CLX, 43).

6a. Stamp seal from Uqair. Ubaid 3 or 4 Phase (Lloyd, 1943, p. 149; drawing after Buchanan).

7. Low hemispheroid seal with design based on division of circle from Gawra, Stratum XII. Early Gawra period (Tobler, 1950, Pl. CLIX, 26).
8. Stamp seal with holes for inlay, Gawra Stratum XII. Early Gawra period (Tobler, 1950, Pl. CLXV, 109).
9. Stamp seal impression with ibex demon from Gawra, Stratum XI. Middle Gawra period (Tobler, 1950, Pl. CLXIII, 81).
10. Stamp seal impression with heads of horned animals from Gawra, Stratum XI. Middle Gawra period (Tobler, 1950, Pl. CLXX, 170).
11. Stamp seal impression with three large horned animals from Gawra, Stratum XI-A. Middle Gawra period (Tobler, 1950, CLXVIII, 155).
12. Stamp seal impression with dogs and horned animals from Gawra, Stratum XI. Middle Gawra period (Tobler, 1950, Pl. CLXVIII, 158, drawing corrected after Buchanan).
13. Stamp seal impression with goat and other animals from Gawra, Stratum IX. Late Gawra period (Tobler, 1950, Pl. CLXIX, 165).

13a. Fragmentary cylinder seal impression from Uruk, Eanna, Level IVb. Late Uruk period (Lenzen, 1950, Pl. 4, 8).

14. Stamp or cylinder seal impression with two figures and animals from Gawra, Stratum IX. Late Gawra period (unpublished), Univ. Museum 33.3.80.

Fig. VII.

1. Stamp seal impression with goats, crossed at necks and horns from Gawra, Stratum VIII. Late Gawra period (Speiser, 1935, Pl. LVIII, 31; drawing corrected after Buchanan).

2. Stamp seal impression with two lions tête-bêche from Gawra, Stratum VIII. Late Gawra period (Speiser, 1935, Pl. LVII, 26).
3. Stamp seal impression with horned animal drawn with three legs, from Gawra, Stratum VIII. Late Gawra period (Speiser, 1935, Pl. LVI, 9; drawing corrected after impressions).
4. Stamp seal impression with tightly dovetailed animal figures from Gawra, Stratum VIII. Late Gawra period (Speiser, 1935, Pl. LVIII, 38; drawing corrected after original impressions).
5. Cylinder seal impression from Uruk, Eanna Level IVb. Late Uruk period (Lenzen, UVB XV, 1959, Pls. 28 c and 30 a, b; here only a part of the impression has been copied).
6. Cylinder seal from Nippur with pigtailed figures. Inanna Temple XVI. Late Uruk period (drawing after photograph kindly supplied by the excavators, Richard C. Haynes and D. P. Hansen).

Fig. VIII.

Map of Mesopotamia after the map reproduced in Delougaz and Lloyd, 1942, with insertion of sites mentioned in the present paper.

NOTE: The following reference was inadvertently omitted from the Bibliography, which follows, as it was originally prepared by the author:

Saggs, H. W. S.

1962 The Greatness That Was Babylon: A Sketch of the Ancient Civilization of the Tigris-Euphrates Valley. New York: Hawthorn Books.

Bibliography

Adams, R. M.

1958 "Survey of Ancient Water Courses and Settlements in Central Iraq," Sumer XIV: 101-3.

1960 "The Origin of Cities," Scientific American (Sept.) 153-68.

Amiet, P.

1961 La Glyptique mésopotamienne archaïque. Paris: Editions du centre national de la recherche scientifique.

1963 "La Glyptique syrienne archaïque," Syria XL: 57-83.

Amiran, Ruth

1961 "The Pottery of the Middle Bronze Age I in Palestine," Israel Exploration Journal 10: 204-25.

Andrae, W.

1922 Die archaischen Ischtar-Tempel in Assur. Wissenschaftliche Veröffentlichung der Deutschen Orient-Gesellschaft, Heft 39.

Balkan, K.

1955 "Observations on the Chronological Problems of the Kārum Kaniš," Türk Tarih Kurumu Yayinlarindan, VII. Seri, No. 28.

Barrelet, Marie-Thérèse

1959 "Notes sur quelques sculptures mésopotamiennes de l'époque d'Akkad," Syria XXXVI: 20-37.

Benson, J. L.

1956 "Aegean and Near Eastern Seal Impressions from Cyprus." In The Aegean and the Near East, Studies Presented to Hetty Goldman, pp. 59-79. Locust Valley: J. J. Augustin.

Bottéro, J..

1957 Textes économiques et administratifs. ("Archives royales de Mari," Vol. VII.) Paris: Geuthner.

Braidwood, R. J., and Braidwood, L. S.

1953 "The Earliest Village Communities of Southwestern Asia," Journal of World History I: 278-310.

1960 Excavations in the Plain of Antioch, Vol. I. ("Oriental Institute Publications," Vol. LXI.) Chicago: University of Chicago Press.

Braidwood, R. J., and Howe, B.

1960 Prehistoric Investigations in Iraqi Kurdistan. ("Studies in Ancient Oriental Civilization," No. 31.) Chicago: University of Chicago Press.

Braidwood, R. J., et al.

1952 "Matarrah, a Southern Variant of the Hassunan Assemblage, Excavated in 1948," Journal of Near Eastern Studies XI: 1-75.

Buchanan, B. W. (See also Hallo, W. W., and Buchanan, B. W., below)

1954 "The Date of the So-Called Second Dynasty Graves of the Royal Cemetery at Ur," Journal of the American Oriental Society 74: 147-53.

1957 "On the Seal Impressions on Some Old Babylonian Tablets," Journal of Cuneiform Studies XI: 45-52, 74-76.

Buringh, P.

1957 "Living Conditions in the Lower Mesopotamian Plain in Ancient Times," Sumer XIII: 30-57.

Carter, T. A.

1964 "Early Assyrians in the Sinjar," Expedition 7: 34-42.

Contenau, G., and Ghirshman, R.

1935 Fouilles du Tépé-Giyan. ("Musée du Louvre, département des antiquités orientales, série archéologique," Vol. III.) Paris: Geuthner.

Crawford, V. E.

1959 "Nippur, the Holy City," Archaeology 12: 74-83.

Dales, G. F., Jr.

1960 "Mesopotamian and Related Female Figurines: their Chronology, Diffusion and Cultural Functions." Ph.D. Dissertation, University of Pennsylvania.

1963 "Necklaces, Bands and Belts on Mesopotamian Figurines," Revue d'Assyriologie 57: 21-40.

Delaporte, L.

1920 Catalogue des cylindres . . . Vol. I. Fouilles et missions (Musée du Louvre) Paris: Hachette.

Delougaz, P.

1933 Plano-convex Bricks and the Methods of their Employment. ("Studies in Ancient Oriental Civilization," No. 7.) Chicago: University of Chicago Press.

1938 "A Short Investigation of the Temple at Al-'Ubaid," Iraq V: 1-11.

1940 The Temple Oval at Khafājah. ("Oriental Institute Publications," Vol. LIII.) Chicago: University of Chicago Press.

1952 Pottery from the Diyala Region. ("Oriental Institute Publications," Vol. LXIII.) Chicago: University of Chicago Press.

1960 "Architectural Representations on Steatite Vases," Iraq XXII: 90-95.

Delougaz, P., and Lloyd, S.

1942 Pre-Sargonid Temples in the Diyala Region. ("Oriental Institute Publications," Vol. LVIII.) Chicago: University of Chicago Press.

Deshayes, J.

1960 Les Outils de bronze, de l'Indus au Danube (IVe au IIe millénaire). ("Institut français d'archéologie de Beyrouth; Bibliothèque archéologique et historique," Vol. LXXI) Paris.

Dossin, G.

1962 "Bronzes inscrits du Luristan de la collection Foroughi," Iranica Antiqua II: 149-64.

Dunand, M.

1945 Biblia grammata. ("République Libanaise, Ministère de l'éducation nationale. Etudes et documents d'archéologie," Vol. II.) Beyrouth.

Dyson, R. H., Jr.

1960 "A Note on Queen Shub-ad's 'Onagers,'" Iraq XXII: 102-4.
1961 "Review of R. J. Braidwood et al., Excavations in the Plain of Antioch." The American Anthropologist 63: 630-41.

Dyson, R. H., Jr., and Young, T. C., Jr.

1960 "The Solduz Valley, Iran: Pisdeli Tepe," Antiquity XXXIV: 19-28.

Egami, N.

1959 Telul eth Thalathat, the Excavation of Tell II, 1956-1957. (Tokyo University Iraq-Iran Expedition, Report I) Tokyo: Yamakawa.

Ehrich, R. W. (ed.)

1954 Relative Chronologies in Old World Archeology. Chicago: University of Chicago Press.

El Wailly, F.

1963 "Tell as-Sawwan," in "Foreword," Sumer XIX: 1, 2. (The comprehensive report on the excavation at Tell-as-Sawwan is being prepared by B. Aboul-Soof.)

Falkenstein, A.

1936 Archaische Texte aus Uruk. ("Ausgrabungen der deutschen Forschungsgemeinschaft in Uruk-Warka," Bd. 2.) Berlin: Commissions-Verlag Harrassowitz.

Falkenstein, A., Edzard, D. O., and Bottéro, J.

1965 "Die altorientalischen Reiche I, Vom Paläolithikum bis zur Mitte des 2. Jahrtausends." In Fischer Weltgeschichte, pp. 13-209. Frankfort a.M.: Fischer Bücherei.

Farkas, Ann L.

1964 "Review of D. J. Wiseman, Catalogue of the Western Asiatic Seals in the British Museum," Vol. I, Bibliotheca Orientalis XXI: 196-97.

Frankfort, H.

1933 Tell Asmar, Khafaje and Khorsabad. ("Oriental Institute Communications," No. 16.) Chicago: University of Chicago Press.

1936 "A New Site in Mesopotamia: Tell Agrab," Illustrated London News, Sept. 12: 432-36.

1937 "Review of C. L. Woolley, Ur Excavations, Vol. II, The Royal Cemetery." Journal of the Royal Asiatic Society: 330-43.

1939 Cylinder Seals, a Documentary Essay on the Art and Religion of the Ancient Near East. London: Macmillan.

1954 The Art and Architecture of the Ancient Orient (Pelican History of Art) Harmondsworth: Penguin).

1955 Stratified Cylinder Seals from the Diyala Region. ("Oriental Institute Publications," Vol. LXXII.) Chicago: University of Chicago Press.

Frankfort, H., Lloyd, S., and Jacobsen, Th.

1940 The Gimilsin Temple and the Palace of the Rulers at Tell Asmar. ("Oriental Institute Publications," Vol. XLIII.) Chicago: University of Chicago Press.

Gadd, C. J.

1963 "The Dynasty of Agade and the Gutian Invasion." In Cambridge Ancient History, Rev. Ed., Vol. I, Chap. XIX. Cambridge, Cambridge University Press.

Garelli, P.

1963 Les Assyriens en Cappadoce. ("Bibliothèque archéologique et historique de l'institut français d'archéologie d'Istanbul," No. XIX.) Paris: Maisonneuve.

Genouillac, H. de

1934 Fouilles de Telloh, Vol. I, Époques présargoniques. Paris: Geuthner.

1936 Ibid., Vol. II, Époques d'Ur IIIe dynastie et de Larsa. Paris: Geuthner.

Ghirshman, R.

1938 Fouilles de Sialk près de Kashan, 1933, 1934, 1937, Vol. I ("Musée du Louvre, département des antiquités orientales," série archéologique, Vol. IV.) Paris: Geuthner.

Goetze, A.

1961 "Early Kings of Kish," Journal of Cuneiform Studies XV: 105-11.

Goldman, H.

1956 Excavations at Gözlü Kule, Vol. II, from the Neolithic through the Bronze Age. Princeton: Princeton University Press.

Gosh, A.

1964 "Archaeology in India," Expedition 6: 12-17.

Haller, A.

1954 Die Gräber und Grüfte von Assur. ("65. Wissenschaftliche Veröffentlichung der Deutschen Orient-Gesellschaft.") Berlin: Verlag Gebr. Mann.

Hallo, W. W.

1964 "The Road to Emar," Journal of Cuneiform Studies XVIII: 57-88.

Hallo, W. W., and Buchanan, B. W.

1965 "A Dated 'Persian Gulf' Seal and Its Implications." In Studies in Honor of Benno Landsberger. ("Oriental Institute Assyriological Studies," No. 16.) Chicago: University of Chicago Press (in press).

Hansen, D. P.

1963 "New Votive Plaques from Nippur," Journal of Near Eastern Studies XXII: 145-66.

Hansen, D. P., and Dales, G. F.

1962 "The Temple of Inanna, Queen of Heaven, at Nippur," Archaeology 15: 75-84.

Heinrich, E.

1936 Kleinfunde aus den archaischen Tempelschichten in Uruk. ("Ausgrabungen der Deutschen Forschungsgemeinschaft in Uruk-Warka," Vol. I.) Leipzig: Commissions-Verlag Harrassowitz.

Herzfeld, E.

1930 Die Vorgeschichtlichen Töpfereien von Samarra. ("Forschungen zur islamischen Kunst II. Die Ausgrabungen von Samarra," Vol. V.) Berlin.

1933 "Aufsätze zur altorientalischen Archäologie II: Stempelsiegel," Archaölogische Mitteilungen aus Iran V/2: 94-102.

Hinz, W.

1963 "Persia, c. 2400-1800 B.C." In Cambridge Ancient History, Rev. Ed., Vol. I, Chap. XXIII. Cambridge: Cambridge University Press.

Hogarth, D. G.

1920 Hittite Seals, with Particular Reference to the Ashmolean Collection. Oxford: Clarendon Press.

Hole, F., and Flannery, K. V.

1962 "Excavations at Ali Kosh, Iran, 1961," Iranica Antiqua II: 7-148.

Hrouda, B.

1957 Die bemalte Keramik des zweiten Jahrtausends in Nordmesopotamien und Nordsyrien. ("Istanbuler Forschungen," Bd. 19.) Berlin: Gebr. Mann.

Jacobsen, Th.

1957 "Early Political Development in Mesopotamia," Zeitschrift für Assyriologie 18 (N.F.): 91-140.

1963 "Ancient Mesopotamian Religion; the Central Concerns," Proceedings of the American Philosophical Society 107: 473-84.

Jacobsen, Th., and Adams, R. M.

1958 "Salt and Silt in Ancient Mesopotamian Agriculture," Science 128: 1251-58.

Kramer, S. N.

1964 "The Indus Civilization and Dilmun, the Sumerian Paradise Land," Expedition 6: 44-52.

Kupper, J.-R.

1963 "Northern Mesopotamia and Syria," Cambridge Ancient History, Rev. Ed., Vol. II, Chap. I. Cambridge: Cambridge University Press.

Le Breton, L.

1957 "The Early Periods at Susa, Mesopotamian Relations," Iraq XIX: 79-124.

Leemans, W. F.

1950 The Old Babylonian Merchant, His Business and His Social Position. ("Studia et documenta ad iura orientis antiqui pertinentia," Vol. III.) Leiden: Brill.

1960 Foreign Trade in the Old Babylonian Period. ("Studia et documenta ad iura orientis antiqui pertinentia," Vol. VI.) Leiden: Brill.

Lees, G. M., and Falcon, N. L.

1952 "The Geographical History of the Mesopotamian Plains," Geographical Journal CXVIII: 24-39.

Legrain, L.

1936 Ur Excavations, Vol. III: Archaic Seal Impressions. London: Oxford University Press.

1951 Ur Excavations, Vol. X: Seal Cylinders. London: Oxford University Press.

Lenzen, H. J.

1941 Die Entwicklung der Zikurrat von ihren Anfängen bis zur Zeit der III Dynastie von Ur. ("Ausgrabungen der Deutschen Forschungsgemeinschaft in Uruk-Warka," Bd. 4.) Leipzig: Harrassowitz.

1950 "Die Tempel der Schicht Archaisch IV in Uruk," Zeitschrift für Assyriologie 15: 1-20.

1951 "Zur Datierung der Anu-Zikurrat in Warka," Mitteilungen der Deutschen Orient-Gesellschaft 83: 1-32.

1955 "Mesopotamische Tempelanlagen von der Frühzeit bis zum zweiten Jahrtausend," Zeitschrift für Assyriologie 17: 1-36.

1960 "Die beiden Hauptheiligtümer von Uruk und Ur zur Zeit der III. Dynastie von Ur," Iraq XXII: 127-38.

1964 "New Discoveries at Warka in Southern Iraq," Archaeology 17: 122-31.

Lewy, Hildegard

1964 "The Assload, the Sack, and Other Measures of Capacity," Revista degli studi Orientali XXXIX: 181-97.

Lewy, J.

1958 "Some Aspects of Commercial Life in Assyria and Asia Minor in the Nineteenth Pre-Christian Century," Journal of the American Oriental Society 78: 89-101.

Limet, H.

1960 Le Travail du métal au pays de Sumer au temps de la IIIe Dynastie d'Ur ("Bibliothèque de la faculté de philosophie et lettres de l'Universite de Liège," Fasc. CLV) Paris: Societé d'édition "Les belles lettres."

Lloyd, S.

1938 "Some Ancient Sites in the Sinjar District," Iraq V: 123-42.

1940 "Iraq Government Soundings at Sinjar," ibid. VII: 13-21.

1943 "Tell Uqair," Journal of Near Eastern Studies II: 131-55.

Lloyd, S., and Safar, F.

1945 "Tell Hassuna: Excavations by the Iraq Government Directorate General of Antiquities in 1943 and 1944," Journal of Near Eastern Studies IV: 255-89.

1947 "Eridu. A Preliminary Communication on the First Season's Excavations January-March 1947," Sumer III: 84-111.

1948 "Eridu. A Preliminary Communication on the Second Season's Excavations 1947-48," ibid. IV: 115-27.

Luschan, F. von, and Andrae, W.

1943 Ausgrabungen in Sendschirli, V. ("Staatliche Museen zu Berlin, Mitteilungen aus den orientalischen Sammlungen," Heft XV.) Berlin.

Mackay, E.

1925-29 Report on the Excavation of the "A" Cemetery at Kish, Mesopotamia, Pt. I; A Sumerian Palace and the "A" Cemetery at Kish, Mesopotamia, Pt. II ("Field Museum of Natural History, Anthropology Memoirs," Vol. I, Nos. 1, 2). Chicago.

1931 Report on Excavations at Jemdet Nasr, Iraq ("Field Museum of Natural History, Anthropology Memoirs," Vol. I, No. 3). Chicago.

Madhlum, T. A.

1960 "The Excavations at Tell-al-Wilayah," Sumer XVI: 62-92 (Arabic section).

Mallowan, M. E. L.

1933 In: Thompson, R. Campbell, and Mallowan, M. E. L. "The British Museum Excavations at Nineveh, 1931-32," University of Liverpool, Annals of Archaeology and Anthropology XX: 71-186.

1936 "The Excavations at Tall Chagar Bazar, and an Archaeological Survey of the Ḫabur Region, 1934-35," Iraq III: 1-86.

1937 "The Excavations at Tall Chagar Bazar and an Archaeological Survey of the Ḫabur Region. Second Campaign, 1936," ibid. IV: 91-177.

1947 "Excavations at Brak and Chagar Bazar," ibid. IX: 1-259.

Mallowan, M. E. L., and El Amin, M.

1950 "Soundings in the Makhmur Plain," Sumer VI: 55-90.

Mallowan, M. E. L., and Rose, J. C.

1935 "Excavations at Tall Arpachiyah, 1933," Iraq II (1935), i-xv, 1-178.

Maxwell-Hyslop, Rachel, K.

1960 "The Ur Jewellery," Iraq XXII: 105-15.

Mecquenem, R. de

1934 Mémoires de la mission archéologique de Perse, Vol. XXV. Paris: Librairie E. Leroux.

Mellaart, J.

1963 "Excavations at Çatal Hüyük," Anatolian Studies XIII: 43-103.

Mellink, Machteld, J.

1963 "An Akkadian Illustration of a Campaign in Cilicia?" Anatolia VII: 101-15.

Moorey, P. R. S.

1964 "The 'Plano-convex building' at Kish and Early Mesopotamian Palaces," Iraq XXVI: 83-98.

Moortgat, A.

1935 "Frühe Bildkunst in Sumer," Mitteilungen der vorderasiatisch-aegyptischen Gesellschaft 40/3.

1940 Vorderasiatische Rollsiegel, ein Beitrag zur Geschichte der Steinschneidekunst. (Staatliche Museen zu Berlin). Berlin: Gebr. Mann. (Reprinted 1966.)

1945 "Die Entstehung der sumerischen Hochkultur." (Der Alte Orient, 43 Band.) Leipzig: Hinrich Verlag.

1960 Tell Chuera in Nordost-Syrien. ("Schriften der Max Freiherr von Oppenheim Stiftung," Heft 4.) Wiesbaden: Harrassowitz.

1965 Tell Chuera in Nord-Ost Syrien, vorläufiger Bericht über die Kampagne 1963 ("Wissenschaftliche Abhandlungen der Arbeitsgemeinschaft für Forschung des Landes Nord Rhein-Westfahlen") in press.

Moortgat-Correns, Ursula

1959 "Bemerkungen zur Glyptik des Diyala-Gebietes," Orientalistische Literaturzeitung LIV: 342-54.

Mortensen, P.

1962 "On the Chronology of Early Village-Farming Communities in Northern Iraq," Sumer XVIII: 73-80.

Nagel, W.

1957 "Ein altassyrisches Königssiegel," Archiv für Orientforschung XVIII: 97-103.

1958 "Glyptische Probleme der Larsa-Zeit," ibid., 319-27.

1959 "Datierte Glyptik in frühdynastischer Zeit," Orientalia (N.S.) 28: 141-62.

1961-64 "Zum neuem Bild des vordynastischen Keramikums in Vorderasien," Berliner Jahrbuch für Vor-und Frühgeschichte 1-4: (1961), 1-125; (1962), 1-83; (1963), 1-61; (1964), 1-74.

Oates, Joan

1960 "Ur and Eridu, The Prehistory," Iraq XXII: 32-50.

Opificius, R.

1961 Das altbabylonische Terrakottarelief. ("Untersuchungen zur Assyriologie und vorderasiatischen Archäologie, Ergänzunsbände zur Zeitschrift für Assyriologie . . . Neue Folge," Bd. 2.) Berlin: W. de Gruyter.

Oppenheim, A. L.

1954 "The Seafaring Merchants of Ur," Journal of the American Oriental Society 74: 6-17.

1957 "A Bird's-Eye View of Mesopotamian Economic History." In K. Polanyi et al. Trade and Market in the Early Empires; Economic History and Theory, pp. 27-37. Glencoe, Ill.: The Free Press.

1964 Ancient Mesopotamia, Portrait of a Dead Civilization. Chicago: University of Chicago Press.

Otten, H.

1951 "Die hethitischen Königslisten und die altorientalische Chronologie," Mitteilüngen der Deutschen Orient-Gesellschaft 83: 47-71.

Özgüç, T.

1955 "Excavations at Kültepe 1954, Finds of Level Ib," Belleten XIX: 64-72.

Parrot, A.

1948 Tello, vingt campagnes de fouilles (1877-1933). Paris: Albin Michel.

1956 Mission archéologique de Mari I. Le Temple d'Ishtar. ("Institut français d'archéologie de Beyrouth. Bibliothèque archéologique et historique," Vol. LXV.). Paris: Geuthner.

1958-59 Mission archeologique de Mari II. Le Palais: 1. Architecture; 2. Peintures; 3. Documents et monuments. ("Institut français d'archéologie de Beyrouth. Bibliotheque archéologique et historique," Vols. LXVII, LXIX, LXX.) Paris: Geuthner.

Perkins, Ann L.

1949 The Comparative Archeology of Early Mesopotamia. ("Studies in Ancient Oriental Civilization," No. 25.) Chicago: University of Chicago Press.

1954 "The Relative Chronology of Mesopotamia." In Ehrich, Robert W., Relative Chronologies in Old World Archeology, pp. 42-55. Chicago: University of Chicago Press.

Porada, Edith

1948 In collaboration with Briggs Buchanan, Corpus of Ancient Near Eastern Seals in North-American Collections. Vol. I The Collection of the Pierpont Morgan Library. ("Bollingen Series," Vol. XIV), New York: Pantheon Books.

1950 "Review of Corpus of Ancient Near Eastern Seals . . ." Journal of Cuneiform Studies 4: 155-62.

1954 "Review of Ur Excavations, Vol. X, L. Legrain, Seal Cylinders . . ." American Journal of Archaeology 58: 339-42.

1957 In "review of Sir Leonard Woolley, Alalakh," by M. J. Mellink, American Journal of Archaeology 61: 396-97.

1958a "Review of Henri Frankfort, Stratified Cylinder Seals from the Diyala Region . . .," Journal of Near Eastern Studies XVII: 62-67.

1958b "Review of Paul Jacobsthal, Greek Pins . . .," Archiv für Orientforschung XVIII: 419-20.

1961 "Review of André Parrot, Le Temple d'Ishtar . . .," Bibliotheca Orientalis XVIII: 160-63.

1962 Alt-Iran, die Kunst in vorislamischer Zeit. ("Kunst der Welt.") Baden Baden: Holle.

1964a "Problems of Interpretation in a Cylinder Seal of the Akkad Period from Iran," Compte rendu de l'onzième recontre assyriologique internationale. Leiden: Nederlands Instituut voor het Nabije Oosten, pp. 88-93.

1964b "The Oldest Inscribed Works of Art in the Columbia Collections," Columbia Library Columns, XIII: 25-33.

Rowton, M. B.

1962 "Ancient Western Asia." In "Chronology," Cambridge Ancient History, Rev. Ed., Vol. I, Chap. VI, pp. 23-69. Cambridge: Cambridge University Press.

Safar, F.

1950a "Eridu: A Preliminary Report on the Third Season's Excavations, 1948-49," Sumer VI: 27-38.

1950b "Pottery from Caves of Baradost," ibid.: 118-23.

Salonen, A.

1939 Die Wasserfahrzeuge in Babylonien. ("Studia Orientalia ed. Societas Or. Fennica," Vol. VIII/4.) Helsinki.

Schüller, A.

1963 "Die Rohstoffe der Steingefässe der Sumerer aus der archaischen Siedlung bei Uruk-Warka." In Lenzen, UVB XIX: 56-58.

Sollberger, E.

1959-60 "Byblos sous les rois d'Ur," Archiv für Orientforschung XIX: 120-22.

Speiser, E. A.

1932-33 "The Pottery of Tell Billa," Museum Journal XXIII: 249-83.

1935 Excavations at Tepe Gawra, Vol. I: Levels I-VIII. Philadelphia: University of Pennsylvania Press.

Starr, R. F. S.

1937-39 Nuzi, Report on the Excavations at Yorgan Tepa near Kirkuk, Iraq . . . 1927-1931. Cambridge, Mass.: Harvard University Press.

Strommenger, Eva

1960 "Das Menschenbild in der altmesopotamischen Rundplastik von Mesilim bis Hammurapi," Baghdader Mitteilungen I: 1-103.

1964 5000 Years of the Art of Mesopotamia. New York: Abrams.

Stronach, D.

1961 "Excavations at Ras Al 'Amiya," Iraq XXIII: 95-137.

Thompson, R. Campbell, and Hamilton, R. W.

1932 "The British Museum Excavations on the Temple of Ishtar at Nineveh, 1930-31," Annals of Archaeology and Anthropology, University of Liverpool XIX: 55-93.

Tobler, A. J.

1950 Excavations at Tepe Gawra, Vol. II: Levels IX-XX. Philadelphia: University of Pennsylvania Press.

UVB II-XI 1931-40 Vorläufiger Bericht über die von der Notgemeinschaft der Deutschen Wissenschaft in Uruk Warka unternommenen Ausgrabungen. ("Abhandlungen der Preussischen Akademie der Wissenschaften, philosophisch-historische Klasse.") Berlin.

UVB XII-XX 1957-64 Vorläufiger Bericht über die von dem Deutschen Archäologischen Institut und der Deutschen Orient-Gesellschaft aus Mitteln der Deutschen Forschungsgemeinschaft unternommenen Ausgrabungen in Uruk-Warka. ("Abhandlungen der Deutschen Orient-Gesellschaft," Nos. 2-9.) Berlin.

Watelin, L. Ch.

1934 Excavations at Kish, Vol. IV, 1925-1930. Paris: Geuthner.

Wheeler, Sir Mortimer

1953 The Indus Civilization. The Cambridge History of India, Supplementary Volume. Cambridge: Cambridge University Press.

Woolley, Sir C. L.

1934 Ur Excavations, Vol. II: The Royal Cemetery. London: Oxford University Press.

1955 Ur Excavations, Vol. IV: The Early Periods. Philadelphia: University Museum; London: British Museum.

Wright, H. E., Jr.

1955 "Geologic Aspects of the Archeology of Iraq," Sumer XI: 83-91.

Ziegler, Charlotte

1950 Die Tempelterasse von Tel Brak. ("Mitteilungen der Deutschen Orient-Gesellschaft," No. 82.) Berlin.

1953 Die Keramik von der Qal 'a des Haǧǧi Moḥammed. ("Ausgrabungen der Deutschen Forschungsgemeinschaft in Uruk-Warka," Band 5.) Berlin: Gebr. Mann.

ADDENDA TO THE BIBLIOGRAPHY*

Adams, R. McC.

1965 Land behind Baghdad: A History of Settlement on the Diyala Plains. Chicago: University of Chicago Press. (See p. 173, above.)

Braidwood, R. J.

1964 "Further Remarks on Radioactive Carbon Age Determination and the Chronology of the Late Prèhistoric and Protohistoric Near East," Vorderasiatische Archäologie, Studien und Aufsätze, Anton Moortgat . . . Berlin: Mann, pp. 57-67.

Mallowan, M. E. L.

1964 "Ninevite 5," Vorderasiatische Archäologie, Studien und Aufsätze, Anton Moortgat . . . Berlin: Mann, pp. 142-54. (Cf. p. 159, above.)

1965 "The Mechanics of Ancient Trade in Western Asia," Iran III: 1-7. (Cf. p. 136, above.)

*For continuing summaries and bibliographies, see COWA 15, Western Asia.

The Relative Chronology of Mesopotamia. Part II. The Pottery Sequence at Nippur from the Middle Uruk to the End of the Old Babylonian Period (3400-1600 B.C.)

Donald P. Hansen
Institute of Fine Arts
New York University

The following section attempts to summarize the development of south Mesopotamian pottery from the Middle Uruk through the Old Babylonian periods. Hitherto, the chronology of the south was based on the excavations of Warka and the Diyala region. Now, new material is available from Nippur, in the heart of central southern Mesopotamia, from the excavations of the Oriental Institute of the University of Chicago. The function of this section is to provide a new sequence of materials from Nippur from both the Inanna precinct and the areas called TA and TB in Tablet Hill. I hope to show how these materials complement and amplify the chronological structure already determined from the excavations at Warka and the Diyala. There is little foreign influence on the pottery of southern Mesopotamia; however, suggestions will be made for the correlation of the sequences of the north and the south.

To the middle Uruk phase (Eanna VIII-VI) may be linked the beginnings of the Nippur sequence (Inanna XX-XVII). It is impossible to correlate a specific level at one site with a specific level at the other. Single pottery examples and recurring types from Inanna XX-XVII cluster at Eanna VI. This is probably due to the fact that Eanna VI produced more pottery than any other level of the sounding, and hence gives somewhat of a false impression of the pottery development.

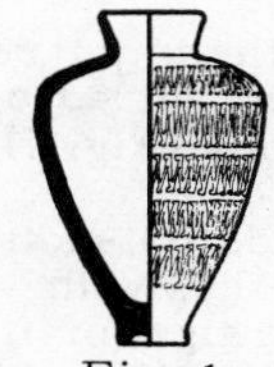
Fig. 1

A small, distinctive jar with an impressed rocker pattern and a wash of a fugitive red paint from a burial in Inanna XIX (Fig. 1) is paralleled almost exactly in Eanna VI (UVB IV, Pl. 19, Da) and Susa Ca (Le Breton, 1957, Fig. 13, 1). The same rocker pattern occurs on a small, buff-

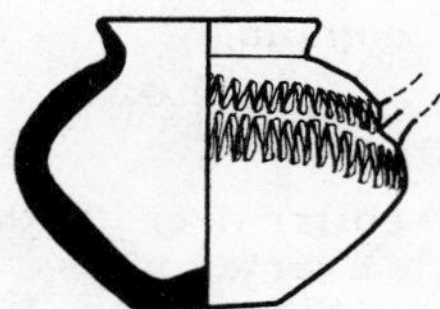
Fig. 2

slipped, handled cup in Inanna XX (Fig. 2). Another distinctive vessel is a shallow dish with straight sides and a pouring spout at the rim. In Inanna XX-XIX, these appear with a creamy buff slip (Fig. 3); a red ware example of the same type occurs in Eanna VI (UVB IV, Pl. 19, <u>Df</u>). Some recurring types and features of Inanna pottery are tabulated below on the left, with rough approximations of the Eanna pottery on the right.

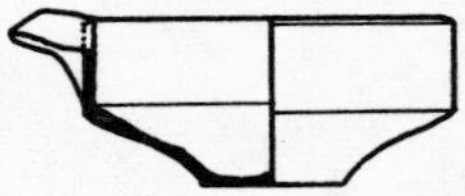

	Inanna	Eanna
red ware	XX-XVI concentration XIX	XIII-IV concentration VI
gray ware	XX-XVII	XIII-IV
gray ware with incised crescent or circles	XVIII-XVII	VIII-VII
beveled-rim bowls (Fig. 4)	XX-XII concentration XX-XV	XII-IV
reserved slip	XIX-ED	
sinuous-sided cups (Fig. 5)	XX-XVI	VIII-V
twisted handles	XVII-XIV	IX-VI
strap-handled cups (Fig. 6)	XX-XIII	VIII (gray) -VI
bottle or jar necks with folded-over rims (Fig. 7)	XVII-XII	VII-III
crude flat-bottom dishes with straight or flaring sides (Fig. 8)	XX-XVII concentration XIX	VII-VI concentration VI
combing	XX-XIV	XI-X
plum red	XVI-JN	VI-JN
collar necks with everted rims (Fig. 9)	XVI-XV	IV

Fig. 3

Fig. 4

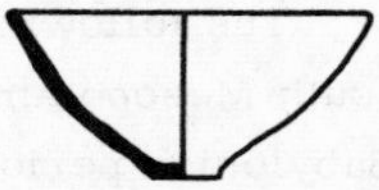

Fig. 5

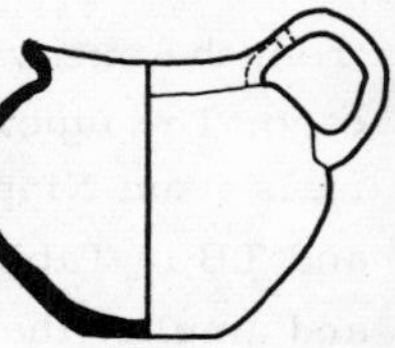

Fig. 6

Fig. 7

Fig. 8

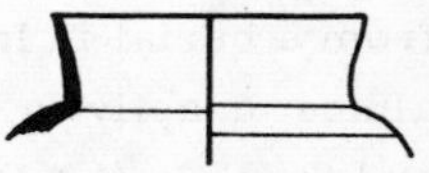

Fig. 9

These correspondences suggest the equation of Inanna XX-XVII with the middle Uruk phase, roughly equivalent to Eanna VIII-VI. In Inanna XX, other parallels with Warka are found (all references are to UVB IV: Pl. 19, *Ac'*, (VI); Pl. 18, *De*, (VII); Pl. 18, *Cu*, (VIII); Pl. 19, *Cw*, (VI). Jars with a "rope" pattern at the shoulder and strap-handled cups with a punctate pattern on the shoulder are found (Fig. 10). A small-handled cup with rocker pattern is apparently like a cup from Susa Bc (Le Breton, 1957, Fig. 10, *5*). It is not known whether the Inanna example had a twisted handle.

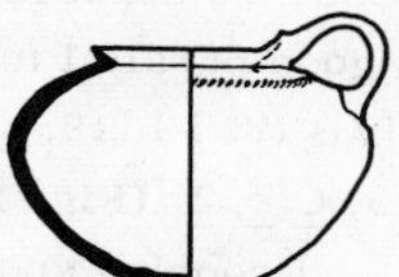
Fig. 10

In Inanna XIX, besides parallels cited above, there are close similarities to Eanna in UVB IV, Pl. 19, *Ag* (VII) gray; Pl. 19, *Bg''*, (VI); Pl. 19, *Ac'* (VI); Pl. 19, *Aw'* (VI) ?; Pl. 19, *Bg'* (VI); Pl. 19, *Ch* (VI). A variety of four-lugged jars in buff ware with a fine buff slip, gray ware, and red wares appear in this level (Fig. 11). Some have punctate designs on the shoulder. A red ware example already has an incised design on the shoulder and tiny raised pellets below the design (Fig. 12). Some of these come from a burial in XIX and may be slightly later, but others of the same type appear in good stratified context. There are no good parallels for the four-lugged jars at Warka. The Inanna examples are close to Susa C a and b pottery (Le Breton, 1957, Fig. 11). In Inanna, the earliest reserved slip appears on a buff ware jar with everted rim in level XIX (Fig. 13). Reserved slip is apparently earlier at Tall-i-Ghazir (Dyson, below, p. 224).

Fig. 11a

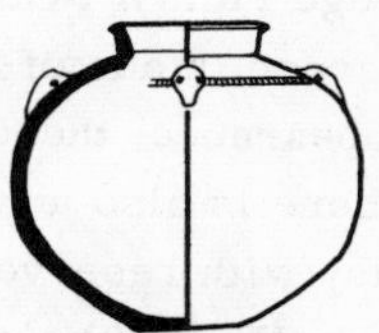
Fig. 11b

Fig. 12

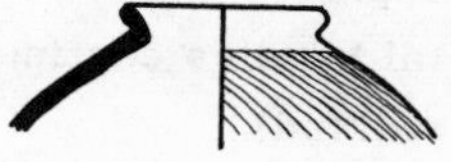
Fig. 13

In Inanna XVIII, the types which started in Level XX continue. A small, thin jar of the Eanna VI type appears; a four-lugged jar with a band of cross hatching on the shoulder (Fig. 14) resembles a four-lugged vessel from Eanna (UVB IV, Pl. 19, *Db*) and from Susa Bd (Le Breton, 1957,

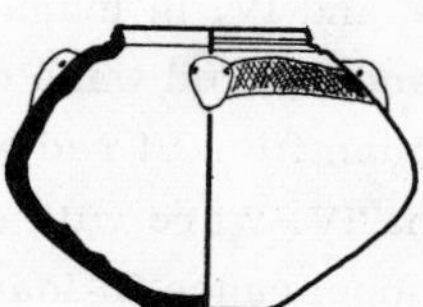
Fig. 14

Fig. 10, 29). The earliest false spout in the Inanna sequence appears in this level (Fig. 15). There is a good parallel to Eanna VI in a jar with rim type UVB IV, Pl. 19, Br'; and "rope" decoration of Pl. 19, C k, 1, (Fig. 16).

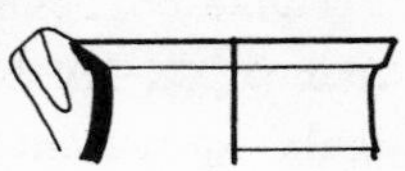

Fig. 15

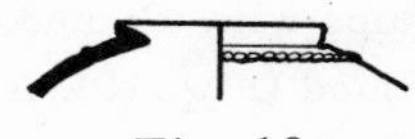

Fig. 16

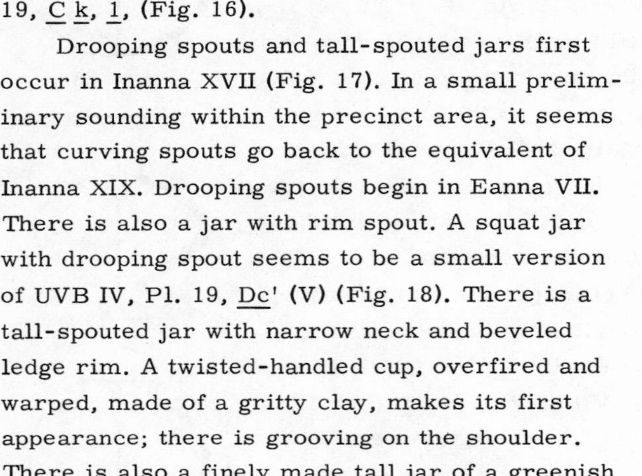

Drooping spouts and tall-spouted jars first occur in Inanna XVII (Fig. 17). In a small preliminary sounding within the precinct area, it seems that curving spouts go back to the equivalent of Inanna XIX. Drooping spouts begin in Eanna VII. There is also a jar with rim spout. A squat jar with drooping spout seems to be a small version of UVB IV, Pl. 19, Dc' (V) (Fig. 18). There is a tall-spouted jar with narrow neck and beveled ledge rim. A twisted-handled cup, overfired and warped, made of a gritty clay, makes its first appearance; there is grooving on the shoulder. There is also a finely made tall jar of a greenish clay with reserved slip on the upper part of the body (Fig. 19). Apparently this was a false-spouted jar. Parallels occur here with Susa C a and b.

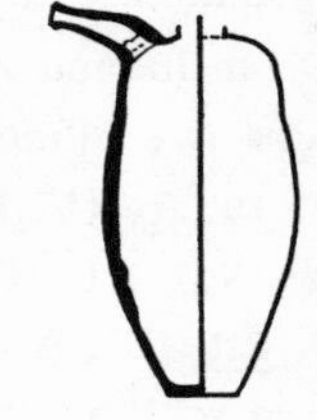

Fig. 17

Red ware four-lugged vessels with tiny pellet appliqués beneath an incised shoulder pattern continue into XVII. Besides the twisted handles of the cups, there also appears a twisted handle applied horizontally to the rim of a jar (horizontal handles continue into XIV, but are no longer twisted).

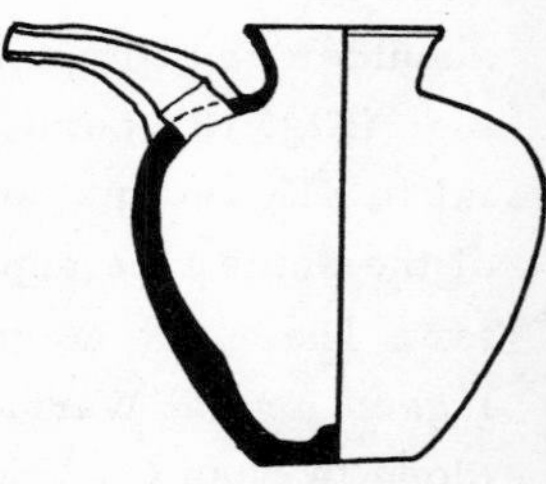

Fig. 18

We have grouped Inanna XVI and XV together in a Late Uruk phase roughly equivalent to Eanna V and IV. In Inanna XVI, the gray ware is gone and the red ware occurs only occasionally. Small quantities of red and gray ware are found in Eanna IV. Ware with a plum-red slip first makes its appearance in Inanna XVI (it first occurs in Eanna VI) and becomes more plentiful in Inanna XV. Some red ware continues into XIV, where red and

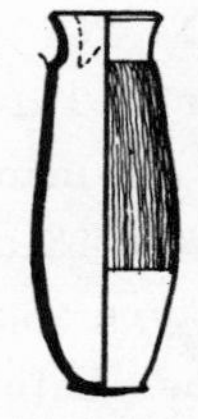

Fig. 19

plum ware are found together. A red burnished ware four-lugged jar continues into XV. Nearly all the rim spouts found in Inanna are concentrated in Level XVI (Fig. 20). In Level XVI appears the first example of an incised criss-cross decoration of triangles on the shoulder of a four-lugged jar (Fig. 21). Such decoration appears on a jar of slightly different form from Eanna IV (UVB IV, Pl. 20, Al'). It has been suggested that the Uruk example is out of place (Perkins, 1949, p. 101). Small-spouted vessels with everted rims continue. In XVI appears a large jar with high shoulder and drooping spout (Fig. 22); an antecedent with straight spout occurs in XVII. The Level XVI example is of the type attributed to Susa Bd by Le Breton. Bottle or jar necks with forms such as UVB IV, Pl. 19, Dv (V), Pl. 20, An (IV) and Pl. 20, Br (III/II) are found. In Inanna XVI begins a "luxury ware" usually made of a fine greenish paste. The Level XVI example is a jar with an incised design on the shoulder and with vertical stripes of reserved slip on the body (Fig. 23). Tall-spouted jars with small neck and folded-over rim continue in XVI. Strap-handled cups and small four-lugged vessels also continue. A common crude ware beaker occurs which is similar to Level IV beaker types in Eanna (UVB IV, Pl. 20, Ay [Fig. 24]).

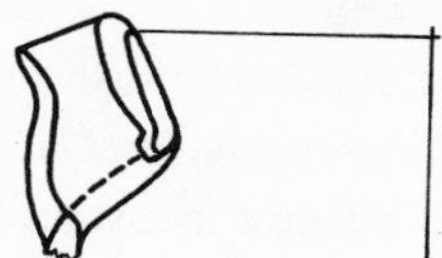
Fig. 20

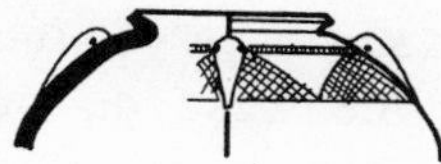
Fig. 21

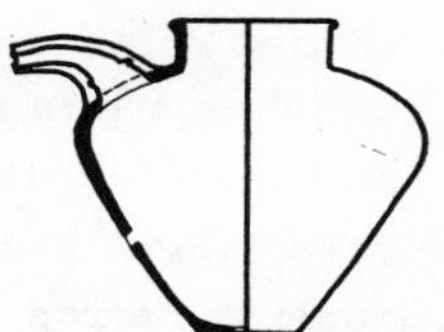
Fig. 22

Fig. 23

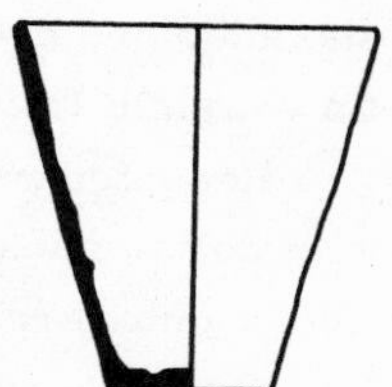
Fig. 24

In Inanna XV, other examples of luxury ware occur. One is a tiny four-lugged vessel made of a greenish paste and with an elaborate incised decoration on the shoulder (Fig. 25). Of the same material is a miniature round-bottom bowl. The walls of this luxury ware are extremely thin, sometimes two millimeters. Although it is more squat, the shape and decoration of the four-lugged vessel are similar to the Susa C a

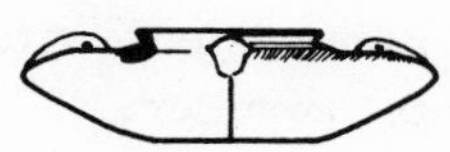
Fig. 25

example of Le Breton (1957, Fig. 11, 21). A small jar with collar and everted rim occurs in the same material (Fig. 26). A variety of spouted jars continues in Inanna XV. Large jars with drooping spouts, collar necks, and slightly everted rims continue from XVI; there are also smaller versions with straight and curved spouts. A small-spouted jar is similar to Diyala B.533.262; the Diyala example has shoulder grooving and is dated to Diyala Protoliterate c (Fig. 27). A bulging hole-mouth jar without lugs appears, and is related in shape to the spouted vessels. A tall ovoid jar with small neck and straight spout is related to a type found in Susa Ca (Le Breton, 1957, Fig. 12, 2), where it appears with a curving spout (Fig. 28). Twisted-handle and strap-handle cups now have more elaborate and more carefully executed patterns on the shoulder. Bases appear which are similar to some from Eanna IV (UVB IV, Pl. 20, Ac). Crude cups or beakers such as found in Eanna IV become more plentiful. A tall jar with a buff slip over a reddish clay has a collar and slightly everted rim (Fig. 29). It is similar in shape to pottery attributed to Susa Cc (Le Breton, 1957, Fig. 11, 39, 45). Another tall jar has four lugs on the shoulder and does not differ greatly from the Susa Ca example (*Ibid.*, Fig. 11, 38) (Fig. 30).

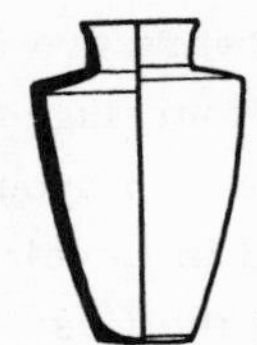

Fig. 26

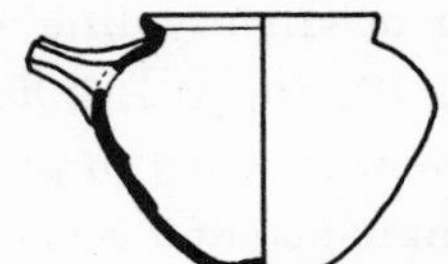

Fig. 27

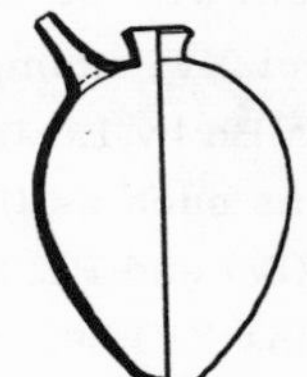

Fig. 28

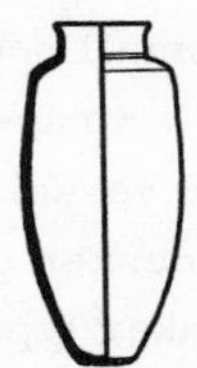

Fig. 29

Fig. 30

Repeated reference has been made to jars with collar necks and slightly everted rims. These rims are confined to Inanna XVI and XV. The type occurs in Eanna IV (UVB IV, Pl. 20, Ap).

In Level XV of Inanna appears the earliest example of a plum-red small-mouth jar with beveled-ledge rim. This becomes common in the next period.

Level XIV marks the beginnings of the Jamdat Nasr period. New types are introduced and certain types decorated with monochrome and polychrome designs appear. Of the types listed on page 202, above, a few continue into the Jamdat Nasr period. Beveled-rim bowls occur but not in great quantity. Reserved slip as a particular feature continues through the Jamdat Nasr period. Twisted handles last into XIV, and strap-handle cups continue into XIII. Bottle or jar necks with folded-over rims continue throughout the period, and ware with a plum-red slip, usually burnished, which started in late Uruk times now becomes the hallmark of the period.

Fig. 31

Fig. 32

Both polychrome (the use of this word follows Delougaz, 1952, p. 35, n. 38) and monochrome pottery appear together in Inanna XIV. The most elaborate polychrome vessels with complicated geometric patterns occur in Level XIII, whereas the floruit of monochrome seems to be in Level XIV. Some shapes of the painted pottery correspond closely to painted pottery vessels in the Diyala (Inanna XIV-Protoliterate c, and Inanna XIII-Protoliterate d). The monochrome continues, however, into XIII.

Fig. 33

A fragment of a large jar with everted rim has shoulder grooving (Fig. 31); this is the first occurrence of its use other than on the strap- and twisted-handle cups. In Levels XIV and perhaps XIII occur small plum-red ware jar caps (Fig. 32) (cf. Diyala, Protoliterate c, B.041.500 and Susa Cb; Le Breton, 1957, Fig. 11, 4). Four-lugged vessels continue of course, and most frequently occur on vessels with painted decoration. A monochrome painted pot introduces the notched raised shoulder ridge (Fig. 33). Spouted jars continue; a new type in Level XIV is a large jar with rounded base. Introduced in this period are large beakers with thickened

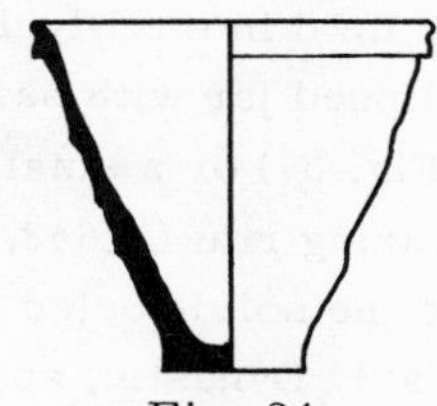
Fig. 34

or overturned rims of a type found in Eanna IV (UVB IV, Pl. 20, Az (Fig. 34)). A buff jar with a beveled-ledge rim and a small base of Inanna XIII is paralleled by a painted version in the Diyala, Protoliterate d (C.536.540). A special variety of beaker found in XIV and XIII has a beveled rim and is paralleled by UVB IV, Pl. 20, Ab (Fig. 35).

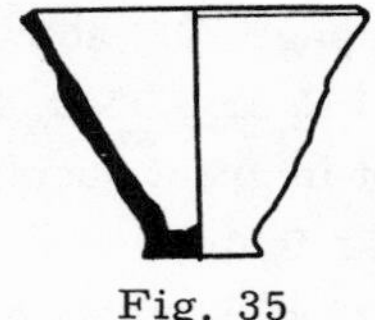
Fig. 35

Level XII of Inanna represents the end of the Jamdat Nasr period and the transition to Early Dynastic. The polychrome painted ware continues, as does a small four-lugged jar with an incised band of decoration on the shoulder. The latter is so similar to late Uruk types that it may well be out of place. Small cups are more frequent; these continue in profusion throughout the Early Dynastic period. In this level occur the first examples of jars with four rim tabs or ledge lugs (cf. Delougaz, 1952, Pl. 63, 13; UVB XIX, Pl. 39, e; UVB IV, Pl. 20, Cc (II/III). This type is characteristic of Early Dynastic I (Fig. 36). Reserved slip on the shoulder of spouted jars becomes more frequent. The reserved slip usually starts on the upper part of the shoulder immediately below a punctate design encircling the upper part of the shoulder. There is one example of a pseudo or mock reserve slip in which a blunt instrument was dragged over the clay to produce a similar effect. Some vessels are paralleled by Protoliterate d in the Diyala, such as a small buff-slipped jar with beveled-ledge rim (C.535.240) (Fig. 37) or a small rounded bowl with slightly flaring rim (B.643.520) (Fig. 38). Two examples of the solid-footed chalice, the hallmark of the Early Dynastic, appear in Level XII (these also appear in Eanna IV).

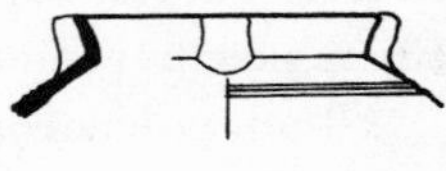
Fig. 36

Fig. 37

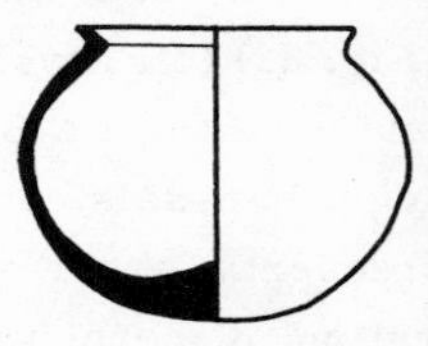
Fig. 38

There are not a great many specific correlations between the pottery of the north and the south for the Uruk and Jamdat Nasr periods. Perkins has conveniently tabulated the correspondences, of which the most distinctive in pottery seem to be gray ware, beveled-rim bowls, handled cups, and ladles.

Levels XI-V of Inanna are assigned to the Early Dynastic period. Levels XI-IX are Early Dynastic I; VIII is Early Dynastic II; and VII-V are Early Dynastic III, however Level VII B may well have been built toward the end of ED II. The length of these periods, as suggested on the chart, is only a surmise.

The Early Dynastic pottery from Inanna well complements the material from the Diyala. Scarlet ware is a characteristic type of painted ware during Early Dynastic I in the Diyala. A few sherds from Inanna XII-X might be scarlet ware; they are so small, however, it is impossible to be sure. It would seem that scarlet ware is basically a local development in the Diyala region, although Delougaz has pointed to connections with Mari and Elam (Delougaz, 1952, pp. 139-41). The pottery hallmark of the first Early Dynastic period is the solid-foot chalice (Fig. 39). The type seems to be concentrated in the middle of ED I; it is less abundant in the first and last levels of the period. No less distinctive for the period is a jar with a single triangular lug (Delougaz, 1952, Pl. 47).

Fig. 39

Almost all the Early Dynastic types of pottery found in the Diyala (Delougaz, 1952) are represented also in Inanna. It is of interest that the burnished gray ware of Early Dynastic I in the Diyala (Delougaz, 1952, Pl. 48) occurs in comparable levels at Inanna in shapes that also imitate stone vessels. The hollow stoppers found in ED I and II in the Diyala (Delougaz, 1952, Pl. 70) are confined to Level X in Nippur. Little pottery from the later Early Dynastic III period has been found in Inanna; the basic pottery types for this period must be determined from the Diyala pottery alone (*ibid.*).

The Akkadian period is not represented in Inanna; it seems to have been completely destroyed by Šulgi's latest construction. We know that a temple of this period once existed, because a mace head of Naramsin dedicated to Inanna was found in the area. Akkadian pottery in TB XIII-XI is not overabundant. Among the major types is a shallow bowl

Fig. 40

with beveled rim, found also at Gawra VI (Fig. 40) and a tall thin-walled beaker frequently found with beveled ledge on the inside of the rim (Fig. 41a). Apparently the type is a continuation of Early Dynastic III pottery (Delougaz, 1952, Pl. 149). Several jars with rounded bottom were found, as well as a beveled-ledge rim with a raised ridge below the rim (Fig. 41b). This type occurs in the Diyala (Delougaz, 1952, Pl. 113, g) and in Gawra VI. A small bottle with rounded base and beveled rim occurs, which also is paralleled in Gawra VI (Fig. 42a). Such bottles start in Early Dynastic times, and continue into Ur III (cf. Delougaz, 1952, Pl. 162). An Akkadian ovoid jar with horizontal ribbing on the shoulder links with Diyala Proto-Imperial, Brak, Nuzi VI-V, and Gawra VI (Perkins, 1954, p. 48, Fig. 42b).

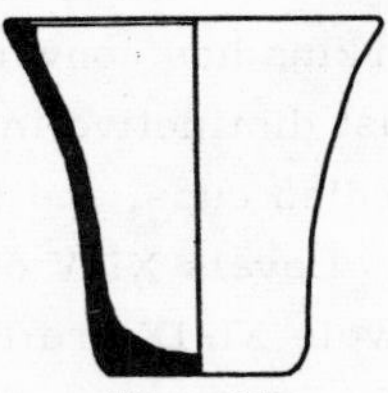
Fig. 41a

Fig. 41b

Fig. 42a

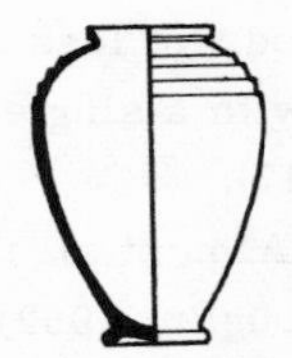
Fig. 42b

In the areas of TA and TB at Nippur, there are some forty different pottery types covering the period from the Third Dynasty of Ur to the end of the First Dynasty of Babylon. These pottery types present a continually evolving series; there are no sharp breaks until the end of the First Dynasty of Babylon. The fact that there is no sharp break in the pottery sequence implies that it is difficult to define this time range from the Ur III through the Old Babylonian Period in precise cultural phases on the basis of pottery, a fact worthy to be noted.

It is impossible to present here all the pottery types and their time ranges in the levels of TA and TB. This will have to await the final publication of the results in McCown and Haines, Nippur I (in press). Haines has kindly allowed me to make use of the evidence mentioned below for the purposes of this paper. Not all the types can be given; hence, the picture presented tends to be somewhat false. It will provide, however, an indication of the pottery development in the south which complements the evidence from the Diyala.

Bowl with sharply flaring sides (Fig. 43).	TB IX-Kassite period concentration Ur III.	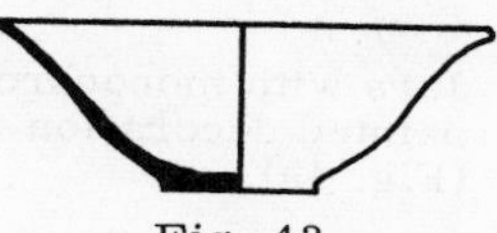 Fig. 43
Low bowl with thick rim (Fig. 44).	TB IX-IV; in the Diyala, the type begins in Akkadian period (Delougaz, 1952, p. 109). A variant with less pronounced rim continues into TB E and TA XI.	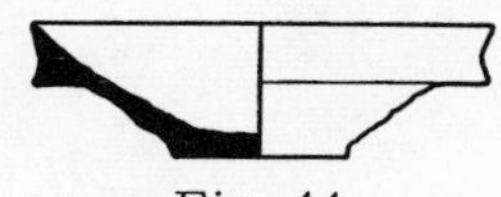 Fig. 44
Small bowl with heavy ledge rim (Fig. 45).	TB VIII-VI. Type B.061.210 of the Diyala. It might begin in Akkadian times (*ibid.*, p. 109).	 Fig. 45
Small round-bottom jar with profile rim (Fig. 46). Others of same type with beveled ledge.	TB XI then in TB VII-II Diyala type B.645.540a. This is related to the Akkadian type, *supra*, Fig. 41*b*.	 Fig. 46
Tall jar with beveled or thickened rim and high shoulder ridge (Fig. 47).	TA XI-III. Equivalent to Diyala types C.208.440 and C.777.340.	 Fig. 47
Ovoid round-bottom jar with shoulder grooving (Fig. 48).	TB IV-I, TA XV-XII.	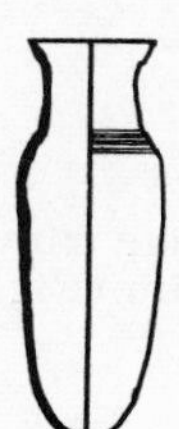 Fig. 48

Jars with monochrome painted decoration (Fig. 49).	TB I-C, TA XII-X.	 Fig. 49
Ovoid jar with collar neck and everted rim. Monochrome painted decoration (Fig. 50).	TB II-C, TA XIII-X.	 Fig. 50
Flat bowl with beveled inner rim (Fig. 51).	TB E-C, TA XI-X.	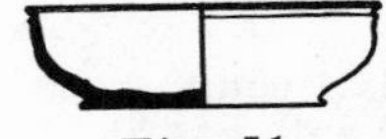 Fig. 51
Small footed cup with thin wall and neckless rim. Painted band on rim (Fig. 52).	TB II-C, TA XIII-X. Related is Diyala B.576.720a (cf. Delougaz, 1952, p. 150, for a discussion of "Hurrian" ware).	 Fig. 52
Ovoid jar with flaring band rim (Fig. 53).	TB III-C, TA XIV-X.	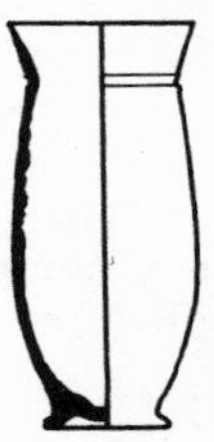 Fig. 53

Tall beaker with monochrome band on rim (Fig. 54)	TB I-C, TA XII-X. Probably related to Diyala B.247.700.	 Fig. 54

Other major types of pottery from the Akkadian through the First Dynasty of Babylon with connections to the north are given by Delougaz (1952, p. 147, n. 138, 139; p. 148, n. 142, 143, 146; p. 149, n. 149; p. 150).*

At Nippur, after the end of the First Dynasty of Babylon, twenty-six pottery types were no longer made, and only three types continued into the Kassite period. This represents a tremendous change and break in Mesopotamian culture. Indeed, with the Kassite period, Mesopotamia begins a completely new phase of its history.

---

*For sources cited in the text, see the Bibliography on pages 189-200.

Problems in the Relative Chronology of Iran, 6000-2000 B.C.

Robert H. Dyson, Jr.
University of Pennsylvania

The relative chronology of Iran is built up in this paper through the systematic comparison of the basic Mesopotamian sequence with stratified assemblages in Iran moving from west to east in order of geographic proximity. In this procedure the great importance of the rugged topography of the country and the question of the reliability of the context of compared materials are two factors which have been kept constantly in mind.

Iran may be divided geographically into a western Zagros Mountain zone running parallel to the Mesopotamian border, a central plateau area bordered on the north and south by mountains and coastal plains, and an eastern zone made up of northeastern Iran, Seistan, and Baluchistan. The relationships between these areas are shown by the pre-industrial caravan routes as given by Le Strange (1905). In any attempt to relate Mesopotamian cultures to Iran, these routes leading from west to east are of paramount interest. There are four major points of access: from the area north of Lake Urmia which adjoins Anatolia and the Caucasus, a route leads southeast toward the central plateau; from northern Assyria via the Kel-i-Shin, Rowanduz, and Little Zab gorges to the area south of Lake Urmia (Solduz and Kurdistan), from which it is possible to move east or southeast to the plateau region; from southern Assyria or Akkad through the Kermanshah Valley system to Hamadan and eastward to the plateau; from Akkad or Sumer southeast between the face of the Kabir Kuh Range and the Tigris marshes to Deloran and Khuzistan. The latter may also be reached by water from southern Sumer. From Khuzistan, it is possible to move northeastward into Luristan and the plateau, or southeastward to the Fars area of the plateau. The routes from the northwest and central Zagros converge around Kazvin-Kashan, from whence it is possible to move eastward along the southern face of the Elburz Range to Meshed. The route through Fars leads southeastward to Baluchistan. There is also a route connecting the Fars area with the Kashan area; another passes along the Caspian shore between the Talish area and Turkistan, with a major link to the plateau via the Safid Rud west of Kazvin and Shahrud east of Damghan. These routes have conditioned the movements of cultures and peoples throughout the history of the area (B.R. 524, 525).

Several discussions of the relative chronology of Iran have previously been published (Childe, 1952; McCown, 1942, 1954; Ghirshman, 1954; Gordon, 1947, 1960; Piggott, 1943, 1950). Each of these papers made a substantial contribution at the time of its presentation. Each was concerned with the major sites of Susa, Tepe Giyan, Tepe Sialk, and Tepe Hissar. Since Relative Chronologies appeared in 1954, information on a number of important additional sites has been made available. These include: in the northwest, Geoy Tepe (Burton Brown, 1951), Hasanlu, Hajji Firuz, and Dalma Tepes (Dyson, 1961; Young, 1962), Yanik Tepe (Burney, 1961, 1962); in the central Zagros, Tepe Sarab, Tepe Siabid, and Deshawar Tepe (Braidwood et al., 1961), Guran Tepe (Crawford, 1963a); in Khuzistan, Ali Kosh (Hole, 1962), a 1954 sounding on the Susa Acropolis (Dyson, n.d.), Tall-i-Ghazir (Caldwell, n.d.), Tchoga Mish (Delougaz, 1964); in the Caspian area, Marlik Tepe (Negahban, 1962, 1964), Yarim Tepe (Crawford, 1963b), Tureng Tepe (Deshayes, 1963), Japanese excavations at several points (Egami, 1960); in the central plateau area, Khorvin-Chandar (Vanden Berghe, 1964), Kara Tepe (Burton Brown, 1962) Ismailabad (Iranian Archaeological Service); in Fars, tepes excavated by Vanden Berghe (1959), Tall-i-Bakun (Egami and Masuda, 1962), Tall-i-Gap (Egami and Sono, 1962), Tall-i-Nokhodi (Goff, 1963, 1964) and Tall-i-Iblis (Caldwell, unpublished). No major work in the range of this paper has been done in the remaining areas of Iran during this time.

In the development of the present study, two facts became apparent early in the process: the need temporarily to abandon the existing theoretical framework and make a fresh review of the basic data for the correlation of the major sites of Susa, Giyan, Sialk, Hissar, and Bakun; and the need for new over-all generalizations which could be used as a starting point for further discussion. The initial step was, therefore, a basic review, the results of which are presented below under "Documentation." The second step was the preparation of Figure 1, using a tentative chronology for the Mesopotamian periods based on a combination of historical, carbon, and estimated dates. The use of such a tentative scale was necessary in order to suggest the relative magnitude of existing gaps. The third step was to indicate in some way in Figure 1 the major relationships between sites and areas. This was accomplished by using arrows to show the directions in which the major cultural impulses in terms of pottery traditions moved. It became evident that the Zagros cultures were immediately related to those of Mesopotamia, although always with their own characteristics, whereas the plateau cultures were distant and derivative. Furthermore, cultures of the north experienced influences from northern Mesopotamia which were not felt in southeastern Iran. Consequently, the northern part of Iran has a history divergent from that of the south. This development had a sound geographical basis as shown in Figure 2. The result is most provocative, in that the various horizons show a repetitive pattern of diffusion which suggests possibilities for the reconstruction of earlier incomplete stages of investigation. A host of problems and questions require discussion, clarification, and new field work.

STYLISTIC AND CULTURAL HORIZONS

Since our general problem is to relate Iranian prehistory to the cultural sequence established in Mesopotamia, the following comments are organized in terms of those periods as a series of related stylistic and cultural horizons spreading eastward through Iran.

Soft Ware Horizon. A very early horizon, probably representing the initial spread of pottery making into Iran, is suggested by the presence of a pre-Jarmo-Sarab ceramic horizon at Tepe Guran in Luristan (Crawford, 1963a) and by the presence of plain burnished buff ware, full of straw temper and fired at a low temperature, at both Hotu and Belt Caves on the Caspian shore in the northeast (Coon, 1957) and at Tall-i-Bakun BI in the southeast (McCown, 1942). On the Caspian shore, this horizon is preceded by a "gazelle Mesolithic"; in the Luristan area, Tepe Asiab provides a local pattern based on shellfish collecting (Braidwood et al., 1961). This horizon may be related in time to the earliest Jarmo ceramic horizon, but there is insufficient evidence to relate it culturally beyond the fact that the earliest Jarmo pottery is a kind of soft ware.

Jarmo-Related Horizon. Material in this stage is found at Tepe Sarab in the Kermanshah Valley (Braidwood et al., 1961), at Tepe Guran (Mortensen, 1964) and in the "Mixed Zone" ceramic levels at Ali Kosh (Hole, 1962) in northwestern Khuzistan. This pottery represents the beginning of the later diffusion pattern from northern Iraq through the central Zagros, and along the western face of the Zagros toward Khuzistan. There is at present no trace of this horizon elsewhere in Iran. The plain ware of this horizon is related to soft ware in technique of manufacture. Sarab culture is characterized by the manufacture of many fat, seated female figurines.

Hassuna-Related Horizon. No purely Hassuna-related levels have been excavated in Iran. The Hajji Firuz culture of the northwest (Young, 1963) may be a derivative from some early Hassuna or Hassuna-like culture in Mesopotamia, since it represents a basic soft ware tradition with Hassuna-like painted elements. A major problem here lies in the nature of the sequence in Mesopotamia between Jarmo and archaic Hassuna—that is, between about 6000 and 5500 B.C. Current excavations at Tell as-Sawwan by the Iraq Department of Antiquities may shed light on this problem (cf. Mortensen, Sumer, 1962, XVIII: 73-80).

A late stage of Hassuna-related materials occurs when the Hassuna culture has already been joined by elements of Samarra (Hassuna IV-V). At this stage, influence enters Iran via the central Zagros and reaches the central plateau, where it may be seen in Sialk I_{1-3}. Between the Hajji Firuz (which has some links to the earlier Sarab) and the Sialk I cultures there is a complete blank in Iran which should cover much of the Hassuna period in Mesopotamia.

Halaf-Related Horizon. As might be expected, influence from the Halaf culture reaches into central Iran along the Kermanshah route affecting Giyan VA and Sialk I_{4-5}. It does not reach the southeast, although some minor influence is felt in Susiana. Classic Halaf reaches the Zagros frontier at Banahilk (Braidwood et al., 1960), but is at present unknown in Iran. In the northwest, following Hajji Firuz, the Dalma culture may extend back into this period, with its origins perhaps in Samarra-Halaf traditions. In the northeast, we have no idea of what culture is present beyond the possibility that the Chalcolithic culture of Yarim Tepe on the Caspian shore may belong here (Crawford, 1963b).

Ubaid-Related Horizon. This horizon marks the first adequately documented major spread of cultural elements through Iran. It begins in the southwestern lowland plains of Khuzistan at Jaffarabad and related sites and evolves locally into Susa A (Le Breton, 1957), which dates to Ubaid 4 times on the basis of recent unpublished work at Susa (Dyson, n.d.) and Tall-i-Ghazir (Caldwell, n.d.). Northward, it spreads through

Luristan to Kermanshah and, from northern Iraq, into northwestern Iran, where it forms the Pisdeli culture. Eastward, it moves out onto the central plateau, where it joins the earlier local traditions of Sialk I forming a distinct northern painted pottery culture—Sialk II—which spreads as far as Hotu Cave on the Caspian shore (Coon, 1957). To the southeast, it penetrates Fars, where it appears at Tall-i-Gap I and other sites (Egami and Sono, 1962). Although displaced at the center by the intrusive Uruk culture of Susa B and C, the Ubaid-related cultures persist until about 3000 B.C. in the northwest (Geoy M) and central Zagros (Giyan VD) and in the central plateau (Sialk III_{7b}). To the northeast, the horizon lingered even later into Hissar IIA, Shah Tepe III, and early Tureng Tepe—all probably beginning Early Dynastic in date. A similar retardation seems to have occurred in the southeast, where the Ubaid tradition progressed through Tall-i-Gap II and Bakun AIII. There is some evidence from Stein to suggest that it persisted until the appearance of (late Early Dynastic) Susa Dc-d elements in the area (Stein, 1937). Recent unpublished work by Caldwell at Tall-i-Iblis will probably clarify this question.

Uruk-Jamdat Nasr-Related Horizon. This horizon appears relatively abruptly in the southwestern plains of Khuzistan (only a short transition exists), where it completely displaces the older Ubaid-related painting tradition with plain wares. It appears at Tchoga Mish, Susa, and Tall-i-Ghazir. From this base it then penetrated to the plateau, possibly by way of the Deshawar area in the Kermanshah Valley, to Sialk IV. If it reached the plateau by this route, it would occupy the gap between Giyan VD and IV. On the other hand, it is not impossible that it went east over the very difficult high passes or even around the south through Fars (no material reported). The presence of quantities of beveled-rim bowls at Deshavar not many miles from Giyan, and at Giyan itself (unpublished), suggests the first of these possibilities. Notwithstanding, the painting tradition probably survived in surrounding areas of the Zagros. This Uruk-Jamdat Nasr horizon seems to have met far greater resistance than did the earlier ones, since it never reached the northwest, the northeast, or the southeast (although Stein, 1937, does mention the presence of buff-colored plain wares which he did not pick up). Why was this penetration of the plateau so limited?

Early Dynastic-Related Horizon. This is the second major period of general west-east diffusion and the last before the emergence of the historic period in Khuzistan and the disruption of the pattern through the incoming of elements from the north in the second millennium. The starting point of this horizon again appears to be Susa, where the painting tradition reasserted itself (Susa D). From this area the impulse moved northward through Luristan to the Kermanshah area (Giyan IV) and still farther north to its ultimate limit in Hasanlu VII (Dyson 1958), where it is dated by C-14 to about 2100 B.C. At Sialk, there is some evidence to suggest that period IV lasted into the Early Dynastic, but the evidence is inconclusive and the sequence ends. The horizon apparently never established itself effectively on the northern plateau beyond the Zagros area. Paralleling the northward spread, it also went southeast, where it is manifest at Bampur and Khurab and finally Kulli. As already mentioned, there is some evidence in Stein to suggest that the earlier painted-ware tradition may have continued to this time.

Northern Gray Ware Horizon. The west-east pattern undergoes a major change in the north for the first time (except for limited earlier intrusions at Geoy and Yanik Tepes in the northwest) with the appearance at Shah Tepe, Tureng Tepe, and Yarim Tepe, along the Caspian and Hissar on the adjoining plateau, of a gray ware horizon which at first overlaps the terminal painted wares and then quickly develops characteristics of its own. Although there is no disconformity at Hissar, there is an apparent change of cultural pattern which in temporal terms parallels the late Early Dynastic, Akkadian, and Ur III periods in Mesopotamia. The origin and meaning of this horizon in the northeast is one of the outstanding problems of Iranian archaeology. With its establishment on the plateau at Hissar, the stage is set for a gradual diffusion westward and southward which forms the major pattern of the second millennium, joined sporadically by intrusions from the northwest, and finally, near the end of the millennium, by major intrusions southward from the Caucasus. The events which follow the end of the Hissar sequence are beyond the scope of this paper.

DOCUMENTATION

The sequence in the southwest plains of Khuzistan depends upon materials from five sites: Ali Kosh (Hole, 1962), Jaffarabad (Le Breton, 1947, 1957), Susa (Le Breton, 1957; Dyson, n.d.), Tall-i-Ghazir (Caldwell, n.d.), and Tchoga Mish (Delougaz, 1964). In the published material, the site of Jaffarabad provides the only approximation of a sequence from early ceramic to Susa A. The following interpretive schemes have been proposed for Jaffarabad and neighboring sites.

<table>
<tr><th>Vanden Berghe
(1952b)</th><th>Le Breton
(1957)</th><th>McCown
(1942, 1954)</th></tr>
<tr><td rowspan="2">Group A</td><td>Susiana a: Jaff.I 6-3.5 m.</td><td>Jaffarabad Aspect</td></tr>
<tr><td>Susiana b: Jowi 8-5.0 m.</td><td rowspan="2">Jowi Aspect</td></tr>
<tr><td>Group B</td><td>Susiana c: Jaff.II 3.5-2.0 m.</td></tr>
<tr><td rowspan="2">Group C</td><td>Susiana d: Upper Bendibal and Buhallan</td><td>Bendebal Aspect</td></tr>
<tr><td>Susiana e: Jaff.III 2.0-0. m.</td><td>Susa I Aspect</td></tr>
</table>

Since these sites were not stratigraphically excavated, there is no general agreement on their ordering. Only one—Jaffarabad—offers even a tentative ordering of materials between Ali Kosh and Susa A, since it alone contains a lower, middle, and upper range of objects. These have been grouped arbitrarily by absolute depth into periods I, II, and III. Related site materials can be fitted into this order by tentative stylistic arguments which await proper excavation for confirmation.

This sequence pinpoints one of the major problems of Iranian chronological discussions: the tendency to rely almost exclusively upon design parallels (sometimes of the most tenuous nature) to the exclusion of shape, non-ceramic objects, and basic technology. Such overemphasis results from the fact that much of the Iranian material consists only of sherds from surface collections, limited soundings, or isolated specimens in collections. In most instances plain wares have been excluded in favor of more interesting painted wares. The difficulty in using this material is compounded by the demonstrable longevity of some of the design motifs and their independence of movement in relation to pottery shapes and other types of objects. In this respect it is necessary to reemphasize the principle of dating an assemblage by the latest parallels present, since there is some tendency to stress earlier parallels at the expense of later ones in order to allow Iran to compete with other areas in the antiquity of its cultural achievement.

Jaffarabad I - Ubaid 2 - Samarra - Hassuna (Le Breton, 1957; cf. Lloyd and Safar, 1945)*

Parallels are mainly with Ubaid 2 and Samarra-Hassuna. (a) Pottery shapes: (1) low bowls with incurving rims (Fig. 5, 18; cf. Fig. 2, 11); (2) carinated bowls (Fig. 5, 22; cf. Fig. 1, 7, and Oates, 1960, type 10); (3) bowls with trough spouts (Fig. 5, 23; cf. Oates, 1960, type 2); (4) ring-based pots (Fig. 5, 2; cf. 7); (5) dishes on fenestrated stands (Fig. 5, 5; cf. 10); (6) milk jars (Fig. 5, 1; cf. Fig. 6). (b) Decorative techniques: (1) reserve decoration; (2) painted and scratched decoration; (3) bowls ornamented inside and out (Fig. 5; cf. Oates, 1960, and Lloyd and Safar, 1945); (c) Design parallels: (1) cruciform pattern of Ubaid 1 and Samarra bowls; (2) triangular pattern in reserve around outside, as on Ubaid 2 bowls; (3) swastika patterns.

Jaffarabad II - Ubaid 3 (Le Breton, 1957)

Parallels are mainly with Ubaid 3. (a) Pottery shapes (89 N.1). (b) Design parallels: (Fig. 6, 22-24, 26-29). Themes common to Iranian pottery for millennia first appear: birds, animals, human beings. Parallels to Gawra XVIII also occur (Fig. 6, 39).

Jaffarabad III - Ubaid 3-4? (Le Breton, 1957; cf. Oates, 1960)

Jaffarabad III, Susiana d, and Susa A materials are nowhere stratigraphically ordered, nor is there any adequate distinction between them in terms of foreign parallels. The latter occur in Ubaid 3 and 4, but with no indication of relative positioning within that time range (Fig. 7); for example, a ring-based goblet of Susiana d (Oates, 1960, type 13) is found at Eridu in Ubaid 2 and 4, whereas a flaring goblet of Susiana d (Oates, 1960, type 17b) is found only in 4. If Susiana d actually precedes Susa A, as suggested by Le Breton, it should, when redefined by excavation, belong to late 3 or early 4 in view of the Ubaid 4 dating of Susa A (see below).

Susa A - Ubaid 4 - Gawra XIII-XII (Le Breton, 1957; cf. Oates, 1960)

Parallels are mainly with Ubaid 4 and Gawra XIII-XII. (a) Pottery shapes: (Fig. 7 and p. 92) specific forms include jars with spouts and basket handles (Oates, 1960, type 15), a bottle form (*ibid.*, type 22,

---

*Documentation in paragraphs following headings refers to texts noted in heading unless otherwise stated.

Eridu cemetery only), and a pedestal bowl (ibid., type 24, at Uqair). (b) Design parallels: (see Fig. 7). (c) Stamp seal parallels: animal themes and linear designs as in Gawra XIII, hemispheric form, size, decorative disposition, geometric stylization, and sparse use of the drill as in Gawra XII (p. 93); (d) Metal objects: full use of copper as in Gawra XII, a celt and pin providing specific parallels (Fig. 9; cf. Tobler, 1950, XCVIIIa).

When did Susa A end? Le Breton (1957, pp. 64-98) conjectures with McCown (1942, p. 39) that it was near the time of, or just before, Warka XIII. In an unpublished sounding made in 1954 on the eastern edge of de Morgan's Grande Tranchée (Dyson, n.d.), a phase (strata 40-32) of pure painted buff ware of Susa A type was followed by a later phase (strata 32-23) in which the painted ware was co-extant with a thin-walled, simple form of beveled-rim bowl. Stratum 23 contained little painted ware, but did have sherds of Early Red Ware (a compact, burnished, slipped or unslipped red ware occurring commonly in flat-bottom bowl shapes from stratum 40 onward). In stratum 21, true coarse beveled-rim bowls appeared with pottery of typical Early Uruk type as seen in Warka XIII-XII. At unpublished Tall-i-Ghazir (Caldwell, n.d.), there was also a "Transitional" phase (floors 7-10) between the Susa A "Painted Buff Ware" phase (floors 1-7) and the "Early Uruk" phase (floors 10-15) of Warka XIII relation. Both sites clearly show the presence of a transitional stage (equivalent in time to Warka XV-XIV) overlying the pure Susa A deposit. The latter should, therefore, date to Ubaid 4.

Susa B - Warka XII-VII: Early and Middle Uruk (Le Breton, 1957)

In the 1954 sounding, a sharp decline of Painted Ware occurs in stratum 23 leaving the Early Red Ware as the main decorated ware for one stratum. Sherds show some Warka XIII parallels. This stratum essentially equals Le Breton's Ba-Bb (McCown's B1) and Ghazir "Transitional" (floors 7-10). No building level occurs in the 1954 area, but one is present in the Acropolis II sounding immediately southeast. A lump of oxidized copper occurs in this level, which also marks the end of the early beveled-rim bowls.

Stratum 22 sees the loss of the Early Red Ware and the full appearance of classic Uruk type plain wares. Ring bases occur in 22, Bc (Fig. 10, 16) and Warka XIII. Tubular spouts link Bc (Fig. 10, 15) and Warka XIII. True beveled-rim bowls appear in 21, Bc (B2, McCown), and Warka XII. Thus, strata 22-20 (and building levels J and K) would seem to approximate Bc and Ghazir "Early Uruk" (floors 10-15) and "Middle Uruk" (floors 15-27). Le Breton's division between Bc and Bd must be accepted on the basis of the relative position of the graves rather than upon the pottery, which, as published, does not substantiate the division (Fig. 10).

The remains of the next five strata, 19-15, represent Bd (B3, McCown). One building level, G, is included, and clay jar sealings without seal impressions occur in 18. Strata 19-15 and Bd are linked by the presence in each of ring bases (Fig. 10, 32), nose lugs (Fig. 10, 29), impressed patterns of triangular elements (Fig. 10, 8), spouted jars (Fig. 10, 18, 19, 23), flaring rim (Fig. 10, 17, 19), short, fat spouts (Fig. 10, 13, 14), and short necks (Fig. 10, 22, 24). Warka VIII cups appear in 19 and Bd (Fig. 10, 7) and the same levels reveal the onset of the floruit of true Uruk Red Wares. Reserve Slip appears for the first time in 15. Straight spouts link Bd (Fig. 10, 10) with Warka VIII-VI. In general this range correlates with Ghazir "Late Uruk" (floors 27-35) excepting that Reserve Slip begins at that site in the preceding period. Vessels with nose lugs and crosshatching also link Ghazir to Bd. A general correlation with Warka VIII-VII seems acceptable for the Bd materials.

Susa C - Warka VI-III: Late Uruk - Jamdat Nasr (Le Breton, 1957)

Strata 14-1 and building levels A-F in the 1954 sounding correspond to Le Breton's Ca period. Cups with twisted handles appear in 8-9. According to Le Breton (1957, Fig. 10, 8, 5) these occur in Bd and possibly even Bc; Caldwell notes them as probably beginning in the "Late Uruk" at Ghazir—along with bottle-neck jars with down-bent spouts. Bottle-neck jars occur at Warka from VI through IV, with the latter being closest to the ones in 8-9. Le Breton places these in Cb (Fig. 12, 5-7). Such contradictions are probably due to the erroneous assignment of inadequately stratified specimens to the higher rather than the lower levels adjoining them. A clay jar sealing bearing the impression of a cylinder seal found in 14 is of Susa C (Fig. 22) and Warka IV-V type. A calcite bowl fragment occurs in 8-9. In 6, a sherd from a flaring neck appears to be from one of the spouted vessel types seen in Ca (Fig. 11, 2-4) and Warka V. Other parallels link Ca to Ghazir "Proto-Elamite" (floors 35-38): trough spouts with painted bands (Fig. 13, 6), teapots (Fig. 13, 3), down-bent spouts, fine rope decoration, and fine impressed patterns. A straight spout in 7 has a parallel in Warka VI. At Ghazir, polychrome and hollow-footed chalices first appear in this period. The general range is that of Warka VI-IV.

In period Cb (C, McCown), Jamdat Nasr type cylinder seals and rare sherds of polychrome provide the date. Metal objects from graves high in the level include copper pins with decorative heads and inlaid jewelry (Fig. 27, 5, 6). Their assignment to Cb by Le Breton, if correct, makes them among the oldest examples of their kind reported. The decorative technique of the pins is paralleled in the Early Dynastic period in the A Cemetery at Kish (Eliot, 1950) and in the Royal Cemetery at Ur (Woolley, 1956, Pl. 27, p. 40). The technique of jewelry inlay occurs also in a grave at Telloh in mixed Jamdat Nasr-Early Dynastic context (Perkins, 1949, p. 148) and at Ur in the Early Dynastic Royal Cemetery (Woolley, 1934). With the exception of these possibly intrusive metal objects, Susa Cb seems to be Jamdat Nasr in date.

In period Cc, seal styles correspond closely to Jamdat Nasr types but are of a regional type with stylized designs. Le Breton (p. 108, Fig. 26) points out that there are one hundred of these known from Susa, eighty from the Diyala, and twenty from Nineveh, indicating a diffusion from Susa northwest along the overland route to northern Mesopotamia. Pottery now includes rare true black-and-red Jamdat Nasr polychrome sherds and a variety of forms related to Protoliterate d (Fig. 11, 42-45), Jamdat Nasr, and Telloh E (Fig. 11, 36, 38). Stage Cc is thus also well connected with the Jamdat Nasr of Mesopotamia.

Susa C - Sialk IV (Le Breton, 1957; cf. Ghirshman, 1938)

Parallels are as follows.

Ca: (a) trough-spouted vessels (Fig. 13, 6; cf. LXXXVIII, S.40, S.52, S.115); (b) deep and shallow beveled-rim bowls (p. 97; cf. XXVI, 7a, 7b).

Cb: (a) lugged vessels (Fig. 12, 12; Fig. 13, 7b; cf. XXVII, 2); (b) down-bent spouts (Fig. 12, 7; cf. LXXXIX, S.43d); (c) trough spouts (cf. Ca:a); (d) lugged vessels (Fig. 13, 7; cf. XC, S.45); (e) beveled-rim bowls (cf. Ca:b); (f) Proto-Elamite tablets of Cb type (p. 104; cf. XCII, XCIII).

Cc: (a) shouldered red ware jars (Fig. 11, 45; cf. LXXXIX, S.80, S.483); (b) cylinder seals of Cb-Cc type (Fig. 23; cf. XCIV, S.89); (c) "Proto-Elamite" tablets of Cc type (p. 104; cf. XCII, S.28); (d) pins with decorated heads (inexact parallel) (Fig. 27; cf. XCV). A parallel between

Sialk IV and Gerzean is provided by a knot-headed pin (XCV, S.1602b, cf. Childe, 1952, Fig. 53, 1). In general the parallels indicate a range for Sialk IV of at least Susa Cb-Cc, which in turn equals the Jamdat Nasr period. The two stages may be reflected stratigraphically at Sialk where the Cb type tablets occur in IV_1 and the Cc tablets in IV_2. The section (Ghirshman, 1938, LIX) shows building level IV_1 filled with its own collapse, an erosion surface (duration?), a subsequent fill from a neighboring structure (collapse or trash), IV_2, and finally two graves dug into this fill from above.

When did Sialk IV end? There is some evidence that it lasted into the Early Dynastic period: (a) small bowl of E.D. II to Post-Early Dynastic type (XC, S.33; cf. Delougaz, 1952, Pl. 146, B001200a); (b) cylinder seal types classified in the Diyala as E.D. I or II but of Jamdat Nasr style (XCIV, S.89, S.54; cf. Frankfort, 1955: Pl. 23, 234; Pl. 81, 856; Pl. 83, 877); (c) motif of deer with branching antlers occurs in Diyala in above context only; (d) fly amulet (XXXIa; cf. University Museum Collection, E.D. III); (e) cloisonné technique (XXXIa; cf. Woolley, 1934, Pls. 133, 138, E.D. III); (f) gold or silver foil used over bitumen core (XXIa; cf. Woolley, 1934, Pl. 140, E.D. III); (g) pins with decorated heads including a double-spiral-headed pin of a type dated in Anatolia to 2600-2300 B.C. (Lloyd, 1956, pp. 56-57). The caution already expressed regarding the dating of similar cloissoné jewelry at Susa applies equally here to the hoard dug into the floor of structure IV_1: the hoard may be somewhat later than its surrounding context.

The date of the end of Sialk IV seems to fall in Early Dynastic times, and may provisionally and conservatively be set at the beginning of E.D. II although it may have been considerably later.

Sialk IV - Gawra XII-XA (Ghirshman, 1938; cf. Tobler, 1950)

Apart from the parallels between Sialk IV and Susa, there are also relations with Gawra. (a) Oval, high-shouldered jar, Gawra XA (LXXXIX, S.483; cf. CXLVIII, 432). (b) Double-hole mouth pots, Gawra XI, XIA, and Nuzi (XC, S.77; cf. CXLVIII, 434; CXLIII, 356, and Starr, 1937, Pl. 42p). (c) Splayed copper celt of Susa A type, Gawra VI, Chalcolithic, and E.B. II in Anatolia (XCV, S.535; cf. Speiser, 1935, XLVIII, 8; Lloyd, 1956, pp. 56-57); celts with flat rather than rounded butts occur in Gawra XI and XII (Tobler, 1950, XCVIII, 1 and 2). (d) Small stone cosmetic jars, Gawra XIII-XIA (XCI, S.5; cf. CLXXX, 63, 65). (e) Stone mace heads of Sialk IV shape, Gawra XII (XCV, S.487; cf. CLXXVII, 33) and grooved mace head (XCV, S.4, S.49; cf. CLXXVII, 30). (f) Motif of deer with branching antler on seals, Gawra XII-XA (XCIV, S.54; cf. CLXVI, 124-26; CLXIX, 160).

These parallels indicate contacts with the Gawran of northern Iraq equated by Perkins to Uruk and Jamdat Nasr in the south. Most of these parallels lie in the Late Uruk range, which suggests that Sialk IV may have begun slightly before the end of that period, with its main relationship occurring during the Jamdat Nasr period of the south and ending sometime in Early Dynastic times.

Susa D - Early Dynastic (Le Breton, 1957)

The analysis of Susa D materials is given by Le Breton (1957). Parallels establishing cross-correlations occur as follows. Da, pottery with non-fast polychrome decoration, is closely related to the Scarlet Ware of E.D. I in the Diyala sites, as are some jar lugs (XXVI:5-7). Db, a new form of large jar with a more or less oval profile with plastic ridges on the shoulder and body, is related to E.D. II shapes; an alabaster bowl is like an E.D. II bowl at Khafaje (p. 120 and XXVI, 9-12). (This is the period of the Susa II style of "composed scenes.") Dc, a regional stylization of natural forms, has influence southeastward to Kulli in Baluchistan; themes of eagle and chariot form a link to E.D. III art; a corrugated jar (Fig. 36, 6) and carinated vases in plain ware have parallels in E.D. III pottery; seal impressions are vaguely like Fara or the SIS 8-4 style at Ur; Le Breton says a bent-tang spearhead cannot be later than Dc (Fig. 41, 1); pins of Kish Cemetery A type possibly belong here (Fig. 41, 15) or in the following period, Dd, which corresponds to later E.D. III. In Dd, chariot burials and new glyptic types occur; pottery is monochrome with special forms (Fig. 35, 9, 11, 13); the famous Style II cachette is assigned here (containing cylinder seals as late as E.D. III in type). In Dc, Dd monochrome designs decline in favor of incised and plastic decoration, the "goddess handle" (Fig. 36, 10) provides a close parallel to the "Proto-Imperial" handle type in the Diyala; pedestal bowls appear as new types; hammered copper begins to replace cast copper, as it did at this time in Mesopotamia.

TEPE GIYAN

The earliest materials at Giyan lie below building level IV from

Mesopotamia	Warka	Ghazir* (Caldwell)	Susa (Le Breton)	Susa (McCown)	Susa* (Dyson)
Jamdat Nasr	III	. . . . .	Cb	C	. . . . .
Late Uruk	VI-IV	"Proto-Elamite"	Ca	. . . . .	14-1
Middle Uruk	VIII-VI	"Late Uruk"	Bd	B3	19-15
Early Uruk	XIII-IX	"Middle Uruk" "Early Uruk"	Bc	B2	20-22
	XV-XIV	"Transitional"	BaBb	B1	23
Late Ubaid	XVIII-XVI	"Buff Ware"	A	A	24-32 Late 40-33 Early

*Tentative terminology.

-7.50 meters to virgin soil at -19.0 meters. McCown (1942, p. 13) has divided this deposit into phases VD, VC, VB, and VA in descending order on the basis of external parallels. Beginning with VD, a synchronism is possible between objects in the fill (the tombs in the fill belong to IV) and Sialk III_{6-7b}.

Giyan VD - Sialk III_{6-7b} (Contenau and Ghirshman, 1935; cf. Ghirshman, 1938)

The following parallels may be noted:

(a) stemmed goblets painted with solid bands and/or inverted line triangles (Pl. 65, top, Pl. 58, row C, item 5; cf. LXXI, S.111, S.1771; Pl. 58, C, 6; cf. LXX, LXXI; Pl. 37, 11; cf. LXX, S.155, S.97; LXXI, S.1759 for shape); (b) Spotted leopards with single front and back legs walking in a row (Pl. 60, D, 5; cf. LXXXI, A15, C2; LXVII, S.137).

Two cylinder seals (Pl. 38, 16, is probably a cylinder bead rather than a true seal) are probably intrusive since they occur only later at Gawra (VII) and Susa (C). Note the similarity of the animal figure (Pl. 60, 21) to that on a stamp seal from Gawra VIII (Tobler, 1950, CLVIII, 36) and Susa B (Le Breton, 1957, Fig. 15, 5).

Sherds with painted birds are from periods II and IV, and show the disturbed nature of the fill of upper VD. In view of the dating of Sialk IV, VD and Sialk III_{6-7b} can date no later than the end of the Late Uruk period.

Giyan VC - Gawra XII-XI (Contenau and Ghirshman, 1935; cf. Tobler, 1950)

A variety of parallels link Giyan VC levels and Gawra XII-XI. (a) Stamp seal motifs: (1) human beings, Gawra XI, XIA (Pl. 38, 22; cf. CLXIII, 88; Pl. 38, 24; cf. CLXIII, 86); (2) scorpions, Gawra XII-X (Pl. 38, 27; cf. CLXX, 181-84); (3) quartered pattern, Gawra XI (Pl. 38, 41; cf. CLIX, 20); (4) animal and man, Gawra XIII-XI (Pl. 35, 5; cf. CLXIV, 94, 97); (5) geometric designs, Gawra XII-XI (Pl. 38, 11; cf. CLVIII, 7; Pl. 38, 32; cf. CLX, 45, 47; Pl. 38, 43; cf. CLXXI, 9). (b) Stamp seal carving technique: quartered pattern, Gawra XIA (VI, 4, b; cf. CLX, 31). (c) Stone: weights or gaming pieces, Gawra XIA, Susa B-C (Pl. 37, 24; cf. CLXXIX, 53, and Mecquenem, 1943; Fig. 22, 8, 9). (d) Metal objects: (1) cast copper rectangular celt, slightly splayed form in Gawra XII-XI, exact form in Sialk III_5 and Susa A (V, 1; cf. XCVIIIa, 1 and 2; Ghirshman, 1938: LXXXVI, S.183; Le Breton 1957, Fig. 9); (2) copper awls with rectangular section—compare older form in Gawra XVII, identical form in Sialk III_4 (Pl. 37, 19; cf. XCVIII, 6 and Ghirshman, 1938: LXXXIV S.240. (e) Pottery designs: (1) stars in the background of painted designs, Gawra XIIA (Pl. 55, D, 2; cf. CXXXVI, 280); (2) four-legged leopards, Gawra XII-XI (Pl. 57, A, 5; cf. CXXXV, 265; LXXXIII, c). (Similar leopards appear in Sialk III_{4-5} [Ghirshman, 1938, LXXX, B, 1]; birds, of dissimilar type, first appear in Gawra XII [Pl. 49, A, 2; Pl. 51, A, 5; cf. CXXXIV, 252]. McCown presents four identical Halaf parallels [1942, Fig. 11, 55, 90, 91, 95] and six Ubaid [ibid., Fig. 13, 38, 46, 127, 165, 168, 208]; two of these are of the same design [ibid., Fig. 13, 38; cf. Fig. 11, 91] and are not useful, leaving three Halaf and five Ubaid parallels. The latter are drawn from Gawra XIII and Ur Ubaid I [equated to Eridu XII and later; Oates, 1960, p. 41].) (f) Pottery shapes: ring-based bowls most common in Gawra XII, Susa A (Pls. 48, B, 1; 49, C, 1; cf. CXXIV and Le Breton, 1957, Fig. 7, 17, 21).

The general evidence suggests a dating of Ubaid 4 - Early Uruk for Giyan VC with relations to Susa A, Gawra XII-XI, and Sialk III_{4-5}.

Giyan VB - Ubaid 3 (Contenau and Ghirshman, 1935; cf. Tobler, 1950)

Giyan VB consists mainly of sherds found in four meters of fill below a building level at -13.50 meters. Parallels follow. (a) Metal objects: simple copper pins without heads, which first appear at -16.0 meters, compared to first copper of different shape in Gawra XVII, same shape in Sialk I_3 and II (p. 44; cf. XCVII, 5, 6 and Ghirshman, 1938, LII, 56, 57). (b) Seals: pyramidal round-faced stamp seal, Gawra XIII (Pl. 38, 45; cf. p. 178). (c) Pottery designs: McCown documents eight identical Ubaid parallels (1942, Fig. 13, 82, 85, 90, 115, 130, 158, 160, 170), of which three are also given in Halaf context (ibid., Fig. 13, 90, 82, 115; cf. Fig. 11, 53, 15, 50).

Two of the remaining five Ubaid parallels are from Gawra XIII, one from Gawra XV, and two from Arpachiya. McCown's Figure 13, 130, design may be found in Gawra XV used vertically (Tobler, 1950, CXLIX, 449), a more exact parallel than the one given in McCown's Figure 11, 18. Southern parallels include one from Ur Ubaid I (no. 160), which also occurs in Gawra XVI and Arpachiyah. Five identical parallels are offered for the Halaf period (ibid., Fig. 11, 15, 50, 51, 53, 89), three of which, as pointed out above, occur in Ubaid context as well. Two parallels are offered for Samarra, only the first of which is exclusively of that period (ibid., Fig. 12, 40, 43). A typical Dalma Ware design occurs in VB (Pl. 44, b, 6). Dalma Ware is found in the Lake Urmia basin. At the type site near Hasanlu, it was associated with an imported Ubaid bowl (Young, 1963) bearing a design known from Siabid (personal communication, F. R. Matson). The levels at both sites are dated by C-14 to about 4200 B.C. Impressed ware also is found at Dalma Tepe, Siabid, and basal Giyan (although it is not reported by the excavators). Sherds of this type occur only during this period, and provide an important link with the north.

On the basis of the relative strength of exclusive patterns (5 in Ubaid, 2 in Halaf, 1 in Samarra), the relative position below VC (Ubaid 4 - Early Uruk), and the other evidence, it may be concluded that VB dates properly to Ubaid 3 times.

Giyan VA - Halaf (Contenau and Ghirshman, 1935)

The lowest deposit at Giyan is related to the Halaf period by three designs (McCown, 1942, Fig. 11, 26, 28, 48) from Arpachiyah TT 6-9 and Gawra XIX and the N.E. Base. Only two designs link VA and Samarra (ibid., Fig. 12, 11, 28). There seems little basis, therefore, in view of the dating of the succeeding level to Ubaid 3 and the presence of Halaf parallels, for dating this level earlier than the later Halaf period. The almost total lack of any Samarran material at Giyan seems significant in view of its strength in the area at the time of Sialk I_{1-3} (see below). Samarran influence seems to have moved forcefully southward along the western Zagros through Khuzistan to Fars. Only the excavation of a site covering the periods between Tepe Sarab and Giyan VA can clarify the parallel situation in the central Zagros area.

Giyan VD - Giyan IV Gap (Contenau and Ghirshman, 1935)

The nature of the transition between Giyan V and IV remains obscure, owing to the mixed nature of the fill of VD as reported. McCown (1942, p. 48) has argued that a considerable gap exists between the two, representing the time of the Susa C - Sialk IV contact. D. H. Gordon (1947), on the other hand, has argued that no gap exists, but that the painting tradition continued into IV. This latter alternative is attractive in that this tradition probably did persist in the mountain area, to reappear in Susa D. The evidence is less than convincing, however, owing to the presence of the beveled-rim bowl site of Deshawar, which implies the presence of an Uruk stage in the sequence. Indeed, sherds of beveled-rim bowls have been picked up at Giyan itself (University Museum collection). The only excavated evidence at Giyan which might indicate this period consists of the two cylinder seals in VD already mentioned and a four-lugged vessel from an indeterminate level of VD (Pl. 68, upper right) which is comparable to one from Susa Cb (Le Breton, 1957, Fig. 11, 29) which McCown compared to an E.D. II form but which Delougaz (1952) says is unreliable chronologically. Thus, there is nothing positive by which a Jamdat Nasr period occupation can be demonstrated. Given the evident mixture of II, IV, and VD sherds in these levels, Gordon's arguments for a stylistic continuum are insufficient to prove the point.

Giyan IV (Contenau and Ghirshman, 1935)

Since there is an apparent stylistic shift in the painted pottery of IV from naturalistic to geometric design, paralleling a similar shift at Susa in D period, it is possible to analyze the graves into typological groups without regard to their absolute depths (meaningless measurements in the absence of a knowledge of the contours of the surface from which they were dug). In such an analysis three major divisions emerge which, interestingly enough, turn out to have an ascending order of average depth. These groups, which differ from those proposed by Vanden Berghe (1956, p. 51), are: IVA, graves (the term "graves" is used here for simple inhumations, "tombs" for burial structures) 119, 117, 116, 114, and 113, -9.50 to -8.20 m., with terminal graves 111, 109, and probably 118 at -7.80 m.; IVB, graves 110, 108, and 102, -7.80 to -7.50 m., and graves of Tepe Djamshidi IV; IVC, graves 115, 112, 107, 105, 103, 101 (reported in period III), -8.30 to -7.50 m., Tepe Djamshidi IV grave 15, with terminal graves 106 and 100 (reported in period III), -7.60 to -7.50 m., and Djamshidi III tombs 8, 9, and 10, and graves 6 and 7 (which lack tripods but contain associated painted flat-bottomed bowls).

The graves of IVA lack all metal objects, and contain at least one flat-bottomed bowl of burnished red ware and one or more shouldered vessels with triple "bird comb" designs painted in black in a decorative zone around the shoulder. These triple "bird comb" motifs are separated horizontally by triangle, circle, or zigzag elements. The decorative zone is usually bordered by two bands of diagonal or wavy lines above and one below. The rim is commonly painted black, and bases graduate from flat to rounded. The terminal graves of the group show some degeneration in design, in that the "bird comb" has been reduced from three to two elements. One terminal grave—109—contains a vessel with a vertical "tooth" pattern (Pl. 31, 109, 1) found at Susa in closely comparable form in De (Le Breton, 1957, Fig. 35, 17), where it occurs between panels of vertical lines between an upper wavy line border and a lower border of a single stripe. The concept of the "tooth" pattern in simpler form begins in Dc and continues in Dd (Le Breton, 1957, Pl. XXVI, 14, and Fig. 35, 12). Shapes are related but not identical. Ridges around vessel shoulders along with flaring rims provide another link (cf. Pl. 32, 113, 1 and 2; Le Breton, 1957, Fig. 35, 12, etc.). Since De is dated to "Proto-Imperial" or post-Early Dynastic, the evidence suggests that group IVA dates mainly to E.D. III in Mesopotamian terms.

In the Giyan IVB grave group, the shift to geometric patterns is almost complete with crosshatched rhomboids, black-filled small tooth patterns (Pl. 31, 110, 2), and bands of crosses at the shoulder carination (Pl. 32, 115, 3). Shapes now tend to be taller proportionally, and have a flare at the lower part of the body. The squat shapes of Djamshidi IV seem to link to those of grave 118 at Giyan at the end of IVA and with those of IVB which carry new patterns. Some vases still retain the decorative zone without the "bird comb" element (Pl. 31, 108, 7; Pl. 102, 1 and 2; Pl. 80, 16, 1; Pl. 79, 11, 1). These vessels have parallels at Susa (Pl. 102, 1 and 2; cf. Le Breton, 1957, Fig. 35, 15), but are, unfortunately, unstratified at that site. Vanden Berghe interprets some of these designs as degenerate renditions of the earlier eagle patterns from Giyan (1956, pp. 50-51). The shapes, painted designs, and placement of design appear in the Painted Orange Ware of Hasanlu VII, dated about 2100 B.C. by C-14. The forms should be somewhat older at Giyan. An Akkadian dating for Giyan IVB would accommodate the suggested E.D. III dating of IVA and the C-14 dating of related material at Hasanlu. The combined evidence indicates a spread of basic forms and style northward from Elam to the southern shore of Lake Urmia. It is important for future comparative purposes to note the occurrence in IVB of a vessel of red and black polychrome combined with incision (Pl. 31, 110, 1). Schaeffer points out (1948, p. 463) that the stemmed goblets with single loop handles, reported from grave 108, are unknown elsewhere in the Near East before 2000 B.C., thus suggesting that group IVB may date in part to that time. This conclusion is further supported by a cylinder seal from grave 102 which, he says, is paralleled at Ras Shamra and Çatal Hüyük in Syria at approximately 2000 B.C. (Schaeffer, 1948, p. 462). Metal forms which now appear in the graves can be paralleled elsewhere in Akkadian or Ur III levels. A socketed ax head, a flat tanged blade with single rivet, and copper toggle pins find parallels in 'Amuq J (Braidwood and Braidwood, 1960, Fig. 351, 9, 6, 3, and 4), Gawra VI (Speiser, 1935, XLCIII, 3; XLIX, 1; XL, 8), Tell Brak Sargonid (Mallowan, 1947, XXXI, 11, 3-5), Tell Billa V (Speiser, 1933, p. 21; Levy and Burke, 1959, Table 1, p. 9). Annular bracelets occur in Gawra VI (Speiser, 1935, L, 12), as do straight pins with decorated segmented heads (ibid., L, 11). A unique socketed spearhead (Pl. 31, 110, 5) has related types at Chagar Bazar lower 1, Mishrifé grave 1, Baghouz, and Ras Shamra (Schaeffer, 1948, p. 463) dating to 2100-1900 B.C.

The final group of graves—IVC—is characterized by vessels with bulging bodies and single ridges around the necks. Naturalistic patterns are now totally replaced by simple geometric patterns. Sometimes a strap handle and/or spout is added to the basic form. Flat-bottomed burnished red bowls continue from IVA. The general impression is one of slowly evolving shapes with a gradual shift in design style. The only possibly useful object correlations are deep tripod pots in terminal graves 106 and 100, double-ended cast bronze bells, ribbed copper buttons, single roll-headed pins, and a bent-tang spearhead. The concept of deep tripod pots appears for the first time in Troy III, El Hammam, and Til Barsib (Tell Ahmar) between 2100-1900 B.C. (Schaeffer, 1948, Figs. 166, 79, and 81). These shapes represent the first appearance of a comparable vessel form, but are not identical. Of the two cast bells attributed to IVC, one is from mixed IV-II fill (Pl. 37, 10) and the other is from grave 105 (Pl. 30), which consists only of a vase and no body and which may, therefore, be no grave at all. The fact that the nearest parallels for three-dimensional open-work bronze casting in the Caucasus and Talish areas all date later than the middle second millennium casts further doubt on their dating. The single roll-headed pin type (Pl. 79, 15) has parallels in Gawra VII and VI (Speiser, 1935, LXXXII, 14, 16) and in 'Amuq J (Braidwood and Braidwood, 1960, Fig. 351, 1 and 2). The form later becomes common in the Talish and Caucasus areas (Schaeffer, 1948, Fig. 217, 13; Fig. 236; Fig. 281, 9; Fig. 296, 16; Fig. 303, 3, 8) as well as at Shah Tepe III (ibid., Fig. 318, 11) and Sialk B (ibid., Fig. 254, 12). Bent-tang spearheads (Pl. 32, T.112, 3) have a wide geographic and temporal occurrence (Cyprus, Ras Shamra, Ahmar, Tarsus, Megiddo, Gaza, Kara Hasan-Carchemish, Alaca, Georgia, Hissar, Marlik, and Susa—Schaeffer, 1948, Figs. 199, 197, 82, 172, 145, 121, 80, 179, 293, 239; Negahban, 1962b, Fig. 19; Susa—Le Breton, 1957, Fig. 41, 1). The later forms are specialized in various ways, and commonly have buttons on the end of the bent tang. The Susa spearhead is the simplest, typologically speaking, and the oldest, dating not later than Dc or Early Dynastic, according to Le Breton (1957, p. 119). The forms most nearly similar to Giyan after Susa are those of Georgia and Kara Hasan-Carchemish, which are dated by Schaeffer to between 2000 and 1850 and between 2300 and 2000 B.C. respectively. The Hissar IIIC spearheads are distinctly more developed in type. The copper square-ribbed buttons are found in grave 107 (Pl. 31, 107, 8) and Djamshidi tomb 10 (ibid., Pl. 78). Elsewhere these buttons are known only in later context: Maralyn Deresi (Caucasus), Tulu and Djonii (Talish), and Hasanlu IV (Schaeffer, 1948, Fig. 275, 13; Fig. 236, 15; Fig. 233, 31; Hasanlu unpublished). The copper button, the single roll-headed pin, and the bent-tang spearhead all indicate a relationship with the bronze-using stone cist tomb cultures of northwestern Iran of the late second and early first millennia B.C. It is not without significance that a major innovation in burial custom—the building of cist tombs—appears at this moment at Giyan, since the same custom makes its appearance at scattered points across northern Mesopotamia, often associated with bent-tang spearheads and pedestal bowls (e.g., Tell Ahmar, Kara Hasan-Carchemish). At Giyan, the tombs are rare, and it is not until after 1000 B.C. that a full-scale cultural pattern connected with such tombs establishes itself in the area.

The majority of the parallels drawn for the terminal IVC materials fall within a range of from about 2100 to about 1900 B.C. Since IVC follows immediately upon IVB, a date of perhaps 2000-1900 or 1800 would seem most acceptable (Schaeffer, 1948, p. 464, argues that all of period IV should date between 2000 and 1800 B.C.). Tepe Djamshidi III graves 3, 4, and 5 closely follow Giyan IVC and provide a terminal date for the series through the presence in grave 3 of a haematite cylinder seal of First Dynasty of Babylon type, about 1750 B.C.

TEPE SIALK

Sialk I_{1-3} - Hassuna IV-V (Ghirshman, 1938; cf. Lloyd and Safar, 1945)

Sialk I_{1-3} is stylistically related to Hassuna IV-V—the Hassuna-Samarran period—through design (but not shape) parallels. Among these are: crosshatched (XL, A, 2; cf. Fig. 11, 3, 24) or chevron (XL, D, 7; cf. Fig. 1, 7, 10) borders; hanging short lines (XL, A, 4; cf. Fig. 17, 19); hanging crosshatched triangles (XL, A, 3; cf. Fig. 11, 2, 4); hanging single-line triangles (XL, B, 8; cf. Fig. 13, 11, 12, 14); a multiple-line zigzag zone (XL, D, 3, 16; XLI, A, 9; cf. Fig. 12, 15); a row of crosshatched triangles parallel but below the rim (XL, A, 4; cf. Fig. 11, 10); rows of solid triangles one above another (XL, D, 14; cf. Fig. 13, 16, 22; Fig. 14, 13); the use of large solid dots (XL, C, 5; cf. Fig. 12, 11, 13, 19, 22; Fig. 17, 6); the use of barred lines (XLII, D, 1; XLIV, B, 8; cf. Fig. 16, 12; Fig. 17, 1, 15). A rotating cross in the bottom of a bowl (XLIV, c, 14) betrays classic Samarran influence. Especially important is the use of hanging solid triangles around the rim (XLIII, B, 10, 14, 15, D, 7; XLIV, A, 11, B, 8, 12, D, 3), which are found also at Hajji Firuz and on two sherds of Hotu Cave Soft Ware (University Museum collection). The pottery at all three sites is burnished, straw tempered, and buff or red colored, showing a common technique of manufacture although with local shapes.

Sialk I_{4-5} - Halaf (Ghirshman, 1938; cf. Contenau and Ghirshman, 1935)

Typical Halaf grid patterns are present both at Sialk and in Giyan VA (XLVI, A, 12, C, 7, and so on; cf. Pl. 41, a, 5, b, 1, 6, and so on). A copper needle, projectile point, and coil show the presence of copper (also in I_3), known elsewhere from Halafian context at Arpachiyah (Mallowan, 1956, p. 2), Chagar Bazar 12 (Mallowan, 1936, p. 27), Tell Halaf (Oppenheim, 1931, p. 215). Earlier copper is now known from Çatal Hüyük in Anatolia. The use of red ocher in burials at Sialk is paralleled in the mass burials at Hajji Firuz (Young, 1962, p. 707) and the "Gazelle Mesolithic" of Belt Cave (Coon, 1951, p. 79).

Sialk II - Halaf - Ubaid 3 (Ghirshman, 1938; cf. Contenau and Ghirshman, 1935).

Several pottery shapes of Sialk II compare closely to those of Giyan VA: a deep beaker (XLV, S.1603; cf. Pl. 42, b, 7), a bowl with incurving rim (XLV, S.1402; cf. Pl. 42, a, 8), and possibly a bowl with a slightly everted rim (XLVII, D, 10; cf. Pl. 43, a). Halafian grid patterns occur at both sites (LI, D, 16; cf. Pl. 41, 13), as do parallel lines painted down the sides to the base of vessels (XLV, S.1394; cf. Pl. 42, 14). In support of a correlation with the Halaf period, McCown provides six parallels, four of which are exclusively Halafian (McCown, 1942, Fig. 11, 20, 80-82) and two of which occur also in Ubaid context (*ibid*., Fig. 11, 17, 22; cf. Fig. 13, 130, 84). Additional Ubaid parallels are given for an unstratified sherd (*ibid*., Fig. 13, 209) and a generalized zigzag pattern (*ibid*., Fig. 13, 126).

Sialk III - Ubaid 4 - Uruk (refer also to Giyan V discussion, above)

Sialk III_{1-3} follows almost immediately after Sialk II, and necessarily dates to Ubaid 4. With III_3 the red ocher burials end, and with III_{4-5} many cultural innovations occur indicating strong cultural influence from Mesopotamia. These innovations include: (1) the introduction of the potter's wheel, known in the Uruk period of Susa B and Gawra IX; (2) the introduction of the technique of casting copper, known already in the Halaf at Arpachiya, according to Mallowan (1956, p. 2), and in Gawra XII and Susa A; and (3) the appearance of stamp seals in quantity with obvious relationships to seals at Giyan and Gawra. Two similar patterns of quartered design occur at Gawra in the Ubaid period (Ghirshman, 1938, LXXXVI, S.231; cf. Tobler, 1950, CLVIII, 15; LXXXVI, S.259, S.117; cf. CLIX, 26). The presence of the potter's wheel and a socketed hoe with a parallel from Susa B (Ghirshman, 1938, LXXXIV, S.251; cf. Le Breton, 1957, Fig. 27, 1) seems to indicate that the Ubaid elements in Sialk III_{4-5} were in use in the Early Uruk period. Here then is additional evidence for the cultural lag from west to east, as already suggested in the discussion of Giyan VC. Sialk III_6 finds a specific link to the Middle Uruk period of Warka VII and Telloh in the form of a spouted jar (Ghirshman, 1938, LXIX, S.135; Perkins, 1949, pp. 100, 105, and Fig. 12, 10), whereas Sialk III_7 has a link with Tell Billa VII in the form of a stemmed, carinated chalice (Ghirshman, 1938, LXX, S.1770; cf. Speiser, 1933, XLIX, 3). The possibility of a slight gap between Sialk III_{7b} and IV is indicated by what seems to be an erosion surface between the two in the published section (Ghirshman, 1938, LIX).

TEPE HISSAR

Hissar IA - Sialk III_{1-3} (Schmidt, 1937; cf. Ghirshman, 1938)

Parallels follow. (a) Pottery shapes: flaring-sided (III, H.3446; cf. LXIII, S.369), vertical-sided (III, H.2046; cf. LXIV, S.227), and globular high ring-stand vessels (III, H.1522; cf. LXII, S.412). (b) Designs: vertical groups of lines on the ring stands (III, H.2446; cf. LXII, S.654).

The presence of stamp seals indicates IA is not earlier than III_{1-3}; the absence of wheel-made pottery, that it is not later.

Hissar IB - Sialk III_{4-5} (Schmidt, 1937; cf. Ghirshman, 1938)

Parallels follow. (a) Pottery shapes: slightly carinated cups (V, H.3464; cf. LXIV, S.248, III_4), flaring cups (IV, H.2091; cf. LXIV, S.1782, III_3), a high ring stand with nearly vertical walls (IV, H.4719 cf. LXVIII, S.174, III_5). (b) Designs: ibexes with stars encircled by their horns placed between unilateral ladders (V, H.3464; cf. LXXX, A, 12, $III_{4 \text{ or } 5}$), a horizontal chevron row over barred lines (IV, H.2060; cf. LXXVIII, C, 5, III_4), stacked birds (VI, DH 44, 10, 3; cf. LXXX, D, 5, III_{4-5}), horizontal snakes (V, DH 36, 14b; cf. LXXIX, B, 17, 18, III_{4-5}), rows of birds (VI, DH 34, 10, 31; cf. LXXIX, D, 19), rows of unjoined circles (IV, H.3066; cf. LXXX, B, 11, III_{4-5}), and rows of dancers (Schmidt, 1933, LXXXVIII, H d23; cf. LXXV, 1, 7, III_{4-5}). (c) Seals: round dome-shaped seal with perforated tab (XV, H.3829; cf. LXXXVI, S.232, III_4; cf. Susa B), a rectangular seal with perforated tab (XV, H.4708; cf. LXXXVI, S.246, III_5). (d) Metal objects: round conical-headed copper pins (XVI, H.2972, 3053 cf. LXXXIV, S.168, S.1774, III_4).

The appearance of wheel-made pottery occurs in IB and III_4. Nearly all Hissar designs occur at Sialk, but not vice versa.

Hissar IC - Sialk III_{6-7b}, IV (Schmidt, 1937; cf. Ghirshman, 1938)

Parallels follow. (a) Pottery shapes: carinated vessels on high ring stands with flaring rims (X, H.3052; cf. LXVII, S.1810, III_6) or nearly straight sides (IX, H.3046; cf. LXVII, S.69, III_6), chalice (X, H.4637 and XXII, H.4498; cf. XC, S.1689, IV), carinated bowl on high ring stand (IX, H.4527, XXV, H.5056; cf. XC, S.244, IV), small chalice of Gawra VII (X, H.802; cf. Speiser, 1935, LXV, 58). (b) Designs: two-legged leopards in "skid" position (VII, H.3366; cf. LXVII, S.137, III_6 and LXXXI, A, 15, III_7), extremely stylized leopards (VIII, H.5136; cf. LXXXI, C, 2, LXXXII,

C, 10, III_{7-7b}), painted jar with vertical patterns of unilateral ladders and wavy lines (XI, H.4695, H.3474; cf. XC, S.1681, IV). (c) Seals: use of the drill (XV, H.3428; cf. LXXXVI, S.129, III_6), two design parallels (XV, H.4450; cf. LXXXVI, S.1739, III_5; XV, H.3376; cf. LXXXVI, S.78), double button seals similar to one in Gawra XI (XV, H.3435, H.3726, and so on; cf. Tobler, 1950, CLX, 42). (d) Metal objects: splayed cast copper celt (XVI, H.4176; cf. XCV, S.535, IV), hammered copper knife blade (XVI, H.3483; cf. LXXXV, S.127, S.1735, III_5, and XCV, S.76, IV)—similar blades appear first in Gawra VI (Speiser, 1935, XLIX, 1)—hemispherical-headed pins (XVI, H.4495; cf. LXXXIV, S.1774, III_5).

Contacts are strongest during Sialk III_6, after which the chalices of the two sites diverge in type largely through the introduction of new types at Sialk. Hissar IC should, therefore, begin in Late Uruk times and, on the basis of some parallels with Sialk IV, extend into the Jamdat Nasr period. Thus, in the extreme northeast, the earlier painted pottery tradition persisted long after its demise in the west. The chalice parallels at Billa and Gawra which are clearly Iranian in origin also indicate the later persistence of the painting tradition in the north. Additional evidence for the later dating of Hissar IC comes from Ward (1954, pp. 137-38), who points to the presence of thin black polished ware at Chashmi Ali (near Teheran) associated with Hissar IC materials. He compares this to the Alishar Chalcolithic black ware (3000-2600 B.C.; Lloyd, 1956) and to the reported black ware from Early Dynastic Mesopotamia.

Hissar II - Shah Tepe III-IIB - E.D. I-III (Schmidt, 1937; cf. Arne, 1945)*

Hissar IIB may be linked to the border of Shah Tepe III and IIB by parallels. (a) Pottery shapes: low, slightly carinated jars (XXVI, H.1822; cf. Fig. 301b) and cylindrical fruit-stand stems without thickening at the top (XXV, H.5119; Arne was unable to reconstruct complete vessels, p. 238). (b) Pottery decoration: studded surfaces (XXVI, H.4783; cf. Fig. 301a). (c) Beads: triangular-shaped (LXVIII, H.2107; cf. Fig. 611b, III). (These also occur in the jewelry hoard of Sialk IV [LXVIII, H.2107; cf. Ghirshman, 1938, XXX, 1] along with teardrop-shaped beads [XXXII, H.2187; cf. Ghirshman, 1938, XXX, 1]. The date of this hoard has been questioned above as being probably Early Dynastic. The beads at Shah

*The materials of Hissar II and III and sites in the south need more study than has been possible here. The following material may be taken as a beginning in their reanalysis.

Tepe, Hissar, and Sialk are all of lapis lazuli. Square beads with the corners pierced diagonally have a range of from Jamdat Nasr to E.D. II in Mesopotamia [Schmidt, 1933, CVIII, H.1202; cf. McCown, 1942, p. 51, Fig. 14].) (d) Metal objects: double-spiral-headed pins (XXIX, H.4856; cf. Ghirshman, 1938, XCV, S.1602e, IV; cf. Lloyd, 1956, pp. 56-57).

At Sialk, the date of the pins is in question (see above). In Anatolia, where they are more reliably stratified, they date to 2600-2300 B.C. In summary, the scanty evidence suggests an Early Dynastic II-III date for Hissar IIB on the basis of the correlation with Shah Tepe (the beginning of Shah Tepe IIB is dated on various evidence by the excavator to about 2700-2600 B.C., particularly through parallels with stemmed fruit bowls of the Alishar Chalcolithic and side-spouted biconical jugs from Yortan Kelembo; Arne, 1945, p. 242). Period IIA at Hissar would then cover later Jamdat Nasr and E.D. I (i.e., late Sialk IV and perhaps later).

Hissar IIIB (Schmidt, 1937)

Scattered parallels for objects in Hissar IIIB may be drawn. (a) Pottery shapes: flat-bottomed bowls (XXXVIII, H.4227; cf. Arne, 1945, Fig. 364, Shah IIB), trough spouts (XXXVII, H.5040; cf. *ibid*., Fig. 223, IIB), spouted pot (XXXVIII, H.5089; cf. *ibid*., Fig. 249, IIB), rim spout (XXXVIII, H.4970; cf. Fig. 366, IIB). (b) Pottery decoration: pattern burnishing (XXXVII, H.3987, H.3841; cf. *ibid*., Figs. 173, 266, and so on, IIB). (c) Seals: a cylinder seal bearing a scene of groom and chariot has been compared to Jamdat Nasr types (Schmidt, 1937, p. 309), but almost the same scene appears in seals of Hasanlu IV, 1000-800 B.C. (cf. *Archaeology* 16 (1963): 132). (d) Beads: gold sheet beads with central tube may be compared with similar beads from Ur dating from E.D. III to Ur III (LXVI, H.2360-61; cf. Woolley, 1934, Fig. 70, p. 371, types 16, 19); amulet beads occur in E.D. III, Akkadian, and rarely in Ur III context at Ur (Figs. 133-34; cf. Woolley, 1934, p. 375). (e) Metal objects: a copper blade with midrib and simple bent tang without button on the end may be compared to similar blades with two slots which occur in Troy III, Tarsus E.B. III, Alaca (Schaeffer, 1948, Figs. 168, 173, 176); bent-tang blades *with* buttons on the ends appear in Cyprus at the end of Early Cypriote period (Pls. L, H.2023, H.2024, LI, H.3855; cf. *ibid*., Fig. 199); cast shaft-hole ax-adz (XLIV, H.3577, LII, H.2710; range from Hissar III to Shalmaneser II; cf. Deshayes, 1960, type A2, 116); chisels

(LII, H.3562; cf. Speiser, 1935, LXXXII, 2, Gawra VIII-III; Woolley, 1934, type 1, Pl. 229, E.D. III); curved copper ornament (XLVI, H.2810; cf. Contenau and Ghirshman, 1935, Pl. 32, T.112, 4, Giyan IVC). embossed copper strip (LIV, H.4112; cf. ibid., Pl. 30, T.104, 1, Giyan IVB-C). (f) Stone: oval arrowheads (XLIII, H.1800, H.1884; cf. Speiser, 1935, XXXVIII a 13-16, Gawra VII-III).

The general range of dates involved in these Hissar IIIB parallels is from Early Dynastic III to the Third Dynasty of Ur. Since Hissar IIIA must be accommodated before IIIB and after IIB (E.D. II-III), IIIA would seem to belong to the first half of this time, or roughly to the Akkadian period. This position fits well for the typological position of the simple bent-tang blade without ridge-stop or button. The blade (Schmidt, 1933, CIII, H.1040; 1937, p. 119) falls typologically between the Susa Dc blade (E.D. III or earlier) and the Giyan IVC blade (Ur III), which has a slight ridge-stop (cf. Le Breton, 1957, Fig. 41, 1; Contenau and Ghirshman, 1935, Pl. 32, T.112: 3). The period Hissar IIIB would then seem to fall approximately in the early part of the Third Dynasty of Ur. Such a position is supported by the C-14 date for comparable material at Yarim Tepe: 2166±249 B.C. (P-508).

Hissar IIIC (Schmidt, 1937)

Parallels with other sites follow. (a) Pottery shapes: a number of shapes provide parallels with Shah Tepe IIa - cylindrical jar (XLIII, H.3313; cf. Arne, 1945, Fig. 416); concave-sided, flat-bottomed bowl (XLII, H.3493; cf. ibid., Fig. 368); side-spouted jar (XLI, H.4296; cf. Fig. 394); globular jar (XLI, H.3490; cf. ibid., Figs. 381, 395); single-handled pot (XLI, H.5235; cf. ibid., Fig. 407); canteen jar (XL, H.4219; cf. Fig. 408). (b) Pottery decoration: appliqué snake and lug handles on canteen jar (XL, H.3522; cf. Fig. 409). (c) Beads: etched carnelian (XXXV; cf. Arne, 1945, Fig. 612b, IIa; Woolley, 1934, p. 374, E.D. III - Ur III); the main bead types of IIIC, which include pentagonal (LXVI, H.3216), oval (LXVIII, H.3594), and lenticular (LXVII, H.3591, H.3593) banded agate types parallel beads of "Second Dynasty" or Ur III context at Ur (as shown by a reanalysis of the University Museum Ur collection in 1955, which used pottery and seal evidence for the revision of assigned grave periods; the materials are on exhibition but the argument is as yet unpublished); amber beads first appear (possibly traded from the Aegean). (d) Stone: alabaster columns (LIX, H.3523, H.2248; cf.

Arne, 1945, Fig. 586, IIa). (e) Metal objects: copper blades with ridge-stopped bent tangs and buttons occur at Ras Shamra, 2200 and 1900 B.C. (LI, H. 3230, H. 3242; cf. Schaeffer, 1948, Fig. 55); stiletto lances are related to types found at Tell Ahmar - Til Barsib and Soli (near Mersin), which date to 2200-1900 B.C. (L, H.3229, 3231; cf. *ibid*., Figs. 82, 174); bidents might perhaps be compared to tridents of post-Akkadian date at Ur (Woolley, 1934, PG 1846, 1850).

In general, the metal parallels suggest a date in the range of 2200-1900 B.C. The correlation of IIIC and Shah Tepe IIa^1 supports a date of 2000-1800 B.C. based on the independent evidence used by the excavator of that site for dating IIa^1 (Arne, 1945, pp. 307 ff.). At the present time there seems little sound evidence in support of a terminal date for IIIC later than 1900 or at most 1800 B.C., although such a possibility cannot be ruled out.

Bakun BII - Giyan VB (McCown, 1942; cf. Contenau and Ghirshman, 1935)

On typological grounds, Bakun BI still appears to be the oldest assemblage in Fars. The one available C-14 date is 4220 ± 83 B.C. (P-438). This plain ware assemblage is overlaid by the painted ware of Bakun BII. Bakun BII designs tend toward running horizontal patterns (McCown, 1942, Fig. 10, 32, 33, 40, 49; Fig. 11, 19, 29, 44, 47, 56, 60, 132; Fig. 12, 26, 55, 72, 77, 109-13) and are related to those of Giyan VB (*ibid*., Fig. 11, 29; cf. Pl. 44, 2, b; Fig. 11, 47; cf. Pl. 43, 3, c, d and Pl. 44, 4, d; Fig. 11, 60; cf. Pl. 47, 4, d; Fig. 12, 77; cf. Pls. 44 [first animals appear] and 47, 2, d [metopes and animals]). Numerous parallels also occur in Arpachiyah TT 6-10 and Sialk II_2 - III_1 (McCown, 1942, Figs. 10-12). This BII culture is followed after another hiatus (McCown, 1942, p. 23) by the Bakun AI culture (Langsdorf and McCown, 1942, Pl. 22, 1, 6; Pl. 31, 4; Pl. 32, 10; Pl. 33, 4; Pl. 36, 4; Pl. 38, 25; Pl. 42, 5, 9; Pl. 44, 7; Pl. 45, 2; Pl. 47, 7, 9; Pl. 48, 12, 13, 15; Pl. 49, 8, 11; Pl. 51, 9; Pl. 53, 13; Pl. 59, 13; Pl. 62, 7; Pl. 67, 4, 5, 7; Pl. 68, 1; Pl. 69, 4, 13, 15; Pl. 71, 7; Pl. 72, 4, 18; Pl. 73, 1, 4, 7, 15; Pl. 76, 4, 15, 16; Pl. 78, 2, 3, 4, 7, 8, 25-28). Elements such as human figures, fish, and ibexes are present which have earlier appeared in Susiana b-c material (Le Breton, 1957, Fig. 6, 31, 33, 38). In general the elaborate style of AI is a first stage of the Ubaid 4- Bakun AIII culture. Shapes include deep bowls with flaring sides and short-necked jars of Ubaid 3 type (Langsdorf and McCown, 1942: Pl. 31, 4 and 44; cf. Oates, 1960, type 11b).

Gap Ia - Bakun BII-AI (Egami and Sono, 1962; cf. Langsdorf and McCown, 1942)

The available information of the ceramics of Tall-i-Gap Ia (levels 17-16) may be reconstructed from the report as follows. (a) Shapes: bowls with flaring sides and ring bases (Fig. 31, 1) or flattened bases (Fig. 26, 8; Fig. 29, 5; Fig. 30, 4; Fig. 31, 5, 6); vases with straight flaring sides (Fig. 24, 7) or with slightly everted rims (Fig. 24, 8); bowls with almost vertical sides (Fig. 21, 2; Fig. 22, 7; Fig. 23, 4, 5, 8); short-necked jars (Fig. 11, 2; Fig. 25, 2) and other vessels (Fig. 11, 6; Fig. 17, 3, 5). (b) Designs: (Egami and Sono, 1962, table 1, designs IVb, V, VI, VII, VIIIb, IXa, IXe, Xa, Xc, Xd, XIf, XIIe, XIII, XIVe, XV, XVIa, XVII, XVIII, and Pl 14, 4; Pl. 15, 4; Pl. 19, 3; Pl. 21, 5; Pl. 24, 5-8; Pl. 25, 1; Pl. 29, 4; Pl. 32B, 1, 3; Pl. 32A, 2, 3, 5, 10; Pl. 34B, 3, 5, 6; Pl. 34A, 3, 6, 11; Pl. 36B, 1, 2, 5, 6; Pl. 37B, 3-6; Pl. 37A, 6, 7; Pl. 38B, 2, 6; Pl. 39B, 2, 7, 9, 10; Pl. 39A, 9, 12). The Ia style, which continues through IIb_1 (levels 9-7) is characterized by continuous horizontal patterns set between two or more parallel lines which are often bordered by wider stripes. The rectilinear design elements stress cross-hatched triangles, lozenges, squares, and rectangles. Animals, birds, and human beings are rarely represented. In 1b (levels 15-13) the quartered circle pattern is added (ibid., Pl. XXXIXA, 1-3), whereas in IIb_1 rows of birds appear (ibid., Pl. XXXVIB, 4). Of the 1a designs, at least 8 may be found in Bakun BII (ibid., design V; cf. McCown, 1942, Fig. 11, 29; Xd cf. 11, 132; Xc cf. 10, 33; Pl. XXIV, 8 cf. 10, 32; Fig. 23, 3 cf. 11, 19; 29, 5 cf. 12, 72; Pl. XXIV, 7 cf. 21, 12; Pl. XXXIIB, 1 cf. 12, 77; Pl. XXXIIA: 3 cf. 12, 26) and 9 in Bakun AI (Egami and Sono, 1962, table 1, design IVb cf. Langsdorf and McCown, 1942, Pl. 33, 4; Pl. 38, 25; Pl. 48, 13; Pl. 76, 16; V cf. Pl. 49, 9; VII cf. Pl. 49, 11; Xa cf. Pl. 53, 13; XIII cf. Pl. 67, 4; Pl. 76, 9; XIVa cf. Pl. 45, 2; Pl. XXXIXB, 7 cf. Pl. 38, 25; Pl. XXXVIIB, 3 cf. Pl. 31, 4; Pl. XXXVIB, 1 cf. Pl. 69, 4). Gap 1a would appear to fill the Bakun BII—AI hiatus. It has a C-14 date of 4096 ± 175 B.C. (Location: GAT-1/17). Pottery spindle whorls provide a further specific parallel to Sialk II (Egami and Sono, 1962, Pl. XL, 12, 13; cf. Ghirshman 1938, Pl. LII, 1, 4).

Gap IIb_1 - Bakun AIII - Susa A

By the period of Gap IIb_1 (levels 9-7) the 1a style has been replaced by a style using the contrast of broad and narrow lines for effect (e.g.,

Egami and Sono, 1962, Pl. XXIII, 2), triangular patterns (ibid., Pl. XXXIIIB, 3; Fig. 24, 9), and goats with sweeping horns (ibid., Pl. XXXVB, 1). Parallels are with Bakun AIII (ibid., Pl. XXXIXA, 5 cf. Langsdorf and McCown, 1942, Pl. 30, 1; Pl. XXXIXB, 12 cf. Pl. 37, 6; Pl. XXXVB, 1 cf. Pl. 69, 16 and Pl. 73, 8; Pl. XXXIIIB, 3 cf. Pl. 57, 13 and Pl. 58, 2; Pl. XXXIIIB, 4 cf. Pl. 25, 25). Short spouts appear in IIb_2 (levels 6-5); (Egami and Sono, 1962, Pl. XXIX, 8, 10 cf. Langsdorf and McCown, 1942, Pl. 15, 6), and there is an increase of deep bowls with curved sides and tall drinking vessels with ring bases (Egami and Sono, 1962, Fig. 28, 4 and Fig. 12, 5). McCown (1942, pp. 25-26, Fig. 10 and notes) has shown that in part Bakun AIII overlaps Susa A but that it is also contemporary with Sialk III_{4-5} with increasing design (but not shape) similarity with Sialk III_{6-7b}. The ceramic evidence, therefore, suggests that the development began in Ubaid 4 times (i.e., Susa A) and ran into the Uruk period (i.e., Sialk III_{4-7b}). Such a dating would fit the thesis of a local florescence in painting based on the Ubaid tradition in general, but occurring somewhat later than the main body of that tradition in a slightly marginal area. Other objects provide some support for this idea. Sling stones occur in Gawra XI (Langsdorf and McCown, 1942, Pl. 85, 6, 7 cf. Tobler, 1950, Pl. CLXXXI, 95); perforated stone sledge hammers occur in Gawra XI and XII (Langsdorf and McCown, 1942, Pl. 84, 1 cf. Pl. CLXXVIII, 42, 43), while similar mace heads are in Gawra XII (ibid., Pl. 84, 19, 20 cf. Pl. CLXXVII, 33, 34). Lapis lazuli first appears in Sialk III (Ghirshman, 1938, p. 56) and Gawra X (Tobler, 1950, pp. 95-96). It occurs in Bakun AIII in the form of beads (Langsdorf and McCown, 1942, Pl. 84, 11, 15, 17). Alabaster vessels, common in Bakun A, first appear in Sialk III_5 (Ghirshman, 1938, Pl. LXXXV, S. 1799). The sharp profiles and flaring rims recall the stone vessels from the "Jamdat Nasr" graves at Ur (Langsdorf and McCown, 1942, Pl. 81, 11 cf. Woolley, 1956, Pl. 66, J.N. 44; Pl. 81, 12 cf. Pl. 67, J.N. 62; Pl. 81, 1 cf. Pl. 66, J.N. 3). Stamp seals from Bakun A show three traits of special interest: (1) Scalloped edges as seen in Giyan VC (Schmidt, 1939, Fig. 93, TBA 539 cf. Contenau and Ghirshman, 1935, Pl. 35, 7, 8; Langsdorf and McCown, 1942, Pl. 8, 12 cf. Egami and Masuda, 1962, Pl. 14, 1) and Gawra XIA (Tobler, 1950, Pl. CLX, 31). (2) The "carving" technique which accompanies scalloped edges. (3) The use of a border of radial lines as a frame, found elsewhere only in Susa A (Schmidt, 1939, Fig. 93: TBA 501, 474 cf. Le Breton, 1957, Fig. 8, 5, 9). One shape and design parallel links Bakun A and

Susa A (Schmidt, 1939, Fig. 93, TBA 412 cf. Le Breton, 1957, Fig. 8, 5); a second shape parallel links Bakun A, Giyan VC, and Susa B (Langsdorf and McCown, 1942, Pl. 81, 17 cf. Contenau and Ghirshman, 1935, Pl. 35, 3 cf. Le Breton, 1957, Fig. 15, 1). Still a third occurs in these three contexts and Gawra XIA (ibid., Pl. 81, 29 cf. Pl. 35, 6 cf. Fig. 15, 9, 11; cf. Tobler, 1950, Pl. CLVIII, 10). The parallels to Gawra XIA and Susa are especially important in view of the late Sialk III parallels of design as indicating the later persistence of the Bakun assemblage.

The metal evidence is less conclusive. A hammered copper blade from AIV finds inexact parallels in Sialk III_{2-5} (Schmidt, 1939, Fig. 92, TBA 288 cf. Ghirshman, 1938, Pl. LXXXV, S. 127, S. 312, S. 1735) and Hissar IC (Schmidt, 1937, Pl. XVI, H. 3483, H. 3408). A needle from Bakun AI may be compared to examples from Susa A, Sialk III_1, and Hissar IB (Schmidt, 1939, Fig. 92, TBA 35 cf. Le Breton, 1957, Fig. 9 cf. Ghirshman, 1938, Pl. LXXXIV, S. 1408; cf. Schmidt, 1937, Pl. XVI, H. 3469). A rectangular-section awl is perhaps comparable to those from Giyan VC, Sialk III_4, and Hissar IB (Schmidt, 1939, Fig. 92, TBA 152 cf. Contenau and Ghirshman, 1935, Pl. 37, 19 cf. Ghirshman, 1938, Pl. LXXXIV, S. 240 cf. Schmidt 1937, Pl. XVI, H. 3658). These comparisons all lie in the Ubaid 4 - Early Uruk period.

Following this material at Tall-i-Gap are the levels (4-1) of period IIc the painted pottery of which shows that this tradition continued on into the Uruk period and was not terminated by the red wares of Bakun AV which must be even later in date.

Mushki - Djarii B - Sialk III_{1-3} (Vanden Berghe, 1952a; cf. Ghirshman, 1938)

Related to this Bakun-Gap painted ware are the sherds from Mushki and Djarii B reported by Vanden Berghe (1954a, pp. 400-401; 1959, p. 42). The material at the two sites is contemporary, and it is said to have been found at the bottom of more than ten sites in the area. It is suggested that it precedes Bakun-Gap type material (Vanden Berghe, 1954a, p. 402), although the exact details are unpublished, making it impossible to see what phase of the Bakun-Gap sequence is involved. Stylistically, the designs point to contacts with Sialk III (but see Vanden Berghe, 1954b, who argues for Sialk I): scale patterns first appear in III_1 (Fig. 28, 18 cf. Pl. LXXVIA, 1, 2, 7); curlicues on patterns, in III_1 (Fig. 28, 19 cf.

Pl. LXXVIB, 11, 21, 22); negative zigzags, in III$_1$ (Vanden Berghe, 1952a, Fig. 28, 3 cf. Pl. LXXVIA, 8, d, 1); unilateral ladder, in III$_{2-3}$ (Fig. 28, 14; cf. Pl. XXVIIC, 11); line and dot constructions, III$_4$ (Fig. 28, 18 cf. Pl. LXIV, S. 248). Running horizontal patterns bordered by two or three lines begin to appear in Sialk II, but are common in III. If the Mushki-Djarii B material underlies Bakun BII material which has been related to Giyan VB, the Mushki material might well be equal in time to Sialk II and Giyan VA (i.e., late Halaf and Ubaid 3), forming a link between the earlier Samarran style with its horizontal patterns and running designs and the later Sialk III style by way of Fars. On present evidence the question must be left open.

Kaftari and Qal'eh Cultures

Following the Bakun-Gap sequence is a further sequence established at three sites (Vanden Berghe, 1954a and b, 1959). The first two cultures seem to predate 2000 B.C.: the Kaftari culture (Tall-i-Shogha III, the deepest layer, Vanden Berghe, 1954a, p. 403; 1959, Pl. 51) and the Qal'eh culture (Tall-i-Shogha II; Tall-i-Taimuran IV; Tall-i-Qal'eh II; *ibid*., Pls. 52, 53, 57). The Qal'eh culture may tentatively be dated to the late third millennium stylistically. Its characteristic patterns of wavy lines occur prominently on vessels of Susa Dc to post-D (Le Breton, 1957, Fig. 35, 7-11, 14, 15, 17). Other elements are crosshatched fish (Susa Dd cachette, *ibid*., Fig. 40) and swimming birds (Susa D, *ibid*., Fig. 35, 15; and tomb 102, Giyan IVB; see text p. 25). Parallels in shape include large bowls with ring bases and flat rims found in Susa De (*ibid*., Fig. 35, 10), Badhora tomb 12 (Contenau and Ghirshman, 1935, Pl. 82) and Djamshidi II, tomb 1 (*ibid*., Pl. 73); globular jars with short necks as seen in Susa D, Giyan IVB, tomb 102. A theriomorphic bird vessel on a stemmed foot has some points in common with another from E.D. II context (Delougaz, 1952, Pl. 94a). In general the evidence would seem to indicate the period between E.D. III and 2000 B.C. for the Qal'eh culture.

Underlying the Qal'eh wares are the sherds assigned to the Kaftari culture, which should thus be about E.D. III or earlier, but not as early as the terminal Bakun-Gap tradition of the Uruk period. This Jamdat Nasr—E.D. I-II range of the Kaftari culture would be equivalent to the Sialk IV and Hissar II period, which, as we have seen, is poorly known in Iran. The type of goblet base (Vanden Berghe, 1959, Pl. 51a, 2a and 2b), the checkerboard, and crosshatched bands—all occur in Sialk IV as surviving elements of the older painting tradition, but few final conclusions can be drawn from such evidence.

Nokhodi I-II

At about the same time as the Kaftari culture (which contains red ware along with the painted) another red and gray ware assemblage appears at Tall-i-Nokhodi (Goff, 1963, 1964). A few tentative parallels may be pointed out. Carinated drinking vessels with loop handles in burnished red ware occur in tombs 118 and 119 of Giyan IVA (Contenau and Ghirshman, 1935, Pls. 33, 34 cf. Goff, 1964, Fig. 7, 7), where they seem to be at the end rather than the beginning of a development. Loop handles on vessels first appear in Shah Tepe IIa_1 in coarse ware, and are dated to about 2000 B.C. (Arne, 1945, Figs. 271, 273). Tall, hollow-stemmed vessels occur in Sialk III_7 and IV (Goff, 1963, Fig. 8, 36 cf. Ghirshman, 1938, Pl. LXXI, S. 59; Pl. XC, S. 244) and Giyan VD (Contenau and Ghirshman, 1935, Pl. 58, 3 e f). Carinated drinking vessels are known from Sialk III_7 and IV and Jamdat Nasr (Goff, 1963, Fig. 8, 30 cf. Ghirshman, 1938, Pl. LXXIII, S. 112 and Pl. XL, S. 31 cf. Mackay, 1931, Pl. LXVII, 14). Gray ware bowls with incurved rims are found at Gawra VI (Goff, 1963, Fig. 8, 13 cf. Speiser, 1935, Pl. LXVII, 87, 99). Carinated bowls (with ring bases) occur in Gawra VII (Goff, 1963, Fig. 8, 15, 23 cf. Speiser, 1935, Pl. LXV, 52). A stemmed flint arrowhead may be compared to those from Hissar IIIC and Anau III (Goff, 1964, Fig. 8, 5 cf. Schmidt, 1933, Pl. CXLIIIA, H. 722 cf. Pumpelly, 1908, Fig. 384). A metal hammer is of a type thought not to date before the middle third millennium on stylistic grounds (Deshayes, 1958; Goff, 1964, Fig. 8, 1). The shape of a copper pin is curiously close to a copper object from Susa Dd (Goff, 1963, Fig. 7, 6 cf. Le Breton, 1957, Fig. 41, 17) whereas an asymmetrical copper knife has a parallel in Anau III (Goff, 1963, Fig. 7, 7 cf. Pumpelly, 1908, Fig. 273). The general evidence points toward the middle of the third millennium B.C. as a possible date for the new material. It is also linked by the red ware, the shapes of incurving rims on bowls, and an unbaked clay seal to the red ware culture of Bakun AV. Perhaps in the not too distant future the relationships of these new assemblages will be put on a firm stratigraphic foundation.

Radiocarbon Dates in Iran: 6000-2000 B.C. (5,730 years half life)

Southern Iran:	B.C.
Tall-i-Bakun B I	4220 ± 83 (P-438)
Tall-i-Gap I	4096 ± 175 (Gak-197)
Tall-i-Gap II	3653 ± 124 (Gak-198)
Western Iran:	
Tepe Sarab, S 5	6245 ± 101 (P-466)
Tepe Sarab, C 1	5923 ± 92 (P-467)
Tepe Sarab, S 4	5883 ± 99 (P-465)
Hajji Firuz, D 15	5537 ± 89 (P-455)
Hajji Firuz, V	5152 ± 85 (P-502)
Dalma Tepe	4216 ± 90 (P-503)
Tepe Siabid	4039 ± 85 (P-442)
Pisdeli Tepe II, 10	3857 ± 88 (P-505)
Pisdeli Tepe II, 5	3734 ± 83 (P-504)
Pisdeli Tepe I	3666 ± 165 (P-157)
Rezaiyeh Road Tepe (Pisdeli ware)	3659 ± 74 (P-866)
Geoy Tepe K3	2574 ± 146 (P-199)
Hasanlu VII	2280 ± 140 (P-194)
Hasanlu VII	2184 ± 138 (P-191)
Hasanlu VII	2142 ± 139 (P-188)
Hasanlu VII	2121 ± 138 (P-189)
Hasanlu VII	2121 ± 138 (P-190)
Northern Iran:	
Belt Cave, Pot. Neo.	6378 ± 742 (C494, 495, 523)*
Hotu Cave, pre-Pot. Neo.	6358 ± 515 (CC Hs-n)
Belt Cave, 21-28	6294 ± 427 (C 492, 547)*
Belt Cave, pre-Pot. Neo.	6070 ± 340 (P-26)*
Belt Cave, Neo.	5544 ± 268 (P-19)*
Hotu Painted Ware (= Sialk II)	4756 ± 438 (P-45)*
Hotu Painted Ware (= Sialk II)	4623 ± 438 (P-36)*
Yarim Tepe Bronze 4	2166 ± 249 (P-508)

*Old solid carbon dates.

B.C.
2200
2300
2400
2500
2600
2700
2800
2900
3000
3100
3200
3300
3400
3500
3600
3700
3800
3900
4000
4100
4200
4300
4400
4500
4600
4700
4800
4900
5000
5100
5200
5300
5400
5500
5600
5700
5800
5900
6000
6100
6200
MESOPOTAMIA
POST-AKKADIAN (Guti, etc.)
AKKADIAN
POST-E. DYN.
EARLY DYNASTIC III
EARLY DYNASTIC II
EARLY DYNASTIC I
JAMDAT NASR (Protolit. c–d)
LATE URUK (Protolit. a–b)
EARLY URUK (Warkan)
UBAID 4 (Late)
UBAID 3 (Ubaid)
UBAID 2
Halaf
SAMARRA Halaf
UBAID 1
SAMARRA HASSUNA
HASSUNA
? (also Hassuna) ?
JARMO
NORTHWEST ZAGROS
Geoy K (from north)
Geoy M
Pisdeli
N. UBAID
Dalma
? ?
Hajji Firuz
? ?
CENTRAL ZAGROS
Giyan IVB
Giyan IVA
SUSA D
? ?
?Deshawar?
URUK? SUSA C
Giyan VD
Giyan VC2
Giyan VC1
Siabid
Giyan VB
UBAID-JAFF.
Giyan VA
HALAF
? ?
Sarab
JARMO
Guran
SOUTHWEST PLAINS
ELAMITE (historic)
Susa De
Susa Dc–d
SUSA D
Susa Db
Susa Da
Susa Cb–c
SUSA C
Susa Ca
URUK
Susa B
Susa A
?Bendebal
?Buhallan
Jaff. II
UBAID
?Jowi
Jaff. I
SAM. HAS.
? ?
Ali Kosh (upper)
?JARMO
SARAB
CENTRAL PLATEAU
? ?
Sialk IV
Sialk III6–7b
Sialk III4–5
Sialk III1–3
Sialk II1–3
Sialk I4–5
HALAF
Sialk I1–3
? ?
NORTHEAST PLATEAU
Hissar IIIB
Hissar IIIA
Hissar IIB
Hissar IIA
Hissar IC
Hissar IB
Hissar IA
SIALK III
? ?
CASPIAN SHORE
Bronze Age 4
Yarim Tepe Bronze Age 5–12
Yarim Tepe Late Chalcolithic
? ?
Hotu Painted Ware
SIALK II
Yarim Tepe Early Chalcolithic?
? ?
Hotu Soft Ware
Belt Neolithic
SOFT WARE
Belt Mesolithic (aceramic)
SOUTHEAST PLATEAU
Bampur
SUSA D
Khurab
? ?
Bakun ? III
Tall-i-Gap II
Tall-i-Gap I
UBAID
Bakun BI (Soft Ware)
? ?
? ?

Fig. 1

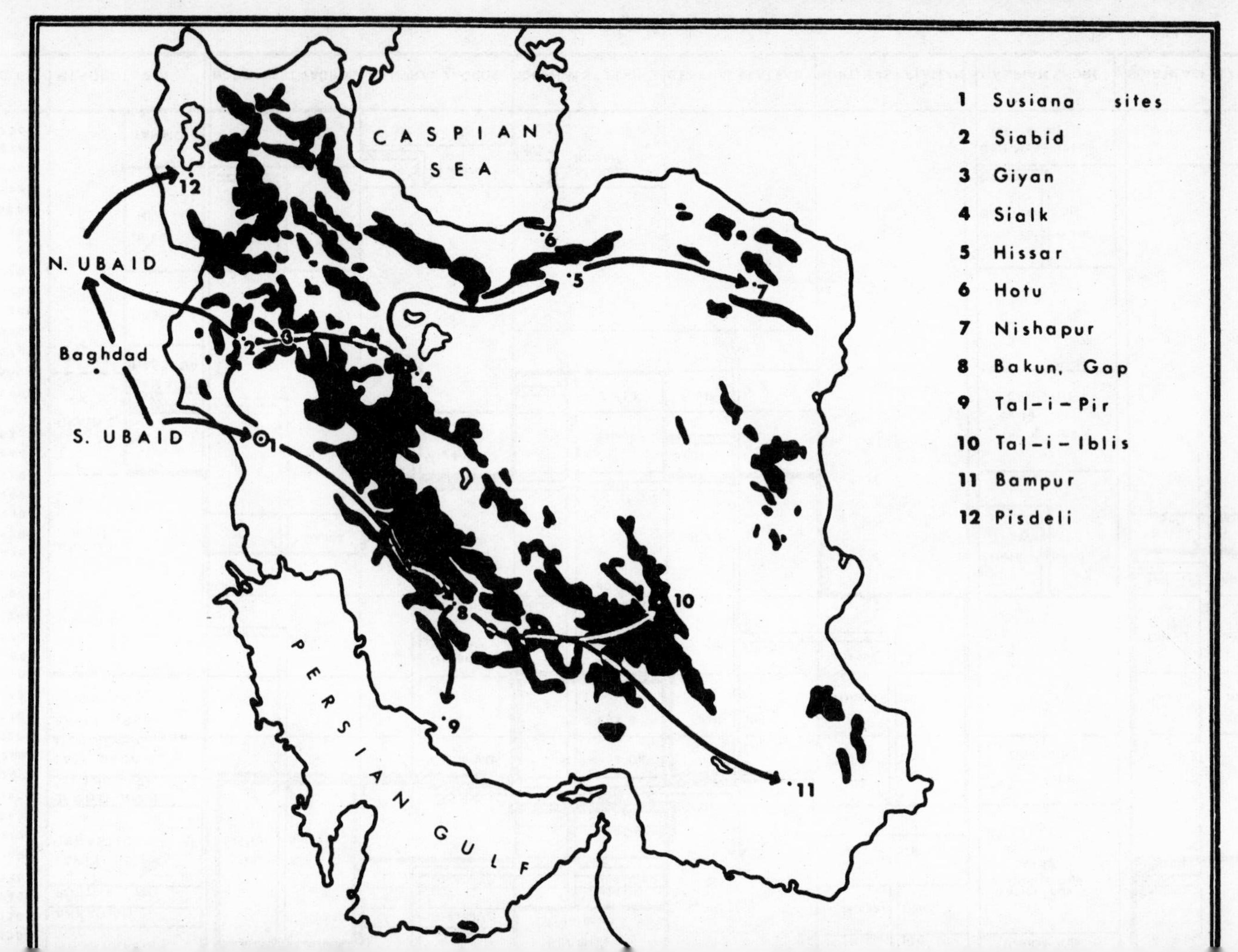
CASPIAN SEA
PERSIAN GULF
N. UBAID
S. UBAID
Baghdad
1 Susiana sites
2 Siabid
3 Giyan
4 Sialk
5 Hissar
6 Hotu
7 Nishapur
8 Bakun, Gap
9 Tal-i-Pir
10 Tal-i-Iblis
11 Bampur
12 Pisdeli

Fig. 1. Relative chronology of Iran from 6000-2000 B.C. as reconstructed in text. Arrows show ongoing ceramic traditions; solid lines mark approximate beginning and end of major ceramic horizons. Southeast Plateau column should be read as if next to Central Plateau. Caspian shore is an isolated unit.

Fig. 2. Map of Iran showing the direction of movement of cultural impulses derived ultimately from the Ubaid culture of Mesopotamia. Similar movements may be reconstructed from Fig. 1 for the Uruk and Early Dynastic periods.

The following should now be integrated with the foregoing discussion: Peder Mortensen, 1964, Sumer XX; Frank Hole, et al., 1965, Current Anthropology 6: 105-6; Kent Flannery, 1965, Science 147: 1247-56.

Bibliography

Arne, A. J.

1945 Excavations at Shah Tepe, Iran. Stockholm: Statens Etnografiska Museum.

Braidwood, Robert J., and Braidwood, Linda S.

1960 Excavations in the Plain of Antioch, I. ("Oriental Institute Publications," No. LXI.) Chicago: University of Chicago Press.

Braidwood, Robert J., and Howe, Bruce

1960 Prehistoric Investigations in Iraqi Kurdistan. ("Studies in Ancient Oriental Civilization," No. 31.) Chicago: University of Chicago Press.

Braidwood, Robert J., Howe, Bruce, and Reed, Charles A.

1961 "The Iranian Prehistoric Project," Science 133: 2008-10.

B.R. 524

1944 Iraq and the Persian Gulf. ("Geographical Handbook Series.") London: Naval Intelligence Division of the British Admiralty.

B.R. 525

1945 Persia. ("Geographical Handbook Series.") London: Naval Intelligence Division of the British Admiralty.

Burney, Charles A.

1961 "Excavations at Yanik Tepe, Northwest Iran," Iraq XXIII: 138-53.

1962 "The Excavations at Yanik Tepe, Azerbaijan, 1961," ibid. XXIV: 134-49.

1964 "The Excavations at Yanik Tepe, Azerbaijan, 1962: Third Preliminary Report," ibid. XXVI: 54-61.

Burton Brown, T.

1951 Excavations in Azarbaijan, 1948. London: John Murray.

1962 "Excavations in Shahrigar, Iran," Archaeology 15: 27-31.

Caldwell, Joseph

n.d. Notes on Tall-i-Ghazir supplied to the author.

Childe, V. Gordon

1952 New Light on the Most Ancient East. London: Routledge and Kegan Paul.

Coon, Carleton S.

1951 Cave Explorations in Iran, 1949. Philadelphia: University Museum.

1957 The Seven Caves. New York: Knopf.

Contenau, George and Ghirshman, Roman.

1935 Fouilles de Tépé Giyan. Paris: Paul Geuthner.

Crawford, Vaughn E.

1963a "Excavations in Iraq and Iran," Archaeology 16: 290-91.
1963b "Beside the Kara Su," Bulletin Metropolitan Museum of Art, April, pp. 263-73.

Deshayes, Jean

1958 "Marteaux de Bronze Iraniens," Syria XXXV: 284 ff.
1960 Les Outils de Bronze, de l'Indus au Danube, II. Paris: Geuthner.
1963 "Rapport préliminaire sur les deux premières campagnes de fouilles à Tureng Tépé," Syria XL: 85-99.

Delougaz, Pinhas

1952 Pottery from the Diyala Region. ("Oriental Institute Publications," No. LXIII.) Chicago: University of Chicago Press.
1964 Communication given at the American Oriental Society, New York, April, 1964.

Dyson, Robert H. Jr.

1958 "Iran, 1957: Iron Age Hasanlu," University Museum Bulletin 22: 25-32.
1961 "Excavating the Mannaean Citadel of Hasanlu," Illustrated London News: 534-37.
n.d. "Excavations on the Acropolis at Susa and Problems of Susa A, B, and C." MS, Ph.D. thesis for Harvard University (in progress).

Egami, Namio

1960 "The Reports of the Society for Near Eastern Studies in Japan," Orient 1: 1-53.

Egami, Namio, and Masuda, Seiichi

1962 The Excavations at Tall-i-Bakun, 1956. Tokyo: Institute for Oriental Culture, University of Tokyo.

Egami, Namio, and Sono, Toshihiko

1962 The Excavations at Tall-i-Gap, 1959. Tokyo: Institute for Oriental Culture, University of Tokyo.

Eliot, Henry Ware

1950 Excavations in Mesopotamia and Western Iran. Cambridge (Mass.): Peabody Museum.

Frankfort, Henri

1936 Progress of the Work of the Oriental Institute in Iraq, 1934/35. ("Oriental Institute Communications," No. 20.) Chicago: University of Chicago Press.
1955 Stratified Cylinder Seals of the Diyala. ("Oriental Institute Publications," No. LXXII.) Chicago: University of Chicago Press.

Ghirshman, Roman

1938 Fouilles de Sialk, I. Paris: Geuthner.

1954 *Iran*. Baltimore: Penguin Books.

Goff, Clare

1963 "Excavations at Tall-i-Nokhodi," *Iran* I: 43-70.
1964 "Excavations at Tall-i-Nokhodi, 1962," *Iran* II: 41-50.

Gordon, Col. D. H.

1947 "Sialk, Giyan, Hissar and the Indo-Iranian Connection," *Man in India* XXVII: 196-241.
1960 *The Prehistoric Background of Indian Culture*. 2d ed. Bombay: N. M. Tripathi.

Hole, Frank

1962 "Excavations at Ali Kosh, Iran, 1961," *Iranica Antiqua* II: 7-147.

Langsdorf, Alexander, and McCown, Donald E.

1942 *Tall-i-Bakun* A. ("Oriental Institute Publications," No. LIX.) Chicago: University of Chicago Press.

Le Breton, Louis

1947 "Note sur la céramique peinte aux environs de Suse et à Suse," *Mémoires, Mission Archéologique en Iran* XXX: 120-219.
1957 "The Early Periods at Susa, Mesopotamian Relations," *Iraq* XIX: 79-124.

Le Strange, G.

1905 *The Lands of the Eastern Caliphate*. Cambridge: Cambridge University Press.

Levy, M., and Burke, J. E.

1959 "A Study of Ancient Mesopotamian Bronze," *Chymia* (University of Pennsylvania Press) 5: 37-50.

Lloyd, Seton

1956 *Early Anatolia*. Baltimore: Penguin Books.

Lloyd, Seton, Safar, Fuad, and Braidwood, Robert J.

1945 "Tell Hassuna," *Journal of Near Eastern Studies* IV: 255-89.

Mackay, Ernest

1931 "Report on Excavations at Jemdet Nasr, Iraq," *Anthropologica Memoires of the Field Museum* I: 217-303.

Mallowan, M. E. L.

1936 "The Excavations at Tall Chagar Bazar," *Iraq* III: 1-85.
1947 "Excavations at Brak and Chagar Bazar," *ibid*. IX: 1-259.
1956 *Twenty-five Years of Mesopotamian Discovery*. London: Britis School of Archaeology in Iraq.

McCown, Donald E.

1942 The Comparative Stratigraphy of Early Iran. Chicago: University of Chicago Press.

1954 "The Relative Stratigraphy and Chronology of Iran." In Relative Chronologies in Old World Archeology, pp. 56-68. Ed. Robert W. Ehrich. Chicago: University of Chicago Press.

Mecquenem, Roland de

1943 "Fouilles de Suse 1933-1939," Mémoires, Mission Archéologique en Iran XXIX: 5-34.

Mortensen, Peder

1964 "Excavations at Tepe Guran, Luristan." II. "Early Village-Farming Occupation," Acta Archaeologica XXXIV: 110-21.

Negahban, Ezat O.

1962a "The Wonderful Gold Treasures of Marlik," Illustrated London News (April 28), 663-64.

1962b "Further Finds from Marlik," ibid. (May 5), 699-701.

1964 "A Brief Report on the Excavation of Marlik Tepe and Pileh Qal'eh," Iran II: 13-20.

Oates, Joan

1960 "Ur and Eridu, the Prehistory," Iraq XXII: 32-50.

Oppenheim, Baron Max von

1931 Tell Halaf. New York: Putnam.

Perkins, Ann L.

1949 The Comparative Archaeology of Early Mesopotamia. ("Studies in Ancient Oriental Civilization," No. 25.) Chicago: University of Chicago Press.

Piggott, Stuart

1943 "Dating the Hissar Sequence—the Indian Evidence," Antiquity XVII: 169-82.

1950 Prehistoric India. Harmondsworth: Pelican Books.

Pumpelly, Raphael

1908 Explorations in Turkestan, Expedition of 1904. I. Washington: Carnegie Institution of Washington.

Schaeffer, Claude F. A.

1948 Stratigraphie Comparée. London: Oxford University Press.

Schmidt, Erich F.

1933 "Tepe Hissar Excavations," Museum Journal XXIII: 323-483.

1937 Excavations at Tepe Hissar, Damghan 1931-1933. Philadelphia: University of Pennsylvania Press.

1939 Tall-i-Bakun. ("Oriental Institute Communications," No. 21), pp. 121-29. Chicago: University of Chicago Press.

Speiser, E. A.

1933 "The Pottery of Tell Billa," Museum Journal XXIII: 249-83.
1935 Excavations at Tepe Gawra, I. Philadelphia: University of Pennsylvania Press.

Starr, Richard F. S.

1937 Nuzi, II. Cambridge (Mass.): Harvard University Press.

Stein, Sir Aurel

1937 Archaeological Reconnaissances in North-western India and South-eastern Iran. London: Macmillan and Co.

Tobler, Arthur J.

1950 Excavations at Tepe Gawra, II. Philadelphia: University of Pennsylvania Press.

Vanden Berghe, L.

1952a "Archaeologische opzoekingen in de Marv Dasht Vlakte (Iran)," Jaarbericht Ex Oriente Lux 12: 211-20.
1952b Revue Archéologique XXXIX: 1-21.
1954a "Archaeologische Navorsingen in de Omstreken van Persepolis, Jaarberichte Ex Oriente Lux 13: 394-408.
1954b Overdruk uit de Gentse Bijdragertet de Kunstgechiedenis XV.
1956 "De Beschilderde Ceramiek in voor-azie van de oudste tijdentot 2000 voor onze Jaartelling," ibid. XVI.
1959 L'Iran Ancienne. Leiden: E. J. Brill.
1964 La Nécropole de Khurvin. Istanbul: Nederlands Historisch-Archaeologisch Instituut in het nabije oosten.

Ward, Lauriston

1954 "The Relative Chronology of China through the Han Period." In Relative Chronologies in Old World Archeology, pp. 130-41. Ed. Robert W. Ehrich. Chicago: University of Chicago Press.

Woolley, Sir Leonard

1934 Ur Excavations II. London and Philadelphia: Trustees of the British Museum and the University Museum.
1956 Ur Excavations IV. London and Philadelphia: Trustees of the British Museum and the University Museum.

Young, T. Cuyler, Jr.

1962 "Taking the History of the Hasanlu Area Back Another Five Thousand Years," Illustrated London News, 707-9.
1963 "Dalma Painted Ware," Expedition 5: 38-39.

A Suggested Chronology for Afghanistan, Baluchistan, and the Indus Valley

George F. Dales
University Museum
University of Pennsylvania

In Relative Chronologies in Old World Archeology, Baluchistan was included as a peripheral adjunct to the study of Iran (McCown, 1954). It is now possible, thanks to a number of major new excavations, to cast Afghanistan and Baluchistan in their proper role as the homeland for the development of the various cultural, social, and economic experiments that provided the necessary antecedents for the rise of civilization in the Indus Valley. During the earliest periods most of the stimuli were demonstrably from the Near Eastern area, but it was the gradual adaptation and transformation of these stimuli to a distinctive South Asian pattern that produced the unique Indus (Harappan) civilization (Fairservis, 1961b).

The two pioneering syntheses of this material (Piggott, 1950; Gordon, 1958), although still useful, reflect the shortcomings of having to rely almost exclusively on stylistic and typological comparisons of unstratified archaeological evidence. The result was that until very recently the entire chronological structure for early South Asia was based on a few comparisons with Near Eastern parallels.

The present paper offers a new synthesis incorporating the results of the most recent excavations in our area. Emphasis is placed on establishing a sound chronological framework for the area based on internal evidence. Foreign parallels are introduced only at the end of the paper, where a correlation with the Iranian and Mesopotamian sequences is presented. The attempt here is to build the internal framework on the correlation of total assemblages of archaeological materials. Several modifications of the earlier chronological schemes that were compelled to rely almost exclusively on ceramic comparisons will be evident. The material is presented here in terms of a succession of "phases." The phases refer to cultural horizons consisting of distinctive material assemblages and representing specific levels of cultural, social, and economic development. Divisions between phases are determined by major changes throughout the total assemblage. Such changes may represent internal development—or decline—or result from foreign intrusions. Subdivisions of the phases will undoubtedly be required as more detailed information is accumulated. Abstract alphabetical designations for the phases are used rather than socioeconomic, technological, or other labels that may or may not prove valid as our knowledge of the phase dynamics increases.

The horizontal lines dividing the phases in the chronological chart are for convenience only. To be more accurate they should slant upward to reflect the "sloping horizon" of cultural level from west to east. The phase descriptions show that many elements of the early assemblages—down to our Phase E—appear first in Afghanistan and subsequently spread through Baluchistan to the Indus Valley. The few available radiocarbon dates suggest the same pattern.

Space limitations prevent the inclusion of the crucial late and post-Harappan periods. Consequently references to the important recent discoveries in India are omitted. This is not altogether an unhappy circumstance. It is, in fact, a bit premature to discuss these periods, because current research is forcing a complete re-examination of factors responsible for the decline and end of the Indus civilization.

The following synthesis would have been impossible without the use of unpublished materials so generously offered by J.-M. Casal, F. A. Khan, A. H. Dani, L. Dupree, B. K. Thapar, W. A. Fairservis, and R. L. Raikes. The interpretation placed on this material is, however, the sole responsibility of the author.

PHASE A

Phase A encompasses the initial stages of human habitation in our area—the early Stone Ages—and is beyond the scope of this paper. For recent researches see, for example, Dupree and Howe (1963), Puglisi (1963), Sankalia (1963), Wheeler (1959).

PHASE B

For sake of convenience, Phase B may be labeled "Neolithic." The crucial stage in human development, when man evolved from a hunter-gatherer to a settled food producer, is as yet not clearly defined in South Asia. Archaeological evidence suggesting such a stage is widely separated in geographical area and absolute date. Furthermore, there is a serious lack of definition in the identifications of stone tool assemblages.

Neolithic artifacts are reported from Afghanistan by Dupree (1964) in a stratified context at Ghar-i-Mar (Snake Cave) near Aq Kupruk, one of many caves discovered in the limestone hills on the northern edge of the Hindu Kush. Situated as they are on the southern side of the Oxus Plain, the caves were strategically located on a main east-west route connecting Central Asia and northern Iran with the Peshawar district of northern West Pakistan, Swat, and Kashmir. Two phases of Neolithic are represented, the lower cave deposit yielding no pottery. Dupree stresses that on the present limited evidence this is not to be construed as a "pre-pottery Neolithic" horizon—so far it is merely "non-ceramic." The upper Neolithic levels yielded two types of pottery: a coarse lime-tempered ware; and a fine, handmade, burnished, yellow-buff ware, evenly fired throughout, with bands of incised wedgelike decorations around the shoulder. In addition there are sickle blades, polished bone points, charred grain, and large pockets of snail shells. Two radiocarbon dates average about 5100 B.C. and 5300 B.C. for the upper Neolithic. No comparable material is known from this area or in the Near East generally. However, the Russian archaeologist S. P. Tolstov has seen the material, and notes similarities with Neolithic material from Turkmenia dated by the Russians to about 5000 B.C. (Dupree, 1964).

Neolithic tools are reported by A. H. Dani (private communication, now published; see note, p. 284, below) from the upper levels of a cave in the Sanghao Valley (Mardan district) above Peshawar, West Pakistan. Dani has also made abundant surface collections of polished Neolithic tools during surveys in Swat and in Dir and Bajaur districts north of Peshawar. It remains to be seen whether these finds are to be associated with the early Neolithic horizon of the Near East or with the much later Neolithic assemblages of Kashmir and India.

In close geographical proximity to the Peshawar area is the site of Burzahom (Burzhom, Burjhama) near Srinagar (Kashmir), where a Neolithic settlement has recently been excavated (Indian Archaeology, 1960-61, p. 11; Lal, 1963, p. 217; Sankalia, 1963, pp. 243-44). Reported are "neolithic celts," bone awls, pottery, and cooking vessels. A few sherds of wheel-made burnished red ware are reported as well as "handmade, mat-impressed, steel grey" pottery. The latter, which has mat impression on the base only, is not the same as the "basket-marked" ware of Baluchistan (Fairservis, 1956, p. 259, Fig. 52) with which it has been compared (DeCardi, 1959, p. 19). Radiocarbon dates of about 1900 B.C. and similarities in the over-all assemblages indicate that the Kashmir "neolithic" is more closely connected with the belated "neolithic" of India (Allchin, 1963; Dani, 1960) than with the earlier Near Eastern Neolithic assemblages.

The chronological framework for northern and central Baluchistan has been tied to a relatively limited series of trenches at Kili Ghul Mohammad and Damb Sadaat in the Quetta Valley of West Pakistan (Fairservis, 1956 and 1959). The published evidence is, however, subject to an interpretation at variance with that presented by the excavator. The interpretation offered here seems to agree more consistently with other recently acquired information from Afghanistan and the Indus Valley. It is impossible to present a detailed discussion of the problem here, but a summary statement is essential in view of the key position the material holds in current studies.

The Quetta sequence as presented by the excavator is based on a quantitative analysis of ceramic finds—a type of analysis adopted from New World archaeological studies of mainly one-period sites that yield only ceramic materials. Basically, the analysis as offered by Fairservis is founded on the statistical maximal occurrences of pottery types. These occurrences are plotted on graphs and the successive cultural "periods" designated by brackets that encompass what appear to be the major ceramic horizons. The period descriptions are then compiled, including the other non-ceramic finds associated with levels falling within each period bracket. It is these Quetta period designations that have conditioned the chronological terminology of Baluchistan in recent years.

A re-evaluation of this material using the following criteria yields quite a different period structure for Baluchistan: (1) initial appearance of ceramic types as opposed to maximal occurrences, (2) relative time-distribution of <u>all</u> types of excavated materials rather than only ceramics, and (3) period divisions based on the distribution of the total assemblage (insofar as it is known). The chart illustrates the differences in the Quetta sequence when analyzed from these two approaches. A major change is that the so-called KGM II period, supposedly characterized by crude handmade and basket-marked pottery, does not exist as a separate entity. The published graphs (Fairservis, 1956, Figs. 60-61) show twelve different pottery types occurring within the KGM II range—of these, ten are wheel-made! This, combined with the occurrences of the non-ceramic materials of the same levels, shows that KGM II and III are in fact a well-defined cultural unit corresponding to our Phase C—the earliest Chalcolithic horizon of Baluchistan. This conclusion is supported by the Anjira sequence of Kalat (DeCardi, 1959 and 1964).

Equally important is the degree to which the designation "pre-pottery Neolithic" can be accepted for the KGM I period. Considering the cultural implications involved in light of the limited size of the pit from which the KGM evidence was derived, it seems safer to follow Dupree's example for his Afghanistan cave material and designate KGM I as merely "non-ceramic" on present evidence.

PHASE C

Phase C represents the first discernible period of settled village life in our area. It is identifiable from Mundigak in Afghanistan, eastward into the Quetta, Zhob, and Loralai districts of northern Baluchistan, and southward into the Kalat area of central Baluchistan. It is not yet evident in southern Baluchistan or in the Indus plain.

Metal objects appear for the first time (Fairservis, 1956, p. 231; Casal, 1961a, p. 245), but the continued use of stone and bone for implements suggests that this is an early Chalcolithic horizon. Throughout the phase, stone tool types become progressively more limited and refined so that by the end of it we have the fine parallel-sided blades that are so characteristic of the succeeding phases. Ground alabaster bowls make their appearance (Mundigak, Kili Ghul Mohammad). Crude, clay, humped bull figurines occur at Mundigak, apparently as the forerunners of the well-made bull figurines of the next phase found here and in northern Baluchistan.

The pottery industry blossoms during this phase with the introduction of the potter's wheel. At Mundigak as much as 90 per cent of the pottery is wheel-made. At the Quetta sites, seventeen of the twenty-two pottery types in the KGM II-III range are wheelmade. The most distinctive painted pottery motifs for comparative purposes are dot-tipped hanging triangles (Fairservis, 1956, Fig. 50B, and 1959, Fig. 63; Casal, 1961a, Fig. 49 with solid triangles instead of dots) and dot-tipped six- or eight-armed star designs (Fairservis, loc. cit.; DeCardi, 1959, Fig. 2, and 1964, Pl. I, A,2-3). The occurrence—albeit rare—at Mundigak of bichrome painted ware, decorated in panel patterns (Casal, 1961a, Fig. 50, 21 and 29), heralds the introduction of this distinctive painted pottery tradition into South Asia (see Phase D). Specialized surface treatment of pottery is another characteristic Phase C feature. Basket-marked ware, apparently produced by forming wet clay liners inside bowl-shaped or vertical-sided baskets, is restricted to this phase (Fairservis, 1956, Fig. 52; DeCardi, 1959, Pl. V, 1, and 1964, Pl. I, A, 6). The earliest of three varieties of "wet ware"—apparently created by dabbing the outside of vessels while the clay is wet to roughen the surface—occurs in northern Baluchistan (Fairservis, 1956, Fig. 59A). This so-called Kechi Beg variety of "wet ware" continues through our Phases D and E, and is thus not so precise a chronological indicator as the other two varieties that begin in Phase D.

A most important ceramic type for comparative purposes is Togau ware (DeCardi, 1950; 1959 superseded by 1964). It is useful, not only because of its wide distribution, but also because its major phases of stylistic development are verified by stratified excavations. These phases, developing from an original naturalistic style of painting animal and human representations to a purely abstract style, have been designated by DeCardi as Togau A, B, C, D. The last three belong to the early part of our Phase D (see below). Unfortunately, all sherds of Togau A style were surface finds at both Siah and Anjira in the Surab Valley (Kalat), where the later stages were so well defined. Stylistically, DeCardi places Togau A in the upper levels of her Anjira Period II (our Phase C). This placement is corroborated by the finding of similar sherds in Period I, 3, at Mundigak (Casal, 1961a, Fig. 49, 11). This tie also helps confirm the theory of a northern origin for the Togau ware and for related traditions (see Phase D).

PHASE D

A period of vitality and expansion is now witnessed at Mundigak (Afghanistan) and in northern Baluchistan. The initial appearance of permanent settlements in southern Baluchistan occurs, and is apparently connected with the spread of the bichrome-polychrome painted pottery traditions through Afghanistan, Baluchistan, and down to the foothills bordering the Indus Plain (Amri). Also involved may be the spread of the humped bull into the Indus Valley. During this phase we see the first permanent settlements in the Indus Plain itself—for example, at

Kot Diji in the south (Khan, 1958 and n.d.; Pakistan Archaeology, 1964, pp. 39-43), in the Bahawalpur region (Field, 1959; Pakistan Archaeology, 1964, pp. 35-36), and throughout northern Rajasthan in India (reports in Indian Archaeology; Sankalia, 1963), especially at Kalibangan (Lal, 1962; Thapar, 1963). Although interaction is to be seen at the earliest stages between the highland and the plains settlements, they seem to have sprung basically from different traditions. The origin of neither is as yet certain, but much of the evidence does point to the northwest —to Afghanistan and possibly beyond.

The internal chronology of this phase in Baluchistan—concerned with the early spread of the painted pottery "hill-cultures"—is tenuous, but hopefully less so than when Piggott made his pioneering synthesis in 1950. Of prime importance is the spread of the multicolored pottery tradition—either bichrome (red-black) or polychrome. These two varieties are at first found together in the northwest in Mundigak III (Casal, 1961a, pottery Nos. 49, 76, 85-87, 100, 120), but have distinctly separate geographical distributions in the south. Polychrome decoration—especially Nal ware—is found in the Baluchistan uplands, whereas bichrome decoration—termed Amri ware—is more concentrated in the foothills and the areas bordering the Lower Indus Plain. It is important to remember that although the painting styles are separate and distinctive, there are many striking similarities between some of the pottery shapes and even some of the painted motifs. Furthermore, both the Nal and Amri "cultures" are noteworthy for their absence of animal and anthropomorphic clay figurines—a characteristic lacking at all sites in our Phase D except for Mundigak (see below).

Present evidence suggests that the multicolor tradition arrives from the West, through the Mundigak area, and that the bichrome variety occurs earliest (Mundigak I, 4-5), during the latest part of our Phase C. The recent discovery of an atypical bichrome site at Pirak, near Sibi (Raikes, 1963), adds an important but problematic element. The site, situated at the eastern end of the Bolan Pass route, is directly on the path connecting the Mundigak-Kandahar area with the Lower Indus Plain. Pirak ware is coarse, heavy, and apparently shaped differently from, Amri pottery. The painting technique is different, and so are the designs. Pirak ware may represent the earliest form of bichrome decoration in our area. At Amri itself, Pirak-style sherds are reported from "a deep layer of the Amri culture" (Casal, in Raikes, 1963, p. 60, n. 2).

One of the common motifs on the inside of Pirak bowls is the same type hanging triangle that is characteristic of the inside of bowls of Mundigak I and KGM II-III (our Phase C). That actual examples of Pirak ware were not found in the early Mundigak levels below those containing Amri-style bichrome sherds is probably an accident of discovery. In fact, one bichrome vessel from Period III, 4 (Casal, 1961a, Fig. 56:85) with oblique and triangular designs does recall the Pirak style. Thus it seems likely that Pirak bichrome (and a closely related ware discovered by a Pakistan Department of Archaeology survey at Spina Ghundai in the Quetta-Pishan district) is the forerunner of the long-lived multicolor pottery tradition of Baluchistan. The more westerly relations of Pirak ware—possibly in northern Mesopotamia—require investigation.

French excavations at Amri (1959-1962) have provided one of the few stratigraphically excavated pre-Harappan through Harappan sequences (Casal 1961b and 1964; and see note, p. 284, below). The earliest period, with four subdivisions, belongs to the Amri culture. The earliest level of the period, on virgin soil, is characterized by pottery of Togau C type, thus providing a solid tie with central and northern Baluchistan. Bichrome ware is present but in the minority, and, as mentioned above, some of it reportedly resembles Pirak ware. The appearance of the humped bull on painted pottery of the last phase of the Amrian period (Casal, 1964, Fig. 9A) may herald the introduction of that most important animal to the Indus Valley. The Intermediate Period at Amri (our Early Phase E) has architectural and ceramic connections with Afghanistan (Mundigak IV, 1) that add credence to the suggested relationship between the earliest inhabitants of Amri and the older cultural groups of northern Baluchistan and Afghanistan. Further confirmation for the relative position of the bichrome tradition is seen at Kot Diji, the only stratigraphically excavated site of the pre-Harappan and Harappan periods in the Lower Indus Valley (Khan, 1958 and n.d.; Casal, 1960; *Pakistan Archaeology*, 1964, pp. 39-43; final report in press). A few sherds with typical Amri-like bichrome panel designs were found in the pre-Harappan levels.

The probable common origin of Amri bichrome and Nal polychrome was mentioned earlier. Why the basic tradition split, with part of the population moving down into the Indus Valley and the rest moving into the medium altitude zones (elevation 1,000-1,300 meters) of Baluchistan, is unknown. It did apparently happen, however, with the result that the two branches developed quite different cultural, economic, and social systems. It has been suggested that the Nal people became dependent on a combination of farming and animal husbandry while retaining a degree of nomadic mobility, whereas the Amri people became sedentary agriculturalists and urban dwellers and thereby contributed more directly to the civilization-making process in the Indus Valley (cf. Raikes, 1964).

The chronological position of the Nal material has not been so secure as the Amrian. This is because of the lack of stratigraphically excavated sites in Baluchistan and also partly because of a misinterpretation of the relative ages of two groups of materials at Nal (Hargreaves, 1929). It has been assumed (e.g., Piggott, 1950; Gordon, 1958) that the cemetery (Area A) was later than the occupational levels excavated on the upper parts of the site (especially Areas D and F). Present comparative evidence points, however, to the opposite sequence. Nal cemetery-like pottery shapes appear as early as Mundigak III, 1 (e.g., Casal, 1961a, Fig. 53, Nos. 55-56). Polychrome decoration, similar to that from the Nal cemetery, also appears in Mundigak III. This, together with the close relationship between the Nal polychrome and Amri bichrome traditions, places the Nal cemetery in our Phase D. Further confirmation is offered by the similarity between the gray-ware bowls decorated with white painted loops found with the Nal polychrome and the Kechi Beg White-on-Dark Slip ware of the Quetta area (Fairservis, 1956, p. 257) that is also assigned to this phase. At Anjira, Nal-like polychrome appears in late Period III and continues through IV. Significantly it occurs with Togau D in Period III, the final stage of Togau ware in which it has developed into a painted gray-ware variety. Furthermore, Togau B and C wares are associated at Siah and Anjira with bichrome wares that have been compared by DeCardi with "Kechi Beg" bichrome of the Quetta area, which is itself a relative of Amri bichrome.

The other material from Nal, mainly from occupation levels in the upper parts of the site, is paralleled at other sites only in our Phase E. The cups from Chamber 6, Area D, have counterparts at Mundigak IV. One of the two vessels from Area F (Hargreaves, 1929, Pl. XIX, 13) is identical in shape and decoration with the Quetta area "Sadaat" ware of our Late Phase E. Painted clay humped bull figurines, a copper stamp seal and lapis lazuli beads from the same Nal contexts also confirm a Phase E date. Furthermore, the popularity of red-ware vessels painted with black designs in the non-cemetery Nal pottery parallels the same tendency at such sites as Mundigak IV and Rana Ghundai III_c_ of our Phase E. The relative sequence of the Nal material is also confirmed by the current French excavations at Nindowari, Ornach (see Phase E).

The use of painted gray-ware pottery was popular during Phase D. It appears in several local varieties—some of which have already been mentioned. At the Quetta sites, a Faiz Mohammad variety was described (Fairservis, 1956), but has been reclassified as a variant of a more general category—Faiz Mohammad Painted Ware (Fairservis, 1959, p. 374)—because of the wide variation in the colors of the wares and painted designs. The true gray variety is nonetheless distinctive enough to serve as a useful comparative item, the more so because of its wide distribution throughout Baluchistan. At Mundigak, painted gray ware occurs as early as III, 1 (Casal, 1961_a_, Fig. 52:45). Painted and unpainted examples from IV, 1, include a sherd of typical Faiz Mohammad variety (_ibid_., Fig. 87, 355). Mention has already been made of the final stage (D), at Anjira in central Baluchistan, in the development of the painted Togau ware wherein the ware is characteristically gray. Sherds of the Faiz Mohammad variety of gray ware were found on the surface of the site.

The so-called "Quetta" ware (Fairservis, 1956, pp. 254-56, 259-61), with its distinctive bold painted decorations, provides valuable comparative material for the Afghanistan-northern Baluchistan areas, to which it seems to be confined. It occurs during our Phases D and Early E, subsequent to which it is better termed "Sadaat" ware (see Phase E).

Of surface-treated wares, the Kechi Beg variety of Phase C continues alongside two new varieties: "Quetta Wet" ware (Fairservis, 1956, p. 269, Fig. 59) and "Quetta Circle-stamped" (_ibid_., p. 270). All three varieties occur in the Zhob-Loralai area (Fairservis, 1959, p. 376). In central Baluchistan, "Quetta Circle-stamped" was found on the surface at Anjira (DeCardi, 1959, Pl. V, 12) and is apparently post-Period IV at the site. In Anjira III and IV is a "granulated" or sandy slipped ware that may anticipate the "wet ware" technique (_ibid_., p. 21, and 1964, Pl. II, B, 11).

The most characteristic pottery of the Indus Plain sites during this phase has been termed Kot Diji ware after the site where it was first identified in a stratified context. This fine wheel-made pottery is found in all the pre-Harappan levels at Kot Diji, below the defenses at Harappa, on the surface of many sites in Bahawalpur and Rajasthan, and in the pre-Harappan levels at Kalibangan. Scattered examples of Kot Diji ware are reported from northern Baluchistan and Afghanistan: Mundigak III, 5, to IV, 2 (Casal 1961a, Types 101, 102, 249). It is too early to be certain about the original relationship between the plains and the highland cultural groups, but the pottery distributions suggest a considerable amount of interaction of some type other than military. Just how early the Kot Dijian settlements go back is not certain, but they do, on comparative grounds, begin sometime during our Phase D. The "Antecedent" or pre-Harappan period at Kalibangan in northern Rajasthan with its Kot Diji-like pottery probably starts during our Phase D also. The final publications on Kalibangan, Kot Diji, and Amri should provide keys to many of the basic questions concerning the development of civilization in South Asia.

Non-ceramic materials provide additional criteria for setting up our Phase D. Metal-working shows signs of progressing, but is still in an early stage of development. Copper-bronze spearpoints, eyed needles, and pins occur in Mundigak II-III. One of the pins has a double-volute head with the spiral in the opposite direction to that of the later type so widespread throughout the Near East and the Mediterranean (Casal, 1961a, Fig. 139, 4). Shaft-hole axes and adzes are found at Mundigak III, 6, but have no Baluchistan or Indus parallels at this period. Metal tools —rarely found as yet—apparently replace stone tools during this phase except for the fine parallel-sided flint blades that become so popular throughout Baluchistan and in the Indus Valley and continue through Phase E. At the Quetta sites, stone scrapers, cores, and the like disappear with the end of our Phase C (Fairservis, 1956, pp. 234 ff.). Flint arrowheads, basically of laurel-leaf shape, are common at Mundigak (Casal, 1961a, pp. 235 ff., Fig. 137, Pl. XXXVIIE) and in the pre-Harappan levels at Kot Diji.

That no metal is reported from stratified contexts at sites in the Zhob-Loralai districts of northern Baluchistan, such as Rana Ghundai and Sur Jangal (Fairservis, 1959), is probably due to the limited nature of the investigations. Metal finds from contemporary sites in central and southern Baluchistan are scarce, but at Amri metal fragments are reported from the earliest levels (Casal, 1964, correcting 1961b, p. 25; and now the final report, p. 27). Traces were also found in the pre-Harappan levels (just how early is uncertain) of Kot Diji.

It is significant that clay figurines are found during this phase only in Afghanistan and the Near East. Painted humped bull figurines are common in Mundigak III (Casal, 1961a, pp. 252 ff., Pl. XL), having appeared first in I, 3 (our Phase C). Their priority at Mundigak over Baluchistan and the Indus Plain may have relevance to the question of the origin of this species. The humped bull figurines reported from Nal (Hargreaves, 1929, p. 33) are said to be from Areas A (cemetery) and D (later occupation), but in the description of the grave groups no mention is made of figurines. It is probable that the Area A figurines also belong to the later occupation (our Phase E), in which such objects are common. Anthropomorphic clay figurines are also found only in Afghanistan and in the Near East during Phase D. They appear first in Mundigak II, 3, in two types: pillar-based with outstretched arms, and a flat fiddle-shaped type with prominent breasts. Both are crude when compared with the Phase E figurines.

In our area, stamp seals with concentric geometric designs first appear in Afghanistan. Stone examples come from Mundigak II, 2, and III (Casal, 1961a, p. 256 and Pl. XLV, A, 2-6). Bone seals are also found (ibid., No. 7, plus three other examples). Stone examples were found at Deh Morasi Ghundai II a and c (Dupree, 1963, p. 99). Copper seals do not occur until Phase E.

PHASE E

We are now on the threshold of "civilization"—in the final stages of development that lead to the establishment of the large urban settlements in the Indus Valley and to what is called the Indus or Harappan civilization. It is a complex phase throughout our area, and the developmental picture is anything but clear. Only a working hypothesis is offered here. Many features and trends recall the Late Uruk-Jemdet Nasr (Protoliterate) phase in Mesopotamia. The analogy—in terms of cultural development, not in specific material objects or in absolute dates—may be useful, at least until research progresses beyond its present initial stages.

Scanty as the current evidence is, it seems valid to distinguish between an early and late part of this phase. We first see the transition from villages to towns, with fortified citadels (Mundigak and Kot Diji). At Mundigak, there was a "palace" and a "temple" in IV, 1. A violent destruction ends IV, 1, after which the fortifications fell into disrepair. Similarly at Kot Diji, the defenses fell into disuse during the late part of this phase. At the Quetta sites the ceramic and non-ceramic material supports a distinct division between Fairservis' Damb Sadaat II and III periods (see below). From Afghanistan to the Indus Plain, there is a growing popularity of red ware or red slipped ware decorated with black painted designs, especially evident during Late Phase E, whereas the multicolored painted pottery traditions of our Phase D (e.g., Nal and Amri) gradually die out or are transformed during Early Phase E. The appearance of potter's marks (earliest at Mundigak IV, 1, and the Quetta sites in Damb Sadaat II) may suggest the beginnings of writing. At least, they first appear at a time that corresponds with a hypothetical Early Harappan period.

A few specific comparative points must be mentioned—first, the Damb Sadaat (DS) II-III sequence for the Quetta area and eastern Afghanistan. DS III sees the transition from the bold geometrically painted designs typical of "Quetta" ware to the more curvilinear, flower-like (or bucranium-like?) "Sadaat" style (e.g., Casal, 1961a, Fig. 75, 250, Fig. 82, 302; Fairservis, 1956, Fig. 61a,f). This distinction was noted by L. Alcock (in Fairservis, 1956) but was not emphasized by Fairservis. The "Sadaat" painted style has important comparative features. The general trend to favor naturalistic motifs over geometric ones seems to appear at Mundigak (IV, 1) before it does so in the Quetta area, but, because of the close geographical relationship and the relatively small amount of material from Damb Sadaat, it is best not to press this point. The floral or bucranium-like motif provides a solid link between this northern area and the post-cemetery pottery from Nal (see Phase D). The motif is also common at Nindowari in the Ornach Valley, where it is reportedly on pottery associated with that of typical Kulli style (J.-M. Casal, personal communication).

Clay animal figurines, which appeared initially at Mundigak as early as Phase C but were conspicuously absent from Baluchistan, are now seen at the Quetta sites (horse or ass in DS II, painted humped bulls in DS III), in the post-cemetery levels at Nal (painted humped bulls), with the Intermediate Period at Amri, and with the pre-Harappan period at Kot Diji. The cultural significance of this rather sudden spread of the making of humped bull figurines and the depicting of these animals on painted pottery needs investigation.

The style employed in depicting animals (and birds) on painted pottery of Early Phase E provides a valuable comparative element for reconstructing the internal chronology of our area and for assessing the chronological connections with southern Iran and Mesopotamia. Compare Intermediate Period Amri (Casal, 1961b and 1964, Fig. 9), Mundigak IV, 1 (Casal, 1961a), Damb Sadaat II (Fairservis, 1956, designs 432, 433), Kulli and Mehi (Stein, 1931, passim), Susa D (LeBreton, 1957, Pl. XXVI and Fig. 35), and Umm an-Nar (Abu Dhabi) off the Trucial Coast (Thorvildsen, 1963, Fig. 23).

Female representations are another important addition to the clay figurine catalogue. These appeared initially at Mundigak during the preceding phase, but are introduced to Baluchistan with the Damb Sadaat II period in the Quetta area (Fairservis, 1956, pp. 224-25, Figs. 16 a-c and 17 a,i). Fragmentary examples occur farther north in Loralai, but are all surface finds (Fairservis, 1959, Fig. 13 b,c). This particular figurine type has bent legs, huge breasts, and elaborate necklaces. No heads have been found with these seated figures. A clue to the appearance of the missing heads may be derived from similar figurines at Namazga Tepe, Turkmenia. With Damb Sadaat III a different type of female figurine appears—designated the "Zhob Mother-goddess" (Fairservis, 1956, pp. 224-26, Fig. 16, d-g)—which was first discovered in the Zhob-Loralai area (Stein, 1929, Pls. IX, XII, XVI). These figures are characterized by their ghostly faces, pedestal or pillar bases, elaborate necklaces, and breasts less prominent than those of the Quetta figures. They are found at Mundigak IV, 1-2 (Casal, 1961a, Pl. XLI, 8, 9). The differences in style and level between these Mundigak examples suggests that the IV, 1, examples display the type of head originally found on the Quetta figures and that the IV, 2, example typifies the Zhob variety. Other types of female figurines found in Mundigak IV have parallels farther west (e.g., ibid., Pls. XLI, 4-6, and XLII, 10-16). Many female figurines were found at Kulli and Mehi (Stein, 1931, Pls. XXII and XXXI). Their pillar-shaped bodies, elaborate necklaces, indifferent treatment of the breasts, hollow eyes, and some of the headdresses suggest a close generic relationship with the Zhob figurines (cf. especially Stein, 1931, Pl. XXXI, Mehi III.4.2 and I.9.7a). The Kulli type figurines represent the earliest known occurrence of female representations in southern Baluchistan.

This leads to a discussion of the relationship of the Nal (polychrome), Kulli, and Amri "cultures." It seems possible on present evidence that the Kulli "culture" of southern Baluchistan, with its important south Iranian and Mesopotamian parallels (Piggott, 1950, p. 96; and now Thorvildsen, 1963), was a late development out of the basic Nal complex. The areal distributions of Nal (polychrome) and Kulli sites overlap, but there is a definite altitudinal difference in the zones occupied by these two groups. Nal settlements are found in the medium altitude zone of from 1,000 to 1,300 meters, whereas the Kulli settlements are found in the lower altitude zone, to 700 meters (Raikes, 1964, and personal communications). Many similarities are seen between the Nal (polychrome) and Amri pottery repertoires, in both shapes and painted designs. This suggested relative time relationship between Nal (polychrome), Kulli, and Amri culture settlements is partly supported by reports from the current French excavations at Nindowari in the Ornach Valley (Casal, personal communication). Here post-cemetery (non-polychrome) Nal-type pottery having the distinctive floral or bucranium "Sadaat" motif is found in association with typical Kulli pottery. During the first two seasons at Nindowari, only a single sherd of Nal polychrome and no Amrian was found.

As for the Kulli "culture" itself, its position in relation to the mature Harappan civilization of the Indus Valley and its role in connection with south Iran, the Persian Gulf, and lower Mesopotamia are still intriguing problems. Much has been written about the supposed contemporaneity of the Kulli culture with at least part of the Harappan period. Piggott (1950) considered the two to be contemporary. D. H. Gordon (1958, p. 52) followed Piggott, and further considered the Harappan-like pottery shapes found in Kulli contexts to be actual imports from the Indus Valley. Wheeler has been more cautious. He raises the question whether Harappan motifs at Kulli and the presence of the Harappan "sacred brazier" among the Kulli shapes is due to direct interaction or whether "the former is in a true sense antecedent and proto-Harappan" (1960, p. 13). The recent description of monumental stone structures in the Las Bela district of southern West Pakistan (Fairservis, 1961b,c,d; Bacon, 1963) could be used in support of the idea of Kulli over Harappan priority. Some of these remains are reportedly associated with Kulli objects and some with mature Harappan materials, suggesting a time difference between the two assemblages. But again we are faced with one of the basic deficiencies in our knowledge of the pre- and Early Harappan sequence. The hypothetical Early Harappan period has yet to be clearly defined (see, e.g., Casal 1961c; Fairservis, 1961b,c,d). Although what may be described as proto-Harappan elements are present at many of the sites from Afghanistan to the Indus Valley, one still gets the impression that at stratigraphically excavated sites such as Amri and Kot Diji the mature Harappan imposes itself on the long-established pre-Harappan settlements. Even at Kalibangan, where there is an "Overlapped" period between "Antecedent" and Harappan, the Harappan objects in the mixed contexts seem to be of mature Harappan character as known from the large Indus Valley sites. One method of solving this dilemma would be to excavate the lowest levels at a site such as Mohenjo-daro.

One indirect bit of evidence supporting the supposition that Kulli and Harappan were at least partly contemporary is the presence of Harappan fortified seaports along the Makran coast of West Pakistan (Dales, 1962; Pakistan Archaeology, 1964, pp. 36-37) and the heavy concentration of Kulli sites in the Kej Valley paralleling the Makran coast (e.g., Field, 1959). Present evidence indicates no significant cultural Phase in this coastal area immediately after the Kulli period. If the Harappan seaports were post-Kulli, why then would they have been such formidable defensive establishments? At present it seems that the Kulli people—apparently hostile to the Harappans—are the only raison d'être for the elaborate Harappan establishments. A new element has, however, recently entered the picture which tends to support the idea that the Kulli people were in fact the middlemen in the trade and cultural contacts between the Harappans and Mesopotamia. The discovery of typical Kulli materials on the island of Umm an-Nar (Abu Dhabi) off the Trucial Coast in the Persian Gulf (Thorvildsen, 1963) and the lack of Harappan remains that far west suggest that the Kulli people were the carriers of goods between the Persian Gulf and the Harappan seaports now known to exist as far west as the present Pakistan-Iran border. Additional research into this question is obviously of prime importance. Such research should involve a thorough survey of the southern coast of Iran and an attempt to define better the material and stylistic development of the Harappan civilization. The relative date of the Harappan seaports in the total life cycle of the Harappan civilization is crucial, but attempts to determine this precisely through comparative studies of pottery from the coastal sites with that published from the large Indus Valley sites are so far inconclusive.

To return to the details of Phase E, it is noteworthy that stamp seals are now made of copper (e.g., Mundigak, Casal, 1961a, Pl. XLV,

B; and post-cemetery Nal, Hargreaves, 1929, Pl. XV,d). Clay house models (?) or compartmented boxes are found in corresponding levels at Mundigak (Casal, 1961a, Fig. 130:6) and in the Quetta area (Fairservis, 1956, pp. 226-28, Fig. 21), and further study may show a direct relationship between such clay objects in the north and the incised compartmented stone vessels of the contemporary Kulli culture in the south (e.g., Stein, 1931, Pl. XXVIII, Mehi I.6.4). The latter vessels have been the object of considerable discussion (Piggott, 1950, pp. 110-11; Gordon, 1958, p. 48; Wheeler, 1960, p. 87), because of their possible relation to incised gray-ware vessels from southeastern Iran and similarly decorated gray stone vessels from Early Dynastic contexts in Mesopotamia (Delougaz, 1960). In addition, there may now be included incised pottery vessels from Cairn II at Umm an-Nar in the Persian Gulf (Thorvildsen, 1963, Fig. 20). Unfortunately, the parallels for these distinctive vessels are not securely dated at the Indus Valley end, since they are reported from both the upper and lower levels at Mohenjo-daro.

The introduction of lapis lazuli—usually in the form of beads—into Baluchistan can be dated to the early part of Phase E, although examples occurred at Mundigak considerably earlier (first in I, 4). It occurs in Baluchistan, at Damb Sadaat II (Fairservis, 1956, p. 230), at Nal in post-cemetery contexts (Hargreaves, 1929), at Kulli and Mehi (Stein, 1931), and possibly in Seistan (Site 109, Fairservis, 1961a, Fig. 35, B). Bronze pins (cosmetic sticks?) with double-volute heads occur at Mundigak IV (Casal, 1961a, p. 249, Fig. 139, 18). They also occur sporadically in the large Indus sites, but their wide distribution in time and space (throughout the Near East and Mediterranean) discredits them at present as reliable relative dating criteria (the same is true of pins with animal heads). Hollow clay balls, with either painted or incised decorations, are found at both Mundigak and the Quetta sites throughout Phase E. These are paralleled at the Indus sites, but it is again a question which part of the Harappan cycle they belong to. A striking—and anachronistic—parallel is provided by identical pottery traps or cages for small animals. These occur in Mundigak IV, 1 (Casal, 1961a, types 314, 314a) and Mohenjo-daro "Upper Levels" (Mackay, 1938, p. 427, Pl. LIV, 16, 17, 20-22; Pl. CVII, 22).

The most spectacular parallel between Mundigak and the Indus Valley is a sculptured stone male head from Mundigak IV, 3—our Late Phase E (Casal, 1961a, p. 255, Pls. XLIII, XLIV). Stylistically, it is closely related to the rare examples of statuary from Mohenjo-daro (Marshall, 1931, Vol. III, Pls. XCVIII, XCIX). The Mohenjo-daro examples are said to belong to the Late Period of the site.

PHASE F

Phase F should include, first of all (Early Phase F), the period of the mature Indus (Harappan) civilization as we know it from Mohenjo-daro (Marshall, 1931; Mackay, 1938), Harappa (Vats, 1940; Wheeler, 1947), and Chanhu-daro (Mackay, 1943). Detailed syntheses of these reports have been made by Piggott (1950), Gordon (1958), Mode (1959), and Wheeler (1959, 1960, 1961), and need not be repeated here. Late Phase F should correspond with the Late Harappan period—the period of decline, eventual abandonment of the large Indus Valley sites, and the shift of focus to the southeast into Gujarat. As explained at the beginning of this paper, this final Harappan period is not discussed here, not merely because of space limitations, but also because it would be premature at this time when our whole concept of the decline and end of the civilization is undergoing a radical readjustment.

FOREIGN PARALLELS

Only those objects that are sufficiently distinctive to warrant an assumption of "contact" are cited here, and comparisons are made with those foreign sites that are in the closest geographical proximity. The initial appearance of each item is stressed—not its duration. Despite the paucity of comparative materials, a pattern is beginning to emerge. During Phases C and D the principal contacts were via the northern overland routes (see map). With Phase E southern contacts (perhaps by coastal sea trade) became popular, and by Phase F most of the contacts were via the southern routes. Phases A and B are still too little known to warrant detailed comparisons. Reference should be made to Dyson's chronological chart for Iran (see p. 249). Foreign parallels and dating are discussed by Piggott (1950), Gordon (1958), Wheeler (1960), Khan (1955), and Mode (1961).

<u>Phase C</u>:

1. Metal (appears in the western part of our area): in Iran, Hissar IA, and earlier at Sialk.
2. Potter's wheel: Mundigak I, 2; in Iran, Hissar IB, Sialk III,4.

3. Togau "A" naturalistic painted decoration on pottery: Anjira II; Mundigak I,3; in Iran, Sialk III,4-5.
4. Dot-tipped rosettes on painted pottery: Kili Ghul Mohammad II-III; in Iran, Hissar IC, Bakun AIII, Sialk III, 1-5.
5. Crude stone "weights" with handles: Mundigak I,5; in Iran, Hissar IC.
6. Clay bull figurines: Mundigak only; in Iran, Hissar I.
7. Parallel-sided flint blades (appear at end of phase): in Iran, Hissar I, Sialk III.
8. Alabaster vessels: Mundigak I; in Iran, Sialk III, 5-7.

Phase D:

1. Gray ware (plain or painted): Mundigak III; Nal cemetery (with polychrome); Anjira III (Togau D); in Iran, Hissar IIA.
2. Pedestaled (hollow base) pottery bowls: Mundigak III; Rana Ghundai II (Zhob district); in Iran, Hissar IC-IIA.
3. Shaft hole ax and adz: Mundigak III,6; in Iran, Sialk III,4 (adz).
4. Clay animal-figurines, painted bulls: Mundigak II; in Iran, Hissar IC.
5. Clay female figurines, crude, pillar-based, outstretched arms: Mundigak II,3; in Iran, Hissar IIA.
6. Stamp seals, compartmented, non-metallic materials: Mundigak II; in Iran, Hissar IA, Sialk III,4.

Phase E:

1. Stamp seals, compartmented, metal: Mundigak IV, 1; in Iran, Hissar IIB.
2. Metal pins, double-volute head: Mundigak IV, 3; in Iran, Hissar IIB, Sialk IV.
3. Clay female figurines, pillar base, fanlike arms, painted: Mundigak IV,3; in Iran, Bakun A.
4. Animal style on painted pottery: Mundigak IV,1; Kulli; in southern Iran and southern Mesopotamia, Susa D period; in Persian Gulf, Umm an-Nar.
5. Incised stone and gray-ware vessels: southern Baluchistan; in Persian Gulf, Umm an-Nar; in lower Mesopotamia, various sites (mainly of Early Dynastic date).

Phase F:

1. Indus style stamp seals: mature Harappan sites; in Mesopotamia, Tepe Gawra VI "Akkadian" in north, Tell Asmar "Akkadian" in central, and various other sites in central and south (mainly Akkadian to Larsa period contexts).
2. Gaming dice: Harappan sites; in Mesopotamia, Tepe Gawra VI "Akkadian."
3. Clay figurines, fat males with movable arms: Chanhu-daro (Harappan levels); in southern Mesopotamia, Nippur "Isin-Larsa" levels (unpublished).

RADIOCARBON DATES

The figures given here are all B.C. dates calculated on the new half life of 5,730 years. Old solid carbon samples—marked *—have been further increased by a 200-year factor to correct for the Suess effect (information from University of Pennsylvania radiocarbon laboratory). Note that in the recent articles by Agrawal (1964) and Lal (1963) this 200-year factor was not added.

REFERENCES: Agrawal (1964); Agrawal, et al. (1964); Broecker, et al. (1956); Kusumgar, et al. (1963); Lal (1963); Ralph (1959); Stuckenrath (1963). The unpublished Ghar-i-Mar dates are through the courtesy of L. Dupree.

	B.C. Dates	Laboratory designations
Phase A:		
Northern Afghanistan		
Ghar-i-Mar (Snake Cave)		
"Mesolithic"	ca. 6700	Hv-425
Phase B:		
Northern Afghanistan		
Ghar-i-Mar (Snake Cave)		
Ceramic Neolithic	ca. 5270	Hv-428
Ceramic Neolithic	ca. 5080	Hv-429
Northern Baluchistan		
Kili Ghul Mohammad I	3712 ± 515	L-180A*
Kili Ghul Mohammad I	3688 ± 85	P-524
Kashmir		
Burzahom		
Neolithic Phase I	1850 ± 130	TF-13
Neolithic Phase I	1540 ± 110	TF-15
South India		
Utnur		
Neolithic, sub-period IB	2295 ± 155	BM-54
Phase C:		
No dates		
Phase D:		
Northern Baluchistan		
Damb Sadaat I	2528 ± 361	L-180B*
Lower Indus Valley		
Kot Diji		
Level 14, Early KD culture	2605 ± 145	P-196
Phase E:		
Northern Baluchistan		
Damb Sadaat II	2559 ± 202	P-522
Damb Sadaat II	2425 ± 412	L-180C*
Damb Sadaat II	2425 ± 361	L-180E*
Damb Sadaat II	2200 ± 76	P-523

Southern Baluchistan		
Niai Buthi (Las Bela)		
Kulli culture	1900 ± 65	P-478
Lower Indus Valley		
Kot Diji		
Level 5, Late KD culture	2335 ± 155	P-179
Level 5, Late KD culture	2255 ± 140	P-180
Level 4, Late KD culture	2090 ± 140	P-195
Phase F:		
Lower Indus Valley		
Mohenjo-daro		
Late Level	1760 ± 115	TF-75
Northern Rajasthan (W. India)		
Kalibangan		
Lower Middle Harappan	2062 ± 103	TF-145
Lower Middle Harappan	2031 ± 103	TF-147
Middle Harappan	1964 ± 103	TF-151
Middle Harappan	1939 ± 103	TF-139
Late Harappan	2095 ± 115	TF-25
Late (mid.?) Harappan	2045 ± 75	P-481
Late Harappan	1902 ± 103	TF-150
Gujarat (W. India)		
Lothal		
Period A - Harappan		
Phase IIIB	2005 ± 115	TF-27
Phase IIIB	1995 ± 125	TF-26
End of Phase IIIB	2010 ± 115	TF-22
Phase IVA	1900 ± 115	TF-29
Post Harappan		
Gujarat (W. India)		
Lothal		
Period B		
Phase VA	1865 ± 110	TF-23
Phase VA	1810 ± 140	TF-19

Published dates for Mundigak (Casal, 1961a) are unreliable. New samples, unpublished, have been run.

	AFGHANISTAN				BALUCHISTAN	
	NORTH	KANDAHAR		SEISTAN	QUETTA AREA	
CULTURAL PHASES	Ghar-i-mar (Snake Cave)	Mundigak	Deh Morasi Ghundai	Surface Survey	Revised Sequence	Fairservis Sequence
F		?	?	?	?	
E Late		IV 3	III	↑	DS III "Sadaat"	Period G3 DS III
		IV 2	IIc ?			Period G2 DS II, upper levels
E Early		IV 1	IIb IIa	↓	DS II "Quetta"	Period G1 DS II
D		III 6 5 4 3 2 1	?		DS I ? KGM IV	Period H2 KGM IV- DS I
		II				
C		I 6 5 4 3 2 1	?		KGM III KGM II	Period H1 KGM III; Period I KGM II
B	Ceramic Neolithic / Non-ceramic Neolithic		I ?		? KGM I ?	Period J KGM I
A	Mesolithic Palaeolithic?					

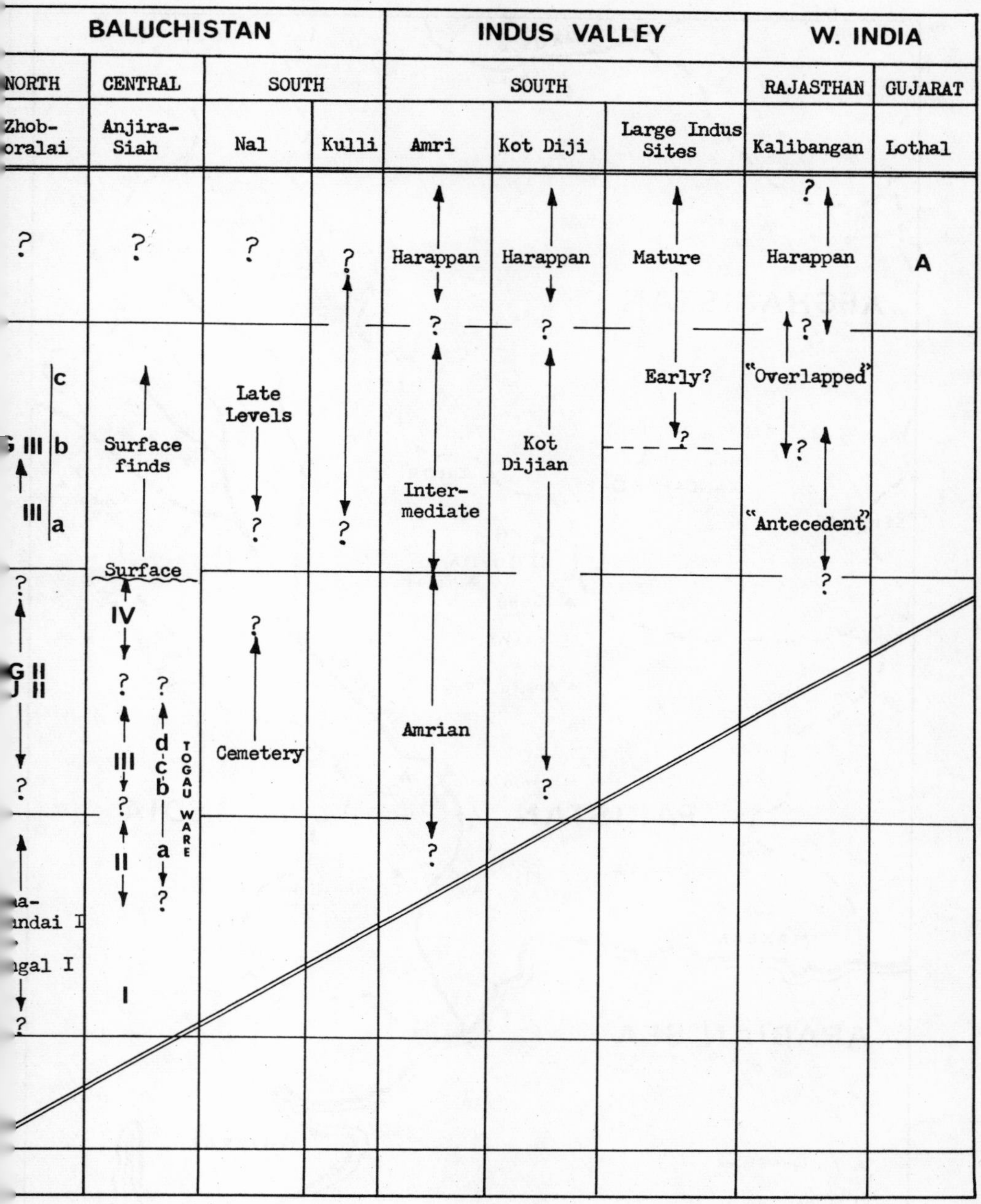

BALUCHISTAN				INDUS VALLEY			W. INDIA	
NORTH	CENTRAL	SOUTH		SOUTH			RAJASTHAN	GUJARAT
Zhob-oralai	Anjira-Siah	Nal	Kulli	Amri	Kot Diji	Large Indus Sites	Kalibangan	Lothal
?	?	?	?	Harappan ?	Harappan ?	Mature	? Harappan ?	A
c G III b III a	Surface finds Surface	Late Levels ?	?	Intermediate	Kot Dijian	Early? ?	"Overlapped" ? "Antecedent" ?	
? IV G II J II ?	IV ? ? III ? ? d c b TOGAU WARE	? Cemetery		Amrian	?			
a- ndai I gal I ?	II ? a ? I			?				

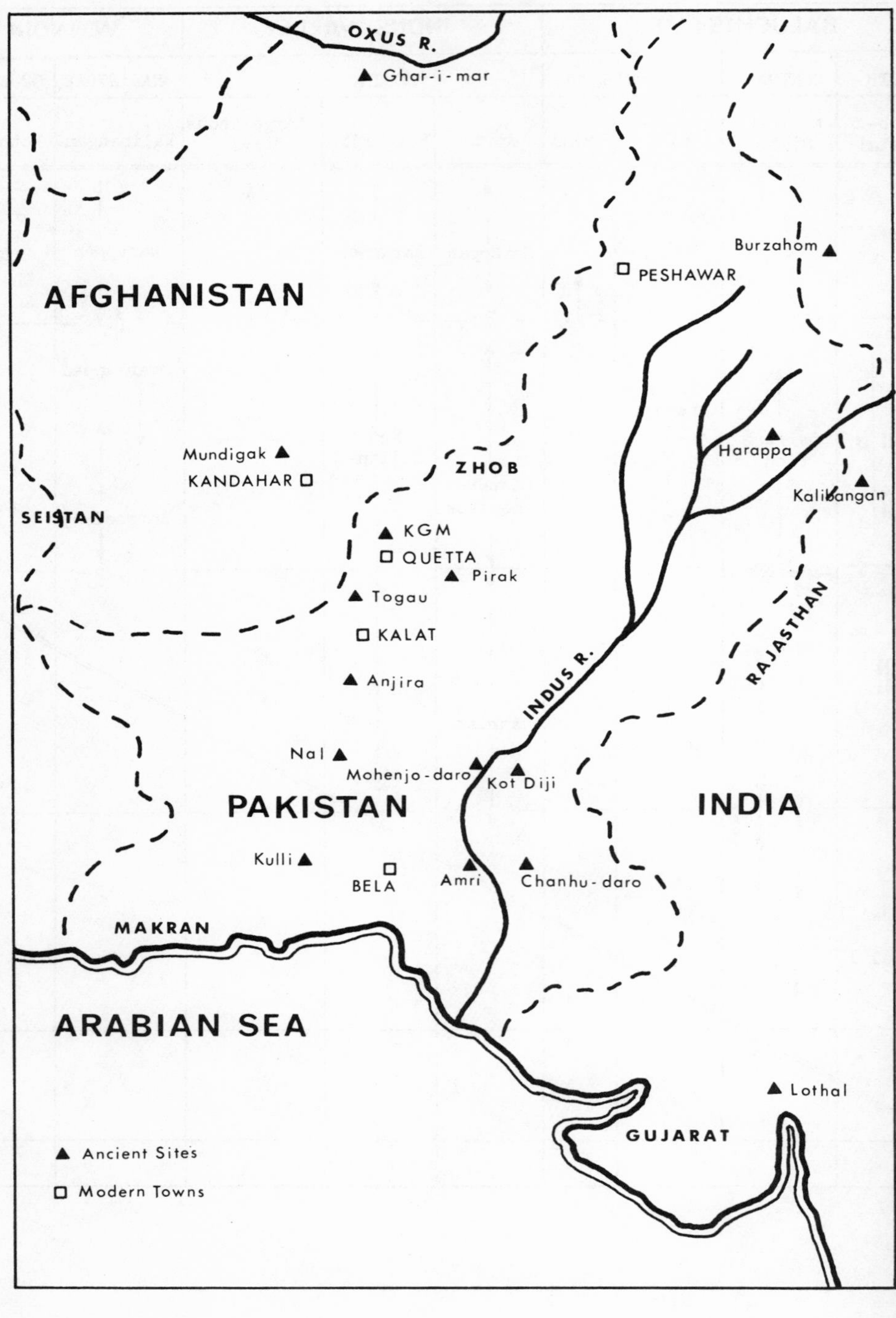
OXUS R.
Ghar-i-mar
AFGHANISTAN
PESHAWAR
Burzahom
Mundigak
KANDAHAR
ZHOB
Harappa
Kalibangan
SEISTAN
KGM
QUETTA
Pirak
Togau
KALAT
Anjira
INDUS R.
RAJASTHAN
Nal
Mohenjo-daro
Kot Diji
PAKISTAN
INDIA
Kulli
BELA
Amri
Chanhu-daro
MAKRAN
ARABIAN SEA
Lothal
GUJARAT
Ancient Sites
Modern Towns

Bibliography

(For Iranian sites, see R. H. Dyson's Bibliography, pp. 252-56, above)

Agrawal, D. P.

1964a "Harappa Culture: New Evidence for a Shorter Chronology," Science 143: 950-52.

Agrawal, D. P., Kusumgar, S., Lal, D., and Sarna, R. P.

1964 "Tata Institute Radiocarbon Date List II," Radiocarbon 6: 226-32.

Allchin, F. R.

1963 Neolithic Cattle-Keepers of South India. Cambridge: Cambridge University Press.

Bacon, E.

1963 "Bridge to the Ancient East: The New Knowledge of Early Afghanistan." In Vanished Civilizations, pp. 251-78. New York: McGraw-Hill.

Broecker, W. S., Kulp, J. L., and Tucek, C. S.

1956 "Lamont Natural Radiocarbon Measurements III," Science 124: 154-65.

Casal, J.-M.

1960 "Archéologie pakistanaise les fouilles de Kot-diji," Arts asiatiques VII: 53-60.

1961a Fouilles de Mundigak. ("Memoires de la Delegation archéologique française en Afghanistan," Tome XVII.). 2 vols. Paris: Librairie C. Klincksieck.

1961b "Rapport provisoire sur les fouilles exécutées à Amri (Pakistan) en 1959-1960," Arts asiatiques VIII: 11-26.

1961c "Les debuts de la civilisation de l'Indus à la lumière de fouilles récentes." In Comptes rendus des séances de l'année 1960, pp. 305-16. Paris: Académie des Inscriptions et Belles-Lettres.

1964 "Fresh Digging at Amri," Pakistan Archaeology I: 57-65.

Dales, G. F.

1962 "Harappan Outposts on the Makran Coast," Antiquity XXXVI: 86-92.

Dani, A. H.

1960 Prehistory and Protohistory of Eastern India. Calcutta: K. L. Mukhopadhyay.

DeCardi, B.

1950 "On the Borders of Pakistan: Recent Exploration," Journal of the Royal India, Pakistan and Ceylon Society 24: 52-57.

1959 "New Wares and Fresh Problems from Baluchistan," Antiquity XXXIII: 15-24.

1964 "British Expeditions to Kalat, 1948 and 1957," Pakistan Archaeology I: 20-29.

Delougaz, P.

1960 "Architectural Representations on Steatite Vases," Iraq XXII: 90-95.

Dupree, L.

1963 Deh Morasi Ghundai: A Chalcolithic Site in South-Central Afghanistan (Anthropological Papers of the American Museum of Natural History, Vol. L, Part 2).

1964 Notes on Ghar-i-Mar supplied to the author.

Dupree, L., and Howe, B.

1963 "Results of an Archaeological Survey for Stone Age Sites in Northern Afghanistan (1)," Afghanistan 2 (Historical Society of Afghanistan): 1-15.

Fairservis, W. A., Jr.

1956 Excavations in the Quetta Valley, West Pakistan (Anthropological Papers of the American Museum of Natural History, Vol. XLV, Part 2).

1959 Archaeological Surveys in the Zhob and Loralai Districts, West Pakistan (ibid., Vol. XLVII, Part 2).

1961a Archaeological Studies in the Seistan Basin of Southwestern Afghanistan and Eastern Iran (ibid., Vol. XLVIII, Part 1).

1961b The Harappan Civilization—New Evidence and More Theory (American Museum Novitates, No. 2055) New York.

1961c "Possible Light on the Indus Valley Civilization: Huge Sites in Baluchistan Recently Discovered and Awaiting the Spade," Illustrated London News, August 26, 324-27.

1961d Baluchistan Find: Ruins of a 4,000 Year Old Culture Still Standing in West Pakistan. Natural History, LXX (6): 22-29.

Field, H.

1959 An Anthropological Reconnaissance in West Pakistan, 1955 (Papers of the Peabody Museum, Harvard University, Vol. LII).

Gordon, D. H.

1958 The Prehistoric Background of Indian Culture. Bombay: Bhulabhai Memorial Institute.

Hargreaves, H.

1929 Excavations in Baluchistan 1925. (Memoirs of the Archaeological Survey of India, No. 35) Calcutta.

Indian Archaeology: A Review. Archaeological Survey of India.

Khan, F. A.

1955 "Fresh Sidelights on the Indus Valley and the Bronze Age Orient," Annual Report of the Institute of Archaeology (University of London), pp. 51-68.

1958 "Before Mohenjo-daro: New Light on the Beginnings of the Indus Valley Civilization from Recent Excavations at Kot Diji," Illustrated London News, May 24, 866-67.

n.d. Preliminary Report on the Kot Diji Excavations: 1957-58. Department of Archaeology, Karachi.

Kusumgar, S., Lal, D., and Sarna, R. P.

1963 "Tata Institute Radiocarbon Date List I," Radiocarbon 5: 273-82.

Lal, B. B.

1962 "A New Indus Valley Provincial Capital Discovered: Excavation at Kalibangan in Northern Rajasthan," Illustrated London News, March 24, 454-57.

1963 "A Picture Emerges—an Assessment of the Carbon-14 Datings of the Protohistoric Cultures of the Indo-Pakistan Subcontinent," Ancient India, Nos. 18 and 19 (1962 and 1963), pp. 208-21.

McCown, D. E.

1954 "The Relative Stratigraphy and Chronology of Iran." In Relative Chronologies in Old World Archeology, ed. Robert Ehrich, pp. 56-58. Chicago: University of Chicago Press.

Mackay, E. J. H.

1938 Further Excavations at Mohenjo-daro. Delhi: Government of India.

1943 Chanhu-daro Excavations, 1935-36. New Haven: American Oriental Society.

Marshall, Sir John

1931 Mohenjo-daro and the Indus Civilization. London: Arthur Probsthain.

Mode, H.

1959 Das Frühe Indien. Stuttgart: Gustav Kilpper Verlag.

1961 The Harappa Culture and the West (Calcutta Sanskrit College Research Series, No. XVI, Studies No. 6).

Pakistan Archaeology

1964 Number I. Department of Archaeology, Pakistan.

Piggott, S.

1950 Prehistoric India. Harmondsworth: Pelican Books.

Puglisi, S. M.

1963 "Preliminary Report on the Researches at Hazar Sum (Samangan)," East and West (Rome), XIV (1-2), 3-12.

Raikes, R. L.

1963 "New Prehistoric Bichrome Ware from the Plains of Baluchistan (West Pakistan)," East and West, XIV (1-2), 56-58.

1965 "Physical Environment and Human Settlement in Prehistoric

Times in the Near and Middle East: A Hydrological Approach," East and West, XV (3-4), 179-93.

Ralph, E. K.

1959 "University of Pennsylvania Radiocarbon Dates III," Radiocarbon Supplement, I, 45-58.

Sankalia, H. D.

1963 Prehistory and Protohistory in India and Pakistan. Bombay: University of Bombay.

Stein, Sir M. A.

1929 An Archaeological Tour in Waziristan and Northern Baluchistan (Memoirs of the Archaeological Survey of India, No. 37). Calcutta.

1931 An Archaeological Tour in Gedrosia (ibid., No. 43). Calcutta.

1937 Archaeological Reconnaissances in North-Western India and South-Eastern Iran. London: Macmillan & Co., Ltd.

Stuckenrath, R.

1963 "University of Pennsylvania Radiocarbon Dates VI," Radiocarbon 5: 82-103.

Thapar, B. K.

1963 Notes supplied to the author.

Thorvildsen, K.

1963 "Burial Cairns on Umm an-Nar" (in Danish with English summary), KUML 1962 (Denmark), pp. 191-219.

Vats, M. S.

1940 Excavations at Harappa. Calcutta: Government of India Press.

Wheeler, Sir R. E. M.

1947 "Harappa 1946: The Defences and Cemetery R.37," Ancient India, No. 3, pp. 58-130.

1959 Early India and Pakistan. New York: Frederick A. Praeger, Inc.

1960 The Indus Civilization. Supplement to The Cambridge History of India, 2d rev. ed.

1961 "Ancient India." In The Dawn of Civilization, ed. S. Piggott, pp. 229-52. New York: McGraw-Hill.

Since submitting the original manuscript, the final report on the Amri excavations has appeared. See Casal, J.-M., Fouilles d'Amri. ("Publications de la Commission des Fouilles Archéologiques.") 2 vols. Paris: Libraire C. Klincksieck. 1964. Also new is Ancient Pakistan: Bulletin of the Department of Archaeology, University of Peshawar. Vol. 1 (1964) which contains "Sanghao Cave Excavation" by A. H. Dani (pp. 1-50) and "Stone Vases as Evidence of Connection between Mesopotamia and the Indus Valley" by F. A. Durrani (pp. 51-96).

New excavations were conducted at Mohenjo-daro during the winter of 1964-65. See G. F. Dales, "New Excavations at Mohenjo-daro," Archaeology 18, Number 2 (Summer, 1965) and Expedition 7, Number 4 (Summer, 1965).

The Relative Chronology of the Aegean in the Stone and Early Bronze Ages

Saul S. Weinberg
University of Missouri

So great have been the changes in the prehistory of the Aegean, as well as of neighboring countries, since the first symposium on Relative Chronologies was held at the end of 1952, that there will be only sporadic resemblances between the picture drawn then (Weinberg, 1954) and that presented here. Most important has been the great lengthening of our vista, first with the discovery of an Aceramic Neolithic assemblage in Thessaly in 1956 (Milojčić, 1960), and then with the finding in the same region in 1958 of Middle and Late Palaeolithic remains (Milojčić, 1958). From Thessaly to the Peloponnesos (Leroi-Gourhan, 1964) there is now clear evidence of the presence of Middle Palaeolithic stone industries related to the Levalloiso-Mousterian of continental Europe; from a cave in Chalcidice came a Neanderthal skull of the same period (Kokkoros and Kanellis, 1960). The almost simultaneous finding of similar material in Level XII of the rock shelter at Crvena Stijena in Montenegro (Brodar, 1958, pp. 62-63) indicates one step in the route down the Balkan peninsula into Greece, and forms the earliest of many newly established ties between Greece and Yugoslavia. In Yugoslavia, these remains have been co-ordinated with the first phase of the Würm glaciation. Upper Palaeolithic industries found in Epirus in 1962 and 1963 (Higgs, 1963, pp. 2-3) have been likened to those of Germany, Hungary, and the U.S.S.R., and placed toward the end of the first warmer oscillation between Early and Main Würm. The material from the Seidi Cave in Boeotia, dug in 1941 (Stampfuss, 1942) and tested again in 1956, combines Aurignacian, Magdalenian, and Gravettian features, suggesting a Late Palaeolithic, or perhaps even a Mesolithic, date. Similar material came from Levels VII-V at Crvena Stijena (Brodar, 1957, p. 55; 1958, pp. 62-64) late in the main phase of the Würm glaciation. Other Late Palaeolithic-Mesolithic industries are now known not only from many places on the mainland of Greece but from the island of Skyros in the north Aegean (Theochares, 1959b, pp. 323-25) and possibly from both Zakynthos (Zapfe, 1937) and

Kephallenia (Petrocheilos, 1959; Marinatos, 1960) in the Ionian Sea, pointing up the early date at which travel by sea developed in the Aegean; on Skyros, obsidian, probably from Melos, is already present, suggesting not only travel by sea but sea-borne commerce over considerable distances.

Whether or not Greece played any part in the revolution that changed man from a food-gatherer to a food-producer is far from evident at present, but it has been clear since 1956 (Milojčić, 1960) that the Aceramic Neolithic type of culture which has become so well known in the Near East during the past fifteen years existed on the Greek main land as well. Only three sites in Thessaly—Argissa (Milojčić, Boessneck and Hopf, 1962), Sesklo, and Soufli (Theochares, 1958b)—have been excavated, but surface finds suggest that other sites in Thessaly and possibly in Attica as well (Milojčić, 1960, pp. 328-31) were settled in this early period. The material assemblage—with its typical microlithic industries in flint and obsidian, its abundant use of both large and small bone tools, its stone pounders, "palettes" and "ear-plugs"—is certainly related to that of the Near Eastern centers, but there is lacking the rich development of a polished stone industry which produced bowls, bracelets, beads, and pendants of a high order of competence. Only the "ear-plugs" in Greece are occasionally of the high quality obtained by the grinders and polishers of stone at Jarmo (Braidwood and Howe, 1960, pp. 45-46) and other Near Eastern settlements. Although in both regions the first settled communities are of the Aceramic Neolithic period, the small Greek huts—often partly dug into the ground, sometimes supported on a framework of wooden posts—cannot compare with the elaborate architectural development at Jericho (Kenyon, 1960, pp. 43-44, 48) and Khirokitia (Dikaios, 1953, pp. 14-195) or even the large mud houses of Jarmo (Braidwood and Howe, 1960, pp. 40-43). On the other hand, the agriculture and domestication of animals that was the economic basis for the settlements in both regions was much the same. Despite the far more primitive nature of the material assemblage in Greece, there are sufficient similarities with that of the Near Eastern Aceramic phase to relate the two; that of Greece was probably an offshoot from the Near East. To the north, in Yugoslavia, Level IV at Crvena Stijena (Benac, 1957a, pp. 48-50; 1958, pp. 41-42) produced a material culture much like that of the Thessalian Aceramic culture.

The arrival of Neolithic potters in Greece seems to have been sudden and widespread, but Theochares now believes that Sesklo shows continuity (Theochares, 1963). The three Thessalian sites which have Aceramic strata were taken over by the pot-producers; from Macedonia in the north to Laconia in the south, from Skyros in the east to Messenia in the west, the new settlers are in evidence at numerous sites. Not only the presence of pottery, already in a well-developed form, but the complete difference in both the stone and bone industries from those of the Aceramic Neolithic period, preclude a local development from the Aceramic to the Ceramic, or Early Neolithic, period. At the three Thessalian sites where both occur, there may well have been a leveling of the sites by the pottery users, which would then have deprived us of some of the record of the earlier period. At twenty-eight sites, levels of the Early Neolithic period have been excavated, although sometimes in limited trial digs; at least ten more surface finds indicate that such early material is present. Even considering the degree to which archaeological reconnaissance has lagged in western Greece, there is still a marked preponderance of sites not only in the eastern part of the country but on the coast and up the valleys leading from it, giving a distinct orientation both eastward and seaward.

Culturally, Greece of the Early Neolithic period presents a "*koiné*" not achieved again in Neolithic times; Crete, however, may be in a separate tradition. Although pit dwellings may still have been in use at the beginning of the Early Neolithic, the architecture of the period was largely rectangular from the beginning, with walls at first of mud or wattle and daub on a framework of wooden posts, but later of mud brick, sometimes even on stone foundations in upper levels of the Early Neolithic period. A fortification ditch more than two meters deep protected the Early Neolithic settlement at Soufli (Theochares, 1958*b*, p. 80). The twelve-meter—square structures at Nea Nikomedeia (Rodden, 1964, p. 564), about which the smaller houses cluster, indicate the height of architectural achievement for the period. Moreover, the unusual size and position of these structures and the exceptional nature of the finds from them indicate a special purpose—as a cult place but perhaps as the chief's house as well. In these buildings, as everywhere in the earliest Early Neolithic levels of mainland sites, occur standing female steatopygous figurines of clay with arms bent and hands on or under the breasts. Everywhere the earliest figurines were the most "naturalistic"; by the end of the Early Neolithic period, stylization was already marked.

A fragment of one such figure found on hardpan at Pyrasos has four "buttons" on the left shoulder—a clear indication of clothing represented in a manner that can be paralleled exactly at Tell Halaf, as Theochares noted (1959a, p. 65). Also from on hardpan at Pyrasos comes a seated nude male figure of clay (Theochares, 1959a, pp. 64-65). Characteristic of all these figurines are the slit "coffee-bean" eyes, to use Rodden's term (1962, p. 285), an imitation of the cowrie shells at home in the Near East but not in the Aegean; such shells were already used for eyes in the plastered skulls of the Pre-ceramic Neolithic period at Jericho (Kenyon, 1960, p. 52). Stone human figurines are absent from Early Neolithic deposits on the mainland. Clay figures of animals are common, but especially noteworthy are two beautifully modeled greenstone frogs and part of a third, from Nea Nikomedeia (Rodden, 1962, p. 286; 1964, p. 604). From the same site also come a bull's head attachment to a pot, the head of a goat, and the head of a bird. Five anthropomorphic vessels with faces modeled just beneath the rim are also from Nea Nikomedeia; Rodden (1964, p. 566) has likened these to the painted, or modeled and painted, vases from Hassuna of the Samarra period (Lloyd and Safar, 1945, p. 281), and Hacılar (Mellaart, 1960, pp. 103-4) respectively. A drinking cup in the form of a woman's head from Hacılar VI (Mellaart, 1961, p. 66) is earlier than the painted examples, and is perhaps a closer parallel to the modeled faces on the vases from Nea Nikomedeia.

In 1952 we had no evidence of burial methods of the Early Neolithic period, but we now have twenty-nine graves—all single interments, except for the mother and two children buried together in a pit at Nea Nikomedeia (Rodden, 1962, p. 286). All the burials are simple inhumations in a roughly dug pit, with the body in a strongly flexed position, usually lying on the side; however, two at Nea Nikomedeia lie on the back (Rodden, 1962, p. 286; 1964, pp. 605-7), and the one burial at Argissa lies prone (Milojčić, 1959, p. 9). In only one grave—at Lerna (Caskey, 1958, p. 138)—were there any grave goods (a small hemispherical bowl of gray-black burnished ware), but at both Nea Nikomedeia and Argissa it was observed that pieces of meat had probably been placed in some of the graves, as indicated by animal bones found there.

The earliest material assemblage that includes pottery also includes baked clay stamp seals with linear geometric motifs, except for one seal from Argissa of the "Protosesklo" phase which seems to portray a leaf (Milojčić, 1956, p. 164). Somewhat later must be the steatite stamp seal from the middle of Level I at Pyrasos (Theochares, 1959a, pp. 66-67), an exact parallel to which was found at Philia; an almost identical clay seal comes from Tsangli, and another is from Nea Nikomedeia (Rodden, 1964, fig. 20, center)—all these have designs of a maeandroid nature. That the cutting and polishing of stone was a competence possessed by these Early Neolithic settlers, although it was lacking in their predecessors of the Aceramic Neolithic period, is demonstrated by the frequency with which fragments of beautifully worked stone vases (in addition to the frogs and seals already cited) occur from the earliest levels of the period at numerous sites (Theochares, 1956, pp. 24-25). So too, the fully polished celt—whether ax, adz, or chisel—occurs from the very beginning of the pottery Neolithic; at Nea Nikomedeia axes as much as 0.20 m. long were found in the large central structure (Rodden, 1964, p. 604). Almost as large are some of the heavy conical pestles from the Early Neolithic phase at Elateia (Weinberg, 1962, p. 205). Mortars, millstones, hammerstones, and polishing slabs occur. The finely polished stone studs, or "nose-plugs," from Nea Nikomedeia (Rodden, 1962, p. 285; 1964, p. 604, fig. 17) are a thinner and finer version of the "ear-plugs" of the Aceramic phase; Rodden suggests that they were placed as decoration in the hair, as indicated by a figurine from Pyrasos (Theochares, 1959a, pp. 65-66).

The chipped-stone industry is quite different from that of the Aceramic phase, consisting largely of blades of both obsidian and flint or chert. Although no obsidian was found in the Early Neolithic levels at Nea Nikomedeia (Rodden, 1962, p. 277), it is common to the south. Flint was used for scrapers as well as for blades. Large and broad blades are common at Lerna (Caskey, 1957, p. 160) and at Nea Makri (Theochares, 1956, p. 26), but elsewhere the blades are rather thin and not long. The limited repertory of stone tools was supplemented by some bone implements, largely awls and needles but also fishhooks, spatulas, and spoons or small ladles. In this period the bone tools were well polished. The only weapons known from the Early Neolithic are clay sling bullets (Weinberg, 1962, pp. 202-3), usually merely dried in the sun or around the hearth rather than baked. These are ubiquitous from the beginning of the Early Neolithic; in many places they occur in later periods as well. The unbaked clay "spools" at Elateia (Weinberg, 1962, pp. 203-4) also belong largely to the Early Neolithic period, and are present from its beginning;

they are not recorded elsewhere. The Early Neolithic clay lamp from Elateia (Weinberg, 1962, p. 204)—if indeed it is a lamp—is unique. Pierced disks made from pottery fragments, more or less well rounded, occur at many Early Neolithic sites, and were most likely used as spindle whorls (Weinberg, 1962, p. 204). There may even be loom weights from Nea Nikomedeia, a site which has produced ample evidence of weaving in impressions on pottery of what may be fine woolen textiles (Rodden, 1964, p. 605); also from this site are abundant impressions of matting and basketry (Rodden, 1964, p. 606, figs. 9-10).

Just as in the features of the Early Neolithic material culture described above we are able to establish with much greater certainty than was possible twelve years ago the important diagnostic features, so too we now know in greater detail just what the first pottery in Greece was like and how pottery developed within the Early Neolithic period. Both at Argissa (Milojčić, 1959, p. 7) and Sesklo (Theochares, 1962a, p. 43) in Thessaly and at Elateia in central Greece (Weinberg, 1962, pp. 167-72), at the bottom of the Neolithic accumulation have been isolated strata (as much as a meter deep at Elateia) bearing only unpainted wares, sometimes monochrome but often variegated. Every shade—from dark gray, through gray-brown, brown, red-brown, red, red-buff, buff to light buff, and even cream or white—occurs in both monochrome or variegated wares. At the beginning, the fabric is more often black at the core, but thoroughly fired pieces do occur. Almost everywhere the earliest shapes are hemispherical bowls and globular, collared jars; small pierced lugs, set either horizontally or vertically, are the only form of handle. Flat bottoms or ring bases, varying from very low to high; slightly everted lips, often separated by a groove; the beginnings of a carination at the belly; hole-mouthed jars—all these begin early, if in fact they are not present in the original repertory. Certainly there was a considerable development of shape, as well as much improvement in firing methods, guaranteeing a better control over the production of fairly light surface colors, before painting began. The first painted patterns were applied directly on the surface of the vase (Weinberg, 1962, pp. 175-76), the patterns being largely simple linear ones or solid filled triangles. When, soon after, white or cream slip came into use as the background for painted patterns, it became possible to use both coarser and darker fabrics for the painted ware. At most other Early Neolithic sites a few such painted sherds occurred from the beginning. Considering both the frequency with which Greek prehistoric strata are telescoped and the ever present possibility that a few painted sherds might infiltrate from above, it can now be generally accepted that the earliest Neolithic pottery in Greece was unpainted and that painting began after a few centuries of settlement in Greece; the C-14 dates at Elateia (Weinberg, 1962, p. 207) suggest a span of some four hundred years for the lowest meter of deposit, which contained no painted pottery.

In 1952, we could relate the Early Neolithic material culture of Greece only generally with "the time of Hassuna, the pre-Halaf of the Amuq, the Mersin Late Neolithic" (Weinberg, 1954, p. 98). Now, our more precise knowledge of the period in Greece, and especially the discovery of rich Neolithic and Chalcolithic cultures in Anatolia, at Çatal Hüyük (Mellaart, 1962, 1963) and at Hacılar (Mellaart, 1958, 1959, 1960, 1961), result in much closer and more exact parallelisms. On the basis of comparisons of the features of the Greek Early Neolithic—as we now know it from its very beginnings—with these newly found Anatolian cultures, it seems that the Early Neolithic of Greece most closely resembles the latest phases of the Early Neolithic at Çatal Hüyük but is probably earlier than the earliest phases of the Late Neolithic at Hacılar (there may be a gap in this Anatolian sequence). The unique occurrence in some quantity at Nea Makri (Theochares, 1956, pp. 10-14), from the lowest levels of its Early Neolithic deposit, of pottery decorated with white-filled incisions has with good reason been likened by Theochares to such wares in Levels XXV and XXIV (Late Neolithic and Proto-Chalcolithic) at Mersin. Mellaart would equate this latter level at Mersin with the earliest level at Hacılar (Mellaart, 1961, p. 75), thus affording a welcome check on our general equation. The painted pottery of Nea Nikomedeia, which occurs in the lower stratum (Rodden, 1962, p. 284), is possibly the only painted ware in Greece which shows close similarities with that of Hacılar, especially with that of Levels V-II, which are dated about 5400-5000 B.C. (Mellaart, 1961, p. 74). A check within Greece is given by the finding at Elateia, on next to the lowest floor above hardpan, of a sherd of imported Corinthian variegated ware (Weinberg, 1962, p. 207); two more fragments were found on a somewhat higher floor at Elateia (loc. cit.), showing the parallelism of the pre-painted pottery series in Phokis and the Corinthia. At its upper end, the Early Neolithic sequence of Greece can be tied in with that of Yugoslavia through the common occurrence of "Barbotine" and "Cardium" wares, which appear in the "Vorsesklo" phase in northern Thessaly just before the beginning of the Sesklo period, particularly at Otzaki, at the sites of Zelena Pećina (Benac, 1957b, pp. 89-92) and Crvena Stijena-Level III (Benac, 1957a, pp. 47-48; 1958, p. 41) in Herzegovina, and Gornja Tuzla-Stratum VIb (Čović, 1960-61, pp. 133, 136) in Bosnia.

The slow but steady development of the Early Neolithic material culture of the Greek mainland was interrupted, especially in the Peloponnesos but also in Attica, Boeotia, and Euboea, by the appearance of a new and quite different kind of pottery: Neolithic Urfirnis ware. At Lerna there is an actual physical division between the Early Neolithic and the Middle Neolithic strata, formed by a scattering of small pebbles (Caskey, 1957, p. 160), below which the glazed ware does not occur. Lerna II has fully two meters of deposit and as many as eight building levels (ibid., p. 156), only at the top of which occurs a scattering of Late Neolithic sherds and a few Late Neolithic graves sunk down into the Middle Neolithic deposits; these are the remnants of Late Neolithic habitational debris which had mostly been swept away by leveling operations in Early Helladic times. No other site yet excavated offers a comparable Middle Neolithic accumulation, although rich remains of the period occur at many sites. It is the pottery which is most obviously new and different. The fabric is thoroughly fired, hard and often very thin; the shapes, although including globular jars, are most often much more highly contoured than were those of the Early Neolithic period. High bases, widely splaying bowls, high concave rims, thickened incurved rims, long tubular lugs—all are part of the new repertory. Replacing the polished slips is a wash, often brushed on, which when fired has an inherent luster. The upper part of the vase—shoulder and collar or rim—commonly bears linear patterns painted with the same glaze, which may have been intentionally varied in thickness to provide a polychrome effect. The repertory of designs is large, but the design elements remain simple.

In the first version of this paper, the Neolithic Urfirnis wares were likened to Halaf pottery (Weinberg, 1954, p. 98). Not until the Greek ware had been carefully examined (in 1957) by Perkins was it possible to document this likeness in detail as to shape, glaze, and decorative patterns (Perkins and Weinberg, 1958; Weinberg, 1961). It is to early Halaf ware, rather than to the more highly developed features of late Halaf pottery, that Perkins found the Neolithic Urfirnis ware of Greece to be similar. Together with the new type of pottery is found a new and more svelte type of standing female figurine, exemplified especially by the fine figure found in the third level from the top of the Middle Neolithic accumulation at Lerna (Caskey and Eliot, 1956). This figure was completely covered with a highly burnished red slip, but numerous other clay female figurines with many of the same features are completely decorated with painted designs in the Neolithic Urfirnis technique. In 1952, we knew only the upper parts of such figurines (Holmberg, 1944, pp. 115-16; Weinberg, 1948, pp. 199-200; Weinberg, 1954, p. 98), or at least the few pieces known from below the waist had been inverted; Lerna II has now yielded the entire lower part of such a figurine (Caskey, 1958, Pl. 36, d, e) and several single legs. The arms apparently extended outward from the shoulder, elbows were bent, and hands held close against the thigh on either side of the pubic triangle. Figurines decorated in lustrous paint are common at Tell Halaf, but they are of the squatting type (Schmidt, 1943, pp. 99-100). Rarer is a standing type with painted designs which appeared in Halafian levels at Arpachiyah (Mallowan and Rose, 1935, p. 82, Fig. 45, 1). Standing female figures with painted designs also came from later levels at Hacılar (Mellaart, 1958, pp. 144-47, Fig. 10; 1961, pp. 54-55, Fig. 13), but the stance with hands on thighs seems without parallel. Both the Urfirnis pottery and the figurines, then, are of Near Eastern derivation and of the time of the early Halaf period. Vessels with deeply scored interiors that perhaps occurred in the latest Early Neolithic levels at Lerna and were then common throughout Lerna II (Caskey, 1957, p. 159, Pl. 48, e; 1958, p. 139, Pl. 38, b) find their closest parallel in the "husking trays" of Hassuna which, while beginning early in the Hassuna phase, continued into the Samarran and even the Halaf periods (Lloyd and Safar, 1945, p. 277, Fig. 3, 8-10, Pl. XVIII, 1). There seems little doubt, then, as to when the Middle Neolithic period began in the Peloponnesos and wherever else Neolithic Urfinis ware appears in quantity—Attica, Boeotia, and Euboea.

Caskey noted a marked difference in the character of the habitation levels between Lerna I and II (Caskey, 1957, p. 160; 1958, pp. 138-39). In the Early Neolithic period the habitations were chiefly of wattle and daub on post frames, but a few stone foundations were found in one area. Such houses often burned, forming an accumulation composed largely of successive layers of ash and carbonized matter. The Lerna II houses of mud brick on stone foundations left debris that was chiefly of decomposed mud bricks. These Middle Neolithic houses often underwent repeated repairs and rebuildings. The foundations were made of small irregular pieces of rough breccia held together by red clay, giving them great strength. The rooms (generally from one to three in number) were usually small, but the walls were straight and the corners often true. In many rooms there were short internal buttresses. Floors were of trodden earth covered with red or yellow clay, and similar clay was used to line pits. Rectangular one-room houses with stone foundations were found in the Middle Neolithic level at Hageorgitika as well. The floors were of trodden earth; some houses had round or rectangular fixed hearths. It thus seems clear that a change in building methods accompanied the change in pottery that marks the beginning of the Middle Neolithic period.

Although there seem to be no burials in the accumulation of Lerna II, there is one associated with the Middle Neolithic deposits at Hageorgitika. This consists of a small oval pit dug in hardpan (measuring 0.60 m. by 0.36 m., and 0.20 m. in depth), in which the secondary burial of the bones of an adult was found (Fürst, 1932). Secondary burials, again associated with Neolithic Urfirnis ware, were found also at Prosymna, the bodies were apparently partly burned and the bones then assembled and deposited in small pits hollowed out of hardpan (Blegen, 1937, pp. 26-28); at Hageorgitika, there were no traces of burning. The evidence is still limited, but what we have indicates the introduction of an entirely different method of burial in the Middle Neolithic period, at least in the Peloponnesos. Secondary burial was not characteristic of the Hassuna or Halaf cultures (Perkins, 1949) of the Near East, but in Anatolia such burials were standard at Çatal Hüyük throughout the Early Neolithic period (Mellaart, 1963, p. 95). Although all the Late Neolithic and Early Chalcolithic burials at Hacılar are simple inhumations in a contracted position, secondary burial occurs at Mersin in the Early Chalcolithic Level XX (Garstang, 1953, p. 77); in Level XIX, the lowest of the Middle Chalcolithic levels showing strong Halafian influence, two instances seem to indicate cremation (Garstang, 1953, p. 111). Garstang suggests, however, that this may be the result of a holocaust caused by the Halafian invaders. It would certainly seem possible that the Halafian culture, perhaps in a provincial Syro-Cilician form, which brought the Neolithic Urfirnis ware to Greece was also responsible for the new burial practices of secondary burial with or without cremation.

In Thessaly, we find a somewhat different situation. Although Neolithic Urfirnis ware is now known from Thessalian sites, its stratigraphic position at Pyrasos indicates an arrival late in the Thessaly A period (Theochares, 1959a, pp. 52-54). A similar situation has been noted at Elateia in Phokis, where the advanced type of Chaeronea ware, which parallels the Thessaly A painted wares, is entirely developed before Neolithic Urfirnis ware occurs; even then the latter is found in only limited quantities (Weinberg, 1962, pp. 179-80). Conceivably, there may have been some delay in the appearance of Neolithic Urfirnis ware north of Boeotia; its appearance there would have been secondary from Greek sources to the south, but it cannot have been a long delay. It would now seem more likely that the Thessaly A period began earlier than did the Middle Neolithic farther south; for this there are several other indications. One is the appearance at Otzaki of a number of fragments of bowls in the tondo of which are whirl patterns like those which are almost the trade-mark of Samarran pottery (Milojčić, 1959, p. 42, Fig. 12, 6; the particular piece illustrated is from the Middle Sesklo phase; letter of December 3, 1958, from Milojčić). Further, Otzaki has produced several examples of a type of rectangular, often almost square, mud-brick house with internal buttresses, usually two on each wall (Milojčić, 1959, p. 12, Figs. 2-4); this type of house was known previously only from Tsangli (Wace and Thompson, 1912, pp. 115-21) in Greece, and nowhere outside it. Now, however, an entire area of closely packed houses with internal buttresses, some exactly like those in Thessaly, has been uncovered in the burned level 2B at Can Hasan in the Konya Plain (French, 1963, p. 35, Fig. 1); the phase is transitional from Early to Middle Chalcolithic, and is equated through imports with Mersin Levels XXI-XX (French, 1963, p. 37), immediately before the Halaf phase (Garstang, 1953, p. 2). From Otzaki it seems clear that the Tsangli type house goes back at least into the Middle Sesklo phase, giving another tie between Middle Sesklo and the Samarran phase of the Near East. We repeat that internal buttresses occurred in several houses of Lerna II, but until plans are published it is impossible to be certain that the type is the same as that of Thessaly and Can Hasan.

There remains for discussion the evidence for separating the Thessaly A period from its antecedents and for making it a separate phase that can be termed Middle Neolithic. Although most recently Theochares (1962a, p. 47; 1963) would consider everything at Sesklo after the preceramic phase and before the Dimini phase as one long Early Neolithic period divided stratigraphically into five subperiods (Theochares, 1962a, p. 41), he still notes that the architecture of Level IV, corresponding to the old Thessaly A phase, is of mud brick on stone foundations, whereas no stone foundations appeared earlier (Theochares, 1962a, p. 42). It is generally true in Thessaly that stone foundations appear first in Phase A. Milojčić notes that with the new architecture of the Sesklo period at Otzaki begin the new Thessaly A types of painted pottery (Milojčić, 1959, p. 12); the level immediately below had contained "Barbotine," "Cardium," and monochrome wares. These wares do not occur south of Larisa and Magoulitsa (Papadopoulou, 1958, p. 44); in southern Thessaly, it is largely monochrome wares which precede the abundant appearance of the Thessaly A painted wares. Surely, there is continuity and some holdover of older types, but it is equally clear that something new is happening. Very probably, what is new is caused by a foreign impulse with Samarran relationships; it seems sufficient to make some division here to designate the Thessaly A culture as Middle Neolithic.

The situation in Phokis is different from that in its neighboring regions to both north and south. The sites in the Kephissos Valley are more remote than the regions already considered, and offer less evidence of direct contact with, or influence from, the Near East; rather, the influences seem to have come from within Greece. There is a long, slow development of the painted pottery called Chaeronea ware, marked by extreme conservatism in shape (Weinberg, 1962, p. 179). Only when the more complicated patterns, with imitations of the Thessaly A "flame," begin to appear can we know that we are in the time of the Middle Neolithic period of Thessaly. Later, the appearance of Neolithic Urfirnis ware (Weinberg, 1962, p. 180) reflects the Peloponnesian or Boeotian Middle Neolithic phase. The change seems to be little more than that noted in the pottery.

A number of facts indicate that intrusive cultural elements made their appearance throughout Greece well before the end of the Sesklo phase in Thessaly and the corresponding Middle Neolithic culture to the south. At Otzaki, alongside one of the houses of the Tsangli type, but later in origin, is a two-room rectangular house with an entrance in the middle of one of the short walls and antae extending beyond this wall. In front of one of the antae was a post hole (Milojčić, 1955, p. 167), thus presenting a typical megaron plan. One other house with the same plan was found also in the late Sesklo level at Otzaki (Milojčić, 1959, p. 12).

With still another architectural level of the late Sesklo phase above, there can be no doubt that the megaron was introduced into Thessaly well before the end of the Sesklo period. That the megaron was an Anatolian house type, with a long history in that region, is now made clear from the excavations at Beycesultan, where the earliest preserved megaron belongs to the end of the Late Chalcolithic phase (Lloyd and Mellaart, 1962, pp. 25-26); its history in the Early Bronze Age was already well known at Troy, where it goes back to the beginning of the settlement (Blegen, 1963, p. 48). We do not know how much earlier the megaron existed in Anatolia, but there is every likelihood that it came thence to Greece.

It was apparently Grundmann who first recognized in Thessaly the occurrence, in the late phase of the A period, of a large quantity and variety of black burnished wares with sharply carinated forms and often decorated with white paint, pattern burnishing, and plastic additions (Grundmann, 1932, pp. 109-12, Beil; XXIV-XXVI). Kunze, too, recognized that at Orchomenos this type of black burnished ware—his group A2—belonged in the middle phase of the Neolithic period (Kunze, 1931, pp. 47-48). At Corinth, such wares were found in deposits that otherwise contained only Neolithic Urfirnis and gray monochrome pottery; from this it was evident that both the gray and black wares came into use in what was later to be termed the Middle Neolithic period (Weinberg, 1937, pp. 511-12; 1947, p. 175). The recent excavations at Elateia in Phokis have found a large group of material (from the pit in Trench 3) which shows a similar association of wares and is, further, totally without the Neolithic matt-painted ware which, as we shall see, was the herald of a new period—the Late Neolithic—throughout Greece (Weinberg, 1962, pp. 186-95). The place of these black wares in Thessaly has been more strictly defined as a result of excavations in the 1950's. It is clear that there are two groups of black wares there: the earlier one with which we are now concerned, and another group belonging to the end of the Late Neolithic period. At Arapi-Magula, the earlier black wares, in several varieties, were found in the lower level with the gray ware and matt-painted wares, whereas the stratum above produced the so-called Arapi wares (Milojčić, 1955, pp. 187-88; 1959, pp. 14-16), which Milojčić equates with the first phase of the Dimini or Thessaly B period. From Kouphovouno at Volo, however, it is clear that the earlier type of black wares is associated with the last of the Thessaly A painted wares—with matt-painted and early polychrome wares—but is earlier than the true Dimini ware (Theochares, 1958a, pp. 6-7); in both places these wares look like imports from central Greece. It seems clear, then, that in most of Greece the last phase of the Middle Neolithic period witnesses the arrival in quantity of variously decorated, black polished wares, which were totally foreign to the normal types of Middle Neolithic pottery. Long called "Danubian," these wares should now be more correctly called "Anatolian," because the relations would certainly seem to be with the Late Chalcolithic culture, as best known now from Beycesultan (Lloyd and Mellaart, 1962, pp. 71-115); a more western manifestation of this culture, such as appears at Tigani in Samos, may be responsible for these wares on the Greek mainland. The black wares occur already in the lowest level at Beycesultan, contemporary with the Halaf period in the Near East, which makes their association with Halaf-derived wares in Greece completely probable (Lloyd and Mellaart, 1962, pp. 112-13, chart). With both the megaron and black polished wares appearing toward the end of the Middle Neolithic period, apparently from the same region of western Anatolia, it is tempting to associate their arrival in Greece, just as they are associated at Beycesultan, but for this there is as yet no evidence. On the other hand, the pit in Trench 3 at Elateia contained enough of a four-legged vase of black polished and incised ware to allow a reconstruction, which has made possible the establishment of close ties with the Danilo and Kakanj cultures of west-central Yugoslavia (Batović, 1959, 1960-61; Benac, 1960-61; Korošec, 1958, 1964; Weinberg, 1962, pp. 190-95).

Possibly the arrival of the new cultural features described above should be considered as marking the beginning of a new phase—Late Neolithic. This would be logical in that the megaron and black polished and gray wares continued in use for the rest of the Neolithic period. However, the old established distinction between Thessaly A and Thessaly B has prevailed, so that it is the appearance throughout Greece in quantity of matt-painted wares which heralds the Late Neolithic period. These are the B3δ and B3ε wares of western Thessaly (Wace and Thompson, 1912), but they occur also in eastern Thessaly; Theochares has established at Kouphovouno that they, together with the polychrome B3β and B3γ pottery, occur before the typical Dimini wares (Theochares, 1958, pp. 6-8); the same was true at Arapi-Magula farther north (Milojčić, 1955, pp. 188-91). Both the matt-painted and the polychrome wares are plentiful in central Greece (Kunze, 1931, pp. 38-44, Pls. XX-XXII, XXIV-XXVI), in Attica (Theochares, 1956, p. 22; Zervos, 1963, Fig. 843), and in the Peloponnesos (Weinberg, 1937, pp. 513-15). Here again, Perkins has been able to document the similarities in fabric, shapes, paint, and patterns between the matt-painted ware of Greece and the Ubaid ware of the Near East, especially in its more provincial Syro-Cilician manifestation (Perkins and Weinberg, 1958; Weinberg, 1961). The polychrome wares, too, with patterns in polished red and matt black colors, find analogies with polychrome wares of Syro-Cilicia that belong in the transitional phase from Halaf to Ubaid (Garstang, 1953, Figs. 92, 6; 93, 5). The beginning of the Late Neolithic period in Greece must then be equated with Mersin Level XVI, and its duration with Levels XV-XII B.

To call this Late Neolithic phase in Greece—or even in Thessaly alone—the Dimini phase, is a misnomer, since it is now clear that the flowering of the Dimini culture was a localized manifestation restricted almost entirely to southeastern Thessaly and beginning well after the Late Neolithic period, as defined here, was under way throughout Greece. Both the Volo (Theochares, 1958a, p. 8) and the Larisa areas (Milojčić, 1959, p. 19, chart) furnish stratigraphic evidence for this fact. The suggestions made in 1952 about the Cycladic connections—and possible Cycladic origin—of many features of the Dimini culture seem even more pertinent now, and can be further documented. For one thing, we have recently begun to learn of a Late Neolithic phase on some of the islands, especially in graves found on the Kephala promontory of the island of Keos (Caskey, 1962, pp. 264-66). At this latter site, there have now been found several examples of a type of scooplike vessel with wide-band handle which divides near the front (Caskey, 1964a, Pl. 46, e, f); the whole vessel is covered with maeandroid incised patterns. The only example known previously came from the south slope of the akropolis of Sesklo, in doubtful context. Tsountas felt that it belonged to the Thessaly B period but that it came from a foreign workshop (Tsountas, 1908, pp. 206-7); it now seems most probable that the workshop was in the islands, very possibly on Keos itself. We know too little yet of this island Late Neolithic culture—traces of which have also been found on Mykonos and at the northern end of Antiparos (Belmont and Renfrew, 1964) and now await excavation—to establish its relations with the Early Cycladic culture, but it would seem to be the latter's immediate predecessor. The Dimini culture, contemporary with the Late Neolithic phase on the islands, may also have been contemporary in part with its Early Cycladic successor.

To the latest phases of the Late Neolithic period in Thessaly, Milojčić has assigned the Larisa culture and the Rachmani culture; the first is characterized by variously decorated black polished wares, the second, by "crusted" ware. The reappearance of the black polished wares seems valid only for Thessaly; to the south they appear to have been in continuous use throughout the Late Neolithic period, as were the gray wares. It is highly probable that new varieties of these wares developed in this period, possibly outside Greece; some kinds of pattern-burnished wares belong to the end of the Late Neolithic period, as recently re-established at Eutresis (Caskey and Caskey, 1960, pp. 131, 134). A type of red-brown pattern-burnished ware, long known from Prosymna (Blegen, 1937, pp. 375-76), is now known from Corinth as well (Robinson and Weinberg, 1960, p. 250). Red-brown is the predominant color in the pattern-burnished pottery of Besika Tepe in the Troad, where it must date to immediately before Troy I (Lamb, 1932, pp. 125-28). The gray-black type of pattern-burnished ware is characteristic of Kumtepe Ib in the Troad, again just before the beginning of Troy I (French, 1961, pp. 102-3, 112-13). It is clear, too, that at the very end of the Late Neolithic period there appeared, especially in the Corinthia and Argolid, a new type of polychrome ware in which patterns in orange-red paint are outlined with a dark grayish-blue paint. Gonia (Blegen, 1930-31, pp. 69-70, Pl. II) and Prosymna (Blegen, 1937, pp. 373-74, Figs. 628-31, Pl. III) produced this ware in quantity; it occurred at Corinth as well (Weinberg, 1939, p. 599), where its position at the end of the Late Neolithic period is established (Kosmopoulos, 1948, pp. 37, 56). This ware is very different from the polychrome wares of the beginning of the Late Neolithic period, which use the red and black separately in their decorative patterns. If the late polychrome ware is as closely connected with Dimini B3β ware as is thought, then Dimini must indeed come down to the end of the Late Neolithic period. In Thessaly, the last manifestation of this period is the "crusted" ware ($\Gamma 1\gamma$ and $\Gamma 1\delta$)—the typical pottery of what Milojčić has named the Rachmani culture (Milojčić, 1959, pp. 18-19)—but the ware occurs in southern Thessaly at Pyrasos (Theochares, 1959a, p. 58, Pls. I, IIa). At Lerna in the Argolid, two graves, which are almost the sole survivors of a Late Neolithic level that was swept away by Early Helladic settlers, have yielded vases and fragments of another form of "crusted" ware (Caskey, 1958, p. 137; 1959, p. 205). Here we seem clearly faced with the arrival of Balkan pottery types in peninsular Greece for the second time, the first having been the "Barbotine" and "Cardium" wares that came at the end of the Early Neolithic period. Schachermeyr (1955, p. 135) has given their lineage in the Lengyel, late Vinča, and Gumelnitza cultures. Also of Gumelnitza derivation are the graphite-painted and incised wares known in quantity at Dikili Tash in eastern Macedonia, which Theochares (1961, p. 95) dates before the beginning of Troy I, as does French (1961, p. 118, Fig. 3).

Before turning to a consideration of the Early Bronze Age in the Aegean, I must mention the Neolithic period on Crete. However, with a large-scale excavation at Knossos only recently completed and published thus far only in brief notices, it is safest to reserve judgment for the present. The restudy of the Neolithic material from the earlier excavations (Furness, 1953) shed much new light, and seemed to confirm the Anatolian derivation of the culture as against possible relations with early dark-faced wares of Syro-Cilicia (*ibid*., p. 134). On the basis of material from the new excavations, J. D. Evans (1960, p. 111) has connected the earliest pottery with West Anatolian Late Chalcolithic pottery tradition. Elsewhere (Evans, 1963, p. 29) he says that the earliest pottery suggests settlement from northwestern Asia Minor; at the same time he reports a C-14 date from the lowest level of 6100 B.C. ± 150 years (6341 B.C. when corrected for the new half life). A derivation from the Late Chalcolithic culture of west Anatolia seems most reasonable, but this could hardly have been before the mid-fifth millennium B.C.; such a derivation would go far to explain the complete lack of painted pottery in Crete to parallel that of the Early and Middle Neolithic periods of the Greek mainland. It is possible that the C-14 date is valid for the lowest level (Stratum X) but that there is a long gap between it and Stratum IX, the first in which pottery appears (J. D. Evans, 1964*a*). In its latest phase, the Cretan Neolithic pottery includes pattern-burnished ware, high tab handles, and other features which relate it to the assemblage found at Tigani on Samos in particular but which are present in variant forms in most of the Aegean at the end of the Late Neolithic period.

The priority of the Early Bronze Age phase in the Cyclades over that of either the Greek mainland or Crete seems as valid now as it did in 1952 (Weinberg, 1954, p. 94). It now appears, however, that the separation of the Early Cycladic period into an early "Pelos" phase and a later "Syros" phase is artificial, and that the two may be contemporaneous in the southern and northern Cyclades respectively. Indeed, examples of vases of both phases are present in the small group of tombs found at Kambos on Paros (Varoucha, 1925-26); the frying pan found there belongs to what Bossert considers an earlier group, with incised rather than stamped spirals (Bossert, 1960). Even the stamped spiral or concentric-circle decoration occurs in the earliest Early Helladic I deposits on the mainland. Although Bossert believes that such stamped decoration may date earlier on the mainland than in the islands, the excavators of Early Helladic sites are quite explicit in stating that there are obvious imports from the Cyclades in the earliest E. H. deposits, indicating at least a migration route over the Cyclades for the bearers of the first Bronze Age culture of the mainland and possibly even an origin in the Cyclades (Weinberg, 1954, p. 94), From new evidence gathered at both Lerna (Caskey, 1958, p. 132, Pl. 35, d-f) and Eutresis (Caskey and Caskey, 1960, p. 164, Pl. 48), it would seem that the beginning of the E.H. II phase may have been the result of another movement from or across the Cyclades. In considering possible origins of the Early Cycladic culture—or cultures—the parallelisms with the Ghassulian culture cited in the first version of this paper (Weinberg, 1954, pp. 94-96) can now be even better documented. Ghassul has now been put in its proper place toward the end of the Chalcolithic period, and the related Beersheba phase has yielded rich material remains which include a pyxis type reminiscent of the Cyclades (Perrot, 1955, Pl. 16, A-B) and incised decoration (although on stone vessels), which is also similar to that on vases of the "Pelos" group (ibid., p. 79). What were referred to earlier as Ghassulian "bird-vases" (Weinberg, 1954, p. 95) are like the churns of the Beersheba culture (Perrot, 1955, p. 82, Fig. 16, 5); the top of one comes from an E.M. I tomb at Kanli Kastelli near Herakleion (Alexiou, 1951, Pl. 14, 2, 17), which also contained many vases common to the southern Cyclades. The finding of a cemetery with contracted burials in cist graves at Iasos on the Carian coast (Levi, 1961-62, pp. 555-71) offers a possibility of connections with the Cyclades, although the vases from the graves show no close relationship with Early Cycladic wares. Nothing has appeared since 1952 to change my belief that the Early Bronze Age ended at about the same time on the Greek mainland, in the Cyclades, and in Crete, and that this was at about the end of Dynasty XI in Egypt and a little before the end of Troy V (Weinberg, 1954, p. 90).

The arrival of the first metal-users on the mainland—the beginning of the E.H. I period—is marked by the complete disappearance of all the pottery types characteristic of the Late Neolithic phase. At sites occupied in both phases there may be a mingling of types, but the many newly founded settlements show only the monochrome ware, often red-slipped and polished, of the new E.H. I period. Besides the Cycladic connections, there are the general relationships with Anatolia previously documented (Weinberg, 1954, p. 93). French now sees closer relations between the typical E.H. I bowls and those of late E.B. 1 and E.B. 2 at Beycesultan (French, 1961, p. 117). However, since French equates E.B. 1 at Beycesultan with Troy I (ibid., p. 118, chart), E.H. I should be related to early E.B. 1. Despite his long argument to the contrary (ibid., pp. 119-20), the occurrence of E.H. Urfirnis ware in middle Troy I cannot be altered, and E.H. I must antedate the appearance of Urfirnis ware, with which E.H. II begins. Much of French's argument hangs on the occurrence in middle Troy I of what he presumes to be E.H. III painted wares. They are not; rather, they are the kind of painted ware which appears in E.H. II, most probably coming from the Cyclades, whence they could also have come to Troy. In no way do they alter the basic equation that E.H. II must begin by middle Troy I. Nor is there validity to French's objection that E.H. II becomes too long a period if it begins by middle Troy I; the long duration of E.H. II has already been repeatedly emphasized by Caskey (1960, p. 288). The supposed undue compression of the Thessalian Neolithic sequence (French, 1961, p. 119) is also largely imaginary; the stringing out of an entire sequence of Late Neolithic cultures (ibid., p. 118, chart) is highly unlikely. Instead, there are probably a number of localized aspects that are co-existent in Thessaly, as they certainly seem to be in central and southern Greece. Between the first appearance of the Late Neolithic matt-painted wares and the end of the period, probably at about the time of the beginning of Troy I, there is almost a millennium; more is hardly needed. Lastly, French (ibid., p. 119) takes at face value the C-14 dates for Eutresis, although Caskey has observed that they are too low (Caskey, 1960, p. 164). There is no indication that French accepts the low dates for the Beycesultan Late Chalcolithic 1 and 3 phases, which were reported at the same time as the Eutresis dates and by the same laboratory (Kohler and Ralph, 1961, p. 360). In fact, it has become increasingly clear that C-14 dates for the third millennium, and probably for the latter part of the fourth millennium as well, are generally much too low. Perhaps the physicists will eventually be able to explain the cause of this discrepancy; for the moment, however, it would seem best to ignore the C-14 dates when they are in clear conflict with solid archaeological evidence. This is exactly what has been done by the excavators of Beycesultan (Lloyd and Mellaart, 1962, pp. 19, 23), whose scheme French has used as the basis for his chronological table (1961, p. 118); it would certainly be inconsistent to insist on using them for Eutresis, especially after the excavator has pointed out that they are too low. The C-14 dates cannot be taken as reason for discarding the basic equation that E.H. II begins by middle Troy I. Rather, it would now seem correct to date Troy I together with the E.B. 1 period at Beycesultan, which would place the beginning of Troy back a few centuries into the fourth millennium. As a result, E.H. I should probably begin also before 3000 B.C.; it may have ended by the turn of the millennium.

As stated above, the E.H. II phase probably began also with a movement of peoples from or across the Cyclades, since there is a new series of Cycladic imports on the mainland, often at settlements founded only at this time. Lerna is the most important of the E.H. II foundations, and the beginning of the site is marked by imports of Early Cycladic pottery (Caskey, 1958, p. 132, Pl. 35, d-f). In addition, the settlement was soon fortified in a manner that is best paralleled at Chalandriani on Syros (ibid., pp. 132-36). At Ayios Kosmas on the coast of Attica, where Caskey believes the Early Helladic occupation belongs almost entirely to the E.H. II phase (Caskey, 1963, p. 14), the burial practices are completely Cycladic in character (ibid., p. 13; Mylonas, 1959, pp. 64-120). The objects from the graves are also particularly close to those from Early Cycladic graves (ibid., Figs. 140-151, 163). The difference between the types of pottery deposited in the graves and those used in the settlement is most clear here (ibid., p. 155). There is, then, good reason for believing that at the beginning of E.H. II the mainland population was increased by migrations from, rather than just across, the Cyclades. The sauceboat, which may rightly be called the type artifact of the E.H. II phase, is most likely also of Cycladic origin; the Urfirnis glaze that is characteristic of the period may have come with it. The sauceboat fragments, as well as fragments of other vessels in Urfirnis ware that occur in middle Troy I, indicate that the phase began about, or not very long after, 3000 B.C.

The deep accumulation of Lerna III comprises at least six building levels, most of which contain such substantial structures as the fortifications and the "House of the Tiles." Nowhere else on the mainland do we have similar evidence of wealth and power such as must have been concentrated in the person of the rulers of Lerna who lived in the successive palaces. On the mainland, only the great tholos at Tiryns is comparable (Caskey, 1960, p. 288); a building of similar construction under the temple in the Heraion on Samos (Milojčić, 1961, p. 27), as well as large megara there (ibid., p. 23) and in Troy II (Blegen, 1963, p. 64, Fig. 15), give evidence of a general prosperity in the Aegean in the middle phase of the Early Bronze Age of which we had little previous evidence. That all this wealth and power ended in a catastrophic destruction is clearly documented at Lerna (Caskey, 1963, p. 17), as it is at most other mainland sites of the E.H. II period (Caskey, 1960, p. 301); Caskey would attribute this destruction to a foreign invasion (loc. cit.). Troy II was similarly destroyed by violence and fire (Blegen, 1963, p. 89), as were Beycesultan at the end of E.B. 2 (Lloyd and Mellaart, 1962, p. 56), Polatlı at the end of its Phase II (Lloyd and Gökçe, 1951, p. 54), and Tarsus at the end of E.B. 2 (Goldman, 1956, p. 347). These destructions completely across Turkey are clearly related; I believe that the general destruction at the end of E.H. II, now established by Caskey for the Greek mainland, is also closely related both in time and in cause to that in Turkey. The time would be about 2300-2200 B.C. The excavators of Beycesultan believe that only the Indo-European invasion can be co-ordinated with the destruction at the end of E.B. 2 (Lloyd and Mellaart, 1962, p. 241) and Caskey (1960, p. 302) hints at the same cause in Greece. I believe there can now be little doubt but that the first wave of Indo-Europeans reached the Peloponnesos between 2300 and 2200 B.C.

Lerna IV gives us the best picture we have of E.H. III—the final phase of the Early Bronze Age in Greece (Caskey, 1960, pp. 293-97): smaller houses of megaron type, often with one apsidal end; numerous bothroi; some wheel-made pottery; much of the pottery decorated with dark glaze paint on a light ground, but a few examples with white patterns on a dark ground; new pottery shapes—especially two-handled bowls—which are often of the same fabric as gray Minyan ware; clay anchor-like objects. Lerna IV is in part contemporary with Troy IV, as indicated by exports in both directions (ibid., p. 297). The position of the "red-cross bowls" as a type artifact for the end of the Early Bronze Age both in the Aegean and across Turkey (Weinberg, 1954, p. 89) remains valid, and is actually strengthened by finds at Beycesultan (Lloyd and

Mellaart, 1962, p. 264, chart); the date is not later than the twentieth century B.C. Within this century, probably nearer its beginning, some sites not destroyed at the end of E.H. II—Eutresis, for example—were burned; in others, a more gradual but still fundamental change in material culture took place as the Middle Bronze Age began (Caskey, 1960, pp. 302-3). Only with the beginning of the Middle Helladic period (Lerna V) is Middle Minoan Ia pottery found, which clearly indicates that E.H. III and M.M. Ia overlap little if at all (*ibid*., pp. 299, 303). In the Cyclades, it is the change from Phylakopi I to II that Caskey equates with the change from Lerna IV to V (*loc. cit*.).

During the past decade, the Early Bronze Age of Crete—Early Minoan—has suffered everything from slight truncation to complete annihilation. Fortunately, new evidence produced during this time has resulted in the resurrection of at least E.M. I and II and most probably of III as well. With such uniformity of development evident everywhere else in the Aegean, as well as throughout Turkey, it would be absurd to have Crete following a completely different course; fortunately, this can be proved not to be true. From both a well at Knossos (Hood, 1961-62, pp. 92-93) and the sealed lower stratum of Tomb II at Lebena (Alexiou, 1961-62, p. 89) have come pure E.M. I deposits, which are in agreement in showing that the E.M. I assemblage included the Pyrgos style of pattern-burnished ware and the Ayios Onouphrios style of dark-on-light painted pottery. The tomb contained also a large number of examples of light-on-dark painted ware. Jugs—with either high cylindrical neck and two handles or beaked spout and one handle—are the chief shape in the painted ware. Although high-footed bowls of dark ware, often pattern-burnished, occur in the well, they are absent from the E.M. I deposit in the tomb. The cylindrical "Cycladic" pyxis with feet and cover is common in the tomb; some pyxides of the Cycladic type on a high conical foot and with pierced vertical lugs have the dark-on-light painted decoration. The pattern-burnished wares, often termed sub-Neolithic, must indeed be a local flourishing of the technique later than its general prevalence in the Aegean; the high-footed cup is a shape not previously common to this ware. It is, however, the dark-on-light painted wares that are completely new to Crete in both shape and decoration. The beaked spouts and plug handles have always been considered as pointing to Anatolia, but the painted technique was as foreign to E.B. 1 and E.B. 2 in Anatolia as it was to Neolithic Crete. Nor does the Greek mainland offer any painted ware in E.H. I or II, except for imports from the Cyclades (Caskey, 1960, p. 292) in E.H. II. The Cycladic painted technique is as much in need of explanation as is that of Crete; being very likely later than that of Crete, it may in fact be derived from there. Perhaps, as in the Early Cycladic culture (Weinberg, 1954, pp. 94-96), we must turn again to the southeast corner of the Mediterranean, where at the very end of the fourth millennium, a similar technique of pottery painting occurs: in Egypt just before and during Dynasty I (Kantor, 1954, p. 5, Fig. 1), and in Palestine at the end of the Chalcolithic period (Kenyon, 1960, p. 88, Fig. 12); the tubular spouted forms of Crete are also here. In First Dynasty Egypt, Evans found parallels to the goblets on high flaring bases (Evans, 1921, p. 48). The beginning of E.M. I should thus fall at about the beginning of Dynasty I in Egypt. However, the Early Cycladic culture was already well formed by that time, since the E.M. I assemblage in Crete contains typical pyxides of the "Pelos" group of the southern Cyclades.

A completely different pottery assemblage represents E.M. II in the upper layer of Tomb II at Lebena (Alexiou, 1961-62, p. 89). The variegated Vasiliki ware prevails; there are globular covered pyxides with incised decoration; the first stone vases appear, as do the large covers with handles—which I believe to be mirrors—the Cretan equivalent of the Cycladic "frying pans." Vasiliki ware marks the E.M. II level at Knossos too (Hood, 1961-62, p. 93); there are also goblets on fairly high feet as well as the legs of cooking pots, which did not occur in the E.M. I well. Alexiou (1961-62, p. 90) would now class as E.M. II everything from other tombs in the Mesara previously ascribed to E.M. I, together with what was called E.M. II. E.M. II must then have been a long period, as was E.H. II, with its beginning going back almost to the start of the third millennium—as indicated by Evans (1921, p. 80) in his search for the prototypes of the exaggerated spouts of the period—and its end occurring at about the time of the destruction of Troy IIg, to judge from the similarities in the gold jewelry from the Troy treasures and the Mochlos tombs (Weinberg, 1954, p. 92).

It is now thought, on the evidence of both the tombs at Lebena (Alexiou, 1961-62, pp. 90-91) and the recent stratigraphic excavations at Knossos (Hood, 1961-62, pp. 93-94), that E.M. III and M.M. Ia are one and the same thing. Yet to eliminate E.M. III entirely would create a large gap. I have already mentioned that M.M. Ia pottery occurs at the beginning of Lerna V, but not in Lerna IV (Caskey, 1960, pp. 299, 303), which Caskey equates with the First City at Phylakopi; Lerna V and Phylakopi II are taken to be contemporary. It is of interest to note, then, that in both the light-on-dark and the dark-on-light pottery of the First City the design is rectilinear (Atkinson et al., 1904, Pl. X), whereas in that of the Second City curvilinear and spiraliform designs are common (ibid., Pl. XIII). There is thus suggested a division, which is also outlined by Hood (1961-62, pp. 93-94), who finds at Knossos vast quantities of material which probably cover a long period of time and are capable of subdivision into two distinct phases. The earlier—which, he suggests, might be called E.M. III—shows no trace of polychromy, no spiraliform designs; both occur in the second phase—which would then be termed M.M. Ia. Although this division would demand a redefining of the assemblages belonging to E.M. III and M.M. Ia, it is preferable, I believe, to a lumping together of all this material in a single E.M. III - M.M. Ia phase The newly defined E.M. III phase would run parallel with Lerna IV (E.H. III) on the mainland; the M.M. Ia phase is the Cretan equivalent of the beginning of Lerna V (M.H.). Note that in this new scheme there is no painted spiraliform decoration in Crete or the Cyclades during the time of E.H. III; we have long been at a loss to understand how the mainland E.H. III painted ware, both light-on-dark and dark-on-light, remained strictly rectilinear in its decorative patterns if Crete and the islands already used spiraliform decoration. This is no longer a problem, and the three areas are again seen to run parallel in their development, as would be expected. E.M. III, like E.H. III and E.C., must have ended early in the twentieth century B.C. Three Egyptian scarabs of Dynasty XII, associated with M.M. Ia remains in the Lebena tombs (Alexiou, 1961-62, p. 91), confirm that M.M. Ia cannot have begun before 1991 B.C.; another scarab, of late Dynasty XII or early Dynasty XIII (about 1750 B.C.), found in an M.M. IIb deposit at Knossos (Hood, 1961-62, p. 96), warns against putting the beginning date of M.M. Ia too late in the twentieth century B.C.

Thus it is possible now, even more than in 1952 (Weinberg, 1954, p. 99), to demonstrate the parallelism between the general development in the Aegean, beginning with the Aceramic Neolithic period, and in the Near East. The Aegean was the recipient of repeated waves of migration from Anatolia and Syro-Cilicia in particular as well as of cultural influences that came independently of actual migrations. Much more sporadic were movements of people and cultural influences from the Balkans or beyond;

the cultural movements from Greece northward, which have not concerned us here, seem to have been both steady and strong. What is particularly new in the past decade is our knowledge of early Anatolia and of its relations with the Aegean. New, too, are the absolute dates afforded by the C-14 method, from which we have derived a completely new idea of the early beginnings of the Neolithic cultures, in the Aegean as everywhere else. We have also a totally different concept of the rate of development of these early societies, now seen to have been extremely slow, especially in the Neolithic period but also in the Early Bronze Age. What is clear, however, is that the whole of the eastern Mediterranean area developed more or less together, with little or no lag from one place to another. Communications would seem to have been good as early as the seventh millennium, possibly indicating that the sea was already the easier and more frequented way. If such a picture is true for the eastern Mediterranean as a whole, it must be even more so for the smaller area of the Aegean. Here, despite local differences due in part to the difficulty of internal communications, the general development that was largely dependent on external communications was essentially the same, first in the various parts of the mainland and then, once the islands were inhabited, throughout the whole region.

This in outline is the present picture. If the lines are drawn with less hesitation than in 1952, it is because of the acquisition of much new knowledge during that time. To do more than outline at this stage would be foolhardy, since there are still great voids and large gaps. No region of Greece can yet be considered to be well explored, and for no region is the knowledge of its prehistoric cultures at all complete. Even basic surface surveys are still required for most regions of Greece, and for few regions is there yet a reliable stratigraphic sequence. We need at least one Lerna in every part of Greece. We are far from achieving that goal, and there is much new knowledge to be obtained everywhere. The next decade should see even greater changes and improvements in our knowledge of prehistoric Greece than did the last. There is much to do for a whole new generation of walkers and workers.

CARBON-14 DATES FOR THE NEOLITHIC PERIOD AND EARLY BRONZE AGE IN GREECE[1]

Neolithic Period - Greek Mainland

Nea Nikomedeia[2]

Q-655	Charcoal from near original ground level.[3]	6475 ± 150 B.C.

Elateia[4]

GrN-2973	Charcoal from floor at -3.10 m., next to lowest floor above hardpan.	5754 ± 70 B.C.
GrN-3037	Charcoal from floor at -2.70 m.	5630 ± 90 B.C.
GrN-3041	Charcoal from floor at -2.55 m.	5455 ± 100 B.C.
GrN-3502	Charcoal from floor at -2.30 m., with earliest painted pottery.[5]	5301 ± 130 B.C.

---

1. Each date given is adjusted for the higher half life of 5730 ± 40, and in all of them the Suess correction had already been taken into account.

2. Godwin, H., and Willis, E. H., "Cambridge University Natural Radiocarbon Measurements V, Radiocarbon 4 (1962): 69.

3. The date seems to this author at least a thousand years too high. It is not mentioned in Radiocarbon 4 (1962), 69, or in the excavation report (Rodden, 1962, p. 276) that three years before the excavation took place the site had suffered by the removal of a large part of its eastern half, down to the level of the surrounding plain, during road-building operations, and that subsequently the area to be excavated had been cultivated by shallow, scratch ploughing (Rodden, 1962, p. 268). As a result, there was less than a meter of fill above hardpan and the possibilities of contamination from ground water were great. Although more samples for C-14 determinations were taken during subsequent seasons, the circumstances were the same; only when samples are taken from beneath the full depth of the mound, and well away from the contaminated areas, will they command greater confidence.

4. Vogel, J. C. and Waterbolk, H. T., "Groningen Radiocarbon Dates IV," Radiocarbon 5 (1963): 182-83.

5. Another part of the same sample had been tested earlier (GrN-3039) and had given a date of 6537 ± 110 B.C., while from the same sample the "humus" fraction (GrN-2454) gave a date of 4611 ± 80 B.C. The former is too high, the latter too low, but it would seem that the new analysis of selected material in GrN-3502 is in line with the other dates given above. Another sample (GrN-2933), which was from the -1.55 m. level and which had been labeled as suspect and was not scheduled for testing, gave a date of 6537 ± 75 B.C. Both these very early dates are so similar to that obtained from the single sample from Nea Nikomedeia as to suggest that the high date of the latter may also have been due to contamination.

Neolithic Period - Crete

Knossos[6]

BM-124	Charcoal from lowest level above bedrock.	6341 ± 180 B.C.
BM-126	Charcoal from near top of Early Neolithic level.	5260 ± 180 B.C.

Early Bronze Age - Greek Mainland

Eutresis[7]

P-307	Charcoal from deposit 1.17 m. above datum (E.H.I - Group III)	2623 ± 64 B.C.
P-306	Charcoal from deposit ca. 1.5 m. above datum (E.H.I - Group IV)	2633 ± 75 B.C.
P-317	Charcoal from House L, ca. 2.5 m. above datum (E.H. II - Group VIII)	2386 ± 64 B.C.

Lerna[8]

P-321	Charcoal from floor of burned room, 4.7 m. above sea level, before House of the Tiles (Late E.H. II).	2108 ± 68 B.C.
P-312	Charcoal from Corridor IV, House of the Tiles (Late E.H. II).	2005 ± 72 B.C.
P-318	Charcoal from Corridor IV, House of the Tiles (Late E.H. II).	2242 ± 72 B.C.
P-319	Charcoal from Corridor IV, House of the Tiles (Late E.H. II).	2149 ± 66 B.C.
P-320	Charcoal from burnt debris over NW part of House of the Tiles (Late E.H. II-Early E.H. III).	2097 ± 65 B.C.
P-300	Charcoal from just above burnt debris of the House of the Tiles (Early E.H. III).	2036 ± 61 B.C.

6. Barker, H., and Mackey, J., "British Museum Natural Radiocarbon Measurements IV," Radiocarbon 5 (1963): 104-5.

7. Ralph, E. K., and Stuckenrath, R., Jr., "University of Pennsylvania Radiocarbon Dates V," Radiocarbon 4 (1962); 149. The dates seem on the whole to be too low, the first one (P-307) especially so.

8. Ralph and Stuckenrath, op. cit., pp. 149-50. Whereas P-318 is not far from the expected date, most of the others are as much as two to four hundred years too low. Caskey has already expressed some scepticism with regard to them (Caskey, 1963, p. 18).

P-299	Charcoal from Bothros 8, Area BH (Early E.H. III).	1912 ± 97 B.C.

Early Bronze Age - East Aegean

Chios[9]

P-273	Charcoal from wooden beam found ca. 2 m. below surface (Troy I level).	2149 ± 97 B.C.

9. Ralph and Stuckenrath, op. cit., pp. 151-52. The date is more tha five hundred years too low, and one would like to have confirmation from other samples and, if possible, from other laboratories as well. The latter would be desirable for all Early Helladic samples, for at present we have only the results of the Pennsylvania laboratory for all Aegean Bron Age material.

Balkans	Northern Greece	C. Greece Peloponnesos	Cyclades	Crete	Troad	Anatolia	Cilicia	Mesopot.	Egypt	
	MB	MH (Lerna V)	MC (Phylakopi II)	MM Ia	Troy VI		MB		Dyn. XII	
		EH III (Lerna IV)	EC III (Phylakopi I)	EM III	Troy V Troy IV Troy III	EB 3B EB 3A	EB 3			2000
	EB	EH II (Lerna III)	EC II (Chalandriani)	EM II	Troy II Troy I	EB 2	EB 2	ED		
Graphite Ware - - →										
Crusted Ware - - →		EH I	EC I	EM I			EB 1		Dyn. I	3000
	Dimini			LN	Kum Tepe Ib Besika Tepe	EB 1		Proto-Literate	Gerzean	
	(Thessaly B)	LN	LN	MN		L. Chal. 4				
	LN				Kum Tepe Ia			Ubaid		
	← - -	← - -	Matt-painted	Ware - -	- -	L. Chal. 3 - -	- -	- -	Amratian	
Danilo + Kakanj cultures ← - -	4-legged vases - - →						Mersin XVI			4000
← - -			Megaron - -	EN - -	- -	L. Chal. 2			Badarian	
	MN (Thessaly A)	MN				L. Chal. 1		Halaf		
	← - -		Neolithic	Urfirnis Ware - -	- -	- -	- -			
← - -			Buttressed	Houses - -	- -	Can Hasan 2b	Mersin XIX			5000
← - -			Samarran	whirl patterns - -	- -	- -	- -	Samarra		
Cardium + Barbotine Wares - - →						E Chal.				
	EN	EN ← - -	White-filled	Incised Ware	- -	- -	Mersin XXIV	Hassuna		
						LN				
										6000
Crvena Stijena Level IX ← - -	Aceramic Neolithic	Aceramic Neolithic? - -	- -	? - -	- -	EN				
						Hacilar Aceramic		Jarmo Aceramic		
										7000

Bibliography

Alexiou, S.

1951 "Prōtominōïkai taphai para to Kanli-Kastelli Hirakleiou," Krētika Chronika 5: 275-94.

1961-62 "Oi prōtominōïkoi taphoi tēs Lebēnos kai ē exelexis tōn proanaktorikōn rhythmōn," ibid. 15-16: 88-91.

Atkinson, T. D., et al.

1904 Excavations at Phylakopi in Melos. ("Society for the Promotion of Hellenic Studies, Supplementary Paper," No. 4.) London: Macmillan.

Batović, Š.

1959 "Neolithische Siedlung in Smilčić," Diadora 1: 5-26.

1960-61 "Station néolithique a Smilčić," ibid. 2: 31-115.

Belmont, J. S., and Renfrew, C.

1964 "Two Prehistoric Sites on Mykonos," American Journal of Archaeology 68: 395-400.

Benac, A.

1957a "Crvena Stijena—1955 (Stratum I-IV)," Glasnik zemaljskog muzeja u Sarajevu N.S. XII: 19-50.

1957b "Zelena Pećina," ibid. XII: 61-92.

1958 "Crvena Stijena—1956 (Stratum I-IV)," ibid. N.S. XIII: 21-42.

1960-61 "Spuren der kultischen Bestattung im Neolithikum des adriatischen Gebietes," Diadora 2: 5-11.

Blegen, C. W.

1930-31 "Gonia," Metropolitan Museum Studies III: 55-80.

1937 Prosymna: The Helladic Settlement Preceding the Argive Heraeum. Cambridge: Cambridge University Press.

1963 Troy and the Trojans. London: Thames and Hudson.

Bossert, E.-M.

1960 "Die gestempelten Verzierungen auf frühbronzezeitlichen Gefässen der Agäis," Jahrbuch des deutschen archäologischen Instituts 75: 1-16.

Braidwood, R. J., and Howe, B.

1960 Prehistoric Investigations in Iraqi Kurdistan. ("Studies in Ancient Oriental Civilization," No. 31.) Chicago: University of Chicago Press.

Brodar, M.

1957 "Crvena Stijena—1955 (Stratum V)," Glasnik . . . Sarajevu N.S. XII: 51-55.

1958 "Crvena Stijena—1956 (Stratum V-XIV)," ibid. N.S. XIII: 43-64.

Caskey, J. L.

1957 "Excavations at Lerna, 1956," Hesperia XXVI: 142-62.
1958 "Excavations at Lerna, 1957," ibid. XXVII: 125-44.
1959 "Activities at Lerna, 1958-1959," ibid. XXVIII: 202-7.
1960 "The Early Helladic Period in the Argolid," ibid. XXIX: 285-303.
1962 "Excavations in Keos, 1960-1961," ibid. XXXI: 263-83.
1964a "Investigations in Keos, 1963," ibid. XXXIII: 314-35.
1964b "Greece, Crete, and the Aegean Islands in the Early Bronze Age," Cambridge Ancient History, I, Chapter XXVI(a). Cambridge: Cambridge University Press.

Caskey, J. L., and E. G.

1960 "The Earliest Settlements at Eutresis: Supplementary Excavations, 1958," Hesperia XXIX: 126-67.

Caskey, J. L., and Eliot, M.

1956 "A Neolithic Figure from Lerna," Hesperia XXV: 175-77.

Chavaillon, N. and J., and Hours, F.

1964 "Une industrie paléolithique du Péloponnèse: Le Moustérien de Vasilaki," Bulletin de correspondance hellénique 88: 616-22.

Čović, B.

1960-61 "Rezultati sondiranja na preistoriskom naselju u Gornjoj Tuzli," Glasnik . . . Sarajevu N.S. XV-XVI: 79-139.

Dakaris, S., Higgs, E. S., and Hey, R. W.

1964 "The Climate, Environment and Industries of Stone Age Greece: Part I," Proceedings of the Prehistoric Society 30: 199-244.

Dikaios, P.

1953 Khirokitia. London: Oxford University Press.

Evans, A.

1921 The Palace of Minos. I. The Neolithic and Early and Middle Minoan Ages. London: Macmillan.

Evans, J. D.

1960 "Excavations in Neolithic Levels at Knossos," Fasti Archeogici XV: 110-11.
1962-63 Report on Results of Excavations at Knossos. Archaeological Reports, p. 29.
1964a "Excavations in the Neolithic Settlement of Knossos, 1957-60. Part I," Annual of the British School at Athens 59: 132-240.
1964b "Excavations in the Neolithic Mound of Knossos, 1958-60," Bulletin of the Institute of Archaeology, University of London 4: 34-60.

French, D. H.

1961 "Late Chalcolithic Pottery in North-West Turkey and the Aegean," Anatolian Studies XI: 99-141.

1963 "Excavations at Can Hasan: Second Preliminary Report, 1962," ibid. XIII: 29-42.

Furness, A.

1953 "The Neolithic Pottery of Knossos," Annual of the British School at Athens 48: 94-134.

Fürst, C. M.

1932 Über einen neolithischen Schädel aus Arkadien ("Lunds Universitets Årsskrift," N.F. Avd. 2. Bd. 28. Nr. 13). Lund: Ohlssons Buchdruckerei.

Garstang, J.

1953 Prehistoric Mersin. Oxford: Clarendon Press.

Goldman, H.

1956 Excavations at Gözlü Kule, Tarsus. II. From the Neolithic through the Bronze Age. Princeton: Princeton University Press.

Grundmann, K.

1932 "Aus neolithischen Siedlungen bei Larisa," Athenische Mitteilungen 57: 102-23.

Higgs, E. S.

1963 "A Middle Palaeolithic Industry in Greece: Preliminary Report," Man, 63: 2-3.

Holmberg, E. J.

1944 The Swedish Excavations at Asea in Arcadia. Lund: G. W. K. Gleerup.

1964a "The Appearance of Neolithic Black Burnished Ware in Mainland Greece," American Journal of Archaeology 68: 343-48.

1964b The Neolithic Pottery of Mainland Greece. ("Göteborgs Kungl. Vetenskaps- och Vitterhets-Samhälles Handlingar," Sjätte följden, Ser. A, Band 7, No. 2). Göteborg: Wettergren and Kerbers Forlag.

Hood, M. S. F.

1961-62 "Stratigraphic Excavations at Knossos, 1957-61," Krētika Chronika 15-16: 92-98.

Kantor, H. J.

1954 "The Chronology of Egypt and Its Correlations with That of Other Parts of the Near East in the Periods before the Late Bronze Age." In Relative Chronologies in Old World Archeology, pp. 1-27. Ed. R. W. Ehrich. Chicago: University of Chicago Press.

Kenyon, K.

1960 Archaeology in the Holy Land. New York: Praeger.

Kohler, E. L., and Ralph, E. K.

1961 "C-14 Dates for Sites in the Mediterranean Area," American Journal of Archaeology 65: 357-67.

Kokkoros, P., and Kanellis, A.

1960 "Découverte d'un crâne d'homme paléolithique dans la péninsule chalcidique," L'Anthropologie 64: 438-46.

Korošec, J.

1958 The Neolithic Settlement at Danilo Bitinj: The Results of Excavations Performed in 1953. Zagreb: Yugoslav Academy of Sciences and Arts.

1964 Danilo und die Danilo-Kulturgruppe: Ergebnisse der Ausgrabungen in Jahre 1955. Ljubljana: University of Ljubljana.

Kosmopoulos, L. W.

1948 The Prehistoric Inhabitation of Corinth. Munich: Münchner Verlag.

Kunze, E.

1931 Orchomenos. II. Die neolithische Keramik. Munich: Verlag der bayerischen Akademie der Wissenschaft.

Lamb, W.

1932 "Schliemann's Prehistoric Sites in the Troad," Praehistorische Zeitschrift XXIII: 111-31.

Leroi-Gourhan, A.

1964 "Découvertes paléolithiques en Élide," Bulletin de correspondance hellénique 88: 1-8.

Leroi-Gourhan, A., and Chavaillon, J. and N.

1963 "Paléolithique du Péloponèse," Bulletin de la société préhistorique française LX: 249-65.

Levi, D.

1961-62 "Le due prime campagne di scavo a Iasos (1960-1961)," Annuario della Scuola Archeologica di Atene XXXIX-XLV: 505-71.

Lloyd, S., and Gökçe, N.

1951 "Excavations at Polatli," Anatolian Studies I: 21-75.

Lloyd, S., and Mellaart, J.

1962 Beycesultan. I. The Chalcolithic and Early Bronze Age Levels. London: British Institute of Archaeology at Ankara.

Lloyd, S., and Safar, F.

1945 "Tell Hassuna: Excavations by the Iraq Government Director General of Antiquities in 1943 and 1944," Journal of Near Eastern Studies IV: 255-89.

Mallowan, M. E. L., and Rose, J. C.

1935 "Excavations at Tall Arpachiyah, 1933," Iraq II: 1-178.

Marinatos, S.

1960 "Lithina ergaleia ek Kephallēnias," Archaiologikon Deltion 16: 41-45.

Mellaart, J.

1958 "Excavations at Hacılar: First Preliminary Report," Anatolian Studies VIII: 127-56.

1959 "Excavations at Hacılar: Second Preliminary Report, 1958," ibid. IX: 51-65.

1960 "Excavations at Hacılar: Third Preliminary Report, 1959," ibid. X: 83-104.

1961 "Excavations at Hacılar: Fourth Preliminary Report, 1960," ibid. XI: 39-75.

1962 "Excavations at Çatal Hüyük: First Preliminary Report, 1961," ibid. XII: 41-65.

1963 "Excavations at Çatal Hüyük, 1962: Second Preliminary Report," ibid. XIII: 43-103.

1964 "Excavations at Çatal Hüyük, 1963: Third Preliminary Report," ibid. XIV: 39-119.

Milojčić, V.

1955 "Bericht über die Ausgrabungen auf der Otzaki-Magula, 1954," Archäologischer Anzeiger, pp. 157-82.

1956 "Bericht über die Ausgrabungen auf der Gremnos-Magoula bei Larisa 1956," ibid., pp. 141-83.

1958 "Die neuen mittel- und altpaläolithischen Funde von der Balkanhalbinsel," Germania 36: 319-24.

1959 "Ergebnisse der deutschen Ausgrabungen in Thessalien, 1953-1958," Jahrbuch des Römisch-Germanischer Zentralmuseums Mainz 6: 1-56.

1960 "Präkeramisches Neolithikum auf der Balkanhalbinsel," Germania, 38: 320-35.

1961 Samos. I. Die prähistorische Siedlung unter dem Heraion, Grabungen 1953 und 1955. Bonn: Habelt Verlag.

Milojčić, V., Boessneck, J., and Hopf, M.

1962 Die deutschen Ausgrabungen auf der Argissa-Magula in Thessalien. I. Das präkeramische Neolithikum sowie die Tier- und Pflanzenreste. (Beiträge zur ur- und frühgeschichtlichen Archäologie des Mittelmeer-Kulturraumes, 2.) Bonn: Habelt Verlag.

Mylonas, G. E.

1959 Aghios Kosmas. An Early Bronze Age Settlement and Cemetery in Attica. Princeton: Princeton University Press.

Papadopoulou, M. G.

1958 "Magoulitsa: Neolithikos synoikismos para tēn Karditsan," Thessalika 1: 39-49.

Perkins, A., and Weinberg, S. A.

1958 "Connections of the Greek Neolithic and the Near East," American Journal of Archaeology LXII: 225.

Perkins, A. L.

1949 The Comparative Archeology of Early Mesopotamia ("Studies in Ancient Oriental Civilization," No. 25). Chicago: University of Chicago Press.

Perrot, J.

1955 "The Excavations at Tell Abu Matar, near Beersheba," Israel Exploration Journal 5: 17-40, 73-84, 167-89.

Petrocheilos, I.

1959 "Spēlaiologikai erevnai eis Kephallēnian," Deltion Hellēnikēs Spēlaiologikēs Hetairias 5: 23-70.

Robinson, H. S., and Weinberg, S. S.

1960 "Excavations at Corinth, 1959," Hesperia XXIX: 225-53.

Rodden, R. J.

1962 "Excavations at the Early Neolithic Site at Nea Nikomedeia, Greek Macedonia (1961 Season)," Proceedings of the Prehistoric Society XXVIII: 267-88.

1964 "A European Link with Chatal Hüyük: Uncovering a 7th Millennium Settlement in Macedonia, Part I - Site and Pottery," Illustrated London News, Apr. 11, pp. 564-67"; Part II - Burials and the Shrine," ibid., Apr. 18, pp. 604-7.

Schachermeyr, F.

1955 Die ältesten Kulturen Griechenlands. Stuttgart: W. Kohlhammer Verlag.

Schmidt, H.

1943 Tell Halaf. I. Die prähistorischen Funde. Berlin: de Gruyter.

Stampfuss, R.

1942 "Die ersten altsteinzeitlichen Höhlenfunde in Griechenland," Mannus 34: 132-47.

Theochares, D. R.

1956 "Nea Makri: Eine grosse neolithische Siedlung in der Nähe von Marathon," Athenischer Mitteilungen 71: 1-29.

1958a "Neolithika ek tēs periochēs tēs Iolkou," Thessalika 1: 1-15.

1958b "Ek tēs Prokerameikēs Thessalias," ibid. 1: 70-86.

1959a "Pyrasos," ibid. 2: 29-68.

1959b "Ek tēs Proïstorias tēs Euboias kai tēs Skyrou," Archeion Euboikōn Meletōn 6: 279-328.

1961 "Makedonia. Dikili-Tas (Hellēnikos tomeus)," Ergon: 82-95.

1962a "Thessalia. Sesklon." ibid.: 39-48.

1962b "Apō tē neolithikē Thessalia: I," Thessalika 4: 63-83.

1963 "Sesklo." Ergon: 27-35.

Tsountas, Ch.

1908 Ai proïstorikai akropoleis Dimēniou kai Sesklou. Athens: Sakellariou.

Varoucha, E. A.

1925-26 "Kykladikoi taphoi tēs Parou," Archaiologikē Ephēmeris: 98-114.

Wace, A. J. B., and Thompson, M. S.

1912 Prehistoric Thessaly. Cambridge: Cambridge University Press.

Weinberg, S. S.

1937 "Remains from Prehistoric Corinth," Hesperia VI: 487-524.

1939 "Excavations at Corinth, 1938-39," American Journal of Archaeology XLIII: 592-600.

1947 "Aegean Chronology: Neolithic Period and Early Bronze Age," ibid. LI: 165-82.

1948 "A Cross-section of Corinthian Antiquities (Excavations of 1940)," Hesperia XVII: 197-241.

1951 "Neolithic Figurines and Aegean Interrelations," American Journal of Archaeology LV: 121-33.

1954 "The Relative Chronology of the Aegean in the Neolithic Period and the Early Bronze Age." In Relative Chronologies in Old World Archeology, ed., R. W. Ehrich, pp. 86-107. Chicago: University of Chicago Press.

1961 "Halafian and Ubaidian Influence in Neolithic Greece," Bericht über den V. internationalen Kongress für Vor- und Frühgeschichte, Hamburg, 1958, p. 858. Berlin: Mann.

1962 "Excavations at Prehistoric Elateia, 1959," Hesperia XXXI: 158-209.

1965 "The Stone Age in the Aegean," Cambridge Ancient History, I, Chapter X. Cambridge: Cambridge University Press.

Zapfe, H.

1937 "Spuren neolithischer Besiedlung auf Zante," Wiener prähistorischer Zeitschrift 24: 158-63.

Zervos, C.

1963 Naissance de la civilisation en Grèce. Paris: Editions "Cahiers d'Art."

The Chronology of the Northwestern Mediterranean

Donald F. Brown
Council for Old World Archaeology
Cambridge, Massachusetts

The area covered in the present survey includes Italy, Sicily, the Aeolian Islands, Sardinia, and the Iberian peninsula. The heaviest emphasis is placed on the first three regions, because of the more abundant evidence of cultural change throughout the subdivisions of each period and the more complete stratigraphic sequences revealed in these regions.

A chronological rather than geographical order of presentation is followed, with the Neolithic subdivided into Early, Middle, and Late phases, and ending with the Eneolithic period, which in some areas encroaches upon the Early Bronze Age.

LOWER NEOLITHIC

In the western Mediterranean as a whole, the earliest agricultural, pottery-using cultures are those characterized by the use of wares decorated by impression before firing. The makers of this ware usually lived in hut villages, but occasionally in caves, and had a stone industry consisting principally of unretouched or partly retouched blades made of flint or occasionally obsidian.

Two rough areal divisions can be made in the impressed pottery; an eastern, and a western. In the eastern division—comprising the eastern and southern coast of Italy (Marche, Apulia, Lucania, Calabria), Sicily, Malta, and the Aeolian Islands—the pottery is decorated with rows of impressions covering almost the entire surface and made with a variety of tools: impressions made by shell edges (frequently the *Cardium*), ends of sticks, and finger nails, as well as imbricated effects produced by finger tips and pinched decoration made by thumb and forefinger. This impressed ware is often called Molfetta ware, after a village site near the Pulo di Molfetta in Apulia. The Sicilian variety—called Stentinello ware—is analogous in its simpler forms, but the decorative style includes a highly original and characteristic form consisting of masses of parallel grooves, often white-filled, as well as curious eye motives. In the western division—which includes primarily the Mediterranean coast of Spain, southern France, Corsica, and Liguria—there dominates a properly called "cardial" ware.

There has been much speculation on the origin of these impressed wares and the cultures of which they are a part. Since impressed ware begins the sequence of Neolithic cultures in both divisions, it seems likely that, despite their minor differences, they are roughly contemporaneous and stem from the same source; the Near East. Bernabò Brea (1956, pp. 185-94), the first to document this hypothesis, found analogies in the lowest Neolithic strata of sites at the eastern end of the Mediterranean (Tell Judeideh, Mersin, Ras Shamra, and Hama) as well as others further inland (Chagar Bazar, Arpachiyah, and Nineveh). In these sites, the upper levels of which could be dated to Halaf and to later periods, the Neolithic pottery included impressed wares exhibiting some of the simpler motives of the western impressed wares.

If the Near East is the source, or at least the inspiration, of the impressed wares, we must speculate on the route by which this idea reached the West. A northern route by way of Greece is quite possible, but we have little evidence. In the pre-Sesklo culture of Thessaly the dominant ware is impressed, but in many sites it is already associated with painted decoration on the same pots (Larissa, Argissa, Rachmani). On the islands of the west coast of Greece impressed ware appears in several sites, notably Aphiona on Corfu and Choirospilia on Levkas.

It is debatable whether the impressed ware of the Starčevo culture has any direct relation to that of Italy; the principal similarity is in only one type of dectoration—finger pinching—which is scarcely enough evidence for the establishing of connections. Also, between the Starčevo area and the Adriatic there is a coastal culture which shows a close relationship to the southern Italian sites in pottery and industry (Benac, 1961, pp. 76 ff.). The main sites—Crvena Stijena, Cres, Zelena Pećina, and Smilčić—can be best interpreted as outposts of the Italian impressed ware culture.

Transmission of influences from the East to the Iberian peninsula by way of North Africa, a theory long maintained by scholars, now seems unlikely. In Egypt there are no sites in which impressed ware is the dominant trait. The earliest impressed ware, with punched marks below the rims of the pots, is from Merimde, which is roughly contemporaneous with Fayum A, which is dated by radiocarbon at 4145 B.C. (Arnold and Libby, 1950). But we have earlier dates for impressed ware in Italy: Grotta dei Piccioni, 4484 B.C.; Grotta Leopardi, 4825 B.C. (Ferrara, 1961).

At Redeyef in Tunisia occurs a simple impressed decoration on pot rims. Only in the zone of Oran is impressed ware at all abundant, but the decorative motives do not closely resemble those of either the Spanish cardial wares or the south Italian impressed wares. The cardial ware in Morocco no longer seems to be the origin of the related Spanish ware, although they both are part of the same Mediterranean phenomenon. As Tarradell points out (1960, p. 55), the cardial decoration is nearly absent in the Andalusian caves, where one would expect to find it if impressed ware crossed the Strait of Gibraltar from Morocco to the Iberian peninsula.

A useful compilation of information on north African cultures is Forde-Johnston's Neolithic Cultures of North Africa (1959).

It would seem that although the north African material substantiates the general movement of impressed ware cultures through the Mediterranean from the East, it does not strengthen the idea of a land route as opposed to a sea route. The almost uniformly coastal and insular distribution of impressed pottery in the western Mediterranean leads one to the hypothesis of transmission from the Near East by sea.

The date of the impressed ware cultures in the West can be expressed only vaguely. In the stratified sites of the East, impressed strata usually lie above the pre-ceramic or mesolithic layers and underlie the painted pottery levels. In the Orient, the latter are represented by Halaf type pottery and in Greece by Sesklo painted ware, both of which must have come into being as early as the beginning of the fifth millennium.

The duration of the impressed wares varied markedly from region to region. In southern Italy and Sicily they lasted well into the Middle Neolithic period, which was dominated in Italy by painted pottery cultures. In Spain, the coastal cave culture with pottery decorated in Monserrat style, which is similar to that of southern France (Châteauneuf-les-Martigues) and to Liguria (Arene Candide), lasted to the beginning of the Eneolithic, when new traits involving megalithic architecture made their appearance. In areas only slightly influenced by the new cultures, the impressed pottery style persisted for a long time.

Stratigraphic evidence for the position of the impressed wares is limited but satisfactory. In Apulia, unmixed impressed ware strata are found in the lower level of the Caverna del Guardiano at Polignano a Mare, in the lower stratum of Torre a Mare, and the lowest level of Coppa Nevigata (Bernabò Brea, 1956, p. 164). It occurs alone in many one-period sites in Apulia, but in others it appears with painted wares.

In the Aeolian Islands, impressed pottery appears at the base of the stratigraphic series made up from a number of interlocking sites, but it first appears already associated with red band painted ware at Castellaro Vecchio (Bernabò Brea, 1956, p. 169). In Liguria, the Caverna delle Arene Candide (Bernabò Brea, 1956) is indispensible for the establishing of the cultural sequence in the northern part of our area. Here the unmixed impressed strata (25-28) lie above Mesolithic occupation levels and below those containing square-mouthed pottery of the succeeding culture. Comparable stratigraphy (Escalon de Fonton, 1956) is found in sites near the Mediterranean coast of southern France (Châteauneuf-les-Martigues, for example).

MIDDLE NEOLITHIC: SOUTHERN ITALY

At a certain point in the development of the impressed ware cultures in Italy, a new influence entered, again coming from the East: painted pottery, which spread over much of the area occupied by the impressed wares.

Various attempts have been made to classify the various styles of south Italian painted wares and to arrange them in chronological order, usually on the basis of artistic development or of association in unstratified sites with presumably earlier or later material (Rellini, 1934; Stevenson, 1947). We now have a fairly reliable scheme, thanks to the work of Bernabò Brea (Bernabò Brea and Cavalier, 1960) in the Aeolian Islands, and fortified by stratified sites in the Abruzzi (Radmilli, 1959, and 1962, pp. 95-97).

The earliest style of painted ware consists of pots decorated with wide red bands or flames, which are found in the Castellaro phase on Lipari associated with impressed ware. The same association is found in the lowest level (VI) of the Grotta dei Piccioni in the Abruzzi (Radmilli, 1962, p. 95) underlying a layer (V) containing Ripoli ware, which belongs to the next phase of the Middle Neolithic.

Associated with the red band ware in many sites of Apulia is a dark monochrome scratched ware with a variety of motives such as checkerboards, zigzags, and hatched triangles. Frequently the scratched lines are minutely serrated, produced by a rocker technique. Scratched and painted designs rarely appear on the same pot. This type of decoration is found sporadically in central Italy, but appears again in Liguria in the square-mouthed pottery levels of Arene Candide. The relationship between these two centers of scratched wares is not at all clear.

A distinctive but rare trait of this period is the surrounding of villages with a defensive trench, as in the Matera region at Murgecchia, Tirlecchia, and Murgia Timone. In Sicily, the corresponding phase is indicated by several sites of the Stentinello culture which produced occasional sherds of red band ware (Megara Hyblaea, Stentinello with defensive trench).

The second style of painted pottery is that of the Felci-Ripoli phase, named after a cave site on the Isle of Capri and a hut village in the Valle della Vibrata in the Abruzzi. Decoration is polychrome and of two principal types: black-bordered red flames, and geometric motives bordered by a frame of parallel lines containing a row of dots. This style can be found in the lowest layers of the acropolis of Lipari, above which are two later types of painted ware (Bernabò Brea and Cavalier, 1960).

The position of Ripoli ware in the sequence of painted wares remains slightly dubious. If we equate it with Felci and the equivalent phase on Lipari, then it should follow the red band ware and precede the third style of Neolithic painted pottery: the Serra d'Alto ware. On the other hand, if we take into account the presence at Ripoli of bifacially worked flint points, some with tangs, which are characteristic of the Eneolithic period, it would seem to be later than Serra d'Alto. Furthermore, in the Grotta dei Piccioni in the Abruzzi the Ripoli layer is said to contain Lagozza ware, which is a Late Neolithic ware in the north of Italy. This layer is above a layer (VI) containing red band ware and below an Eneolithic layer (IV) with Remedello-Ortucchio pottery. Elements of the Ripoli culture are said to have extended as far north as Liguria, Lombardia, and Emilia; there is no evidence of any massive migration of Ripoli traits, but only occasional painted sherds.

The third and possibly latest style of painted pottery arose in the same general area as the others: Apulia and the Materano. It is named Serra d'Alto after a site near Matera in which this style predominates. The term "fine painted ware" was used by Peet to describe this ware.

The pottery is decorated variously with rows of painted triangles, hatched triangles, concentric squares, step designs, fragments of spirals, and a tremolo bordered by two straight lines. The ribbon handles are frequently surmounted by animal protomes, and there is also a characteristic folded back ribbon handle as well as elongated spool-shaped lugs.

In the Lipari sequence, the Serra d'Alto ware follows the Felci style ware and precedes the monochrome Diana ware, which is dated to the Upper Neolithic. There are traces also in Sicily, particularly in elaborate handles found in the Palermo area, and in Campania at La Starza (Trump, 1960).

The origins of the painted pottery cultures are still obscure. Since there is nothing comparable to the north, west and south, the east seems to be the only direction from which these cultures—or at least the idea of painting—came. Indeed, the distribution of painted pottery favors this assumption, since the greatest concentration of sites is in the southeastern part of the peninsula. Certain analogies are immediately apparent in the succession of Neolithic cultures in Greece. The Sesklo period has bichrome decoration, which may represent the same stage as the red band ware in Italy, whereas the spirals and meanders of the Dimini pottery which followed are reminiscent of the Serra d'Alto ware.

MIDDLE NEOLITHIC: CENTRAL AND NORTHERN ITALY

While the painted pottery cultures were evolving in southern Italy, cultures of different character and origin were developing in central and northern Italy. For central Italy we can say nothing about the Early Neolithic; only in the Middle Neolithic is there found definite evidence: from the Grotta Patrizi at Sasso Furbara in Lazio (Radmilli, 1962, p. 104). In this burial cave, the associated incised pottery was so much like that of the Fiorano culture of northern Italy that Radmilli has called the whole complex the Sasso-Fiorano culture.

The northern branch is represented by the type site of Fiorano Modenese in Emilia as well as by the long known Reggian hut villages of Albinea, Rivaltella, Castelnuovo-Sotto, and Calerno.

To F. Malavolti we are indebted for the main synthesis of Neolithic sites in Emilia (Malavolta, 1951). He distinguishes two Middle Neolithic phases in Emilia: the Fiorano and the succeeding Chiozza phases, followed by a Late Neolithic Pescale phase. In my own study of this material I had combined the Fiorano and Chiozza phases and had placed Pescale in a later phase as did Malavolti.

Bernabò Brea (1956, p. 201) considers the Fiorano culture to be synchronous with strata 21-24 of Arene Candide, which contain pottery *a bocca quadrilobata* (with four-lobed rims), although this form does not appear in the Fiorano culture. At the moment, the Fiorano seems isolated except for its connection with Sasso, unless we include it in the Chiozza culture.

The second phase in Emilia is represented by the Chiozza culture, named after the type site of Chiozza di Scandiano in Reggio-Emilia. (It is also called the square-mouthed pottery culture.) At this point in the progression of cultures in the area we can detect a certain unity extending from Liguria to Venezia, marked by the presence of several traits thought by Bernabò Brea to be of Danubian II origin: chiefly square-mouthed pots (*a bocca quadrata*), terracotta idols, and clay stamps (*pintadere*).

The Danubian influence is seen most clearly, not in the eastern or central part of northern Italy, but in Liguria in several cave sites—particularly Arene Candide levels 20-17, where all the characteristic traits are found. The strata in question lie above those containing the lobe-rimmed vases (*vasi a bocca quadrilobata*) and below those (13-9) containing material of the succeeding Lagozza culture. In other parts of northern Italy, the evidence is more fragmentary. Square-mouthed bowls, rather than vases, are found at Vayes and Alba in Piemonte, in some lake dwellings of the Varese area of Lombardia, and at Quinzano and other sites near Verona. *Pintadere* are found in Venezia Giulia.

Scratched ware, associated in the south with red band painted ware, is also found in the north, particularly in Liguria. At Arene Candide, it is most frequent in levels 20-17, which may be synchronous in the south with the Serra d'Alto phase, in which scratched ware reaches a maximum.

MIDDLE NEOLITHIC: IBERIAN PENINSULA

The Middle Neolithic in Spain is represented, according to present scanty evidence, only by a survival of the Spanish impressed ware culture along the Mediterranean coast from Catalonia to Gibraltar and the Atlantic coast of Portugal. In Catalonia, the only other truly Neolithic culture is the Fossa culture which is characterized by single flexed burials, a smooth dark pottery and occasional square-mouthed pots.

UPPER NEOLITHIC: SOUTHERN ITALY

In the sequence found on the Aeolian Islands, the Serra d'Alto layer of the Castello in Lipari is overlain by a thin stratum of the Diana culture, named after an adjacent site in the plain in which great quantities of material pertaining to this period were excavated. The Diana culture, typified by a monochrome red ware with elongated tubular or spool-shaped handles, seems to be a final stage in the development of painted pottery, with a tendency toward simplification of all elements.

The distribution of this culture is extensive. In Sicily, the long known site of Marmo has almost identical pottery. The later sites of the Serra d'Alto culture have many pots on which thin spool-shaped handles of Diana shape have replaced the ribbon handles. Sites near Taranto (tombs of Scoglio del Tonno and the Masseria Bellavista) have pottery of the same form but of less refined design than those at Contrada Diana on Lipari. On Malta, Diana pottery is found associated with material of the Skorba and Zebbug phases.

Since there are no likely sources in adjacent areas of the Mediterranean, it is possible that the Diana culture is merely a regional development—or degeneration—of the long established painted pottery cultures. Diana ware has been found as far north as Umbria, where, in a Neolithic village site at Norcia, Diana ware is found associated with Lagozza ware (Calzoni, 1939, pp. 37 ff.).

UPPER NEOLITHIC: NORTHERN ITALY

Although there is clearly a survival of the Chiozza culture and Danubian influence in many sites, the Upper Neolithic is marked in northern Italy by the introduction of traits of a new culture—Lagozza, named after a village situated in a small, now dry lake, near Besnate in the province of Varese, Lombardia.

The Lagozza sites have a wide distribution throughout the lake and moraine area of Lombardia, with influences extending to Liguria and south into the peninsula as far as Toscana (Grotta all'Onda) in the west and Abruzzi (Grotta dei Piccioni) in the east. Except for these curious offshoots, the culture is essentially a lake-dwelling one, with villages built on the margins of lakes on artificial earth platforms reinforced with beams and piles. At the Lago di Varese, the settlement is constructed on an artificial island in the lake (Isolino)—a warning to those who insist that lake dwellings must be lake-side ones. However, there now seems to be no evidence for platforms raised above ground or water, as was once thought.

Relations of this culture—with its black polished pottery equipped frequently with string-hole lugs or lugs with multiple perforations, of which the "panpipe" lug is a characteristic variant—are definitely with the west and north, in contrast with those of the preceding cultures. Such close similarities exist between the Lagozza culture and the Chassey culture of France and the Cortaillod of Switzerland that these can all be assigned to the same general complex of cultures. Caves and some open sites of southern France reveal clear levels of the Lagozza culture.

In Spain, the Lagozza influence extends into Catalonia, where the Fossa graves show evidence of an industry of flint blades retouched on one side as in the typical Lagozza industry. At the site of Sabadell, there are cups of typical Lagozza form and workmanship with string-hole lugs.

For the chronological position of the Lagozza culture, we return to Arene Candide, where pottery typical of this culture, including vessels with panpipe lugs, are found in levels 13-9 overlying the square-mouthed pottery layer of Chiozza and Danubian affinity. In central Italy, the Grotta dei Piccioni (Abruzzi) has a stratified deposit in which layer V contained wares identified as of Ripoli and Lagozza derivation. Underlying this is a middle layer with red band ware, and above is a layer of Eneolithic pottery. In our present scheme, in which Ripoli precedes Serra d'Alto, the Ripoli ware appears here much too late. If, however, we take my original assumption that Ripoli follows Serra d'Alto, it would be closer in period to the Lagozza culture.

The evidence for relating the Lagozza culture to southern Italy is slight but not insignificant. A tie with the Aeolian Islands is the previously mentioned association of Lagozza and Diana ware at Norcia in Umbria. There is other evidence in the Aeolian Islands (Bernabò Brea, 1956, p. 223). In the strata of the Piano Conte culture, which succeeds the Diana culture and stands on the threshhold of the Eneolithic period, there are numerous carinated bowls of characteristic Lagozza form with lugs, some of which are multi-perforated in a manner reminiscent of the panpipe lug. If these analogies are correct, then the Lagozza influence reached Lipari at the beginning of the Eneolithic period.

The origin of the Upper Neolithic Lagozza culture is not clear. It seems likely, however, that it is an overflow from the Chassey-Cortaillod area.

ENEOLITHIC PERIOD: GENERAL

The beginning of the Eneolithic is marked by a greater change in culture than in any of the preceding periods after the introduction of agriculture. Italy, the islands of the western Mediterranean, France, and the Iberian Peninsula all show the influence of new ideas and traits, particularly new religious ideas expressed in megalithic architecture, collective burals, idols, weapons of copper and their imitations in flint, new forms of pottery, as well as the beginnings of towns.

The cause of such a cultural upheaval can be traced to the eastern Mediterranean, where the Aegean and Anatolian cultures had developed to such a point that they sought trade, raw materials, and possibly colonization in the west. The result was the development of new cultures in all the areas of our survey.

ENEOLITHIC: SICILY AND AEOLIAN ISLANDS

Since the cultures of Sicily during the Eneolithic period are so numerous and their interrelations so complex, it will be necessary to deal with them in a rather simplified and general manner. The chief cultures in this period are, in order of date, the Serraferlicchio, S. Ippolito, Conca d'Oro, and Castelluccio.

First, however, we must bring the Lipari sequence up to date (Bernabò Brea and Cavalier, 1960). Following the Diana culture occurred the Piano Conte culture, characterized by a channeled ware without handles. Some of the pottery, as mentioned above, has Lagozza analogies, and some tunnel handles are reminiscent of the Eneolithic Rinaldone pottery on the mainland. Ties with Sicily are indicated by the presence of Serraferlicchio sherds and Piano Conte ware in sites in Sicily. Above the Piano Conte levels on Lipari are remains of the Piano Quartara culture of the later Eneolithic, with similarities in pottery to Early Helladic sauce boats and in handles of some pots to the elbow handles of the Polada culture in northern Italy, which probably began in the Eneolithic period. Above the Piano Quartara levels there exists material of the Capo Graziano culture, which ends the Eneolithic or begins the Aeolian Bronze Age.

In Sicily, there is good stratigraphic evidence for arranging the various cultures in the site of Chiusazza in the Syracuse region. In this cave, seven periods are represented, from Greek to Diana. Above the Diana level are successive strata containing pottery of San Cono-Piano Notaro, Conzo, Serraferlicchio, Malpasso, Castelluccio, and Thapsos styles (Bernabò Brea, 1957, pp. 73-74). The sequence of most of the major cultures in southern and southeastern Sicily is thus confirmed by stratigraphy.

The San Cono-Piano Notaro culture seems to bridge the Neolithic and Eneolithic periods; its pottery shows some forms of the earlier Stentinello culture. Conzo pottery is a polychrome ware with as yet a limited distribution in Sicily. Of greater importance is the culture of Serraferlicchio, with its shiny black-on-red pottery, which Bernabò Brea (1956, p. 288) thinks was derived from the late Neolithic of Greece but with some Early Helladic influences.

The site of Malpasso, with collective tombs and red monochrome ware of possible Anatolian inspiration, is another source of evidence for the eastern origin of the Sicilian Eneolithic period. At S. Ippolito near Caltagirone, a site consists of several villages which cover a time span from the Neolithic to the Iron Age. Much of the pottery belongs to the Eneolithic and is a painted ware with many Eastern characteristics, such as small ovoid flasks of Cypriote type with obliquely cut mouths.

In the Palermo area developed the Conca d'Oro culture with its oven tombs and pottery, which seems to have evolved from the San Cono-Piano Notaro incised ware.

In this period the Spanish form of the bell beaker was introduced into western Sicily, at Torrebigini and at sites in the Palermo area such as Villafrati and Termini Imerese. At Villafrati, the bell beakers are associated with pottery of the Capo Graziano culture style of the Aeolian Islands. Metal objects also appear in the Conca d'Oro sites of Villafrati, Carini, and Capaci.

The Castelluccio culture, which terminates the Eneolithic and ushers in the Bronze Age, has been studied for a long time. It is essentially the Siculan I of Orsi's terminology. This is a culture of small towns with extensive cemeteries of rock-cut collective tombs containing large numbers of skeletons. The characteristic painted hourglass mugs have analogies with Early Helladic tankards and Cappadocian ware of around 1800 B.C. A curious trait is the bossed bone plaque, several of which have been found in tombs at Castelluccio. Remarkably similar ones have turned up in Troy II, in a Middle Helladic level at Lerna, and at Hal Tarxien in Malta. Carvings on tomb entrances are reminiscent of carvings on Western megalithic structures.

The relation of the Maltese cultures to those of Sicily is not clear. The original sequence of cultures on Malta established by Evans (1953) was based largely on the assumption of typological evolution, strengthened by some stratigraphy. The order of cultural phases from Ghar Dalam through Mgarr, Zebbug, Ggantija, and Tarxien to Tarxien Cemetery has been revised more than once by Trump as the result of stratigraphic excavations and radiocarbon dating (Trump, 1961). Trump's latest views (1963) equate Ghar Dalam with Stentinello in Sicily, a new phase called Skorba, and part of Zebbug with Diana; Mgarr now follows Zebbug; the remaining phases retain their previous order. Unfortunately, of seven radiocarbon dates (Trump, 1963), two clash decidedly with other similarly derived dates for the same period (Tarxien Cemetery, 1930 B.C., 2535 B.C.; Zebbug, 2690 B.C., 3050 B.C.), and the single Ggantija date of 3290 B.C. is much too early for the present location of this phase in the sequence. Thus, until Trump's laudable attempts to establish the sequence on the basis of excavation and radiocarbon dates result in a more stable picture, we cannot make good use of the tempting Maltese data. Both Bernabò Brea (1960) and Evans (1959, 1960), who disagreed on the interpretation of the original sequence, will have to revise their views in the light of the new evidence.

ENEOLITHIC: CENTRAL ITALY

Since the Eneolithic of southern Italy is relatively unknown, the few sites with oven tombs (Torre Castelluccia near Taranto, and Murgia Timone in the Materano) being a reflection of the cultures to the north, we move to central Italy. Here the Eneolithic period is represented by two main facies: the Gaudo facies (Sestieri, 1946, 1947) centered in Paestum in Campania, and the Rinaldone facies centered in Lazio.

Both facies are characterized by oven-shaped tombs, daggers of copper, pottery bottles, flint daggers, and triangular tanged points—but there are differences. The Gaudo sites have styloid daggers of flint which are flaked on only one surface; the bottles have strap handles rather than subcutaneous stringholes; and there are certain unique forms, such as askoid pots and double bowls connected by a stirrup handle. The Rinaldone daggers are bifacially flaked, and in the type site there is a stone battle ax as well as several stone mace heads. Both facies are represented only by cemeteries or single tombs.

Bernabò Brea (1956, p. 257) suggests that the nearest analogies to the Gaudo pottery types are in the final phases of Troy I, in Troy II and III, at Poliochni in Lemnos, and in Thermi.

For Rinaldone there are no good analogies outside Italy. The battle ax, found only at the type site, is not really characteristic of the culture, although stray shaft-hole axes have been found elsewhere in Italy. The oven tombs seem to be an extension of the megalithic tomb as in Sicily, ultimately derived from Cyprus and the Cyclades. There is, however, an obvious relationship of Rinaldone to the Eneolithic culture of Remedello to the north in Lombardia.

ENEOLITHIC: NORTHERN ITALY

Across the Apennines in northern Italy, the related Remedello culture appeared at approximately the same time as the Rinaldone culture. These peoples shared some traits: the use of copper for flat metal axes and ribbed daggers, bifacial flaking of flint daggers, and tanged triangular points. Burial rites were, however, different since the Remedello cemeteries in Lombardia consist of single trench graves instead of single or multiple burials in oven tombs. Pottery is rare and its relations vague, but at the sites of Cà di Marco, Santa Cristina, and Roccolo Bresciani there occurred sherds of typical bell beakers of central Spanish style. Two objects of silver were found: a crutch-headed pin at Fontanella, and a lunula at Villafranca Veronese.

The origin of the Remedello culture is obscure. The mode of burial—a single contracted skeleton in a trench—is known from earlier periods in the area. The stone industry, representing weapons only, could well represent a change in armament rather than an influx of immigrants. Since no habitation sites are yet known, it is tempting to consider that there is some relationship between the Remedello cemeteries and the early Polada lake dwellings. The bell beakers may have come in by trade. We know of Spanish bell beakers in western Sicily. There is definite beaker influence in Sardinia, but the absence of bell beakers in the area between Sardinia and Lombardia leave the route an open question.

In Toscana at the Grotta all'Onda, there were found V-bored buttons of antimony as well as copper daggers. These buttons are characteristic of the Bell Beaker culture. Hence we could postulate a route from Sardinia to Toscana to Lombardia. A coastal route from Spain to Lombardia is unlikely, since there are no beakers in southern France and Liguria. Bernabò Brea, however, sees similarities in several decorative motives of the scarce Remedello pottery and that of Fontbouïsse in southern France, and hence favors this route for the introduction of bell beakers into Italy (Bernabò Brea, 1956, p. 259). Acanfora has given the most recent comprehensive treatment of the Remedello culture (1956) and of the bell beakers in Italy (1955).

ENEOLITHIC: SARDINIA

Although there is limited evidence for earlier periods in Sardinia, the Eneolithic period is represented by a striking development of megalithic monuments represented by dolmens, stelae, and rock-cut tombs (domus de janas) of considerable size and complexity (Zervos, 1954). There are also several important cave sites and at least one necropolis of cist burials. Evidence for distinct cultures is accumulating, but so far there is little stratigraphic foundation for arranging them in chronological order.

From the welter of cultural traits we can see that Sardinia must have been an important way station for influences traveling in various directions. It must have played a part in the transmission of the custom of collective burial to the West from the eastern Mediterranean. In the opposite direction, it had something to do with the expansion of the influence of bell beakers from Spain to northern Italy. In addition, there are cultural relations with France.

The principal sites of the Eneolithic period are collective cave burials and rock-cut collective tombs. The Grotta di San Bartolomeo near Cagliari, which was excavated in the latter part of the nineteenth century (Colini, 1898), revealed an uncertain stratigraphy containing material of the Eneolithic period, including carinated bowls with hatched ribbon designs similar to those of Villafrati in Sicily. There were indisputable bell beakers and tripod bowls decorated in beaker style, accompanied by a copper flat ax and copper daggers of Western European style. The burial cave at San Michele, Ozieri (Taramelli, 1915), contained some similar material and tunnel handles like those found on Malta in the Tarxien phase.

The chief center for rock-cut tombs is Anghelu Ruju (Taramelli, 1909), where some forty or more examples have been found. The earliest of these date from the Eneolithic period and contain a combination of elements from the east and west, among which are beakers of Spanish type, Western European copper daggers, V-bored buttons, a variety of flint points recalling both Spain and the Remedello culture, and marble idols imitating early Cycladic types. Bell beakers are also found in the rock-cut tomb of Cuguttu and the tomb of Marinaru.

A different burial practice is offered by the necropolis of Li Muri near Arzachena in Galluro, where stone-lined trench graves are each surrounded by a funerary circle of stones. Outside the circles are small stone cists.

After the Eneolithic period, there developed the Nuragic culture which lasted from the fifteenth century B.C. to Roman times.

ENEOLITHIC: IBERIAN PENINSULA

At some point in the Late Neolithic or early Eneolithic, new influences from the Near East appeared at several points along the coast (Almeria, mouth of the Guadalquivir, and possibly the Tagus). Whether the Almerian culture was in existence before this time is debatable. Although Almagro (1961) places the Almerian in his Neolithic II and Childe considers it of Neolithic date, Bernabò Brea (1956, p. 291) assigns the earliest sites—El Garcel and Tres Cabezos—to the early Eneolithic. Tarradell (1960) stresses the fact that only the cave cultures and Catalonian Fossa culture lack such Eneolithic traits as towns, collective burials, use of metal, and idols. He points out (ibid., p. 63) that the earliest Almerian sites have circular tombs with collective burials and the characteristic Eneolithic flint industry of triangular points with secondary flaking.

If the mature Almerian culture is of Eneolithic date, there exists the problem of reconciling its position with respect to the Western Neolithic cultures with which it has been generally assumed to be related: Lagozza, Chassey, Cortaillod, Michelsberg, and Windmill Hill. If we accept the early radiocarbon dates obtained for these cultures, and if we accept the common assumption that the Western Neolithic spread north and east from Spain, then the movement from Spain must have taken place long before the Almerian culture acquired Eneolithic traits. A more satisfactory explanation is that of Almagro (1961, p. 50), who derives the Western Neolithic cultures from the Danube. The Almerian would be an extension into Spain of the Chiozza and Lagozza cultures of northern Italy. We find occasional square-mouthed pots, characteristic of the Chiozza culture and levels 17-20 of Arene Candide, in the Catalonian Fossa Grave culture (Fletcher, 1960), which Almagro associates with the Almerian. According to this view, the Almerian culture would be one of the last rather than the first of the Western Neolithic cultures. The Eneolithic elements that appear in the Almerian would thus fit into place. Tarradell (1960, p. 63), however, argues effectively against the supposed relation between the Almerian culture and the Catalonian Fossa Grave culture, stressing in particular the contrast between the Almerian collective burials and the Catalonian single burials.

The important site of Los Millares is by general consent placed in the Eneolithic, or Bronze I of Almagro's terminology. This is an extraordinary site consisting of a large town fortified by a ditch and a wall with semicircular bastions. The cemetery outside the town contains more than a hundred tombs, of which about sixty-five are tholos tombs. Present at Los Millares are bifacially flaked arrow points and copper tools, painted pottery, pottery with eye motives, and imported ivory. Set apart from the Los Millares material is that of many surrounding sites—mostly tombs—which contained trapeze-shaped points, stone axes, and other Neolithic traits. Blance (1961, pp. 192 ff.) considers Los Millares, Vila Nova de S. Pedro (a similarly bastioned site in southern Portugal), Almizaraque, and Alcalá to be towns alien to the native cultural tradition. She finds many comparisons with the eastern Mediterranean in fortification, tomb types, pottery (particularly stroke burnished wares), and other traits. Copper ax and dagger types have analogies with the Cyclades and Crete. These parallels are with sites of Early Cycladic I, which ended around 2400 B.C. The presence of bell beakers in both Los Millares and Vila Nova de S. Pedro (upper level) suggests a long period of occupation, unless we raise the date of the bell beaker complex considerably.

Arribas (1960, p. 94) places the arrival of the Near Eastern traits at about 2300 B.C., and suggests that a second wave may have led to the construction of the large tholoi of Los Alcores, Antequera, and Rambla de Gor in Granada, which resemble the princely tombs of the Mycenaean period. We have a problem in reconciling the dating of the Iberian tholoi with those of the Aegean, since most of the latter range from Late Helladic I to III, and the Mycenaean treasuries are of LHIII date. Thus, the earliest Aegean tholoi date from around 1600 BC, whereas the late dating of Los Millares to 2000-1700 B.C. by Santa Olalla is still too early to allow an Eastern origin of the large Western tholoi. It would be more satisfactory to derive the Western tholoi from the circular passage graves which appeared as an early manifestation in Spain of the Near Eastern collective tomb.

Another problem of the Iberian Eneolithic is the origin and spread of the bell beaker complex. Whether this represents a group of itinerant traders, as Childe suggests, we do not know. Bell beakers are found in all types of megalithic tombs and in settlements belonging to other cultures. Not all the diagnostic elements of the complex—which include wrist guards, V-bored buttons, stone arrow straighteners, and tang-and-barb arrowheads of flint, Western European tanged copper daggers, and regionally different beakers—are present in all areas. The area of this complex includes the major countries of Western Europe. We do not know in which part of this area the bell beaker complex originated, and there are proponents for a central European origin as well as an Iberian origin. The majority opinion favors Spain, where it is tempting to drive the beaker from the much earlier Spanish impressed ware culture. It does seem certain, however, that the beaker complex arose in the Eneolithic period, since the earliest associations in the south are always with Eneolithic groups, such as the Remedello culture in Italy, the Late Eneolithic Villafrati site in Sicily, and the Eneolithic Los Millares civilization in Spain.

CHRONOLOGICAL TABLE

The appended table of cultural successions and relationships has been kept as simple as possible. The period names are essentially those used by Bernabò Brea (1956); the names of the cultures, a few of which represent distinct pottery styles rather than clearly defined cultures, are terms in common use. In arranging the French and Swiss sequences, I have taken into consideration the table constructed by Professor Homer Thomas for his West European section of the present volume. Nevertheless, it has been impossible to reconcile with complete satisfaction the dating of the Italian cultures and those of the Iberian peninsula with the early dating of some French sites. Since complete agreement is lacking on the succession and dating of the cultures of the Iberian peninsula, their arrangement on this table reflects principally their relationships to the Italian cultures.

The column of radiocarbon dates (Ferrara *et al.*, 1959; Ferrara *et al.*, 1961) was added to the already prepared table, and the agreement between the two is remarkably satisfactory. The absolute dates have been corrected according to the formula, BP x 1.03 - 1950, which takes into account the new half-life of carbon 14 (Godwin, 1962, p. 984).

NORTHWESTERN MEDITERRANEAN

PERIOD	SPAIN, FRANCE SWITZERLAND	N. ITALY		C. ITALY	S. ITALY	SICILY	AEOLIAN IS.	RADIOCARBON (BP x 1.03 - 1950)
		ARENE CANDIDE LEVELS						
1400 FULL ENEOLITHIC 2000	LOS MILLARES BELL BEAKER		REMEDELLO and POLADA	RINALDONE	PROTO-APENNINE ANDRIA	CASTELLUCCIO VILLAFRATI and BELL BEAKERS	CAPO GRAZIANO	1400 Barche di Solferino 1491 $\pm$ 115 (Polada) 2000
ENEOLITHIC 2600	BELL BEAKER HORGEN - S.O.M. ALMERIAN	5-8	REMEDELLO and POLADA	RINALDONE	GAUDO	CONCA D'ORO S. IPPOLITO SERRA-FERLICCHIO	PIANO QUARTARA PIANO CONTE	Asciano (Rinaldone) 2425 $\pm$ 115 Piccioni (Remedello infl.) 2485 $\pm$ 105 2600
UPPER NEOLITHIC 3200	CHASSEY B CORTAILLOD EGOLZWIL SPANISH FOSSA GRAVES	9-13 LAGOZZA	LAGOZZA	LAGOZZA and DIANA (NORCIA)	DIANA LATE SERRA D'ALTO	S. CONO and PIANO NOTARO MARMO (Red Monochrome)	DIANA (Red Monochrome)	Piccioni (Lagozza) 2963 $\pm$ 110 Lagozza 2988 $\pm$ 90 Zebbug (Diana) 3050 $\pm$ 150; 3190 $\pm$ 150 3200
LATE MIDDLE NEOLITHIC 3800	MICHELSBERG CHASSEY A SPANISH IMPRESSED	17-20 BOCCA QUADRATA	CHIOZZA	SASSO	SERRA D'ALTO	STENTINELLO and SERRA D'ALTO TRACES	SERRA D'ALTO	Isolino (Chiozza) 3535 $\pm$ 180 Petescia (M. Neol) 3610 $\pm$ 145 Isolino (Chiozza) 3750 $\pm$ 144 3800
EARLY MIDDLE NEOLITHIC 4400	S. FRENCH IMPRESSED SPANISH IMPRESSED	21-24 BOCCA QUADRILOBATA	FIORANO	SASSO	FELCI-RIPOLI (RED BAND)	STENTINELLO and RED BAND	FELCI-RIPOLI CASTELLARO (RED BAND & IMPRESSED)	4400
LOWER NEOLITHIC 5000	S. FRENCH IMPRESSED SPANISH IMPRESSED	25-28 LIGURIAN IMPRESSED			MOLFETTA (IMPRESSED)	STENTINELLO		Piccioni (impr. & red band) 4484 $\pm$ 130 Leopardi (Figulina & impr.) 4825 $\pm$ 135 5000

Acanfora, M. O.

1955 "Sui vasi campaniformi dell'Italia settentrionale," Rivista di Scienze Preistoriche 10: 38-46.

1956 "Fontanella Mantovana e la cultura di Remedello," Bullettino di Paletnologia Italiana 65: 321-85.

Almagro, Martin

1961 "La secuencia cultural de la peninsula iberica del Neolitico al Bronce final," Boletín del Seminario de Estudios de Arte y Arqueologia (Valladolid) 27: 45-59.

Arnold, J. R., and Libby, W. F.

1950 Radiocarbon Dates. Chicago: University of Chicago, Institute for Nuclear Studies.

Arribas, Antonio

1960 "Megalitismo peninsular," Primer symposium de prehistoria de la peninsula iberica, pp. 69-99. Pamplona.

Benac, A.

1961 "Les influences méditerranéennes sur le néolithique des Balkans du nord-ouest," Bericht V Internat. Kongress für Vor- und Frühgeschichte, pp. 75-83. Hamburg.

Bernabò Brea, L.

1956 Gli scavi nella Caverna delle Arene Candide, parte prima, gli strati con ceramiche. Vol. 2. Bordighera.

1957 Sicily before the Greeks. New York: Praeger.

1960 "Malta and the Mediterranean," Antiquity 34: 132-37.

Bernabò Brea, L., and Cavalier, M.

1960 Meligunís-Lipára, Vol. I. Palermo.

Blance, Beatrice

1961 "Early Bronze Age Colonists in Iberia," Antiquity 35: 192-201.

Calzoni, U.

1939 Bullettino di Paletnologia Italiana n.s. 3: 37 ff.

Colini, G. A.

1898 Bullettino di Paletnologia Italiana 24: 253 ff.

Escalon de Fonton, M.

1956 "Préhistoire de la Basse Provence," Préhistoire 12: 1-159.

Evans, J. D.

1953 "The Prehistoric Culture Sequence in the Maltese Archipelago Proceedings of the Prehistoric Society 19: 41-94.

1959 Malta, pp. 42-43 (table). New York: Praeger.

1960 "Malta and the Mediterranean," Antiquity 34: 218-20.

Ferrara, G., Fornaca-Rinaldi, G., and Tongiorgi, E.

1961 "Carbon-14 Dating in Pisa—II," Radiocarbon 3: 99-104.

Ferrara, G., Reinharz, M., and Tongiorgi, E.

1959 "Carbon-14 Dating in Pisa," Radiocarbon Supplement 1: 103-10.

Fletcher, Domingo

1960 "Vasos de boca cuadrata en la península ibérica," Festschrift für Lothar Zotz, pp. 145-50. Bonn.

Forde-Johnston, J. L.

1959 Neolithic Cultures of North Africa. "Liverpool Monographs in Archaeology and Oriental Studies." Liverpool.

Godwin, H.

1962 "The Half-life of Radiocarbon 14." Nature 195: 984.

Malavolti, F.

1951 "Appunti per una cronologia relativa del neo-eneolitico emiliano," Emilia Preromana 3.

Radmilli, A.

1959 "Gli insediamenti preistorici in Abruzzo," L'Universo 39.

1962 Piccola guida della preistoria italiana. Firenze: Sansoni.

Rellini, Ugo

1934 La piu antica ceramica dipinta in Italia. Roma.

Sestieri, P. C.

1946 "La necropoli preistorica di Paestum," Rivista di Scienze Preistoriche 1: 245-66.

1947 "Nuovi risultati degli scavi nella necropoli preistorica di Paestum," Rivista di Scienze Preistoriche 2: 283-90.

Stevenson, R. B. K.

1947 "The Neolithic Cultures of South-East Italy," Proceedings of the Prehistoric Society n.s. 13: 85-100.

Taramelli, A.

1909 "Alghero," Monumenti Antichi 19: 409 ff.

1915 Notizie degli Scavi, 130.

Tarradell, M.

1960 "Problemas neoliticas," Primer symposium de prehistoria de la peninsula iberica, pp. 45-65. Pamplona.

Trump, David

1960 "Scavi a la Starza, Ariano Irpino," Bullettino di Paletnologia Italiana 69-70: 221-31.

1961 "Skorba, Malta and the Mediterranean," Antiquity 35: 300-3.

1963 "Carbon, Malta and the Mediterranean," *ibid*. 37: 302-3.

Zervos, C.

1954 *La civilisation de la Sardaigne du début de l' éneolithique à la fin de la période nouragique*. Paris.

The Archaeological Chronology of Northwestern Europe

Homer L. Thomas
University of Missouri

The revival of French interest in the Neolithic period since World War II makes it possible to undertake a survey of western European chronology from the end of the Mesolithic to the beginning of the Bronze Age. The work of Piggott (1953, 1954a, 1954b), Bailloud and Meig de Boofzheim (1955), Arnal and Burnez (1958), and Giot (1960a), as well as that of many others, has laid new foundations for an understanding of the Neolithic in France. A real revolution has come out of the new studies on the Dutch beakers, particularly from their dating through the radiocarbon method at Groningen. In the British Isles, the work of Isobel Smith, at Windmill Hill (Smith, 1960), together with the recent excavations at West Kennet and the Hurst Farm, has brought major modifications in the archaeological system developed by Fox (1947), Childe (1947), and Piggott (1954a). Needless to say, any chronological study in the area of western and northern Europe must depend upon regional surveys of the thousands of finds that have accumulated in the course of the past hundred and fifty years, subject of course to the control of excavations at key sites. Works such as Daniel's excellent surveys of the megalithic tombs of France, England, and Wales (1950, 1960) and Henshall's corpus (1963) of Scottish megalithic materials are typical of regional studies useful for chronological studies. The investigation of the history of climate and flora in the British Isles, the Netherlands, and Switzerland is of particular importance for chronology because of the large number of sites which now have good pollen-analytical fixes. These materials together with the increasing number of radiocarbon dates, particularly for British and Dutch sites, make it possible to undertake a tentative reconsideration of the archaeological chronology of northwestern Europe. This study is an attempt to determine the value of radiocarbon dates for chronology over a wide geographic area and their validity in relation to the various relative chronologies which have been developed for the various regions of northwestern Europe. It must be noted, however, that the archaeological coverage, area by area, from the Pyrenees to the north of Scotland and from the upper Danube to the Atlantic is still uneven, making it difficult to undertake any form of archaeological synthesis which cuts across several regions.

The Early Neolithic Cultures

The first Neolithic cultures to reach the forest lands of western Europe were brought by people with a Cardial Ware pottery, who were spreading along the coasts of the Mediterranean, and others with a Danubian culture, who penetrated well into northern France from Rhenish bases. During the time of the Atlantic climate, which had induced a forest environment, these two groups of Neolithic settlers pushed into lands occupied by Mesolithic peoples.

The Cardial Ware culture occurs on both sides of the Mediterranean in Greece, coastal Yugoslavia, southern Italy, Liguria, southern France, eastern and southern Spain, and along the coast of North Africa from Tunisia to Morocco (see above, Brown, pp. 321-24). In southern France, it is called the Châteauneuf culture by Bailloud and Mieg de Boofzheim (1955, pp. 68-72) and the Montserratian by Arnal and Burnez (1958, pp. 8-14). This culture, which did not spread beyond Provence, was found above a Tardenoisian level in the Abri Châteauneuf-les-Martigues (Bouches-du-Rhône) (Escalon de Fonton, 1956, pp. 41-106). A similar stratigraphic position can be observed in other sites of the Midi. At the Grotte de Fontbrégoua (Var), the Cardial Ware assemblage has its best analogies with that of the Lower Neolithic level at Arene Candide (levels 28-25) on the Italian Riviera (Arnal and Brunez, 1958, p. 12; Bernabò Brea, 194 pp. 131-54). Pittioni (1962, pp. 155-69) and many others would tie these levels to the Early Neolithic Cardial Ware horizon in Italy, which can be placed in the fifth millennium on the basis of C-14 dates from Penne Di Pescara (Abruzzi), where charcoal from a central hearth of a Lower Ne lithic house (Pi-101), was dated 4825 ± 135 B.C. (Ferrara, 1961, p. 100), and from the Grotta dei Piccioni (Pi-46), where a sample from an early Middle Neolithic level was dated 4484 ± 130 B.C. (Ferrara, 1961, pp. 100-101). It must be noted that all radiocarbon dates in this paper are corrected for the new half life of C-14 (Godwin, 1962, p. 984). These dates suggest that the Cardial Ware cultures reached southern France not long before the Danubian culture penetrated into the Paris Basin (see below, p. 345).

The Danubian culture moved westward from the Rhineland as far as the Seine, the middle Loire, and perhaps the Channel Islands, and southward into northern Switzerland. In eastern France, the Danubian culture paralleled the development in the Rhineland; in the Paris Basin, the relatively few finds of pottery suggest that by the time this culture reached the Seine and the Loire, it was already in a late phase. Unhappily, the Danubian of the Paris Basin cannot be fixed stratigraphically in relation to the subsequent Chassey culture (Bailloud and Mieg de Boofzeim, 1955, pp. 48-50).

The Danubian culture also penetrated into northern Switzerland, where it is known from one settlement site at Gächlingen in Canton Schaffhausen (Guyan, 1953, pp. 68-70). It is possible that the early Danubian culture, characterized by early Bandkeramik, reached eastern France and northern Switzerland at the same time as it did the Netherlands. In any event, it can hardly date before the culture of the Danubian sites of Dutch Limburg, which is now placed as early as 4400 B.C. by radiocarbon determinations (see below, pp. 373-74).

Although the Danubian culture penetrated into lands still occupied by Tardenoisian collectors, it apparently, as in the Netherlands, did not influence the local Tardenoisian or play any role in the formation of the subsequent Campignian culture of northern France and Belgium. As in the Low Countries, it vanished without leaving a heritage to later cultures (De Laet, 1959, pp. 54-55, 70-71). On the other hand, northernmost Switzerland became incorporated in the Danubian sphere; here the early Danubian is known from both Bandkeramik and Stroked Ware, and is followed as in south Germany by a Rössen occupation (Vogt, 1961, p. 462). The well-known Danubian cultures of the Rhineland, which were concentrated in the Rhine-Main Basin and downstream in the northern Rhine province, can be followed through an early to a late phase, to which can be tied the intrusive Rössen culture. Culturally, the Rhine Basin belongs to central Europe, which in this paper will be considered only when this area is important for establishing chronological horizons in western Europe (Buttler, 1938; Quitta, 1960).

Mesolithic cultures continued to dominate much of western Europe, since the Cardial Ware culture penetrated only into the Midi, and northern France was settled only lightly by Danubian settlers (Clark, 1962, pp. 97-111). A number of radiocarbon determinations (of which only a few can be given here) clearly indicate that the Mesolithic collecting cultures lasted through the fifth and into the fourth millennium B.C. In Switzerland, bone from the Birsmatten-Basishöhle near Laufen in Canton Bern, which came from Tardenoisian layers I and II (B-234, B-235), dated 3560 ± 120 and 3519 ± 240 B.C., indicating that Mesolithic cultures still dominated central and, very likely, western Switzerland long after the Danubian peasants had settled to the north (Gfeller, Oeschger, and Schwarz, 1961, p. 23). The late survival of the Mesolithic in relation to the incoming Neolithic is also supported by radiocarbon dates for material from Asturian, Breton, and British Mesolithic contexts. The Asturian culture of northern Spain and southwestern France is dated by a wood sample from Mouligna (Q-314) in the Basses-Pyrénées. Its date—3210 ± 130 B.C. (Godwin and Willis, 1960, p. 70)—is surprisingly late. Charcoal from a Mesolithic kitchen midden at La Torche in Brittany (GrN-2001) was dated 4199 ± 80 B.C. (Vogel and Waterbolk, 1963, p. 176), clearly indicating that the Breton Mesolithic was contemporary with the Danubian of the Paris Basin and Netherlands. Organic mud found with Tardenoisian artifacts in a pool at Stump Cross in Yorkshire (Q-141) was dated 4745 ± 310 B.C. (Godwin and Willis, 1959, p. 69). The British Tardenoisian date and comparable Dutch dates tend to support Waterbolk's suggestion that areas such as the Netherlands were abandoned by Tardenoisian peoples with the disappearance of open lands brought about by the spread of Atlantic forests. This would have occurred well before the Danubian occupation (Waterbolk, 1962, pp. 232-34). Nevertheless, the Swiss Tardenoisian, French Asturian, and Breton Mesolithic dates support the contention that the Mesolithic survived in remaining open areas in France and Switzerland during the period of the first Neolithic of west ern Europe.

In northern France, the Low Countries, and the British Isles, the Tardenoisian was gradually replaced by Mesolithic Forest cultures, which were better adapted to the new Atlantic environment. The Campignian culture of northern France, which is related through its flint ax and pick types to the Lower Halstow culture of the British Isles and the Ellerbek-Ertebølle cultures of southern Scandinavia, can be dated to the time of the Tardenoisian (De Laet, 1958, pp. 55-58; Schwabedissen, 1962, pp. 260-62). At sites such as those of the forest of Montmorency in the Paris Basin, it is found stratified above, or possibly between, Tardenoisian I and II, tending to indicate the interpenetration of the two cultures and the late survival of Tardenoisian (Giraud, Vaché, and Vignard, 1949, pp. 336-38; Daniel and Daniel, 1953, pp. 236-37). The earliest Neolithic horizon of western Europe may therefore be placed in the fifth and fourth millennia and defined in terms of intrusive Cardial Ware and Danubian Neolithic cultures, surviving Asturian and Tardenoisian Mesolithic cultures, and the new Forest cultures of the north. All these cultures had made suitable adaptations to the environmental conditions induced by the Atlantic climate.

The Western Neolithic Cultures

The first Neolithic to establish itself on a more permanent basis in northwestern Europe has for a long time been defined in terms of Windmill Hill (England), Chassey (France), Cortaillod (Switzerland), and Lagozza (Italy) cultures. The discovery of the Egolzwil culture, as well as the difficulty of defining the relations of both the Chassey and Windmill Hill cultures, has forced a revision of this simple equation of cultures once so important for chronology. The Chassey culture, which is found throughout France, is interpreted from two quite different points of view. On the basis of stratigraphy in southern France, this culture can be traced through two main phases: Chassey A (decorated pottery, square-mouthed vessels, pottery stands), found at sites such as La Madeleine in the south and Camp de Chassey and Fort Harrouard in the north; and Chassey B (plain pottery, Pan-flute handles) (Arnal and Burnez, 1958, pp. 14-36). Bailloud and Mieg de Boofzheim (1955, pp. 97-116; Bailloud, 1961a, pp. 494-98) point out that such a division for the whole of France into phases is doubtful on present stratigraphic evidence, and that for the time being this culture should be dealt with in regional terms.

In southern France, two phases are clearly defined at Roucadour (Lot) and La Madeleine (Hérault) (Arnal, Bailloud, and Riquet, 1960, pp. 117-19). I cannot here consider the complicated stratigraphy of sites such as Châteauneuf-les-Martigues and Fraischamp, which indicate that Chassey overlapped the evolved Cardial Ware and preceded the Horgen-S.O.M. and Bell Beaker cultures (Escalon de Fonton, 1956, pp. 103-6). The relations of the Chassey culture with Arene Candide are important for chronology. Arnal and Burnez (1958, pp. 14-36) are probably right in connecting Chassey A with Arene Candide levels 24-14, on the basis of square-mouthed vessels, and Chassey B with levels 13-9, despite Bernabò Brea's contention that only these latter levels parallel the Chassey in France (Bernabò Brea, 1946, pp. 60-130; 1956, pp. 246-47).

If Chassey A may be correlated with Arene Candide levels 24-14, and thus with the Middle Neolithic Chiozza-Matera horizon in Italy, then the Chassey B may be tied on the basis of levels 13-9 at Arene Candide with the Lagozza horizon in northern Italy (see above, Brown, pp. 328-30). The succession of Chassey A and B in southern France is supported not only by stratigraphy and relationships with Italy but by radiocarbon dates. At Roucadour, Thémines (Lot), there is a succession of Cardial or Impressed Ware, early Chassey, and late Chassey occupations (Arnal and Burnez, 1958, p. 30). Level C, which has Cardial or Impressed Ware, is dated by the Gif-sur-Yvette Laboratory to 4157 ± 150 B.C., a date which supports the synchronisms given above; Levels B1 and B2, which belong to the early and late Chassey respectively, had samples dated to 3385 ± 140 and 2448 ± 125 B.C. (Coursaget, Giot, and Le Run, 1960, p. 147).

In northern and eastern France, there is little stratigraphy for the Chassey culture; in the west, the Early Neolithic pottery that is found from the Garonne northward into Brittany is classified as Chassey by many archaeologists, but elements in the Er Lannic and Bougon styles reveal other influences which probably come from Iberia or represent a development of the Chassey-Matera decorative style (Bailloud, 1961a, pp. 496-97; Giot, 1960a, pp. 30-31). Few traits in the northern and eastern groups are specifically useful for chronology. The plats à pain (baking plates) of the Paris Basin are similar to plates found in Michelsberg context (see below, p. 352). There are also Rössen elements at Chassey sites in eastern France, but it is difficult to place them within Chassey development. The presence of copper objects at Chassey sites suggests how late this culture lasted.

As we have seen, the beginning of the Chassey culture can be fixed within the chronological framework of western Europe through its ties with Italy. Chassey A in the south and early Chassey in the north should go back to the time of the Middle Neolithic levels at Petescia in central Italy and of Isola Virginia, in Lake Varese, in northern Italy. Carbonized acorns from the occupation level at Petescia (Pi-28) date 3609 ± 145 B.C. wood from the platform of the Isola Virginia lake dwelling (Pi-38) dates 3535 ± 180 B.C. (Ferrara, Reinharz, and Tongiorgi, 1959, pp. 106-7). In Brittany, pottery which, if not related, must be close in time to the early Chassey has been found in the first passage graves as well as in Early Neolithic long mounds, which scarcely antedate the passage graves. Char coal (GrN-1968) from the chamber of the passage grave at Ile-Carn (Finistère) was dated 3436 ± 75 B.C.; charcoal (GrN-1966) from a contemporary settlement at Curnic (Finistère) was dated 3550 ± 60 B.C. (Vogel and Waterbolk, 1963, p. 186; Giot, 1960b, pp. 38-50). The Ile-Carn date is supported by C-14 dates for twig charcoal (GsY-64) from a passage grave in the Sept Iles archipelago (Côtes du Nord): 3205 ± 150 (Old Laboratory) and 3369 ± 130 and 3591 ± 135 B.C. (New Laboratory) (Coursaget, Giot, and Le Run, 1962, pp. 139-40).

A date as early as 3600-3500 B.C. for the beginning of the Chassey culture correlates well with its relative chronological position in relation to both Italy and Brittany, but the long accepted Chassey-Cortaillod synchronism must be reinterpreted in light of the discovery of the Egolzwil culture in central Switzerland. This culture, known from sites such as the settlement of Egolzwil III (Vogt, 1951, pp. 193-215), can be tied chronologically by imports or copies to the middle Rössen culture, which had penetrated into northern Switzerland. It cannot be connected with the Cortaillod culture of western Switzerland, and its pottery is difficult to connect with either Cardial Ware or Chassey pottery (Vogt, 1961, pp. 466-68). The C-14 measurements for material from Egolzwil (K-115, 116, 118, 121) give an average date of 3086 ± 90 B.C. (Tauber, 1960, pp. 6-7). This date, together with the Rössen connections, indicates that Egolzwil was earlier than the Cortaillod, which is often dated to the time of the contraction of the Swiss lakes in late Atlantic/early Sub-Boreal times (ca. 3100 B.C.). The middle Rössen contacts provide another chronological check, because this culture can be dated to the middle of the fourth millennium in central Germany (see below, pp. 377-78). Rössen probably also formed an element (along with eastern elements) in the Schussenried culture of southwestern Germany, which is also known from Lutzengütle in Liechtenstein (Vogt, 1945, pp. 151-60), where it is found stratigraphically below a level with late Michelsberg elements. At Ehrenstein, in Württemberg, wood samples from an early Michelsberg-Schussenried settlement (H-125-107, H-61-149) dated 3406 ± 200 B.C. and 3344 ± 130 B.C. (Münnich, 1957, p. 197; Zürn, 1958, pp. 75-92). Recent Berlin measurements of samples from Ehrenstein (Bln-54, 70, 71) gave similar dates: 3344 ± 80, 3447 ± 100, and 3406 ± 100 B.C. (Kohl and Quitta, 1963, pp. 294-95). Early Michelsberg, in turn, overlapped late Rössen in the Rhineland. These dates and connections suggest that Egolzwil culture must belong to the last half of the fourth millennium

B.C. Isolated finds of Schussenried pottery from the Aisne region (Arnal and Burnez, 1958, p. 68) and from the lowest levels of the Camp de Château (Jura) (Bailloud and Mieg de Boofzheim, 1955, p. 126) suggest that Schussenried might be correlated with the early Chassey culture, a correlation supported by both Italian and Breton C-14 dates. In light of these connections it may be postulated that early Chassey in France, Egolzwil in central Switzerland, and middle Rössen, Schussenried, and early Michelsberg, which overlap in southwestern Germany and the Rhineland (Scollar, 1959, pp. 105-10), belong to the same chronological horizon, which on the basis of radiocarbon determinations may be dated 3600-3000 B.C.

Although the Chassey B of southern France can be correlated with the Italian cultures, the later Chassey phases in northern France are more difficult to establish within the framework of western European chronology because of the lack of stratigraphy. Southern Chassey B is linked with levels 13-9 at Arene Candide and the Lagozza culture of northern Italy (see above, Brown, p. 329). A wood piling from the Upper Neolithic settlement at Lagozza di Besnate (Pi-34) has been dated 2987 ± 90 B.C. (Ferrarra, 1961, p. 102). This date may be compared with those for carbonized wheat and shells from a Chassey B level at La Madeleine (Hérault). These dates—for the carbonized wheat (L-188A), 2582 ± 500 B.C.; for the shells (L-188D), 3097 ± 400 B.C. (Broecker, Kulp, and Tucek, 1956, p. 160)—show that the Chassey B and Lagozza cultures are of the same period. The later Chassey sites of northern France are difficult to correlate with those of the south. C-14 dates suggest that a few sites can probably be attributed to the time of the Chassey B. The habitation site of Montagne de Lumbres (Pas-de-Calais), which yielded sherds of Chassey pottery that may show Michelsberg influence, has samples dated to 2746 ± 125 and 2540 ± 125 B.C. (Coursaget, Giot, and Le Run, 1961, p. 147). Radiocarbon dates from Mont Joly, or La Brèche-au-Diable, in Calvados (3009 ± 130 and 2942 ± 130 B.C.), which had pottery close to that of Fort Harrouard I, and the camp of Les Matignons in the Charente (2865 ± 160 and 2638 ± 160 B.C.), where the samples came from a burned layer indicating the end of the Chassey occupation, suggest that the later Chassey of northern France fell within the first half of the third millennium B.C. (Coursaget, Giot, and Le Run, 1960, pp. 147-48). The same is true of the habitation site of Restudo, Saint-Pever (Côtes-du-Nord), where samples from a layer of cinders and charcoal (GsY-56) dated 3024 ± 140 (New Laboratory) and 3004 ± 140 (Old Laboratory), if the traces of settlement found at this site can be attributed to the Chassey (Coursaget, Giot, and Le Run, 1962, p. 141).

The Chassey culture penetrated into southwestern Switzerland, where there are no Cortaillod sites. Here it is found at a number of sites, including "Sur le Grand Pré" near Saint-Léonard in Canton Wallis (Sauter, 1957, pp. 136-49). Soil formed from the decomposition of wood from this Neolithic settlement (B-232) dated 2942 ± 100 B.C. (Gfeller, Oeschger, and Schwarz, 1961, p. 23), which is in agreement with French radiocarbon dates for the later Chassey. Few connections can be found between the later Chassey and the Cortaillod cultures of western Switzerland, despite their close proximity to one another (Vogt, 1961, pp. 474-77). Nevertheless, radiocarbon dates from Cortaillod sites clearly indicate that they were contemporary. C-14 dates for numerous samples from the Cortaillod settlement at Burgäschisee, near Seeburg in Canton Bern (B-116-118A), range from 3035 ± 110 to 2674 ± 90 B.C. (Oeschger, Schwarz, Gfeller, 1959, pp. 140-41). Wood samples from the Cortaillod site at Escalon in the Jura (Gro-672, 970) date 2355 ± 130 and 2777 ± 80 B.C. (Vries and Waterbolk, 1958, p. 1553; all Groningen dates are corrected as suggested in Radiocarbon V [1963], 164).

Although there is no space here to evaluate the Cortaillod-Chassey connections with the Chamblandes culture of Switzerland, their relations with the Michelsberg culture must be considered because of the widespread connections of the latter, which have significance for chronology. The Michelsberg culture probably derived from the Chassey culture of eastern France and spread eastward into the Rhineland and western Germany. Here it overlapped and gradually displaced the Rössen and Schussenried cultures (Scollar, 1959, pp. 110-20); the alternative theories of Vogt, Becker, Driehaus, and others are considered here and in a more recent article of Scollar (1961, pp. 519-48). The Michelsberg culture penetrated also into the Bodensee and Aar Valley area of northern Switzerland, where it is known from a great many older finds. Its chronological position, however, is best determined at sites such as Thayngen-Weier in Canton Schaffhausen (Guyan, 1955), where it is found in association with Cortaillod (younger Cortaillod, as defined by von Gonzenbach, 1949). Wood (B-43, 44, 45) from this site gave the following C-14 dates: 2880 ± 130, 2880 ± 180, and 2973 ± 130 B.C. (Oeschger, Schwarz, and Gfeller, 1959, p. 140). This is in full agreement with the Cortaillod and southern French Chassey B dates. The Michelsberg of Thayngen-Weier is regarded by Scollar (1959, p. 97) as slightly later than the earliest phase of the Classic Michelsberg of the Middle Rhineland and contemporary with the Pfyn culture of northeastern Switzerland and Liechtenstein, where it is an element in the upper level of Lutzengütle. Scollar would equate the Pfyn culture with Jevišovice C 2 in Moravia (see below, Ehrich, p. 435). Jevišovice C 2 may in turn be equated with the Bohemian Siřem phase of the Funnel Beaker culture or its chronological equivalent, and through it with the late Baalberg and early Salzmünde phases of central Germany, whose beginning may be dated to about 3000 B.C. (see below, p. 380, and Ehrich, p. 435).

Scollar (1959, pp. 105-15) derives the Classic Michelsberg from the eastern French Chassey on the basis of pottery, bone, stone, and flint tool types. He proposes that the Chassey culture pushed eastward about the time of the Chassey A/B transition and evolved into the Michelsberg by taking over elements such as the handled jug, necked flask, and footed bowl from the older Danubian cultures of the Rhineland. C-14 dates, however, indicate that the Chassey A/B transition took place in southern France not much before 3000 B.C., and that Chassey A or early Chassey may go back as early as 3600 B.C. The Ehrenstein Michelsberg date suggests that the Classic phase goes back as early as 3400 B.C. The Classic Michelsberg is connected with the early Chassey by a unique trait, the *plat à pain*, which occurs at sites such as the Camp de Catenoy and Fort Harrouard (Philippe, 1927; Bailloud, 1961*b*, pp. 509-13). This correlation is supported by climatic evidence, since the Michelsberg culture arose and spread during the environmental change which accompanied the gradual shift from an Atlantic to a Sub-Boreal climate. This shift in environment, which must have begun before the end of Atlantic times, brought open conditions, which encouraged the rise of cattle-herding so typical of the Michelsberg and Windmill Hill cultures. All this would indicate that early Michelsberg began about 3400 B.C., and that it was in a developed phase when it is known in Switzerland about 3000 B.C. Archaeological connections and C-14 dates given above indicate that the Chassey B culture of southern France, the Cortaillod culture of western and central Switzerland, the Pfyn culture of northeast Switzerland, the later Michelsberg culture of northern Switzerland and western Germany, and the later phases of the Chassey culture of northern and eastern France cannot be dated much before 3000 B.C. These cultures lasted to the time of the Horgen and Seine-Oise-Marne cultures, the beginning of which can be tied to the time of the intrusion of the Corded Ware cultures from the east, around 2600 B.C. (see below, pp. 388-92).

Radiocarbon dates for earlier Neolithic settlement material and from relevant bog profiles indicate that a change is necessary in our concept of the development of the Neolithic in the British Isles (Clark, and Godwin, 1962, pp. 21-22). Present archaeological work in the British Isles permits only tentative conclusions about the character of the Neolithic period. C-14 dates from sites such as the early encampment at Windmill Hill (BM-73, 3107 ± 150 B.C.) and the causeway camp at Hembury (BM-130, 3303 ± 150, BM-136, 3395 ± 150, and BM-138, 3488 ± 150 B.C.), which are in the south of England, as well as from the lakeside settlement of Ehenside Tarn in Cumberland (C-462, 3162 ± 300 B.C.) and the Neolithic settlement layers at Shippea Hill in the Cambridgeshire Fens (Q-525/6, 3055 ± 120 B.C.), suggest that the first Neolithic reached England in the latter part of the fourth millennium, perhaps as early as 3500 B.C. (Barker and Mackey, 1961, p. 42; Barker and Mackey, 1963, p. 106; Fox, 1963, pp. 228-29; Libby, 1955, p. 88; Godwin and Willis, 1961, pp. 70-71; Clark and Godwin, 1962, pp. 10-23). Radiocarbon dates from Irish sites suggest that it was equally early in Ireland (Watts, 1960). C-14 dates of 3509 ± 170 B.C. for charcoal (D-38) from the Larnian kitchen-midden layer with Neolithic elements on Dalkey Island (County Dublin), of 3498 ± 170 B.C. for charcoal (D-36) from a hearth with Bann flakes and fragments of polished stone axes found at Newferry (County Antrim), and of 3220 ± 170 B.C. for charcoal (D-37) from a layer with Neolithic sherds beneath the large cairn at Knockiveagh (County Down)—all suggest that the Neolithic must have penetrated into the northwestern part of the British Isles as early as 3500 B.C. (McAulay and Watts, 1961, p. 32). The reinvestigation of the Clyde-Carlingford chambered cairn at Monamore on the island of Arran, which is a long gallery divided into three segments by two high septal slabs, has produced a carbon sample (Q-675) dating its second phase as early as 3313 ± 110 B.C. (Mackie, 1964, pp. 52-54). The C-14 dates (Gro-901, 901a) for charcoal from the long barrow at Durrington Walls, Wiltshire —3018 ± 80 and 3009 ± 50 (De Vries, Barendsen, and Waterbolk, 1958, p. 135)—suggest that the long barrow also goes back before 3000 B.C. This high chronology for the beginning of the Neolithic in the British Isles is supported by radiocarbon dates for the Atlantic/Sub-Boreal boundary, which is usually correlated with the beginning of the Neolithic (Godwin, Walker, and Willis, 1957, p. 364; Clark and Godwin, 1962, pp. 10-23).

The radiocarbon evidence is clear, but unfortunately there are few sites for which there are both C-14 dates and sufficient archaeological material to permit anything beyond speculation about continental origins and connections. Only Hembury and related sites in the south of England, which have been regarded as representing an early phase of the Windmill Hill culture, do have some connections with the continent. The causewayed camp at Hembury and the trumpet lugs of the Hembury pottery have analogies in the Chassey culture. The long barrow of Durrington Walls, which may date from the end of the Early Neolithic and before the mature Windmill Hill culture, must be related to similar ones in Brittany. The long barrow at Saint-Just (Ille-et-Vilaine) must derive from the same prototype as the English ones (Giot and Milon, 1954b, pp. 401-3). A similar long barrow, with Chassey connections, was found at Le Quillio (Côtes-du-Nord) (Giot, 1956, 187-88). Until there is further excavation, we can only speculate that the C-14 dates and these few continental connections suggest that a western Neolithic culture related to the early Chassey reached and spread rapidly through the British Isles sometime after 3600-3500 B.C.

The mature Windmill Hill culture, which represents a full adaptation to island conditions, still has many links with northern France. Its causewayed camps have general analogies with those of the Chassey culture (such as the Camp de Chassey), and its pottery has over-all affinities to the Chassey and Cortaillod pottery (Piggott, 1954a, pp. 376-77; Clark and Godwin, 1962, p. 22). At Windmill Hill itself, charcoal (BM-74) from the primary silt of the ditches of the causewayed camp, which was erected long after the Early Neolithic encampment had been abandoned, dated 2715 ± 150 B.C. (Barker and Mackey, 1961, p. 42). The recently excavated long barrow of Nutbane, which is placed in the time of the fully developed Windmill Hill culture, has yielded a charcoal sample (BM-49) which has been dated to 2870 ± 150 B.C. (Barker and Mackey, 1960, p. 28; Morgan and Ashbee, 1958, pp. 104-6). The Windmill Hill culture continued to the time of the Beaker cultures. Its development was marked by the emergence of regional styles of pottery, such as Abingdon, Ebbsfleet, and Mildenhall (Case, 1956; Clark, 1960). The Peterborough wares, such as Ebbsfleet, Mortlake, and Fengate, were formerly regarded as products of a Secondary Neolithic, but are now considered as pottery styles which developed within the Windmill Hill culture (Isobel Smith's unpublished work is summarized by Piggott, 1961, pp. 567-71, and referred to in a report of the conference on the Windmill Hill culture and aspects of the British Neolithic, April 6-8, 1962; see Antiquity 36 [1962], 215). This regionalism is of itself indicative of a fully mature culture. Surprisingly, a radiocarbon date for wood from Ebbsfleet (BM-113)—2849 ± 150 B.C.—suggests that the Ebbsfleet style had evolved early (Barker and Mackey, 1963, p. 105). On the other hand, Beaker elements found in the Mortlake and Fengate wares suggest that they belong to a much later phase. Although the mature Windmill Hill culture paralleled the later Chassey, Cortaillod, and later Michelsberg cultures, it seems to have had few contacts with them. It is particularly difficult to see any connection with the Michelsberg, Funnel Beaker or Pitted Ware cultures. If the Michelsberg culture derives from the Chassey, as Scollar proposes (1959, p. 115), the traits shared by Windmill Hill and Michelsberg can be explained in terms of a common parentage. Pitted Ware and Funnel Beaker influences from Scandinavia, which were postulated by so many British archaeologists to explain the rise of the Peterborough pottery styles, are now eliminated, thanks to the work of Isobel Smith (summarized by Piggott, 1961, pp. 567-69); instead, the Peterborough pottery is explained as a local development of the Windmill Hill culture. The British Isles were, however, far from isolated from the continent; shortly after the early Neolithic had established itself—or perhaps even while it was penetrating into the British Isles—megalithic peoples began to settle along the coasts of western Britain.

The Megalithic Cultures

Archaeological work in Brittany and western Britain clearly indicates that the first megalithic tombs were built at the same time or not long after these lands were occupied by the first Neolithic settlers. Unfortunately, most of the megalithic monuments along the Atlantic coasts are difficult to date on archaeological grounds, since they were used over and over and then plundered in later times.

There are rare exceptions, such as the passage grave on the Ile-Carn (Finistère), which is fortunately of an early type. This early type is found mainly on the southern coast of Brittany, but also at other places along the coast from the mouth of the Loire to Normandy and the Pas-de-Calais (Giot and Millon, 1954a, p. 404; Giot, 1960a, pp. 42-54). A charcoal sample from the Ile-Carn passage grave (GrN-1968) dated 3436 ± 75 B.C. (Vogel and Waterbolk, 1963, p. 186), which dating is supported by the measurements of the Gif-sur-Yvette Laboratory for the passage grave in the Sept-Iles archipelago (GsY 64, 3105 ± 150 [Old Laboratory], 3369 ± 130 and 3591 ± 135 B.C. [New Laboratory]) (Coursaget, Giot, and Le Run, 1962, pp. 139-40). These dates suggest that "Iberian" colonists were spreading along the Atlantic coast and reached Brittany at about the same time as the Neolithic settlers who built the long mounds of the interior and coastal areas of Brittany. This conclusion is also supported by the common pottery style of the long mounds and the passage graves. Once established in Brittany, the older passage graves continued in use into the Bronze Age. The Er Lannic and Bougon pottery styles, whose decoration was inspired by those from the Iberian peninsula, may mark a later phase than the first undecorated wares. Still later stages and external contacts are indicated by the appearance of the Scandinavian collared flask and the Iberian bell beaker as well as elements similar to those of the S.O.M. culture, which is known from the gallery graves and rock-cut tombs of the Paris Basin. Relative chronology is difficult because stratified finds are rare. The recent excavations at Barnenez in Finistère uncovered a group of eleven passage graves under a common barrow (Giot, 1958, pp. 149-53). The chamber of passage grave D provided one of the rare exceptions: a lower level with Western Neolithic and Bell Beaker pottery and an upper level with pottery of the flower-pot type which must belong to the time of the S.O.M. culture. This chance bit of stratigraphy suggests that the Chassey survived into Bell Beaker times and that the S.O.M. culture is relatively late. The correlation of the coastal Passage Grave culture with the Neolithic culture characterized by burials made in long mounds is partly supported by the C-14 dates (GsY-89) of 3066 ± 125 and 3282 ± 130 B.C. for cist Y of the long barrow of Mont-Saint-Michel at Carnac (Morbihan) (Coursaget, Giot, and Le Run, 1962, p. 140). The long mounds of Brittany, like the related long barrows of Britain (no attempt is made here to discuss the many theories concerning their origins), continued in use for nearly as long a period as the passage graves. The long mound of Saint-Just (Ille-et-Vilaine) has been dated 2437 ± 120 B.C.; the barrow of Kermené (Morbihan), which has Late Neolithic pottery with S.O.M.

affinities, is placed at 2190 ± 110 B.C. (Coursaget, Giot, and Le Run, 1961, p. 148; Coursaget, Giot, and Le Run, 1960, p. 148).

The relative chronology of other French megalithic groups is the subject of much controversy. Aside from the passage graves of the Gard and Hérault, which must be of Almerian origin, the other megalithic groups are characterized by rock-cut and gallery graves, probably originally introduced into southern France from the western Mediterranean during the time of the Chassey culture. Only a brief mention can be made of the wide diffusion of gallery graves, which spread from the Midi to southwestern France, into the tableland (*Causses*) of the Massif Central and via the Rhone Valley or western France to northern France, where they became a trait of the S.O.M. culture. In the south of France, they began in Chassey times, spread during the period before the Bell Beaker culture, and continued into the Bronze Age (Daniel, 1960, pp. 191-212). Once accepted, the megalithic tomb continued in use by the peoples of the successive Neolithic and Chalcolithic cultures of France.

The megalithic culture of western Britain is also known from both gallery and passage graves, whose grouping and dating are as complicated as those of the French groups. The gallery graves of the Severn-Cotswold group of southeastern England and of the Clyde-Carlingford group of southwestern Scotland and northern Ireland may go back well into the fourth millennium, to judge by the radiocarbon date from the chambered cairn at Monamore on Arran (see above, p. 353). Pottery, leaf points, and mound shapes indicate that they were used during the time of the mature Windmill Hill culture (Piggott, 1954*a*, pp. 122-92). Recent excavations—such as those at Fussell's Lodge long barrow, which has a trapezoidal mound like those of the gallery graves along the west coast (Morgan and Ashbee, 1958, pp. 106-11), and at West Kennet long barrow, whose facade is like that of one or two late Clyde-Carlingford tombs—clearly support such a synchronism (Piggott, 1958, pp. 235-42). The plain Beacharra A wares of the early Clyde-Carlingford group tie with Windmill Hill; the subsequent Beacharra B wares, with channeled and incised ornament, connect southward with similar wares in France and Spain. The Beacharra C ware, which marks the end of the use of these tombs, must now be placed in the Beaker period (Piggott, 1961, p. 571). The lateness of the use of these tombs is supported by C-14 dates. A charcoal sample from the forecourt of the horned cairn at Ballyutoag in County Antrim (D-48) has been dated 2293 ± 300 B.C. (McAulay and

Watts, 1961, p. 34), while charcoal (Q-675) found immediately under the blocking pavement of Monamore dated 2365 ± 110 B.C. (Mackie, 1964, pp. 52-54). C-14 dates for the Lough Gur culture of south Ireland support the assumption that the Clyde-Carlingford culture paralleled the Windmill Hill culture and persisted into Beaker times. Dates of 2880 ± 240 and 2592 ± 240 B.C. have been determined for charcoal samples (D-40, D-41) from the lower pre-Beaker level of a house (Circle L) at Knockadoon near Lough Gur (County Limerick) (McAulay and Watts, 1961, p. 33). This level, which has Lough Gur I or Limerick ware, should belong to the time of Beacharra B. Charcoal (D-39) from a somewhat later habitation site on Geroid Island near Lough Gur, which has Lough Gur II or Knockadoon pottery, dated 2262 ± 140 B.C. (McAulay and Watts, 1961, pp. 32-33; Watts, 1961, p. 113). It belongs to the time of the Beacharra C wares and the latest use of the gallery graves (see Case, 1961 for the most recent survey of the Irish Neolithic pottery styles).

The gallery graves and the Beacharra and Lough Gur Neolithic lasted through the Beaker period to the time of the arrival of the Passage Grave peoples who built the Boyne tombs. Charcoal (D-43, D-42) from the burned ground surfaces and from the filling of a ditch at the site of the passage grave at Tara, which presumably antedated the erection of the tomb, dated 2437 ± 160 and 2252 ± 160 B.C.; charcoal (D-44) from the tomb dated 2046 ± 150 B.C. (McAulay and Watts, 1961, p. 33). This latter date, which fits well with the Beaker dates in England and the Netherlands, marks the beginning of the Passage Grave phase in Ireland. It is further supported by the discovery of Loughcrew or Carrowkeel pottery, which is typical of the Boyne culture, in association with classic Bell Beaker at Moytirra in County Sligo and by other Bell Beaker finds in Ireland (Watts, 1960, p. 115; Paor, 1961, pp. 653-60). The Boyne tombs, whose Loughcrew ware recalls the Beacharra C ware, continued into the time of the Wessex Bronze Age (Piggott, 1954_a_, pp. 193-222).

The megalithic groups of western and northern Scotland are difficult to date. Some tombs of the Hebrides probably derive from the Clyde-Carlingford group about the time of the Beacharra B wares and lasted until the time of the Boyne tombs, to judge from stone balls found in both the Hebridean and Irish tombs. Passage Grave influence may lie behind the rise of the megalithic tombs found in the north of Scotland and the Orkney Islands, but their Unstan pottery developed from the "secondary" Neolithic culture of Britain, to judge from its stab-and-drag decoration.

One more group must be mentioned: the so-called Medway tombs of Kent, which have survived in fragmentary condition. Although some of these with both long and square barrows are like tombs in other parts of Britain, a few with low mound fitted with a peristalith and covering a single burial chamber are like the Dutch and German Hun's Beds (Evans, 1950, pp. 63-81).

The megalithic passage graves and gallery graves of Atlantic Europe seem to go back almost to the beginnings of the Neolithic. In France, they were often used by successive cultures within a single region, and seem to have been in use from Chassey times through the Beaker age into the Bronze Age. Some groups, such as those of Brittany and the Midi, began early; others, such as the gallery and rock-cut tombs associated with the S.O.M. culture of northern France, date to Beaker times. In the British Isles, the Severn-Cotswold and Clyde-Carlingford groups probably began in the early Neolithic, paralleled in the western parts of the British Isles the mature Windmill Hill culture, and lasted into Beaker times. The Irish passage graves began much later—in the Beaker age—and lasted into the full Bronze Age.

The Cultures of the Beaker Age

The Late Neolithic of the continent and the British Isles began with the diffusion of the Bell Beaker culture from Spain, which must have begun as early as 2400 or even 2500 B.C., to judge from radiocarbon dates for this culture in the Netherlands. Here, where the Michelsberg and Funnel Beaker cultures dominated the land until the arrival of the Bell Beaker peoples, there are a number of C-14 dates for material associated with this incoming culture. The earliest Bell Beaker context dated by this means is at Anlo in the province of Drenthe. Charcoal from a flat grave containing two all-over-corded beakers (GrN-851) and from a pit associated with a similar grave (GrN-1976) dated 2314 ± 70 and 2133 ± 50 B.C. (Vogel and Waterbolk, 1963, p. 180). Beakers of this type, which occur mainly in Belgian and Dutch Limburg and only occasionally in Drenthe, represent a Bell Beaker group which had already fallen under the influence of the Corded Ware culture (De Laet, 1958, pp. 98-101). Since the Bell Beaker peoples must have been settled in the Low Countries for at least a short period before such a hybrid type of pottery could have arisen (notwithstanding the rapidity of change in Bell Beaker styles), a date of 2500 - 2400 B.C. is not high for the beginning of the

Bell Beaker occupation of the Low Countries.

The Beaker cultures of the Low Countries (De Laet, 1958, pp. 97-106; van der Waals and Glasbergen, 1955, pp. 5-46) are important for the chronology of the Late Neolithic in the British Isles. The B-Beaker pottery group, whose remains are found stratified in the upper levels of camps at Windmill Hill and Maiden Castle and in secondary deposits of long barrows—such as Giant's Hill long barrow in Lincolnshire (Piggott, 1954a, pp. 104-9)—belong to the Pan-European or classic Bell Beaker type. This group is contemporary with the later Windmill Hill pottery of Abingdon and Mortlake type. The marine transgression which ended human occupation in the Fenland occurred between 3150 and 2500 B.C., when the transgression reached its maximum (Godwin and Willis, 1961, pp. 65-72; Godwin, 1961, pp. 315-16; these dates have been corrected roughly for the new half life of C-14). The absence of Beaker pottery in the Fenland sites suggests that B-Beaker peoples did not reach the British Isles until after 2500 B.C. The Rinyo-Clacton henge monument of Arminghall (Norfolk), which has yielded a rusticated type of pottery occasionally associated with Beaker ware, is dated 2503 ± 150 B.C. by a sample (BM-129) from the center of an oak post (Clark, 1936, pp. 19-23; Barker and Mackey, 1963, p. 105). This date, which allows 120 years for the age of the oak, supports the hypothesis that both B-Beaker and Rinyo-Clacton came from the continent about the middle of the third millennium B.C. The long survival of B-Beaker is indicated by its presence with Windmill Hill, A-Beaker, Rusticated, and Rinyo-Clacton wares on the submerged land surface of Essex (Smith, 1955) and by a C-14 date of 1912 ± 150 B.C. for a B-Beaker hearth at Antofts Windy Pit in Yorkshire (BM-6) (Barker and Mackey, 1960, p. 28). Rinyo-Clacton also survived into the second millennium, to judge from a C-14 date of 1961 ± 275 B.C. for a sample (C-602), from Hole 32 of Stonehenge I (Libby, 1955, pp. 88-89).

About 2000 B.C. C-Beaker peoples from the Netherlands crossed the North Sea to settle in northeastern Britain. Van der Waals and Glasbergen (1955, p. 5) have related the C-Beaker to Dutch types immediately preceding the rise of the Veluwe Beaker. Charcoal from a grave at St. Walrick (GrN-2996) and a charred post from a burial at Bennekom (Gro-326) dated Veluwe Beakers 1866 ± 80 B.C. and 2030 ± 180 B.C. respectively, suggesting that the prototype for the C-Beaker dated before 2000 B.C. in the Netherlands (Vogel and Waterbolk, 1963, p. 182; De Vries, Barendsen, and Waterbolk, 1958, p. 135).

Beaker peoples spread out over the British Isles, reaching even to Ireland. Their adaptation to the island environment may well be signaled by the rise of the A-Beaker, whose development paralleled that of the Veluwe Beaker. The A-Beaker, which was current at the time of the influence of the Dutch Pot Beaker to be seen in Fengate ware, is dated by a charcoal sample (BM-133) from Fifty Farm in Suffolk to 1964 ± 150 B.C. (Piggott, 1961, pp. 568-70; Barker and Mackey, 1963, pp. 105-6). The ascendancy of the Beaker culture over the heterogeneous cultures of Late Neolithic Britain may well be marked by the erection of Stonehenge III, which is dated to 1830 ± 150 B.C. by a sample of red deer antler from the base of the clean chalk filling of the ramp leading to Stonehole 56 of the Great Trilithon (BM-46) (Barker and Mackey, 1960, p. 27). The Beaker age in the British Isles, which must go back to 2500-2400 B.C., lasted until the Wessex culture, which marks the beginning of the Bronze Age (see Piggott, 1963, pp. 53-91, and Savory, 1963, pp. 25-52, for recent discussions of the Beaker controversy).

During the Beaker age in the Netherlands and Britain, the S.O.M. and Horgen cultures replaced the late Chassey in France; the passage graves continued in Brittany, but were now in their Bell Beaker phase. The Horgen-S.O.M. cultures, which seem to have been more impoverished than the cultures they replaced, may be divided into at least four regional groups: the S.O.M. culture of northern France, the Vienne-Charente culture of the Loire area, the Horgen culture of eastern France and Switzerland, and the poorly known Roucadour culture of southern France. The gallery graves (_allées couvertes_) and rock-cut tombs of the S.O.M. culture may be placed chronologically by their tanged daggers and beads brought by Bell Beaker trade and by their connections with the Bell Beaker and Corded Ware cultures in the Low Countries. Some archaeologists maintain that S.O.M. influence extended via Westphalia (where there is a group of porthole gallery cists) as far as Scandinavia. A C-14 date for animal bone from the settlement contemporary with S.O.M. at Hekelingen in southern Holland (Gro-684) is 2252 ± 85 B.C. (De Vries and Waterbolk, 1958, p. 1553), a date in full agreement with the relative dating of the S.O.M. culture in the Low Countries suggested by the presence of battle axes and pot beakers in one or two Belgian sites (De Laet and Glasbergen, 1959, pp. 107-12). In the Vienne-Charente area, the Horgen-S.O.M. culture is known from the Loire type of _allées couvertes_, which yield a flint assemblage—which is different but which connects this culture with the northern S.O.M. culture—and bits of copper that must come from Bell Beaker trade (Bailloud, 1961*a*, p. 500; Arnal and Burnez, 1958, p. 40). The true Horgen culture is found only in eastern France and Switzerland. Its chronological position is fixed by stratigraphy at Chalain in the Jura, where it lies above a Cortaillod level (Bailloud, 1961*a*, pp. 500-1). The Horgen is always found above Cortaillod levels in central and western Switzerland and stratified above the Pfyn culture in northeastern Switzerland (Vogt, 1961, pp. 485-86). In the south of France, the Roucadour culture (which has both Chassey B and Horgen elements) is stratified above an earlier Chassey B level in the Madeleine Cave in Hérault. Wood samples from the Horgen level at Escalon in the Jura (Gro-949) date 2520 ± 60 B.C. (De Vries and Waterbolk, 1958, p. 1553), suggesting that it began before the expansion of the Bell Beaker culture and the invasion of Switzerland by Corded Ware peoples. The spread of the Horgen culture did not put an end to the Chassey culture in the south of France. The latter continued in cultures such as the Fontbouïsse of the lower Rhone (whose sites yield both Bell Beakers and Horgen pots), the impoverished Ferrières culture of Languedoc, the Couronne culture of Provence, the Rodez culture of the *Causses* of the Massif Central, and the Peu-Richard culture of the lower Charente (Arnal and Burnez, 1958, pp. 75-89; Bailloud, 1961, pp. 501-4). The survival of Chassey derivatives in the south is fully supported by C-14 dates from the cave of Trou-Arnaud (Drôme) (2302 ± 135 B.C.) and the cave of the Perte du Cros (Lot) (2458 ± 125 and 2288 ± 125 B.C.) of the Chassey culture, and from the Camp de Briard (Charente) (2521 ± 137 B.C.) of the Peu-Richard culture (Coursaget, Giot, and Le Run, 1961, pp. 147-48; *ibid.*, 1960, p. 147; *ibid.*, 1961, p. 147).

The complexity of Late Neolithic France was further increased by continuation of the Megalithic and the spread of the Bell Beaker peoples, who established themselves in Catalonia and the eastern Pyrenees, whence their influence extended through much of southern France; it can also be seen in the megalithic hypogee of the Arles group. In the second major Bell Beaker region of France—Brittany—the beakers occur in both the late passage graves and the *allées couvertes*. The Boulannais group in Pas-de-Calais marks their movement toward the Low Countries, but the Alsatian and Burgundian groups must be connected with the Beaker cultures of the Rhineland (Bailloud, 1961, pp. 504-7). The mixed Horgen-S.O.M.-Bell Beaker cultures of the Late Neolithic—actually Chalcolithic—period lasted until the intrusion of the Tumulus culture into eastern and northern France and the rise of the Rhone Valley Bronze culture, both of which have Straubing-Adlerberg-Aunjetitz connections. In Brittany and western France, the hybrid and mixed cultures of the Late Neolithic lasted even longer, preserving older ways as late as Middle Bronze times (Sandars, 1957).

In Switzerland, the Horgen culture was only slightly influenced by the Bell Beaker culture, which as a cultural entity reached only as far as Basel, to judge from recent finds (Vogt, 1961, p. 487). A late Corded Ware culture penetrated into northern Switzerland, but does not seem to have disturbed the Horgen culture in the west and south, which gradually took over a Bronze Age economy.

To summarize, the Beaker Age, which may have begun as early as 2500-2400 B.C., was dominated by the spread of the Horgen-S.O.M. cultures and the movements of the Bell Beaker peoples. Nevertheless, the picture is complicated by the survival of older Neolithic traditions in the Windmill Hill cultures of Britain, the late Chassey-like cultures of southern France, and the late megalithic cultures along the Atlantic coasts of Britain and France. Although radiocarbon dates give some idea of absolute chronology, they are of little value for determining when these heterogeneous Late Neolithic cultures gave way to Bronze Age cultures. This determination depends upon our dating of the Bronze Age cultures of central Europe and Italy, which must be established archaeologically—ultimately in terms of the historical chronology of the Near East (Thomas, 1961, pp. 805-9). Radiocarbon dates, which often have large probable errors, give only approximations.

In this paper, the radiocarbon method of dating is largely taken for granted in an attempt to determine its effect upon our conception of the chronology of western Europe. The inherent limitations of C-14 dates, which have been widely discussed in recent years, do not permit exact dating. Nevertheless, these dates do suggest that one must return to the high chronology proposed in the past upon the basis of varve dating in northern Europe (Pittioni, 1949, pp. 99-100). The high chronology suggested by the C-14 dates fits very well with the chronologies recently proposed on the basis of radiocarbon determinations for southwestern Asia and the Aegean. Even more important, the chronology here proposed fits with the relative chronology developed through many years by archaeological methods.

B.C.	Brittany	N.France	S.France	Switzerland	Switzerland	SW.Germany
			BRONZE AGE	CULTURES		
						ADLERBERG
2000						
	Kermené 2190 ± 110		Trou-Arnaud 2302 ± 125 Perte du Cros 2288 ± 125 2458 ± 125			
	St.Just 2437 ± 120		Roucadour 2448 ± 125 Camp Briard 2521 ± 137	Escalon 2520 ± 60		BELL BEAKER &
2500	BELL BEAKER	S.O.M.		HORGEN	CULTURE	CORDED WARE
	St.Michel 3066 ± 125 3282 ± 130	Lumbres 2540 ± 125 2746 ± 125	St.Léonard 2942 ± 160	Escalon 2355 ± 130 2770 ± 80		
	LONG MOUND Ile Carn 3436 ± 75	Matignons 2638 ± 160 2865 ± 160 Mont Joly 2942 ± 130 3009 ± 130	Madeleine 2483 ± 500 3097 ± 400	Burgäschisee 2674 ± 110 3035 ± 110	Thayngen 2880 ± 130 2973 ± 130	
3000	Sept-Iles 3205 ± 150 3369 ± 130 3591 ± 135	Restudo 3004 ± 140 3024 ± 140	CHASSEY B	CORTAILLOD	PFYN MICHELSBERG	
	PASSAGE GRAVES		Mouligna 3210 ± 130			Ehrenstein 3344 ± 130 3406 ± 200 3447 ± 100
	Curnic 3550 ± 60		Roucadour 3385 ± 140			
				EGOLZWIL		MICHELSBERG &
3500	EARLY NEOLITHIC	CHASSEY	CHASSEY A	Birsmatten Basishöhle 3519 ± 240 3560 ± 120		SCHUSSENRIED
						RÖSSEN
4000	La Torche 4199 ± 80		Roucadour 4157 ± 150			
		DANUBIAN & CAMPIGNIAN				DANUBIAN
4500			CARDIAL			
				MESOLITHIC		

B.C.	Netherlands	S.England	E.England	N.England	W.Britain	Ireland
	St.Walrick 1866 ± 80 Bennekom 2030 ± 180	Stonehenge III 1830 ± 150 I 1961 ± 275	Fifty Farm 1964 ± 150	Antofts Windy Pit 1921 ± 150		
2000	VELUWE	A-BEAKER	A-BEAKER	C-BEAKER		2046 ± 150
	Hekelingen 2252 ± 85 (S.O.M.)					Tara 2252 ± 160 2437 ± 160
						BOYNE
	Anlo 2133 ± 50 2314 ± 70		Arminghall 2503 ± 150		Monamore 2365 ± 110	Geroid Isle 2262 ± 140 Ballyutoag 2293 ± 300
2500	BEAKER	B-BEAKER			BEACHARRA C	LOUGH GUR II
		Windmill Hill 2715 ± 150				
		Nutbane 2870 ± 150	Ebbsfleet 2849 ± 150			Lough Gur 2592 ± 240 2880 ± 240
		Durrington Walls 3009 ± 80 3030 ± 50				
3000			Shippea Hill 3055 ± 120	Ehenside 3162 ± 300	BEACHARRA B	LOUGH GUR I
		Windmill Hill 3107 ± 150			Monamore 3313 ± 110	Knockiveagh 3220 ± 170
		Hembury 3303 ± 150 3395 ± 150 3488 ± 150				Newferry 3498 ± 170
					BEACHARRA A	Dalkey 3509 ± 170
		WINDMILL HILL			CLYDE-CARLINGFORD	
3500					SEVERN- COTSWOLD	
4000						
	Sittard 4013 ± 140 4333 ± 140 4436 ± 150					
	DANUBIAN					
4500						
	MESOLITHIC					

Bibliography

Arnal, J., and Burnez, C.

1958 "Die Struktur des französischen Neolithikums auf Grund neuester stratigraphischer Beobachtungen." In 37.-38. Bericht der römisch- germanischen Kommission, 1956-1957, pp. 1-90. Berlin.

Arnal, J., Bailloud, G., and Riquet, R.

1960 "Les styles céramiques du néolithique français," Préhistoire 14: 1-200.

Bailloud, G.

1961a "Les civilisations énéolithiques de la France." In L'Europe à la fin de l'âge de la pierre, pp. 493-508. Prague: Éditions de l'Académie tchécoslovaque des Sciences.

1961b "Les disques et terre cuite ('plats-à-pain') dans le néolithique français." In ibid., pp. 509-13.

Bailloud, G., and Mieg de Boofzheim, P.

1955 Les civilisations néolithiques de la France. Paris: Éditions A. et J. Picard et Cie.

Barker, H., and Mackey, J.

1960 "British Museum Natural Radiocarbon Measurements II," Radiocarbon Supplement 2: 26-30.

1961 "British Museum Natural Radiocarbon Measurements III," Radiocarbon 3: 39-45.

1963 "British Museum Natural Radiocarbon Measurements IV," ibid. 5: 104-8.

Bernabò Brea, L.

1946 Gli scavi nella caverna delle Arene Candide. Bordighera: Istituto di Studi Liguri.

1956 Gli scavi nella caverna delle Arene Candide II. Bordighera: Istituto internazionale di Studi Liguri.

Broecker, W. S., Kulp, J. L., and Tucek, C. S.

1956 "Lamont Natural Radiocarbon Measurements III," Science 124: 154-65.

Buttler, W.

1938 Der donauländische und der westische Kulturkreis der jüngeren Steinzeit. ("Handbuch der Urgeschichte Deutschlands," Vol. 2.) Berlin.

Case, H.

1956 "Neolithic Causewayed Camp at Abingdon," Antiquaries Journal 36: 11-30.

1961 "Irish Neolithic Pottery Distribution and Sequence," Proceedings of the Prehistoric Society N.S. 27: 174-233.

Childe, V. G.

1947 Prehistoric Communities of the British Isles, 2d. ed. London: Chambers.

Clark, J. G. D.

1936 "The Timber Monument at Arminghall, and Its Affinities," Proceedings of the Prehistoric Society N.S. 2: 1-51.
1960 "Excavations at the Neolithic Site at Hurst Fen, Mildenhall, Suffolk," ibid. N.S. 26: 202-45.
1962 "A Survey of the Mesolithic Phase in the Prehistory of Europe and South-west Asia," Atti del VI Congresso delle Scienze Internazionale Preistoriche e Protostoriche I: 97-111.

Clark, J. G. D., and Godwin, H.

1962 "The Neolithic in the Cambridgeshire Fens," Antiquity 36: 10-23.

Coursaget, J., Giot, P. R., and Le Run, J.

1960 "C-14 Neolithic Dates from France," Antiquity 34: 147-48.
1961 "New Radiocarbon Dates from France," ibid. 35: 147-48.
1962 "A Fresh Series of Radiocarbon Dates from France," ibid. 36: 139-41.

Daniel, G.

1950 The Prehistoric Chamber Tombs of England and Wales. Cambridge: Cambridge University Press.
1960 The Prehistoric Chamber Tombs of France. London: Thames and Hudson.

Daniel, M., and R.

1953 "Les gisements préhistoriques de la vallée du Loing," L'Anthropologie 57: 209-39.

Escalon de Fonton, M.

1956 "Préhistoire de la Basse-Provence," Préhistoire 12: 1-159.

Evans, J. H.

1950 "Kentish Megalith Types," Archaeologia Cantiana 63: 63-81.

Ferrara, G., Fornaca-Rinaldi, G., and Tongiorgi, E.

1961 "Carbon-14 Dating in Pisa II," Radiocarbon 3: 99-104.

Ferrara, G., Reinharz, M., and Tongiorgi, E.

1959 "Carbon-14 Dating in Pisa," Radiocarbon Supplement 1: 103-10.

Fox, A.

1963 "Neolithic Charcoal from Hembury," Antiquity 37: 228-29.

Fox, C.

1947 The Personality of Britain, 4th ed. Cardiff: National Museum of Wales.

Gfeller, C., Oeschger, H., and Schwarz, U.

1961 "Bern Radiocarbon Dates II," Radiocarbon 3: 15-25.

Giot, P. R.

1956 "Le Quillio, Cotes-du-Nord, IVe circonscription préhistorique, Informations," Gallia 14: 187-88.

1958 "The Chambered Barrow of Barnenez in Finistère," Antiquity 32: 149-53.

1960a Brittany. ("Ancient Peoples and Places," Vol. 13.) London: Thames and Hudson.

1960b "Une station du néolithique primaire armoricain, Le Curnic en Guissény (Finistère)," Bulletin de la société préhistorique française 57: 38-50.

Giot, P. R., and Millon, Y.

1954a "Ploudalmézeau, Finistère, IVe circonscription des antiquités préhistoriques, Informations," Gallia 12: 404.

1954b "Saint-Just, Ille-et-Vilaine, IVe circonscription des antiquités préhistoriques, Informations," ibid.: 401-3.

Giraud, E., Vaché, C., and Vignard, E.

1949 "Les industries de la forêt de Montmorency," L'Anthropologie 53: 336-38.

Godwin, H.

1961 "The Croonian Lecture, Radiocarbon Dating and the Quaternary History in Britain," Proceedings of the Royal Society, Series B, Vol. 153: 287-320.

1962 "Half-Life of Radiocarbon," Nature 195: 984.

Godwin, H., Walker, D., and Willis, E. H.

1957 "Radiocarbon Dating and Post-glacial Vegetational History: Scaleby Moss," Proceedings of the Royal Society, Series B, Vol. 147: 352-66.

Godwin, H., and Willis, E. H.

1959 "Cambridge University Natural Radiocarbon Measurements I," Radiocarbon Supplement 1: 63-75.

1960 "Cambridge University Natural Radiocarbon Measurements II," Radiocarbon 2: 62-72.

1961 "Cambridge University Natural Radiocarbon Measurements III," ibid. 3: 60-76.

Guyan, W.

1953 "Eine bandkeramische Siedlung in Gächlingen (Kt. Schaffhausen)," Ur-Schweiz 17: 68-70.

1955 Das jungsteinzeitliche Moordorf von Thayngen-Weier. ("Monographien zur Ur- und Frühgeschichte der Schweiz," Vol. 2.) Basel.

Henshall, A. S.

1963 The Chambered Tombs of Scotland, Vol. 1, Edinburgh: Edinburgh University Press.

Kohl, G., and Quitta, H.

1963 "Berlin-Radiokarbondaten archäologischer Proben. I," Ausgrabungen und Funde, Nachrichtenblatt für Vor- und Frühgeschichte 8: 281-301.

Laet, S. J. De

1958 The Low Countries. ("Ancient Peoples and Places," Vol. 5.) London: Thames and Hudson.

Laet, S. J. De, and Glasbergen, W.

1959 De voorgeschiedenis der Lage Landen. Brussels: J. B. Wolters.

Libby, W. F.

1955 Radiocarbon Dating. 2d. ed. Chicago: University of Chicago Press.

Mackie, E. W.

1964 "Two Radiocarbon Dates from a Clyde-Solway Chambered Cairn," Antiquity 38: 52-54.

McAulay, I. R., and Watts, W. A.

1961 "Dublin Radiocarbon Dates I," Radiocarbon 3: 26-38.

Morgan, F. de M., and Ashbee, P.

1958 "The Excavations of Two Long Barrows in Wessex," Antiquity 32: 104-11.

Münnich, K. O.

1957 "Heidelberg Natural Radiocarbon Measurements I," Science 126: 194-99.

Nougier, L. R.

1950 Les civilisations campigniennes en Europe occidentale. Le Mans: Ch. Monnoyer.

Oeschger, H., Schwarz, U., and Gfeller, C.

1959 "Bern Radiocarbon Dates I," Radiocarbon Supplement 1: 133-43.

Paor, M. de

1961 "Notes on Irish Beakers." In Bericht über den V Internationalen Kongress für Vor- und Frühgeschichte Hamburg, pp. 653-60. Berlin: Verlag Gebr. Mann.

Philippe, J.

1927 Cinq années de fouilles au Fort-Harrouard, 1921-1925. ("Bulletin de la société normande d'études préhistoriques," 25.)

Piggott, S.

1953 "Le néolithique occidental et le chalcolithique en France: Esquisse préliminaire," L'Anthropologie 57: 401-43.

1954a The Neolithic Cultures of the British Isles. Cambridge: Cambridge University Press.

1954b "Le néolithique occidental et le chalcolithique en France: Esquisse préliminaire," L'Anthropologie 58: 1-28.

1958 "The Excavations of the West Kennet Long Barrow, 1955-6," Antiquity 32: 235-42.

1961 "The British Neolithic Cultures in Their Continental Settings." In L'Europe à la fin de l'âge de la pierre, pp. 557-83. Prague, Éditions de l'Académie tchécoslovaque des Sciences.

1963 "Abercromby and After, The Beaker Cultures of Britain Reexamined." In Culture and Environment, Essays in Honour of Sir Cyril Fox, pp. 53-91. Ed. I. LL. Foster and L. Alcock. London: Routledge and Kegan Paul.

Pittioni, R.

1949 Die urgeschichtlichen Grundlagen der europäischen Kultur. Vienna: Franz Deuticke.

1962 "Italien, urgeschichtliche Kulturen." In Realencyclopädie der classischen Altertumswissenschaft, Supplementband 9, pp. 106-371. Ed. Pauly-Wissowa.

Quitta, H.

1960 "Zur Frage der ältesten Bandkeramik in Mitteleuropa," Praehistorische Zeitschrift 38: 1-38, 153-88.

Sandars, N. K.

1957 Bronze Age Cultures in France. Cambridge: Cambridge University Press.

Sauter, M. R.

1957 "La station néolithique et protohistorique de 'Sur le Grand Pré' à Saint-Léonard (distr. Sierre, Valais), Note préliminaire," Archives suisses d'anthropologie générale 22: 136-49.

Savory, H. N.

1963 "The Personality of the Southern Marches of Wales in the Neolithic and Early Bronze Age." In Culture and Environment. Essays in Honour of Sir Cyril Fox, pp. 25-52. Ed. I. LL. Foster and L. Alcock. London: Routledge and Kegan Paul.

Schwabedissen, H.

1962 "Northern Continental Europe." In Courses toward Urban Life, pp. 254-66. ("Viking Fund Publications in Anthropology," No. 32.) New York: Viking Fund.

Scollar, I.

1959 "Regional Groups in the Michelsberg Culture," Proceedings of the Prehistoric Society 25: 52-134.

1961 "The Late Neolithic in Belgium, Western Germany and Alsace." In L'Europe à la fin de l'âge de la pierre, pp. 519-48. Prague: Éditions de l'Académie tchécoslovaque des Sciences.

Smith, I.

1955 "Late Beaker Pottery from the Lyonesse Surface and the Date of the Transgression," Eleventh Annual Report of the Institute of Archaeology (University of London).

1958 "The 1957-58 Excavations at Windmill Hill," Antiquity 32: 268-69.

1960 "Radiocarbon Dates from Windmill Hill," ibid. 34: 212-13.

Tauber, H.

1960 "Copenhagen Natural Radiocarbon Measurements III, Corrections to Radiocarbon Dates Made with the Solid Carbon Technique," Radiocarbon 2: 5-11.

Thomas, H. L.

1961 "The Significance of Radiocarbon Dating for the Bronze Age Chronology of Central Europe." In Bericht über den V. Internationalen Kongress für Vor- und Frühgeschichte Hamburg, pp. 805-9. Berlin: Verlag Gebr. Mann.

Vogel, J. C., and Waterbolk, H. T.

1963 "Groningen Radiocarbon Dates IV," Radiocarbon 5: 163-202.

Vogt, E.

1945 "Die Ausgrabungen auf dem Lutzengütle bei Eschen, 1945," Jahrbuch der historischen Verein . . . Liechtenstein 45: 151-60.

1951 "Das steinzeitliche Uferdorf Egolzwil 3, (Kt. Luzern), Bericht über die Ausgrabungen, 1950," Zeitschrift für schweizerische Archäologie und Kunstgeschichte 12: 193-215.

1961 "Der Stand der neolithischen Forschung in der Schweiz (1960)." In L'Europe à la fin de l'âge de la pierre, pp. 459-88. Prague: Éditions de l'Académie tchécoslovaque des Sciences.

von Gonzenbach, V.

1949 Die Cortaillodkultur in der Schweiz. ("Monographien zur Ur- und Frühgeschichte der Schweiz," Vol. 7.) Basel.

Vries, H. de, Barendsen, G. W., and Waterbolk, H. T.

1958 "Groningen Radiocarbon Dates II," Science 127: 129-37.

Vries, H. de, and Waterbolk, H. T.

1958 "Groningen Radiocarbon Dates III," Science 128: 1550-56.

Waals, J. D. van der, and Glasbergen, W.

1955 "Beaker Types and Their Distribution in the Netherlands," Palaeohistoria 4: 5-46.

Waterbolk, H. T.
1962 "The Lower Rhine Basin." In *Courses toward Urban Life*, pp. 227-53. ("Viking Fund Publications in Anthropology," No. 32.) New York: Viking Fund.

Watts, W. A.
1960 "C-14 Dating and the Neolithic in Ireland," *Antiquity* 34: 111-16.

Zürn, H.
1958 "Eine jungsteinzeitliche Siedlung bei Ehrenstein, Kr. Ulm/Donau." In *Neue Ausgrabungen in Deutschland*, pp. 75-92. Verlag Gebr. Mann.

Addendum:

Since this paper went to press, a few radiocarbon dates have been published which further support the chronology outlined here. These include radiocarbon dates: of 3303 ± 250 B.C. (MC-7) and 3426 ± 230 B.C. (MC-8) for the Chassey levels VII and X of the grotte de la Madeleine (J. Thommeret and J. L. Rapaire, "Monaco Radiocarbon Measurements I," *Radiocarbon* 6 [1964]: 195); of 3591 ± 120 B.C. (Q-770) for the Mesolithic/Neolithic transition at Ringneill Quay, Co. Down (H. Godwin and E. H. Willis, "Cambridge University Natural Radiocarbon Measurements VI," *Radiocarbon* 6 [1964]: 127); and of 2942 ± 100 B.C. (K-539) and 3107 ± 100 (K-540) for the Michelsberg occupation at Thayngen-Weier (H. Tauber, "Copenhagen Radiocarbon Dates VI," *Radiocarbon* 6 [1964]: 224-25). All these dates agree well with similar or related dates given above in this paper.

Several useful studies have appeared since this study was prepared. Among these are J. G. D. Clark, "Radiocarbon Dating and the Spread of Farming Economy," *Antiquity* 36 (1965): 45-48, and R. Riquet, J. Guilaine and A. Coffyn, "Les Campaniformes français," *Gallia Préhistoire* 6 (1963): 63-128. One must agree with Clark that many more Carbon-14 dates are needed, but can radiocarbon dates ever provide more than a rough check, accurate within perhaps a range of from one to three centuries? Except for areas with firm historical chronologies, archaeological chronology will continue to depend not only upon traditional archaeological methods but upon the ethno-historical assumptions behind each chronological system.

The Archaeological Chronology of Northern Europe

Homer L. Thomas
University of Missouri

In the years since World War II, the relative chronology of the Neolithic cultures of northern Europe has undergone a series of revolutionary changes. These changes are largely the result of the new chronology advanced by Swedish and Danish archaeologists for the Neolithic of Scandinavia, the discovery of early Bandkeramik in the Netherlands, and the impact of the use of the C-14 method. For the most part the recent work has proceeded along regional lines. Nevertheless, new concepts of cultural development have grown out of the work of Becker (1947, 1961b) on the Danish Neolithic, of Schwabedissen (1958; 1962, pp. 262-65) on Schleswig-Holstein, and of De Laet and Glasbergen (1959), and others on the Low Countries. The efforts of these archaeologists have put down the foundations for a new structure for northern European chronology.

The Early Neolithic

The first Neolithic culture to reach the northern plains of Europe—which extend from the Low Countries through northern Germany to Poland—was the Danubian I culture, the oldest Bandkeramik. The discovery of sites such as Sittard (Modderman, 1955, pp. 13-21), Geleen (Waterbolk, 1959, pp. 121-61), and others in Dutch Limburg clearly shows that the earliest Neolithic in the Netherlands was not only as old as the earliest phases of Köln-Lindenthal in the Rhineland, but, to judge from the absence of Notenkopfkeramik, as old as that of the Middle Danubian lands. It is clear that one can no longer assume a slow diffusion from the southeast through the loess lands to the northwest (Waterbolk, 1962, pp. 236-37). The Danubian peasants with their Bandkeramik not only reached the lower Rhineland, but penetrated at the same time into central Germany along the valley of the Elbe and into eastern Germany and western Poland along the valley of the Oder (Quitta, 1958a, pp. 173-77; 1960, pp. 11 ff.). Sites on the lower Oder indicate that Danubian I penetrated almost to Stettin on the edge of the Baltic. C-14 dates for material found in the Limburg sites indicate that it reached the northwestern frontier of the Danubian region as early as the middle of the fifth millennium B.C.[1] Measurements of charcoal samples from Sittard (Gro-320, Gro-422, Gro-423) give the following dates: 4333 ± 140 B.C., 4013 ± 190 B.C., and 4436 ± 150 B.C. (De Vries, Barendsen, and Waterbolk, 1958, pp. 134-35; see _Radiocarbon_ V [1963], 164 for correction of Groningen dates). Dates close to these were also determined for charcoal samples from similar Danubian contexts at Geleen and Elsloo (see table 1). Radiocarbon determinations made on charcoal samples from Westeregeln near Magdeburg and Zwenkau-Harth near Leipzig were respectively 4436 ± 200 B.C. (De Vries, 1954, p. 1140) and 4394 ± 70 B.C. (GrN-1581, Vogel and Waterbolk, p. 184; Quitta, 1958_b_, pp. 177-79), indicating that the Danubian was just as early in central Germany. Recently, additional determinations have been made at Berlin for samples from the early to middle phases of the _Bandkeramik_ settlement at Westeregeln (Bln-92, 4374 ± 100 B.C.; Bln-42, 4276 ± 100 B.C.) (Kohl and Quitta, 1963, pp. 293-94). To judge from radiocarbon dates (Bln-66, K-555) of 4127 ± 100 and 4065 ± 120 B.C. for the early Stroked Ware phase at Zwenkau-Harth, the Danubian I lasted until the end of the fifth millennium B.C. (Kohl and Quitta, 1963, p. 294; Tauber, 1960_b_, p. 22). Palynological investigations of peat profiles near Sittard and Geleen showed that the Danubian villages belonged approximately to the time of the first appearance of grains of _Plantago lanceolata_, an indicator of the onset of agriculture and datable to the period of Atlantic climate (Vogel and Waterbolk, 1963, pp. 198-99). These new finds from the Netherlands and central Germany clearly suggest that the earliest Neolithic to reach the plains of northern Europe is to be placed as early as the second half of the fifth millennium B.C. This is in agreement with the dating of the _Bandkeramik_ cultures in east central Europe (cf. Ehrich, p. 440, below).

In northern Europe, the Danubian peasants must have encountered Mesolithic peoples still living by means of hunting and fishing. Waterbolk has argued that with the disappearance of the open lands of the Boreal period the Mesolithic population had largely abandoned the Netherlands, leaving the land free for settlement by the Danubian people (Waterbolk, 1962, pp. 234-35); yet the upper level of the Tardenoisian site

---

1. All dates in this paper are corrected for the new half life of C-14 (Godwin, 1962, p. 984) and, when known, for the Suess effect and other published laboratory corrections.

of Zonhoven has trapezes made from fragments of Neolithic polished axes. In view of the possible late survival of the Tardenoisian, it is difficult to say whether the axes derive from a Danubian or a later Neolithic settlement. The early Danubian sites of Dutch Limburg (which are tied to Köln-Lindenthal I-II) and the later Danubian sites of Dutch Limburg and the related settlements of the Hesbaye area near Liège (Omalian culture, which can be linked to Köln-Lindenthal III-IV) seem to show relatively little contact with Mesolithic culture, to judge from their flint inventories. Much the same applies to the Danubian groups in central Germany. Strangely, these peasants seem to have left little in the way of an inheritance for their successors in the Netherlands (Waterbolk, 1962, p. 237).

During the later Atlantic period, Schleswig-Holstein and Denmark were occupied by the Ellerbek-Ertebølle culture—now known from inland as well as coastal kitchen middens—which has a conical-based pottery, domesticated animals, and some elements of agriculture, if one can trust grain imprints on a few vessel fragments. Schwabedissen would derive these "Neolithic" elements from western Europe, since the pottery has general similarities with the Michelsberg and Almerian pottery, and the picks and axes are similar to those of the Campignian culture of northern France and Belgium (Schwabedissen, 1962, pp. 260-63). Wood from both the upper and lower layers of the Ellerbek cultural occupation at Rüde (Y-471, Y-441a) in Schleswig-Holstein gives the same C-14 date, 3838 ± 50 B.C. Wood (Y-160) from the 1951 excavations was dated 3910 ± 70 B.C. (Barendsen, Deevey, and Gralenski, 1957, p. 911). At Rüde, the pollen age was Atlantic. A radiocarbon date of 4291 ± 200 B.C. was determined from wood found at Ellerbek (Y-440) near Kiel (*ibid*., p. 911). The C-14 and pollen-analytical determinations clearly indicate that the Danubian and the Ellerbek-Ertebølle cultures belong to approximately the same period and climatic phase; the Ellerbek-Ertebølle cultures, which Schwabedissen has called Proto-Neolithic, probably began somewhat later than the Danubian *Bandkeramik* cultures. This is in agreement with the varve dates of 4000-3000 B.C. for the Ertebølle culture (Jaździewski, 1961, p. 100).

The succeeding archaeological horizon in northern Europe is characterized by the Funnel Beaker (*Trichterbecher*), which appears in its earliest form in southern Scandinavia, northern Germany, Czechoslovakia, and Poland. Since World War II, many theories have been advanced to explain the origin of the Funnel Beaker culture. Only the aspects of these theories which have an immediate bearing upon chronology can be considered here. The discovery of the Funnel Beaker settlement at Store Valby in Zealand clearly established that this culture was intrusive in Scandinavia and not a development of the Scandinavian Mesolithic. Becker, in his report on Store Valby, pointed out that this culture is intrusive in both northern Germany and Scandinavia and probably derives from eastern Europe (Becker, 1954, pp. 155-65, 187-92). In his fundamental study of the Northern Neolithic, which was published in 1947, he had already proposed that the Funnel Beaker cultures probably derived from the southeast (Becker, 1947, pp. xv-xvi). More recently, he has suggested that the region of their origin should be placed in the area north of the Tripolye-Cucuteni cultures (Becker, 1961a, p. 69; 1961c, pp. 599-600). Nevertheless, theories of a Mesolithic origin for the Funnel Beaker culture have continued (Troels-Smith, 1953, pp. 42-43; Schwabedissen, 1958, pp. 35-42; 1962, pp. 260-66), and Evžen and Jiří Neustupný (1961, p. 86) derive the Funnel Beaker culture from the Lengyel culture of the middle Danubian basin and connect both with the Indo-Europeans. Mildenberger (1953, pp. 77-87) would also derive the Funnel Beaker from south-central Europe. Theories such as these are not of direct importance for chronology, but they underlie the concepts used by archaeologists in constructing chronological systems (Jażdżewski, 1961, pp. 73-100 gives a recent summary of these theories).

In Scandinavia, the beginning of the Funnel Beaker culture can be established on the basis of the finds at Store Valby. Unfortunately, these finds are not dated by either C-14 or pollen-analytical determinations. Store Valby pottery, which defines the beginning phase of the Funnel Beaker culture—Phase A pottery—has been found in association with Ertebølle pottery at Mulbjerg (Mul I) on Zealand. The average of the radiocarbon determinations on a variety of samples from Mulbjerg (K 123-127, 129, 131-132) places its occupation at about 2963 ± 80 B.C. (Tauber, 1960a, p. 7). Pollen-analytical studies indicate that this occupation dates after the decline of the Ulmus curve and before the spread of Plantago lanceolata—that is, above the Atlantic/Sub-Boreal boundary. The Mulbjerg date is in agreement with the Uppsala dates of U-47, 3011 ± 205 B.C. and U-46, 2880 ± 175 B.C., for samples from the Early Neolithic level at Vätteryd in Skåne, which is also fixed pollen-analytically immediately above the Atlantic/Sub-Boreal boundary (Olsson, 1959, p. 97; Tilander,

1958, pp. 91-102). The Mulbjerg and Vätteryd dates are supported by Godwin's date of 3150 B.C. (if one corrects his date of ca. 3000 B.C. for the new half life of C-14) for the Atlantic/Sub-Boreal boundary (Godwin, Walker, and Willis, 1957, p. 364; Godwin, 1961, p. 388). It must be remembered that Mulbjerg is an Ertebølle and not a Funnel Beaker A site, and that it has a complicated stratigraphy, making it extremely difficult to date (Tauber, 1958, pp. 59-69). The C-14 dates of 3668 ± 245 B.C. for charcoal and hazelnut shells from the mixed Ertebølle-Early Neolithic site at Elinelund 71 (U-48) in Skåne (Olsson, 1959, p. 97), and of 3344 ± 115 and 3220 ± 105 B.C. for wood and charcoal from the early Funnel Beaker level at Heidmoor (H-29-146, H-30-145) in Schleswig-Holstein (Münnich, 1957, p. 197) suggest higher dates for the beginning of the Early Neolithic in the north. These higher dates, which are in agreement with those for the contemporary Ertebølle culture (see above), would place the beginnings of the Early Neolithic within the late Atlantic climatic phase, which is also indicated by palynological evidence.

Unfortunately, the beginning of the Funnel Beaker culture is difficult to define in northern Germany, Poland, and Czechoslovakia. In northern Germany, the early Funnel Beaker culture is known only from finds of single vessels in Mecklenburg and Pomerania which are difficult to date. The same is true of the Polish finds, except for those from Sarnovo, which came from a pit found below a burial assigned to the fully developed Funnel Beaker culture, usually equated with Funnel Beaker C in south Scandinavia (Chmielewski, 1952, pp. 53 ff.). These isolated Funnel Beakers found in northern Germany and western Poland cannot be separated into A and B types, although considered together they are closer stylistically to the A types (Becker, 1961b, pp. 591-92). Neustupný (1961b, pp. 317-18) has postulated a Funnel Beaker A phase in Bohemia and Moravia, largely upon the basis of the depot find of pottery at Božice. Driehaus and Pleslová (1961, p. 361) point out that Neustupný's Funnel Beaker A and Zápotocký's Funnel Beaker A/B phases (1957, pp. 206-35) for Bohemia and Moravia rest largely upon the Božice find and a few isolated vessels. Although these finds do not permit a clear definition of the early Funnel Beaker culture in Bohemia and Moravia, they probably date before the early Baalberg culture of central Germany, which is here correlated with the Funnel Beaker B phase in Scandinavia. This would place the beginning of the Funnel Beaker culture in the period of the Rössen culture of central Germany, the earliest Michelsberg culture of western

Germany, the Tiszapolgár culture of Slovakia, and the Lengyel culture of western Hungary—a dating that would agree with the Scandinavian evidence which indicates that the early phases of the Funnel Beaker culture overlapped the Ertebølle culture and date to the late Atlantic period. In terms of absolute chronology, the Funnel Beaker culture began in Scandinavia and Germany well before 3000 B.C.—perhaps as early as 3600 B.C., to judge from the Heidmoor and Elinelund dates. Such a date is in agreement with C-14 dates not only for the late Atlantic period but for the Rössen and early Michelsberg cultures, which are contemporary with the early Funnel Beaker culture on archaeological grounds as well.

The subsequent development of the Funnel Beaker culture must be followed separately in southern Scandinavia, northern Germany, and central Germany. Its development in Poland, Bohemia, and Moravia is dealt with elsewhere in this volume (see Ehrich, pp. 435-36).

In Scandinavia, the development of the Funnel Beaker culture has been divided into four phases—A-D—the earliest found in association with Late Ertebølle, the latest extending into the period of the passage graves which mark the beginning of the Middle Neolithic. Following Phase A, which is best defined by the assemblage at Store Valby, Phase B is characterized by finds from the settlement at Havnelev in Zealand and the single burial found in an oval pit or earth grave at Birring in Jutland (Mathiassen, 1940, pp. 3-16; Brøndsted, 1960, pp. 147-48). Various relationships can be established within southern Scandinavia. B type pottery turns up in Ertebølle sites such as Strandegaard, indicating that a late Ertebølle culture still lingered on and indeed, in terms of other sites, continued perhaps as late as Funnel Beaker D culture. The Dwelling Places of southern Scandinavia have yielded Funnel Beaker pottery, but it is often difficult to distinguish whether it belongs to A or B phase (Becker, 1961*b*, p. 590). There are no traits with external connections except for the baking plates of Phases A and B, which are similar to those of the Michelsberg culture (see above, p. 352).

Funnel Beaker C phase, which marks the end of the Early Neolithic, is known from a vast number of finds, which indicate the rise of at least three regional groups in Denmark and three or four in Sweden. This is the period of the appearance of the *dysse* (or dolmen) that was generally covered by a round barrow or, if there is more than one tomb, by a long barrow. The *dysse* consists of small chambers with square, rectangular or five- or six-sided plans. Until recently, the dysse has been ascribed to outside influence, but Becker (1947, pp. 264-69; see also Daniel, 1959, pp. 52-57) has shown that they could have evolved out of the use of boulders in flat cist graves. Since the dysse must not be regarded as a western creation, external connections must be established on the basis of finds such as the copper disks of Salten and the stone axes with splayed blades found at various sites in southern Scandinavia (Becker, 1947, fig. 54; Childe, 1958, p. 180). The Salten disks are similar to ones found at Brześć Kujawski (Jordansmühl culture), in the Stollhoff depot (Bodrogkeresztúr culture), and in the Rumanian Hăbăşeşti depot (Lomborg, 1962, pp. 5-10), and must therefore be connected to the time of Bodrogkeresztúr culture (Troy I-II) and might be connected through the middle Danubian basin even with related ornamental types at Troy II. The splayed ax blades, which must be regarded as imitations of metal ax types current in Hungary as early as the Bodrogkeresztúr culture, might be considered as a distant reflection of the great commercial expansion of Early Dynastic III and Akkadian times in southwestern Asia. The collared flasks which had appeared in phase B, the knob-hammer axes which are certain in phase C, and the thin-butted stone axes are important not only for internal correlations but also for connections with the Funnel Beaker cultures in northern and central Germany. The Funnel Beaker D phase belongs to what is really the first phase of Middle Neolithic Ia, since its pottery can be correlated with that found in the settlement at Troldebjerg (Winther, 1935). The earth grave is now seldom used and the five- or six-sided dysse is dominant, but there are as yet none of the passage graves which characterize the fully developed culture of the Middle Neolithic (Becker, 1961b, pp. 588-89).

In northern and central Germany, the early Funnel Beaker culture is defined by finds of A/B pottery which suggest that northern Germany and southern Scandinavia shared a common culture at the beginning of the Early Neolithic. In phase B, the two regions were probably developing along separate lines, anticipating the regionalism of phase C (Becker, 1947, xii-xiii). The regionalism which arose in Funnel Beaker C phase can be traced in northwestern, northeastern, and central Germany. The Holstein-Hannover group of northwestern Germany was characterized by both flat graves and rectangular dolmens under long barrows, which have yielded funnel beakers, collared flasks, and a late style of decoration (Dehnke, 1940, pp. 140-53). In northeastern Germany, there are local groups such as the Molzow and Zarrenthin, which are characterized by local styles of pottery (Jażdżewski, 1932, pp. 90-91). The Baalberg group of central Germany is of particular importance because of its connections with other central European cultures. Unfortunately, its chronological position within central Germany and its specific relationships with Bohemia and Moravia are difficult to establish. Mildenberger (1953, pp. 49-51) assumes that the Baalberg culture must be correlated with phase C in the north and was succeeded by the Salzmünde culture. On the other hand, Fischer (1951, p. 104; 1961, pp. 416-17; see also Driehaus and Pleslová, 1961, pp. 247-52; Preuss, 1961, pp. 405-13) holds that the Baalberg continued into a late phase which paralleled the Salzmünde. These theories are based upon the analysis of geographic distribution of these central German cultures and the stratigraphy of their burial tumuli. At Baalberg itself, the Funnel Beaker material comes from a ground grave of a tumulus with later burials of Walternienburg II-Bernburg I, Globe Amphorae, and Corded Ware cultures (Höfer, 1902, pp. 16-49; Mildenberger, 1953, pp. 23-25). The beginning of the Baalberg culture overlapped the late Rössen and Gatersleben cultures, which had replaced the Danubian culture in central Germany. The contemporary Bohemian Baalberg group can be linked with the Schussenried culture, which overlaps the early Michelsberg in western Germany (E. F. Neustupný, 1961b, pp. 314-16). Michelsberg elements penetrated into central Germany, where they occur in Jordansmühl-related cultures datable to Baalberg times. Late Michelsberg is found as a distinct culture in Bohemia, where it is connected with the Siřem or later Baalberg group (Scollar, 1959, pp. 97-100; see also below, Ehrich, p. 435, for discussion of Siřem phase), confirming the earlier tie between Baalberg, Schussenried, and early Michelsberg. The Salzmünde culture and presumably the later Baalberg culture can be connected with the late Jordansmühl culture, which has two-handled tankards, cylindrical ribbon bracelets, spectacle spirals, and small disks with embossed ornament that must derive from the southeast at the time of the Bodrogkeresztúr culture (Childe, 1958, p. 123). Similar connections of the Scandinavian Funnel Beaker C phase would support an equation of the C groups in southern Scandinavia with the Salzmünde and later Baalberg in central Germany. This web of interrelations suggests that Scandinavian Funnel Beaker B phase is to be connected through the earlier Baalberg culture with the Schussenried and early Michelsberg cultures, whereas the Scan dinavian Funnel Beaker C phase is to be linked through the Salzmünde and later Baalberg cultures with the later Michelsberg, late Jordansmühl, and Bodrogkeresztúr cultures. Unfortunately, it is difficult to correlate the development in central Germany with that proposed for Bohemia and Moravia by E. F. Neustupný (1956, pp. 66-69; 1961a, pp. 441-57) and Zápotocký (1957, pp. 206-35; see also Driehaus, 1959, pp. 53-65; and Ehrich, pp. 435-36, below).

There are several C-14 dates for Schussenried, early Michelsberg, Rössen, and Salzmünde cultures that have importance for the synchronisms given above for the Funnel Beaker B and C phases. In view of the early Baalberg connections, the Ehrenstein (H-125-107 and H-16-149) dates of 3406 ± 200 and 3344 ± 130 B.C. (Münnich, 1957, p. 197) for the Schussenried and early Michelsberg cultures suggest that the beginning of the Funnel Beaker B phase might go back to about 3400-3300 B.C. This date is supported by the Wahlitz date (Gro-433) of 3509 ± 200 B.C. (De Vries, Barendsen, and Waterbolk, 1958, p. 135) for the Rössen culture, the later phases of which survived into the period of the early Baalberg culture. This would also fit with the presumed connection between Michelsberg and Funnel Beaker A and B phases, and is supported by the new dates recently reported from a Salzmünde site in central Germany. Two charcoal samples from the ditch before the palisade of the Salzmünde settlement on the Dölauer Heide near Halle (Bln-64, 53) gave dates of 2973 ± 100 and 2818 ± 100 B.C. (Kohl and Quitta, 1963, p. 290; Behrens, 1963, pp. 18-21). These dates for Salzmünde are contradicted by the Mogetorp date of 3708 ± 135 B.C. for the Vrå culture, regarded as contemporary with Funnel Beaker C phase (Olsson, 1959, pp. 93-94), but here the cultural attribution or the C-14 date may be in error. On the other hand, a sample from the settlement site of Ćmielów, which is usually equated with Funnel Beaker C phase, has been dated by the Cologne Laboratory to 2865 ± 110 B.C. (Jażdżewski, 1961, pp. 99-100). The connections of the Funnel Beaker C phase of Scandinavia, the Salzmünde, later Baalberg, Siřem, and Jordansmühl groups with the Bodrogkeresztúr culture indicate that the C phase must last until the middle of the third millennium B.C. As a rough estimate, made on the basis of C-14 dates and the southeastern connections, the cultures of Funnel Beaker C phase may be placed in the first half of the third millennium B.C.

The Megalithic Cultures

In Scandinavia, the Middle Neolithic began with the appearance of the megalithic passage grave, which most scholars regard as an introduction from the west because of its excellent Portuguese and Breton prototypes (Daniel, 1959, pp. 55-59). The relative chronology of the Scandinavian Middle Neolithic is based upon the pottery from a series of short-lived settlements in Denmark: Troldebjerg and Klintebakke defining Middle Neolithic Ia and Ib, and Blandebjerg, Bundsø, Lindø, and Store Valby defining Middle Neolithic II-V. The pottery of each of these settlements, which is fixed typologically in relation to the pottery of preceding and subsequent settlements, can be used to date finds associated with pottery from passage graves and occasionally from hoards (Becker, 1961b, pp. 585-94).

The famous Danish hoard of Bygholm, which was found near Horsens, in Jutland, has long been used to determine the relative date of the beginning of the Passage Grave period, since it is securely fixed to Middle Neolithic Ia. This hoard consists of four copper axes, two copper arm spirals, and a copper dagger with a midrib on one side that is similar to daggers found in Portuguese megalithic tombs. Unhappily, the Bygholm hoard is far from diagnostic, since the Portuguese connection is difficult to fix chronologically and the arm spirals might well have been current as early as the Funnel Beaker C phase.

The beginning of the Middle Neolithic is ambiguous as it is defined, because Middle Neolithic Ia, which is defined by pottery from the settlement of Troldebjerg (Winther, 1935), is still associated with dysse, not passage graves. The passage grave began in the Middle Neolithic Ib period, when pottery such as that found in the settlement of Klintebakke was current (Becker, 1961b, pp. 588-89; Berg, 1951). Unfortunately, this pottery is transitional in character, consisting partly of pottery of Funnel Beaker type—now classified as D phase—and partly of new types such as a footed bowl and a broad ladle. In this pottery, we see the beginning of densely furrowed decoration. There are few types which can be connected with similar types abroad, but the footed bowl is similar to the Middle Danubian footed bowl. Middle Neolithic II offers little more in terms of external connections. The pottery which is in the so-called "Grand Style" has its closest similarities in the Walternienburg pottery of central Germany. External relations are equally limited for Middle

Neolithic III. Its pottery decoration and more rounded pottery profiles have been explained in terms of Bell Beaker influence. In the latter part of Middle Neolithic III, the Single Grave culture appeared in Denmark and southern Sweden, providing a chronological point of contact of great importance (Becker, 1961b, pp. 589-90; Brøndsted, 1960, pp. 202-43).

The Passage Grave culture of Sweden closely follows the Danish pattern of development, although Early Neolithic elements tended to linger longer than in Denmark. There is little that is important for external chronological connections except that the tanged and barbed arrowheads found in the Fjärrestad passage grave (Kaelas, 1952, pp. 165-75) date to Middle Neolithic III, since these points have been connected with the intrusion of Bell Beaker influence.

Internal development is difficult to follow in Sweden because of the rise of Sub-Neolithic cultures, which can now be dated to as early as the first stages of the Middle Neolithic at sites such as Henninge Bro (Thomas, 1961, p. 810) and Jonstorp (Bagge, 1951b, pp. 50-51). These cultures, which have been called Dwelling Place, Pitted Ware, and Secondary Neolithic, occur in southern, central, and western Sweden and in southern Norway. They represent the acculturation of Neolithic elements by late Ertebølle peoples (Thomas, 1961, pp. 809-13). The Pitted Ware cultures which spread through Scandinavia during the late Passage Grave period are regarded as a Secondary Neolithic by Thomas, but Becker has argued that they represent an intrusion from the Russian woodlands (Becker, 1950, pp. 153-263). In any event, these cultures and those of the Arctic north, which cannot be dealt with here, are not of major importance for the relative position of the Scandinavian Passage Grave culture in the chronology of northern Europe.

Aside from the passage graves, which have obvious western European connections, several synchronisms can be used to place the early Passage Grave period within the framework of a wider European chronology. The form of the first southern Scandinavian passage graves is similar to those of Portugal and Brittany, and their connection with western Europe is reinforced by the dagger of the Bygholm hoard. Unhappily, however, these similarities are so general that they have little chronological value. The early passage graves of Brittany are now dated by radiocarbon determinations to about 3500-3400 B.C. (see above, pp. 355-56), but such a dating is of little value for fixing the beginning of the Scandinavian passage graves. The dating of the Passage Graves period must rest upon archaeological synchronisms. The similarity of the Middle Neolithic II pottery with the Walternienburg, which immediately followed the Salzmünde or derived, along with Salzmünde, from the Baalberg (Preuss, 1961, p. 408), suggests that Middle Neolithic I must be tied to later Salzmünde times, since Funnel Beaker C has been connected with early Salzmünde on the basis of the Siřem-Jordansmühl synchronism and southeastern connections. The long accepted equation of Walternienburg and Middle Neolithic II would fit well into the relative chronology of central and northern Europe, since Walternienburg gave way to the Saxo-Thuringian Corded Ware culture, and the related Single Grave culture appeared in Scandinavia in the succeeding Middle Neolithic III period. The Corded Ware cultures, which extend across the whole of central Europe and form a convenient chronological horizon, can go back as early as 2600 B.C. on the basis of radiocarbon determinations for material found in Corded Ware context in the Netherlands. In view of the long period covered by the Corded Ware cultures, such dates are of little value in fixing the chronology of Middle Neolithic III. Bell Beaker elements in Middle Neolithic III provide a much better chronological indication, if one can assume that Bell Beaker influence reached the Netherlands and Scandinavia at about the same time. C-14 dates place the first appearance of the Bell Beaker in the Netherlands about 2300 B.C., perhaps as early as 2500 B.C. (see above, pp. 359-60). Such a date for the middle of the Passage Grave period suggests that this culture probably occupied the last half of the third millennium. This would fit with a terminal date of about 2500 B.C. for the Funnel Beaker C phase, and would be supported by the Sub-Boreal dating of the whole Passage Grave period. The C-14 dates of 2623 ± 120 and 2571 ± 120 B.C. from Tustrup (K-727, K-718) and of 2612 ± 120 B.C. from Ferslev (K-717) in Denmark, which date samples belonging to the beginning of the Middle Neolithic, support the dating given here that was based upon archaeological synchronisms (Tauber, 1964, pp. 217-18; these dates became available while this paper was in press).

The megalithic passage graves, which are found from the northern Netherlands across northern Germany as far as the Oder, can be divided into western, eastern, and central groups. The western group (Netherlands, northwestern Germany, and Holstein), consisting of rectangular chambers which became increasingly longer in proportion to width, can be traced through three phases of development. The early group of northwestern German passage graves—or, as they are more usually called, Hunenbetten—yields ladles and footed bowls with Tiefstich ornament (Dehnke, 1940, pp. 23-24) which are similar to those of the Middle Neolithic Ib in the north, but they also have collared flasks (Dehnke, 1940, p. 141), which are typical of Funnel Beaker C phase but are absent in Middle Neolithic I in the north. Although the early passage graves of the Netherlands lack the Scandinavian ladle and footed bowl, their pottery, according to a recent study by Lüüdik-Kaelas (1955, pp. 47-79), goes back to the Funnel Beaker C phase. Older theories—such as that of Dehnke (1940, pp. 175-80), which assumes a parallel development between northwestern Germany and Scandinavia from a common Funnel Beaker A/B culture, and of Sprockhoff (1938, pp. 20-24), which holds that the distinctive passage grave of northwest Germany evolved and spread from Holstein—will not resolve this dilemma. Evidence clearly suggesting that the Dutch and northwestern German megalithic graves are earlier than the Scandinavian led De Laet (1958, p. 86) to conclude that it would be necessary to reconsider how the passage grave reached Scandinavia.

The distinctive Passage Grave culture of the Netherlands, northwestern Germany, and Holstein has a completely different origin from that of Scandinavia. The first traces of the Tiefstich ornament which is so characteristic of the pottery of these passage graves are found in the Salzmünde culture along with the so-called Trommel vessel, which must be the prototype of the footed bowl that subsequently spread to both the Dutch and northwestern German and the Scandinavian Passage Grave cultures (Fischer, 1951, pp. 98-104; Childe, 1958, p. 190). The Dutch and northwestern German megalithic tomb might well represent a local adaptation of a western megalithic type in an area occupied by a Funnel Beaker culture. It could then have spread eastward into Holstein and Mecklenburg, where the earliest passage graves can be shown to be later than those of Hannover. There is no question of Scandinavian influence, since the northern type of passage grave did not reach south of the river Eider in Schleswig-Holstein (Sprockhoff, 1938, p. 19). The northwestern German passage grave may well have reached Mecklenburg-Pomerania in a simplified form, often covered with a trapezoidal mound, when the dysse was still in use in Schleswig-Holstein. The pottery found in these graves is of Funnel Beaker type, not far removed from Baalberg types, to judge from cup forms. In turn, these Mecklenburg-Pomeranian graves may well have inspired the wedge-shaped or trapezoidal mounds of Kujavian type found eastward from the Oder into Poland. Unfortunately, most of the Kujavian mounds are undatable, but at Gaj there is a settlement with Funnel Beaker C ware covered by a Kujavian barrow (Neustupný, 1961a, pp. 444-45). This would suggest that the Kujavian barrows are later than their prototypes in Mecklenburg and Pomerania.

The attribution of the beginning phase of the Dutch and northwestern German passage graves to the period before the Scandinavian passage graves is supported by C-14 dates. A radiocarbon determination for a small quantity of charcoal from a flat grave containing two funnel beakers found under the mound of a megalithic grave at Odoorn in Drenthe (GrN-2226) was 2777 ± 80 B.C. (Vogel and Waterbolk, 1963, p. 177). It provides a terminus post quem for the Passage Grave culture in the Netherlands. Since the first pottery of Funnel Beaker type to be found in the Netherlands, where it occurs in passage graves, cist graves, and flat graves, is of C type, the Odoorn date may indicate that the intrusion of the western megalithic into the Netherlands cannot have been long after 2777 B.C. Such a chronology would fit well with that projected here for the Scandinavian Funnel Beaker C phase, the Salzmünde, later Baalberg, and late Jordansmühl cultures. Interestingly, bronze fragments and a high footed bowl from an early passage grave at Drouwen (Hunebed D.-19) and two copper spirals from a similar grave at Buinen (Hunebed D.-28) have excellent connections in the late Jordansmühl culture (De Laet, 1958, pp. 87-88; Giffen, 1925, I, pp. 56-60, 79-81). The subsequent development of the Passage Grave culture can be followed as far as the intrusion of the Corded Ware cultures into the Netherlands and to the period of the later Tiefstichtonwäre in northwestern Germany, which was paralleled by the Walternienburg pottery in central Germany and the degenerate Passage Grave wares in northeastern Germany (Knöll, 1959, pp. 152-55).

The Corded Ware and Single Grave Cultures

The Single Grave and Corded Ware cultures, which are found throughout transalpine Europe, form a cultural horizon of great importance, but because these cultures developed over such a long period this horizon must be used with considerable care when applied to chronological problems. The beginning phase of these cultures in northern Europe is probably indicated when they appear as intrusive elements in the later Passage

Grave culture of the Netherlands and northwestern Germany, the Walternienburg-Bernburg culture of central Germany, and the later Passage Grave culture of southern Scandinavia. In time, these cultures, which were everywhere characterized by their single burials (generally under tumuli), corded pottery, and battle axes, came to dominate all of northern Europe.

In Scandinavia, the first phase of the Single Grave culture, which has strong ties with the Corded Ware cultures to the south, is found intrusive in Jutland and southern Sweden. It has just enough contact with the coastal megalithic Passage Grave culture to indicate that the early Bottom Grave phase, as it is called in Jutland, and the Continental, as it is called in southern Sweden, can be dated to Middle Neolithic III. The subsequent upper Bottom Grave and lower Ground Grave subphases, which occur in Jutland and spread to the Danish islands during the lower Ground Grave phase, can be dated by pottery contacts to Middle Neolithic IV. In Sweden, this is the period of the Early Swedish Single Grave culture, when the so-called boat-ax variety of battle ax was fully developed. It has been compared by many authors with a copper version found in eastern Russia, but this comparison is not specifically useful for chronology. The final phase of the Single Grave culture in southern Scandinavia is known from the upper Ground Graves and Upper Graves of Denmark and the Younger Swedish group, which are linked to Middle Neolithic V. This phase has numerous foreign connections. Copper axes, double stone axes, and flint daggers are taken to indicate relations with Bohemia and the middle Danube, where imports of amber beads are taken as reflexes of the trade with the north. Exports of amber to Britain, France, and Brittany were part of a trade which brought back Irish halberds and bell beakers (Brøndsted, 1960, pp. 265-85; Becker, 1961b, p. 592). None of these types have sufficiently narrow time ranges abroad to make them specifically useful in the construction of an absolute chronology. Bell beakers, for example, were current over a long period of time in western and central Europe. Their importation into Scandinavia was limited; only four have been found in Denmark. The bell beaker from the passage grave at Bigum in Denmark seems late, and possibly derives from central Europe (Brøndsted, 1960, p. 309). There are C-14 dates for a Bell Beaker level at Heidmoor in Schleswig-Holstein. Wood from immediately below this level (H-28-33) dated 2139 ± 170 B.C., whereas carbonized wood from immediately above (H-27-25) dated 1881 ± 150 B.C., suggesting that bell beakers were current in this area during the twentieth century B.C. (Münnich, 1957, p. 197), Such a date would be in full agreement with C-14 dates for the later Beaker cultures in western Europe. These Heidmoor dates, together with the Dutch date of 2500-2300 B.C. for the beginning of the Bell Beaker phase in the north, are suggestive of the possible chronological range of the Single Grave culture and Middle Neolithic III-V. They are partly supported by a C-14 date of 1830 ± 130 B.C. for a charcoal sample from the main settlement at Nesvikja II (T-162) in western Norway, which is assigned to the latter part of the Middle Neolithic (Nydal, 1960, p. 94). C-14 dates such as the Dutch date of ca. 2500-2300 B.C., which might fix the beginning of Bell Beaker influence in the north, and the Heidmoor and Nesvikja dates, which fall in the latter part of the Middle Neolithic, probably in Middle Neolithic V, are only suggestive of the chronological range of the Single Grave culture and Middle Neolithic III-V. Many more radiocarbon dates are needed before the absolute dates suggested in Table I are anything more than guesses. (See Malmer, 1962, pp. 677-821 on the difficulties of correlating the Single Grave culture with the Passage Grave and Pitted Ware cultures).

The latter part of the Middle Neolithic in Scandinavia was an age of increasing complexity, and it is often difficult to separate Passage Grave, Single Grave, and Pitted Ware elements. In Sweden, finds from Fagervik III suggest that Single Grave-Battle Ax peoples came into contact with the Pitted Ware culture as it was reaching its classic phase (Bagge, 1951a, pp. 57-118). Whatever their origin, the peoples of the Pitted Ware culture raided into northeastern Denmark and were the intermediaries in the flint trade with the Arctic north (Becker, 1950, p. 271). These diverse elements were already beginning to coalesce toward the end of the Middle Neolithic, foreshadowing the more unified Cist Grave culture of the Late Neolithic period, which is usually equated with the period of the Únětice culture in central Europe.

On the northern European plain, Corded Ware cultures extend from the Netherlands eastward across Germany into Poland. Although many theories which have been advanced concerning their origins have bearing upon the chronology of these cultures and the relative chronology of northern Europe, here it can only be postulated that the Single Grave and Corded Ware cultures arose in eastern Europe and spread by various routes to the west (see recent summary of Sturms, 1961, pp. 779-86).

The Globe Amphorae episode, which is so important for this problem and is marked by burials in central Germany—as in the Baalberg barrow—must be linked to east Europe (Ehrich, p. 438; Gimbutas, p. 490, below).

After the Corded Ware peoples had settled on the northern plains, distinct regional groups of their culture emerged in Saxony and Thuringia, along the Oder, in northwestern Germany, and in the Netherlands. Only the Saxo-Thuringian and Dutch groups are adequately established in terms of relative chronology. The relative chronological position of the Corded Ware culture (Mildenberger, 1953, pp. 23-47) is established by the sequence of Baalberg, Walternienburg II/Bernburg I, Globe Amphorae, and Corded Ware burials in the Baalberg barrow; of Bernburg, Corded Ware, and Aunjetitz (Únětice) in the Helmsdorf barrow; and of Baalberg, Corded Ware, Globe Amphorae, and Aunjetitz burials in the Defflinger barrow, together with similar sequences of burials in more than thirty other such barrows in central Germany. Without considering the complicated question of the correlations of its phases of internal development, it is clear everywhere that the Corded Ware culture overlapped the late Walternienburg-Bernburg culture and preceded the Aunjetitz—or Únětice—and was more or less contemporary with Globe Amphorae and late Bell Beaker in central Germany. The Corded Ware culture along the Oder has beakers similar to those of the Saxo-Thuringian group, but it lacks the amphorae. On the other hand, flower pot vessels link it with the late Single Grave culture in Denmark, suggesting it survived until the eve of the Bronze Age.

It is generally believed that the Corded Ware peoples spread westward from central Germany into Hannover and Westphalia, where pottery similar to that of the Saxo-Thuringian group turns up in late passage graves along with Bell Beaker wares. In the Netherlands, where Corded Ware culture can now be shown to have preceded the Bell Beaker, the earliest pottery from both flat graves and barrows is exactly like that of western and central Germany. The Corded Ware culture, which established itself mainly in the region near Veluwe in the eastern Netherlands, can be traced through five phases (De Laet, 1958, pp. 97-99). The first phase is marked by beakers with a slender S-profile and a small protruding foot, which can be dated by radiocarbon determinations. The C-14 date for charcoal associated with an early beaker with protruding foot at Anlo (GrN-1855) is 2602 ± 55 B.C., a very high date. Charcoal from the central grave at Ede (Gro-330), which yielded a similar early beaker, dated 2370 ± 120 B.C.; determinations on charcoal from a grave at Schaarsbergen (Gro-318) with similar pottery yielded again a high date of 2618 ± 320 B.C. (Vogel and Waterbolk, 1963, p. 180; De Vries, Barendsen, and Waterbolk, 1958, p. 135). High dates such as those of Ede and Schaarsbergen suggest that the Corded Ware peoples had certainly reached the Netherlands by 2600 B.C. It may well be that the Corded Ware culture, with its pastoral economy, had filtered slowly across Europe and had reached the Netherlands as early as this date. In central Germany, the stratigraphy of many of the barrows, such as those at Bohlen-Zeschwitz and Burgorner, indicates that the Corded Ware and Walternienburg cultures might well be contemporary (Mildenberger, 1953, pp. 26-27). The situation of Walternienburg settlements on heights which were probably fortified suggests that they existed in troubled times. On the other hand, the presence of corded ware in the late passage graves of Hannover suggests that there was no sudden destruction of older cultures. As a working hypothesis, it might be postulated that the Corded Ware culture probably filtered into central and northern Europe over a long period and did not become dominant until much later. Such a time might be fixed at the point when there is clear Corded Ware influence upon the Bell Beaker culture. The earliest C-14 date for such influence is for charcoal from a flat grave at Anlo (GrN-851) which has two all-over-corded beakers (Vogel and Waterbolk, 1963, p. 180). This date—2314 ± 70 B.C.—suggests that the Corded Ware peoples did not become dominant until the late twenty-fourth century B.C. These radiocarbon dates suggest that Corded Ware cultures may well have begun to spread westward across Europe between 2600 and 2400 B.C., and achieve some sort of consolidation between 2400 and 2300 B.C. An attribution of the earliest Corded Ware to as early as 2600 B.C. on the basis of the Dutch dates is further supported by a recently determined date of 2438 ± 70 B.C. for charcoal (GrN-4065) from the burnt floor of a house at Homolka. This house belongs to a late phase of the Řivnáč culture, which overlapped the fully developed Corded Ware culture (I am indebted to R. Ehrich for information concerning this date). In some areas such as southern Scandinavia, they may not have become a factor until much later, if the later Middle Neolithic actually dates to the latter part of the third and early second millennia B.C. Once established, these Corded Ware-Single Grave cultures continued until the rise of the Únětice-Aunjetitz culture in central Europe and the consolidation of the Cist Grave period in southern Scandinavia, whose beginning dates are subject to as much controversy as those presented in this paper.

These high dates for the Corded Ware cultures were indeed alarming to me, as were many others in this paper upon first encounter. The dates for the Corded Ware cultures seem, however, to fit with new archaeological evidence that is coming to light in southeastern Europe, the Aegean, and the Near East and which can only be noted here. The date of the first expansion of the peoples of the southern Russian steppe may well be reflected in the movement of the peoples who destroyed Troy I (ca. 2600 B.C.) and ultimately accounted for the spread of Troy I culture not only into southwestern Anatolia (Beycesultan XVI) but westward into Macedonia, where they introduced the Early Bronze Age (Mellaart, 1962, p. 23; see above, Weinberg, p. 305). This high date for the first expansion of Corded Ware peoples also fits well with the time of the arrival of the Grey Ware culture in northern Iran (Hissar II), which is now dated to the time of the late Early Dynastic period in Mesopotamia (see above, Dyson, p. 240). The assignment of the first expansion of steppe peoples (who must have already developed a pastoral economy) to the early third millennium is further supported by climatic evidence. The full impact of the Sub-Boreal climate, which began about 3100 B.C. (see above, p. 349), would not have been felt immediately, but well before the middle of the third millennium its effect must have produced an environment more suitable to the nomad than the peasant. The later and more important expansion of steppe peoples which brought the consolidation of their cultures in central and northern Europe has been placed here as early as 2400-2300 B.C. on the basis of C-14 dates. Such a dating is in conflict with a carbon date of 2715 ± 65 for charcoal (GrN-1995) but in agreement with a date of 2262 ± 160 B.C. for wood (Bln-29) from grave I of tumulus I at Baia-Hamangia in Rumania (Quitta, 1960, p. 184; Kohl and Quitta, 1963, p. 297; Vogel and Waterbolk, 1963, p. 184). It should be noted that the Groningen date is probably too high. The Baia-Hamangia ocher grave probably belonged to the Usatovo culture, whose expansion put an end to the Gumelnitza culture and may lie behind the movement of peoples who brought about the destruction of Troy II (ca. 2300/2200 B.C.) (Mellaart, 1960, p. 276); see above, Weinberg, p. 305; and below, Ehrich, pp. 438-39). This same movement must be related in some way to the destruction levels marking the end of Early Helladic II in Greece. It is now generally assumed that these destructions mark the arrival of the Indo-Europeans in the Aegean world (Caskey, 1960, p. 301). This high chronology for the movements of peoples of the steppe, long recognized as Indo-Europeans and horse nomads, is further supported by the appearance of the horse in the Aegean (oral communication from Paul F. K. Åström) and the Near East before 2000 B.C. The appearance of the horse in the Near East in the late third millennium must be assumed from Emery's report of the discovery of horse bones from the Nubian fortress of Buhen, which is dated to the Middle Kingdom (Emery, 1959, p. 250).

This tentative chronology of the Neolithic cultures of northern Europe has been put forward in order to determine in a preliminary way how the new C-14 dates co-ordinate with our archaeological evidence. Of course, many more C-14 dates are needed before a firm chronology can be achieved, but archaeological theory and evidence must not be neglected in chronological studies. The radiocarbon dates provide at best only a rough guide for chronology because of difficulties growing out of this method of dating. Nevertheless they do suggest that there must be a general revision of many of our theories of cultural origin and development. The radiocarbon dates for northern Europe indicate that the cultures of Neolithic man flowed one into the other. We must not expect in actuality the sharp boundaries we use in our tables. Radiocarbon dating will probably never provide a basis for a chronology consisting of a series of water-tight compartments such as was demanded in the past by system-minded archaeologists.

B.C.	Climate	Schleswig &	Denmark and South Sweden		C.Sweden
		LATE NEOLITHIC	LATE NEOLITHIC		Nesvikja 1830 ± 130
2000		1881 ± 150 Heidmoor 2139 ± 170	V		
			IV SINGLE GRAVE CULTURE		CLASSIC PITTED WARE
			III Ferslev 2612 ± 120		
			II Tustrup 2571 ± 120		
2500			I 2623 ± 120 MIDDLE NEOLITHIC		EARLY PITTED WARE
			Mulbjerg 2963 ± 80	Vatteryd 2880 ± 175 3011 ± 205	
3000		C	C		Vrå
	SUB-BOREAL				
		Heidmoor 3220 ± 105 3344 ± 115	B		
				Elinelund 3668 ± 245	
3500		A/B FUNNEL BEAKER	A EARLY NEOLITHIC		Mogetorp 3708 ± 135
		Rüde 3838 ± 50 3910 ± 70			
4000					
		Ellerbek 4291 ± 200			
		ELLERBEK	ERTEBØLLE		
4500		MESOLITHIC			
	ATLANTIC				

B.C.	Rhineland	Netherlands	N.Germany	C.Germany	N.W.Poland	S.Poland
	ADIERBERG		LATE NEOLITHIC	AUNJETITZ	"AUNJETITZ"	TOMASCHOW
2000						
		Anlo 2314 ± 70 Ede 2370 ± 120 Schaarsberg-en 2618 ± 320 Anlo 2602 ± 55		CORDED WARE GLOBULAR AMPHORA WALTERNIEN-BURG	RADIAL WARE CORDED WARE GLOBULAR AMPHORA	ZLØTA
	BELL BEAKER					
2500	CORDED WARE	BEAKER	CORDED WARE	↑	E	
		Odoorn 2777 ± 80			D	
		PASSAGE GRAVES	PASSAGE GRAVES	Dölauer H. 2818 ± 100 2973 ± 100		Ćmielów 2865 ± 11
3000			C	SALZMÜNDE	C	
	MICHELSBERG			BAALBERG		
3500			A/B FUNNEL BEAKER	Wahlitz 3509 ± 200	A/B FUNNEL BEAKER	
				Zwenkau 4065 ± 120 4127 ± 100		
	RÖSSEN			GATERSLEBEN STROKED WARE RÖSSEN		
4000						
		Sittard 4013 ± 140 4333 ± 140 4436 ± 150		Zwenkau 4394 ± 70 Westeregeln 4276 ± 100 4374 ± 100 4436 ± 200	DANUBIAN	
	DANUBIAN	DANUBIAN		DANUBIAN		
4500						
			MESOLITHIC			

Bibliography

Bagge, A.

1951a "Fagervik, ein Rückgrat für die Periodeneinteilung der ostschwedischen Wohnplatz und Bootaxtkulturen aus dem Mittelneolithikum," Acta Archaeologica 22: 57-118.

1951b "Settlements, Houses, Fortifications; Stone Age and Bronze Age." In Swedish Archaeological Bibliography, 1939-1948, pp. 44-59. Uppsala.

Barendsen, G. W., Deevey, E. S., and Gralenski, L. J.

1957 "Yale Natural Radiocarbon Measurements III," Science 126: 908-19.

Becker, C. J.

1947 "Mosefundne Lerkar fra yngre Stenalder." In Aarbøger for nordisk Oldkyndighed og Historie, pp. 1-318.

1950 "Den grubekeramiske Kultur in Danmark." In ibid., pp. 153-274.

1954 "Stenalderbebyggelsen ved Store Valby i Vestsjaelland." In ibid., pp. 127-97.

1961a "Aktuelle Probleme der Trichterbecherkultur." In Bericht über den V Internationalen Kongress für Vor- und Frühgeschichte Hamburg, pp. 68-73. Berlin: Verlag Gebr. Mann.

1961b "Probleme der neolithischen Kulturen in Nordeuropa vom Anfang der Trichterbecherkultur bis zum Auftretten der Schnurkeramiker." In L'Europe à la fin de l'âge de la pierre, pp. 585-94. Prague: Éditions de l'Académie tchécoslovaque des Sciences.

1961c "Über den Ursprung von Michelsberg und der Trichterbecherkultur." In ibid., pp. 595-601.

Behrens, H.

1963 "Mehrgliedrige Grabenanlage um Siedlung der Salzmünder Kultur bei Halle (Saale)," Ausgrabungen und Funde, Nachrichtenblatt für Vor- und Frühgeschichte 8: 18-21.

Berg, H.

1951 "Klintebakken. En boplads fra yngre stenalder på Langeland." In Meddelelser fra Langelands Museum, pp. 7-18. Rudkøbing.

Brøndsted, J.

1960 Nordische Vorzeit, I. Steinzeit in Dänemark. Neumünster: Karl Wachholtz Verlag.

Caskey, J. L.

1960 "The Early Helladic Period in the Argolid," Hesperia 39: 285-303.

Childe, V. G.

1958 The Dawn of European Civilization. 6th ed. New York: Knopf.

Chmielewski, W.

1952 "Zugadnienie grobowców Kujawskich w świetle ostatnich badan," Biblioteka Muzeum Archeologicznym w Łodzi 2.

Daniel, G.

1958 The Megalithic Builders of Western Europe. New York: Praeger.

Dehnke, R.

1940 Die Tiefstichtonware der Jungsteinzeit in Osthannover. ("Veröffentlichungen der urgeschichtlichen Sammlungen des Landesmuseums zu Hannover," Vol. 5.) Hildesheim and Leipzig.

Driehaus, J.

1959 "Die Gliederung des böhmischen und mährischen Jungneolithikums als forschungsgeschichtliches Problem," Germania 37: 53-65.

Driehaus, J., and Behrens, H.

1961 "Stand und Aufgaben der Erforschung des Jungneolithikums in Mitteleuropa." In L'Europe à la fin de l'âge de la pierre, pp. 233-75. Prague: Éditions de l'Académie tchécoslovaque des Sciences.

Driehaus, J., and Pleslová, E.

1961 "Aspekte zur Beurteilung des Äneolithikum Böhmen und Mähren." In L'Europe à la fin de l'âge de la pierre, pp. 361-78. Prague: Éditions de l'Académie tchécoslovaque des Sciences.

Emery, W. B.

1959 "A Master-Work of Egyptian Military Architecture of 3900 Years Ago: The Great Castle of Buhen in the Sudan - New Discoveries, Including the Earliest Horse Known in Egypt," Illustrated London News (September 12), 250-51.

Fischer, U.

1951 "Zu den mitteldeutschen Trommeln," Archaeologia Geographica 2: 98-105.

1961 "Zum Problem der spätneolithischen Gruppenbildung an Saale und mittlerer Elbe." In L'Europe à la fin de l'âge de la pierre, pp. 415-29. Prague: Éditions de l'Académie tchécoslovaque des Sciences.

Giffen, A. E. van

1925 De Hunebedden in Nederland, I. Utrecht: A. Oosthoek.

Godwin, H.

1961 "The Croonian Lecture, Radiocarbon Dating and the Quaternary History in Britain," Proceedings of the Royal Society, Series B, Vol. 153: 287-320.

1962 "The Half-Life of Radiocarbon 14," Nature 195: 984.

Godwin, H., Walker, D., and Willis, E. H.

1957 "Radiocarbon Dating and Post-glacial Vegetational History: Scaleby Moss," Proceedings of the Royal Society, Series B, Vol. 147: 352-66.

Hinsch, E.

1955 "Tragtbegerkultur-Megalitkultur." In Årbok, Universitetets Oldsaksamling. Oslo.

Höfer, P.

1902 "Baalberge." In Jahresschrift für die Vorgeschichte der sächsisch-thuringischen Länder, 1, pp. 16-49.

Jażdżewski, K.

1932 "Zusammenfassender Überblick über die Trichterbecherkultur," Praehistorische Zeitschrift 23: 77-110.

1961 "Kultura Pucharów Lejkowatych," Prace I Materiały, Muzeum Archeologicznego i Etnograficznego w Łodzi 6: 73-100.

Kaelas, L.

1952 "En Klockbägarpilspets från Fjärrestadsgånggriften Skåne," Fornvännen 47: 165-75.

Knöll, H.

1959 Die nordwestdeutsche Tiefstichkeramik und ihre Stellung im nord- und mitteleuropäischen Neolithikum. ("Veröffentlichungen der Altertumskommission in Provinzialinstitut für westfalische Landes- und Volkskund," Vol. 3.) Münster.

Kohl, G., and Quitta, H.

1963 "Berlin-Radiokarbondaten archäologischer Proben. I." Ausgrabungen und Funde, Nachrichtenblatt für Vor- und Frühgeschichte 8: 281-301.

Laet, S. J. De

1958 The Low Countries. London: Thames and Hudson.

Laet, S. J. De, and Glasbergen, W.

1959 De voorgeschiedenis der lage Landen. Brussels: J. B. Wolters.

Lomborg, E.

1962 "Zur Frage der bandkeramischen Einflüsse in Südskandinavien," Acta Archaeologica 33: 1-38.

Lüüdik-Kaelas, L.

1955 "Wann sind die ersten Megalithgräber in Holland entstanden?" Palaeohistoria 4: 47-79.

Malmer, M. P.

1962 Jungneolithische Studien. ("Acta Archaeologica Lundensia," Series in 8°, No. 2.) Lund.

Mathiassen, T.

1940 "Havnelev-Strandegaard. Et Bidrag til Diskussionen om den yngre Stenalders begyndelse i Danmark." In Aarbøger for nordisk Oldkyndighed og Historie, pp. 1-55.

Mellaart, J.

1960 "Anatolia and the Balkans," Antiquity 34: 270-78.

Mildenberger, G.

1953 Studien zum Mitteldeutschen Neolithikum. ("Veröffentlichungen des Landesmuseum für Vorgeschichte Dresden," Vol. 2.) Leipzig.

Modderman, P. J. R.

1955 "Een bandceramische nederzetting te Sittard, Limburg," Berichten van de Rijksdienst voor het Oudheidkundig Bodemonderzoek 6: 13-21.

Münnich, K. O.

1957 "Heidelberg Natural Radiocarbon Measurements I," Science 126: 194-99.

Neustupný, E.

1956 Chronologie préhistorique de la Tchécoslovaquie. Prague: Département de Préhistoire, Musée national de Prague, 1956.

1961a "Contributions to the Eneolithic Period in Poland." In L'Europe à la fin de l'âge de la pierre, pp. 441-57. Prague: Éditions de l'Académie tchécoslovaque des Sciences, 1961.

1961b "Die westlichen Kulturen in böhmischen Äneolithikum." In ibid., pp. 313-20.

Neustupný, Evžen and Jiří.

1961 Czechoslovakia before the Slavs. London: Thames and Hudson.

Nydal, R.

1960 "Trondheim Natural Radiocarbon Measurements II," Radiocarbon Supplement 2: 82-96.

Olsson, I.

1959 "Uppsala Natural Radiocarbon Measurements I," Radiocarbon Supplement 1: 87-102.

Preuss, J.

1961 "Die chronologische Stellung der Baalberger, Salzmünder, und Walternienburger Gruppe innerhalb der Trichterbecherkultur Mitteldeutschlands." In L'Europe à la fin de l'âge de la pierre, pp. 405-13. Prague: Éditions de l'Académie tchécoslovaque des Sciences.

Quitta, H.

1958a "Bandkeramische Kultur," Ausgrabungen und Funde, Nachrichtenblatt für Vor- und Frühgeschichte 3: 173-77.

1958b "Die bandkeramische Siedlung Zwenkau-Harth, Kr. Leipzig," ibid., 177-79.

1960 "Zur Frage der ältesten Bandkeramik in Mitteleuropa," Praehistorische Zeitschrift 38: 1-38, 153-88.

Schwabedissen, H.

1958 "Untersuchung mesolithisch-neolithischer Moorsiedlungen in Schleswig-Holstein." In Neue Ausgrabungen in Deutschland, pp. 26-42. Berlin: Verlag Gebr. Mann.

1962 "Northern Continental Europe." In Courses toward Urban Life, pp. 254-66. ("Viking Fund Publications in Anthropology," No. 32.) New York: Viking Fund.

Scollar, I.

1959 "Regional Groups in the Michelsberg Culture," Proceedings of the Prehistoric Society 25: 52-134.

Sprockhoff, E.

1938 Die nordische Megalithkultur. ("Handbuch der Urgeschichte Deutschlands," III.) Berlin and Leipzig.

Sturms, E.

1961 "Die Herkunft der Becher-Bootaxt-Kultur." In Bericht über den V Internationalen Kongress für Vor- und Frühgeschichte Hamburg, pp. 779-86. Berlin: Verlag Gebr. Mann.

Tauber, H.

1958 "Difficulties in the application of C-14 results in Archaeology," Archaeologia Austriaca 24: 59-69.

1960a "Copenhagen Natural Radiocarbon Measurements III: Corrections to Radiocarbon Dates Made with the Solid Carbon Technique," Radiocarbon Supplement 2: 5-11.

1960b "Copenhagen Radiocarbon Dates IV," ibid. 2: 12-25.

1964 "Copenhagen Radiocarbon Dates VI," Radiocarbon 6: 215-25.

Thomas, S. E.

1961 "Secondary Development in the South Swedish Neolithic." In Bericht über den V Internationalen Kongress für Vor- und Frühgeschichte Hamburg, pp. 809-13. Berlin: Verlag Gebr. Mann.

Tilander, I.

1958 "Pollen-analytical Investigation of Two Prehistoric Levels at Vätteryd." In Meddelanden från Lunds universitets historiska museum, pp. 91-102.

Troels-Smith, J.

1953 "Erteb*ø*llekultur-Bondekultur." In Aarbøger for nordisk Oldkyndighed og Historie, pp. 5-62.

Vogel, J. C., and Waterbolk, H. T.

1963 "Groningen Radiocarbon Dates IV," Radiocarbon 5: 163-202.

Vries, H. de

1954 "Measurements of Age by the Carbon 14 Technique," Nature 174: 1138-41.

Vries, H. de, Barendsen, G. W., and Waterbolk, H. T.

1958 "Groningen Radiocarbon Dates II," Science 127: 129-37.

Waterbolk, H. T.

1958-59 "Die bandkeramische Siedlung von Geleen," Palaeohistoria 6-7: (1958-1959), 121-61.

1962 "The Lower Rhine Basin." In Courses toward Urban Life, pp. 227-53. ("Viking Fund Publications in Anthropology," No. 32.) New York: Viking Fund.

Winther, J.

1935 Troldebjerg I. Rudkøbing.

Zápotocký, M.

1957 "K Problému počatků kultury Nálevkových Pohárů (Zum Problem der Anfange der Trichterbecherkultur)." Archeologické rozhledy 9: 206-35.

Addendum:

Several radiocarbon dates have become available since this paper was sent to press. A few of the more important ones might be mentioned, such as the two Copenhagen dates for late Ertebølle culture. Wood from Christiansholms Mose was dated 3519 ± 100 B.C. (K-729) and 3581 ± 100 B.C. (K-750) (Tauber, H. "Copenhagen Radiocarbon Dates VI," Radiocarbon 6 [1964]: 217). Seeds from a Younger Linienbandkeramik occupation of Dresden-Neckern dated 4174 ± 100 B.C. and 4154 ± 100 B.C. (Bln-73, Bln-73a); rotten wood from Grave 4, Burial Mound 6, which probably belonged to the Corded Ware culture, dated 2108 ± 100 B.C. (Bln-65) (Kohl, G., and Quitta, H., "Berlin Radiocarbon Measurements I," Radiocarbon 6 [1964]: 309-11). All these dates agree well with similar or related dates given above in this paper.

It is regretted that articles such as Aner Ekkehard, "Die Stellung der Dolmen Schleswig-Holsteins in der nordischen Megalithkultur," Offa

20 [1963]: 9-23; Reinhard Schindler, "Rössener Elemente im Frühneolithikum von Boberg," Hammaburg 13 [1961]: 9-29; and C. J. Becker, "Sen-neolitikum i Norden, Aktuelle problemer," Tor X [1964]: 131-34 were not in hand in time for consideration in this study.

The material in the two columns N. W. Poland and S. Poland on the chronological chart for northern Europe should be regarded as only tentative. They have been added to aid in the correlation of the northern cultures with those of eastern and east central Europe (See: Ehrich, chart pp. 444-47; Gimbutas chart, p. 494).

Geographical and Chronological Patterns in East Central Europe

Robert W. Ehrich
Brooklyn College of the
City University of New York

Despite the change of name, the area here treated as east central Europe is the same as that covered in my earlier paper (Ehrich, 1954). The new term is more consonant with current practice and accords well with Teleki's (1953) description, the only difference being that I have included parts of Austria and do not discuss Poland and Albania.

Since 1954, when Relative Chronologies in Old World Archeology appeared, there has been so much archaeological activity in the region, accompanied by so much change in the archaeological picture, that a complete rewriting of my original contribution has become necessary. Much of the general development is now somewhat clearer and perhaps more comprehensible; but for the nonspecialist in the area and for the beginning student the whole has become more complex and more difficult to grasp, since, with the increase in information, many more detailed and specific questions have arisen. This paper is therefore primarily intended as a general introduction to the Neolithic and Eneolithic periods and to a lesser extent to the Bronze Age of the area, with lesser concern for a specific site-by-site evaluation of direct imports and other evidences for cross-dating, the details of which can be found in the literature. Archaeological sequences and cross-ties are, of course, an integral part of the discussion, but a too specific analysis at this point would obscure the forest by paying too much attention to the individual trees. It is too much to hope that anyone will be completely happy with the result, particularly with regard to his own area of specialization, but it is high time for such an effort to be made.

Among the sources of confusion are the following.

(1) This is the European shatter belt and, although there is a growing body of publication in German, French, English, Italian, or Russian, the mass of information is still available only through brief summaries in those languages when they accompany the Czech, Slovakian, Hungarian,

Serbian, Croatian, Slovenian, Macedonian, Bulgarian, and Rumanian texts.

(2) Because of the sharply observed present political boundaries, the terminology applied to the various cultures and groups has become needlessly complicated. Thus, in different countries the same culture complex may carry completely different names based on different eponymous sites, or may have the same basic name modified by regional or language variants. For example, Yugoslavian Starčevo is the general equivalent of Hungarian Körös and Rumanian Criş.

(3) Intense archaeological activity has resulted in various revisions of earlier major studies, and much earlier terminology is now awkward, inapplicable, or dropped from use. Thus, although one may have to refer to what was written twenty to fifty years ago, he must translate it into current usage.

(4) Many present-day studies have a strong local focus and are limited to areas within national boundaries, or tend to be schematic without much reference to geographic entities. Although many political boundaries do follow natural geographic divisions, some of them do not, as, for example, the Banat.

(5) The degree of archaeological activity and of publication has been exceedingly uneven, and our knowledge is spotty.

(6) We are frequently faced with semantic difficulties—as when the use of such words as "culture" and "group" is not clear—and the meaning is consequently obscure.

We thus have basic problems in accessibility through the languages used, an unnecessary degree of confusion in appellation, changes in terminology that make continuity between older and newer literature more difficult to manage, and, beyond broad and general distinctions and local focus of interest, a tendency to ignore geographic regions as entitites.

THE GEOGRAPHICAL SETTING (See Map, p. 443)

For the purposes of this symposium, my treatment encompasses the entire drainage of the middle and lower Danube basins and includes certain fringe areas as well. Although the key concept in the organization of this paper is that the archaeological picture can best be understood with due reference to geographical entities, it has been necessary to utilize some of the more familiar political units and to relate and rearrange their subdivisions according to need. I have already expressed my view that culture areas and culture boundaries on various levels of magnitude persist or reappear during the course of culture history (Ehrich, 1956, 1961), and this theme is one of my underlying suppositions.

Beginning in the north, Bohemia as the western province of Czechoslovakia is a fringe area, geographically distinct from the rest of the country. It is diamond-shaped, enclosed by low, worn, not difficult mountain ranges or heights on all four sides. Of great significance is the fact that it includes all the upper waters of the Elbe and its tributaries, the Vltava (Moldau), Ohře (Eger), Jizera (Iser), and the like, and that it has no other drainage. It consists of the lower-lying, fertile loess lands of the north, open to influences through the Elbe gap, and also from the Glatzer depression, across the Sudetens on the northeast; a western basin in the Plzeň area, often influenced or penetrated from across the Erzgebirge on the northwest side; and a rugged, inhospitable plateau to the south, deeply trenched by the Vltava (Moldau). Little contact seems to have taken place across the Böhmerwald (Česky Les) on the southwest, but considerable influence and influx crossed the Czecho-Moravian Heights from Moravia to the east and southeast.

Although not a part of the Danube drainage, neither does Bohemia culturally belong with the North European Plain, in spite of the fact that the Elbe traverses it to the northwest, nor does it really belong with the German areas to the west, although it is geologically a part of the Hercynean system. As a geographico-cultural fringe area, it provides many chronological links between the Danube basin, the North European Plain, and western Europe.

East of Bohemia lies the middle Danube drainage. Here is another source of potential confusion, for there are two Morava rivers, both of which are tributaries of the Danube. One flows southward, its broad, fertile valley forming the central Czechoslovakian province of Moravia; the other starts above the headwaters of the Vardar and flows northward through Yugoslavia. For purposes of clarity, we emphasize the province of Moravia when discussing the Czechoslovakian river Morava (German March), and the Morava Valley when speaking of the Yugoslavian one.

The north end of Moravia crosses the low divide separating the upper Morava from the Oder drainage, thus forming the Moravian corridor through which cultural impulses, diffusion, and migration from the south moved northward to the Oder system or to debouch on to the North

European Plain, with an occasional reflux or southward penetration. As a settlement area, the southern loess land of the broad Moravian plain, both topographically and culturally, was usually related to the Little Alföld of northwest Hungary, the Burgenland, and to the Danube Valley of Lower Austria, westward as far as the Enns River area.

Although outliers may have reached the Traun and Salzach, even as far as Salzburg, beyond this point the cultural systems belong with the Alpine foreland, Bavaria, and southeast Germany. The Enns River area, then, forms the rough western edge of our area (Pittioni, 1954, 1960; Willvonseder, 1934, p. 188).

Along the east side of Moravia the westernmost ridges of the Carpathian system swing northward and then eastward in a large, flat arc of parallel ranges to form the structure of Slovakia. To some extent the present Polish-Czechoslovakian border follows the watershed between the Danube drainage and those of the Oder and Vistula systems which flow northward to the Baltic. The three parallel ranges of the High Tatra, the Low Tatra, and the Slovakian Ore Mountains are separated by the Váh (Waag) and Hron (Gran) rivers, which flow westward in broad, flat valleys and then bend southward to flow directly into the Danube. South of the Slovakian Ore Mountains is the Danube Valley which physiographically belongs with the north Hungarian plain.

Further east, the more complex mountainous areas of east Slovakia and Ruthenia are laced by the headwaters of various affluents of the Tisza and by the Tisza itself. Wheeling eastward, then southward, and then returning westward as the Transylvanian Alps to form the north border of the Danube Valley, the folded ranges of the Carpathian arc set off the mountainous Transylvanian basin from the Moldavian plateau, the plain of eastern Rumania, and from the lower Danube Valley. It is highly significant with relation to cultural distributions that, with the exception of the Olt—which breaches the mountain wall and drains its southeastern part—the entire drainage system of Transylvania is westward to the Tisza via the Körös (Criş) and Maros (Mureş) systems, and only ultimately to the Danube.

Beyond the mountains on the east, the Siret and Prut rivers run parallel to the Carpathian ranges and flow into the Danube near its mouth. These define the Rumanian province of Moldavia, which is the eastern border of the area treated in this paper. However, the culture patterns of this strip belong, for the most part, with those of Bessarabia and are found eastward, at least as far as the Dniester, usually to the Southern Bug, and the Tripolye culture extends to the Dnieper (Passek, 1962a, Figs. 1-6; Gimbutas, p. 460, below). As with the two Morava rivers, it is necessary to point out that there are two Bug rivers. The Western Bug flows into the Narew and is a part of the eastern drainage system of the Vistula, thus eventually reaching the Baltic. Part of its course coincides with part of the current eastern boundary of Poland. The Southern Bug (or Boh), on the other hand, flows southward through the southern Ukraine to empty into the Black Sea not far from the mouth of the Dnieper.

Except for the upper Olt region of southeastern Transylvania, the middle Danube drainage takes in the entire territory lying within the Carpathian arc, the hilly area of Transdanubia west of the Danube to the foot of the Alps, and the entire western and southern drainage area of the Danube itself, including the eastward-flowing Drave and Save and the northward-flowing Morava of Yugoslavia, together with their extensive dendritic systems. The division between the middle and lower Danube basins is the Iron Gate, running between Oršova and Turnu-Severin.

Within this vast area, a few geographico-cultural divisions are not only recognizable, but are critical in organizing and interpreting the archaeological materials. To begin with, a major north-south division is formed by the originally inhospitable and treacherous area between the Danube and the Tisza. Although not well explored, it seems to have remained almost uninhabited until Bodrogkeresztúr (Middle Copper Age) times. The east Hungarian plain was linked to the interior of Transylvania, but its segments, as marked by the Maros and Koros, show differences from south to north. The southernmost area of this strip below the mountains and lying between the Danube, Tisza, and Temes rivers, is known as the Banat. It is flat, fertile, and now forms the western corner of Rumania, the northeast corner of Yugoslavia, and a small part of southeast Hungary, with their respective political boundary lines traversing it.

West of the Danube, the Bakony Hills and Lake Balaton provide another boundary zone running northeast-southwest. This region too is not well explored, but there are differences between what is found in the loess plains to the north and in the hilly country to the south. Not surprisingly, the Burgenland immediately to the west draws from both areas.

Further to the south and southwest, the upper drainages of the Drave and Save systems form an area of composite culture, made up in varying degrees of elements pushing upstream from the east, Transdanubian ones working southward around the eastern flank of the Alps, northward diffusion from the regions south and southwest of the Save, and occasional characters that seem to have penetrated from the upper Danube across the Alpine passes. The nucleus of this east Alpine region takes in most of Carniola, Carinthia, Styria, part of northwest Croatia, and adjacent territories.

A further major division is the watershed along the Dinaric Alpine slopes of western Yugoslavia. The cultures of the Adriatic drainage tie closely to the littoral complex, and are related to Italy and to other parts of the Mediterranean. With few exceptions, there is no cultural relationship and little contact between the Adriatic side and the plateaus and river valleys across the mountains which ultimately drain into the Danube.

Eastward, the Vardar and Morava river valleys, often bruited as a cultural and migratory pathway, served as a settlement area in which the cultures were composite (containing elements that were independently diffused), and was generally a zone of division between east and west.

Below the Iron Gate the lower Danube flows through a broad plain, defined on its north by the Transylvanian Alps and on its south by the long Balkan ranges of the Stara Planina. Here the Danube itself seems to be a unifying feature in the cultural landscape, for within this broad trough there is usually little difference in what is found in Rumania to the north and in Bulgaria to the south. Cultural divisions run from north to south, a major one in Rumania being the Olt drainage which divides Oltenia from Muntenia. In Bulgaria the archaeological patterns are only beginning to emerge. There seems to be a culture boundary somewhere in the neighborhood of the Isker River, separating the cultures of the western part of the lower Danube from those of the eastern part. A southern limit during the earlier periods seems to lie along the Rhodope Mountains south of the Marica rather than along the Stara Planina which served during later times. South of the Rhodopes the streams flow into the Aegean. Our archaeological knowledge of Greek and Turkish Thrace is so limited as to be almost unusable. (After this paper had gone to press, my attention was called to an article by Srejović [1963] in Archaeologia Iugoslavica in which he makes use of the same type of geographical approach to his historical interpretation of the Vinča culture and utilizes much the same boundaries and subareas of Yugoslavia and the lower Danube that I have outlined above.)

Some General Archaeological Considerations

In our discussion, it will become evident that there is a marked difference in the degree to which various territories have been explored. It is particularly unfortunate for our purpose that the most critical area of all has seen the least research and is the least known. This is the band that runs westward from the Bosporus to the Adriatic, forming the boundary zone between the major culture areas of continental Europe and the north Mediterranean. It includes Turkish and Greek Thrace, the major parts of Greek and Yugoslavian Macedonia, and the mountain systems that stretch across to and encompass Albania. Cross-dating between the Balkans and the Aegean is seriously hampered by the lack of work in this intervening region, and although much has been said about links across it, the gap is too wide to allow out-of-hand acceptance of most of the cited resemblances or to arrive at satisfactory or convincing interpretations.

A characteristic of most of the middle Danube and Bohemian areas is the paucity of stratified sites. The majority show occupation of a single period only and, where stratified sites do occur, the levels tend to be thin and often disturbed. This is a temperate zone, where the buildings were of wood which rotted away to leave thin strata. Heavy deposits are not, for the most part, characteristic, although they do occur in the Herpály culture and later in the Hungarian Bronze Age.

The lack of deep, stratified deposits with comfortably thick and relatively undisturbed layers has meant that many of the various sequential and chronological interpretations have of necessity been based on geographical distributions, intrusive finds, sequences of disturbance, and typology. Thus, in specific instances we frequently face the question of whether we are dealing with age differences, regional variants, or a combination of both. Furthermore, as indicated in the earlier volume, although there is generally a ratio between the age of an excavation and the degree to which it is unreliable, even some modern excavations raise questions, not only about technique, but about the interpretation of impeccably excavated sites. Thus, the appearance of two distinguishable complexes in the same stratum may indicate contemporaneity, or one may represent a small earlier layer thoroughly disturbed and churned into the ground by a later group who occupied the same site shortly afterward. Even when such mixed material is found in pits which are closed units, it may indicate contemporaneity, contamination, or possibly backfill by the later group. In other words, without deeply stratified sites, the repeated finding of a situation and the isolation of complexes in separate sites is necessary before we can discard alternative possibilities in favor of a fairly definite interpretation that will stand. Even a clearly stratified sequence can be highly misleading, as witness the discussion of the site of Tószeg below (pp. 434-35). Small-scale sounding or salvage operations, although often extremely helpful, can also add to the confusion if not interpreted with caution.

In this paper we use the term "culture" to mean the way of life of a coherent group of any size, whether it be extended to encompass broad similarities or limited to a nexus of very minute ones. A "pottery group," as here conceived, is not necessarily equated with a culture, but refers to different types or kinds of pots that are repeatedly found in association with each other.

The word "complex" denotes a basic cluster of traits usually found together, in either cultural or group patterns, but which may diffuse as linked elements—such as given types of pots—or perhaps only certain typical ceramic characters together with recognizable stone or bone forms, burial types, and the like. It thus includes not only the concept of a characteristic assemblage but also the shifting combinations of its traits.

A further difficulty lies in the nomenclature of general periods. In the different regions of our area, different categorical terms often describe related cultures or groups that equate in time. Thus, some cultures classed as Eneolithic in Bohemia have counterparts called Bronze Age in Hungary. I therefore divide this treatment into three periods labeled Early, Middle, and Late, for I think it preferable to use descriptive words rather than Childe's numbered sequence, which is tantamount to the same thing but which gives a false sense of accuracy and tends to obscure the real problems of time relationships or lack thereof.

Although the same geographical divisions appear and reappear, they are often temporarily obliterated or lost from view, and an organization by time with the repetition of spatial considerations thus seems preferable to a spatial organization with the recurrence of time units.

Furthermore, since this paper is primarily descriptive of geographical distribution and time sequence rather than of origins, migrations, and diffusions, I have reversed the order of presentation that might seem preferable in historical terms in order to provide the maximum degree of integration with the adjacent chapters. The discussions thus generally move from west to east, tying first to Thomas' two papers which precede it, and then to Gimbutas' paper which follows. This arrangement has the further advantage of matching the discussion to the comparative table, the columns of which fall into rough geographic position with Bohemia on the west and the Karanovo sequence of south Bulgaria on the east.

REGIONAL COMPLEXES BY PERIOD

Early Period

Pre-pottery Neolithic. Although there is now some discussion as to the presence of an aceramic Neolithic in the Balkans and in Central Europe, this seems to be based on similarities in the typology of stone tools with pre-pottery cultures outside the area (see Weinberg, p. 286, above). The occurrence of domesticated animals or plants with the cultural inventory is not convincingly demonstrated, and no good dating has yet appeared to justify the conclusions drawn. Crvena Stijena, it should be noted, lies on the Adriatic slope and belongs in the Mediterranean sphere. We need more definite and specific evidence before the presence of an aceramic Neolithic becomes unequivocally acceptable.

Although such an association may eventually be attested, various elements in the technological inventory might have spread by independent trait or trait complex diffusion without migration and without the technique of domestication. There is also a question as to whether the similarities of the tool types cited actually define relationship, either by migration or diffusion, or whether we have here a generic Mesolithic pattern (see Lichardus and Pavúk, 1963, for a discussion and pertinent bibliography on this question, and Nicolăescu-Plopşor, 1959, for a rejection of Berciu's suggestion that pre-pottery Neolithic exists at Baile Herculane [Berciu, 1958, p. 99]).

Ceramic Neolithic—Regional Patterns

(1) The Center, South, and Southeast. The groups of this area seem to be closely related and, for the most part, occupy the heart of the region. Although those of the southeast may be either the earliest or relatively late, the central area is the best known.

(a) The Körös-Criş-Starčevo complex. The finding of Körös and Starčevo material throughout Rumania and across to the drainage of the Southern Bug (Berciu, 1961a, pp. 104-5; 1961c, p. 560) makes it advisable to add the term Criş to the name of the complex. It should be explained here that the Körös culture takes its name from the Körös River. Körös is the Hungarian form, Criş the Rumanian. Starčevo, on the other hand, is a village in the Yugoslavian part of the Banat. Initial general studies of the Körös culture (Kutzián, 1947) and of Starčevo (Arandjelović-Garašanin, 1954b) have served as the basis for further work and for generalization. The division into periods rests partly on a doubtful statement by Fewkes that at Starčevo painted wares appeared later than unpainted (Ehrich, 1954, pp. 111 ff.) and partly on the finding by Arandjelović-Garašanin of some difference between the upper and lower parts of the deposit of Pit 5a at Starčevo. For the most part, however, chronological distinctions were based on typology (e.g., Milojčić, 1949) and left the uneasy question of whether the Starčevo phases might not have reflected relatively contemporaneous group differences rather than distinctly chronological ones. Although this question still persists to some extent, Zaharia (1962), writing on the soundings at Leţ in Transylvania, reports two distinguishable layers overlying the foundations of an earlier hut. All three of these deposits contained Criş material, and she equates Leţ II and III with Starčevo II and III. She thus logically assumes a correlation between Leţ I and Starčevo I. It should also be noted that she questions (p. 48) the interpretation of a pre-Criş or proto Criş culture tentatively based on a presumed association of pottery with microlithic implements at Dîrtu (Nicolăescu-Plopşor, 1959; Berciu, 1961c, p. 560). (Also, see Trogmayer, 1964, on Körös Chronology.)

The picture of this complex is not yet clear, although the gaps are being rapidly filled. With few exceptions, the Körös sites in Hungary lie along the left bank of the Tisza northward from the Maros (Mureş) junction to that of the Körös, and are found along the drainages of both tributaries into Transylvania. The Körös culture sites contain little, if any, painted pottery, and in this feature particularly they differ from the Starčevo sites farther south. These latter lie in the Danube plain and in the Banat; it is the Starčevo group with painted pottery that extends westward along the Danube and up the Save and Drave rivers into Slavonia. In Transylvania, on the other hand, some Criş sites contain painted pottery and others do not. So far no stratigraphic relationship between these has been observed, so we are still faced with the question of whether there really is a time difference involved or whether the Transylvanian sites are contemporaneous representatives of the Körös and Starčevo variants, the latter having entered the basin by way of the Maros River.

In general the areas of western Slavonia and those to the west of it are not well explored, and neither the westward extent of the Starčevo culture nor whether incised wares penetrated southward into Slovenia and western Slavonia is yet known.

South of the Save, sites with Starčevo culture appear along the Drina and some of its tributaries, the southernmost lying on the Lim near Berane. Westward they approach Bosnia, and tentatively it seems that their elements may go as far as the Adriatic watershed. In any event, no Starčevo sites or traits as such seem to have crossed this boundary, either directly westward or southward across the mountains from the Lim-Drina headwaters to the next river systems, which flow either southward to Lake Scutari or westward to the sea.

Between the littoral complex, which also includes Zelena Pećina and Lisičići on the seaward side, and the unpainted Starčevo wares of the highlands a basic technical distinction is that the characteristic Starčevo barbotine wares do not cross the boundary going westward and, conversely, the cardial wares of the coast do not appear in the uplands. There are, of course, other differences in form and decoration. The so-called fingernail and finger-impressed wares (which are really _Stichverzierung_) occur in both complexes.

Eastward along the south boundary, it is not at all surprising that the west Macedonian wares of Pelagonia in the Bitolj district relate to the south (M. Garašanin, 1959), or that on the Vardar drainage the settlements at Zelenikovo and Vršnik, although containing Starčevo elements, seem to be of somewhat mixed character. Since Vršnik has four strata containing material described as Starčevo, it is almost unique, for a single level seems to be the rule (M. and D. Garašanin, 1961). Galović (1964, p. 27) dates the lower level of Zelenikovo to Vršnik III (Starčevo II) and Olynthus—(probably II-III; cf. Ehrich, 1954, pp. 122-23).

(b) The Kremikovci complex. The eastern boundary of the Starčevo complex is not yet clearly defined, nor is the composition and extent of the related West Bulgarian Kremikovci group to the east. This complex seems closely related to that of Starčevo, with some differences in the paint, designs, and forms. It is known primarily from surface collections and from small test and salvage excavations, and our picture is shadowy. Its boundaries seem to run from the right bank of the Morava, or at least from the drainage along its eastern side, eastward to the Isker Valley in north Bulgaria. It apparently reached the Morava via the Nišava, whence it spread up and down stream. Gaul (1948, pp. 18, 33, 35) reported "scraped ware" sherds, apparently burnished over paint, of Kremikovci type, from two sites on the upper Struma, suggesting a southern limit beyond the Nišava. It is not clear whether sites reported as of the Criş culture, on the plain to the north of the Danube and opposite the Kremikovci area, really belong to the general Transylvanian Criş pattern, or whether they are a part of the Kremikovci sphere as one would expect.

(c) Karanovo. At the site of Karanovo, which lies in the Marica (Maritza) Valley to the north of the Rhodopes, Georgiev (1961) has isolated and described seven major strata, each with various recognizable levels. The earliest—Karanovo I—contains a variety of pottery forms together with some white-on-red painted wares which help to equate it, at least roughly, with Kremikovci and Starčevo-Körös-Criş. In Karanovo II, the painted wares are lost; but since some distinctive shapes—usually unpainted but sometimes painted in Karanovo I—continue in unpainted form into Karanovo II, the painted wares of Karanovo I are certainly a part of that complex. Again, the distribution of this culture is not clear, but it apparently reaches westward to the Isker drainage to border on the Kremikovci area, in which occasional Karanovo finds seem to be intrusive. It may also extend northward to the Danube, and eastward to the Dobrudja, perhaps even to the Black Sea coast.

(2) The Fringes.

(a) The Adriatic drainage. Here the complexes of the various periods are completely separate from those of the highlands, and the sites of the coastal strip and the off-lying islands link essentially with the circum-Adriatic and Italian complexes. Early impresso wares at Smilčić (Batović, 1959), Early Danilo (J. Korošec, 1963), Crvena Stijena III and Zelena Pećina III (Benac, 1957a, 1957b, 1962: 68-75), the Island of Cres (Mirosavljević, 1962), and the Slovenian littoral (J. Korošec, 1960b) extend this group along the western side of Yugoslavia.

(b) The west, north, and east: the Band Ceramics. Fringing the Körös-Criş area, the band ceramic or incised ware groups present a complex pattern of their own. Where they occur, they are usually the earliest manifestations of Neolithic culture and—with the exception of eastern Rumania and perhaps eastern Slovakia, a few stray finds east of the Tisza and in Transylvania, and in the Vinča complex of Yugoslavia, where it is intrusive—the distribution of these two major ceramic groups is mutually exclusive. In rough terms, we can characterize the groups already treated as southeastern and the incised or linear wares as central European. The actual point of origin of this family is obscure, for it appears in strength in early forms both in Germany and in western Czechoslovakia. Because of various traits such as the shoe last celt, loess land patterns of life, and the early excavation of the stratified site of Vinča, this complex has unfortunately acquired the label of Danubian I (Buttler, 1938; Childe, 1929, pp. 36-66; 1947, pp. 97-102, 105-8) although only a few outlying sites, most of them late, are actually in the Danube drainage.

Although not completely satisfactory as a scheme, we can divide the cultures of the Band Ceramics tradition into two periods: Linear (also known as Incised, Volute, volutová, rubanée) and Stroked (Stichbandkeramik, vypíchaná, pointillée), or Ia and Ib respectively. Buttler comments on the relative uniformity of this culture, but isolates a series of local styles in Germany. In central and southeastern Europe, on the other hand, many recognizable differences in the groups of Linear or Incised wares are now attributed to time distinctions and phases, although many are also geographically distinct and evidence is accumulating that some are contemporaneous. The point of actual origin or the original center of diffusion is not at all clear.

The chronological position of Central European Linear Wares with relation to the Körös-Starčevo complex is also not yet definitely established. Although Tichý (1960) agrees with Soudský (1956) that Volute pottery appears in Bohemia before Starčevo III, and thus probably equates with Starčevo II, the few available radiocarbon dates have not, so far at least, confirmed this equation. On the other hand, Homer Thomas has pointed out (personal communication) that radiocarbon dates for Band Ceramics in the west (p. 345) fall so close to those from central Europe that a rapid expansion or migration must have taken place at this time. (See pp. 440-41, below, and Thomas pp. 364-65, above.)

In our area, the oldest facets of this complex occur in: Bohemia, where the central and northern loess lands were apparently well settled; Moravia; and in the Little Alföld of northwest Hungary, where the Linear Wares seem relatively old in type. The Austrian, Slovakian, and Hungarian distributions, by geographical position alone, seem peripheral, although supposedly early types are now reported for eastern as well as western Slovakia (Pavúk and Lichardus, 1964). Not surprisingly, pottery of this complex, relatively late, appears in Lower Austria westward as far as the Enns River cultural boundary; South German Linear, followed by the Stroked Ware, Münchshöfen variant, occupies Upper Austria (Hell, 1954; Pittioni, 1954, 1960).

In Hungary, the older Linear Wares lie west of the Danube, and cluster in the flatlands north of the Balaton-Bakony zone. To the south, only a handful of sherds is yet known, and although these may be early in type, their marginal distribution marks them as either incidental or late. Since this area is not well explored, their chronological relationships with other cultures and their southern limit, which could well lie along the upper Drave or even in westernmost Slavonia, are unknown. Their present distribution must be noted, however, for in southwest Hungary our picture of the Early Neolithic is almost nonexistent, as is also true in northwest Yugoslavia.

In northwest Hungary and southwest Slovakia, principally along the Danube, stretches the Zseliz group, described as a middle or late phase of Linear. The terms "early," "middle," and "late" in this context vary from author to author, and depend upon whether the Šarka type is considered as a late phase or as a transitional one, and on whether one recognizes three or five phases. Still further west, in the Bükk Mountains of northern Hungary and across the mountains in eastern Slovakia in the upper drainage area of the Tisza, lies the center of the elaborately decorated Bükk pottery (bukovohorská in Slovakian), which may be divisible into phases but which generally seems to be a late marginal group. Until recently the Bükk ceramics were thought to be the earliest Neolithic in east Slovakia, but it has now been reported that an east Slovakian Linear Ware, thought to be an old type, precedes Bükk, serves as its foundation, and survives as an entity to coexist with it (Novotný, 1958, pp. 15 ff.; Lichardus, 1962). Cross-finds of Zseliz and Bükk are well established (Milojčic, 1951, pp. 122 f.; E. B.-Thomas, 1956, pp. 56, 57), and Novotný reports (1958, pp. 21, 23, 24) further cross-finds with young spiral meander, Szilmeg, and Tisza. Music note (Notenkopf) wares seem probably contemporary.

Across the northern part of the Great Hungarian Plain, east of the Danube Elbow, another group of incised wares is now appearing. This is called the Alföld Linear, but opinions vary as to whether it is merely a late type of Linear or an early form of Tisza, which it also resembles.

In Transylvania, only a few isolated, scattered, Linear sherds appear (e.g., Vlassa, 1959), but on the Rumanian plains east of the Carpathians, sites with incised wares of the late music note type have been found in quantity on the lower lands between the Siret and the Prut, and these extend southward, progressively thinning out, to the neighborhood of the Ialomiţa River drainage. Here, for the most part, they seem later than the Criş culture which has also been found in this area, particularly in view of the stratigraphy at Perieni (Petrescu-Dîmboviţa, 1957). (For a general discussion of the Moldavian distribution of this Late Linear music note group, together with a distribution map, see Comşa, 1959a; for the easternmost distribution of Linear Wares, to the Dniester and the Southern Bug, see Passek, 1962a, Fig. 2, and Gimbutas, pp. 464-65, below.)

Although the known distribution of these eastern sites runs only to Volhynia, it is generally agreed that the most probable path of diffusion was northward into Poland through the Moravian corridor, then down the Oder and Vistula (Wisła) rivers toward the Baltic, with one branch working east and south, traveling up the Western (Polish) Bug—or perhaps some other eastern tributary of the Vistula such as the San—to enter the Dniester and eventually the Prut drainages. The map accompanying Novotný's article on this subject (1959) bears arrows which show this route extremely well. (The reader must be warned, however, that the English summary of the Czech article completely reverses the direction of flow.)

With regard to this discussion of the Band Ceramics, there are still a few untidy but important ends remaining. The first of these is the group appearing in Vinča A-C, marked by spiral and meandric incised bands filled with punctate dots. Compared to the linear wares further north, and by virtue of its stratigraphic position, this would seem to represent a relatively late intrusion of Band Ceramic people southward and eastward below the lower bend of the Danube. Tichý (1962), in discussing the Linear Wares of Moravia, places such decoration in his Younger or Period II phase, and equates it with music note. Since much of the long-lived Vinča complex has an Anatolian look, it seems possible to envision a mixture of two ceramic traditions that probably reflects the presence of two ethnic strains in the population. No site with only Band Ceramic pottery is known from this area, so admixture must have taken place. Since Vinča pottery without the presence of Band Ceramics is known from eastern Yugoslavia, and in the absence of any good evidence from southwest Hungary, western Slavonia, and Slovenia, the route, sequence, and means by which the Band Ceramics arrived still present various possibilities.

From Bohemia and Moravia westward, a clearly recognizable pottery complex known as Stroked Ware (*Stichbandkeramik, vypichaná, pointillée*) replaces the earlier Linear. This seems to be a development within the Band Ceramic tradition, for the general cultural pattern shows little change. Although Childe (1947, pp. 106-7) suggests that this change might have taken place in Bohemia, there is as yet no good evidence for this. Despite the fact that the finds at Šarka were formerly considered to represent an intermediate stage, they now seem merely a late stage in the Linear development (Tichý, 1962, p. 304), and the following Stroked complex now appears in phases. In any event, Bohemia and Moravia represent the easternmost concentration of the Stroked Ware complex, and further stray finds beyond this area may be used for cross-dating. To the west, the closest relationships of the Bohemian wares seem to be with the *Winkelband* ceramics of Hinkelstein and, for the later wares, with the Rössen of Saxony and with the groups which wandered westward down the Rhine.

As for the general chronological position, Childe (1929, 1947) categorized this Stroked Ware complex as Danubian Ib, because it continued the so-called Danubian Band Ceramic tradition, but he regarded it as something of a retarded development that actually existed in a Period II context. This is borne out by the cross-finds and contemporaneity of Stroked Ware with Moravian Painted (Steklá, 1960; Zápotocký, 1958; Tichý, 1961, p. 115) and perhaps with the earlier phases of the TRB culture (Houšt'ová, 1960; Zápotocký, 1958), although this latter is much more doubtful. The oldest Stroked Wares occur in Germany, east Bohemia, and Moravia; in Moravia, Lengyel influences overlap those of the middle phase and preclude the appearance of late ones. Late Stroked Ware is lacking in Moravia.

Since the end of the Early Neolithic is irregular in various localities (Vinča A, for example, can certainly be treated as Early Neolithic), and since the cross-dating of later finds from the early periods is significant for the establishment of the beginning of the Middle Neolithic period, further chronological discussion is reserved to follow our treatment of the middle period.

Middle Period

During the Early Neolithic, the Danube-Tisza strip served as an effective boundary zone between two major cultural spheres. In the subsequent period it again served as a boundary between different cultural groups, but its function seems to have been rather as a divider on either side of which there was some northward flow of population, culture, or at least of trait complexes, starting in some degree as far south as northern Yugoslavia.

In Hungary, it was formerly thought that the distribution of the Lengyel culture was limited to the southeastern tip of Transdanubia, but it has now been found throughout the area west of the Danube. Lying in the path of its northward movement, the Little Carpathians served to divert a part of it eastward into the area between their eastern flank and the Nitra River (Neutra), where the Lužianky group belongs essentially to the Lengyel complex but contains other components and has a recognizable identity of its own (Novotný, 1962). The later Ludanice group is thought to have developed from early Lužianky and Moravian-west Slovakian Painted elements. It occupies the same area as the Lužianky group, but extends further eastward to the Ipel (Ipoly, Eipel) (Novotný, 1958; Bognár-Kutzián, 1963, pp. 473-74). Secondary diffusion carried some Lužianky settlements to the edge of the Morava drainage.

To the west, although there was some deflection up the Danube into Lower Austria, most of the movement carried into the loess lands of lower Moravia, where another variant is known as the Moravian Painted group. Elements of this Moravian Painted pottery occur in east Bohemia, and closely related, unpainted assemblages—known as Moravian Unpainted—are found throughout Bohemia, with influences extending into Germany and Poland, sometimes in association with the latest Stroked Wares. In a grave in Prague-Dejvice, a Lužianky type pot occurred with vessels of the middle phase of Stroked Ware. In Bohemia, it is generally the later phase of Moravian Painted that appears with the Stroked Wares; in Moravia, the Stroked Wares occur with the earlier Moravian Painted but not with the later (Steklá, 1960: 38), thus underlining the eastward movement of the Stroked and the westward movement of the Moravian ceramics.

There seems to have been a final drift of Lengyel elements northward through the Moravian corridor into Silesia, where, in unpainted form, they may have become a part of the Jordansmühl (Jordanów) culture, which Scollar (1959) equates in time with Michelsberg. Until recently it was thought that in Bohemia and Moravia there was some intrusion of Jordansmühl groups from the north. However, if the Neustupnýs (1961) are correct, which seems unlikely, the Jordansmühl complex may have taken shape in Bohemia before moving north into Silesia. Since Jordansmühl has been dated as later than Stroked in both Bohemia and Moravia, presumably the Michelsberg type beakers, which enter from the west and reach as far as Prague, belong in the same chronological niche. The present tendency to attribute many central European forms of this period to the TRB complex, including the Michelsberg tulip beakers, confuses the issue rather than clarifies it, particularly since no recent reworking of the Jordansmühl complex has appeared.

South of the Drave, in eastern Slavonia and Syrmia, Vinča and Butmir elements appear earlier than true Lengyel. In western Slavonia and north Bosnia, Lengyel elements seem still later. For the Lengyel and Slavonian cultures at least, J. Korošec (1957, 1958, 1960a, 1960b) sees East Alpine facies in Carniola (Krain), Styria (Steiermark), Carinthia (Kärnten), and western Croatia, where a complex of mixed elements is called the Lasinje culture. (See also P. Korošec, 1963.)

East of the Danube-Tisza strip, the situation seems to be roughly as follows: (a). The earlier Vinča culture (discussed below) covered the Banat upstream as far as the Maros junction and perhaps a little to the north of it, and followed up the Maros into Transylvania, where the site of Tordos is one of its representatives. (b). The early Tisza culture took shape along the east side of that river in the area of the Alföld Linear—that is, from the Maros junction northward as far as eastern Slovakia. Downstream, it seems contemporaneous with Bükk; in the north, it appears to be somewhat later. Early Tisza may equate in time with Late Linear—for example, the site of Lebö (Korek, 1958; Quitta, 1960)—and with Early Lengyel, whereas Late Lengyel equates with Tiszapolgár.

According to Bognár-Kutzián (1963, pp. 506-9), the extent and importance of the Tisza culture has been exaggerated. East of the Tisza to the edge of the mountains, the related Herpály complex took shape, and it is from Herpály and not Tisza that the Early Copper Age culture of Tiszapolgár is derived. Tiszapolgár also penetrated north into eastern Slovakia. She also calls attention to the fact that for some centuries a zone of unpainted pottery tradition occupied the Great Hungarian Plain and separated the painted wares of the Lengyel complex of Transdanubia and the Moravian Painted groups on the west from those of Central Transylvania and of the Cucuteni-Tripolye complex to the east.

The subsequent Middle Copper Age culture of Bodrogkeresztúr evolved by gradual transition and spread widely, reaching southeast Hungary and establishing the first major settlements in the hitherto relatively unoccupied strip between the Danube and the Tisza. Expansion reached into eastern Slovakia, and some groups followed up the rivers into Transylvania. There was, however, little spread of this culture in the south, and none in Transdanubia. (For a map of Bodrogkeresztúr cemeteries, see Patay, 1961, Fig. 1.)

The southern part of the Middle Danube drainage during this period is occupied, for the most part, by the Vinča culture, the distribution of which coincides well with that of Starčevo, part of Körös, and a part of Criş. Although excavations have been carried out on numerous sites in which the Vinča culture occurs, no new work has been done at Vinča itself. The situation with regard to the material remains much the same as in 1954, and although Vasić's detailed field notes are apparently still available for a thorough reworking of the finds, it seems more likely that a control excavation will eventually take place.

As matters now stand, Holste's (1939) sequence of A-D still forms the basis of detailed comparative study; however, for the purpose of broad treatment, it is now common practice to lump together Vinča A and B as Vinča-Tordos (Todos, Turdaş) after the site on the south bank of the Maros in Transylvania, and Vinča C and D as Vinča-Pločnik. This, ironically, approximates a return to Vasić's division of Vinča I and II for the Neolithic deposits, and his Vinča III for the top layers which contain Baden-Kostolac, Vučedol, and other elements. It is from Vinča I and II that the terms Danubian I and II were derived for central Europe, as lamented above, and Childe's Period III for the Eneolithic corresponds to Vinča III (Childe, 1929, pp. 36, 68, etc.).

Although the beginning of Vinča probably overlapped the end of the Starčevo culture, direct evidence for such contemporaneity remains shaky. Srejović (1963) sees a true Old Vinča culture developing in the heart of the Starčevo area along the Danube from the Olt-Isker line to the Save, replacing Starčevo at the core while on the peripheries late Starčevo persisted and was contemporaneous with early Vinča. Where the two cultures are reported as having been found together, certain nagging questions remain. Thus, the presence of Starčevo sherds in Vinča A itself might, so far as we know, have been caused by Vinča A disturbance of a Starčevo level. Likewise, at Ószentiván VIII, Banner and Pârducz (1948, pp. 39 f.) do not seem completely happy with the association that they found. M. Garašanin (1958, p. 8) points out that although Starčevo I and II occurred throughout Serbia and Vojvodina, Starčevo III was limited to the area north of the Danube; he sees this as an indication of at least partial contemporaneity between Vinča A and Starčevo III. Benac (1962b, p. 60) carries this further to explain the sudden appearance of Starčevo III (followed by Vinča B) up the Danube and Save (for example, Gornja Tuzla) to the west. His explanation is that the incoming Vinča people displaced the Starčevo settlers. As a working assumption on the basis of survivals, geographic distributions, and some stylistic associations at the peripheries where Starčevo traditions persisted, we can probably accept this overlap (shown on Benac's table, 1962b, p. 154), but an indisputable closed find, such as a grave that contains elements of both, is still needed.

With regard to the two possible components in the Vinča culture mentioned above, M. Garašanin (1958, pp. 22-23) points out that although the characteristic Vinča punctate bands are fairly common in the Danube Valley and in Transylvania during the Vinča-Tordos phase, they are rare on the southern Morava and appear not at all or only exceptionally in the rest of the south, and that this is true of other forms as well. Srejović (1963) sees the true Early Vinča complex developing in the Starčevo area, with black polished wares, channeling, and other traits diffusing westward from Anatolia.

The west boundary of the Vinča culture is shown by Benac (1959, p. 9; 1962b, p. 66) as running south from Tuzla on an eastern tributary of the Bosna, crossing the watershed on a long, gradual angle to Goražde, near the westernmost bend of the Drina. So far at least, this separates the Vinča sites by a wide space from the cluster of Butmir settlements to the west, most of which lie along the west side of the Bosna. The terrain here is rugged, and the river valleys play a major role.

The above discussion takes on a particular importance when one considers that the two Kakanj sites of Kakanj and Arnautovići are on the Bosna in Butmir territory. At Kakanj, Benac (1962b, p. 42) recognizes barbotine and impresso wares, which he considers to be late Starčevo-Körös, and he assigns them to the period in which Starčevo and Vinča A overlap. The Adriatic type of four-footed vase found with this material certainly relates to Danilo and to the similar ones found by Weinberg (1962) in the late Middle Neolithic of Elateia. Although Holmberg (1964, p. 347) quite properly equates the black ware associated with the four-legged vase in the Elateia bothros with Vinča A, he says that it is Late Neolithic in Greece. Weinberg, however (1962, pp. 181 ff., and pp. 297-98, above), clearly assigns the bothros to the late part of the Middle Neolithic on the grounds that matt painted wares did not appear in it. The wares at Arnautovići, on the other hand, contain elements closer to Butmir, suggesting that it might be slightly later than Kakanj. In general the equations of Kakanj with Vinča A-B, and of Butmir with Vinča B2-D or C-D, if not an exact fit, should be roughly valid.

The origin of the Butmir culture is not a subject for this paper. As an identifiable entity it occupies a geographic range between that of the Vinča culture and the coast, although some Vinča elements may appear south and southwest of it but still east of the Adriatic watershed. On his distribution map, Benac (1962b, p. 67) shows a blank zone for the whole of west Bosnia between the Una and the Vrbas and as far south as the Neretva; he argues that enough exploration has taken place there to indicate little if any settlement in the area during the Neolithic.

On the coastal side, he describes three periods for the Neolithic, the first of which we have briefly mentioned. On the one hand, he ties the impresso wares to Italy, particularly mentioning Arene Candide 23-26; on the other hand, in reviewing the sites of Zelena Pećina and Crvena Stijena, he sees the end of Zelena Pećina III equating with Starčevo II/III and the beginning of Vinča.

The Middle Neolithic is represented here by a number of sites along the Adriatic shore and hinterland and on the islands. The best known of these is Danilo. Relative dating based on the four-legged "cult" vases has already been discussed with regard to Kakanj, and has given us the equation: Elateia Late Middle Neolithic = Danilo = Kakanj = Starčevo III/Vinča A (B). (See also J. Korošec 1958, 1963, and particularly 1962, in which he adds Butmir and equates Danilo III with Lengyel and Hvar Ia with Danilo.)

There are also many Late Neolithic sites, the best known of which are Grapčeva Spilja (Grabak) on Hvar (Novak, 1955) and Lisičići (Benac, 1958). Here again, the coastal complexes are markedly different from those of the hinterland. Benac (1962b, pp. 84-86) sees Hvar and Lisičići as chronologically equivalent, and says that at Lisičići a few Butmir elements are found and that in the Butmir complex an occasional but rare Lisičići trait appears. If this is correct, Late Coastal Neolithic = Butmir Vinča-Pločnik (C-D).

In the Pelagonian plains around Bitolj and Prilep, the Porodin and Crnobuki groups are also suggestive for cross-dating. In general, their closest relations are with Thessaly. Porodin is apparently earlier than Crnobuki, which M. Garašanin (1958, p. 119) places at the end of the Neolithic. Porodin, which he ties to Vinča (presumably C-D, but not clearly stated) on typological grounds, he also correlates with the Arapi level of Thessaly, which falls stratigraphically between classical Dimini and the Larisa phase (p. 118).

M. Garašanin (1958, p. 108), following Grbić, sees a difference between north and south Macedonia during this period. In the south, Greek types, described as Sesklo, follow the Starčevo wares; in the north, Vinča-Pločnik wares, which are not found in the south, overlie the Starčevo wares of North Macedonia. The site of Žegligovo, between the bend of the Vardar and the headwaters of the Morava, has been the present southern limit of known Vinča distribution. The implication here is that Vinča C-D equates with Sesklo, which seems questionable. Galović (1964) now reports late Vinča finds in the scanty material from the upper level at Zelenikovo near Skopje. These are associated with other elements from the Kosovo-Metohija and from the Morava Valley. It is not yet clear whether we should regard Zelenikovo II as representing an extension of the Vinča sphere or as a composite culture in which Vinča traits form a component. Two items that may confuse the issue are: the questionable survival and retention of Starčevo traits in later deposits (Grbić, 1956), and the question of whether there may not be an unrecognized Early Vinča occupation in North Macedonia. For Serbia, D. Garašanin (1954a, p. 23) points out that the crusted wares that mark the distinction between Bubanj I and II follow immediately upon Late Vinča in North Serbia, thus indicating that the Vinča culture persisted longer in the north whereas in the south it was replaced somewhat earlier by Bubanj I.

On the east and to the north of the Danube, carriers of the early Vinča culture spread northward across the Banat and then eastward up the Maros into Transylvania. M. Garašanin (1958) sees a mixed zone in the north Banat—where Vinča and Tisza distributions overlap—and north of this the beginning of the area of Tisza culture. (See also M. Garašanin, 1951, p. 128, where he equates Vinča-Tordos with the beginning of Tisza culture.) In the lower Danube basin, remains of Early Vinča have appeared along the north bank. However, Berciu's (1961c, pp. 42, 560) unequivocal statement that the old Vinča basic culture stretched deep into Muntenia and perhaps to Moldavia may be misleading. Settlements with Vinča culture occupied most or all of western Oltenia to the Jiul and, as a foundation of the Vădastra culture, may have extended into Muntenia at least far enough to occupy the lower Olt drainage. On the other hand, the published material from the soundings at Dudeşti near Bucureşti, which Berciu cites, is not convincing. I do not know the material at first hand, but the illustrations do not seem to show the Vinča type in the usual sense. Vinča traits were perhaps modified in a different cultural setting upstream and then reached the Bucureşti area as a secondary diffusion of a derived complex. Comşa (1959b, pp. 91-98), who reports on this assemblage, refers to Vinča only with regard to analogies for the human figurines found there. It thus seems probable that the original Vinča drift occupied roughly the western territory formerly recognized for it, and that Vinča finds to the eastward represent either secondary or independent trait diffusion. In southwest Oltenia, a recognizable Vinča tradition persists as Vinča-Rast or Rast-Verbicioara I. In east Oltenia and west Muntenia, however, it comes to an end with the beginning of the Vădastra and Boian cultures. (See also Srejović, 1963.)

The east and southeast. In Rumania and Bulgaria, the archaeological situation is uneven, with a wealth of excavation and accessible published material for the former and a sketchy picture for the latter. Because of the numerous cross-ties to the Karanovo levels, this section will extend to the end of the Karanovo-Gumelniţa period, which equates well with the division between Bodrogkeresztúr and Baden, used here as the division between Middle and Late in the middle Danube Basin. The material entered on the correlation table for Rumania is taken largely from Berciu (1961a, p. 123). Much that appears in his regional columns is predictable on the basis of the geographical discussion at the beginning of this paper. (See also Berciu's distribution map, 1961c, p. 44.) However, a few clarifying remarks should be made.

In the plains of the Banat, the Vinča tradition runs unbroken from A to D in the southwest, and similarly elements of the subsequent so-called E level (see below) are indicated. In the eastern Banat, penetration from west Oltenia by people with Sălcuţa culture took place during the Copper Age.

At the west edge of Transylvania, Bodrogkeresztúr follows Tisza I and II, but this terminology must be revised. On Berciu's chart, for the northern plains strip at least, Tisza I should read Herpály and Tisza II should read Tiszapolgár (Bognár-Kutzián, 1963). Since Bodrogkeresztúr traveled up the Maros into Transylvania, the cultures here are the same as those in eastern Hungary. (See also Vlassa, 1964.) Decea Mureşului seems contemporary with Bodrogkeresztúr but seems ethnically to be of the intrusive eastern Kurgan Pitgrave Culture of late Phase II or Phase III (Bognár-Kutzián, 1963, pp. 452-53; Gimbutas, p. 484, below).

In central Transylvania, the sequence is given as Vinča-Turdaş (Tordos), Turdaş (Tordos), and then Petreşti. This suggests that after the Vinča people moved up the Maros and into the basin, the doors were closed behind them by Tisza or Herpály settlers on the plains. Turdaş is a Transylvanian variant of Vinča, probably developed in isolation, and Berciu considers Petreşti to be a survival of Starčevo-Körös elements absorbed into the Turdaş complex to produce a composite central Transylvanian tradition with distinctive painted wares that runs parallel with Cucuteni.

Eastern and southeastern Transylvania—that is, the general area of the upper Olt—with minor differences in infiltration, duplicates the sequence in Moldavia to the east. Dumitrescu (1960, 1963) indicates the basic differences between Precucuteni and Cucuteni, and at Izvoare Vulpe (1957, p. 376) describes Izvoare I 1 as Precucuteni of Boian Giuleşti and Izvoare I 2 as Precucuteni of Tripolye A character. Passek (1961, pp. 155-56) adds Floreşti to the Izvoare I 1 equation. Ariuşd (Erösd) is not now treated as a separate culture, but as a site and as a regional variant of the Cucuteni complex. Although Dumitrescu points out that the southwest edge of the Cucuteni area, symbolized by Ariuşd, borders on the Petreşti area and suggests the derivation of at least some of the Cucuteni painted characteristics from the Petreşti and Gumelniţa groups, it is now usual to consider the Cucuteni complex as a western facet of the Tripolye culture rather than as a strictly local development (Passek, 1962a, Table, pp. 15-16; maps, Figs. 5, 6; Passek, 1962b; for a comprehensive discussion of the Cucuteni-Tripolye cultures see Gimbutas, pp. 460-70 below. See also Dumitrescu, 1963, map facing p. 304 for the adjoining boundaries of the Petreşti, Gumelniţa, and Cucuteni-Tripolye cultures; and Nestor, 1960, for a discussion of Cucuteni periods).

There have been two shifts in the terminology of the Cucuteni sequence. First, Dumitrescu now calls the earliest stage Cucuteni A 1 as preferable to the term Proto-Cucuteni used by others; second, the phase formerly known as Horodiştea-Folteşti I has now been absorbed into the local sequence as Cucuteni IV, and the second phase—now Folteşti II—is the one that relates to Gorodsk-Usatovo (Berciu, 1961c).

In the Middle Neolithic of the Danube plain, Boian and Vădastra have parallel developments and are closely related. Vădastra extends into the west part of Valachia, apparently tied to river drainage patterns, and both Boian and Vădastra are found across the Danube in North Bulgaria (Gaul, 1948, pp. 52-53, 64 ff., 213 ff.).

In the Late Neolithic, not only do Gumelniţa and Sălcuţa occupy adjoining territories and run parallel, but they are so closely related that the question is whether Sălcuţa should be considered a separate culture or merely a variant of Gumelniţa.

In the Rumanian Dobrudja, there have been no finds of anything earlier than Hamangia, and Berciu charts a purely hypothetical Proto-Hamangia which is here omitted, since other elements, such as Karanovo I, could easily have occupied the area.

For the Bulgarian Dobrudja, Mikov thinks that Karanovo I and II are probably earlier there than Hamangia (personal communication), and this is certainly what one might expect. Although the presence of the Hamangia culture is not firmly established, Berciu (1961c, p. 562) reports a typical Hamangia vase in the Burgas Museum that came from Kableškovo, not far from Pomerice in the Burgas region near the middle of the Bulgarian Black Sea coast.

In Bulgaria, although some sites have been extensively excavated, some regions and cultures are known only from surface finds and brief soundings. In west Bulgaria, for example, no excavations of Kremikovci or Vinča wares have taken place. Gaul's early West Bulgarian Painted (Gaul, 1948) is now recognized as Kremikovci and, as such, is distinguished from Starčevo on the one hand and Karanovo on the other; the equation of west Bulgarian Vinča with that across the Danube is guesswork although probable.

On the other hand, the huge mound of Karanovo in the Maritza Valley has been carefully excavated and, because of its deep stratigraphy and well-organized results, is known by the Bulgarians as "our Troy." For the present at least, almost the entire relative chronology of Bulgaria, both internal and external, must be anchored to this sequence. Although the final publication of Karanovo has not appeared, Georgiev's paper (1961) outlines seven levels and concentrates on the relationships between them and with other Bulgarian sites, particularly Yassa (Jasa) Tepe and Kapitan Dimitrievo. Here Georgiev (p. 49) proposes a new and simple consecutive numbering from I to VII, on the grounds that the assemblages are readily distinguishable, to replace the older system of five levels with I and IV divided into two phases each. Since Berciu (1961a, p. 114) uses both systems without explanation, and since Bognár-Kutzián (1963, p. 542) equates Tiszapolgár and Bodrogkeresztúr with Karanovo IV 2 in the older nomenclature (VI in the newer), it seems advisable to give the equations here. Thus Karanovo I = Ia, II = Ib, III = II, IV = III, V = IVa or IV 1, VI = IV b or IV 2, and VII = V. Georgiev is one of the excavators, and this newer system which he proposes should and will be followed. However, we should point out that there does seem to be a continuity in the pottery forms from I to II (old Ia and Ib) with an apparent cultural break between his II and III. In the same way, Level V (old IVa) which Georgiev says can now be distinguished as a separate entity, does contain various elements—such as graphite painting—that mark the succeeding Level VI (IVb) stage. On these grounds we seem to have ethnic continuities in the two sets of periods, so it seems probable that some authors will persist in using the older terminology. One can only hope that anyone who refers to the Karanovo sequence will be explicit about which system he is using.

Berciu's correlation (1961a, 1961b) of the various phases shown for the different Rumanian cultures—Boian with Vădastra, Petreşti with Cucuteni, Gumelniţa and Sălcuţa together with Krivodol—leads one to wonder whether all these divisions may not be somewhat overschematized, and whether the tight correspondence between equivalent numbered phases is not somewhat suspect as an overly neat and orderly pattern. However, in broad terms, the major culture units do seem to run parallel as shown, and the numbered phases are convenient shorthand for indicating such looser terms as early, middle, and late.

At Bubanj, although a layer containing Starčevo material lies below the later deposits, the Bubanj sequence referred to by Berciu (1961b; pp. 128 ff.) equates Bubanj with the identically numbered Gumelniţa, Sălcuţa, and Krivodol phases (abbreviated as GSK) as follows: Bubanj I = GSK IIc, Bubanj II = GSK III, and Bubanj III = GSK IV—this last continuing into the subsequent Coţofeni-Baden period discussed below. Thus, the use of the term Bubanj I in this context refers to the Bubanj-Hum culture only.

In a brief paper, D. Garašanin (1954a) calls attention to a few specimens from Velika Humska Čuka near Niš, excavated by Grbić in 1934. Although the field notes were lost during World War II, she sees Bubanj I as equating with a late phase of Early Helladic, and Bubanj II with Early Middle Helladic, because of the presence of an Early Helladic II-III type cup and two sherds strongly similar to Minyan types. Furthermore, since she equates Vinča-Pločnik (Vinča 4-3 m.) with Bubanj I, Vinča D would then equate with Late Early Helladic. Since Vinča D correlates in turn with Gumelniţa and Karanovo VI, in both of which askoi appear (e.g., Georgiev, 1961, pp. 79-80), the correspondence with Early Helladic II and III rests on two suggestive chains of evidence.

New material, particularly from Lerna as well as from other sites, now carries the Minyan influx into Greece back as early as EH III (Troy II-II), thus making a Bubanj I = EH II and Bubanj II = EH III correlation entirely possible (see Weinberg, pp. 304-5, above).

Although one may question the rhythm of virtually identical cultural fluctuation over such a broad and topographically divided landscape, as seen by Berciu, the close relationship between the Krivodol and Sălcuţa cultures on opposite sides of the Danube is not in dispute. Whether or not these, together with Bubanj on the Morava, form a separate major Western culture—related to, but composed of sufficiently different elements to distinguish it from an eastern Karanovo VI-Gumelniţa complex—is a subject of some disagreement. My own inclination at the present time is to see these cultures as regional subdivisions of a major tradition, with Karanovo VI-Gumelniţa being closely related, and Sălcuţa-Krivodol being almost identical and deserving of a single name. The Thracian and Morava areas may show sufficient admixture with neighboring patterns to warrant distinctive regional modifiers of a basic centralizing term. I do not propose reverting to the old "Bulgarian Mound Culture," but something similar, with co-ordinating qualifiers of geographical significance as distinguished from time phases, is clearly called for.

Since late Karanovo VI equates with Bodrogkeresztúr and is followed by Baden-Kostolac elements in Karanovo VII, the division between these two levels correlates, roughly at least, with the division between Bodrogkeresztúr and Baden in Hungary. This is, therefore, the most convenient time horizon in both the lower and middle Danube basins to mark the division between our Middle and Later periods.

The Later Period

In the middle Danube Basin, following the Bodrogkeresztúr culture, the Baden culture sites cover a much wider area. In his massive study of the Pécel variant of this culture, Banner (1956) shows on his distribution map (p. 136) a heavy concentration of Baden finds in west Hungary from south of Lake Balaton to the angle of the Drave-Danube junction, north of the Bakonys in the entire northwest plain and into lower Austria, eastward across the Danube-Tisza strip—which was first encroached upon in Bodrogkeresztúr times and which now for the first time seems heavily settled—to the banks of the Tisza, extending northward from slightly below the Maros junction. The trans-Tisza area, however, shows few sites south of the Körös River, but between the Körös and the Tisza dense occupation is again indicated. To the north, the Slovakian plain—not surprisingly—continues the pattern, and clusters of settlements follow up the river valleys of the Vah and Hron systems, with sites reaching well back into the arc of the northern Carpathians and rather strongly into south Poland. Other outliers extend into Moravia and Bohemia (Banner, 1956:224), the western edge of the Carpatho-Ukraine and Transylvania; to the south, a few sites stretch eastward across Slavonia and down the Danube. In Rumania, Baden is found only in the Banat and in southwest Transylvania, with a few independently diffused traits extending further.

This culture was first named after a site near Baden in Austria, but it goes by a bewildering number of names in the literature. In Austria, it is sometimes called Ossarn; in Hungary, it is now usually known as Pécel; in Slovakia, Moravia, and Bohemia, it is termed the Cannelated or Channeled Ware culture. "Carpathian" and "Band Handle," although proposed as more comprehensive names, never saw much use. To the south, the Yugoslavs revert to the name of Baden, but qualify a late phase as Baden-Kostolac in accordance with its pottery style admixture. Further to complicate matters, Hungarian and Slovakian archaeologists recognize several regional groups which are named after sites where they were first isolated. On the accompanying table (pp. 444-47), I have indicated these types in parentheses (Kostolac, Viss, Budakalász, Boleráz, Fonyód, Úny, and Bošáca).

The origins of the culture are not understood; there are no good evidences of a development, despite an apparently early form labeled proto-Baden in Hungary. Explanations have ranged from local development from Bodrogkeresztúr and from early Lengyel to invasions from outside: either from the north, for which there is no scrap of evidence, or—with Kalicz as a recent exponent (1963)—from Anatolia. Banner and Bognár-Kutzián (1961) consider present evidence to point to a southern origin, with Kostolac appearing later. They refer to two centers in western and eastern Yugoslavia and a similar division in Hungary. There is a suggestion of two northward diffusion streams: one in a strip extending from the Morava at least as far as the Bodrog, and the other moving up the Danube to its upper elbow (ibid., pp. 28 ff.). Early Baden without admixture of Kostolac decoration has appeared in southwest Hungary and in western Yugoslavia (Dimitrijević, 1962, pp. 257 ff.), and the Baden-Kostolac admixture which characterizes most of the southern distribution is apparently late in the period (M. Garašanin, 1958). Pertinent to this is Benac's report on the site of Pivnica near the Bosna-Save junction (Benac, 1962a), where he found Kostolac type pottery with no Baden association. He dates this as later than Baden-without-Kostolac in the area, and his distribution map (p. 31) suggests a westward trend down the Save, Drave, and Danube and up the Morava and Temes rivers respectively.

Garašanin mentions Baden-without-Kostolac elements found at Rimski Sančevi and Perlez, and cites Baden-Kostolac with Bubanj-Hum Ib at Bubanj. Since the Garašanins equate Bubanj-Hum II with early Middle Helladic on the basis of Minyan-looking sherds, not only Bubanj-Hum I but also Baden-Kostolac must correlate with Early Helladic III and perhaps with the beginnings of Middle Helladic I (M. Garašanin, 1958, p. 43; D. Garašanin, 1954a). However, if these Minyan style sherds should actually be late Early Helladic III in date, these equations must be correspondingly changed. (See Weinberg, p. 305, above.)

In the north, the picture is also not clear. The Boleráz group in west Slovakia has been termed early by E. Neustupný, but is considered later by most others. From the distribution pattern alone, it seems most unlikely that it served as the foundation for the explosive spread of Baden throughout the whole area. The Bošáca type, although also not clearly understood, may follow Baden in its direct form in Slovakia (Novotný, 1958), but is described by Novotná (1961) as containing Kostolac elements and belonging essentially to the late Channeled Ware and thus to the Baden complex. Banner and Bognár-Kutzián (1961) consider it as one of four late regional variants of Baden: Bošáca, Viss, Úny, and Kostolac. Although its center is in the middle Vah Valley, the Bošáca complex spread or diffused westward—some elements crossing the Little Carpathians as far as Uherské Hradiště in eastern Moravia—and occupied southeast Moravia east of the Morava.

Following the Baden horizon in the middle Danube Basin is another widely spread cultural complex of several local facies with different names—subsumed under the title of Vučedol or Slavonian culture although to a great extent the striking elements known from the site of Vučedol itself and from other Slavonian sites such as Sarvaš are lacking. These sites are apparently late, and these names thus seem strictly applicable to a late phase only. For a long time it was an article of faith that the Slavonian wares were either derived from the Laibach Moor (Ljubljansko Barje or Ljubljansko Blato) or formed a part of the same complex; however, the assemblages from there, so often referred to, actually came from several sites of different periods and represent a widely mixed collection, including Vučedol wares. J. and P. Korošec are in the process of trying to unravel it (for example, P. Korošec, 1958-59), so far at least by reference to the material from Ig.

In any event, although the more striking traits are lacking in the north, Bognár-Kutzián (1961, p. 228) says that the less spectacular ones that make up the foundation of the corpus do show a broad consistency during this period and also provide a basis for the groups which follow. Only two locations of this material are known in Serbia itself south of the Danube; the major cluster of characteristic Vučedol sites is in east Slavonia and in western Srem (Syrmia) (Garašanin, 1958, pp. 45 ff.). This suggests that the agglomerations in the north may be, in part at least, derivations from the preceding regional groups to which new elements have been added, and that the more recognizable types of decoration to the south may have developed somewhere in south Pannonia and eastern Slavonia, perhaps under late Lengyel influence (Benac, 1962b, p. 143). Benac (ibid., p. 145) maps Vučedol elements in Bosnia as clustered on the upper Bosna, on the Sana, and across the mountains on the Adriatic coast west of the Cetina River and on the islands of Hvar and Korčula. The drift here thus seems to have been southward and westward from Slavonia as well as into the eastern Alps region, Slovenia, and western Slavonia; the Vučedol traits here are intrusive and should be late in the series.

For the so-called Vučedol culture as a whole, P. Korošec (1961) makes a broad distinction between what she calls pure Slavonian, centered in Slavonia, Srem, southern Transdanubia, Bosnia, and Slovenia, on the one hand, and the broad area in which Vučedol or Slavonian traits diffused.

For Hungary, Kalicz (1962, pp. 12 ff.) identifies three such groups: Vučedol-Zók in Baranya county in south Transdanubia; Makó-Čaka, for which the type site of Makó lies in the southeast near Szeged and that of Čaka (Csaka) is in the northwest near Bratislava; and Niyerség, generally across the north. These seem to begin somewhat earlier than Nagyrév and Hatvan I, but survive and overlap them before disintegrating. (The Kalicz article is entirely in Hungarian, and I am indebted to S. Foltiny for a translation and summary.)

Although the Vučedol-Zók group belongs in P. Korošec's pure Slavonian, Makó-Čaka and Nyirség are groups of the second class, consisting of related substrata of previous local cultures and groups with an overwash of traits that spread even more widely, as shown on her map.

Finds of the contemporary Bell Beaker culture occur only in northwest Hungary; these people apparently came down the Danube no farther than the Budapest area. A few stray sherds have been found a little farther to the east. Their graves are of course numerous in Austria, Moravia, and Bohemia. According to Patay (personal communication), the Budapest group contains Vučedol elements; Kastner (1939) and Willvonseder (1939) reported finding Vučedol and Bell Beaker elements together. This link is further borne out by the occurrence of small Vučedol-type pedestaled bowls or lamps in Řivnáč contexts in Bohemia. Here, although Novotný (1955, p. 58) says that the association of Slavonian with Bell Beaker is not yet definite, it seems highly probable.

In west Slovakia, Točik (1963) describes the Veselé type as belonging to the Eastern Corded Wàre complex and as stretching from the Vah to the Morava. He believes the eastern part of this Veselé group, lying between the Vah and the Nitra, was strongly affected by Nagyrév influences together with associated Bell Beaker and Corded elements, and there developed into the Nitra group. Thus, at least in part and with some overlapping: Nagyrév I = Čaka = Veselé = Bell Beaker = Saxo-Thuringian Corded Ware. Nagyrév II = Early Nitra = Preúnětice. Late Nitra = Late Corded = Early Únětice = Early Straubing = Early Perjámos.

To complete the picture in Hungary, the Gáta-Wieselburg culture develops from the Litzenkeramik (Corded Ware) in the northwest and runs parallel with the Únětice period; across the north, the Nagyrév complex takes shape. Stretching westward from the Ipel, but not so far as the Nitra, the Tokod group is coming to light. Although Bandi (1963) thinks it must be equated with Hatvan II, he also points out that Hatvan II replaces it; thus, it must be limited to the early part of Hatvan II, or it could be partly Hatvan I in date, possibly overlapping late Nagyrév and Nitra as well. In the northeast, Hatvan replaces Nyirség-Zók; in east Hungary, the Otomani culture, characteristic of northwest Transylvania, extends westward; in the southeast, the material from Perjámos, Deszk, and Szöreg forms a group that replaces Óbéba (cf. Foltiny, 1941a, Pl. VI; 1941b, Pls. II and III; 1942, Pl. V; and Patay, 1938, Pl. VI.)

Here a word must be said about Tószeg, which was long considered to offer a classic picture of the Bronze Age sequence (e.g., Tompa, 1937, pp. 64 ff.). Von Márton, who excavated there for many years, died suddenly in 1934. Although interpretations were based on various reports, the material as a whole went unpublished until 1957, when Banner and Bóna completed Márton's manuscript (Banner, Bóna, and Márton, 1957). In the meantime, in 1948 Csalog and Mozsolics carried on a control excavation which they published in 1952 (Acta Hungarica 2), completely revising the older interpretations. The new results are also summarized in Banner, Bóna, and Márton, 1957. The interpretation of the Tószeg sequence went through several changes, but the next to last was: Nagyrév-Perjámos-Hatvan-Füzesabony. The excavations of 1948 demonstrated that the recognition of a Perjámos level was a mistake and that only three levels could be established. Even this last ordering of Nagyrév-Hatvan-Füzesabony is misleading, since Tószeg lies in the zone of geographical overlap between the Hatvan and Nagyrév complexes, which are largely contemporary. Thus, the stratigraphy at Tószeg is valid for that site only. The equation of Hatvan and Nagyrév is, so far as I know, not yet based on actual cross-finds, but rather on correlated sequences in adjoining areas, with Füzesabony overlying both cultures.

Although Bronze Age sequences have emerged in various parts of Hungary, Slovakia, and Rumania, the chronological equations proposed by different scholars show considerable variation. It is not yet clear whether this means that our corpus of material is as yet insufficient to delineate an across-the-board picture, or whether regional differences account for this situation. Únětice, for example, is equated with Hatvan II by some and with Füzesabony by others; the literature reflects the same uncertainty with regard to Otomani.

In my opening section on geography, I pointed out that the peculiar peripheral relation of Bohemia to the Danubian area made it extremely valuable for establishing wider equations. Whether or not we accept the four stages of TRB (that is, TRB A/B, Baalberg, Siřem, Salzmünde) proposed by Zápotocký (1958) for Bohemia and Houšt'ová (1960) for Moravia, Baalberg and Salzmünde elements are clearly discernible. In the course of their article, Driehaus and Pleslová (1961), following Driehaus, give the following equations: 1) Jevišovice C 1 = Salzmünde = first Cannelated = Baden-Pécel; 2) Jevišovice C 2, which is earlier, = Swiss Pfyn and South German Altheim = Siřem. (Driehaus and Behrens, 1961, p. 247.) Pleslová (1961), however, questions the validity of a Siřem phase. Since Baalberg is at least partly older than Salzmünde, it should probably fit here—Baalberg = Altheim = Michelsberg = Jordansmühl—giving a rough equation within which some parts overlap. A point of difficulty is that the various phases of TRB are regional variants that are partly synchronous and partly diachronous (Driehaus and Behrens, 1961, p. 251).

For the next phase, Jevišovice B = Řivnáč = Goldberg III = Middle Corded Ware in Bohemia = at least part of Mondsee-Attersee in Bavaria and Upper Austria, with Cham and the related West Bohemian groups (Plzeň basin) equating with Early B.

Earliest Řivnáč contains Cannelated elements which do not occur in the later phase. At the site of Homolka, the assemblage is marked by Bernburg cups, Vučedol-type footed bowls, and Globular Amphora fragments, thus cross-dating Řivnáč in three different directions. The earlier stages of Řivnáč overlap the late Baden Cannelated sequence at its periphery, where it may be a late survival (Pleslová in Ehrich and Pleslová, in press). Since Early Homolka does not seem to be the earliest Řivnáč, the Driehaus-Pleslová suggestion that Řivnáč actually begins in the gap between Jevišovice C1 and B seems reasonable and seems to find support in the recent results from Brno-Líšeň (Medunová-Benešová, 1964.)

Zápotocký (1961), utilizing various elements including the distinctive ansa lunata, adds Little Poland and Upper Silesian TRB = Złota = Cham to the Jevišovice B = Řivnáč equation.

During the late Eneolithic, Corded Ware, Řivnáč, and Bell Beaker ethnic groups entered the region successively and were at least partly contemporaneous there. Neustupný (1961) equates Older Corded with Řivnáč and Later Corded with Bell Beaker, although admitting some overlap between Late Řivnáč and the early Bohemian Bell Beaker, which is a late phase in Europe as a whole. In this regard, it is of interest to compare the radiocarbon determination of 2438 ± 70 B.C. from Homolka with those from the Netherlands for Bell Beaker and Corded Wares (see Homer Thomas, pp. 359-60, 365, above); although the dates seem uncomfortably high, their relative pattern is consistent. Despite some evidence that the Řivnáč pattern did not survive until the end of the period, as did the Corded and Bell Beaker complexes (Mašek, 1961), some recognizable Řivnáč traits do appear in the Únětice (Aunjetitz) Bronze Age. The proto-Únětice people seem to have been a separate group entirely. On the other hand, there are blends of Bell Beaker and Corded traditions in the formative stages of Únětice.

The Řivnáč group is intrusive in Bohemia, and apparently came from northwest Hungary. Since the Hungarian material is not yet adequately published, we can merely mention possible relations with Čaka-Mako, Hatvan I, or Nagyrév (Pleslová, ms. in Ehrich and Pleslová). The initial phase of the Early Bronze Age Únětice period, which follows immediately upon the late Eneolithic, not only represents a new influx but assimilates surviving elements from the Řivnáč, Bell Beaker, and Corded Ware groups. There has been some change in terminology, and what was formerly called Preúnětice is now known as Early Únětice. Proto-Únětice, on the other hand, is now recognized as an intrusive group, probably from northwest Hungary and apparently related to Prenagyrév (Moucha, 1963).

One point of geographical significance is Hájek's statement (1954) that during the Neolithic and Eneolithic periods, the south Bohemian Plateau was only lightly occupied and that the Únětice (Aunjetitz) there was mixed, showing strong relationships with Straubing, Unterwölbling, and Austrian Aunjetitz. Another is that in Lower Austria, Únětice sites cluster heavily north of the Danube, whereas south of it only Wieselburg occurs in the Vienna basin and east of it, whereas at the same time Unterwölbling appears to the west (Pittioni, 1954, pp. 283-336; 1960, Map V 2 a).

For Yugoslavia, Todorović (1963) bases his conclusions on cross-finds from the excavations at Hissar and at other sites in the Kosovo-Metohija area, and offers the following equations which tend to support those already drawn from other evidence:

(1) Predionica II = Bubanj Hum Ia = Late Vinča = Krivodol IIc = Sălcuţa IIc = Karanovo V.

(2) Hissar Ia = Bubanj Hum Ib = Krivodol III = Sălcuţa III = Karanovo VI.

(3) Hissar Ib = Bubanj Hum Ib-II = Krivodol IV = Sălcuţa IV = Karanovo VI.

(4) Hissar II and Gladnica = Baden Kostolac = Bubanj Hum II = Macedonian Bronze Age = Cernavoda III = Ezero III = Karanovo VII.

Throughout Rumania, the transition between Neolithic and the Bronze Age is marked by the influx of foreign cultures and the diffusion of foreign influences, after which there is a long, slow development from the Early Bronze Age into the Iron Age. During this period, Baden sites extend only into southwest Transylvania via the Maros and into the Banat, with only a few elements reaching Oltenia. Inside the Transylvanian Basin, the picture is not completely clear; the north is vaguely described as Carpathian, which may mean Folteşti II. Eastern elements in an Ocher Grave tumulus, superimposed on a Cucuteni B level, suggest that Horodiştea-Folteşti I (now Cucuteni IV) overlaps into the transition period before being supplanted by Folteşti-Stoicani II. Throughout most of Transylvania—extending westward into the Banat and southward into Oltenia, where it replaces the Sălcuţa sequence—is the Coţofeni complex, which Berciu describes as essentially a local development. He equates this with Baden-Pécel in Hungary and with Cernavoda II in the Dobrudja.

In the next cultural horizon, we find the Schneckenberg group in south Transylvania and the closely related Glina III in Oltenia, both of which contain elements of Eastern Corded Ware. Actually these two terms refer to the same cultural complex in different regions. The group is classed as full Bronze Age but is equated by Kalicz (personal communication) with Hatvan I. In describing the Wietenberg culture, Horedt (1960) calls attention to its riverine distribution, clustered mainly on the upper middle Mureş (Maros) and the upper Someş. Outliers extend along the upper Olt to the southeast, with an occasional western site down the westward-flowing streams. Geographically then, the Wietenberg complex occupies the eastern half of central Transylvania, and the Otomani complex lies west of it. The equations seem to be: Otomani I = Nagyrév = Tószeg A; Otomani II-III or III = Wietenberg = Tószeg B-C = Hatvan I-II. There are gaps in our information, and probably a considerable overlap. Thus, the Glina III-Schneckenberg complex may survive a bit later, since Otomani is also equated with the early part of the Füzesabony culture of Hungary and the late Únětice of Czechoslovakia. In Muntenia and southeast Transylvania, the Tei culture follows Glina III.

In Moldavia, according to Berciu (1961a, p. 120), Globular Amphorae appear stratigraphically before Horodiştea-Folteşti I (Cucuteni IV), which would indicate that these are so much earlier there than in Czechoslovakia that they cannot be used for cross-dating purposes. Dinu (1961), on the other hand, insists that material recently found in Moldavia above a late phase of Gorodsk can be attributed to the Globular Amphora people; he thinks these people belong to the transitional phase between the Eneolithic and Bronze Ages, corresponding to the middle stage of Ocher Graves in tumuli.

In the Dobrudja, the continuation of the Cernavoda complex, which also contains Ocher Graves of apparently Eastern Steppe derivation, corresponds with Ezero in Bulgaria (Berciu, 1961b, p. 127; 1961c, p. 563), which in turn must correlate with Karanovo VII and the other Bulgarian sites with which it is equated.

Absolute Dating

With the possible exception of those for the Linear Wares, the number of radiocarbon determinations for our area is as yet too small and scattered to give a very reliable picture. I regard this method as a coarse-mesh screen which permits of rough equations when repeated or consistent results allow the elimination of moderately deviant to wildly erratic ones. I also take a conservative view, and continue to suspect that there may well be some as yet unrecognized factor that affects the radiocarbon determinations throughout Temperate Europe before 2000 B.C., making them uniformly too old, but at the same time allowing the emergence of a consistent pattern.

In a preliminary report seen too late for discussion or for inclusion in the formal bibliography, N. Vlassa in Dacia n.s. VII, 1963, pp. 485-94, notes the finding at Tărtăria in Transylvania of three pictographic tablets with Uruk-Warka IV and Jemdet Nasr affiliations. He equates their Turdaş context with Early Vinča B1, which, if actually synchronous with it, would make the assumed dates for the Protoliterate of Mesopotamia much too low, or the radiocarbon determinations for European Neolithic much too high. If the thin Turdaş layer should correlate with Vinča B2-C in date, the established pattern would remain pretty much unchanged.

For what they may be worth, a list of relevant determinations is appended. Consistencies with other lists, particularly those of Thomas (pp. 364-65 and 394-95, above), and also internal and external inconsistencies should be noted. Nearly all these dates are reported in Radiocarbon 5 (1963), 6 (1964); Quitta (1960, p. 184); or Kohl and Quitta (1963). All have been corrected to conform to a 5730 ± 40 year half life, as recommended in the Editorial Statement in Radiocarbon 5. Conversion has been effected by multiplying published dates based on a 5570 ± 30 half life by 1.03; A.D. 1950 remains the reference year for converting B.P. dates to B.C.

RADIOCARBON DATES

LAB. NO.	COUNTRY	SITE	CULTURE	DATE
Bln. 75	Hungary	Gyálarét	Körös	5332 ± 100
GrN 2059	Yugoslavia	Gornja Tuzla	Starčevo III	4889 ± 75
Bln. 115	Hungary	Hódmezövásárhely-Kotacpart	Körös	4693 ± 100
Bln. 86	Hungary	Katalszeg	Körös	4611 ± 100
Bln. 119	Hungary	Korlát	Bükk	4683 ± 100
Bln. 57	Czechoslovakia	Žopy	Linear	4672 ± 100
Bln. 102, 102a	Czechoslovakia	Mohelnice	Linear (early)	4585 ± 100
Bln. 123	Hungary	Tarnabod	Linear (Alföld)	4518 ± 100
Bln. 83	Austria	Pulkau	Linear (Music Note)	4451 ± 100
GrN 1546	Yugoslavia	Vinča	Vinča A	4426 ± 60
Bln. 87	Hungary	Zalavár	Linear (Zseliz ?)	4415 ± 100
GrN 2435	Czechoslovakia	Kečovo (Domica)	Bükk	4312 ± 75
Bln. 58	Austria	Mold	Linear (Music Note)	4219 ± 100
Bln. 55	Austria	Winden-am-See	Linear (Music Note)	4168 ± 100
GrN 1986	Rumania	Hamangia-Baia	Hamangia I	4106 ± 70
GrN 1993	Hungary	Tiszapolgár Csöszhalom	Herpály	4070 ± 60
GrN 1537	Yugoslavia	Vinča	Vinča D	4070 ± 160

RADIOCARBON DATES (continued)

LAB. NO.	COUNTRY	SITE	CULTURE	DATE
Bln. 107	Austria	Winden-am-See	Linear (Music Note)	4044 ± 100
GrN 3025	Rumania	Gumelniţa	Gumelniţa A2	3936 ± 70
GrN 1542	Yugoslavia	Banjica	Vinča D	3931 ± 90
GrN 1974	Yugoslavia	Gornja Tuzla	Vinča C	3797 ± 60
GrN 1990	Rumania	Sălcuţa	Sălcuţa	3689 ± 55
GrN 1989	Rumania	Sălcuţa	Sălcuţa	3663 ± 55
GrN 3028	Rumania	Gumelniţa	Gumelniţa A2	3612 ± 90
GrN 1987	Rumania	Vărăşti	Gumelniţa (Boian B)	3570 ± 70
GrN 1985	Rumania	Habaşeşti	Cucuteni A	3539 ± 80
GrN 1982	Rumania	Valea Lupului	Cucuteni B	3148 ± 60
H (no num.)	Austria	Stallegg	Lengyel	2695 ± 200
Bln. 61, 61a	Rumania	Cernavoda	Cernavoda-Ezero I	2628 ± 100
Bln. 62	Rumania	Cernavoda	Cernavoda-Ezero I	2437 ± 100
GrN 4065	Czechoslovakia	Homolka	Řivnáč	2438 ± 70
Bln. 29	Rumania	Baia-Hamangia	Ocher Grave	2262 ± 160
GrN 1995	Rumania	Baia-Hamangia	Ocher Grave*	2716 ± 65

*Wood from the same grave as Bln. 29.

Note on Comparative Table

The accompanying comparative table represents only rough equations; many finer correlations are omitted. The horizontal arrows indicate only the extent of various cultural distributions; they have nothing to do with the direction of diffusion.

In addition to the published sources cited and to much separately acknowledged personal information, the following colleagues kindly drafted charts expressing their views on the sequences and external relationships within their several areas: A. Točik for Slovakia and Moravia; N. Kalicz and P. Patay for Hungary; and V. Mikov for Bulgaria. I am immensely grateful to them. Although they have allowed me to make use of this material, they are in no way to be held responsible for what I have done with it.

ACKNOWLEDGMENTS

During the winter of 1963-64, thanks to a grant from the National Science Foundation, of which the preparation of this paper was one objective, I was enabled to spend some time in Europe to consult with numerous colleagues. Without their co-operation and generosity with regard to active guidance, help, and advice, as well as information and ideas often not yet published, this essay could never have taken its present form. I wish to express my very deep appreciation to A. Točik of Nitra; E. Plesl and E. Pleslová of Prague; I. Bognár-Kutzián, N. Kalicz, J. Korek, and P. Patay of Budapest; D. Berciu, E. Comşa, V. Dumitrescu, I. Nestor, and R. Vulpe of Bucharest; M. Petrescu-Dîmboviţa of Iaşi; V. Mikov, V. Velkov, and R. Katinčarov of Sofia; M. and D. Garašanin and M. Grbić of Beograd; A. Benac of Sarajevo; J. and P. Korošec of Ljubljana and G. Novak, D. Mirosavljević, and Z. Vinski of Zagreb; R. Pittioni of Vienna; and K. Willvonseder of Salzburg. In addition, Stephen Foltiny of the Institute for Advanced Studies at Princeton has been particularly kind and helpful. Of my colleagues in the symposium, I am indebted to Homer Thomas for much information and criticism, and to Saul S. Weinberg and Marija Gimbutas for materials interlocking with that from my own area of study.

Plesl and Pleslová, Thomas, and Foltiny have all read this paper and have made valuable suggestions and criticisms. I alone must be charged with anything amiss.

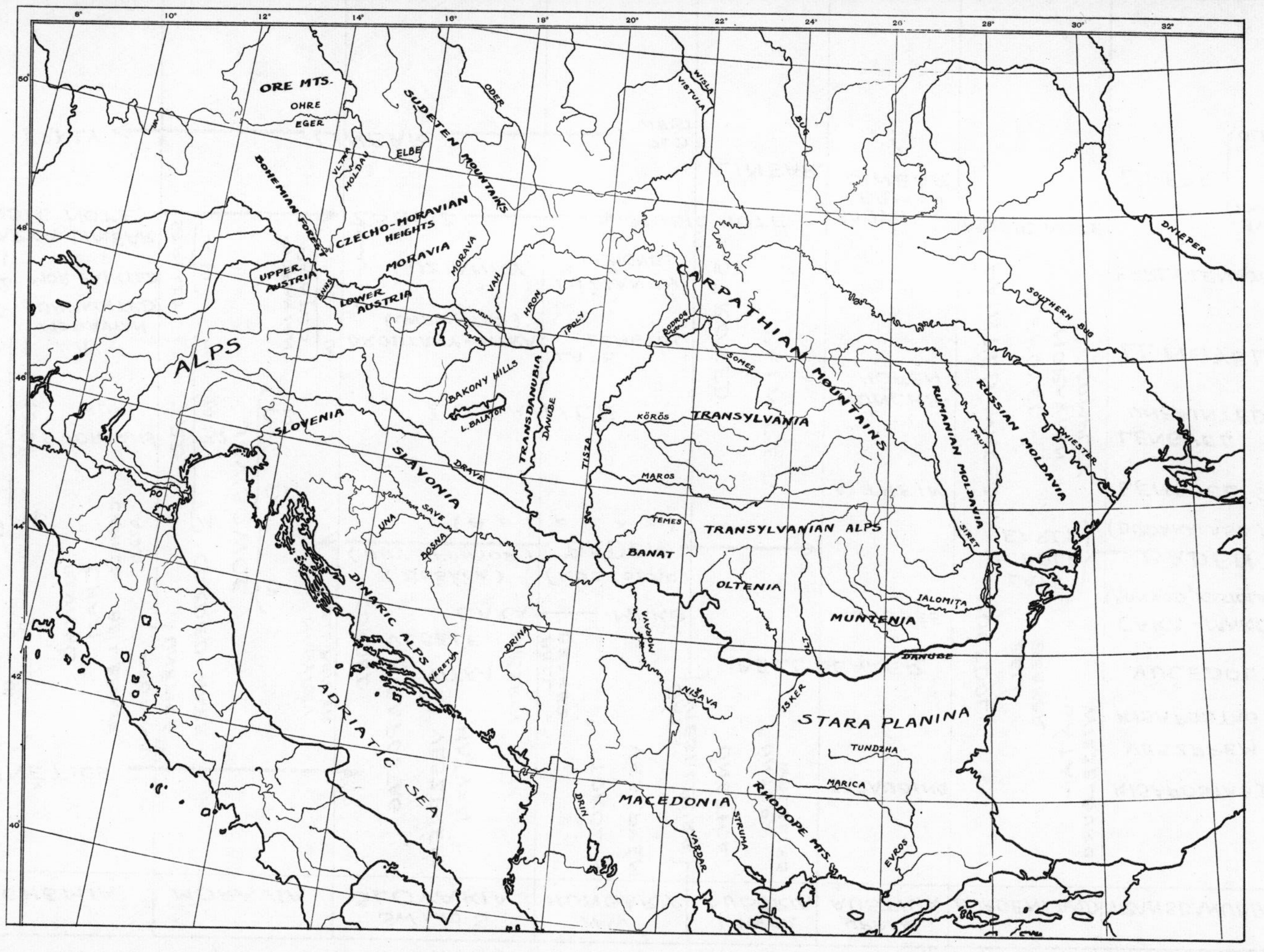
ORE MTS.
OHRE
EGER
BOHEMIAN FOREST
VLTAVA
MOLDAU
ELBE
SUDETEN MOUNTAINS
ODER
CZECHO-MORAVIAN HEIGHTS
MORAVIA
MORAVA
UPPER AUSTRIA
ENNS
LOWER AUSTRIA
VAH
HRON
IPOLY
ALPS
BAKONY HILLS
L. BALATON
TRANSDANUBIA
DANUBE
SLOVENIA
SLAVONIA
DRAVE
PO
UNA
SAVE
BOSNA
DINARIC ALPS
NERETVA
ADRIATIC SEA
DRINA
DRIN
MACEDONIA
VARDAR
STRUMA
RHODOPE MTS.
EVROS
MARICA
TUNDZHA
STARA PLANINA
ISKER
NIŠAVA
MORAVA
TISZA
WISLA
VISTULA
BUG
BODROG
CARPATHIAN MOUNTAINS
SOMES
KÖRÖS
TRANSYLVANIA
MAROS
TEMES
BANAT
TRANSYLVANIAN ALPS
OLTENIA
OLT
MUNTENIA
IALOMIȚA
DANUBE
RUMANIAN MOLDAVIA
SIRET
PRUT
RUSSIAN MOLDAVIA
DNIESTER
SOUTHERN BUG
DNIEPER

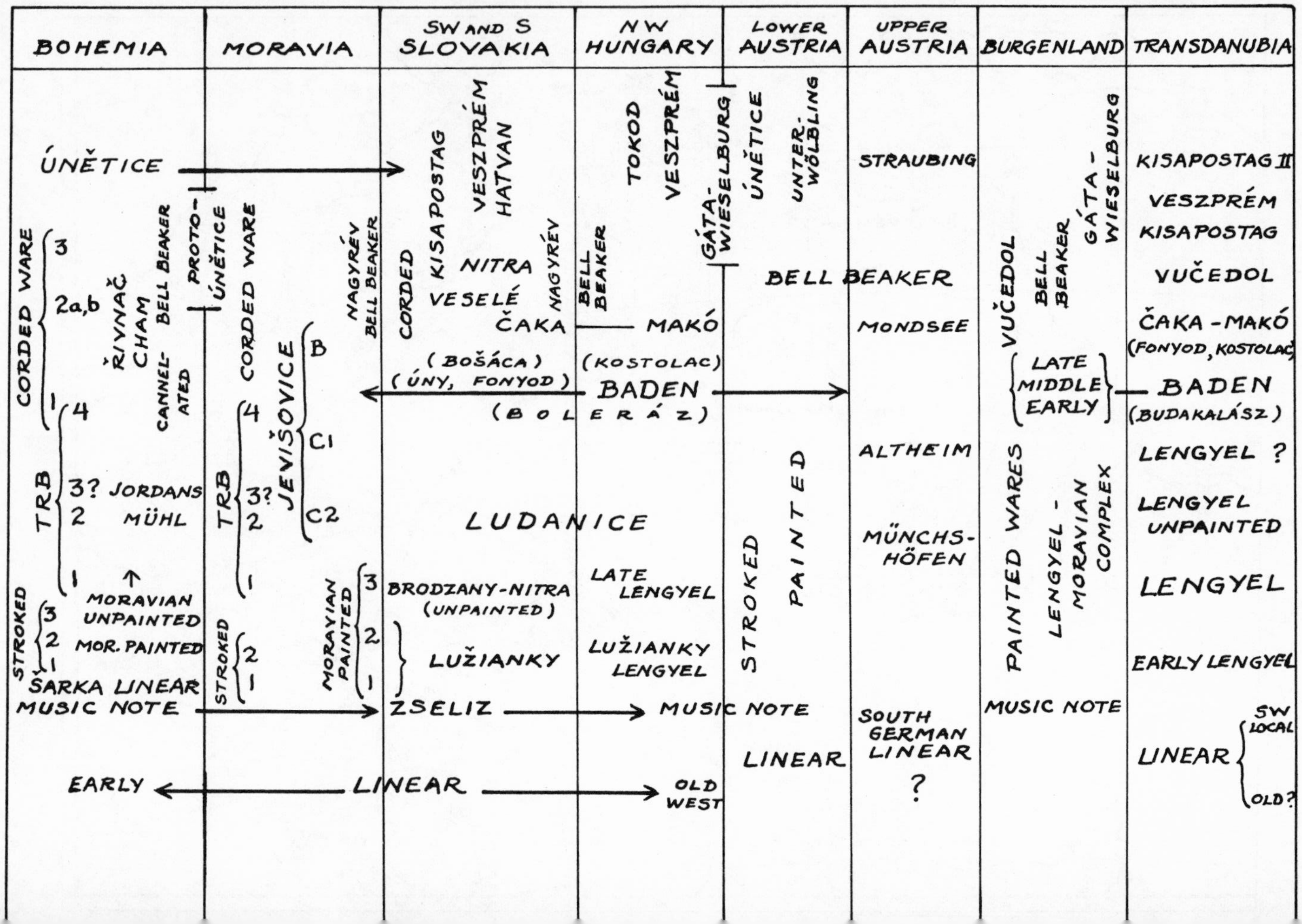

BOHEMIA	MORAVIA	SW AND S SLOVAKIA	NW HUNGARY	LOWER AUSTRIA	UPPER AUSTRIA	BURGENLAND	TRANSDANUBIA
ÚNĚTICE →	PROTO-ÚNĚTICE →	KISAPOSTAG VESZPRÉM HATVAN	TOKOD VESZPRÉM	GÁTA-WIESELBURG ÚNĚTICE UNTER-WÖLBLING	STRAUBING	GÁTA-WIESELBURG	KISAPOSTAG II VESZPRÉM KISAPOSTAG
CORDED WARE {3, 2a,b, 1} ŘIVNÁČ CHAM BELL BEAKER CANNELATED	CORDED WARE NAGYRÉV BELL BEAKER	CORDED NITRA VESELÉ ČAKA NAGYRÉV	BELL BEAKER MAKÓ	BELL BEAKER	BELL BEAKER MONDSEE	VUČEDOL BELL BEAKER	VUČEDOL ČAKA-MAKÓ (FONYOD, KOSTOLAC)
	JEVIŠOVICE {B, C1, C2}	← (BOŠÁCA) (ÚNY, FONYOD)	(KOSTOLAC) BADEN (BOLERÁZ) →	→		{LATE, MIDDLE, EARLY} —	BADEN (BUDAKALÁSZ)
TRB {4, 3? JORDANS, 2 MÜHL, 1}	TRB {4, 3?, 2, 1}	LUDANICE	LUDANICE	PAINTED	ALTHEIM MÜNCHSHÖFEN	PAINTED WARES LENGYEL-MORAVIAN COMPLEX	LENGYEL ? LENGYEL UNPAINTED LENGYEL
STROKED {3 MORAVIAN UNPAINTED ↑, 2 MOR. PAINTED, 1}	STROKED {2, 1} MORAVIAN PAINTED {3, 2, 1}	BRODZANY-NITRA (UNPAINTED) LUŽIANKY	LATE LENGYEL LUŽIANKY LENGYEL	STROKED			EARLY LENGYEL
ŠARKA LINEAR MUSIC NOTE →	→	ZSELIZ →	MUSIC NOTE	MUSIC NOTE	SOUTH GERMAN LINEAR	MUSIC NOTE	LINEAR {SW LOCAL, OLD?}
EARLY ←	LINEAR	LINEAR	→ OLD WEST	LINEAR	?		

TRANSDANUBIA	W / E SLAVONIA	BOSNIA	SOUTHEASTERN ALPINE AREA	SLOVENIA	DALMATIA	PELA-GONIA	SOUTH MACE-DONIA	BUDAPEST	CENTRAL HUNGARY
KISAPOSTAG II			STRAUBING?					FÜZESABONY	VATYA { 3
VESZPRÉM								HATVAN 2	VATYA { 2, 1
KISAPOSTAG			BELL BEAKER WITH VUČEDOL ADMIXTURE					NAGYRÉV	
VUČEDOL { 2, 1	VUČEDOL	VUČEDOL { 2, 1		LAIBACH MOOR (IG) { II, I	VUČEDOL / BELL BEAKER		MACEDONIAN EARLY BRONZE	BELL BEAKER	MAKÓ ZÓK
ČAKA - MAKÓ									
(FONYOD, KOSTOLAC) BADEN (BUDAKALÁSZ) →	(BADEN-KOSTOLAC) →	KOSTOLAC) →	LATE LENGYEL WITH BADEN ADMIXTURE; LASINJA; PÖLSHALS-STRAPPELKOGEL	KANZIANBERG				(ÚNY, KOSTOLAC) BADEN (BUDAKALÁSZ) →	→
LENGYEL ?	LATE LENGYEL			LENGYEL ?					
LENGYEL UNPAINTED	SLAVONIAN-SYRMIAN BUTMIR-VINČA ADMIXTURE	BUTMIR			HVAR	CRNOBUKI	?	BODROG-KERESZTÚR →	→
LENGYEL	LENGYEL (EAST ALPINE)	VINČA			LISIČIĆI	PORODIN		LENGYEL	RELATIVELY UNINHABITED
EARLY LENGYEL		EARLY TUZLA							
								ZSELIZ	
LINEAR { SW LOCAL, OLD?					DANILO; CARDIAL AND IMPRESSO →				
	STARČEVO	STARČEVO		?		STARČEVO	STARČEVO		

BUDAPEST	NORTH CENTRAL HUNGARY	EAST SLOVAKIA	NE HUNGARY	EAST HUNGARY	WEST TRANSYLVANIA	SE HUNGARY	S BANAT SE	SERBIA VOJVODINA	NORTH MACEDONIA	CENTRAL TRANSYLVANIA
FÜZESABONY →	→	3	FÜZESABONY	3	3		VATTINA ↑ VERBICIOARA	↑		WIETENBERG
HATVAN 2 →	→	OTOMANI 2	HATVAN 2	2 OTOMANI	2		MOKRIN	VATTINA	TRANSITION MACEDONIAN BRONZE AGE - BUBANJ	
BELL BEAKER NAGYRÉV	NAGYRÉV	HATVAN ? 1	HATVAN 1B 1A	1	1	PERJÁMOS	PERJÁMOS			
	PRE-NAGYRÉV									
	← NYIRSÉG	ZATIN NYIRSÉG -	ZÓK →	→	→	OBEBA		BUBANJ 3		FURCHENSTICH
(ÚNY, KOSTOLAC)	(BOŠÁCA) (VISS, KOSTOLAC)		(VISS)	(KOSTOLAC)		MAKÓ-ČAKA (KOSTOLAC)	(KOS-TO-LAC) (COTO FENI)	2		
BADEN (BUDAKALÁSZ) →	→	→	→	→	→	→	→	1b	KRIVODOL VINČA-PLOČNIK	COȚOFENI
BODROGKERESZTÚR →	→	→	→	→	(DECEA-MUREȘULUI)	→		D 1a		PETREȘTI 4
← TISZAPOLGÁR →	← TISZAPOLGÁR →	LUCSKA	→	→	↑ (dashed)	TISZAPOLGÁR		C		3 2 1
LENGYEL	TRANSITIONAL	LENGYEL	TRANSITIONAL	TRANSITIONAL	TISZA II	TRANSITIONAL	VINČA	B2		TURDAȘ
ZSELIZ	TISZA	BÜKK POTISKA SZILMEG	BÜKK	TISZA, HERPÁLY AND ALFÖLD LINEAR ←	TISZA I	→ AND ALFÖLD LINEAR		B1 A	VRŠNIK IV	
		YOUNG LINEAR	EARLY BÜKK	PAINTED, ALFÖLD LINEAR?			←	STARČEVO III		
	ALFÖLD LINEAR	BARCA III	ALFÖLD LINEAR	KÖRÖS	STARČEVO-CRIȘ	KÖRÖS			STARČEVO	

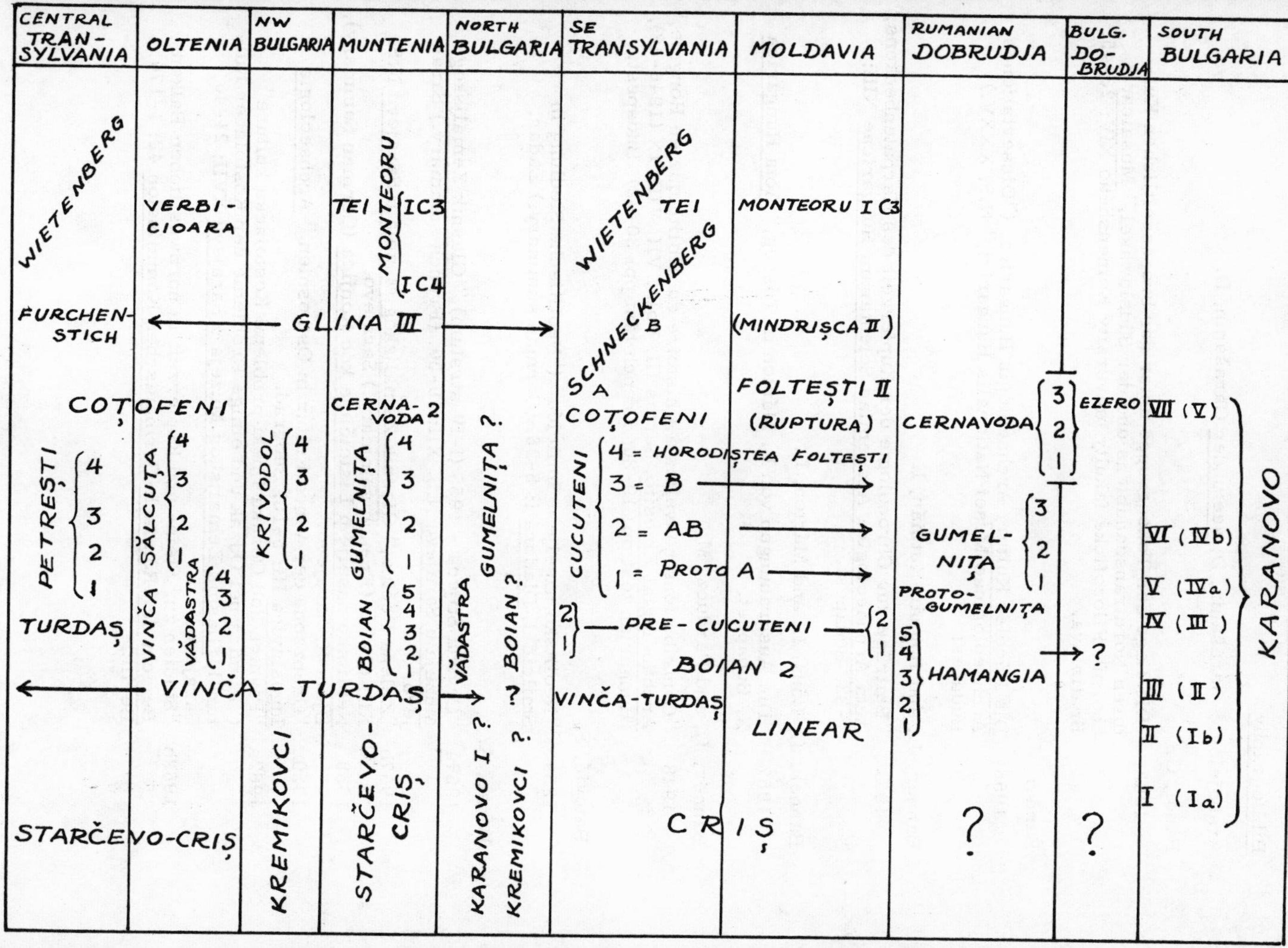

CENTRAL TRANSYLVANIA	OLTENIA	NW BULGARIA	MUNTENIA	NORTH BULGARIA	SE TRANSYLVANIA	MOLDAVIA	RUMANIAN DOBRUDJA	BULG. DOBRUDJA	SOUTH BULGARIA
WIETENBERG	VERBICIOARA		TEI { IC3 MONTEORU		WIETENBERG TEI	MONTEORU I C3			
			IC4		SCHNECKENBERG B				
FURCHENSTICH	← GLINA III →					(MINDRIȘCA II)			
COȚOFENI	COȚOFENI		CERNAVODA 2	GUMELNIȚA ?	A COȚOFENI	FOLTEȘTI II (RUPTURA)	CERNAVODA	3 2 1 EZERO	VII (V)
PETREȘTI 4 3 2 1	VINČA SĂLCUȚA 4 3 2 1	KRIVODOL 4 3 2 1	GUMELNIȚA 4 3 2 1		CUCUTENI 4 = HORODIȘTEA FOLTEȘTI; 3 = B →; 2 = AB →; 1 = PROTO A →		GUMELNIȚA 3 2 1		VI (IVb); V (IVa)
TURDAȘ	VĂDASTRA 4 3 2 1		BOIAN 5 4 3 2 1	VĂDASTRA; BOIAN ?	2 1 — PRE-CUCUTENI →	2 1; BOIAN 2	PROTO-GUMELNIȚA; HAMANGIA 5 4 3 2 1	→ ?	IV (III)
← VINČA – TURDAȘ →				?	VINČA-TURDAȘ	LINEAR			III (II); II (Ib)
STARČEVO-CRIȘ		KREMIKOVCI	STARČEVO-CRIȘ	KARANOVO I ?; KREMIKOVCI ?	CRIȘ		?	?	I (Ia)
									KARANOVO (I–VII)

Bibliography

Arandjelović-Garašanin, D; see under Garašanin, D.

Bandi, G.

1963 "Die Lage der Tokodgruppe unter der bronzezeitlichen Kulturen Nordtransdanubiens und der Südslowakei," Musaica. Sborník Filozofické fakulty univerzity Komenshého XIV: 23-45. Bratislava.

Banner, J.

1956 Die Péceler Kultur, Archaeologia Hungarica. ("Dissertationes Archaeologicae Musei Nationalis Hungarici," N.S. XXXV.) Budapest.

Banner, J., and Bognár-Kutzián, I.

1961 "Beiträge zur Chronologie der Kupferzeit des Karpatenbeckens," Acta Archaeologica Academiae Scientarum Hungaricae XIII: 1-32. Budapest.

Banner, J., Bóna, I., and Márton, L.

1957 "Die Ausgrabungen von L. Márton in Tószeg," Acta Hungarica X. Budapest.

Banner, J., and Parducz, M.

1948 "Contributions nouvelles à l'histoire du néolithique en Hongrie," Archaeologiai Értesitö, Series III, Vols. VII, VIII, IX (1946-48), (Hungarian text pp. 19-30; French text pp. 30-42). Budapest.

Batović, Š.

1959 "Neolitsko naselje u Smilčiću" ("Neolitische Siedlung in Smilčić"), Diadora I: 5-26. (German summary.) Zadar.

Benac, A.

1957a "Crvena Stijena - 1955 (I-IV stratum)," Glasnik Zemaljskog Muzeja u Sarajevu N.S. XII: 19-50. (French summary.) Sarajevo.

1957b "Zelena Pećina," Glasnik Zemaljskog Muzeja u Sarajevu N.S. XII: 61-92. (French summary.) Sarajevo.

1958 Neolitsko naselje u Lisičićima kod Konjica (German Summary), Djela X. Sarajevo.

1959 "Grenzzone der Vinča Kultur in Ostbosnien," Archaeologia Iugoslavica III: 5-10. Beograd.

1962a "Pivnica kod Odžaka i neki problemi Kostolačke kulture" ("Pivnica bei Odžak und einige Probleme der Kostolacer Kultur"), Glasnik Zemaljskog Muzeja u Sarajevu XVII: 21-40. Sarajevo.

1962b "Studien zur Stein- und Kupferzeit in nordwestlichen Balkan," Bericht der Römisch-Germanischen Kommission 42: 1-170. Berlin.

Berciu, D.

1958 "Neolitic preceramic în Balcani." Studii si cercetări de istorie veche IX: 91-98. (French summary.) Bucarest.

1961a "Chronologie relative du Néolithique du Bas Danube à la lumière des nouvelles fouilles fait en Roumanie," L'Europe à la fin de l'âge de la pierre, pp. 101-24. Prague.

1961b "Les nouvelles fouilles de Sălcuţa (Roumanie) et le problème des groupes Bubanj (Yougoslavie) et Krivodol (Bulgarie)," ibid., pp. 125-35. Praguc.

1961c Contribuţii le problemele neoliticului în Romînia în lumina noilor cercetări. (Contribution à l'Etude des problèmes du Néolithique de Roumanie à la lumière des nouvelles recherches.) Bucureşti: Institutul de Arheologia al Academiei R.P.R.

Bognár-Kutzián, I.; see under Kutzián.

Buttler, W.

1938 Der Donauländische und der westische Kulturkreis der jüngeren Steinzeit. ("Handbuch der Urgeschichte Deutschlands," No. 2.) Berlin and Leipzig.

Childe, V. G.

1929 The Danube in Prehistory. Oxford: Clarendon Press.

1947 The Dawn of European Civilization. 4th ed. London: Kegan Paul, Trench, Trubner.

Comşa, E.

1959a "Betrachtungen über die Linearbandkeramik auf dem Gebiet der Rumänischen Volksrepublik und der angrenzenden Länder," Dacia N.S. III: 35-57. Bucarest.

1959b "Săpăturile de la Dudeşti (reg. Bucureşti)" ("Les fouilles de Dudeşti"), Materiale şi cercetări arheologice V: 91-98. Bucureşti: Academia Republicii Populare Romîne.

Dimitrijević, S.

1962 "Prilog stupnjevanju badenske kulture u sjevernoj Jugoslaviji" ("Ein Beitrag zur Stufeneinteilung der Badener Kultur in Nordjugoslawien"), Arheološki Radovi i Rasprave II: 239-61. (German summary.) Zagreb.

Dinu, M.

1961 "Contribuţii la problema culturii amforelor sferice pe teritoriul Moldavei" ("Contribution à l'étude de la civilisation des amphores sphériques sur le territoire de la Moldavie"), Arheologia Moldovei I: 43-64 (French summary). Iaşi.

Driehaus, J.

1961 "Mitteleuropäisches Äneolithikum und balkanische Kupferzeit." L'Europe à la fin de l'âge de la pierre, pp. 353-60. Prague.

Driehaus, J., and Behrens, H.

1961 "Stand und Aufgaben der Erforschung des Jungneolithikums in

Mitteleuropa," L'Europe à la fin de l'âge de la pierre, pp. 233-75. Prague.

Driehaus, J., and Pleslová, E.

1961 "Aspekte zur Beurteilung des Äneolithikums in Böhmen und Mähren," ibid., pp. 361-88. Prague.

Dumitrescu, Vl.

1960 "La civilisation de Cucuteni," Berichten van de rijksdienst voor het oudheitkundig bodemonderzoek (Jaargang, 1959) 9: 6-48. Amersfoort.

1963 "Originea şi evoluţia culturii Cucuteni-Tripolie," Studii şi cercetări istorie veche XIV: 51-78, 285-308. (French summary.) Bucarest.

Ehrich, R. W.

1954 "The Relative Chronology of Southeastern and Central Europe in the Neolithic Period." In Relative Chronologies in Old World Archeology, ed. R. W. Ehrich, pp. 108-29. Chicago: University of Chicago Press.

1956 "Culture Area and Culture History in the Mediterranean and the Middle East." The Aegean and the Near East, ed. S. S. Weinberg, pp. 1-21. New York: Augustin.

1961 "On the Persistences and Recurrences of Culture Areas and Culture Boundaries during the Course of European Prehistory, Protohistory, and History," Berichte über den V Internationalen Kongress für Vor- und Frühgeschichte, Hamburg 1958, item 77, pp. 253-57. Berlin: Gebrüder Mann.

Ehrich, R. W., and Pleslová, E.

In press "Homolka: An Eneolithic Village in Bohemia," Monumenta Archaeologica and also Bulletin of the American School of Prehistoric Research. Prague and Cambridge, Mass.

Foltiny, I.

1941a "A Szöregi bronzkori temetö" ("Das bronzezeitliche Gräberfeld in Szöreg"), Dolgozatok XVII. Szeged.

1941b "Koraréz-és bronzkori temetö Deszken (Torontal M.)" ("Frühkupferzeitliches und bronzezeitliches Gräberfeld in Deszk (Komitat Torontal"), Folia Archaeologica III/IV: 69-88 (German text, 88-98). Budapest.

1942 "A 'Deszk-F' bronzkori temetö" ("Das bronzezeitliche Gräberfeld Deszk-F."), Szegedi Városi Muzeum Kiadvanyai Series II, 3. Szeged.

Galović, R

1964 "Neue Funde der Starčevo Kultur in Mittelserbien and Makedonien," Bericht der Römisch-Germanischen Kommission 1962-1963 43-44: 1-29. Berlin.

Garašanin, D.

1954a "Quelques éléments datant la civilisation de Bubanj-Hum," Archaeologia Iugoslavica I: 19-24. Beograd.

1954b (Arandjelović-Garašanin, D.) Starčevačka kultura. Ljubljana: Univerza v Ljubljani Arheološki Seminar. (French summary.)

Garašanin, M.

1951 "Die Theiss Kultur im jugoslawischen Banat," Bericht der Römisch-Germanischen Kommission 1943-1950 33: 125-32. Berlin.

1958 "Neolithikum und Bronzezeit in Serbien und Makedonien. Überblick über den Stand der Forschung 1958." ibid. 39: 1-130.

1959 "Zur Chronologie des makedonischen Neolithikums," Archaeologia Iugoslavica III: 1-4. Beograd.

Garašanin, M. and D.

1961 "Neolitske naselja 'Vršnik' kaj selo Tarinci" ("L'habitat néolithique Vršnik près de Tarinci"), Zbornik na Štipskiot Naroden Muzej 2 (1960-61): 7-40. (French summary.)

Gaul, J. H.

1948 "The Neolithic Period in Bulgaria." Bulletin of the American School of Prehistoric Research 16. Cambridge, Mass.

Georgiev, G. I.

1961 "Kulturgruppen der Jungstein- und der Kupferzeit in der Ebene von Thrazien (Südbulgarien)," L'Europe à la fin de l'âge de la pierre, pp. 45-100. Prague.

Grbić, M.

1956 "Retention der Starčevo Kultur." Archaeologia Iugoslavica II: 1-9. Beograd.

Hájek, L.

1954 "Jižní Čechy ve starší době bronzové" ("La Bohême méridionale à l'âge du bronze ancien"), Památky archeologické XLV: 115-92. (Russian and French summaries.) Prague.

Hell, M.

1954 "Salzburg in vollneolithischer Zeit. Die Münchshöferkultur," Archaeologia Austriaca 14: 11-34. Vienna.

Holmberg, E. J.

1964 "The Appearance of Neolithic Black Burnished Ware in Mainland Greece," American Journal of Archaeology 68: 343-48.

Holste, F.

1939 "Zur chronologischen Stellung der Vinča-Keramik," Wiener Prähistorische Zeitschrift XXVI: 1-21.

Horedt, K.

1960 "Die Wietenbergkultur," Dacia IV: 107-37. Bucarest: Institut d'Archéologie.

Houšt'ová, A.

1960 Die Trichterbecherkultur in Mähren, Fontes Archaeologici Pragenses 3. Prague: National Museum.

Kalicz, N.

1962 "Északkelet-Mágyarország korabronzkora és kapcsolatai." ("The Early Bronze Age of Northeast Hungary and Its Relationships.") Régészeti Dolgozatok IV, pp. 1-30. Budapest.

1963 Die Péceler (Badener) Kultur und Anatolien, Studia Archaeologica II: Academiae Scientiarum Hungaricae. Budapest.

Kastner, J. F.

1939 "Funde der Vučedol (Laibacher) Kultur und der Glockenbecherkultur von Aspern (Wien, 22 Bez.)," Wiener Prähistorische Zeitschrift XXVI: 117-34.

Kohl, G., and Quitta, H.

1963 "Berlin-Radiokarbondaten archäologischer Proben I," Ausgrabungen und Funde, 8: 281-301, Berlin.

Korek, J.

1958 "Leböhalmi ásatás 1950-ben" ("The Excavation at Leböhalom in 1950"), Archaeologiai Értesitö 85: 132-55. (English summary.) Budapest.

Korošec, J.

1957 "Lengyelska kulturna skupina v Bosni, Sremu, in Slavoniji" ("Lengyel Kulturgruppe in Bosnien, Syrmien und Slawonien"), Arheološki Vestnik VIII: 175-203. (German summary.) Ljubljana.

1958 "Eine neue Kulturgruppe des späten Neolithikums in Nordwestjugoslavien," Acta Archaeologica Academiae Scientarum Hungaricae 9: 83-93. Budapest.

1960a "Drulovka," Zbornik Filozofske Fakultete III, No. 4. Ljubljana.

1960b "Neolit na krasu in v Slovenskem primorju" ("The Neolithic Age in the Slovene Karst Area and in the Slovene Littoral"), Zgodovinski Časopis XIV: 5-34. (English summary.) Ljubljana.

1962 "Neka pitanja oko neolita u Dalmaciji" ("Gewisse Fragen des Neolithikums in Dalmatien"), Diadora II: 13-30. (German summary.) Zadar.

1963 "Relative Chronologie der Danilo Kulturgruppe," Munera Archaeologica Iosepho Kostrzewski, pp. 79-85. Poznan.

Korošec, P.

1958-59 "Kulturna opredelitev materialne kulture na koliščih pri Igu" ("Kultureinreihung der materiellen Kultur in den Pfahlbauten bei Ig"), Arheološki Vestnik IX-X/2: 94-107. (German summary.) Ljubljana.

1961 "Rasprostranjenost slavonske kulturne grupe" ("Expansion du groupe culturel Slavon"), Glasnik XV-XVI: 141-50. Sarajevo.

1963 "Zeitliche und kulturelle Einteilung einiger Funde aus Vinomer." Munera Archaeologica Iosepho Kostrzewski, pp. 129-37. Poznan.

Kutzián, I. Bognár-

1947 The Körös Culture. ("Dissertationes Pannonicae," Ser. II, No. 23.) Budapest.

1961 "Zur Problematik der ungarischen Kupferzeit," L'Europe à la fin de l'âge de la pierre, pp. 221-32. Prague.

1963 The Copper Age Cemetery of Tiszapolgár-Basatanya. Archaeologia Hungarica XLII. Budapest: Hungarian Academy of Sciences.

Lichardus, J.

1962 "Bukovohorská kultúra na Slovensku a jej postaveniu v Karpatskej kotline," Referáty o pracovních výsledcích československých archeologů za rok 1961, pp. 85-89. (In Slovakian but with table.) Smolenice.

Lichardus, J., and Pavúk, J.

1963 "Bemerkungen zum präkeramischen Neolithikum in der Argissa Magula und zu seiner Existenz in Europa," Slovenská archeológia XI: 459-76. Bratislava.

Mašek, N.

1961 "Die Řivnáč Gruppe in Böhmen und ihre chronologische Stellung." L'Europe à la fin du l'âge de la pierre, pp. 327-35. Prague.

Medunová-Benešová,

1964 "Eneolitické výšinne sídliště Stare Zamky v Brně-Líšni" ("Die äneolitische Höhensiedlung Staré Zámky in Brno-Líšeň"), Památky archeologické LV: 91-155. Prague.

Milojčić, V.

1949 Chronologie der jüngeren Steinzeit Mittel- und Südosteuropas. Berlin: Gebrüder Mann.

1951 "Die Siedlungsgrenzen und Zeitstellung der Bandkeramik in Osten und Südosten Europas," Bericht der Romisch-Germanischen Kommission 1943-1950 33: 110-24.

Mirosavljević, V.

1962 "Impresso-Cardium keramika na otocima Cresa, Lošinja i Krka" ("Impresso-Cardium Keramik auf den Inseln Cres, Lošinj und Krk"), Arheološki Radovi i Rasprave II: 175-211. (German summary.) Zagreb.

Moucha, V.

1963 "Die Periodisierung der Úněticer Kultur in Böhmen," Sborník Československé Společnosti Archeologické 3: 9-60. Brno.

Mozsolics, A.

1952 "Die Ausgrabungen in Tószeg im Jahre 1948," Acta Archaeologica 2: 35-69. Budapest.

Nestor, I.

1960 "Zur Periodisierung der späteren Zeitstufen des Neolithikums in der Rumänischen Volksrepublik." Dacia IV: 53-68. Bucarest.

Neustupný, E. and J.

1961 Czechoslovakia before the Slavs. New York: Praeger.

Neustupný, J.

1961 "Zum Stand der relativen Chronologie des Äneolithikums in der Tchechoslowakei," Kommission für das Äneolithikum und die ältere Bronzezeit, Nitra 1958, pp. 43-58. Bratislava.

Nicolăescu-Plopşor, C. S.

1959 "Discuţii pe marginea paleoliticului de sfîrşit şi începuturilor neoliticului nostru." Studii şi cercetări de istorie veche X: 221-37.

Novak, G.

1955 Prethistorijski Hvar: Grapčeva spilja (Prehistoric Hvar: The Cave of Grabak). Zagreb.

Novotná, M.

1961 "Bošácko-kostolacký horizont na stredňom Považí" ("Der Horizont von Bošáca-Kostolac im mittleren Waagtal"), Musaica. Sborník Filozofické fakulty univerzity Komenského XII: 21-34. Bratislava.

Novotný, B.

1955 "Slavónska kultura v Československu" ("Slawonische Kultur in der Tschechoslowakei"), Slovenská archeológia III: 5-69. (Russian and German summaries.)

1958 Die Slowakei in der jüngeren Steinzeit (Pamphlet—text translation of Slovensko v mladšej dobe Kamennej). Bratislava: Slovenská Akadémia Vied.

1959 "Spojení jihozápadního Slovenska se Zakarpatím a Přičernomořím v mladší době kamenné" ("The Communication of Southwest Slovakia with the Transcarpathian and Black Sea Areas in the New Stone Age"), Acta Universitatis Carolinae. Philosophica et Historica 3. Filipův sborník, pp. 13-20. Prague.

1962 Lužianske skupina a počiatky mal'ovanej keramiky na Slovensku. Bratislava: Slovenská Akadémia Vied.

Passek, T. S.

1961 "Problèmes de l'Enéolithique du Sud-Ouest de l'Europe orientale," L'Europe à la fin de l'âge de la pierre, pp. 148-60. Prague.

1962a "Relations entre l'Europe occidentale et l'Europe orientale à l'époque néolithique." VI Congrès Internationale des Sciences Préhistoriques et Protohistoriques. Les Rapports et les Informations des Archéologues de l'URSS (Pamphlet). Moscow: Les Academies des Sciences de l'URSS.

1962b "Relations entre l'Europe occidentale et l'Europe orientale à l'époque néolithique," Atti del VI Congresso Internationale delle Scienze preistoriche e protoistoriche I, pp. 127-44. Firenze: Sanzoni. (Same text as 1962a but without maps; more easily available.)

Patay, P.

1938 "Frühbronzezeitliche Kulturen in Ungarn," Dissertationes Pannonicae II: 13. Budapest.

1961 "A Bodrogkeresztúri kultura temetöi," Régészeti Füzetek, Ser. II, 10. Budapest: Magyar Nemzeti Muzeum.

Pavúk, J., and Lichardus, J.

1964 "Poznámky k vývoju neolitu na Slovensku." Referáty o pracovných výsledcích československých archeologů I: 29-35. Liblice: Československá Akademie Věd. Archeologické ústavy v Praze, Brně, a Nitře.

Petrescu-Dîmboviţa, M.

1957 "Sondajul stratigrafia de la Perieni (reg. Iaşi, r. Bîrlad)," materiale şi cercetări arheologice III: 65-82. Bucureşti.

Pittioni, R.

1954 Urgeschichte des österreichischen Raumes. Wien: Franz Deuticke.

1960 Urzeitliche Besiedlung I, II (7 maps and chart). Österreich-Atlas. V/1 a-d, V/2 a-d. Wien: Österreichischen Akademie der Wissenschaften.

Pleslová, E.

1961 "Zur Entwicklung des Äneolithikums in Böhmen," L'Europe à la fin de l'âge de la pierre, pp. 322-26. Prague.

Quitta, H.

1960 "Zur Frage der ältesten Bandkeramik in Mitteleuropa," Prähistorische Zeitschrift XXXVIII: 1-38, 153-88. Berlin.

Radiocarbon

1963 Vol. 5. The American Journal of Science, Yale University,
1964 Vol. 6. New Haven.

Scollar, I.

1959 "Regional Groups in the Michelsberg Culture: A Study in the Middle Neolithic of West Central Europe," Proceedings of the Prehistoric Society XXV: 52-134. Cambridge, England.

Soudský, B.

1956 "K relativní chronologii volutové keramiky" ("À la chronologie relative de la céramique spiralée"), Archeologické rozhledy VIII: 408-12, 462-63. (French summary.) Prague.

Srejović, D.

1963 "Versuch einer historischen Wertung der Vinča-gruppe," Archaeologia Iugoslavica IV: 5-18.

Steklá, M.

1960 "Vztahy mezi keramikou vypíchanou a malovanou" ("Die Beziehungen zwischen den Mährisch-bemalte Keramik und Stichbandkeramik"), Acta Universitatis Carolinae. Philosophica et Historica 3. Filipův sbornik, pp. 31-38. Prague.

Teleki, G.

1953 "East Central Europe." In The Geography of Europe, ed. G. W. Hoffman, pp. 509-83. New York: Ronald Press.

Thomas, E. B.-(ed.)

1956 Archäologische Funde in Ungarn. Budapest: Corvina.

Tichý, R.

1960 "K nejstarší volutové keramice na Moravě" ("Zur ältesten Volutenkeramik in Mähren"), Památky archeologické LI: 415-41. (German summary.) Prague.

1961 "Einige Bemerkungen zum Neolithikum in der Tschechoslowakei (nach den Forschungsergebnissen seit 1945)," Archaeologia Austriaca 29: 96-122. Vienna.

1962 "Osídlení s volutovou keramikou na Moravě" ("Die Besiedlung mit Voluten- (Linearband) Keramik in Mähren"), Památky archeologické LIII: 245-305. (German summary.) Prague.

Točik, A.

1963 "Die Nitra-Gruppe," Archeologické rozhledy XV: 716-74. Prague.

Todorović, J.

1963 "Die Grabung Hissar und ihre Verhältnisse zum Äneolithikum und den frühen Bronzezeit," Archaeologia Iugoslavica IV: 25-2

Tompa, F. von

1937 "25 Jahre Urgeschichtsforschung in Ungarn, 1912-1936," Bericht der Römisch-Germanischen Kommission 1934/1935, 24/25: 27-114, 117-27.

Trogmayer, O.

1964 "Megjegyzések a Körös-csoport relatív Idörendjéhez" ("Remarks to the Relative Chronology of the Körös group"), Archaeologiai Értesítö 91: 67-86.

Vlassa, N.

1959 "Cultura ceramicii lineare în Transylvania," Studii şi cercetări de istorie veche X: 239-46.

1964 "Contribuţii la cunoaşterea culturii Bodrogkeresztúr în Transilvania" ("Contributions à la connaissance de la culture de

Bodrogkeresztúr, en Transylvanie"), Studii şi cercetări de istorie veche 15: 351-67.

Vulpe, R.

1957 Izvoare: Săpăturile din 1936-1948. Biblioteca Arheologica I. Bucureşti: Institutul de Arheologie al Academiei RPR.

Weinberg, S. S.

1962 "Excavations at Prehistoric Elateia, 1959," Hesperia XXXI: 158-209. Athens.

Willvonseder, K.

1934 "Die Kultur der süddeutschen Urnenfelder in Österreich," Germania 18: 182-89. Frankfort a.M.

1939 "Funde des Kreises Vučedol-Laibach aus Niederdonau und Ungarn," Wiener Prähistorische Zeitschrift XXVI: 135-47. Vienna.

Zaharia, E.

1962 "Considérations sur la civilisation de Criş à la lumière des sondages de Leţ," Dacia N.S. VI: 5-51. Bucarest.

Zápotocký, M.

1958 "Problém periodisace kultury nálevkovitých pohárů v Čechách a na Moravě" ("Problem der Periodisierung der Trichterbecherkultur in Böhmen und Mähren"), Archeologické rozhledy X: 664-700. Prague.

1961 "Einige Fragen des jüngeren böhmischen Äneolithikums," L'Europe à la fin de l'âge de la pierre, pp. 337-47. Prague.

Addendum:

Although seen too late for inclusion in either the discussion or the bibliography, attention should be called to the following pertinent articles by J. Pavúk, J. Lichardus and J. Vladár, V. Němecová-Pavúková, and D. Berciu, on Zseliz, Ludanice, Boleráz, and Cernavoda respectively, in Slovenská Archeólogia XII, 1, 1964; by S. Šiška on Tiszapolgár in XII, 2, 1964; by A. Točik and J. Lichardus on Slovakian painted wares, and J. Pavelčík on Bošáca in Moravia in Památky archeologické LV, 2, 1964; J. Lichardus on linear wares plus some Starčevo material in East Slovakia in Archeologické rozhledy XVI, 6, 1964.

In Dacia, n.s. VII, 1963, N. Vlassa, with regard to Neolithic chronology in Transylvania, reports the finding of three pictographic tablets at Tărtăria, for the significance of which see comment on page 439, above. V. Dumitrescu, also in Dacia VII, writes on the date of early Kurgan expansion, and in Dacia VIII, 1964, discusses synchronisms between Cucuteni and Gumelniţa.

In Danilo in Danilska Kultura (Danilo und die Danilo-Kulturgruppe), Univerza v Ljubljani, Ljubljana, 1964, J. Korošec discusses the Danilo excavations of 1955; and in Poročilo o raziskovanju neolita in eneolita v Sloveniji, Univerza v Ljubljani, Ljubljana, 1962 (German summaries), J. and P. Korošec together with T. Bregant and K. Drobne report on the 1962 excavations on the Laibach Moor near Ig.

The Relative Chronology of Neolithic and Chalcolithic Cultures in Eastern Europe North of the Balkan Peninsula and the Black Sea

Marija Gimbutas
University of California, Los Angeles

This paper covers the relative chronologies of three cultures in eastern Europe—the Cucuteni-Tripolye, the North Pontic, the Kurgan—from the beginning of the food-producing economy in the fifth millennium B.C. to about 2000 B.C. (Bronze Age chronologies of central and eastern European cultures are dealt with in detail in my monograph Bronze Age Cultures in Central and Eastern Europe, 1965.)

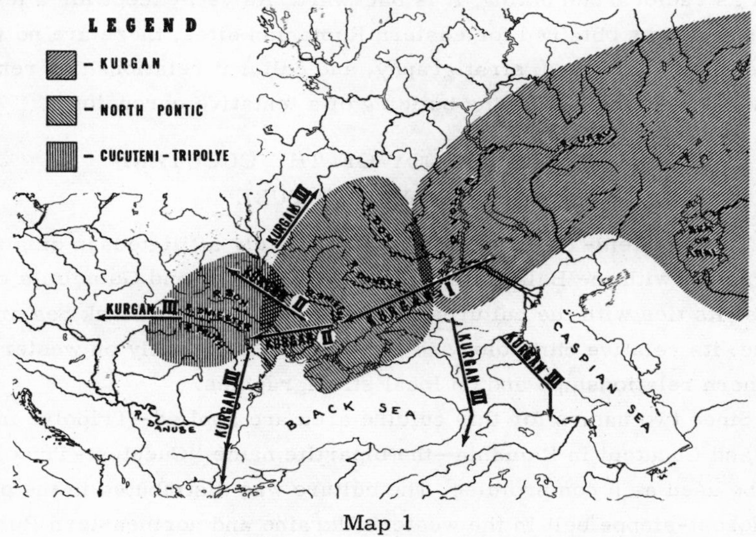

Map 1

The distribution of these cultures, as indicated on Map 1, is north of the Carpathian Mountains, north of the Black Sea, and north of the Caucasus Mountains. This wide strip of land is intersected by large rivers flowing into the Black Sea: the Sereth (Siret), Pruth (Prut), Boh (Southern Bug), Dniester, Dnieper, and Don. All these river valleys were inhabited during Neolithic and Chalcolithic times in spite of the fact that the climate changed from dry to wet and from wet to dry. The faunal and floral remains in habitation sites have proved the existence, throughout most of the period, of forest conditions, particularly by the presence of such animals as elk, beaver, and bear.

In Neolithic and Chalcolithic times, the Volga and the Urals formed no bulwark against Asiatic peoples, and hordes of semi-nomads appeared from beyond the lower Volga. These were the Kurgan people who, in the second half of the third millennium B.C., caused the local cultures to disintegrate. The appearance of these Kurgan people in the North Pontic region dramatically marks a cultural change and is of incontestable value for chronological studies. In countless instances, habitation sites and cemeteries have yielded elements of several different cultures.

Many new chronological phases have come to light as a result of recent excavations in each of the three cultural areas. The old labels must be revised, and new chronological charts must be drawn. This part of Europe can boast of the most rapid spade work, but in other respects, such as radiocarbon dating, it is backward. As yet, except for a few determinations obtained for eastern Rumanian sites, there are no C-14 dates. Climate change, stratigraphy, and cultural relationships remain about the only means for the building of a tentative chronology.

THE CHRONOLOGY OF THE CUCUTENI-TRIPOLYE CULTURE

The Cucuteni-Tripolye culture is definitely affiliated, in origin and character, with the Balkan bloc: Boian, Hamangia, and Gumelniţa cultures. Its ties with the cultures in Russia north of the Black Sea are vague; its relative chronology is therefore based chiefly on western and southern relationships and on local stratigraphies.

Since two names for this culture area are applied—Tripolye in Russia, and Cucuteni in Rumania—the bipartite name "Cucuteni-Tripolye" can be used as a compromise. The culture was distributed in the present forest-steppe belt in the western Ukraine and northeastern Rumania covering the fertile valleys of the Sereth, Pruth, upper and middle Dniester, and Boh (Southern Bug) rivers, and later of the middle Dneiper.

The stratified site of utmost importance for the research of this culture was Cucuteni, in the valley of the middle Pruth. During the excavations of 1909-10, Schmidt came upon traces of two superimposed strata. The lower—A—contained trichrome pottery, and the upper—B—included bichrome. Soon thereafter Schmidt discovered another site in the same area (Dîmbul Morii) with pottery showing an intermediate style between Cucuteni A and B. Consequently, this new phase was labeled "Cucuteni A-B." After Schmidt published his book Cucuteni in der Oberen Moldau, Rumänien in 1932, the knowledge of the Cucuteni A, A-B, and B strata highlighted the future chronological studies. From 1935 to 1940, Radu Vulpe verified the same three strata at Calu (Vulpe, 1937-1940); during the excavations of 1936, 1938, 1940, 1951, and later, thousands of square meters of Cucuteni A-B settlement were revealed at Traian by V. and H. Dumitrescu (V. Dumitrescu, 1941-44; H. Dumitrescu, 1952, 1954, 1955, 1957, 1959). During this same period, new excavations in Rumania proved that Cucuteni A, A-B, and B phases represent merely later developments of the culture and that Cucuteni A was preceded by earlier phases. New light was thrown on the earlier phases by the excavations carried out by Radu Vulpe in 1936 and 1948 at Izvoare near Neamţ in the basin of upper Sereth in Moldavia, during which were discovered a stratum with a more primitive monochrome and incised pottery and several layers with a bichrome pottery called Precucuteni and Protocucuteni respectively (Vulpe, 1957). Finds of Precucutenian character also appeared in other sites such as Traian-Dealul Viei (or Zăneşti), Traian-Dealul Fîntînilor, and Larga Jijiei (see references in V. Dumitrescu, 1959). The Precucuteni sites with unpainted pottery are assumed to have belonged to three consecutive phases: Precucuteni I, II, and III.

Another series of well-excavated sites have been assigned stratigraphically and typologically to the period between Precucuteni and Cucuteni A itself. Vulpe calls them "Protocucuteni," whereas V. Dumitrescu has placed them in the beginning of the Cucuteni A period, Cucuteni A_1 and A_2. The latter author, on typological and stratigraphical grounds, has divided Cucuteni A into four phases: A_1, A_2, A_3, and A_4. Cucuteni A (as of the Cucuteni site) became Cucuteni A_3. To the Cucuteni A_1 and A_2 phases (after Dumitrescu) belong two strata of the Izvoare site—II_1 and II_2 (Vulpe, 1957)—the Frumuşica site excavated by Matasă (Matasă, 1946), a large village of Truşeşti north of Iaşi in Moldavia (Petrescu-Dîmboviţa, 1963), one stratum of the Ariuşd site on the upper Olt excavated before World War I, and Bonteşti between Moldavia and Walachia (V. Dumitrescu, 1927-1932).

To Cucuteni A_3, which equals Schmidt's Cucuteni A, belong other great sites, among them one layer of the most prominent stratified site at Hăbăşeşti, excavated in 1949-50 under the supervision of V. Dumitrescu

(V. Dumitrescu et al., 1954). Other sites with related but somewhat typologically more advanced materials, like Ruginoasa and Fedeleşeni, are grouped by V. Dumitrescu (1963) as Cucuteni A_4. The phase Cucuteni A-B has recently been subdivided into early and late: A-B_1 and A-B_2 (V. Dumitrescu, 1963).

The old Cucuteni B period is also no longer regarded as a short phase. Newly excavated habitation sites, like the fortress of Cucuteni, Draguşeni, Petreni, Valea Lupului in Rumanian Moldavia, have made it possible to subdivide the period into three subphases: B_1, B_2, and B_3 (V. Dumitrescu, 1963).

The following chart summarizes what has been said above, concerning sites in Rumania. It was drawn by V. Dumitrescu (1963) on the basis of both stratigraphy (with Izvoare as a key site) and typology (Table 1).

Table 1

	PHASES	SITES	
12.	Cucuteni B_3	Valea Lupului	
11.	Cucuteni B_2	Cucuteni B_2. Petreni. Şipeniţ. Draguşeni	
10.	Cucuteni B_1	Cucuteni B_1	
9.	Cucuteni A-B_2	Traian - Dealul Fîntînilor	
8.	Cucuteni A-B_1	Corlateni	
7.	Cucuteni A_4		Fedeleşeni
6.	Cucuteni A_3 (Tripolye B_1)	Ruginoasa Hăbăşeşti	Cucuteni A
5.	Cucuteni A_2	Ariuşd. Bonteşti. Frumuşica. Truşeşti Izvoare II_2. Tirpeşti	
4.	Cucuteni A_1	Izvoare II_1. Tirpeşti	
3.	Precucuteni III (Tripolye A)	Tirpeşti	Izvoare I_2, Traian-Dealul Fîntînilor etc.
2.	Precucuteni II	Larga Jijiei	Izvoare I_1. Floreşti
1.	Precucuteni I	Traian-Dealul Viei	

The phases indicated in Table 1 are probably not of equal duration, and some chronological gaps may still exist because the Cucuteni-Tripolyans, like central European upper Danubians, practiced a "shifting agriculture" and did not live permanently on the same spot. In the Cucuteni-Tripolye area, there are no sites like Karanovo or Vinča which have twelve or more meters of cultural debris. However, the typological evolution we now have in this area is striking, and leads us to believe that our knowledge of the development of the Cucuteni-Tripolye culture is nearly complete.

In the Ukrainian SSR, before and after World War II, a number of "Tripolye" villages were excavated, some of which yielded more than one stratum—for instance, Nezvisko (Chernysh, 1962), Darabani (Passek, 1949), Polivanov Jar (Passek, 1951), Soloncheny II (Movsha, 1960), and others.

Passek has published (1949) a chronological classification of the Tripolye culture in which she has classified the vast amount of material from the excavations in the western Ukraine. Her basic classification is Early, Middle, and Late Tripolye with Middle and Late each subdivided into two phases. Early or A equals the late Precucuteni period; Middle or B, the Cucuteni A itself and AB; and the Late or C corresponds to Cucuteni B.

The classification of the "Tripolye" sites is summarized in Table 2.

Table 2

Phases in the Western Ukraine		Stratified and Other Important Sites	Roughly Synchronous with Rumanian Sites of
Tripolye C_I		Polivanov Jar 3 Soloncheny II_3	Cucuteni B
Tripolye B_{II}		Polivanov Jar 2 Nezvisko, upper Soloncheny II_2	Cucuteni A-B
Tripolye B_I	c b a	Soloncheny II_I Nezvisko, lower Polivanov Jar_1	Cucuteni A_3
Tripolye A	b a	Luka Vrublevetskaja Floreshty	Precucuteni III Precucuteni II

The earliest phases of the Cucuteni-Tripolye culture in the basins of the Pruth and the upper Dniester succeed the Linear Danubian culture typified by music note ornamented pottery. The site of Zăneşti, classified as Precucuteni I, has shown persistent influences of the Danubian culture, and the culture layer of Floreshty, a Precucuteni II site on the Reut River, a tributary of the upper Dniester, was one meter above the Linear Danubian deposits. C-14 dates for the music note ornamented Danubian culture cluster in the late part of the fifth millennium B.C. Hence, the Precucuteni period may have started before the middle of the fourth millennium B.C.

The beginning of the Precucuteni is, however, not the beginning of the Neolithic in Moldavia and the western Ukraine. New horizons relevant to the problem of the beginnings of the Cucuteni-Tripolye culture opened with the discovery of early Neolithic sites in the Boh basin (Danilenko, 1957, 1960; Passek, 1962), which antedate the earliest Precucuteni culture.

So far there are only a few C-14 dates for the Cucuteni-Tripolye culture—too few to form a backbone for the chronology. One was obtained from the Cucuteni A_3 site at Hăbăşeşti: 3130 ± 60 B.C.; another from the Cucuteni B_3 site at Valea Lupului: 2750 ± 60 B.C. Both dates were rejected by Dumitrescu (1963) as too early, particularly that of Valea Lupului, which contradicts the facts of cultural relationships that indicate that it can hardly be before 2000 B.C. As corrected for a half life of 5,730 ± 30, these dates are even higher (see Ehrich, p. 441). Before we have more determinations, not much stress can be laid on this method of dating.

The whole cultural evolution throughout the Neolithic and Chalcolithic periods in this part of Europe can be summarized as follows.

The primitive Neolithic period, which covers the earliest Neolithic sites in the Boh basin. In this period, the Rumanian provinces were occupied by people with the Starčevo-Criş culture and later by those with music note ornamented Danubian pottery and by the Boian people of the Giuleşti phase.

The formative Cucuteni-Tripolye period, during which the Cucuteni-Tripolye culture developed its characteristic features with strong influences from the Boian and Linear Danubian cultures. The period covers three consecutive phases typified by excised and incised pottery. In Rumania these phases are known as Precucuteni I-III. On the Ukrainian side, this is Tripolye A.

The classical Cucuteni-Tripolye period, which is characterized by its beautiful bichrome and trichrome pottery and by larger villages. This is a long period comprising many phases of this culture's golden age, cherished for its outstanding painted pottery. A gradual development through its phases distinguished by stratigraphy—Cucuteni A_1, A_2, A_3, A_4, A-B_2, and B_1 to B_3—is undoubted. The disintegration of the culture took place following Cucuteni B, owing to the conquest of the whole Cucuteni-Tripolye area by the Kurgan peoples.

The Primitive Neolithic Period

The chronology of the earliest Neolithic sites with evidence for agriculture in the basin of R. Boh (Skibinets, Sokolets, and Pechera) is indicated by the appearance of Starčevo (Criş, Körös) pottery elements: barbotine decoration, flat bases, and well-polished, very thin-walled pots in the site of Pechera in contrast with large rude pots of local manufacture. The latter were reddish brown in color, tempered with sand and organic substance, and decorated all over with incised, slightly curved, vertical and horizontal ribbons. The presence of Starčevo elements in the third phase of the earliest Neolithic sites in the basin of the Boh indicates their relative contemporaneity with the Starčevo culture. This means that the beginnings of a Neolithic culture in this area started not later than in the early part of the fifth millennium B.C. if we rely on C-14 dates for Starčevo III. Primitive pointed-based pottery and a microlithic flint industry found in the two earlier sites—Skibinets and Sokolets—speak for a local and long lasting process toward a more civilized life (Danilenko, 1962).

The next phase shows a more advanced character with permanent villages and rectangular houses having stone foundations (type sites: Samchin and Savran). Oval or slightly biconical vases with flat bases continued to be decorated with incised ribbons sometimes forming spirals and meanders which find close parallels in the central European Linear Danubian pottery. The similarity in ornament may indicate the contemporaneity of this second phase with the Danubian culture of the late Linear phase during which it expanded from the west to the upper Dniester and the Pruth basins and replaced the Starčevo culture. At Perieni on the upper Pruth, a Danubian settlement overlay the Starčevo layers. As already indicated, Danubian sites typified by music note ornamented pottery are shown by C-14 dating to have belonged to the late fifth millennium B.C.

The position of early Neolithic settlements in the river valleys, on the lowest terraces close to the stream, is an indication of the dry climate of that period since the present spring flood waters usually flow above the level of the earliest Neolithic sites. The period of dry climate in the Pontic region is regarded as coeval with the Boreal period in the Baltic area (Sulimirski, 1961).

The Formative Period

Danubian, Boian, and partly Hamangian influences were responsible for the ensuing formation of the Cucuteni-Tripolye culture during the fourth millennium B.C. The beginning of this period succeeds the late Linear Danubian culture in the Pruth and upper Dniester valleys. The earliest phase of this period was contemporary with the expanding Boian culture of the Giuleşti phase.

The best known sites are those of Izvoare I, Zăneşti (or Traian Dealul Viei), Larga Jijiei, and Traian (Dealul Fîntînilor) in northeastern Rumania, and Floreshty, Luka Vrublevetskaja, Bernovo Luka, and Golerkany in the upper Dniester basin in the western Ukraine. They constitute three consecutive phases: Precucuteni I-III.

Agricultural preoccupations are indicated by antler hoes, saddle querns, and millet grains. Some of the sites yielded domestic animal bones, among which those of cattle, pig, goat, and dog were identified. The important role of domesticated animals is shown also by clay figurines representing bulls, goats, and pigs. Horse bones were found in the village of Luka Vrublevetskaja (Bibikov, 1953, p. 454). Among wild animal bones, those of elk and beaver have been identified. Both species are confined to the forests. The presence of forest fauna and flora is a clear hint of the damper climate which must have succeeded the dry climate of the early Neolithic period. The villages were then founded on the first terraces and not on the low banks of the streams as during the earlier period. Small plots for agriculture must have been cleared by burning shrubs and trees.

Tools were of flint acquired from the Pruth area, obsidian from the volcanic mountains in Transylvania, and of various stones, slate, antler, and bone. Flint and obsidian were used to make knives and end scrapers; other stones, for perforated axes; slate, for small ax-adzes; bone for points and awls. Boar's tusks and elk antlers and teeth were widely used for ornaments.

Copper artifacts appeared in this period. The earliest came from the lowest layer of the Izvoare site, in which an awl having a rectangular section, a needle, and a pendant of copper were found. In 1961, a gigantic hoard was discovered in the village of Karbuna (on the Karbuna River, tributary of the Botna River) in the Moldavian SSR, including 444 copper objects in addition to 408 artifacts of stone, marble, Mediterranean shells, bone, and elk teeth. The hoard, with a total of 852 artifacts, was stored in a large pear-shaped vase covered with a smaller vase, both typical of the Precucuteni III phase (Sergeev, 1962). The hoard is unique in the eastern part of the Balkan Peninsula.

Most of the copper objects were ornaments: four spiral bracelets, a bracelet of eight tubes, fourteen flat pendants of light copper with perforations in the corners, eleven tubular beads, 377 annular and flattened spherical beads, twenty-four schematic anthropomorphic figurines, two disk-shaped plates with perforations and pointillé decoration, and two other simple plates. Among the ornaments were only two copper axes. One was wedge-shaped, rectangular in cross section, 14.5 cm. long. The other, 12.1 cm. long, was a hammer-ax with a large round shaft hole. The edges of both axes were narrow, and the copper from which they were made was softer than stone. This explains why copper axes were rare and why stone axes were used with them. The same hoard included a beautifully made perforated ax of white marble and another ax of slate.

The Karbuna hoard bears witness to commercial relations with the southeastern world, since neither copper, marble, nor Mediterranean shells are native to the Cucuteni-Tripolye area. The imported objects may have reached this culture via the Black and Aegean Seas from Anatolia.

Separate phases of this period were determined on the basis of stratigraphy in Izvoare and Traian as well as on the changing fashions of pottery decoration.

The earliest phase (Precucuteni I) is characterized particularly by pottery with excised and white incrusted ornament having close analogies with pottery of the Giuleşti phase of the Boian culture. Ornamental motifs consisted of incised spiral or straight bands, rows of excised triangles or "wolf's teeth," and checker patterns. Engraved stylized anthropomorphic motifs also appear. From the primitive period the barbotine decoration continued, applied on storage vessels. Alveoli at the end of incised lines recall the note-head ornament on late Danubian pottery. Pots were roughly biconical or pear-shaped in form, and there were also stands and ladles. Lids with cylindrical protuberances were exactly like those in the Boian culture.

The second phase (Precucuteni II) is marked by unquestionable development in pottery. The surface was now well polished. The excised and incised ornament continued, but fluting technique also came into use The space between parallel incisions forming spiral bands was sometimes painted in red.

During the third phase (Precucuteni III), the excised ornament disappeared; incised or punctate lines and fluted ornament predominated. After incision, red painting was frequently applied.

Female and—rarely—male human figurines of clay are the most usual finds aside from pots. Figurines were depicted schematically in a standing or seated position with a cone-shaped or oval head either plain or with roughly indicated facial features, and with the body covered all over with incised or dotted lines, sometimes with indication of necklaces. Female figurines are nearly all of steatopygous type. The upper part of the body is neglected: breasts are rarely shown, hands are lacking. Flat figurines of clay, bone, or copper were extremely schematized being of a pear shape or violin form with roughly indicated head or neck They have perforations on the sides and presumably were originally sew on garments as decoration. Close analogies for the anthropomorphic figurines are in the Hamangia culture in Dobrudja on the Rumanian Black Sea coast which shows direct contacts with Anatolia and the eastern Mediterranean area.

The Classical Period

This period is marked by constant development in all aspects. The growth of population is indicated by a large number of sizable villages. Change of climate toward a warmer and less damp period resulted in better living conditions. Enormous villages are eloquent witnesses to a remarkable evolution in the Cucuteni-Tripolye peasant society.

Villages were founded on the second terraces of rivers at some distance from the water, some on elevated promontories difficult of access but with good visibility over considerable distances. The Cucuteni site itself was situated on a high promontory as was Hăbăşeşti, which had a view of about thirty kilometers. A number of villages were fortified by ditches and perhaps by wooden palisades on the inland side.

A tangible border line between the formative and classical periods is drawn by the appearance of bichrome pottery, soon followed by even more exquisite trichrome that must be considered one of the outstanding achievements of this culture and recognized as thoroughly representative of the main body of Cucuteni-Tripolye materials. Whereas most of the shapes had their prototypes in the Formative period, they had now become more sophisticated, varied, and striking. Basic forms were large pear-shaped vases, beakers, bowls, binocular vases, hollow stands, and ladles with long handles. For chronological studies, the changing pottery style—the transition from bichrome to trichrome and from trichrome back to bichrome, and the constant enrichment of ornamental motifs—is of considerable importance.

Chronological phases of the classical period have been well defined stratigraphically and typologically, primarily by pottery (see Table I).

The mode of pottery painting seems to have spread from south to north: the earliest bichrome pottery is found in sites in western and southern Moldavia bordering on Gumelniţa but is lacking in the Ukraine east of the Pruth River. Dumitrescu, in considering the appearance of painted pottery, regards southern Moldavia and northeastern Walachia as the cradle of the Cucuteni-Tripolye civilization (V. Dumitrescu, 1959).

Pottery of Cucuteni A_1 is characterized by painting in two colors: white and red. Ornamental motifs—bands of spirals between incised lines—were painted in white on a reddish background before firing. Red was also applied next to the incised lines. In addition to incision, fluting technique was also used. Side by side with sophisticated painted and well-fired pottery, a more primitive, porous pottery decorated with ornament in relief was used in this and in all later phases.

During Cucuteni A_2, painted pottery, now in three colors—white, red, and black before firing—was being made in Cucuteni-Tripolye villages of all Moldavia. The black was used instead of incisions for bordering the red and white bands.

In Cucuteni A_3, polychrome pottery reached its climax and its widest distribution. For the first time polychrome pottery appeared as far as the middle Dnieper, where it was found in the eponymous Tripolye settlement. Black border lines were no longer employed, and incision was going out of use.

Technologically, this pottery is surpassed by neither the preceding nor the succeeding. The best examples had very thin walls and, as shown by analyses, the clay was baked at a temperature of 900° C.

During this phase, Kurgan II pottery appears in the Cucuteni-Tripolye sites east of the Dniester.

In Cucuteni A_4, trichrome pottery continued and bichrome pottery of new fashion was introduced; incised decoration was now abandoned.

During Cucuteni A-B, polychrome pottery continued. Foreign elements, however, now made their appearance in the whole Cucuteni-Tripolye area. These elements are represented by a totally different pottery made of clay tempered with crushed shells and stones and decorated with cord and comblike impressions, typical of the Eurasian Kurgan III pottery. The proportion of Kurgan pottery was still small, indicating that Cucuteni-Tripolye villages persisted and were not massively assaulted.

Cucuteni B, with its three subphases, is a definite proof of further Cucuteni-Tripolye existence. Painted pottery did not die out. Being closely related to that of the preceding phase, it manifests changes in that the trichrome pottery becomes less frequent and a bichrome pottery (usually black or chocolate brown on a flesh or cream-colored background) takes its place. The curvilinear designs become somewhat decomposed and meanders disappear completely. In addition to schematic anthropomorphic motifs that are found on some vases of Cucuteni A-B, zoömorphic motifs appear for the first time. The animals portrayed were schematized so much that their identity is not known. From the first glimpse, we get an impression that these animals were dogs or mythical beings reminiscent of dogs. They are organic parts of strictly geometric pottery which fill the empty spaces between curvilinear or straight lines.

During Cucuteni A_3 and particularly during A-B, elements of the Kurgan culture were present, but the old population maintained its characteristic features. After Cucuteni B, the picture rapidly changed. Cultural remains above the Cucuteni B layers in stratified sites indicate that the Cucuteni-Tripolye culture was uprooted. Perhaps there were repeated massive invasions of the Kurgan people or an assimilation of the local people after several centuries of occupation by invaders. Only insignificant islands remained in which the old traditions persisted, tapering off in the course of the following several centuries.

THE CHRONOLOGY OF THE NORTH PONTIC DNIEPER-DONETS CULTURE

This culture has become better known since 1933, when Makarenko published materials on the excavation of the large cemetery of Mariupol' north of the Sea of Azov (Makarenko, 1933). It was long regarded as the only "Neolithic" monument in the area. The cemetery yielded pottery sherds; bull figurines; boar-tusk laminae; pendants of shells, teeth, porphyry, and rock crystal; stone mace heads; flint knives and axes; and other finds indicative of a Neolithic culture. Its date was assumed to be the third millennium B.C. In 1961, I narrowed this date down to the third quarter of the third millennium: between 2500 and 2200 B.C. (Gimbutas, 1961). There are now known almost two hundred Neolithic sites north of the Black Sea which precede the Kurgan (or Pit-grave) culture. The Mariupol' cemetery represents the latest Neolithic phase.

This culture is distributed along the courses of the lower and middle Dnieper, the valleys of the rivers in Volhynia, the banks of the Sejm River, the basin of the Donets, and in the Crimea. The relative chronology can be estimated on the basis of stratigraphy and by the location of the habitation sites, and also, to some extent, by comparisons with the Balkan materials.

The North Pontic Neolithic Dnieper-Donets culture does not belong to the Mediterrano-Balkan cultural sphere, nor does it belong to the Near Eastern bloc. At first it seemed as if this culture were a locally developed phenomenon without much influence from outside except in its latest phases. Its relations with the Neolithic culture of the southern Baltic area's Atlantic period Ertebølle culture cannot be neglected in the light of similarities in both skeletal type and pottery.

The Neolithic people in the lower Dnieper and Donets basins and in the Crimea were of Proto-European Crô-Magnon type. It has been noted that they were not the same people who lived in the same area during the Mesolithic period. The Mesolithic men north of the Black Sea were more gracile, more like the Mediterranean type (Debets, 1955; Konduktorova, 1957; Gokhman, 1958; Stoljar, 1961). Hence there is a possibility that the Crô-Magnon group came to the Black Sea coasts from the north via Poland and the western Ukraine (Volhynia). The question which concerns us here, however, is not the origin but the duration and development of the North Pontic Neolithic.

Since there is not a single C-14 date available for dating the Neolithic strata in this region, investigators must rely heavily on observations of the location and stratigraphy of the sites. Sulimirski has drawn attention to changes of elevation with regard to cultural stratum (Sulimirski, 1961). His study has made it clear that the Mesolithic and Early Neolithic people occupied the lowest terraces of the Dnieper and its tributaries and islands. The climate must have been very dry at that time. The sites of the later Early Neolithic and Middle Neolithic periods still occupied low terraces, but the cultural strata contained a larger proportion of humus, which indicates a slightly damper climate. A change in the character of site locations during the subsequent period marks a further advance of the damper climatic phase: Late Neolithic sites in addition to some from the Middle Neolithic lay on granite rocks high above the river, probably because the water level had risen. It was only after the onset of a drier phase, in the Late Bronze Age, that the low terraces were reoccupied. The same conditions have been observed in the Boh River basin, where the Early Neolithic sites (called Primitive Neolithic; see the section on Cucuteni-Tripolye, pp. 464-66) were located on the lowest terraces.

Two stratified sites in the area of the Dnieper rapids, on the Surskij and Igren (Ihrin) islands, reveal a similar path of climatic change, clearly marked out by Early, Middle, and Late Neolithic materials (Danilenko, 1950; Dobrovolskij, 1959; Gimbutas, 1956). In brief, the stratigraphy of both sites was as follows:

The Early Neolithic sherds of pointed-based large pots, decorated with incisions or scratches, were found in a layer of yellow river sand (in Igren 8, immediately above a Mesolithic cultural layer that included a flint industry of Pontic Tardenoisian character but no pottery). Wild animal bones—red deer, boar, and two breeds of dogs—indicated forest conditions. The people subsisted mainly on hunting and fishing. In the layers containing the early primitive pottery at Igren 8, intercalated layers of Unio and Paludina shells testified to an increase in rainfall great enough to raise the level of the Dnieper and to submerge the whole area.

The Middle Neolithic layers were characterized by pointed-base and flat-based pots decorated with toothlike or comblike impressions and incisions of parallel slanting grooves. These strata in both sites had some humus content and great accumulations of kitchen middens; the pottery calls to mind Ertebølle ware. At Surskij, the Middle Neolithic layer was terminated with a sterile layer of alluvial deposits, indicating a damp period during which the site was abandoned. At Igren, there was a great accumulation of shells.

The Late Neolithic deposits, characterized by flat-based comb-impressed pots, lay in dark sand with a high humus content and no shells. The climate must have become drier again after the very wet phase.

During the Neolithic period the Boreal dry conditions gradually changed into wet conditions much like those of the Atlantic climate around the Baltic Sea. The amount of rainfall increased particularly between the Middle and Late Neolithic periods. Then the climate became drier again.

Until we have C-14 determinations and more material for the synchronization of the Pontic Early Neolithic with materials from the southern Baltic coasts, it will not be possible to establish the beginning date of the North Pontic Neolithic culture, but the best conjecture seems to be the fifth millennium B.C. It seems, however, that the bulk of the North Pontic Neolithic is coeval with the Atlantic period of northern Europe. The whole fourth millennium, and the third to 2300-2200 B.C., must be taken into consideration as a time span for at least the Middle and Late Neolithic periods. Stratigraphy is not yet well worked out as it is in the Cucuteni-Tripolye or Boian-Gumelniţa area. The chronology of the Neolithic culture north of the Black Sea thus still lies in a very general frame.

The above-mentioned stratified sites did not offer sufficient information on the Neolithic economy. Bones of domesticated animals were found at other sites in the lower Dnieper area. Many Late Neolithic sites yielded bones of cattle, pigs, goats, and dogs (Dobrovolskij, 1952; Telegin, 1961b). The presence of domesticated pigs and a small breed of cattle was evidenced in the Middle Neolithic site of Kaja-arasy near Bakhchisaraj in the Crimea (Formozov, 1962). As yet no cereals have been found, but Late Neolithic sites include such finds as mortars and pestles (cf. the cemetery of Nikol'skij in the district of Dniepropetrovsk; Telegin, 1961b, p. 25). The flint and bone tools from all three periods indicate that the people were engaged chiefly in hunting, fishing, and gathering, as well as in some animal husbandry.

Throughout the entire Neolithic culture, the dead were buried in the extended position in trenchlike graves. The growth of population and the settled character of life are shown by the large size of cemeteries starting with Late Neolithic times. For instance, there were 130 graves in the cemetery of Vovnigi (Rudinskij, 1955, 1956; Stoljar, 1961) and 124 graves in that of Mariupol'.

The chronology of the latest Neolithic period is the best defined of all. To it belong the cemeteries of Mariupol', Vovnigi, and Nikol'skij, and the habitation sites of Sobachki and Srednij Stog I in the Dnieper rapids area. All yielded similar finds, and therefore must belong to one period. The several layers of graves in the Mariupol', Vovnigi, and Nikol'skij cemeteries, and some typological variations of ornaments, indicate that the period could not have been of short duration. Its end phase was marked by the appearance of copper ornaments.

Pottery consists of flat-based, barrel-shaped vessels with broad rims or collars decorated all over with incised or stamped lines usually forming a herringbone design or with cord impressions. The Late Neolithic inventory also includes long flint knives, round and long scrapers, leaf-shaped points, polishing tools, chisels, and flake axes, as well as various artifacts: boar's tusk laminae with grooves or perforations and bull figurines; beads made of slate, shell, mother-of-pearl, elk-, deer-, and fish-teeth; mace heads of porphyry and serpentine and pieces of rock crystal. The latest graves in the cemeteries of Mariupol' and Nikol'skij contained copper and gold pendants. The cultural level rose, only to be wiped out by new invaders.

Among the sixty pots of genuine North Pontic Late Neolithic type in the cemetery of Nikol'skij (Fig. 1: 1, 3, 4) were: a small, flat-based, bulging vessel with channeled ornamentation typical of Tripolye A (= Precucuteni III) type (Telegin, 1961b, p. 23, Fig. 3: 4); a round-based pot of a truncated egg shape with a design of small stamped triangles, probably imprinted with the end of a thin stick having a triangular cross section (Fig. 1: 2); and an amphora with a globular body. The latter two represent the earliest shapes of Kurgan pottery, having affinities in the Aral and Caspian area of central Asia and northern Iran. Analogies for such pots are known in the Kel'teminar culture south of the Sea of Aral and in the cave of Dzhebel southeast of the Caspian Sea (references in: Merpert, 1961; Gimbutas, 1961).

This is the first instance in which Precucuteni (Tripolye A) type ware appears in association with Kurgan and Mariupol' types. I have no detailed information about the discovery of the pots in question, but the report by Telegin seems to indicate that the foreign pots could not be separated stratigraphically from the regular North Pontic pots attribut-

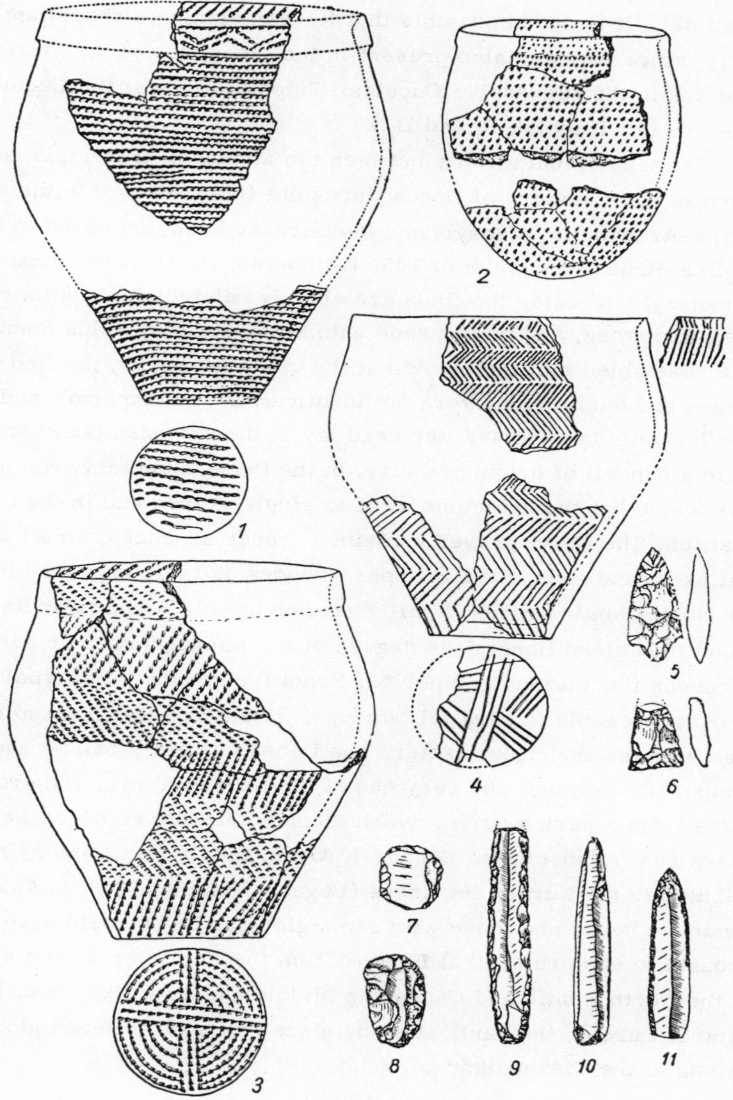

Fig. 1. Pots and flints from a late Neolithic North Pontic cemetery near the village of Nikol'skij, district of Dnepropetrovsk. 1, 3, 4: pots of local North Pontic type. 2: pot of Kurgan I appearance. Scale: 1-4 approx. 4/7; 5-11, 1/3. (After Telegin, 1961b.)

ed to the Late Neolithic. They do belong to the phase which precedes the appearance of copper and gold pendants. Hence the Late Neolithic or Mariupol' period can be equated with Precucuteni III and Kurgan I, if we assume that these pots represent either a cultural exchange or the presence of people belonging to three different cultures in the village of Nikol'skij. It is not impossible that Kurgan elements should appear this early, since they are also present in the late phase of the Mariupol' period and in the successive Cucuteni-Tripolye phases: the Cucuteni A_3 and A-B (or Tripolye B_I and B_{II}).

The typological affinity between the Mariupol' materials and those found in the cemetery of Decea Mureşului (Marosdesce) in the district of Torda-Aranyos in Transylvania has already been discussed in the Prague-Liblice-Brno symposium of 1959 (Gimbutas, 1961). It was observed that in general character the finds are closely related; flint tools, beads of shell and stone, and mace heads with semi-globular bulbs found at one site resembled similar objects at the other. However, the find assemblages and burial rites were not identical. In the Mariupol' and other North Pontic cemeteries, the dead lay in the extended position in trenches in a deposit of bright red clay. In the Decea cemetery, red ocher also was found, but the skeletons were in single graves and in the contracted position. The Decea graves contained copper ax-adzes, small daggers, flat axes, and awls, but no copper weapons or tools appeared in any of the North Pontic graves. Similar copper ax-adzes and tools have been found in eastern Hungary in graves of the Bodrogkeresztúr period, which succeeds the Tiszapolgár period. From the standpoint of typology, it is more reasonable to parallel Mariupol' itself with the Tiszapolgár period than with the Bodrogkeresztúr. The Decea cemetery can be roughly contemporary with only the very end of the Mariupol' era, and probably dates from a period during which steppe elements emerged west of the Black Sea. According to Bognar-Kutzián, the Decea cemetery may be attributed to the Kurgan intruders (Bognar-Kutzián, 1963, p. 453). Globular mace heads and those with semi-globular bulbs could have been brought to eastern central Europe from the Pontic area, and are typical of the North Pontic and Caucasian Middle and Late Neolithic. In eastern central Europe, the earliest stone mace heads of flattened globular shape belong to the Tiszapolgár period.

THE CHRONOLOGY OF THE KURGAN CULTURE

Ten years ago, when I wrote my monograph on the prehistory of eastern Europe, a culture called "Pit-grave" ("Jamna" or "Yamna" in Russian) in the lower Volga and Donets basins was known largely from the excavations by Gorodtsov at the beginning of this century. In 1956 I renamed it the "Kurgan culture" (in English, "Barrow culture") and have used the name ever since. At the present stage of research, the Yamna culture is no longer thought of as a short-lived culture of about 2000 B.C. (or earlier) in the northern Pontic area, but rather as an extensive and long-lasting Eurasian culture that caused momentous changes in the prehistory of Europe and the Near East. The carriers of the Kurgan culture must have been the proto-Indo-Europeans, through whose expansion the greater part of Europe and the Near East became gradually Indo-Europeanized (Gimbutas, 1963).

Study of the chronology of the Kurgan culture has already thrown much light on many confused ideas, such as the theory that the origins of the "Corded" people were in northern, central, or Balkan Europe. It has also shown that the infiltration of the Kurgan elements from the present steppe area of Eurasia into Europe and the Near East was a complicated process over many centuries.

A decade of intensive excavation work has brought great changes in our concept of this culture. It became clearer than ever that this culture was foreign to the area north of the Black Sea and that its origin was in the east, beyond the Donets. Its contemporaneity and coexistence with the Late Neolithic North Pontic (Mariupol') and with four or more phases of the Cucuteni-Tripolye culture have been particularly substantiated by the habitation sites in the Dnieper region. Of exceptional chronological value are the stratified sites of Mikhajlovka in the district of Kherson (Lagodovska, Shaposhnikova, and Makarevich, 1962), Skelja Kamenolomna south of Dnepropetrovsk (Danilenko, 1955), and Moljukhov Bugor in the district of Chigirin on the Tjasmin River west of the middle Dnieper (Danilenko, 1959). The first two were hilltop villages with impressive fortifications. Another important source of Kurgan stratigraphy is the habitation site of Aleksandrija on the Oskol, a tributary of the Donets (Telegin, 1959).

In the symposium of 1959 in Prague-Liblice-Brno, Merpert and I discussed the relative chronology of the Kurgan culture as illuminated by stratigraphical evidence and by contacts with the cultures east and west of the Black Sea. Merpert offered a classification of four periods, I-IV (Merpert, 1961), and I tried to connect the separate Kurgan phases with the cultures on the west and to establish them in terms of relative dates (Gimbutas, 1961). New discoveries continue to support the existence of at least four phases.

For the purpose of simplification, I classify the whole Kurgan sequence into Early, Middle, and Late. The four known phases can be grouped as follows: Early=Kurgan I; Middle=Kurgan II and III; Late=Kurgan IV.

The Early Kurgan Period (Kurgan I)

Kurgan I is known from the earliest pit graves in barrows in the lower Volga region and from a few sites in the Dnieper basin. Truncated egg-shaped pots and globular amphorae with narrow, well-defined necks, made of clay tempered with crushed shells, organic substances, or sand, are the most diagnostic artifacts. This kind of pottery contrasts with that of the North Pontic culture and has its closest analogies in the Dzhanbas-4 site south of the Sea of Aral and also in northern Iran (Vinogradov, 1957; Merpert, 1961). Typological relationships can be traced between the earliest Kurgan ware in the lower Volga area and the earliest pottery in the Middle Urals from the locality called Strelka in the peat bog of Gorbunovo. Strelka represents the lowest cultural stratum, and pollen analysis has shown that it belonged to a wet climatic period (Gimbutas, 1961). One C-14 date from Strelka, published in 1961, is 4800 ± 200 B.P. (Artem'ev et al., 1961). This determination presumably takes into account the Suess effect but is apparently based on a half life of 5,570 years. If adjusted to a half life of 5,730 years, the reading becomes 4944 ± 200 B.P. or 2994 ± 200 B.C.

The first encounter of the Kurgan with the western cultures is indicated by Kurgan I pots in the Late Neolithic cemetery of Nikol'skij. The pit in this cemetery already referred to (p. 474) yielded a pot of Precucuteni III (Tripolye A) type. If this evidence is correct, it may mean that the earliest traces of the Kurgan people on the Dnieper were roughly synchronous with the Precucuteni III phase.

After the initial excavations at Mikhajlovka in 1955, it was believed that the lowest layer, containing the remains of one house with stone foundations, had nothing to do with the middle and upper strata of the site, which represent the main development of the Kurgan culture in the Dnieper region. Excavations resumed in 1960, on the eastern side of the hill, revealed another house and more pottery in the earliest cultural layer (Shaposhnikova, 1961). This house was dug somewhat into the ground, had an oval plan twelve meters long and a pitched roof. In it were found bones of cattle, sheep, and horses, and flat-based pots and narrow-necked globular amphorae. Horizontal cord impressions, incisions with a sharp tool and shallow pits decorated the upper parts, and there were occasional incisions around the bottom. Some sherds with impressed pits and incised zigzags recall Precucuteni III (Tripolye A) kitchen ware.

The amphorae link this type of pottery with the Kurgan ware, found in the steppes around the Sea of Aral. Hence, the lowest layer of Mikhajlovka (Mikhajlovka I) may represent the earliest Kurgan settlers on the mouth of the Dnieper River, and may be roughly synchronous with the cemetery of Nikol'skij. Horse bones in the lowest stratum of Mikhajlovka seem to be the earliest in this region. Horse bones known from the Early Tripolye (Precucuteni III) habitation site at Luka Vrublevetskaja (Bibikov, 1953) probably belong to about the same time horizon, and hence are not an isolated phenomenon. That the horse was brought to Europe by the Kurgan people from the east is more likely than that its breeding was independently started by the Tripolyans in the upper Dniester Valley. The presence of horses is well evidenced in all other Kurgan periods.

Single burials, in which the corpse lies on its back with legs contracted, under a stone or earthen barrow, are known in the lower Dnieper basin—for instance, the barrows of Osokorovka—are possibly synchronous with Mikhajlovka I (Danilenko, 1955, p. 127).

From the above, we can make an inference that the Kurgan people reached the Dnieper in a period coinciding with the end of Precucuteni in Rumanian Moldavia and Tripolye A in the Dniester Valley of the Ukraine.

The Kurgan pastoralists occupied high river banks, living for centuries in the neighborhood of the Cucuteni-Tripolye culture and alongside the North Pontic Dnieper-Donets farmers. The Cucuteni-Tripolye culture had yet to reach its flourishing or classical period and to expand into the area south of Kiev in the middle Dnieper basin. The first culture to feel the burden of the eastern invaders was the North Pontic.

The Middle Kurgan Period (Kurgan II and III)

Kurgan II

Of utmost importance for the establishment of the chronological position of Kurgan II is the presence of Classical Cucuteni-Tripolye polychrome pottery (Cucuteni A_3 and Tripolye B_I) in the Kurgan habitation sites and of Kurgan pottery (unpainted, porous, tempered with shells and sand) in the Cucuteni-Tripolye villages. There are not merely one or two but a number of settlements in which Kurgan II and Cucuteni A_3 (Tripolye B_I) pottery appeared together and were thus proved to be contemporary (Movsha, 1961). Among the outstanding examples are: the Kurgan villages of Srednij Stog II (the upper layer) in the Dnieper rapids area and Moljukhov Bugor (the middle layer) in the district of Chigirin in the basin of the Tjasmin River, west of the Middle Dnieper; and the Tripolyan villages Soloncheny II, Kudrintsy, Kadjevtsy, Nezvisko I, Polivanov Jar I, and Floreshty-Zagotzerno (Danilenko, 1959; Passek, 1962; Merpert, 1961; Chernysh, 1962). Thus, there are indications that the Kurgan and Cucuteni-Tripolye people in the Ukraine moved around and that the Kurgan people occupied Cucuteni-Tripolye lands in the upper Dniester Valley but did not penetrate Moldavia west of the Dniester. The date of the first appearance of the Kurgan elements in the eastern part of the Cucuteni-Tripolye distribution area is the same as that of Cucuteni A_3.

Stratigraphically, Kurgan II materials have been shown to overlie the North Pontic cultural deposits in the following stratified sites: Igren 8 (layer D), Srednij Stog, Moljukhov Bugor, and Aleksandrija. The Kurgan II finds in the latter site were followed by Kurgan III materials that are equivalent to those of Mikhajlovka II. The Kurgan II horizon of Aleksandrija was in the lower part of the so-called "Eneolithic" stratum, in whose upper part appeared finds of Kurgan III type. This lower level has revealed finds of North Pontic and Kurgan character: two types of pottery and two types of graves (Telegin, 1959). They sharply contrast with each other, and speak for the persistence of local North Pontic populations or traditions even at the time when Kurgan culture was already a dominant power in the North Pontic region. The tools and pots exhibit hybrid forms, whereas flint artifacts are not markedly different from the North Pontic Mariupol' types. A typical Kurgan pottery form during this phase was an egg-shaped pot with a pointed bottom and a high, straight neck, decorated with comb stamps, herringbone designs, and cord impressions over the upper part (Fig. 2). The broad necks, comb stamps, and herringbone design are borrowings from the North Pontic culture. Pots were tempered with crushed shells, some organic material, and occasionally with sand or gravel. They were porous, lightweight, and light gray in color. The North Pontic Dneiper-Donets pots, on the other hand, had considerably thicker walls and were entirely covered with decoration.

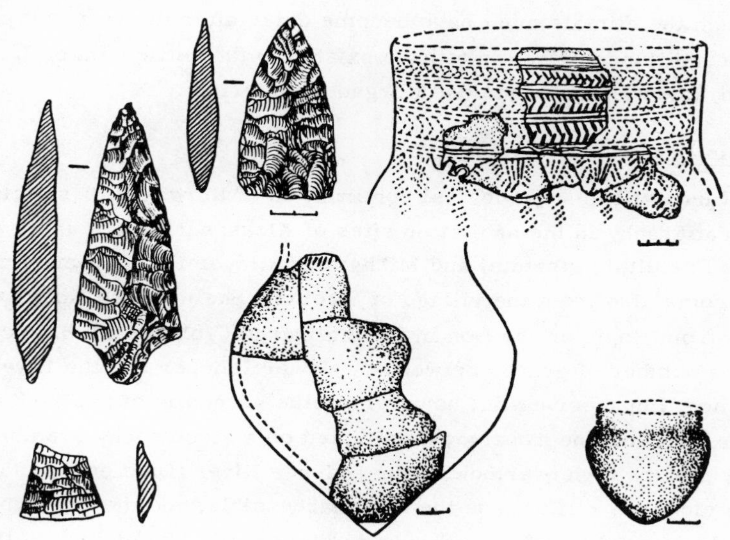

Fig. 2. Flint arrowheads and Kurgan II pots from the lower part of the "Eneolithic" layer in the habitation site of Aleksandrija near Kupjansk, district of Kharkov. Bottom right: pot from a Kurgan II grave. (After Telegin, 1959.)

Graves exhibiting two distinct types—a North Pontic, with the dead in the extended position, covered with red ocher, in deep trenchlike pits, which has analogies in the Mariupol' and Vovnigi cemeteries; and a Kurgan type, with the dead in the strongly contracted position lying on their backs—are presumed to be associated with the same cultural layer (Telegin, 1959, pp. 17 ff.). If this should prove to be true, it would emphatically prove the existence of two different ethnic groups even in one village. Further, the skeletons were representative of two different types: the North Pontic were massive Crô-Magnons; the Kurgan skeletons were of more gracile and narrow-faced type. It seems that the Kurgan II horizon at Aleksandrija bears witness to a troublesome period for the local North Pontic population. The old inhabitants had to adapt themselves to the new rule and culture.

The North Pontic and the Kurgan peoples were both basically small-scale stock breeders, hunters, and farmers. Antler hoes are among the finds of Kurgan II type, and bones of the domesticated horse continue to prove the importance of this animal in the Kurgan economy. During the Kurgan II phase forested conditions still prevailed, as bones of elk, roe-deer, boar, and waterfowl found in Aleksandrija and other sites indicate, although the climate must have become drier after the very wet phase. Such conditions are shown to have existed in the settlement on Igren Island, layer D, which yielded Kurgan II materials.

Kurgan III

Kurgan III is a typological continuation of Kurgan II, best evidenced by stratigraphy in the habitation sites of Aleksandrija (the upper horizon of the Eneolithic stratum) and Mikhajlovka (layer II). Rich materials have come also from the village of Strel'cha Skelja in the Dnieper rapids area, from Repin on the Don in the Stalingrad (Volgograd) district, and from a number of graves between the lower Dnieper and the lower Volga. The most impressive site, however, is the acropolis of Skelja-Kamenolomna south of Dnepropetrovsk, situated on a steep rocky promontory thirty meters high overlooking the Dnieper River (Danilenko, 1955). On three sides the cliffs made the site inaccessible, and the western side was sloping and fortified with a thick stone wall. The plateau of the hilltop had an area of about one hectare. The remains of houses indicated a rectangular or oval plan with stone foundations and timber walls. In the houses and the settlement area were found bones of domesticated animals including the horse, hoes of antler or aurochs horn, flint arrowheads and scrapers, well-polished battle-axes, and other tools. Similar finds were made in other habitation sites. Skelja-Kamenolomna must have been an important tribal center. It contained workshops for polished stone tools, particularly battle-axes made with meticulous care.

The basic ceramic forms continued to be of truncated egg shape, but the bases became either more rounded or flat and necks were not so tall as those of Kurgan II and were sometimes flared. The texture of clay remained typically "Kurgan": light gray in color and tempered with crushed shells plus some mineral and/or organic substance. Predominant were horizontal cord impressions around the shoulders, and pits impressed from inside at the line where shoulders and neck meet (the latter ornament is called in Russian "zhemchuzhnyj"—"pearl ornament") (Fig. 3).

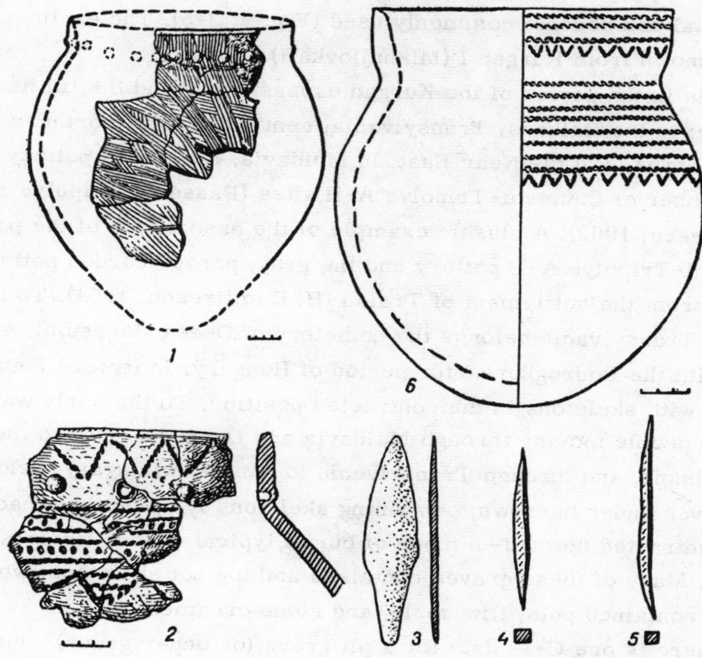

Fig. 3. Kurgan III pots and copper artifacts. 1-5: the upper part of the "Eneolithic" layer in the site of Aleksandrija, district of Kharkov. 6: a pot of Kurgan III type from the district museum in the town of Stalin. (After Telegin, 1959.)

Along with these were rows of incisions or stamps made by a sharp tool and impressions of a whipped cord forming zigzag or herringbone patterns.

The 1960 excavations of the Mikhajlovka settlement have brought to light two horizons of layer II. In the lower horizon, a house contained, along with potsherds with corded and "pearl" ornament derived from pots with flat bases, several painted Cucuteni-Tripolye A-B or early B sherds, defined by the excavator as "late Tripolye" (Shaposhnikova, 1961). The same horizon yielded one copper awl. From earlier excavations in Mikhajlovka II two other copper awls are known. Awls having a rectangular cross-section and a leaf-shaped arrowhead or spearhead of copper were discovered in upper Aleksandrija (i.e., the upper horizon of the

Eneolithic layer, roughly contemporary with Mikhajlovka II), indicating that metal had become commonly used (Fig. 3, 3-5). The earliest copper awl is known from Kurgan I (Mikhajlovka I).

This is the period of the Kurgan expansion beyond the limits of the Ukraine: to the Balkans, Transylvania, central Europe, northern Europe, the Caucasus, and the Near East. In Moldavia, Kurgan III pottery appeared in a number of Cucuteni-Tripolye A-B sites (Passek's Tripolye B_{II}) (V. Dumitrescu, 1963). A classic example of the association of the painted Cucuteni-Tripolye A-B pottery and the gray, porous corded pottery comes from the settlement of Traian (H. Dumitrescu, 1954). To this period in Transylvania belongs the cemetery of Decea Mureşului, synchronous with the Bodrogkeresztúr period of Hungary. In it were found ocher graves with skeletons in the contracted position. To the early wave of Kurgan people moving through Moldavia and Dobrudja down to the southern Balkans, and through Transylvania to northern Hungary, belong the pit graves under barrows, containing skeletons lying on their backs with legs contracted upward—a mode of burial typical of the Middle Kurgan period. Many of these graves contained nothing but skeletons, whereas others contained pots, flint tools, and stone ornaments.

There is one C-14 date for a pit grave (or ocher grave) under a one and a half meters high barrow, discovered at Baia-Hamangia near Istria in the district of Constanţa on the Rumanian Black Sea coast: 2140 ± 160 B.C. (Kohl and Quitta, 1963). Corrected for a half life of 5.730, the date is 2262 ± 160 B.C. (see Ehrich, pp. 439-41). This grave contained a skeleton, a pot, and an ornament made of marble. Peculiar round or flat figurines portraying horses' heads, made of diorite and presumably used as mace heads, discovered in Moldavia, Dobrudja, Transylvania, and Yugoslavia, also must belong to the Kurgan period of expansion (Nestor, 1933, 1955; Popescu, 1937-40; Berciu, 1954). In the local Neolithic and Chalcolithic cultures nothing similar was found, but an analogous portrayal of a horse's head is known from Terek Makhteb near Groznyj in Dagestan, in the eastern Caucasus (Berciu, 1954). The figurine from Salcuţa in northwestern Rumania (Nestor, 1933, Taf. 2, 1, 2; Berciu, 1939, Fig. 74) corresponds in time to the end of the Salcuţa culture (Berciu, 1954). Another sculpture of a horse's head from Casimcea in Dobrudja was found in an ocher grave together with triangular flint points, knife blades, and celts (Popescu, 1937-40), again typical of the Middle Kurgan period. At Lerna in Greece, the destruction layer, probably connected with the coming of the people from the north, is dated to the end of Early Helladic II, which is about 2300 to 2200 B.C. (Caskey, 1960, pp. 285-303; see also Weinberg's paper, above). Great destruction in Anatolia also occurred about 2300 to 2200 B.C. At that time Troy was destroyed, and in Beycesultan the complete disintegration of culture followed the destruction of Layer XIII, dated at 2300 B.C.

The earliest corded ware in northwestern Europe is now dated about 2600 B.C. (see Thomas, pp. 389-90, 394-95, above). However, clear typological ties with Kurgan III types are not yet successfully elaborated. The bulk of Kurgan ware (called early "Schnurkeramik" in central and northern Europe and "Bottom-grave phase" of Denmark) can be equated with Kurgan IV.

Until now the earliest culture of the food-producers in central Russia has been called the "Fat'janovo culture" after a cemetery near Yaroslavl' on the upper Volga. The Fat'janovo graves included stone battle axes and geometrically decorated globular vases together with stone celts and flint knives. New discoveries have proved that the Fat'janovo phase in the middle Volga area (Chuvashia) was already an Early Bronze Age culture with developed local metallurgy (Kakhovskij, 1963). Shaft-hole axes and their bivalve molds have close parallels in the early Timber-grave culture in southern Russia. Hence, the Fat'janovo proper dates from the post-Kurgan IV period, probably from the nineteenth or eighteenth centuries B.C. Around Kiev, and along the upper Dnieper and Desna rivers, the lowest graves in the barrows and a number of habitation sites contained pottery of Kurgan IV appearance (Artemenko, 1963, Fig. 2, 1-11; Fig. 3). This shows that the upper Dnieper basin at the end of the third millennium B.C. was thickly settled by the Kurgan people and that the first immigration must have occurred earlier. Pottery of Kurgan III type appeared in the habitation sites of the Pit-marked Pottery culture in the upper Volga basin, although the fact was not noticed by Soviet scholars. In the site of Lopachi on the Kljaz'ma River, in the district of Vladimir, both Pit-marked and Kurgan III types of pottery were found in the same cultural layer (Zimina, 1963). The Pit-marked Pottery culture of central Russia—a culture of hunters and fishers which precedes the intrusive food-producing Kurgan culture—belongs to the Atlantic climatic period (pollen analysis of the Ljalovo peat bog on the Kljaz'ma River near Moscow with Pit-marked pottery was made forty years ago: Dokturovskij, 1925). It seems that the Kurgan expansion northward up the Dnieper River to the upper Volga basin dates from the Kurgan III period.

On the other side of the Black Sea, a cultural change of a similar nature can be seen in the Caucasus. One of the earliest Kurgan cemeteries in the central part of the northern Caucasus is that at Nal'chik on the upper Terek (Kruglov, Piotrovskij, and Podgaetskij, 1941; Gimbutas, 1956); another is the habitation site of Agubekovo (Krichevskij and Kruglov, 1941). In burial rites, Nal'chik resembles the cemetery of Decea Mureşului in Transylvania and the Kurgan II-III graves in the lower Dnieper region. Decea Mureşului is paralleled in time by the Bodrogkeresztúr period and by Cucuteni-Tripolye A-B. The cemetery of Nal'chik yielded one schematic female figurine made of marl, for which the closest analogies are in the Cucuteni-Tripolye A-B villages—for instance, Kolomiščina II on the Dnieper. In the habitation site at Agubekovo, northwest of Nal'chik, a schematic head was found on a columnar neck with small perforations around it (Gimbutas, 1956, Fig. 25, a), and at Urup site (Urupskaja Stanitsa) a lower part of a similar figurine was found (Markovin, 1959). This again has close affinities in Cucuteni-Tripolye A-B settlements—for instance, in the village of Traian (Dumitrescu and Dumitrescu, 1959, Fig. 9). Flint and polished stone tools found in Agubekovo indicate relationships in the same direction: with the end of the Mariupol' phase and with Cucuteni-Tripolye A-B. Seated figurines of Aegean type, made of alabaster or clay, are known from several places in the Caucasus: from the lowest pit grave in the barrow at Ul' near Majkop and from Kataragač-Tapa between Derbent and Kaja-Kent in the eastern Caucasus (Gimbutas, 1956, Fig. 25). These isolated figurines in the Caucasus, some of which were found in datable contexts, seem to have been brought this far east by people who at that time were familiar with both sides of the Black Sea. Their dispersion reminds us of the horse-head scepters found in Rumania, Yugoslavia, and in the Caucasus. Before this period no artifacts were ever spread so widely.

The Majkop period, or the Early Kuban Copper Age, succeeds that of Nal'chik in the northern Caucasus. The famous royal house graves of Majkop and Tsarskaja, under high barrows, were lavishly equipped. A large quantity of gold, silver, copper, pottery, and stone vases; gold figurines of bulls and lions sewn on garments; gold and silver bull figurines adorning canopies; gold beads and rings; gold, silver, turquoise, and carnelian beads; as well as copper axes, tanged daggers, and spearheads—

all show relations with the royal tombs of Alaca Hüyük and Horoztepe in northern central Anatolia (for description and references, see Gimbutas, 1956; 1963). Horoztepe is dated about 2200 B.C., the graves of Alaca Hüyük at a somewhat earlier period, about 2400 to 2200 B.C. The latter shows ties with Troy II.

Majkop is a peculiar combination of Kurgan and Near Eastern elements: the burial rites are typically Kurgan, the metal forms entirely Mesopotamian, Anatolian, and Transcaucasian. The Kurgan people could not have suddenly imported all the gold, silver, precious stones, and copper of which the Majkop artifacts were made—there must have been previous intimate connections between the northern Caucasus and the southern regions. In an earlier paper (Gimbutas, 1963) I have pointed out that the Kurgan people must have spread down across the Caucasus into the milieu of the Transcaucasian (and eastern Anatolian) culture in a period preceding the Majkop, and must have borrowed many new cultural elements from the Transcaucasian. Since the bull figurines from Horoztepe and Majkop are closely similar, I should like to place the Majkop and Horoztepe royal burials into one time horizon. Hence the date for Majkop: about 2200 B.C. Other ties that indicate the same date for the Majkop period are: in the lower horizon of the stratified settlement of Dolinskoe southwest of Nal'chik, believed to be contemporary with Majkop, there have been found high oval vases with handles that recall jars from the second, third, and fourth settlements of Troy (Kruglov and Podgaetskij, 1941; Gimbutas, 1956, p. 53, Fig. 26, a). The earliest graves of the Kurgan cemetery in Kabardino Park near Nal'chik yielded long T-shaped or "crutch-headed" pins of copper, the prototypes of the later hammer-headed pins (Degen, 1941; Gimbutas, 1956, pp. 63-65). Analogies for these are in Alaca Hüyük, Tomb TM. Large pins with double-spiral ("mouflon horn") heads, also found in the same cemetery, have parallels in Anatolia dated to the end of Troy II or Troy III.

That the Kurgan people were present in the eastern Caucasus before the culture of Majkop type evolved was recently demonstrated by stratigraphic evidence in the Kurgan cemetery at Novyj Arshti near Bamut in Checheno Ingushetija. The earliest graves in the large barrows were similar to those of Nal'chik: corpses buried on the back with the legs contracted upward and covered with ocher. There were no metal artifacts. One of the graves contained white paste beads (Munchaev, 1962). Most graves discovered in this cemetery belonged to the Majkop period.

Chronologically, Majkop can be said to be a representative of the later phase of Kurgan III. However, as soon as the contacts with the Transcaucasian and Anatolian cultures started, the Kurgan culture changed rapidly and pursued its own path. If the cultural level of the Nal'chik cemetery can be compared with that of Kurgan III throughout the Ukraine, it can no longer be compared with the stage of Majkop. With the beginning of Majkop, the northern Caucasian culture is called the Majkop culture—for from that time it maintained its own traits and was an influence zone from, and an outpost of, Near Eastern material culture.

The Late Kurgan Period

Kurgan IV is the last period in the series of a culture which, like a volcano, continued to erupt until its lava covered a great part of Europe and the Near East. The period ended with an increased differentiation of cultures north of the Black Sea and elsewhere in Europe, synchronous with the beginning of the central European Bronze Age and the Timber-grave culture in southern Russia.

Most Kurgan IV materials north of the Black Sea come from Mikhajlovka III. Stratigraphy similar to that of Mikhajlovka was brought to light in several other places. In the lower Volga area, in Barrow II of the cemetery of Bykovo, district of Stalingrad, a grave with pots of Mikhajlovka III type lay immediately above a grave with finds characteristic of Mikhajlovka II. Found in stratum III of Mikhajlovka was a considerable number of copper artifacts: tanged daggers, tanged arrowheads or spearheads, a flat shafthole ax, and awls having a rectangular cross-section.

In the northwestern Caucasus, the excavations by Merpert in 1960 uncovered at Meken two layers: the lower contained globular pottery typical of the Majkop phase, and the upper, that of the Tsarskaja. There is no doubt that the royal stone-cist burials at Tsarskaja in Kuban follow those of Majkop, since it has now been demonstrated by stratigraphy. Typological analysis leads to a similar conclusion. The Tsarskaja copper artifacts have analogies in Hissar IIIC of northern Iran and in the Early Bronze Age sites of Georgia in western Transcaucasia. At this period local metallurgy in the western and northern Caucasus is well evidenced. The Tsarskaja metal forms—tanged daggers and spearheads, flat shaft-hole axes, rings and spiral rings—are prototypes for the Kurgan IV repertory of metal artifacts and therefore should be placed at the beginning of the Kurgan IV period. If Majkop can be dated tentatively to 2200 B.C., Tsarskaja should not be dated later than 2100 B.C.

Kurgan IV pots show more evolved forms, although rounded bottoms were maintained. Necks were short, and handles appeared—perhaps re-

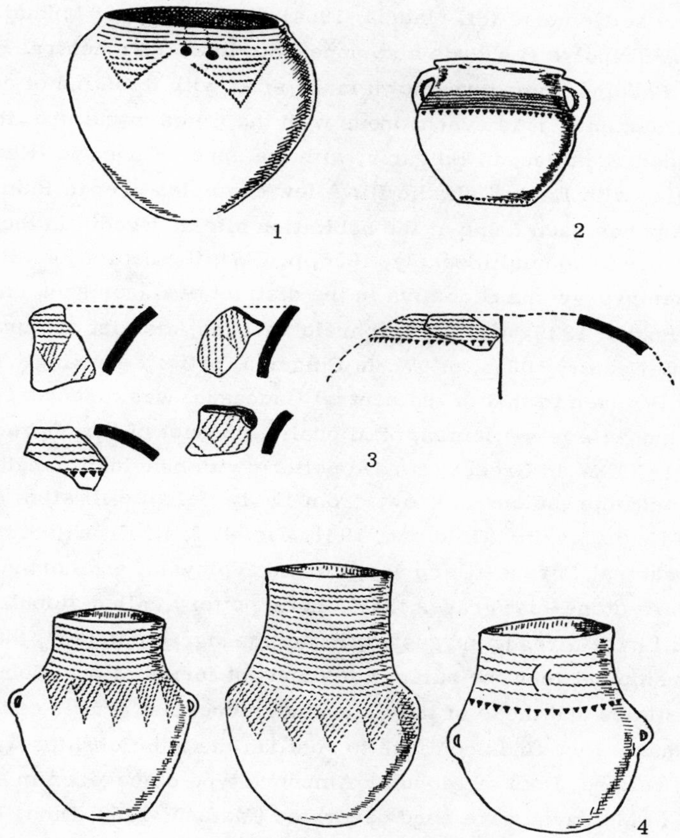

Fig. 4. Kurgan IV pottery from southern Russia, the northern Caucasus, Greece, and central Germany. 1: Chpakovka barrow near Izjum on the Donets, district of Kharkov. 2: the barrow of Tri Kamnja near Kislovodsk, northern Caucasus. 3: corded sherds from Eutresis and Hagia Marina, Greece. 4: "Grosser Stein" barrow near Seifartsdorf, district of Eisenberg, Thuringia. (Reprinted from the author's article in the *Selected Papers of the Fifth International Congress of Anthropology and Ethnology*, Philadelphia, 1956.)

flecting Caucasian influences. The most typical decorative motif consists of corded triangles impressed along the persisting horizontal cord impressions and stampings or incisions made with a sharp tool (Fig. 4). Identical decorative motifs are to be found from between the lower Volga and Transcaucasia to Scandinavia, the upper Rhine, and Greece. Outside the Ukraine, Kurgan IV pottery appears in Cucuteni-Tripolye B (Late Tripolye) settlements (cf. Matasă, 1964). In the layer of Mikhajlovka III, Cucuteni-Tripolye B sherds also appeared. In eastern central Europe and the Balkans, there are known many sites with this kind of corded pottery. In Rumania, it is synchronous with the Coţofeni culture; in Hungary with Baden-Kostolac; in Bulgaria, with the upper Karanovo (Karanovo VII in Greece, with Early Helladic III. A few examples are: in Rumania, corded pottery has been found at the habitation site at Jigodin in the district of Miercurea Ciucului (Székely, 1955, p. 847), the habitation site between Sepsiszentgyörgy and Gidófalva in the district of Háromszek on the Olt River (Roska, 1925), and the Izvoarele kurgans, district of Turda, Transylvania (Nestor, 1933b, p. 67). In Bulgaria, pottery strikingly similar to Kurgan IV (even to that of the central Caucasus) was discovered in the Early Bronze Age settlement of Michalič, district of Svilengrad (Georgie 1961, Pl. XXX). In Greece, corded pottery with hanging triangle motifs an horizontal impressions is known from Early Helladic III sites at Eutresis and Hagia Marina (Goldman, 1931, Fig. 4, 3; H. Frankfort, 1927).

In central Europe—Germany, Poland, Volhynia, and northern Moldavia—are stone-cist graves that contain pottery called globular amphorae. I have already suggested, in my monograph of 1956, the peculiar relationship between the burial rites and pot forms of the Globular Amphora culture and those of the Caucasian stone-cist graves of the Tsarskaja phase. New finds continue to confirm the relationships with the Kurgan culture. Pots of Globular Amphora type discovered in stone-cist graves in Moldavia were cord decorated (Matasă, 1959; Dinu, 1961); some had impressions forming a semicircular design. Identical decoration is to be found on the pottery of Michalič in Bulgaria, on that of Mikhajlovka III and other sites north of the Black Sea, and on that of the central northern Caucasus (Degen, 1941).

In Transcaucasian barrows typical of Kurgan culture, Kurgan IV pots with cord-impressed hanging triangles, skulls and legs of bulls in the corners of the grave, and the skull of a goat or sheep appeared together with local painted pottery. A good example is Lchashen Barrow

No. 6 in the area of Lake Sevan (Khanzadian, 1962).

It is difficult to determine whether Kurgan IV elements were dispersed over a wide area by a renewed expansion at the end of the third millennium B.C. or were a local continuation from Kurgan III times. The remarkable similarity of ornamental motifs would speak in the latter instance for mobility and communication among the Kurgan peoples who were now settled in many areas of the Old World.

This discussion of the four phases of the Kurgan culture as well as their synchronisms with the North Pontic Dnieper-Donets, Cucuteni-Tripolye, Trojan Troy, Helladic, and other cultures are summarized in Table 3.

Each of these Kurgan phases has proved to represent a push westward that reached its climax in Kurgan III. The last centuries of the third millennium B.C. were a time of mixture of cultural elements. The old cultures, such as Cucuteni-Tripolye, Gumelniţa in eastern Rumania and Bulgaria, Funnel-necked Beaker (TRB) in northwestern Europe, Comb-marked Pottery culture in the East Baltic area, and the Pit-marked Pottery culture in central Russia, continued until they merged with and disappeared into the Kurgan culture.

In the early part of the second millennium B.C., a series of localized cultural groups of Kurgan background emerged. In some parts of Europe, as in southern Russia, the Kurgan culture continued; in other parts, as in the Balkans and central and northern Europe, the formation of new cultural groups with Kurgan elements was influenced by the cultural substratum and by natural conditions. At this point, a change in the labels of the archaeological cultures becomes necessary.

In the lower Volga basin, the culture of Kurgan IV character persisted with evidences of local metallurgy from the beginning of the second millennium B.C. The phase which immediately succeeds Kurgan IV in southern Russia is called Poltavka, and can be placed at the beginning of that long-lasting and constantly growing force throughout the Bronze Age: the Timber-grave culture. Solid timber construction in graves is particularly typical of the Timber-grave culture during its classical period between 1800 B.C. and 1100 B.C.

In the eastern Ukraine, north of the Black Sea, in the Crimea, and in the northwestern Caucasus, the Kurgan IV culture also continued, but here more changes occurred. About 2000 B.C., the pit-cave or catacomb type of burial appeared, probably borrowed from the Aegean area. This

Table 3

Periods	Important Kurgan Sites in the Ukraine, South Russia, Northern Caucasus	Synchronous Cultures
KURGAN IV ca. 2100 B.C.	Mikhajlovka III Bykovo II, Meken II Tsarskaja	Coţofeni (W. Rumania) Baden-Kostolac (Hungary) Early Helladic III (Greece) Cucuteni B (Moldavia) Karanovo VII (Bulgaria)
ca. 2200 B.C. KURGAN III ca. 2300 B.C.	Meken I, Majkop (northern Caucasus) Bykovo I Mikhajlovka II Aleksandrija, upper "Eneolithic" Skel'ja Kamenolomna Strel'cha Skel'ja Nal'chik (northern Caucasus)	Early Helladic II (Greece) Troy III, Horoztepe Alaca Hüyük (Anatolia) Cucuteni A-B (Moldavia)
KURGAN II	Igren', layer D Srednij Stog, upper layer Mol'jukhov Bugor, middle layer Aleksandrija, lower part of the "Eneolithic" layer	Cucuteni A_3 (Moldavia) and Tripolye A (W. Ukraine) Late Dnieper-Donets: Aleksandrija (lower part of the "Eneolithic" layer), Mariupol'
KURGAN I	Mikhajlovka I Nikol'skij (pot) Earliest barrows in the lower Dnieper basin Berezhnovka, lower Volga	Late Dnieper-Donets Precucuteni III (Moldavia) Tripolye A (W. Ukraine) Kel'teminar (Dzhanbas 4) in Kazakhstan

form appeared only in the Ukraine whereas in the eastern Crimea, the Caucasus, and the Volga region, the construction of rectangular house-graves continued. Pottery and metal forms were enriched through Caucasian influences. This North Pontic Bronze Age culture, tied to the Caucasus and to the Near East, continued through the stone-cist period and was characterized by ridged pottery in the lower Dnieper and Don area. Gradually, it was destroyed by the Timber-grave peoples. About 1100 B.C. the Timber-grave people appeared in the lower Dnieper region, and by the end of the eighth century B.C. their occupation of the Black Sea area was completed. These peoples (probably the Proto-Scythians) followed the steps their ancestors (=the Kurgan peoples) had taken some two thousand years earlier in their westward expansion to the Black Sea and to central Europe.

In central and east central Europe north of the Carpathian Mountains, in the Baltic area and central Russia, the following groups formed during the Early Bronze Age (in European terminology):

Únětice, in central Europe along the upper Danube and north of the middle Danube, succeeded several phases of Corded Pottery and was strongly influenced by the Nagyrév, Pecica (or Pécska) and Incrusted Pottery cultures from the south and by the Bell Beakers. Its beginning about 1800 B.C. equates with the end phase of the catacomb period north of the Black Sea and the Poltavka in the lower Volga area.

Bilopotok, north of the Carpathians, succeeded an early Corded phase with some substratum elements derived from the Cucuteni-Tripolye culture.

Monteoru, in eastern Rumania north of the Carpathians and in east-Transylvania, succeeded Cucuteni B and several phases of the Kurgan culture in the former Cucuteni-Tripolye territory.

Baltic Corded, between the Oder River in the west to southwestern Finland in the northeast, had a close relationship with the Northern Area Corded and the upper Dnieper Corded Pottery groups.

Central Russian Fat'janovo, in the forested zone in the early second millennium B.C., developed into at least three cultural variants: the upper Dnieper, the Fat'janovo proper in the upper Volga area, and the Balanovo in the middle Volga area.*

The general chronology of the cultures in question and the neighboring ones is given in Table 4.

*Although it came to hand too late to be treated in this paper, a recent important article by Artemenko (1964) should be called to attention.

Table 4

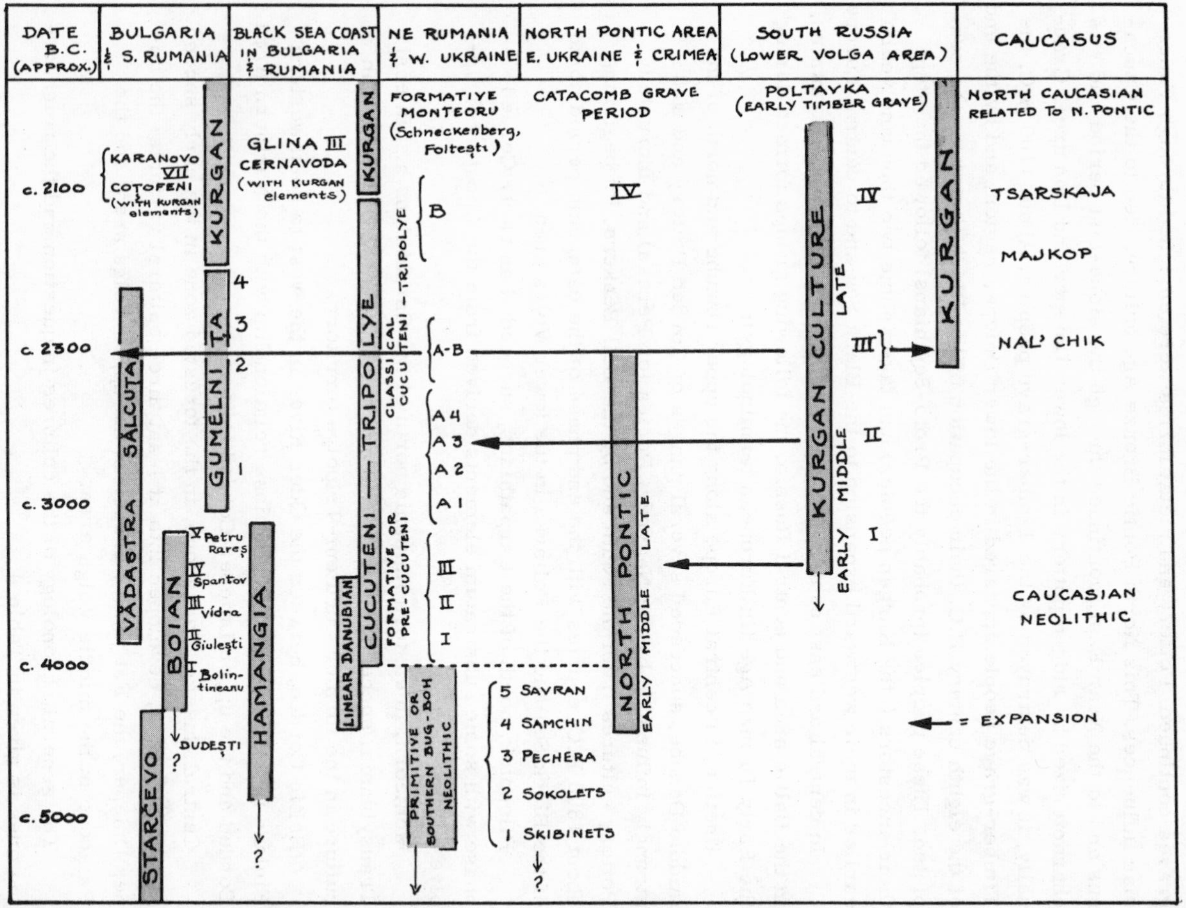
DATE B.C. (APPROX.)
BULGARIA & S. RUMANIA
BLACK SEA COAST IN BULGARIA & RUMANIA
NE RUMANIA & W. UKRAINE
NORTH PONTIC AREA E. UKRAINE & CRIMEA
SOUTH RUSSIA (LOWER VOLGA AREA)
CAUCASUS
c. 2100
c. 2300
c. 3000
c. 4000
c. 5000
KARANOVO VII
COTOFENI (WITH KURGAN elements)
KURGAN
GUMELNITA
1
2
3
4
VĂDASTRA
SĂLCUTA
BOIAN
V Petru Rareș
IV Spantov
III Vidra
II Giulești
I Bolintineanu
DUDEȘTI
?
STARČEVO
GLINA III
CERNAVODA (WITH KURGAN elements)
HAMANGIA
?
KURGAN
CUCUTENI — TRIPOLYE
LINEAR DANUBIAN
FORMATIVE MONTEORU (Schneckenberg, Foltești)
B
CLASSICAL CUCUTENI - TRIPOLYE
A-B
A 4
A 3
A 2
A 1
FORMATIVE OR PRE-CUCUTENI
III
II
I
PRIMITIVE OR SOUTHERN BUG-BOH NEOLITHIC
CATACOMB GRAVE PERIOD
IV
NORTH PONTIC
EARLY MIDDLE LATE
5 SAVRAN
4 SAMCHIN
3 PECHERA
2 SOKOLETS
1 SKIBINETS
?
POLTAVKA (EARLY TIMBER GRAVE)
KURGAN CULTURE
EARLY MIDDLE LATE
IV
III
II
I
NORTH CAUCASIAN RELATED TO N. PONTIC
KURGAN
TSARSKAJA
MAJKOP
NAL' CHIK
CAUCASIAN NEOLITHIC
= EXPANSION

Bibliography

Abbreviations

MIA — Materialy i Issledovanija po Arkheologii SSSR. Akademija Nauk SSSR, Moscow.

KSIA — Kratkie Soobshchenija Instituta Arkheologii Akademii Nauk USSR, Kiev.

KSIIMK — Kratkie Soobshchenija o Dokladakh i Polevykh Issledovanijakh Instituta Istorii Material'noj Kul'tury Akademii Nauk SSSR, Moscow (now: Kratkie Soobshchenija Instituta Arkheologii).

SA — Sovetskaja Arkheologija, Moscow.

SĖ — Sovetskaja Ėtnografija, Moscow.

Artemenko, I. I.

1963 "Srednedneprovskaja kul'tura" ("The Middle Dnieper Culture"), SA 2: 12-37.

1964 "Neoliticheskie stojanki i kurgany ėpokhi bronzy bliz s. Khodosovichi gomel'skoj obl. BSSR" ("Neolithic Habitation Sites and Bronze Age Kurgans near the Village of Khodosovichi, District of Gomel', Byelo Russia"). Pamjatniki Kamennogo i Bronzovogo Vekov, Akademija Nauk SSSR, pp. 31-87.

Artem'ev, V. A., Butomo, C. V., Drozhzhin, V. M., and Romanova, E. N.

1961 Rezul'taty opredelenija absoljutnogo vozrasta rjada arkheologicheskikh i geologicheskikh obraztsov po radiouglerodu (C 14). (Results of Age Determination of Archaeological and Geological Objects According to C-14 Dating.) SA 2.

Berciu, D.

1939 Arheologia preistorică a Olteniei. Ramuri Craiova.

1954 "Asupra problemei aşa-nu-mitelor sceptre de piatră din R.P.R." (Résumé in French: "Sur la question des ainsi dits 'Sceptres' de pierre de la République Populaire Roumaine"), Studii şi cercetări de istorie veche V: 539-49.

Bibikov, S.

1953 "Rannetripol'ske poselenie Luka-Vrublevetskaja na Dnestre" ("Early Tripolye site Luka-Vrublevetskaja on the Dniester"), MIA 38.

Bichir, Gh. I.

1958 "Un mormînt cu ocru la Cîrna" (Résumés in Russian and French: "Une tombe à ocre à Cîrna"), Studii şi cercetări istorie veche IX: 101-12.

Bodjanskij, A. V.

1956 "Rozkopki Mar'ïvs'kogo ta Fedorivs'kogo mogil'nikov u Nadporizhzhi" ("Excavations of the Marivka and Fedorivka cemeteries in the Dnieper rapids area"), Arkheologichni pam'jatki URSR VI: 179-81.

1961 "Lysogorskij neoliticheskij mogil'nik" ("The Neolithic Cemetery of Lysa Gora"), KSIA 11: 32-37.

Bognár-Kutzián, I.

1963 The Copper Age Cemetery of Tiszapolgár-Basatanya. Budapest: Akadémiai Kiadó.

Chernysh, E. K.

1962 "K istorii naselenija ėneoliticheskogo vremeni v srednem pridnestrov'e. Po materialam mnogoslojnogo poselenija u s. Nezvisko" ("A Contribution to the History of the Eneolithic Settlement in the Middle Dniester Area. Based on Materials of the Stratified Site at Nezvisko"), MIA 102: 5-85.

Danilenko, V. M.

1950 "Do pitannija pro rannij neolit pivdennoj naddniprjanshchini" ("A Contribution to the Question of the Early Neolithic in the Northern Part of the Lower Dnieper Region"), Arkheologija VII: 119-51.

1955 "O rannikh zven'jakh razvitija stepnikh vostochnoevropejskikh kul'tur shnurovoj keramiki" ("The Early Phases of the Development of the East European Corded Pottery Culture in the Steppe Area"), KSIA IV: 126-28.

1957 "Issledovanija neolitichesbikh pamjatnikov na Juzhnom Buge" ("The Excavations of Neolithic Sites on the Boh River"), Arkheologija X (Kiev).

1959 "Arkheologicheskie issledovanija 1956 goda v Chigirinskom rajone" ("Archaeological Investigations of 1956 in the District of Chigirinsk, Middle Dnieper Area"), KSIA 8: 13-21.

1962 "Arkheologicheskie issledovanija v zonakh stroitel'stva GES na Iuzhnom Buge" ("Archaeological Investigations in the Area of the Construction of State Electric Station on the Southern Bug River in 1950 and 1960). KSIA 12: 23-27.

Debets, G. F.

1955 "Cherepa iz ėpipaleoliticheskogo mogil'nika u s. Voloshskogo" ("Skulls from the Epipolaeolithic Cemetery of Voloshsk"), SĖ 3: 62-73.

Degen, B. E.

1941 "Kurgany v Kabardinskom parke g. Nal'chika" ("Kurgans in the Kabardino Park of the City of Nal'chik"), MIA 3: 213-317.

Dinu, M.

1961 "Contribuţii la problema culturii amforelor sferice pe teritoriul Moldovei" (Résumé in Russian and French: "Contribution à l'étude de la civilisation des amphores sphériques sur le territoire de la Moldavie"), Arheologia Moldovei I: 43-64.

Dobrovolskij, A. V.

1949 "Vos'ma Igrins'ka neolitichna stojanka" ("The Igren No. 8 Neolithic Site"), *Arkheologichni pam'jatki* URSR II: 243-51. (Kiev.)

1954 "Mogil'nik v s. Chapli" (The Cemetery in the Village of Chapli"), *Arkheologija* IX: 106-17.

Dokturovskij, V.

1925 "Opredelenija vozrasta Ljalovskoj stojanki po pyltse v torfe" (Résumé in German: "Die Pollenanalyse aus der Kulturschicht bei Lialovo"), *Russkij Antropologicheskij Zhurnal* XIII: 83-84.

Dumitrescu, Hortensia

1927-32 "La station préhistorique de Ruginoasa," *Dacia* III-IV.

1952-59 ("Results of the Excavations of the Site at Traian") In *Studii şi cercetări de istorie veche* III (1952): 121-40; IV (1953): 45-68; V (1954): 35-68; VI (1955): 459-86; and in *Materiale şi cercetări arheologice* III (1957): 115-28 and V (1959): 189-202.

1961 "Connections between the Cucuteni-Tripolie Cultural Complex and the Neighbouring Eneolithic Cultures in the Light of the Utilization of Golden Pendants," *Dacia* N.S. V: 69-93.

Dumitrescu, Hortensia, and Dumitrescu, Vladimir

1959 "Săpăturile de la Traian-Dealul Fîntînilor," *Materiale şi cercetări arheologice* VI: 157-78. (With Russian and French summaries.)

Dumitrescu, Vladimir

1941-44 "La station préhistorique de Traian," *Dacia* IX-X.

1958 "Les fouilles de Hăbăşeşti et quelques-uns des problèmes de la civilisation de Cucuteni-Tripolye," *Památky archeologické* 49: 265-96.

1959 "La civilisation de Cucuteni," *Berichten van de rijksdienst voor het oudheidkundig bodemonderzoek* 9: 7-48.

1963 "Originea şi evoluţia culturii Cucuteni-Tripolie," *Studii şi cercetări de istorie veche* XIV: 51-78, 285-308. (In Rumanian with summaries in Russian and French.)

Dumitrescu, Vladimir, and collaborators

1954 Hăbăşeşti. *Monografie arheologică* (Bucharest).

Formozov, A. A.

1962 "Neolit Kryma: Chernomorskogo poberezh'ja Kavkaza." ("The Neolithic in the Crimea and the Black Sea Coast of the Caucasus"), *MIA* 102: 89-149.

Frankfort, H.

1927 *Studies in Early Pottery of the Near East. II.* ("Occasional Papers," No. 8.) London: Royal Anthropological Institute of Great Britain.

Georgiev, G. I.

1961 "Kulturgruppen der Jungsteinzeit und der Kupferzeit in der Ebene von Thrazien (Südbulgarien)," L'Europe à la fin de l'âge de la pierre, pp. 45-100.

Gimbutas, M.

1956 The Prehistory of Eastern Europe. Part I. American School of Prehistoric Research, Bulletin No. 20. Cambridge, Mass.

1961 "Notes on the Chronology and Expansion of the Pit-grave Kurgan Culture," L'Europe à la fin de l'âge de la pierre, pp. 193-200.

1963 "The Indo-Europeans: Archeological Problems," American Anthropologist 65: 815-36.

Gokhman, I. I.

1958 "Paleoantropologicheskije materialy iz neoliticheskogo mogil'nika Vasil'jevka-2 v Dneprovskom Nadporozh'e" ("Palaeoanthropological Materials from the Neolithic Cemetery of Vasil'jevka-2 in the Area of the Dnieper Rapids"), SE 1: 25-29.

Goldman, H.

1931 Excavations at Eutresis. Cambridge, Mass.: Harvard University Press.

Kakhovskij, V. F.

1963 "Churachikskij Kurgan v Chuvashii" ("The Barrow of Churachiki in Chuvashia"), SA 3: 169-77.

Khanzadian, E. V.

1962 "Lchashenskij kurgan No. 6." ("The Barrow No. 6 from Lchashen"), KSIA 91: 66-71.

Khavljuk, P. I.

1959 "Stojanki razvitogo neolita v severnoj chasti srednego techenija juzhnogo Buga" ("Sites of Developed Neolithic in the Northern Part of the Middle Boh"), KSIIMK 65: 169-74.

Kohl, G., and Quitta, H.

1963 "Berlin-Radiokarbondaten archäologischer Proben. I," Ausgrabungen und Funde 8: 281-301.

Konduktorova, T. S.

1957 "Paleoantropologicheskie materialy iz mezoliticheskogo mogil'nika Vasil'evka-1" ("Palaeoanthropological Materials from the Mesolithic Cemetery of Vasil'evka-1"), Sovetskaja Antropologija 2: 207-10.

Krichevskij, E. Ju. and Kruglov, A. P.

1941 "Neoliticheskoe poselenie bliz g. Nal'chika" ("The Neolithic Site near the Town of Nal'chik") MIA 3: 51-63.

Kruglov, A. P., Piotrovskij, B. B., and Podgaetskij, G. V.
1941 "Mogil'nik v g. Nal'chike" ("Cemetery in the City of Nal'chik"), MIA 3: 67-147.

Kruglov, A. P., and Podgaetskij, G. V.
1941 "Dolinskoe poselenie u. g. Nal'chika" ("The Habitation Site of Dolinskoe near the City of Nal'chik"), MIA 3: 143-213.

Logodovskaja, O. F.
1955 "Mikhajlovskoe poselenie i ego istoricheskoe znachenie" ("The Habitation Site of Mikhajlovka and Its Historical Significance"), KSIA 4: 119-22.

Logodovska, O. F., Shaposhnikova, O. G., and Makarevich, M. L.
1962 Mikhajlivske posselenija (The Settlements of Mikhajlovka). (In Ukrainian.) Kiev.

Makarenko, M.
1933 Marijupil'skij mogil'nik (The Cemetery of Mariupol). Kiev.

Makarevich, M. L.
1955 "Raskopki pervogo Mikhajlovskogo poselenija" ("The Excavations of the First Settlement of Mikhajlovka"), KSIA 4: 122-24.

Markovin, V. I.
1959 "Glinjanaja statuetka iz stanitsy Urupskoj" ("A Clay Figurine from the Site of Urupskaja"), KSIIMK 76: 108-11.

Matasă, C.
1946 Frumuşica. Village préhistorique à céramique peinte dans la Moldavie du Nord. Bucharest.
1959 "Descoperiri arheologice în raionul Piatra Neamţ." (Summaries in Russian and French: "Découvertes archéologiques dans le district de Piatra Neamţ.") Materiale şi cercetări arheologice V: 723-33.
1964 "Aşazarea eneolitică Cucuteni B de la Tîrgu Ocna-Podei (raionul Tîrgu Ocna, reg. Bacău)," Archeologia Moldovei, II-III: 11-66. (With résumés in Russian and French.)

Merpert, N. Ja.
1961 "Ėneolit stepnoj polosy evropejskoj chasti SSSR" ("Eneolithic in the Steppe Zone of the European Part of the USSR.) (With a French translation: "L'enéolithique de la zone steppique de la partie européenne de l'U.R.S.S.") L'Europe à la fin de l'âge de la pierre, pp. 161-92.

Movsha, T. G.
1960 "Tripolskoe zhilische na poselenii Soloncheny II" (A Tripolyan House in the Habitation Site of Soloncheny II"), Zapiski Odesskogo Arkheologicheskogo Obshchestva (Odessa).
1961 "O svjaz'jakh plemen tripol'skoj kul'tury so stepnymi pleme-

nami mednogo veka" ("A Contribution to the Question of the Contacts between the Tripolye and Steppe Tribes in the Copper Age"), SA 2: 186-99.

Munchaev, R. M.

1961 "Drevnejshaja kul'tura severo-vostochnogo Kavkaza" ("The Most Ancient Culture of the Northeastern Caucasus"), MIA 100.

1962 "Pamjatniki majkopskoj kul'tury v Checheno-Ingushetii" ("Sites of the Majkop Culture in Checheno-Ingushetia"), SA 3: 176-98.

Nestor, I.

1933 "Der Stand der Vorgeschichtsforschung in Rumänien," 22. Bericht der Römisch-Germanischen Kommission 1932, pp. 11-182.

1955 "Sur les débuts de la métallurgie du cuivre et du bronze en Roumanie," Nouvelles études d'histoire presentées au Xe congrès des sciences historiques Rome 1955 (Bucarest), pp. 47-63.

Passek, T. S.

1949 "Periodizatsija tripolskikh poselenii" ("The Chronological Classification of the Tripolye Sites"), MIA 10.

1951 "Tripol'skoe poselenie Polivanov-jar" ("A Tripolyan Habitation Site of Polivanov-Jar"), KSIIMK 37: 41-64.

1960 "Rezul'taty arkheologicheskikh raskopok u s. Floreshty v Moldavii," Materialy i Issledovanija po Arkheologii Jugo-zapada SSSR i Rumynskoj Narodnoj Respubliki (Kishinev).

1961 "Rannezemledel'cheskie (tripol'skie) plemena Podnestrov'ja" ("Early Agricultural Tripolye Tribes in the Dniester Basin"), MIA 84.

1962 "Relations entre l'Europe Occidentale et l'Europe Orientale à l'époque néolithique," Atti del VI Congresso Internazionale delle Scienze Preistoriche e Protostoriche, Vol. I, pp. 127-44. Florence.

Petrescu-Dîmboviţa, M.

1963 "Die wichtigsten Ergebnisse der archäologischen Ausgrabungen in der neolithischen Siedlung von Truşeşti (Moldau)," Prähistorische Zeitschrift XLI: 172-86.

Petrescu-Dîmboviţa, M., et al.

1964 "Şantierul arheologic Cucuteni-Băiceni (r. Paşcani, reg. Iaşi), Materiale şi cercetări arheologice.

Piotrovskij, B.

1962 "The Aeneolithic Culture of Transcaucasia in the Third Millennium B.C." VI. Int. Congress of Prehistoric and Protohistoric Sciences. Reports and Communications by Archaeologists of the U.S.S.R. Moscow.

Popescu, D.

1937-40 "La tombe â ocre a Casimcea," Dacia VII-VIII: 85-91.

Roska, M.

1925 "Über die Schnurkeramik in Siebenbürgen," Prähistorische Zeitschrift XVI: 85-86.

Rudinskij, M. Ja.

1955 "Vovnigskie pozdneneoliticheskie mogil'niki" ("The Late Neolithic Cemeteries of Vovnigi"), KSIA 4: 147-51.

1956 "Pervshij Vovniz'kij piz'noneolitichnij mogil'nik" ("The First Late Neolithic Cemetery of Vovnigi"), Arkheologichni pam'jatki URSR VI: 151-61.

Schmidt, H.

1932 Cucuteni in der Oberen Moldau, Rumänien. Berlin-Leipzig.

Sergeev, T. P.

1962 "Rannetripol'skij klad u s. Karbuna" ("Early Tripolye Hoard near the Village of Karbuna"), SA 1: 135-51.

Stoljar, A. D.

1955 "Marjupol'skij mogil'nik kak istoricheskij istochnik" ("The Cemetery of Marjupol' as a Historical Source"), SA 23:16-38.

1961 "Ob istoricheshikh kornjakh kul'tury nadporozhskogo neolita" ("A Contribution to the Ethnohistory of the Neolithic Culture in the Area of Dnieper Rapids"), Issledovanija po Arkheologii SSSR, pp. 34-46. University of Leningrad.

Sulimirski, T.

1961 "The Climate of the Ukraine during the Neolithic and the Bronze Age," Archeologia XII: 1-18. (Warsaw.)

Székely, Z.

1955 "Contribuţie la cronologia epocii bronzului in Transilvania" (Résumé in French: "Contribution à la chronologie de l'age du bronze en Transylvanie"), Studii şi cercetări de istorie veche VI: 843-63.

Telegin, D. Ja.

1957 "Tretij Vasiljevskij mogil'nik" ("The Third Cemetery of Vasil'jevka"), KSIA 7: 9-12.

1959 "Ėneoliticheskoe poselenie i mogil'nik u khutora Aleksandrija" ("An Eneolithic Settlement and Cemetery at the Village of Aleksandria"), KSIA 9: 10-20.

1960 "Raskopki neoliticheskikh stojanok v ust'e r. Oskola" ("Excavations of Neolithic Sites at the Mouth of R. Oskol"), MIA 79: 176-87.

1961a "K voprosu o Dnepro-Donetskoj kul'ture" ("A Contribution to the Problem of the Dnieper-Donets Culture"), SA 4: 26-40.

1961b "Nikol'skij mogil'nik ėpokhi neolita-medi v nadporozh'e.

Predvaritel'noe soobshchenie" ("The Neolithic and Copper Age Cemetery at Nikol'skij in the Dnieper Rapids Area"), KSIA 11: 20-31.

Vinogradov, A. V.

1957 "K voprosu o juzhnykh svjazjakh kel'teminarskoj kul'tury" ("A Contribution to the Problem of Southern Affinities of the Kel'teminar Culture"), SĖ 3: 25-42.

Vulpe, R.

1937-40 "Les fouilles de Calu," Dacia VII-VIII: 13-68.

1957 Izvoare: Săpăturile din 1936-48. Bucharest: Biblioteca de Arheologie. (With summaries in Russian and French.)

Zimina, M. P.

1963 "Stojanka Lopachi" ("The Site of Lopachi"), SA 1: 278-83.

Relative Chronologies of China to the End of Chou

Kwang-chih Chang*
Yale University

In his paper for Relative Chronologies in Old World Archeology, the late Lauriston Ward pointed out that "thanks to the archeological work of recent years, it is impossible to escape the conviction that China, in spite of its remote position, has always been in more or less intimate, though indirect, contact with the West and that many of the fundamental elements of Chinese culture had their origin in the countries near the Mediterranean Sea" (Ward, 1954, p. 130). He observed also that for two reasons it was "extremely difficult to assign accurate dates to the early Chinese cultures on the basis of Western traits which they contain." The first was that "the parallels [between China and the West] are usually general in their nature and do not yet permit close and accurate dating in terms of the prehistoric and early historic culture sequences in the Near East and Europe" (*ibid*., pp. 133-34). The second was that "in most cases probably these traits were not diffused directly from Iran, let us say, to the North China plain but passed gradually through Central Asia, from people to people and with many modifications en route, until they ultimately reached China . . . [and therefore] it is impossible to know in each case how long it took for the diffusion from west to east" (*ibid*., p. 140).

During the fifteen years since 1949, when Ward's latest sources appeared in print, drastic changes have taken place in Chinese archaeology both in outlook and in substance. The impossible situation with which Ward was faced in dating the early Chinese cultures *according to the Western traits they contained* remains with us. But we are fortunate enough today to have a much better knowledge of the early Chinese culture sequences themselves than we had a decade and a half ago, and this knowledge has expanded from the North China plains to most of the Chinese territory (K. C. Chang, 1963*a*). Thus we have an improved light

*Asia Studies Grantee, American Council of Learned Societies and the Social Science Research Council, 1963-64.

upon two aspects of the prehistoric chronology of China. First, there is now a sounder basis for re-examining the local background of those traits that were believed to have been imported. Second, the native sequences of cultural contexts in which the Western traits occurred are better established. Accordingly, in this review of the relative chronologies of China,[1] there will be a shift of emphasis from that adopted in Ward's article. Rather than attempt to date the Chinese sequences in terms of the Western traits that occurred in them at various time intervals, this paper will endeavor to characterize a number of cultural units in prehistoric China, as established by archaeology, and to place these units in a time-space framework based upon internal evidence. A correlation can then be made between the Chinese sequences and the sequences in contiguous eastern, southern, and northern areas, as well as in the West, according to either absolute chronology, or relative synchronism, or both.

NORTH CHINA

"The starting point for any attempt to date the early archeological remains of the Far East must be the critical use of the Chinese historical records" (Ward, 1954, p. 130). Such records started with two historic dynasties, Shang and Chou. Reliable, absolute dates are available for the segment of the Chou Dynasty after 841 B.C. The beginning date of Chou and the beginning and ending dates of Shang are problematical, and the different chronological systems vary from one another by a few decades or even centuries (Table 1).

In Ssu-ma Ch'ien's Shih Chi ("Historical Memoirs"), events before the first year of the Kung Ho Era were charted by the author under his San Tai Shih Piao ("Table of Reigns of the Three Dynasties"). Those immediately following the same year were charted under his Shih Erh Chu Hou Nien Piao ("Table of Years of the Twelve Lords"). The dividing year, the first year of the Kung Ho Era, has been reliably put at 841 B.C. The absolute chronology of events before 841 B.C. has to be inferred from various kinds of conflicting evidence.

There are two principal kinds of evidence, calendrical and accumu-

1. For general and documented discussions on the prehistoric chronologies in China, see C. M. An, 1959a, 1959b; K. C. Chang, 1959, 1963a; CKKHY-KKYCS, 1962; S. C. Hsu, 1960; H. P. Shih, 1959; C. C. T'ung, 1957. References to document the discussions in the present article are not given if they can be found in K. C. Chang, 1963a.

TABLE 1

Some Early Historical Dates of North China

Dynasty	Subdivisions	Events	Absolute Dates (B.C.)
Shang		Founding of dynasty by T'ang	? 1514-1722+
		P'an Keng moves capital to An-yang	? 1291-1397
		Wu Wang conquest	? 1018-1122
Chou	Western Chou	First year of the Kung Ho Era	841
		P'ing Wang moves capital to Lo-yang	770
	Eastern Chou		
		Ch'in unification	221
Ch'in			

lative. The former consists of records in ancient texts of fixed astronomical events (such as solar and lunar eclipses and the lunar cycles) in correlation with the reigning years, months, or dates of particular kings before 841 B.C. According to such evidence, several chronological systems have been proposed by Chinese and Western scholars for the period before 841 B.C. (Tung, 1951; Ch'en, 1945), but any careful examination inevitably leads to the conclusion that the facts conflict, and the systems based upon them are therefore inconclusive. In a word, a generally acceptable, absolute chronological system for China before 841 B.C. does not exist.

This does not mean, however, that the approximate dates of the major historical events before 841 B.C. are not known. The most important date to be determined is the year in which Wu Wang of Chou conquered the last king of Shang, known variably as Chou, Shou, or Ti Hsin, and thereby founded the Chou Dynasty. No fewer than eleven dates have been proposed for this major event: 1122, 1116, 1111, 1070, 1067, 1066, 1050, 1047, 1030, 1027, and 1018 B.C. (T. P. Tung, 1951; Chou, 1961). Some of these, such as 1122, 1111, 1050, 1027, and 1018, may have been reconstructed on firmer grounds than others, but there is no one, in my opinion, that stands out and can be accepted as <u>the</u> most reliable. Any one of these five or six relatively reliable dates may serve as the terminal date of the Shang Dynasty, and its first year can then be calculated. <u>Chu Shu</u> or the <u>Bamboo Annals</u>, as quoted in <u>Shih Chi Chi Chieh</u>, says that from T'ang through Shou the Shang Dynasty lasted 496 years, and several other sources put the figure variously at "more than 500 years," "600 years," or "more than 600 years." Thus, the first year of Shang could be as recent as 1514 B.C. (1018 B.C. + 496 years) or as early as 1722+ B.C. (1122 B.C. + 600+ years). During the reign of the Shang another year is of importance—the year in which P'an-Keng moved his capital to An-yang, where extensive ruins dating from the Shang period have been well excavated. The <u>Bamboo Annals</u> (different versions are quoted in various sources) put this event at 273 or 275 years before the end of the dynasty, and thus it could be as early as 1397 B.C. (1122 B.C. + 275 years) or as late as 1291 B.C. (1018 B.C. + 273 years).

When did the historical period begin in North China? The first historical dynasty with archaeologically recovered, written records describing its own events is the Shang. Although the archaeological remains of the Shang writings at An-yang are no earlier than 1397 B.C. at the earliest, we have good reason to accept the beginning of this whole dynasty as falling between 1514 and 1800 B.C. At present I accept this interval as the beginning of the historical period in China. In the traditional, legendary history of China, a Hsia Dynasty precedes the Shang, and its duration has been variably given as 431, 432, 471, or 472 years, which would place the beginning of the Hsia at 1945 B.C. at the latest or 2194+ B.C. at the earliest. Ssu-ma's <u>Shih Chi</u> gives a rather detailed description of the Hsia events together with a complete royal genealogy. Since Ssu-ma's records of the Shang have been borne out almost in their entirety by archaeological findings, one may suspect that the substantiation of the Hsia Dynasty by archaeological evidence will be more or less a matter of time. Before that happens, however, the beginning dates of the Shang must serve our purpose. By the term "prehistoric," therefore, we refer to the pre-Shang period of cultural development within the confines of the Shang civilization in North China.

The earliest archaeological site now known in China is the one dating from the Early Pleistocene period near the village of Hsi-hou-tu, in

Jui-ch'eng County, southwestern Shansi (Chia and Wang, 1962, p. 25). Palaeolithic assemblages have been discovered in many places in North China (mainly in Shansi, at Choukoutien, and in the Ordos) from Middle and Upper Pleistocene deposits, and a fairly complete sequence of Palaeolithic cultural and human development in this area has been established (K. C. Chang, 1963b; 1962a). Since the chronological problems of the Palaeolithic period can be discussed only in geological terms, these are not our concern. After the last glacial stage came to a close and before the historic period began, North China was the stage for the following successive cultures:

1) Postglacial hunter-fishers
2) The Sheng-wen horizon
3) The primary village-farmers: Yangshao horizon
4) The stratified village-farmers: Lungshan horizon

The chronological problems of these successive cultures will be discussed briefly below.

Postglacial Hunter-Fishers

So-called Mesolithic remains have been brought to light in North China at no more than one or two places (K. C. Chang, 1963a, pp. 39-46). Their microblade character indicates continuity from the Upper Palaeolithic, but recognizable prototypes of characteristically Neolithic artifacts are few, suggesting a considerable gap between these cultures and the earliest known food-producing cultures.

The Sheng-wen Horizon

In 1954, Ward speculated upon the likelihood of a ceramic horizon in North China preceding the known Neolithic cultures:

> . . . all the Neolithic sites of North China, Red Pottery and Black Pottery alike, contain another ceramic ware, characterized by mat-marking and cord-marking; this ware is closely related to pottery found widely extended in eastern Asia, from Siberia in the north to Indochina and Malaya in the south. Accompanying this pottery in North China are also polished stone celts, identical with those which are associated with the mat-marked and cord-marked pottery of Siberia, Indochina, and Malaya. If these relationships are valid, it must have taken a considerable time to produce such a wide diffusion of these traits through the eastern half of Asia, and one must assume that the first appearance of this type of pottery and the polished stone celts in the North China plain antedated the comparatively late development of the painted pottery and black ware in that area. The proof of this would lie in the discovery of sites containing

mat-marked pottery and polished stone celts, without either painted pottery or black ware. So far, no such sites have been reported in North China . . . . Yet it seems almost inevitable that such sites will ultimately be found—and this is all the more likely, since we know of no archeological remains to fill the great interval of time between the "Upper Cave" of Chou-k'ou-tien and the first appearance of the Red Pottery culture. Accordingly, it seems best, on the basis of existing evidence, to break down the Neolithic of the North China plain into three cultures: a hypothetical Early Neolithic culture, which was followed in time by two late Neolithic cultures, Red Pottery and Black Pottery . . . ." (Ward, 1954, p. 133).

This "Early Neolithic" remains "hypothetical," but information unavailable to Ward has shed more light on it. As early as 1934, Hsü Ping-ch'ang of the National Peiping Academy excavated at Kou-tung-ch'ü, near Pao-chi in central Shensi, a cultural stratum that underlay a Red Pottery layer and yielded cord-marked pottery and polished stone celts but was without either painted or black pottery (P. C. Hsü 1935). The published descriptions of the site are inadequate, and the stratigraphic evidence is not entirely convincing. But other sites of a like nature have been discovered in the past decade in other regions (Chang, 1959), and it appears that this hypothetical Neolithic phase is on the verge of being substantiated. The term "Sheng-wen (cord-marked pottery) horizon" has been coined by me (1959); its chronological position in preceding the Yangshao and its characterization by cord-marked ceramic ware are both considered probable, but whether or not it indicates a food-producing culture is unclear. It is likely that the ultimate solution of the problem of the origin of food production in North China depends to a large extent upon future exploration within the Sheng-wen horizon.

The fact that cord-marked pottery occurred early and widely in east Asia has important chronological bearing. In northeast Asia in both the maritime (Kidder, 1959, p. 61) and the taiga (Michael, 1958, p. 39) areas the earliest ceramic ware appears to be the textile-marked (cord- and "net"-marked) pottery with characteristic pointed bottoms made by the sub-Neolithic hunter-fishers with a microblade cultural substratum. Clusters of radiocarbon dates convincingly indicate that this ceramic tradition existed in Japan as early as 9000 B.C. at the latest (Beardsley, 1962, p. 3; Chard, 1963). Together with the fact that cord-marked pottery appeared in southeast Asia in late Hoabinhian and Bacsonian assemblages, the early occurrence of this ceramic ware in northeast Asia suggests a rather early date for the hypothetical Sheng-wen horizon in North China, a possibility which is particularly significant in raising the ceiling of upper limits for dating the subsequent "late" Neolithic cultures.

Primary Village Farmers: Yangshao Horizon

The first well-defined Neolithic culture stage of North China is the Yangshao, to which more than a thousand discovered sites can be assigned, sites distributed in the Nuclear Area of North China and its immediate neighborhood—western and northern Honan, southwestern Hopei, southern and central Shansi, central Shensi, and eastern Kansu, in the valleys of the middle Huangho, the lower Fenho, the Weishui, and the T'aoho. Remains at these sites—mostly on river terraces in the western highlands of North China—indicate moderate-sized village occupation, pig husbandry, and slash-and-burn cultivation of millet; in short, the beginning of effective food production by village farmers, although hunting-fishing-collecting remained to play important local roles in the subsistence patterns (K. C. Chang, 1963a). These sites are grouped into a broadly contemporary archaeological horizon primarily on the basis of their ceramic remains. The Yangshao pottery was handmade and primarily reddish in color. Predominant surface treatment was the impression on the external surface of cord marks and marks of other textiles such as baskets and mats. Designs in black pigment were frequently painted on the reddish surface or on a white slip. Characteristic vessel forms are round- or flat-bottomed bowls, jars, and beakers and pointed-bottom jars. Variations in the ceramic ware of the Yangshao divide the sites further into several phases. The following phases are currently distinguished: Miao-ti-kou I, Pan-p'o, Ma-chia-yao, and Panshan-Mach'ang (An, 1959b; An, *et al.*, 1959; CKKHY-KKYCS, 1962; Ma, 1961; Shih, 1959; 1962). Miao-ti-kou I centers in western Honan but spreads into southern Shansi and eastern Shensi. The Pan-p'o phase is typically represented in the lower Weishui valley of central Shensi, but extends into the Huangho valley of western Honan in the east and eastern Kansu in the west. Both the Ma-chia-yao and the Panshan-Mach'ang phases are confined to eastern Kansu. Stratigraphical evidence at Ma-chia-yao in Lin-t'ao County (H. C. Chang, 1958), eastern Kansu, indicates that the Kansu phases are later in time than the phases to the east, and the stratigraphic evidence at Hsia-meng-ts'un in Pin County, central Shensi (S. K. Li, 1962), suggests that the

Pan-p'o phase preceded the Miao-ti-kou I in time.[2] Other Yangshao sites in northern Honan, southwestern Hopei, and central Shansi have yet to be clearly defined in terms of ceramic phases, and their chronological relationships with the above phases are to be determined (*cf.* Yang, 1962). The intra-horizon chronological problems of the Yangshao will remain one of the focal points of North Chinese Neolithic archaeology for some time to come.

Available archaeological evidence suggests that the earliest Yangshao sites occurred in eastern Shensi, western Honan, and southwestern Shensi—the Nuclear Area where the hypothetical Sheng-wen horizon is considered to have originated. Later Yangshao phases spread toward the east into the eastern fringes of the North China western highlands and westward into eastern Kansu and Chinghai. The time span of this development remains unknown, and the absence of any absolute dates that can be determined from the Yangshao sites (such as C-14 dates) makes it totally impossible to assign any dates to any part of the Yangshao sequence. All we can say is that the Yangshao development took place in North China between the Sheng-wen horizon (which *could* be as early as, if not earlier than, 9000 B.C., if its relationship with the earlier segments of the Japanese Jomon can possibly be regarded as contemporary) and the beginning of the next Lungshan horizon.

Can absolute dates for the Yangshao be plausibly projected in terms of any "Western" traits it may contain? Any archaeologist reasonably familiar with both Chinese and Western Neolithic and Chalcolithic remains will not fail to notice a considerable number of "similarities" between these two areas. When the study of Chinese Neolithic archaeology was still in its infancy in the 1920's and 1930's, it was only natural for scholars, who knew the western Asian materials much better, simply because there was much more to be known, to jump at the assumptions that all Chinese Neolithic traits similar to Near Eastern traits came into China from the Near East, and were, therefore, later in time than their Near Eastern counterparts. Such assumptions have gradually become suspect, however, in the face of two new pieces of information: (1) The Chinese Neolithic had both a distinctive life of its

2. The relative chronology of the Pan-p'o and Miao-ti-kou phases of the Yangshao horizon cannot, however, be considered settled. For recent controversies over this problem, see: An, 1959*b*, 1961; An *et al.*, 1959; S. C. Chang, 1961; Fang, 1963; J. T. Wu, 1961; Yang, 1961, 1962.

own, most of which was not similar to that of the Near East except in very broad terms, and also a long history of internal development; and (2) the Neolithic culture in the Far East, insofar as its ceramic components are concerned, could have begun at the same time as, if not earlier than, the Neolithic culture in the Near East. In view of these new considerations we must distinguish the following four kinds of East-West similarities: (a) convergence or parallel and independent development; (b) probable relationship with undetermined direction of diffusion; (c) probable relationship with a West-to-East direction of diffusion; and (d) probable relationship with an East-to-West direction of diffusion. Determination among these various alternatives is therefore a prerequisite for any chronological consideration of specific traits, but it is apparent that such determination is, unfortunately, never easy nor is it often clear-cut.

Diffusions between the two regions concerned are probably best demonstrated by certain cultivated plants and domestic animals. Although there is no inherent reason why specific plants or animals could not have been domesticated by men more than once in widely separated areas—the pig may possibly be a case in point, as suggested by the possible independent domestication of pigs in such a small and marginal food-producing area as the Liaotung Peninsula (Kanaseki *et al*., 1943)—yet we can have no reason at the moment to doubt that wheat, cattle, sheep, and goats, remains of which were found at a few Yangshao sites in North China (K. C. Chang, 1963*a*, pp. 59-60), were introduced from the Near East, where local histories of their domestication have been well documented archaeologically. On the other hand, millet, though occurring in the Near East and Europe, was the staple crop of the Yangshao farmers and was probably first domesticated by them and was subsequently introduced into western Asia. Owing to the long persistence in time of these plant and animal remains in both China and the Near East, they are of little chronological significance.

More specific East-West similarities that were probably more limited in time and are thus of greater chronological value are some ceramic features. Cord-marked pottery, as observed by Ward (1954, p. 134), was extremely rare in the Near East, and was probably intrusive from its Far Eastern center of distribution. But since the great antiquity of cord-marked pottery in the Far East has now been established by C-14 tests, its date of occurrence in the Near East has little more than supporting significance. The "painted pottery" as a ceramic category that has often been used to show the China-West relationships at this period clearly serves poorly, if at all, for such purposes. More useful are some specific decorative designs and vessel forms. Several scholars (Arne, 1925; Andersson, 1943; Bachhofer, 1935; Sirén, 1929, vol. I, p. 11) have attempted to compare certain painted decorative motifs on pottery of Anau, Tripolye, and Yangshao, but most of the similarities are such simple and isolated decorative elements that the historical connections suggested by them are rather superficial and dubious.

The Yangshao pottery of North China has seldom been compared with the earliest painted pottery of Mesopotamia. Probably this is because scholars feel that the Hassuna-Halaf painted pottery is too distant from the Yangshao both in time and in space. Actually, this need not be so. The distance between Tell Hassuna and Kansu is about 3,150 miles by air, and that between Anau and Kansu, 2,400 miles. If the Anau-Kansu ties are considered possible with a few finds between these two places to serve as links, then the Hassuna-Kansu ties are equally credible. As to the time distance, the date of Kansu Yangshao is not known, and the possibility remains that it could have been early, as mentioned above. It is necessary to point out these facts, because striking similarities between the Panshan-Mach'ang phase of Kansu and the Tell Hassuna assemblage of Mesopotamia can be found.

I want to draw attention to the similarity between the human figure on the neck of a jar excavated from level V at Tell Hassuna and three similar pieces purchased by Andersson in the Pan-shan area (Fig. 1). The use of a human head for the top of the vessel and the tattoo pattern consisting of parallel short strokes on the cheeks are both indicative of artistic or even ritual ideas that could hardly be accidentally shared by two widely separated archaeological assemblages. Another similarity is the use of cowrie shell-shaped designs as the leading decorative motif on urns. Elsewhere I have suggested that these designs at Pan-shan were possible depictions of the female vagina which carried ritual significance (K. C. Chang, 1960). _If_ the Hassuna design has any like meaning, then the connection between it and the one from Pan-shan would be one of both form and meaning, and one that carries weighty historical significance.

It cannot be overstressed that the Hassuna and the Panshan-Mach'ang phases are, on the whole, characterized by widely different

Fig. 1. Right, above and below: Pan-shan figurines, after Palmgren, 1934, Pl. XIX; Center: Hassuna sherds, after Lloyd and Safar, Pl. XVII, 2; Left, above: Halaf ware, after Childe, 1953, Pl. XVII; Left, below: Hassuna sherd, after Lloyd and Safar, Fig. 14.

features of stone industry and ceramics. The similarities mentioned above indicate at most cultural contacts between them, despite the great distance involved, but there is no inherent evidence to suggest the direction of the cultural flow. Whatever the direction, if these similar features resulted from contact, this would mean that the Pan-shan phase could be as early as the sixth millennium B.C., in which the Hassuna has been placed (Braidwood, 1958, pp. 1924-25), and that the Pan-p'o and Miao-ti-kou I phases, which have been stratigraphically demonstrated to be earlier than the Kansu phases, could be even earlier—a conclusion in no way at odds with the current understanding of the North China Neolithic sequence.

Not to confuse the issue, however, but to jar our complacency, if any, in such dating techniques, I might point to another specific similarity between a Syrian "churn" and a "canteen" of the Pan-p'o phase in Shensi (Fig. 2). The former was unearthed from a tomb considered to be of the fourth millennium B.C. (Perrot, 1961), but the latter dates from a period earlier than the Kansu phases which, as "demonstrated" above, could be as early as the sixth millennium B.C.! To be sure, the uses of these vessels were probably quite different in Syria and in North China—the Shensi piece was hardly a "churn," whatever it was—but their forms are strikingly similar.

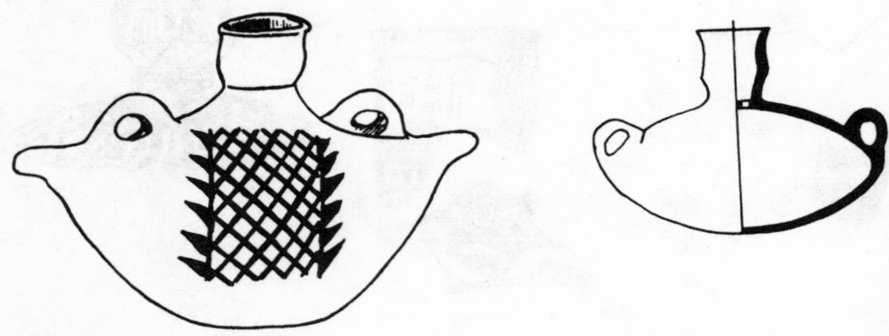

Fig. 2. Left: "Canteen," North China; after CKKHY-KKYCS, Pl. VI, no. 2; Right: "Churn," Syria, after Perrot, 1961, Fig. 39, no. 1.

Aside from the West, the Yangshao also shared occasional similar features with Neolithic cultures in Siberia and South China. But these latter areas often depend for their chronologies upon the Yangshao dates. V. Elisséeff maintains that "taking into account the forms of the jade and paste (jade?) ornaments and the disks of the cylindrical tubes that appear in the Yangshao culture, it can be assumed that this culture and that of Glaskovo [of Lake Baikal] were contemporary (17th-12th cent. B.C.)" (1960, p. 18). He seems to have overlooked the fact that in giving absolute dates to the Glaskovo complex, Soviet archaeologists relied heavily upon Andersson's estimates of the Yangshao dates (Okladnikov, 1950: 137-38). In short, outside parallels have not proved positively helpful in dating the Yangshao stage of North China Neolithic.

Stratified Village Farmers: Lungshan Horizon

When Ward wrote his article on China for Relative Chronologies a decade ago, he voiced the unanimous opinion of Chinese archaeologists at that time that the Red Pottery and the Black Pottery cultures "were largely contemporary, though in certain cases the Red Pottery culture may be considered the earlier of the two" (1954, p. 133). The most notable development in Neolithic archaeology in the past ten years has been a reappraisal of the relationship between these two cultures, which has led to the hypothesis, gradually being accepted by Chinese archaeologists in general, that the Red Pottery culture and the Black Pottery culture were essentially two stages of the same Neolithic culture tradition, the latter having developed from the former (K. C. Chang, 1959).

This hypothesis is based upon a number of considerations, typological and stratigraphical. The new Neolithic culture of North China—referred to as the Black Pottery or the Lungshan—marks a further development within the Yangshao context of village farmers who evolved into a more sophisticated culture and a more complex social order at the village level, and who greatly expanded their territory and became quite differentiated in their cultural styles. A new kiln construction and firing technique led to the predominance of gray and black pottery in place of the red, and the social complexity of the Lungshan villagers—"stratified village-farmers" in my terminology (K. C. Chang, 1962b)—must be taken into account in the increasing complexity of ceramic forms and function. Painting as a medium of decoration went out of vogue, although cord-, mat-, and basket-marked surfaces remained. Stamped and impressed geometric patterns gained popularity owing to the introduction of the paddle-and-anvil technique. Tripods of several kinds and bowls on pedestals are significant forms that gained great popularity at this time.

This new Neolithic culture had a much wider distribution than the Yangshao: in addition to the Nuclear Area it expanded into the eastern lowlands of North China and the hills and river valleys of South China, where rice was probably added to the crop list. In fact, the Lungshan sites found in a large area of China clearly delineate a horizon style in the American usage of the term, and this apparently resulted from an explosive expansion of population. Social differentiation and the growing prevalence of warfare must be concomitant features. In the vast Lungshan area, a number of local phases came into being, such as Miao-ti-kou II, Shensi, Shansi, Honan, the Pohai Bay, the Hanshui, the Huai, and the Southeastern Coastal. Stratigraphical evidence in western Honan has demonstrated conclusively that in the Nuclear Area the Miao-ti-kou II phase immediately followed the Yangshao and was followed by the Honan Lungshan phase which immediately preceded the Shang civilization of the area. Stylistic and chronological correlations render likely the hypothesis that the rapid Lungshan expansion from the Nuclear Area took place during the time span of the Miao-ti-kou II phase and that later Lungshan phases developed independently in the various areas (K. C. Chang 1963a).

The chronological problems of the Lungshan are no less complex than the Yangshao, but its lower time limits coincide with the beginning of the historical period in a large part of North China. In Chengchou and Loyang in western and northern Honan, cultural assemblages have recently been brought to light to serve as intermediate phases between the Honan Lungshan and the earliest recognizable Shang Dynasty remains (*ibid.*). The remaining unknown factors are beginning dates of the Lungshan stage as a whole, and these cannot be determined until and unless C-14 dates become available. Characteristic Lungshan pottery forms—such as tripods (Loehr, 1952, p. 43, Fig. 11) and bowls with perforated pedestals (Heine-Geldern, 1950, Figs. 1-5)—have been found in Near Eastern sites of comparable age, such as Tepe Hissar, and the stamped-earth village walls of the Lungshan have been compared with the pisé construction of the Near East. Indeed, Heine-Geldern (1950, 1956, 1959) contends that the "Lungshan Culture" had an Eastern Caspian origin. But the coastal "Lungshan Culture" that Heine-Geldern compared with the Eastern Caspian counterparts is now known to be a later phase whose derivation from the Miao-ti-kou II phase in the Nuclear Area has been all but demonstrated. The similarities between the coastal Lungshan phase and the Eastern Caspian culture are interesting because they are difficult to explain, but at the present they do not add anything significant to our knowledge of the Lungshan chronology.

SOUTHEAST CHINA

Neither Mesolithic nor Yangshao Neolithic remains have been brought to light in southeast China (from Shantung Peninsula down to the Pearl Delta) up to the present time. Aside from a small number of sites in the southern fringes of the area—eastern Kwangtung and Taiwan—where a sub-Neolithic occupation probably intrusive from the southwest is indicated by chipped and polished stone implements and cord-marked pottery, the extensive occupation of southeast China in postglacial times seems to have been accomplished by farmers with a Lungshanoid culture who in all likelihood were immigrants from North China during the Lungshan stage of the Neolithic, a stage marked by growing and expanding populations. The Lungshanoid stratum of this area was directly overlain by assemblages with geometric impressed pottery and bronze artifacts, both attributable to Shang and Western Chou influences from the north. During these early historic periods, islands of Shang and Western Chou civilizations gradually pushed their way southward into the Geometric area, and by about 700 B.C. several native civilizations became established here and were known in the historical records as Wu, Yüeh, and Ch'u.

Thus, the prehistoric chronology of southeast China is broadly divisible into a Lungshanoid horizon, beginning at an unknown date but lasting until the end of the second millennium B.C.; a Geometric horizon, spanning the last centuries of the second millennium and the first centuries of the first millennium B.C.; and an Eastern Chou horizon, extending through the remaining centuries of the first millennium and continuing until the Ch'in and Han conquests in the third and second centuries B.C.

The prehistoric culture history of southeast China is intimately related to the early chapters of Pacific prehistory. It is widely believed that the recent rapid expansion of the Mongoloid races in eastern Asia was an event closely related to the spreading of agriculture (Birdsell, 1951). The newly established archaeological facts that the first southeast Chinese coastal inhabitants were emigrants from the Lungshan in North China and that the Neolithic northern Chinese skeletons exhibit closer similarities to modern Oceanic Mongoloids than to the present-day northern Chinese (Li, 1962; Yen, 1960) are both significant in shedding light on the early history of the Proto-Malays of the western Pacific. The radiocarbon dates obtained from Neolithic sites in eastern Malaysia, Micronesia, and Polynesia (Shutler, 1962) are thus of great interest in suggesting possible time ranges for the Neolithic farmers on the continent.

SOUTHWEST CHINA

Unlike the eastern part of South China, the southwest (south of the Tsinling Mountains and west of the Pearl Delta) had a long and uninterrupted record of hominid occupation throughout the Pleistocene period, and its postglacial culture history is above all characterized by the long persistence of a native culture tradition or a complex of native culture traditions that exhibited distinctive features and considerable resistance to rapid and facile assimilation by the high cultures and civilizations pushing in from North China.

Mesolithic sites have been found widely in the southwest, divisible into a pebble-tool tradition (similar to the southeast Asian Hoabinhian) and a flake-tool tradition coexisting at different localities. Pottery characterized mainly by the cord-marked variety, which apparently indicates contacts with North China of the Sheng-wen horizon, first appeared in the archaeological record in sub-neolithic contexts in association with continuing Mesolithic stone implements. Painted and black-gray wares subsequently made sporadic appearances, mainly along the northern and eastern peripheries, probably indicating contacts with the Neolithic North and southeast China, and fully agricultural assemblages yielding remains of millet and rice have also been brought to light. But apparently sub-Neolithic and Neolithic southwestern cultures existed side by side for a considerable length of time, during which Shang and Western Chou influences are indicated by isolated findings, until the Eastern Chou period of the middle of the first millennium B.C. in the northern part of the area and until the late Eastern Chou and early Han periods of the late first millennium B.C. in the southern part. The stimulation brought about by the impact of the Eastern Chou and Han civilizations upon southwest China was probably responsible for the emergence of Bronze-Iron Age native civilizations throughout the area late in the first millennium B.C.

Southwest China surely cannot be separated from Indochina in culture history, and the Indochinese prehistoric sequence of Mesolithic (early Hoabinhian)-sub-Neolithic (late Hoabinhian and Bacsonian)-Neolithic-Bronze-Iron Age (Dongsonian) parallels the southwestern Chinese development, and any chronological assessment of both sequences must depend to a large extent upon the known archaeology and early historic documents of both North and southeast China. To the west, the southeast Asian Neolithic complex apparently was related to the Andhra-Karnatak Culture of south India. The discoveries of rice, millet, and silk at Nevasa and Nevdatoli, carbon-dated approximately 2500 to 2000 B.C. (Sankalia, 1962a, 1962b), are of great interest in the problem of India-southeast Asia Neolithic contacts and chronologies.

NORTHWEST CHINA

Although it is a vast area and was presumably of great importance in early East-West communications, northwest China (western Kansu, Chinghai, and Sinkiang) is practically a terra incognita in prehistory. Non-ceramic microlithic sites, few and far between, have been found, but these tell a poor story of the Mesolithic population in this region. Ceramic assemblages are divisible into Eastern and Western varieties, the former recalling late Yangshao characteristics of eastern Kansu and the latter resembling the Keltiminar remains in Khazakstan immediately to the west of Sinkiang. If one ventures to generalize on the basis of the few data available (cf. Y. C. Li, 1962), one might see here a long persistence of Mesolithic and sub-Neolithic cultures, receiving transitory Neolithic influences from both the East and the West, until the seventh century B.C. when the militant nomads arose to become the masters of the steppe. If East and West had extensive contacts during the Neolithic and the Bronze Age, they presumably were made in the main via northwest China, but so far there is little evidence for contact in the archaeological record of this region. Any generalizations will probably prove to have been grossly unwise when northwest China is finally explored by archaeologists.

EASTERN MONGOLIA AND MANCHURIA

Postglacial non-ceramic assemblages have been found in Manchuria and seem to belong to the widespread northeast Asian microlithic substratum. Subsequent ceramic assemblages exhibit connections with both East and West: Manchurian finds fall into the Maritime flat-bottomed pottery tradition, but eastern Mongolian industries show greater similarities with the Lake Baikal tradition and the steppe microliths to the west. Yangshao influences from North China reaching eastern Mongolia and the southwestern extremes of Manchuria are the first markers of relative chronology, and agriculture and animal husbandry penetrated into this area as far north as the natural environment permitted during both Yangshao and Lungshan times. The Western Chou established a few outposts in eastern Mongolia, and the first extensive Sinicization of southern Manchuria was not achieved until the Eastern Chou period, to which many so-called Eneolithic sites in this region should probably be dated (T'ung, 1962).

REMARKS

Bishop stated more than thirty years ago that "Northern China forms an integral part of the north temperate zone of the Old World. It is, moreover, connected with Western Asia and Eastern Europe by a long but continuous belt of steppe presenting no transverse barriers to migration, whether faunal or human. It cannot, therefore, be treated as a region apart, save in a very limited and subordinate sense" (1933, p. 389). The archaeological research carried out during the past thirty years has proved that this view is no longer tenable. Culture contacts between North China and western Asia and eastern Europe during prehistoric and early historic times are both presumable and probable, but in discussing the origins of the Far Eastern civilizations, their developmental process, and their chronological problems, North China must be treated as a region apart. It had a long history of essentially self-sufficient cultural development, and its early cultures were the main precursors of cultural events taking place in the entire area west from the T'ien-shan and the Yenisei and east to the circum-Pacific areas. Any chronological assessment of archaeological assemblages within this area can ill afford to lose sight of this basic fact. North China's prehistory and early history provide the basic yardstick for chronologists working in the eastern half of Asia.

Unfortunately, this yardstick up to now has been rather imprecise. The beginning dates of the Northern Chinese sequence can only be inferred in broad terms from the geological chronology and radiocarbon dates of areas other than China, which may indirectly reflect the pertinent time ranges in China. The ending dates of the sequence, however, are more precisely known. Between these two poles we have relative sequences and approximate durations, but no absolute dating. From the Mesolithic to the historic, North China culture history can be broken down into at least the following major cultural segments: Sheng-wen, Pan-p'o, Miao-ti-kou I, Miao-ti-kou II, and Honan Lungshan, each of which is susceptible to further and minor subdivisions.

For Chinese prehistory, therefore, we are in possession of a considerable amount of building material as well as a general framework of time-space relationships of cultural phases. In precisely what manner this framework should be placed in relation with, and in proportion to, other areas of the Old World must depend upon two sets of new evidence that are yet unavailable: a significant number of radiocarbon dates in order to place the Chinese Neolithic phases within an absolute chronology, and a much better knowledge of the prehistory of both the Chinese and Russian Turkestans, which alone can tie the two pyramids of ancient Asian civilizations together in a chronological as well as historical sense.

Before these two sets of evidence are brought to bear on the problem, efforts to correlate positively and precisely the prehistoric Chinese sequence with the Near East must be regarded as unwarranted.

Bibliography

An, Chih-min

1959a "The Major Achievements in the Neolithic Archaeology of China," Wen-wu, 1959, no. 10, pp. 19-23.

1959b "A Preliminary Discussion on the Neolithic Culture of the Huangho Valley," K'ao-ku, 1959, no. 10, pp. 559-65.

1961 "Remarks on the Analysis of the Decorative Patterns of the Painted Pottery of Miao-ti-kou," K'ao-ku, 1961, no. 7, pp. 385-87.

An, Chih-min, and others

1959 Miao-ti-kou and San-li-ch'iao. Peiping: Science Press.

Andersson, J. G.

1943 "Researches into the Prehistory of the Chinese," Bulletin of the Museum of Far Eastern Antiquities (Stockholm), no. 15

Bachhofer, L.

1935 "Der Zug nach dem Osten," Sinica-Sonderausgabe, pp. 101 ff., Frankfort: China-Institut der Universität.

Beardsley, Richard K.

1962 COWA Survey and Bibliography, Area 17: Far East (Japan), no. 2. Cambridge, Mass.: Council for Old World Archaeology.

Birdsell, Joseph B.

1951 "The Problem of the Early Peopling of the Americas as Viewed from Asia." In Papers on the Physical Anthropology of the American Indian, pp. 1-68. Ed. W. S. Laughlin. New York: Viking Fund.

Bishop, Carl W.

1933 "The Neolithic Age in Northern China," Antiquity 7: 389-404.

Braidwood, Robert J.

1958 "Near Eastern Prehistory," Science 127: 1419-30.

Chang, Hsüeh-cheng

1958 "Preliminary Report of Archaeological Reconnaissance in Lin-t'ao and Lin-hsia Counties, Kansu," K'ao-ku T'ung-hsün, 1958, no. 9, pp. 36-49.

Chang, Kwang-chih

1959 "The Chronology of the Neolithic Cultures of China," Bulletin of the Institute of History and Philology, Academia Sinica, 30: 259-309.

1960 "Evidence for the Ritual Life in Prehistoric China," Bulletin of the Institute of Ethnology, Academia Sinica, 9: 253-70.

1962a "New Evidence on Fossil Man in China," Science 136: 749-60.

1962b "Major Problems in the Culture History of Southeast Asia,"

Bulletin of the Institute of Ethnology, Academia Sinica, 13: 1-26.

1963a The Archaeology of Ancient China. New Haven: Yale University Press.

1963b "Prehistoric Archaeology in China: 1920-60," Arctic Anthropology 1: 29-61.

Chang, Shih-ch'üan

1961 "On the Relative Chronology of the Yangshao Remains at Miao-ti-kou and San-li-ch'iao," K'ao-ku, 1961, no. 7, pp. 380-83.

Chard, Chester S.

1963 Personal communication.

Ch'en, Meng-chia

1945 The Chronology of the Western Chou. Chungking: Commercial Press.

Chia, Lan-p'o, and Wang Chien

1962 "The Present Status and Prospect of the Palaeolithic Studies in Shansi," Wen-wu, 1962, nos. 4/5, pp. 23-27.

Childe, V. Gordon

1953 New Light on the Most Ancient East. New York: Praeger.

Chou, Fa-kao

1961 "Certain Dates of the Shang Period," Harvard Journal of Asiatic Studies 23: 108-12.

Chung-kuo K'o-hsüeh-yüan K'ao-ku-yen-chiu-suo (CKKHY-KKYCS)

1962 The Archaeology of New China. Peiping: Wen-wu Press.

Elisséeff, Vadime

1960 "Asiatic Protohistory." In Encyclopedia of World Art, vol. 2, pp. 1-39. New York: McGraw-Hill.

Fang, Yin

1963 "On the Problem of the Subdivision of the Yangshao Culture as Viewed from the Analysis of the Painted Pottery of Miao-ti-kou," K'ao-ku, 1963, no. 3, pp. 149-52, 155.

Heine-Geldern, Robert von

1950 "China, die ostkaspische Kultur und die Herkunft der Schrift," Paideuma 6: 51-92.

1956 "The Origin of Ancient Civilizations and Toynbee's Theories," Diogenes 13: pp. 81-99.

1959 "Lungshan Culture and East Caspian culture; a Link between Prehistoric China and the ancient Near East—The Origin and Spread of Writing," International Symposium on History of Eastern and Western Cultural Contacts, pp. 5-23. Tokyo and Kyoto.

Hsü, Ping-ch'ang

1935 "Neolithic Sites Recently Found in Shensi," Bulletin of the Peiping Academy of Science 7: 201-8.

Hsü, Shun-ch'en

1960 "Several Problems on the Neolithic Cultures in the Central Plain" Wen-wu 1960, no. 5, pp. 36-39.

Kanaseki, Takeo, and others

1943 "Yang-t'ou-wa," Archaeologia Orientalis (Tokyo), ser. B, no. 3.

Kidder, J. Edward, Jr.

1959 Japan before Buddhism. New York: Praeger.

Li, Chi

1954 "The Reconstruction of the Ancient History of China and Its Problems," The Democratic Review (Hong Kong) 5: 86-89, 131.

1962 "Some Anthropological Problems of China: Reconsidered," Proc. International Assoc. of Historians of Asia, Second Biennial Conference, Taipei, pp. 1-12.

Li, Shih-kuei

1962 "Preliminary Report of the Further Excavations at the Yangshao Culture Site at Hsia-meng-ts'un in Pin County, Shensi," K'ao-ku, 1962, no. 6, pp. 292-95.

Li, Yü-ch'un

1962 "A Survey of the Archaeological Work of the Uighur Autonomous Region in Sinkiang," Wen-wu, 1962, nos. 7/8, pp. 11-15, 80.

Lloyd, Seton, and Safar, Fuad

1945 "Tell Hassuna. Excavations by the Iraq Government Directorate General of Antiquities, 1943 and 1944," Journal of Near Eastern Studies 4: 255-89.

Loehr, Max

1952 "Zur Ur- und Vorgeschichte Chinas," Saeculum 3: 15-55.

Ma, Ch'eng-yüan

1961 "Some Problems on the Yangshao and the Ma-chia-yao Cultures," K'ao-ku, 1961, no. 7, pp. 375-79.

Michael, Henry N.

1958 "The Neolithic Age in Eastern Siberia," Transactions of the American Philosophical Society, n.s. 48, part 2.

Okladnikov, A. P.

1950 "Neolithic and Bronze Age of the Baikal Region," Materials and Research on the Archaeology of the USSR, no. 18. Moscow and Leningrad: Publishing House of the Academy of Sciences of the USSR. (Trans. by O. Frink, manuscript, Peabody Museum, Harvard.)

Palmgren, Nils

1934 "Kansu Mortuary Urns of the Pan Shan and Ma Ch'ang groups," Palaeontologia Sinica, ser. D, vol. 3, fasc. 1.

Perrot, J.

1961 "Une Tombe a Ossuaires du IVe Millenaire â Azor, près de Tel Aviv," Atiqot (Jerusalem) 3: pp. 1-83.

Sankalia, H. D.

1962a Indian Archaeology Today. New York: Asia Publishing House.

1962b "From Food Collection to Urbanization in India." In Indian Anthropology, pp. 66-104. Eds. T. N. Madan and Gepala Sarana. New York: Asia Publishing House.

Shih, Hsing-pang

1959 "Some Problems in the Archaeological Study of the Primitive Society in the Huangho Valley," K'ao-ku, 1959, no. 10, pp. 566-70.

1962 "Some Problems Pertaining to the Ma-chia-yao Culture," K'ao-ku, 1962, no. 6, pp. 318-29.

Shutler, Richard, Jr.

1962 "Peopling of the Pacific in the Light of Radiocarbon Dating," Asian Perspectives 5: 207-12.

Sirén, Osvald

1929 Histoire des arts anciens de la Chine. ("Annales du Musée Guimet, Bibliothéque d'Art," n.s. Vol. III.) Paris et Bruxelles: Les Editions G. Van Oest.

T'ung, Chu-ch'en

1957 "The Distribution and Chronology of Neolithic cultures in the Middle and Lower Huangho and Yangtze," K'ao-ku Hsüeh-pao, 1957, no. 2, pp. 7-21.

1961 "The Distribution and Chronology of the Primitive Cultures in Manchuria," K'ao-ku, 1961, no. 10, pp. 557-66.

Tung, Tso-pin

1951 "The Date of the Wu Wang Conquest of Chou," Bulletin of the College of Arts (National Taiwan University) 3: 177-212.

Ward, Lauriston

1954 "The Relative Chronology of China through the Han period." In Relative Chronologies in Old World Archeology, pp. 130-44. Ed. Robert W. Ehrich. Chicago: University of Chicago Press.

Wu, Li

1961 "The Yangshao Remains at Miao-ti-kou Should be Later in Time Than San-li-ch'iao," K'ao-ku, 1961, no. 7, pp. 384, 389.

Yang, Chien-fang

1961 "An Analysis of the Decorative Patterns of the Painted Pottery of the Yangshao Site at Miao-ti-kou," K'ao-ku, 1961, no. 5, pp. 266-71.

1962 "The Chronology of the Yangshao and the Ma-chia-yao Cultures," K'ao-ku Hsüeh-pao, 1962, no. 1, pp. 49-80.

Yen, Yen, and others

1960 "Report of the Study of the Neolithic Human Skeletal Materials from Pao-chi," Palaeovertebrata et Palaeoanthropologia, 2, no. 1.

[Underscored page references indicate an entire article or clearly titled section of which the subject is the theme. Numbered and lettered periods, phases, site levels, and the like are also underscored for clarity and ease in reading.]